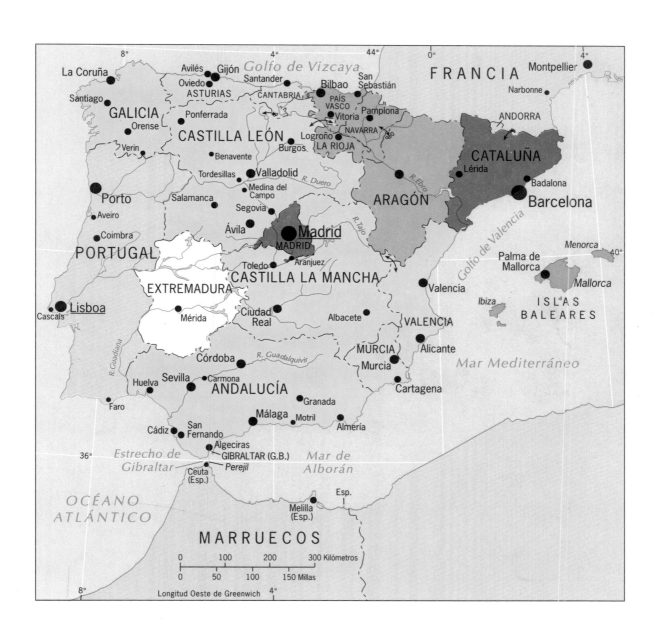

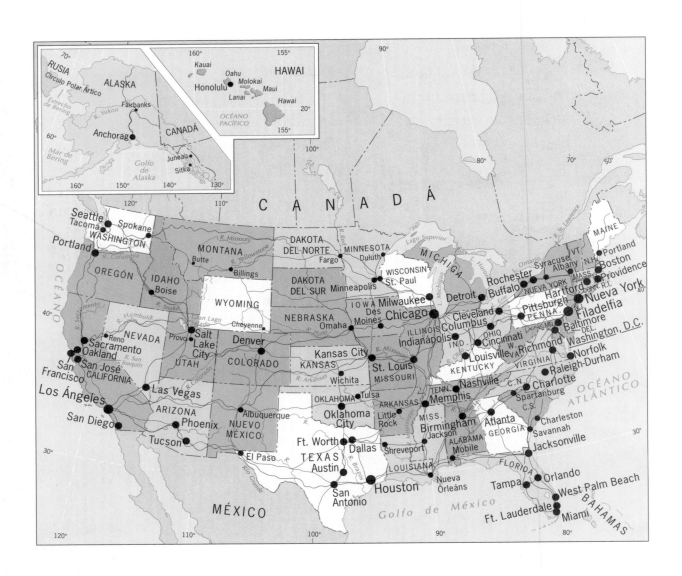

FOR INSTRUCTORS

WileyPLUS is built around the activities you perform in your class each day. With *WileyPLUS* you can:

Prepare & Present
Create outstanding class presentations using a wealth of resources such as PowerPoint™ slides, image galleries, videos, and more. You can even add materials you have created yourself.

Create Assignments
Use the provided question banks, or add your own questions to create assignments based upon text material, class lectures, or additional audio/video content provided in *WileyPLUS*.

Assess your Students' Comprehension
Keep track of your students' progress and analyze individual and overall class results.

Now Available with WebCT, eCollege, and ANGEL Learning!

"It has been a great help, and I believe it has helped me to achieve a better grade."

Michael Morris,
Columbia Basin College

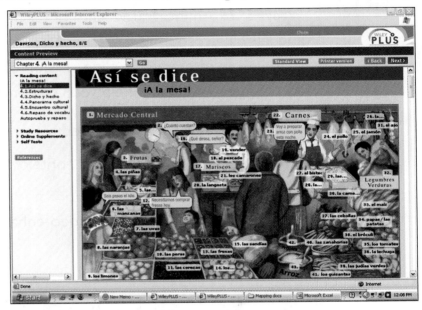

FOR STUDENTS

You have the potential to make a difference!
WileyPLUS is a powerful online system packed with features to help you turn your potential to performance.

- A complete online version of your text, plus other study resources including audio and video-enhanced files to help you understand the material.

With *WileyPLUS* you get:

- Context-sensitive help including visual flashcards, pronunciation guides, and more.
- Tools to help you assess your own comprehension of the concepts under study—including an online gradebook to track your own progress.

- Reinforce and master vocabulary and grammar skills.

Learn more about *WileyPLUS*: www.wileyplus.com/experience

76% of students surveyed said *WileyPLUS* made them better prepared for tests. *

* Based upon over 5000 responses to a survey of students using *WileyPLUS*.

Dicho y hecho

EIGHTH EDITION

Beginning Spanish

Laila M. Dawson

Kim Potowski
University of Illinois at Chicago

Silvia Sobral
Brown University

John Wiley & Sons, Inc.

PUBLISHER	Jay O'Callaghan
DIRECTOR, MODERN LANGUAGES	Magali Iglesias
DEVELOPMENTAL EDITOR	Elena Herrero
EXECUTIVE MARKETING MANAGER	Jeffrey Rucker
SENIOR PRODUCTION EDITOR	William A. Murray
PRODUCTION MANAGEMENT SERVICES	Christine Cervoni, Camelot Editorial Services
EDITORIAL PROGRAM ASSISTANT	Jennifer Mendoza
DIRECTOR, CREATIVE SERVICES	Harry Nolan
COVER DESIGN	Howard Grossman
COVER IMAGES	(left to right) Pacific Stock/SuperStock; Superstock/Punchstock; Corbis/MediaBakery; (border) Cindy Miller Hopkins/Danita Delimont
SENIOR ILLUSTRATION EDITOR	Anna Melhorn
ILLUSTRATION STUDIO	Escletxa, Barcelona, Spain
PHOTO EDITOR	Elle Wagner
SENIOR MEDIA EDITOR	Lynn Pearlman
BICENTENNIAL LOGO DESIGN	Richard J. Pacifico

This book was set in ITC Highlander Book by Creative Curriculum Initiatives and printed and bound by R.R. Donnelley.

This book is printed on acid-free paper.

To order books or for customer service please call 1-800-CALL WILEY (225-5945).

Library of Congress Cataloging in Publication Data:
Dawson, Laila M.
Dicho y hecho: beginning Spanish / Laila M. Dawson, Kim Potowski. —8th ed. p. cm.
Includes bibliographical references and index.
ISBN 978-0-471-76107-5 (cloth)
1. Spanish language—Textbooks for foreign speakers—English.
2. Spanish language—Grammar. I. Potowski, Kim. II. Title.

PC4129.E5D38 2007
468.2'421—dc22
2007042811

AIE ISBN: 978-0-470-17117-2

Printed in the United States of America

10 9 8 7 6 5 4 3 2 1

Laila Dawson

Dicho y hecho, 1e had its beginnings during an 11,000-mile road trip through Mexico in the late 1970's. From that time to the present, **Dicho** has been an integral part of my life journey, with inspiration drawn from my passion for teaching and my love for Hispanic countries and their cultures. I was born in Buenos Aires, Argentina, and attended bilingual schools there and in Mexico City. This foundation led me to graduate studies at the University of Wisconsin and a teaching career, first at Virginia Union University, and then at the University of Richmond, where I helped develop and direct the Intensive Spanish Program. I also accompanied students on study-abroad programs in Spain, Venezuela, Ecuador, and Costa Rica, and on service-learning projects in Honduras.

I proudly dedicate this 8th edition of **Dicho** to my beloved grandchildren, Joel and Maya. And it is with joy that I welcome to this edition two brilliant teachers and authors, Kim Potowski and Silvia Sobral.

Soon after becoming *Licenciada* in English Philology in Spain, I arrived at the University of Illinois at Urbana-Champaign to pursue an M.A. in Teaching English as a Second Language. I faced a classroom for the first time when, a few weeks later, I was assigned to teach advanced English grammar to international students. Both my students and I believed that, as a teacher, I should explain grammar rules and their exceptions, give examples, and correct mistakes. My M.A studies, further graduate work in Spanish Applied Linguistics, and extensive teaching and coordinating experience in the U.S. and Spain proved me wrong. I have come to learn that language learning and teaching are much more complex and exciting processes. **Dicho y hecho, 8e** brings together my experience and that of my co-authors for a text that we hope will facilitate teaching and learning while making it a meaningful, enjoyable endeavor.

Silvia Sobral

Dedico este trabajo a mis profesores, estudiantes y colegas, de quienes sigo aprendiendo, y especialmente a mis padres, Eusebio y Mª de los Ángeles, por enseñarme, inspirarme y apoyarme siempre.

Kim Potowski

I was raised on Long Island, New York, and began my study of Spanish at around the same time the first edition of **Dicho y hecho** was published; my inspirational 10th grade Spanish teacher, Mr. Paul Ferrotti, likely never imagined that his influence would reach the eighth edition twenty-three years later. I majored in Spanish and spent a most memorable and formative year abroad in Salamanca, Spain. After taking a year off to teach Spanish at my alma mater, Washington University in St. Louis, I began graduate studies at the University of Illinois at Urbana-Champaign, where, after a three-year hiatus to teach English in Mexico City and in France, I finished a Ph.D. in linguistics with a specialization in language learning and teaching. I moved to Chicago to work on what eventually became a book about a dual immersion language school, and I've been here ever since, enjoying its rich linguistic and cultural diversity and teaching and learning from a wide variety of students.

I dedicate this book to my husband, Cliff Meece, and my sons Nicolás and Samuel.

Preface

TO THE INSTRUCTOR

Building on a tradition, now beyond its 25th year, the eighth edition of **Dicho y hecho** maintains the features that have made this program extremely successful as a student-centered and user-friendly program, while incorporating an unwavering focus on authentic, purposeful communication and the implementation of input processing instruction, a sound research-based pedagogical approach.

Over 30 years of research in second language acquisition indicate that numerous and varied **input** activities are required *before* asking students to produce **output** using the new structure or vocabulary. **Dicho y hecho**, **8e** not only provides students with sufficient input on new forms and structures before moving them to output, but the Instructor Annotated Edition contains the icons **I** for input and **O** for output to assist them in identifying the nature of these activities.

HALLMARKS OF THE DICHO Y HECHO PROGRAM

A comprehensive and integrated program

With 350,000 satisfied users and counting, **Dicho y hecho** offers a complete program designed to support you and your students as you create and carry out your course. Each chapter, while integrating grammar, vocabulary, and cultural content into a cohesive unit, has been carefully developed to follow a consistent sequence of linguistic and cultural presentations, practice activities, and skill-building tasks.

Diverse and engaging

Dicho y hecho combines a broad array of class-tested and innovative activities (individual, paired, and small group activities) that involve all language skills (listening, speaking, reading and writing) and range from structured to guided and open-ended.

Flexible and easy to adapt

While it focuses on the essentials that beginning students need to master, **Dicho y hecho** is flexible enough to adapt to any kind of course in the curriculum. Whether used on its own, supplemented with traditional materials or with newer technology, it maintains a clear direction for students, and solidly grounds them in the basics of the language.

Focuses on grammar as a means for communication

Grammar is presented with precise, simple explanations and clear visual formats, drawing immediate connections between forms and their communicative use. Carefully sequenced activities take students from understanding input to effectively expressing themselves.

Takes practical, contextualized vocabulary into active use

A selection of varied, practical, and thorough vocabulary is organized within thematic units. Visual and contextual presentations lead to progressive phases of active application that range from identification in the chapter-opening art scenes and input based exercises to personal expression and situational conversations, resulting in more effective acquisition of the new words.

Integrates relevant, varied cultural information throughout

Through an appealing combination of readings, maps, photos, realia, and intriguing *Notas culturales*, **Dicho y hecho** introduces students to the geography, politics, arts, history, and both traditional and contemporary cultural aspects of the countries and peoples that make up the Spanish-speaking world.

HIGHLIGHTS OF THE EIGHTH EDITION

Dicho y hecho, *8e* takes full advantage of its authors' varied and extensive experience as second language learners, teachers, and researchers to incorporate sound, research-based pedagogical principles into *Dicho y hecho*'s teacher and student-friendly program.

- **Authentic communicative activities** are designed to replicate real-world tasks. The activities in *Dicho y hecho* continue to utilize topics that relate to students' lives and interests, but now engage them further, via the content of the activity, to more relevant and meaningful levels of communication. This approach is based on current research in second language acquisition, which shows that language teachers really do not "teach" the language—our job is to provide students with well-structured and well-sequenced opportunities to communicate in the new language and thus develop their internal grammar systems.

- Students are given ample opportunity to make form-meaning connections and work with **comprehension of new linguistic forms (words, structures) before being asked to produce** them. That is, they are presented with and guided through interactions with input before being required to produce output.

- **New design and art** offer a contemporary, dynamic and, most importantly, clear visual setting that enhances *Dicho y hecho*'s user-friendly nature while appealing to today's students' preferences.

- **Thematic vocabulary** is presented in context, either through illustrations or within a highly contextualized text. English translations have been significantly reduced at the presentation stage, thus pushing students to draw the connection between the new word and its referent. In order to ensure appropriate linguistic support for new vocabulary, translations for all new active vocabulary have been added to *Repaso de vocabulario activo* sections at the end of each chapter.

- **Grammar presentations** have been revised and visually enhanced, resulting in simpler, clearer, and more precise information.

- **Expanded instructors' annotations**, now written in Spanish, include comments on the pedagogical basis of certain activities, suggestions on alternative ways to implement activities, follow-up and expansion possibilities, as well as tips on presentation of new grammar.

- **Cultural knowledge and understanding** take a more central role in this edition of *Dicho y hecho*. Cultural content readings have been dispersed throughout the chapter instead of being heavily concentrated at the end. Several have been replaced, while others have been updated to reflect current political, social, and cultural issues in the Hispanic world. New *Notas culturales* are brief boxes on cultural themes in the margins. The importance of cultural content is underscored by a new cultural section in the *Autoprueba y repaso* self-tests at the end of each chapter.

  While still offering focused, updated information on Spanish-speaking countries, this edition seeks to help students arrive at a greater cultural sensitivity through comparison and contrast of their customs, beliefs, etc. and those of different Hispanic groups. There is also a new effort to emphasize the diversity of peoples and cultures within the Spanish-speaking world, which should, in turn, shed light on stereotypes that students may inadvertently hold.

- **Revamped *Situaciones* and new *Investig@ en Internet* sections** encourage students to take an active role in the learning process, to become independent learners, and to think critically.

- **Reading and listening sections** are now accompanied by pre-reading and pre-listening questions that prepare and motivate students for the task at hand, as well as post-reading activities that help students synthesize information and encourage them to reflect on what they just learned.

- In a similar vein, *Entrando al tema*, a new feature at the beginning of each chapter, presents two to three thought-provoking questions designed to get students thinking about the major themes of the chapter.

- *Dicho y hecho* has two new types of videos to expose students to authentic communication and interactions between native speakers of Spanish in the US and abroad, in professional and social settings.

Visual Walkthrough

Overview

The opening of each chapter presents the chapter's goals for communication, structures, vocabulary theme, and the cultural focus.

Entrando al tema

This new feature at the beginning of each chapter, presents two to three thought-provoking questions designed to get students thinking about the major cultural themes of the chapter.

Repaso de vocabulario activo

This alphabetized list of active Spanish vocabulary words and phrases introduced in the chapter, grouped by parts of speech, appears at the end of each chapter. This list is also recorded on the audio program.

Así se dice

Active vocabulary is introduced through illustrations or highly contextualized texts, English translations added only when context may not suffice.

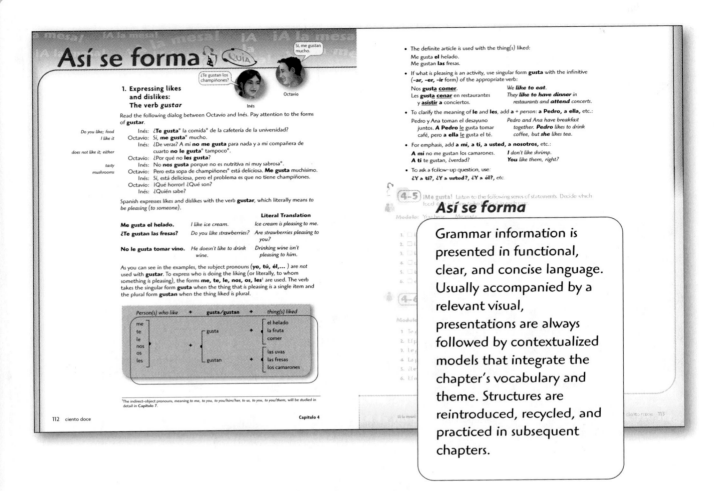

Así se forma

Grammar information is presented in functional, clear, and concise language. Usually accompanied by a relevant visual, presentations are always followed by contextualized models that integrate the chapter's vocabulary and theme. Structures are reintroduced, recycled, and practiced in subsequent chapters.

NOTA DE LENGUA

- **Mucho** and **poco** do not change in gender and number when they modify verbs.

  Comemos **mucho/poco**.   We eat a lot/little.

  When they modify nouns, **mucho** and **poco** do change in gender and number to agree with the noun.

  Comemos **muchas** verduras y **poca** carne.

- Spanish uses the preposition **de** (of) to join two nouns for the purpose of description.

  helado **de** vainilla   vanilla ice cream

  jugo **de** naranja   orange juice

  How many combinations can you come up with?

Notas de lengua

These short notes provide additional details on features of the Spanish language and its use.

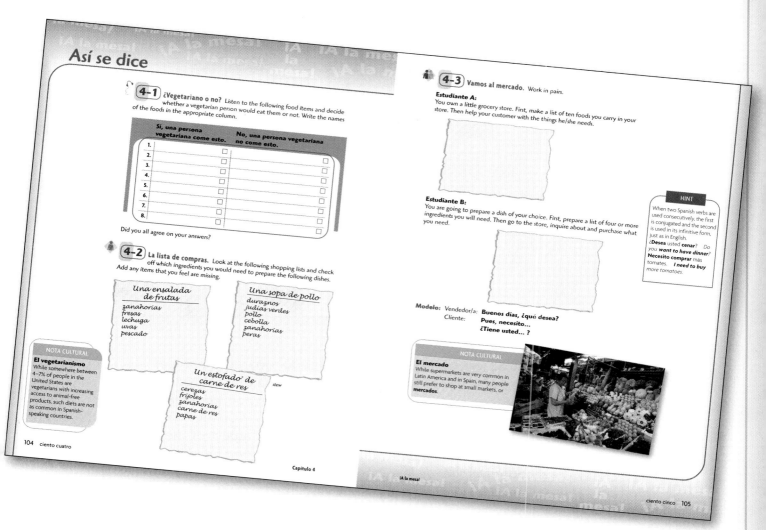

Así se dice

4-1 **¿Vegetariano o no?** Listen to the following food items and decide whether a vegetarian person would eat them or not. Write the names of the foods in the appropriate column.

	Sí, una persona vegetariana come esto.	No, una persona vegetariana no come esto.
1.	☐	☐
2.	☐	☐
3.	☐	☐
4.	☐	☐
5.	☐	☐
6.	☐	☐
7.	☐	☐
8.	☐	☐

Did you all agree on your answers?

4-2 **La lista de compras.** Look at the following shopping lists and check off which ingredients you would need to prepare the following dishes. Add any items that you feel are missing.

Una ensalada de frutas
zanahorias
fresas
lechuga
uvas
pescado

Una sopa de pollo
duraznos
judías verdes
pollo
cebolla
zanahorias
peras

Un estofado² de carne de res   stew
cerezas
frijoles
zanahorias
carne de res
papas

NOTA CULTURAL

El vegetarianismo
While somewhere between 4–7% of people in the United States are vegetarians with increasing access to animal-free products, such diets are not as common in Spanish-speaking countries.

4-3 **Vamos al mercado.** Work in pairs.

Estudiante A:
You own a little grocery store. First, make a list of ten foods you carry in your store. Then help your customer with the things he/she needs.

Estudiante B:
You are going to prepare a dish of your choice. First, prepare a list of four or more ingredients you will need. Then go to the store, inquire about and purchase what you need.

HINT
When two Spanish verbs are used consecutively, the first is conjugated and the second is used in its infinitive form, just as in English.
¿Desea usted **cenar**? Do you *want to have dinner*?
Necesito comprar más tomates. *I need to buy* more tomatoes.

Modelo: Vendedor/a: **Buenos días, ¿qué desea?**
Cliente: **Pues, necesito...**
¿Tiene usted... ?

NOTA CULTURAL

El mercado
While supermarkets are very common in Latin America and in Spain, many people still prefer to shop at small markets, or **mercados.**

Actividades

Vocabulary and grammar presentations are followed by a series of communicative activities moving students from input activities (comprehension-based) to output (production-based) activities. Even simple activities (see 4–1 here) are communicative in that they require students to make meaning-form connections in order to complete the task at hand. Activities are also purposeful in that they lead to an objective (to compare oneself to other students, to decide on something, etc.) beyond "practicing" the new forms.

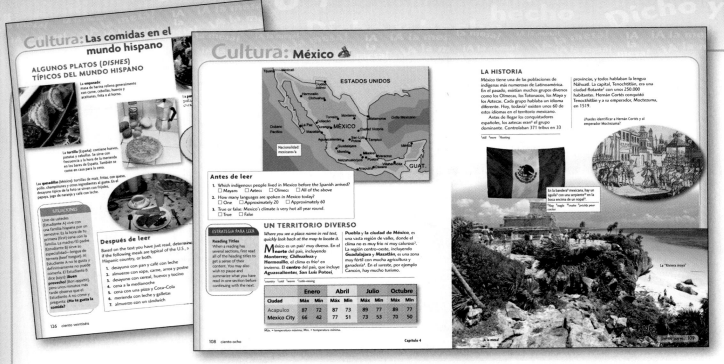

Cultura

Expanded on the web at www.wiley.com/college/panoramas, *Cultura* is an appealing combination of readings, maps, photos, and realia that acquaint students with the geography, history, and other aspects of the various countries and peoples of the Spanish-speaking world. It also includes short readings in Spanish that focus on cultural attitudes and behaviors, and expand one cultural aspect of the chapter theme. These are preceded by a set of pre-reading questions *Antes de leer* and followed by the sections *Después de leer*, consisting in a set of comprehension questions, and/or *Conexiones y contrastes*, where students are required to make cultural contrasts and comparisons to develop an appreciation of their own heritage and culture, as well as those of others.

Notas culturales

These new boxes in the margins present a variety of attention-grabbing bits about people, customs, etc. in the Hispanic world.

NOTA CULTURAL

La comida rápida en el mundo hispano

There are several popular fast-food chains in the Spanish-speaking world, including:

Pollo Campero	Guatemala, Costa Rica, Honduras, Nicaragua, Ecuador, Mexico, El Salvador, the United States
El Pollo Loco	Mexico, the United States
Pans & Company	Spain

In addition, United States fast-food chains that open in other countries often adopt local customs. For example, in Puerto Rico, McDonald's serves **tostones** (*fried plantains*) and in Spain, they serve beer. Even several McDonald's locations in Miami serve classic Cuban sandwiches (ham, pork, Swiss cheese, pickles, and mustard on toasted Cuban-style bread) and the *Dulce de Leche* McFlurry with caramelized, sweetened condensed milk.

Escenas

These brief, situational conversations designed for listening practice employ authentic language to provide concise, practical, and natural contexts in which to apply the chapter's vocabulary and grammar and integrate listening strategies through the use of pre- and post-listening exercises. This section is also recorded on the audio program.

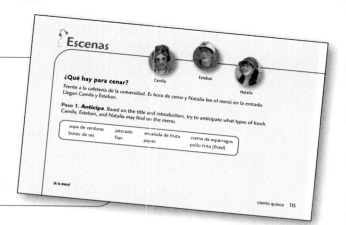

Situaciones

These authentic communicative activities present interactive, often humoristic, problem-solving situations that students have to solve through the creative use of the language.

SITUACIONES

Uno de ustedes (Estudiante A) vive con una familia hispana por un semestre. Es la hora de tu primera (*first*) cena con la familia. La madre/El padre (Estudiante B) sirve su especialidad—lengua de ternera (*beef tongue*). Al Estudiante A no le gusta y definitivamente no puede comerla. El Estudiante B dice (*says*): **¡Buen provecho!** (*Bon appétit*), pero unos minutos más tarde observa que el Estudiante A no come y pregunta: **¿No te gusta la comida?**

Así se pronuncia

This pronunciation component (in Chapters 1– 8 only) presents key points on Spanish pronunciation and spelling and provides listening and oral practice.

Investig@ en Internet

These boxes prompt students to answer a question or find information from the Internet and report back to the class, thus encouraging independent exploration of issues related to the Spanish-speaking world.

Investig@ en INTERNET

Do you know who Frida Kahlo is? Find information about her on the Internet, including some images of her and her work. Be prepared to share this information in class.

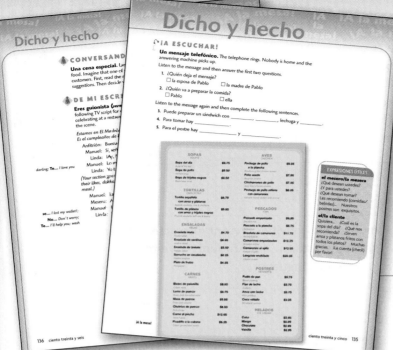

Dicho y hecho

Acclaimed by users and reviewers, *Dicho y hecho* reviews, integrates, and puts into practice all components of the chapter. It features lively listening activities in *¡A escuchar!* (recorded on CD), guided conversations, role play and situational dramatizations in *Conversando*, and varied individual and group writing practice in *De mi escritorio*.

Artes

This section introduces students to a wide variety of Hispanic creative expression, including literary, visual, textile, and folk arts. Some authentic literary reading selections are included here.

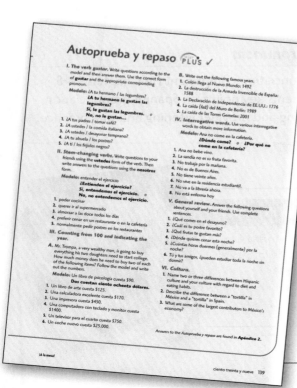

Autoprueba y repaso

These review exercises at the end of each chapter and on the Web are an effective tool for reviewing material and preparing for tests. The answer key that appears in an appendix provides instant feedback. The eighth edition incorporates questions on culture into this review.

The Complete Program

STUDENT TEXTBOOK

Packaged with Textbook Audio CDs

978-0-471-76107-5

The textbook includes 15 thematically based chapters. The Textbook Audio CDs (978-0-470-28549-7) packaged with the text includes the pronunciation materials from the *Así se pronuncia* sections, the *Escenas*, the *¡A escuchar!* activities from the *Dicho y hecho* sections, and the end-of-chapter vocabularies.

ANNOTATED INSTRUCTOR'S EDITION

Packaged with Textbook Audio CDs

978-0-470-17117-2

The Annotated Instructor's Edition contains side notes with suggestions for teaching, meaningful structural exercises, suggestions for varying or expanding communicative activities, and scripts for comprehension activities. These annotations are especially helpful for first-time instructors. The Annotated Instructor's Edition includes CDs (978-0-470-28591-6) that contain the listening activities plus the audio material for the student edition.

ACTIVITIES MANUAL

978-0-471-76106-8

The Activities Manual contains two components:

- A Workbook (also sold separately—978-0-470-12903-6) that links reading and writing, builds vocabulary, practices grammar, and helps students develop personal expression and composition skills. Some activities are self correcting and the answer key appears at the end of the Activities Manual. For a few writing activities, students are directed to write in a journal (notebook, folder) rather than in the workbook itself. Not writing in the workbook accommodates instructors who want longer writing pieces typed and/or want to have students do multiple versions of some writing pieces. It also facilitates review and learning from the writing process.

- A Lab Manual (also sold separately—978-0-470-12902-9) to be used with the Lab Audio Program available on CDs and in WileyPLUS. The Lab Manual includes a variety of contextualized listening comprehension activities.

LAB AUDIO PROGRAM

978-0-470-17331-2

The Lab Audio Program is coordinated with the Lab Manual in the Activities Manual. The audio program is available on CD and in WileyPLUS for students and instructors. The audioscript is included in the Instructor's Resource Manual.

DICHO Y HECHO VIDEO

978-0-470-27874-1

Dicho y hecho has two new types of videos to expose students to authentic communication and interactions between native speakers of Spanish in the US and abroad, in professional and social settings. One of the videos has 15 dialogues tightly connected to the grammar and vocabulary from each chapter. The second video has 15 documentaries featuring real-life people interviewed in authentic settings. The videos contain a variety of characters, with a variety of accents, in a variety of settings; a good way to expose students to different experiences. Also available is the cultural video for the seventh edition.

PLUS WILEYPLUS

www.wiley.com/college/wileyplus

Dicho y hecho is available with *WileyPLUS*, a powerful online tool that provides instructors and students with an integrated suite of teaching and learning resources in one easy-to-use Web site. *WileyPLUS* is organized around the activities you and your students perform in class.

FOR INSTRUCTORS

Prepare & Present: Create class presentations using a wealth of Wiley-provided resources—such as an online version of the textbook, PowerPoint© slides, animations, overviews, and visuals from the Wiley Image Gallery—making your preparation time more efficient. You may easily adapt, customize, and add to this content to meet the needs of your course.

Create Assignments: Automate the assigning and grading of homework or quizzes by using Wiley-provided question banks, or by writing your own. Student results will be automatically graded and recorded in your gradebook. *WileyPLUS* can link the pre-lecture quizzes and test bank questions to the relevant section of the online text.

Track Student Progress: Keep track of your students' progress via an instructor's gradebook, which allows you to analyze individual and overall class results to determine students' progress and level of understanding.

Administer Your Course: *WileyPLUS* can easily be integrated with another course management system, gradebook, or other resources you are using in your class, providing you with the flexibility to build your course, your way.

FOR STUDENTS

WileyPLUS provides immediate feedback on student assignments and a wealth of support materials. This powerful study tool will help your students develop their conceptual understanding of the class material and increase their ability to answer questions.

A "Study and Practice" area links directly to text content, allowing students to review the text while they study and answer. Resources include videos, concept animations and tutorials, visual learning interactive exercises, and links to Web sites that offer opportunities for further exploration.

An "Assignment" area keeps all the work you want your students to complete in one location, making it easy for them to stay "on task." Students will have access to a variety of interactive self-assessment tools, as well as other resources for building their confidence and understanding. In addition, all of the pre-lecture quizzes contain a link to the relevant section of the multimedia book, providing students with context-sensitive help that allows them to conquer problem-solving obstacles as they arise.

A Personal Gradebook for each student will allow students to view their results from past assignments at any time.

Please view our online demo at www.wiley.com/college/wileyplus. Here you will find additional information about the features and benefits of *WileyPLUS*, how to request a "test drive" of *WileyPLUS* for **Dicho y hecho**, and how to adopt it for class use.

WileyPLUS is also available with WIMBA voice recording and multimedia functionality, for qualified adopters.

QUIA ELECTRONIC ACTIVITIES MANUAL WITH GRADEBOOK

978-0-470-12901-2

Quia offers an electronic version of the Activities Manual with its workbook, lab manual, and DVD activities. This electronic version allows instructors to assign work to students that will be automatically graded as well as work that can be manually graded by the professor. Quia also contains a gradebook that allows instructors to view class statistics in a variety of ways and that provides students with individual feedback. Quia activities can be accessed from any computer with an Internet connection.

BOOK COMPANION WEB SITE FOR STUDENTS

www.wiley.com/college/dawson/

The Web site for students contains complimentary self-tests, Internet activities, *Panorama cultural* section, and flashcards.

BOOK COMPANION WEB SITE FOR INSTRUCTORS WITH TESTING PROGRAM AND POWERPOINT SLIDES

www.wiley.com/college/dawson/

The Web site for instructors features an online IRM, including word and computerized versions of exams and digital exam audio files. It also includes image gallery, answer key for the exams and the Lab Manual, audio and video scripts, and PowerPoint presentations.

To the Student

Welcome! You are about to begin an exciting new creative experience. You might think learning a new language is simply memorizing grammatical rules and vocabulary. But learning a new language is actually a creative pursuit that involves getting things done through communication, expressing ideas, and sharing views. Sure, there are technical details that you will need to master. But as you immerse yourself deeper into the Spanish language and culture, you will learn to weave new words, new ideas, and new experiences into your own creative expressions.

To help you along the way, we've assembled a complete program of student course components.

STUDENT TEXTBOOK
Packaged with Textbook Audio CDs

978-0-471-76107-5

The textbook includes 15 thematically based chapters. The Textbook Audio CDs (978-0-470-28549-7) packaged with the text includes the pronunciation materials from the *Así se pronuncia* sections, the *Escenas*, the *¡A escuchar!* activities from the *Dicho y hecho* sections, and the end-of-chapter vocabularies.

ACTIVITIES MANUAL
978-0-471-76106-8

The Activities Manual contains two components:

- A Workbook (also sold separately—978-0-470-12903-6) that links reading and writing, builds vocabulary, practices grammar, and helps students develop personal expression and composition skills. Some activities are self correcting and the answer key appears at the end of the Activities Manual. For a few writing activities, students are directed to write in a journal (notebook, folder) rather than in the workbook itself. Not writing in the workbook accommodates instructors who want longer writing pieces typed and/or want to have students do multiple versions of some writing pieces. It also facilitates review and learning from the writing process.

- A Lab Manual (also sold separately—978-0-470-12902-9) to be used with the Lab Audio Program available on CDs and in *WileyPLUS*. The Lab Manual includes a variety of contextualized listening comprehension activities.

LAB AUDIO PROGRAM
978-0-470-17331-2

The Lab Audio Program is coordinated with the Lab Manual in the Activities Manual. The audio program is available on CD and in *WileyPLUS*.

BOOK COMPANION WEB SITE FOR STUDENTS
www.wiley.com/college/dawson/

The Web site contains complimentary self-tests, Internet activities, *Panorama cultural* section, and flashcards.

Icons in your Textbook

Resources	Activities
PLUS WileyPLUS	Individual
✓ Autoprueba	Pairs
Quia Quía	Group
Video	Instructor-led
Activities Manual	Listening

Acknowledgements

No project of the scope and complexity of **Dicho y hecho, Eighth Edition** could have materialized without the collaboration of numerous people. The author team gratefully acknowledges the contributions of the many individuals who were instrumental in the development of this work.

The professionalism, dedication, and expertise of the John Wiley & Sons, Inc. staff who worked with us have been both indispensable and inspirational. To Jay O'Callaghan, Publisher, who oversaw the administrative aspects of the entire project, bore the ultimate responsibility for its completion, and never failed to be approachable, we are very grateful. We also thank Magali Iglesias, Director of Modern Languages, for the expertise she brings to the project in its pivotal later stages and her role in carrying it into the future. We are also most grateful to William A. Murray, Senior Production Editor, for his expertise, flexibility, creativity, inordinate patience, and dedication to the project. We extend our thanks and appreciation to Elle Wagner, Photo Editor, for facilitating the photo selections that enhance the text. Nor can we neglect to thank Jeffrey Rucker, Executive Marketing Manager, for creating a brilliant advertising program that will position Dicho y hecho favorably in the marketplace, and also many thanks to Wiley's Market Specialists, Tiziana Aime and Elena Casillas, for their enthusiasm, creativity, and dedication in meeting Spanish instructors around the country.

We thank Lynn Pearlman for her creativity in coordinating the outstanding media ancillaries that supplement the text. We would also like to acknowledge everyone at Creative Curriculum Initiatives. Most of all, the authors extend our heartfelt appreciation and most profound gratitude to our wonderful Developmental Editor, Elena Herrero, for her unfaltering devotion to **Dicho y hecho**, her tireless hands-on involvement with us on a daily basis since initial conceptualization of the **Eighth Edition**, her talent, expertise, and diligence in turning a manuscript into a book, her relentless pursuit of perfection, and—most importantly—her friendship and confidence in us as authors.

We are grateful to the loyal users of **Dicho y hecho**, who over the years have continued to provide valuable insights and suggestions. And finally, for their candid observations, their critically important scrutiny, and their creative ideas, we wish to thank the following reviewers and contributors for this edition from across the nation:

Aleta Anderson, *Grand Rapids Community College*; Evelyne M. Bornier, *Louisiana University*; Carmen Chavez, *Florida Atlantic University*; Cristina Cordero, *Cy-Fair College*; Dominick Defillippis, *Wheeling Jesuit University*; Marcella Fierro, *Mesa Community College*; Lucilla Adela González-Cirre, *Cerro Coso College*; Yolanda González, *Valencia Community College*; Andrew Gorden, *Mesa State Community College*; Frozina Goussak, *Collin County Community College*; Agnieszka Gutthy, *Southern Louisiana University*; Eda Henao, *Borough of Manhattan Community College*; Krishauna Hines, *Salem College*; Victoria Ketz, *Iona College*; Cynthia Lepeley, *Heidelberg College*; Iraida H. Lopez, *Ramapo College*; Francisco Martinez, *Northwestern Oklahoma State University*; Sarah McCurry, *Idaho State University*; Dulce Menes, *University of New Orleans*; Nancy Minguez, *Old Dominion University*; Sandra Oakley, *Palm Beach Community College*; Sue Pechter, *Northwestern University*; Federico Perez Pineda, *University of South Alabama*; Michelle Peterson, *Arizona State University*; Karen Schairer, *Northern Arizona University*; Dora Schoebrun Fernández, *San Diego Mesa College*; Nidia A. Schuhmacher, *Brown University*; Francisco Solares-Larrave, *Northern Illinois University*; Benay W. Stein, *Northwestern University*; Linda Tracy, *Santa Rosa College*; Gheorghita Tres, *Oakland University*; Phyllis E. VanBuren, *St. Cloud State University*; Celines Villalba, *University of California – Berkeley*; Joseph R. Weyers, *College of Charleston*.

Laila Dawson

Kim Potowski

Silvia Sobral

	Así se dice	Así se forma

 Go to **WileyPlus** for activities and online version of the text.

	Así se dice	Así se forma

Go to **WileyPlus** for activities and online version of the text.

	Así se dice	**Así se forma**

Go to **WileyPlus** for activities and online version of the text.

1

WILEY PLUS

Nuevos encuentros

By the end of this chapter you will be able to:

- Meet and greet each other
- State where you are from and learn the origins of others
- Describe yourself and others
- Exchange phone numbers, e-mail addresses, and birthdays
- Tell time

Así se dice

- Greetings and expressions of courtesy
- Cognates (Los cognados)
- Numbers from 0 to 99
- The alphabet
- Days of the week and months of the year
- Telling time

Así se forma

- Subject pronouns and the verb ser

Cultura

- Hispanic nationalities and greetings

ENTRANDO AL TEMA

1. What are these people probably saying to each other?
   ¡Hola!   **Gracias.**   **Hasta mañana.**

2. Is there anyone that you kiss on the cheek when you greet them? Would you kiss someone on the cheek whom you just met?

We will explore these questions in this chapter.

Así se dice

Nuevos encuentros

¿Cómo te llamas/ se llama?	*What's your name?*
Me llamo...	*My name is . . .*
Buenos días	*Good morning*
Te/ Le presento a...	*I want to introduce you to . . .*
Encantado/a	*It's nice to meet you*
Mucho gusto	*I'm pleased to meet you*
¿De dónde eres?	*Where are you from?*
Soy de...	*I'm from . . .*

Así se dice

A. Las presentaciones (*Greetings*)

In Spanish, there are two ways of addressing someone and, therefore, there are two equivalents of the English *you*: **tú** and **usted**. In general, use **tú** with classmates, relatives, friends, and others in a first-name basis relationship; use **usted** with professors and other adults in a last-name basis relationship.

Here are some informal and formal greetings and ways of introducing ourselves.

Informal (with classmates)

Hola, me llamo...,
¿Cómo te llamas (tú)?

Formal (with instructor)

Buenos días, me llamo...,
¿Cómo se llama (usted)?

To say you are pleased to meet someone, you can say

Mucho gusto.
Encantado. (*said by males*)/**Encantada.** (*said by females*)

To ask where someone is from, say

Informal

¿De dónde eres?

Formal

¿De dónde es usted?

To say where you are from, say

Soy de...

NOTA DE LENGUA

Spanish uses an upside-down question mark at the beginning of a question and an upside-down exclamation point at the beginning of an exclamation.

¿? = **signos de interrogación**
¡! = **signos de exclamación**

1-1 ¿Quién... ? (*Who . . . ?*) Refer back to pages 4–5 to see who . . .

1. are greeting informally?
   a. Carmen y Alfonso   **b.** Inés y la profesora Falcón

2. is introducing one person to another informally?
   a. Javier   **b.** Inés

3. are introducing themselves?
   a. Linda y Manuel   **b.** Alfonso y Carmen

4. is introducing one person to another formally?
   a. Javier   **b.** Inés

5. is asking about someone's origin informally?
   a. Pepita   **b.** Octavio

B. Más presentaciones

Examine and compare the following conversations. The first introduces some formal greetings and the second presents their informal equivalents, as well as expressions of farewell (**las despedidas**). Expressions in parentheses are possible alternatives (for example, *Good morning vs. Good afternoon*).

Formal

Prof. Ruiz:	**Buenos días, señorita.**	*Good morning, Miss.*
	(Buenas tardes, señora.)	*(Good afternoon, Ma'am.)*
	(Buenas noches, señor.)	*(Good evening, Sir.)*
Susana:	**Buenos días.**	*Good morning. How are you?*
	¿Cómo está usted?	
Prof. Ruiz:	**Muy bien, gracias.**	*Very well, thanks. And you?*
	¿Y usted?	
Susana:	**Bien, gracias.**	*Fine, thanks.*

Informal

Luis:	**¡Hola!**	*Hello!/Hi!*
Olga:	**¡Hola! ¿Cómo estás?**	*How are you?*
	(¿Qué tal?)	*(How's it going?)*
Luis:	**Fenomenal. ¿Y tú?**	*Terrific. And you?*
Olga:	**Regular.**	*OK./So-so.*
Luis:	**¿Qué pasa?**	*What's happening?*
	(¿Qué hay de nuevo?)	*(What's new?)*
Olga:	**Pues nada.**	*Not much.*
	Voy a la clase de historia.	*I'm going to History class.*
Luis:	**Bueno (Pues), hasta luego.**	*Well, see you later.*
	(Hasta mañana.)	*(See you tomorrow.)*
	(Hasta pronto.)	*(See you soon.)*
	(Chao.)	*(Bye./So long.)*
Olga:	**Adiós.**	*Good-bye.*

NOTA DE LENGUA

There is no Spanish equivalent for *Ms*. Use **señora** or **señorita** as appropriate.
- In many Spanish-speaking countries, **tarde** is used while there is still daylight.
- **Buenos días** and **Buenas tardes/ noches** are also used in informal settings, especially the first time you see people during a given day.

NOTA DE LENGUA

You may have noticed that Spanish has two verbs expressing *to be*:
ser → **Soy** de México.
estar → ¿Cómo **está** usted?
You will study **estar** and the differences between **ser** and **estar** in later chapters.

Así se dice

NOTA CULTURAL

In Spanish-speaking countries, women on a first-name basis with each other will greet each other, and will also greet men, with a single light kiss on the right cheek, sometimes accompanied by a handshake. In Spain and some other countries, they will kiss once on each cheek. Men sometimes greet male friends and family with a short hug in addition to a handshake.

When the two people are in a last-name basis relationship, they will use a handshake only.

When people take leave, they tend to repeat the same gestures as when they greeted.

How would the following Spanish-speakers probably greet and take leave from each other?

Susana and Antonio, Perú	One kiss	Two kisses	Handshake only
Juan and Alfonso, México	One kiss	Two kisses	Handshake only
Mr. González and Mrs. Burgos, Chile	One kiss	Two kisses	Handshake only
Elena and Linda, Spain	One kiss	Two kisses	Handshake only

1-2 **¿Formal o informal?** Listen to the following people as they greet each other and indicate whether they are addressing each other in a formal or informal manner.

	Formal	Informal
1.		
2.		
3.		
4.		

1-3 **¿Cómo estás?** Listen to your instructor and choose the appropriate response.

1. **a.** Me llamo Juan. **b.** Hola, ¿qué tal? **c.** Soy de los Estados Unidos.

2. **a.** Muy bien, ¿y tú? **b.** Pues nada. **c.** Gracias.

3. **a.** Fenomenal. **b.** Soy de México, ¿y tú? **c.** Hasta pronto.

4. **a.** Muy bien, gracias. **b.** Pues nada. **c.** Bueno, pues, hasta luego.

5. **a.** ¿Qué pasa? **b.** Buenas tardes. **c.** Chao.

1-4 Las presentaciones.

Paso 1. Move about the classroom and talk to at least five of your classmates and your instructor. Take notes in the chart provided below.

- Greet them (remember to greet your instructor with formal forms!).
- Introduce yourself and learn their names.
- Find out where they are from.
- Say good-bye.

Modelo: Estudiante A: **Hola, me llamo Antonio. Y tú, ¿cómo te llamas?**
Estudiante B: **Me llamo Raquel. ¿Cómo estás?**

Nombre	Es de...

Paso 2. Find one of the classmates you met earlier. Move about the classroom together and introduce him/her to the other classmates you met and to the instructor. Each person should respond to the introduction appropriately.

Modelo: **Roberto, <u>te</u> presento a mi amiga Raquel. Raquel es de...**
Profesor/a, <u>le</u> presento a...

Cognates (*Los cognados*)

Me llamo Pepita. Soy dinámica, atlética y extrovertida. Ah... y soy muy puntual.

Cognates are words that are identical or similar in two languages and have the same meaning. Below you have a list of adjectives (words we use to describe people and things) that are cognates.

Note that some adjectives may be used to describe males or females.

admirable	flexible	materialista	rebelde
arrogante	independiente	optimista	responsable
conformista	inteligente	paciente	sentimental
eficiente	irresponsable	pesimista	terrible
egoísta	liberal	puntual	tolerante

Así se dice

But other adjectives change **-o** to **-a** when referring to a female.

ambicioso/a	dinámico/a	introvertido/a	religioso/a
atlético/a	extrovertido/a	modesto/a	romántico/a
cómico/a	generoso/a	organizado/a	serio/a
creativo/a	impulsivo/a	práctico/a	tranquilo/a

To describe more than one person, add **-s** to adjectives that end in a vowel and **-es** to those ending in a consonant (**admirable** → **admirables**; **sentimental** → **sentimentales**).

NOTA DE LENGUA

To make a negative statement, place **no** before the verb.

No soy estudiante.	I am not a student.

In answering yes/no questions, repeat the **no**.

¿Eres pesimista?	Are you a pessimist?
¡**No, no** soy pesimista!	No, I'm not a pessimist!

1-5 **¿Similares o diferentes?** Can you figure out what the title of this activity is? The words are cognates!

 Paso 1. Read the following sentences and mark whether they are true (**Cierto**) or false (**Falso**) for you. Then add one more sentence using a different cognate from the box above.

		Cierto	Falso
1.	Soy optimista.	✔	
2.	Soy creativo/a.	✔	
3.	Soy serio/a.	✔	
4.	Soy responsable.	✔	
5.	Soy extrovertido/a.		✔
6.	Soy paciente.		✔
7.	_práctica_	✔	

PALABRAS ÚTILES

(Useful words)

también	also
tampoco	neither/ not either

 Paso 2. Work with a partner and compare your answers orally. Then write sentences about your differences.

Modelo: **Soy optimista pero Kate no es optimista.** *o*
Soy optimista y Kate es optimista también (*as well*). *o*
No soy optimista y Kate no es optimista tampoco (*either*).

Así se forma

Natalia y yo somos amigas.

Me llamo Natalia. Soy estudiante y soy de Nuevo México. Soy responsable, generosa y muy independiente.

Identifying and describing people: Subject pronouns and the verb *ser*

In the previous section you used some subject pronouns to address people (**usted, tú**) and forms of the verb **ser** *(to be)*: **¿De dónde *es* usted? ¿De dónde *eres*? Soy de...** Here are some more subject pronouns and forms of **ser**.

Subject pronouns	ser *to be*
yo (*I*)	**soy** estudiante I am
tú (*you, singular informal*)	**eres** inteligente are
usted (Ud.) (*you, singular formal*)	**es** de Bolivia is / are
él (*he*)/**ella** (*she*)	**es** profesor/profesora is / are
nosotros/as (*we*)	**somos** estudiantes we are
vosotros/as (*you, plural informal*)	**sois** inteligentes you all are
ustedes (Uds.) (*you, plural*)	**son** de Panamá they are
ellos (*they, masc.*)/**ellas** (*they, fem.*)	**son** profesores/profesoras they are

- **Vosotros/as** is used only in Spain. **Ustedes** is formal in Spain but both formal and informal in Hispanic America.

- Use subject pronouns only *to emphasize, to contrast,* or *to clarify.* Avoid them otherwise, since Spanish verb endings already indicate who the subject is.

Soy de Cuba.	*I am from Cuba.*
Yo soy de Cuba y **él** es de Chile.	*I am from Cuba and **he** is from Chile.*
Somos estudiantes.	***We are** students.*

- Use the verb **ser** to tell who a person is, where a person is from, and what a person is like.

Natalia **es** estudiante.	*Natalia is a student.*
Es de Nuevo México.	*She is from New Mexico.*
Es muy independiente.	*She is very independent.*

Así se forma

(1-6) **¿Cómo son?** Listen to the sentences your instructor reads. After you hear the first sentence, write *1* next to the photo of the person/people being described. There will be two descriptions for each photo.

Jóvenes pintando un mural en Nueva York.

___ y ___

Hombre indígena ecuatoriano.

___ y ___

La novelista Isabel Allende.

___ y ___

Chicas futbolistas.

___ y ___

(1-7) **Personas famosas.** Using adjectives from the following list, plus others that you can come up with, tell a classmate about the following famous people and two more of your choice.

Modelo: Salma Hayek (actriz)
Salma Hayek *es* una actriz de México.
Es muy bell*a* y dinámic*a*.

atlético/a	creativo/a	famoso/a	popular	bello/a (*beautiful*)
dinámico/a	fuerte (*strong*)	romántico/a	serio/a	rebelde(s)

1. Antonio Banderas (actor)

2. Shakira (cantante)

3. Sammy Sosa (jugador de béisbol)

4. Jessica Alba (actriz)

5. ¿ ... ?   **6.** ¿ ... ?

(1-8) Mi personalidad.

Paso 1. In pairs, greet and introduce yourselves and talk about your origins. Then ask each other *yes/no* questions to determine your personality traits. Take notes, as you will need some of this information later.

Modelo: (*to a male*)   *¿Eres* **(muy) extrovertido?**

           (*to a female*)   *¿Eres* **(muy) extrovertida?**

           (*male responds*)   **Sí, soy muy extrovertido./ No, no soy (muy) extrovertido. ¿Y tú?**

           (*female responds*) **Sí, soy (muy) extrovertida./ No, no soy (muy) extrovertida.**

Paso 2. Walking around the classroom, introduce your classmate to three other students. Tell his/her name, origin, and two personality traits.

Modelo: **Mi amigo/a se llama... o Te presento a mi amigo/a...**
           Es de...
           Es... y...

Paso 3. Tell the class one difference between you and your classmate and two things you have in common. Remember to add **-s** or **-es** to the adjective to form the plural.

Modelo: **(*Partner's name*) es... y yo soy...**
           Él/Ella y yo somos... y...

Así se dice

Expressions of courtesy

Con permiso.	*Pardon me./Excuse me.*
	(to seek permission to pass by someone or to leave)
Perdón./ Disculpe.	*Pardon me./Excuse me.*
	(to get someone's attention or to seek forgiveness)
Lo siento (mucho).	*I'm (so/very) sorry.*
Por favor.	*Please.*
(Muchas) Gracias.	*Thank you (very much).*
De nada.	*You're welcome.*

Así se dice

 1-9 **¡Son muy corteses!** Write the expression from the box below under the appropriate drawing.

| Disculpe | Muchas gracias | Lo siento mucho | De nada | Con permiso |

1. El profesor Marín-Vivar a Natalia y Alfonso

Prof. Marín-Vivar is going to pass by Natalia and Alfonso. What does he say?

_____

2. Rubén a Camila

Rubén wants to speak to Camila, but she is talking with Carmen. What does Rubén say?

_____

3. Esteban a Inés y Pepita

Esteban drops his tray on Inés and Pepita!

_____

4. Linda y Manuel
5. Manuel y Linda

Manuel gives Linda a gift. What does she say?

_____

What does Manuel say to Linda?

_____

 1-10 **Somos muy corteses también.**

 Paso 1. Look at the situations below and write what you would say in each case. Pretend you do not know any of these people, so you need to use formal forms.

1. You excuse yourself before you walk in front of someone.

_____

2. You lightly bump into someone and seek his/her forgiveness.

_____

3. You get someone's attention and ask the person his/her name and where he/she is from.

_____

4. You give someone something of yours, saying **Para usted** (*For you*). Expect a thank you and respond appropriately.

_____

Paso 2. Now walk around the class and perform all four tasks (in any order) using the expressions you wrote.

Numbers from 0 to 99

0 **cero**	10 **diez**	20 **veinte**	30 **treinta**
1 **uno**	11 **once**	21 **veintiuno**	31 **treinta y uno**
2 **dos**	12 **doce**	22 **veintidós**	32 treinta y dos
3 **tres**	13 **trece**	23 veintitrés	. . .
4 **cuatro**	14 **catorce**	24 veinticuatro	40 **cuarenta**
5 **cinco**	15 **quince**	25 veinticinco	50 **cincuenta**
6 **seis**	16 **dieciséis**	26 veintiséis	60 **sesenta**
7 **siete**	17 **diecisiete**	27 veintisiete	70 **setenta**
8 **ocho**	18 **dieciocho**	28 veintiocho	80 **ochenta**
9 **nueve**	19 **diecinueve**	29 veintinueve	90 **noventa**

- **Uno** is used for counting, but before a noun we use the indefinite article **un** (masculine)/**una** (feminine). The same holds true for **veintiuno, treinta y uno,** and so on.

  Un profesor, **una** profesora y **veintiún** estudiantes son de Tejas.
  One (male) professor, one (female) professor, and twenty-one students are from Texas.

- The numbers from 16 to 29 are usually written as one word: **diecisiete, veinticuatro.** Those from 31 on are written as three words: **treinta y tres; cincuenta y seis.**

- Note the numbers that carry accent marks: **dieciséis, veintidós, veintitrés, veintiséis.**

Así se dice

1-11 ¿Correcto o incorrecto?

Paso 1. Listen to some math problems and decide whether the answer is correct or incorrect, or if no answer is given, raise your hand when you are ready to offer a solution.

Paso 2. Now write five simple math problems like the ones you just heard. In pairs, take turns reading your problems to your partner and solving his/hers.

1-12 **Números de teléfono.** In Spanish, the digits of phone numbers are usually given in pairs and the article **el** (*the*) precedes the phone number: **"Es el 4–86–05–72."**

Paso 1. Listen as your instructor reads telephone numbers from the following phone list. Raise your hand when you know whose number was read and tell whose number it is.

Modelo: **Es el número de Juan Millán.**

Paso 2. Now, in pairs, take turns reading phone numbers and identifying the person whose number it is.

PALABRAS ÚTILES

C/ → Calle *Street*
Avda. → Avenida *Avenue*
Pl. → Plaza *Square*

Nombre	Dirección	Teléfono
Antolín, Sonia	c/ Mayor, 34	321.99.02
Cruz, Ángel	Avda. de la Paz, 2	844.93.15
García, Ignacio	c/ Rivera, 20	321.43.36
Gregorio, Javier	c/ Roma, 12	423.15.90
Hernández, Alicia	c/ Aurelio Díaz, 11	655.76.91
Jiménez, Luís	Avda. de América, 43	251.90.02
Landa, Marina	Pl. Abril, 1	630.18.54
Martínez, Elena	c/ Luz, 77	922.37.78
Pérez, Félix	Avda. Juárez, 144	794.47.20
Schuhmacher, Elena	Avda. Pirineos, 22	623.12.97
Sánchez, Raquel	c/ Estrecho, 13	777.85.32
Yuster, Jorge	c/ Los Molinos, 27	209.03.76

The alphabet

The letters of the alphabet (**alfabeto** or **abecedario**) and their names follow. Listen and repeat.

a (a)	Argentina	**j** (jota)	Juárez	**r** (ere)	Puerto Rico
b (be)	Bolivia	**k** (ka)	Nueva York	**s** (ese)	San Salvador
c (ce)	Cuba, Ciudad Real	**l** (ele)	Laredo	**t** (te)	Tegucigalpa
d (de)	Dallas	**m** (eme)	Managua	**u** (u)	Uruguay
e (e)	Ecuador	**n** (ene)	Nicaragua	**v** (ve, uve)	Venezuela
f (efe)	Florida	**ñ** (eñe)	España	**w** (doble ve, doble uve)	Washington
g (ge)	Guatemala, Gerona	**o** (o)	Oaxaca	**x** (equis)	examen, México
h (hache)	Honduras	**p** (pe)	Panamá	**y** (i griega)	Yucatán
i (i)	Iquitos	**q** (cu)	Quito	**z** (zeta)	Zacatecas, Cuzco

> ### NOTA DE LENGUA
>
> The letters **w** and **k** are rare in Spanish and appear mostly in foreign words. The letter **x** is pronounced as "ks" in most words (**examen**), but it is pronounced as "j" in many names of places (**México**) because the sound of "j" was spelled as x in old Spanish and the old spelling is still used.

- The combinations **ch** (**che**) as in **Ch**ile, **ll** (**elle**) as in Mede**ll**ín, and **rr** (**erre**) as in Monte**rr**ey used to be considered letters of the alphabet. You might still find them listed separately in some books!

- You might have noticed that a few letters have two possible pronunciations. You will learn more about these in the next few chapters.

1-13 ¿Cómo se escribe? (*How do you spell it?*)

 Paso 1. Listen to your instructor spell the names of Hispanic cities and write them down.

1. _____	4. _____
2. _____	5. _____
3. _____	6. _____

Paso 2. Choose three cities where Spanish is spoken (check the maps at the end of your textbook) and write them down.

Now work with a partner. Taking turns, spell the names of your cities for your partner and write down the names of the cities he/she spells for you.

Así se dice

1-14 **Mi nombre y mi número de teléfono.** In groups, ask for and give each other your names, phone numbers, and e-mail addresses, using the Spanish alphabet. Write the information accurately, as it will be used later for a Class Directory.

Modelo: Estudiante A: **¿Cómo te llamas?**

Estudiante B: **Me llamo Mónica Smith: m-o-n...**

Estudiante C: **¿Cuál es tu número de teléfono?**

Estudiante B: **Es el cuatro ochenta y seis, cero, cinco, setenta y dos.**

Estudiante D: **¿Cuál es tu dirección electrónica?**

Estudiante B: **Es monica3@dicho.com.**

Days of the week and months of the year

¿Qué día es hoy?

¡Ay, es lunes!

Septiembre

lunes[1]	martes	miércoles	jueves	viernes	sábado	domingo
					1	2
3	4	5	6	7	8	9
10	11	12	13	14	15	16
17	18	19	20	21	22	23
24	25	26	27	28	29	30

└ **el día** ┘   ├ **la semana** ┤   └ el **fin de semana** ┘

- The days of the week are not capitalized in Spanish.

- With the day of the week, the definite article **el** (singular) or **los** (plural) is used to indicate *on*.

  El sábado vamos a una gran fiesta.   ***On Saturday*** *we are going to a big party.*

  Los miércoles vamos al gimnasio.   ***On Wednesdays*** *we go to the gym.*

---

[1]In Hispanic calendars, the week usually begins on Monday.

- The plural of **el sábado** and **el domingo** is **los sábados** and **los domingos.** The other days use the same form in the singular and in the plural: **el lunes** → **los lunes**.

1-15 **El mes de septiembre.** Listen to your instructor and, based on the calendar on page 18, mark whether the statements are true (**Cierto**) or false (**Falso**).

	Cierto	Falso
1.		
2.		
3.		
4.		
5.		

1-16 **¿Qué día es?** In pairs, one of you will choose a day in the month of September from the calendar above and the other will indicate on what day of the week it falls. Take turns.

Modelo: Estudiante A: **¿Qué día es el catorce de septiembre?**
Estudiante B: **Es viernes.**

1-17 **¿Qué opinas? (*What do you think?*)** Complete the statements with the appropriate day(s). Then in groups, share your answers with your classmates. Are your opinions similar?

1. Mi día de la semana favorito es ______________________.
2. El peor (*worst*) día de la semana es ______________________.
3. Tengo (*I have*) muchas clases ______________________.
4. No tengo muchas clases ______________________.
5. Un día malo (*bad*) para exámenes es ______________________.
6. Un día bueno (*good*) para hacer fiestas es ______________________.

NOTA CULTURAL

September 16th is when Mexicans celebrate their independence from Spain in 1821. "Cinco de mayo," which is popular in the United States, is the celebration of an important victory against French invaders in Puebla, Mexico, in 1862.

Así se dice

Pero Alfonso, mi cumpleaños es el 13 de agosto.

Months, dates, and birthdays

¿Cuál es la fecha de hoy?
¿Qué fecha es hoy? (*What's today's date?*)

- To express what day of the month it is, use cardinal numbers (**dos, tres, cuatro, ...**). In Latin America, the first of the month is always expressed with **el primero**. In Spain, **el uno** is used.

  Hoy es (el)[2] cuatro de abril.
  Mañana es (el) primero de abril. (Latin America)
  Mañana es el uno de abril. (Spain)

- To express the month in a date, use **de** before the month. Months are not generally capitalized in Spanish.

  el 25 **de** diciembre   el cinco **de** mayo

- When dates are given in numbers, the day precedes the month.

  4/7 = **el cuatro de julio**

Note the names of the months in this calendar.

ENERO	200 __

L	M	M	J	V	S	D
	1	2	3	4	5	6
7	8	9	10	11	12	13
14	15	16	17	18	19	20
21	22	23	24	25	26	27
28	29	30	31			

FEBRERO	200 __

L	M	M	J	V	S	D
				1	2	3
4	5	6	7	8	9	10
11	12	13	14	15	16	17
18	19	20	21	22	23	24
25	26	27	28			

MARZO	200 __

L	M	M	J	V	S	D
				1	2	3
4	5	6	7	8	9	10
11	12	13	14	15	16	17
18	19	20	21	22	23	24
25	26	27	28	29	30	31

ABRIL	200 __

L	M	M	J	V	S	D
1	2	3	4	5	6	7
8	9	10	11	12	13	14
15	16	17	18	19	20	21
22	23	24	25	26	27	28
29	30	31				

MAYO	200 __

L	M	M	J	V	S	D
	1	2	3	4	5	
6	7	8	9	10	11	12
13	14	15	16	17	18	19
20	21	22	23	24	25	26
27	28	29	30	31		

JUNIO	200 __

L	M	M	J	V	S	D
					1	2
3	4	5	6	7	8	9
10	11	12	13	14	15	16
17	18	19	20	21	22	23
24	25	26	27	28	29	30

JULIO	200 __

L	M	M	J	V	S	D
1	2	3	4	5	6	7
8	9	10	11	12	13	14
15	16	17	18	19	20	21
22	23	24	25	26	27	28
29	30	31				

AGOSTO	200 __

L	M	M	J	V	S	D
			1	2	3	4
5	6	7	8	9	10	11
12	13	14	15	16	17	18
19	20	21	22	23	24	25
26	27	28	29	30	31	

SEPTIEMBRE	200 __

L	M	M	J	V	S	D
						1
2	3	4	5	6	7	8
9	10	11	12	13	14	15
16	17	18	19	20	21	22
23	24	25	26	27	28	29
30						

OCTUBRE	200 __

L	M	M	J	V	S	D
1	2	3	4	5	6	
7	8	9	10	11	12	13
14	15	16	17	18	19	20
21	22	23	24	25	26	27
28	29	30	31			

NOVIEMBRE	200 __

L	M	M	J	V	S	D
				1	2	3
4	5	6	7	8	9	10
11	12	13	14	15	16	17
18	19	20	21	22	23	24
25	26	27	28	29	30	31

DICIEMBRE	200 __

L	M	M	J	V	S	D
						1
2	3	4	5	6	7	8
9	10	11	12	13	14	15
16	17	18	19	20	21	22
23	24	25	26	27	28	29
30	31					

---

[2]A word in parentheses ( ) indicates that it is optional.

Three Kings Day, or **el Día de los Reyes Magos** (*Wise Kings*), is the celebration of the Epiphany, honoring the arrival of the Three Wise Men to Jerusalem: Melchior, Balthazar, and Caspar. It is celebrated twelve days after Christmas (the "twelfth day of Christmas" in the famous Christmas carol). In the Hispanic world, the Three Kings bring gifts to children on this day, although "Santa Clos/San Nicolás" is gaining in popularity in many areas. Children often leave clumps of grass or hay for the Kings' camels to eat after their long journey.

Find out what a **Rosca de Reyes** is and what surprise is baked inside of it!

1-18 **Días festivos.** With the help of a classmate, first identify the month of the following celebrations. Then see how many of them you can give the date for (look at a current calendar).

Modelo: El Día de Navidad es el veinticinco de diciembre.

1. El día de Nochebuena (*Christmas Eve*)
2. El día de Año Nuevo (*New Year's Day*)
3. El Día de los Reyes Magos
4. El Día de los Enamorados (*Valentine's Day*)
5. El Día de la Madre (*Mother's Day*)
6. El Día del Padre (*Father's Day*)
7. El Día de la Independencia de los Estados Unidos
8. El Día del Trabajo (*Labor Day*) en los Estados Unidos

Not all holidays are celebrated equally or on the same dates in different Hispanic countries. For example, Father's Day is celebrated on March 19 in Spain, but on the second Sunday in June in other countries. Mother's Day is always on May 10 in México, May 27 in Bolivia, etc.

Así se dice

1-19 Los cumpleaños (*Birthdays*).

Paso 1. Write the date of your birthday on a small piece of paper using numbers (**día/ mes**) and give it to your instructor.

Paso 2. Your instructor will now give each student one of the pieces of paper. Move around the class to find the person whose birthday is written on it.

Modelo: Estudiante A: **¿Cuándo es tu cumpleaños?**
            Estudiante B: **Mi cumpleaños es el ocho de octubre.**

Paso 3. ¡Dicho y hecho! Tell the class the name of the student whose birthday information you have and when his/her birthday is.

Modelo: **El cumpleaños de Roberta es el ocho de octubre.**

NOTA CULTURAL

In most Hispanic countries, it is common to celebrate your birthday and also your *saint's day* (based on the Catholic tradition). If your parents gave you the name of the saint honored on the day of your birth, then your birthday and your saint's day are one and the same. If they gave you the name of a saint honored on a different day of the year, you have two celebrations! Observe the names of the saints on the January calendar.

ENERO

LUNES	MARTES	MIÉRCOLES	JUEVES	VIERNES	SÁBADO	DOMINGO
◯ LUNA LLENA DIA 1 - 31	◗ C. MENGUANTE DIA 9	◯ LUNA NUEVA DIA 17	◖ C. CRECIENTE DIA 24	**1** LA CIRCUNCISION	**2** SAN BASILIO M.	**3** SAN ANTERO PAPA
4 SAN PRISCO	**5** S.TELESFORO	**6** LOS S. REYES EPIPHANY	**7** SAN RAYMUNDO	**8** SAN APOLINAR	**9** SAN MARCELINO	**10** SAN GONZALO
11 S. HIGINO PAPA	**12** S. ARCADIO M.	**13** S. HILARIO OB.	**14** SAN FELIX M.	**15** SAN MAURO ABAD	**16** SAN MARCELO	**17** SAN ANTONIO ABAD
18 STA. PRISCA V.	**19** SAN MARIO	**20** SAN FABIAN	**21** SAN FRUCTUOSO	**22** SAN VICENTE M.	**23** SAN ALBERTO	**24** SAN FRANCISCO DE S.
25 STA. ELVIRA V.	**26** S. TIMOTEO OB.	**27** STA. ANGELA V.	**28** STO. TOMAS DE A.	**29** SAN VALERIO	**30** STA MARTINA	**31** SAN JUAN BOSCO

1-20 El día del santo.   Look at the calendar page above and find what days these people are celebrating their saints' day.

Modelo: Ángela   **El santo de Ángela es el 27 de enero.**

   1. Elvira   **2.** Gonzalo   **3.** Martina   **4.** Tomás   **5.** Félix

Can you find a saint's day for someone you know?

Telling time

- When you want to know what time it is, ask **¿Qué hora es?** For telling time on the hour, use **es** for *one o'clock* only. Use **son** for all other times.

Es la una.

Son las ocho.

- To state the number of minutes past the hour, say the name of that hour plus (**y**) the number of minutes.

Es la una **y** diez.

Son las cuatro **y** cuarto.
Son las cuatro **y** quince.

Son las diez **y** media.
Son las diez **y** treinta.

Son las once **y** cuarenta³.

- To state the number of minutes before the coming hour, give the next hour less (**menos**) the number of minutes to go before that hour.

Es la una **menos** diez.

Son las nueve **menos** veinticinco.

- To differentiate between hours in the morning, afternoon, and evening, use the following expressions.

Son las seis **de la
mañana.**

Son las seis **de la
tarde.**⁴

Son las diez **de
la noche.**

Es mediodía.

Es medianoche.

---

³In Spanish, trends in telling time have been affected by the popularity of digital watches and clocks. This presentation on telling time reflects these changes.

⁴In most Spanish-speaking countries, **tarde** is used while there is still daylight, and thus may extend until 7:00 P.M. or even 8:00 P.M.

Así se dice

1-21 ¿Qué hora es?

Paso 1. Listen to the times given and identify the clock (**reloj**) that tells each time.

Modelo: You hear: Son las ocho y media de la mañana.

You say: **Reloj 3.**

1. 2. 3. 4.

5. 6. 7. 8.

Paso 2. With a classmate, one of you chooses a clock and tells the time on it. Then the other identifies the clock that tells that time.

Modelo: Estudiante A: **Son las ocho y media de la mañana.**

Estudiante B: **Reloj 3.**

1. 2. 3.

4. 5.

6. 7. 8.

1-22 ¿A qué hora? (*At what time?*) In pairs, each student looks at one of the following TV guides. Ask each other at what time the programs indicated are featured. Do not look at your partner's TV guide! (To avoid temptation, cover it with your hand or a piece of paper.)

Modelo: Estudiante A: [sees program title ***Cero en conducta***]
¿A qué hora es *Cero en conducta*?
Estudiante B: **A las ocho de la noche.**

Estudiante A		Estudiante B	
Horario Univisión		**Televisa. Canal 2 Nacional**	
En la mañana		**En la mañana**	
7:00 A.M. – 10:00 A.M.	Despierta América	6:00 – 9:00	Primero Noticias
10:00 A.M. – 11:00 A.M.	Casos de Familia	9:00 – 12:00	Hoy
11:00 A.M. – 12:00 P.M.	Mujer... Casos de la Vida Real	**En la tarde**	
En la tarde		12:00 –13:30	La Usurpadora
12:00 P.M. – 1:00 P.M	Sueño con Tu Amor	13:30 – 14:30	Nuestra Casa
1:00 P.M. – 2:00 P.M.	Mi Vida Eres Tú	14:30 – 15:00	Noticiero con Lolita Ayala
2:00 P.M. – 3:00 P.M.	El Amor no Tiene Precio	15:00 – 16:00	Espacio en Blanco
3:00 P.M. – 4:00 P.M.	Rebelde	16:00 – 17:00	Mujer... Casos de la Vida Real
4:00 P.M. – 5:00 P.M.	El Gordo y La Flaca	17:00 – 18:00	Las Dos Caras De Ana
5:00 P.M. – 6:00 P.M.	Primer Impacto	18:00 – 19:00	Código Postal
6:00 P.M. – 6:30 P.M.	¡Qué Locura!	**En la noche**	
6:30 P.M. – 7:00 P.M.	Noticiero Univisión	19:00 – 20:00	Amar Sin Límites
En la noche		20:00 – 20:30	Amor Mío
7:00 P.M. – 8:00 P.M.	Heridas de Amor	20:30 – 21:30	La Fea Más Bella
8:00 P.M. – 9:00 P.M.	La Fea Más Bella	21:30 – 22:30	Mundo De Fieras
9:00 P.M. – 10:00 P.M.	Mundo de Fieras	22:30 – 23:30	Noticiero con Joaquín López Doriga
10:00 P.M. – 11:00 P.M.	Historias para Contar	23:30 – 00:00	Tercer Grado
11:00 P.M. – 11:30 P.M.	Primer Impacto Extra		
11:30 P.M. – 12:00 A.M.	Noticiero Univisión		
	—Última Hora		

Estudiante A: Ask your partner about:

1. Mundo de Fieras
2. Hoy
3. Tercer Grado
4. Código Postal
5. Noticiero con Joaquín López Doriga

Estudiante B: Ask your partner about:

1. Noticiero Univisión — Última Hora
2. Historias para contar
3. Casos de Familia
4. Mi vida Eres tú
5. Despierta América

Así se dice

1-23 **El mundo hispano (*The Hispanic world*).** Times on the map below are given according to the 24-hour clock, which is often used for transportation schedules, TV and movie times, class schedules, etc.[5]

Tell what time it is in the following cities according to the information on the map.

Modelo: ¿Qué hora es en San Salvador, El Salvador?

Son las 7:30 horas. *o* **Son las 7 y media de la mañana.**

1. ¿Qué hora es en Lima, Perú?
2. ¿Qué hora es en Buenos Aires, Argentina?
3. ¿Qué hora es en Los Ángeles?
4. ¿Qué hora es en Nueva York?
5. ¿Qué hora es en Madrid, España?
6. ¿Qué hora es en Chicago, Illinois?
7. ¿Qué hora es en Manila, Filipinas?
8. ¿Qué hora es en Malabo, Guinea Ecuatorial?

What do these cities have in common?

NOTA CULTURAL

Spanish is one of the five most spoken languages in the world and it is an official language in twenty-one countries: Argentina, Bolivia, Chile, Colombia, Costa Rica, Cuba, Dominican Republic, Ecuador, El Salvador, Equatorial Guinea, Guatemala, Honduras, Mexico, Nicaragua, Panama, Paraguay, Peru, Puerto Rico (US), Spain, Uruguay, Venezuela.
Spanish was also an official language in the Philippines and it is still spoken in some communities there.

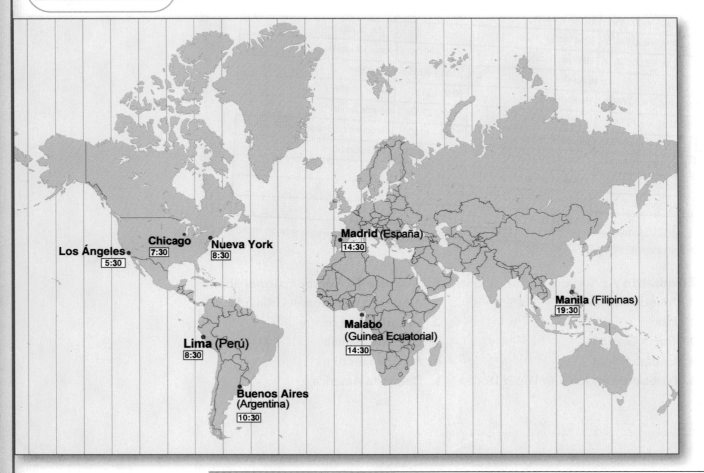

[5]To convert from the 24-hour clock to a 12-hour clock, subtract 12. For example: 14:00 minus 12 equals 2:00 P.M. All A.M. times are the same in both systems.

NOTA CULTURAL

¿De dónde son los hispanos?

When you meet Hispanic people here in the U.S. or travel to a Hispanic country, you will frequently be asked: **¿De dónde eres?** or **¿De dónde es usted?** If you are from the United States, your response would be: **Soy de los Estados Unidos.** or **Soy estadounidense.**

Note that, as with some of the cognates above, several nationalities have two different forms: those ending in **-o** refer to a male, and those ending in **-a**, to a female, such as **mexicano** and **mexicana**. Other nationalities end in a consonant in the masculine form and **-a** in the female form, such as **español** and **española**. Others have only one form, **-e**, such as **estadounidense**.

Turn to the map of the Hispanic world on the back inside cover of your textbook, and become familiar with the names of the countries and their corresponding nationalities. Note that this includes the United States, where soon about 20 percent of the population will be of Hispanic origin![6]

Soy mexicana.

Soy español.

Soy cubano.

Soy estadounidense.

1-24 **Las nacionalidades.** Work in pairs. Read to your partner the sentences on your list of nationalities of famous people. Your partner has to decide (or guess!) whether the statement is true (**Cierto**) or false (**Falso**). Then switch roles. Don't look at your partner's list.

Modelo: Estudiante A: **La artista Frida Kahlo es mexicana.**
Estudiante B: **Es cierto.** *o* **Es falso.**

Estudiante A:

1. El cantante Marc Anthony es puertorriqueño.
2. El ganador (*winner*) del Premio Nobel de la Paz, Óscar Arias, es costarricense.
3. La cantante Shakira es de ecuatoriana.
4. La actriz Jennifer López es estadounidense.
5. La presidenta Michelle Bachelet es chilena.

Estudiante B:

6. La actriz Penélope Cruz es española.
7. La autora Isabel Allende es hondureña.
8. El escritor Gabriel García Márquez es colombiano.
9. El jugador de básquetbol Manu Ginóbili es argentino.
10. El atleta Sammy Sosa es nicaragüense.

---

[6]For a complete listing of nationalities from around the world, see **Apéndice 3**, page A-15.

Así se pronuncia (*It's pronounced like this*)

Becoming familiar with the sounds of Spanish is the first step to an exciting encounter with the world of Spanish language and Hispanic cultures. The information recorded on the CD that accompanies your textbook will help you absorb the basic rules in this section. Soon you will be able to pronounce most Spanish words correctly.

Vowels

Each Spanish vowel has only one basic sound and is represented with one symbol. Spanish vowels are short and clipped, never drawn out. Listen carefully and repeat each sound and the corresponding examples.

a	**Panamá, ala**
e	**bebe, lee**
i	**sí, ni**
o	**solo, loco**
u	**Lulú, cucú**

A. Now listen to and repeat the following words, focusing on the vowels. Do not worry about their meanings.

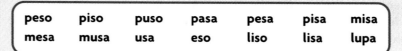

peso	**piso**	**puso**	**pasa**	**pesa**	**pisa**	**misa**
mesa	**musa**	**usa**	**eso**	**liso**	**lisa**	**lupa**

B. Line by line, repeat the following children's verse, Arbolito del Perú (*Little Tree from Peru*). Focus on the vowel sounds.

a, e, i, o, u

Arbolito del Perú.

Yo me llamo... (*add your name*)

¿Cómo te llamas tú?

Diphthongs

A diphthong is a combination of two vowels. In Spanish, the possibilities include: **a, e, o + i, u;** or **i + u;** or **u + i**. The consonant **y** also forms a diphthong when it occurs at the end of a word. Diphthongs constitute one unit of sound. Listen to and repeat the following examples. The symbol in brackets represents the sound of the diphthong.

Sound	Spelling	Examples
[ay]	**ai/ay**	*aire, traigo, caray*
[ye]	**ie**	*cielo, Diego, siempre*
[oy]	**oi/oy**	*oigo, doy, soy*
[ew]	**eu**	*euro, Europa, Eugenia*
[aw]	**au**	*aula, Paula*
[ey]	**ei/ey**	*reina, rey*
[yu]	**iu**	*ciudad, viuda*
[wy]	**ui/uy**	*cuidado, muy*

C. Let's learn to greet people and ask how they are. Repeat the following conversation, paying special attention to the diphthongs.

Estudiante A: B**ue**nos días. ¿Cómo está?

Estudiante B: M**uy** b**ie**n, grac**ia**s. ¿**Y u**sted?

Estudiante A: B**ie**n, grac**ia**s.

Repaso de vocabulario activo

Saludos y expresiones comunes

Greetings and common expressions

Buenos días, señorita/señora/señor.
Good morning, Miss/Ma'am/Sir.

Buenas tardes.
Good afternoon.

Buenas noches.
Good evening.

¡Hola!   *Hello!/Hi!*

¿Cómo está usted? ¿Cómo estás?
How are you?

¿Qué tal?   *How is it going?*

Muy bien, gracias.
Very well, thanks.

Fenomenal.   *Great.*

Regular.   *OK./So-so.*

¿Qué pasa?   *What's happening?*

¿Qué hay de nuevo?
What's new?

Pues nada.   *Not much.*

Le presento a... (*formal*)
I would like to introduce you to . . .

Te presento a... (*informal*)
I want to introduce you to . . .

Mucho gusto.
Nice meeting you.

Encantado/a.
Pleased to meet you.

Igualmente.
Nice meeting you too.

El gusto es mío.
The pleasure is mine.

¿Cómo se llama usted? ¿Cómo te llamas?
What's your name?

Me llamo...   *My name is . . .*

¿De dónde es usted? ¿De dónde eres?   *Where are you from?*

Soy de...   *I am from . . .*

Perdón./ Disculpe.
Pardon me. Excuse me. (≠ Con permiso.)

Lo siento (mucho).   *I am (very) sorry.*

Con permiso.   *Pardon me. Excuse me. (≠ Perdón./ Disculpe.)*

Por favor.   *Please.*

(Muchas) gracias.   *Thank you (very much.)*

De nada.   *You're welcome.*

Adiós.   *Good-bye.*

Hasta luego.   *See you later.*

Hasta pronto.   *See you soon.*

Hasta mañana.   *See you tomorrow.*

Chao.   *Bye./So-long.*

Verbo   *Verb*

ser   *to be*

Los días de la semana
The days of the week

lunes   *Monday*

martes   *Tuesday*

miércoles   *Wednesday*

jueves   *Thursday*

viernes   *Friday*

sábado   *Saturday*

domingo   *Sunday*

¿Qué día es hoy?
What day is it?

el día   *day*

la semana   *week*

el fin de semana   *weekend*

Los meses   Months

enero   *January*

febrero   *February*

marzo   *March*

abril   *April*

mayo   *May*

junio   *June*

julio   *July*

agosto   *August*

septiembre   *September*

octubre   *October*

noviembre   *November*

diciembre   *December*

¿Cuál es la fecha de hoy?/ ¿Qué fecha es hoy?   *What's the date today?*

¿Qué hora es?   What time is it?

la hora   *time/hour*

y/ menos   *and/less*

cuarto/ media   *quarter/half*

de la mañana/ tarde/ noche   *in the morning/afternoon/evening*

Es mediodía./ medianoche.
It's noon./midnight.

Autoprueba y repaso WILEY PLUS ✓

I. Meeting and greeting each other. Complete the conversations. In some cases, there is more than one possible answer.

1. PROFESORA: Buenos días. ¿Cómo estás?
   PEPITA: _____. ¿Y usted?
   PROFESORA: _____.

2. PROFESORA: _____?
   PEPITA: Me llamo Pepita.

3. CARMEN: ¡Hola, Pepita! ¿ _____?
   PEPITA: Regular. ¿Y tú?
   CARMEN: _____.

4. PEPITA: Profesora, le presento a Carmen Martínez.
   PROFESORA: _____.
   CARMEN: _____.

5. PEPITA: ¿Cómo te llamas?
   MANUEL: _____. ¿Y tú?
   PEPITA: _____.
   MANUEL: Encantado, Pepita.
   PEPITA: _____.

6. CARMEN: ¿_____?
   PEPITA: Son las 9:30.
   CARMEN: Pues, tengo una clase ahora. Hasta luego.
   PEPITA: _____.

II. Subject pronouns and the verb *ser*. Tell where the people are from. Write sentences using the correct form of the verb **ser**.

   Modelo: yo / de México; ella / de Panamá
   Yo soy de México pero (*but*) ella es de Panamá.

1. ellos / de Chile; nosotras / de México
2. tú / de Colombia; ustedes / de España
3. Luis / de El Salvador; Juan y Elena / de Honduras

III. Counting from 0 to 99. Tell how much each item costs. Write out the numbers ($ = **dólar/dólares**).

1. los jeans $35.00
2. el suéter $57.00
3. la chaqueta $72.00
4. el sombrero $26.00
5. el video $15.00
6. el CD $9.00

IV. The days of the week. Complete the sentences.

1. Vamos (*We go*) a la clase de español los _____ y _____.

2. Muchos estudiantes van (*go*) a fiestas _____ y _____.

V. Indicating dates. Write the dates in Spanish. Include only the day and the month.

   Modelo: 2/1/08 (día/mes/año)
   Es el dos de enero.

1. 14/2/09
2. 1/4/09
3. 4/7/08
4. 23/11/08
5. 25/12/10

VI. Telling time. What time is it? Give both possible answers when it is a quarter after the hour, such as **Es la una y cuarto.** or **Es la una y quince.**

   Modelo: 1:10 P.M.
   Es la una y diez de la tarde.

1. 1:15 P.M.
2. 9:30 P.M.
3. 5:50 P.M.
4. 11:40 P.M.
5. 12:00 P.M.

VII. General review. Answer the questions in complete sentences.

1. ¿Cómo te llamas?
2. ¿Cómo estás?
3. ¿Eres inflexible y arrogante? ¿Eres responsable y generoso/a?
4. ¿De dónde eres?
5. ¿Cuál es la fecha de tu cumpleaños?
6. ¿Qué día es hoy?
7. ¿Qué hora es?
8. ¿A qué hora es la clase de español?

VIII. Culture. Answer the following questions.

1. How would a male and a female student greet each other in Argentina? And in Spain?
2. What is the **Día de los Reyes Magos** and when is it celebrated?
3. What is a person's **Día del santo**?

Answers to the *Autoprueba y repaso* are found in **Apéndice 2**.

La vida universitaria

By the end of this chapter you will be able to:

- Talk about computers, the language lab, and the "smart" classroom

- Talk about where you are going on campus

- Talk about your class schedule

- Talk about activities related to university life

Así se dice	Así se forma	Cultura	Dicho y hecho
• La vida universitaria • ¿Adónde van? • ¿Cuándo... ?	**1.** Nouns and articles **2.** **Ir** + **a** + destination **3.** The present tense of regular **-ar** verbs **4.** The present tense of regular **-er/-ir** verbs; **hacer** and **salir**	• Puerto Rico • La vida universitaria en el mundo hispano • Artes musicales: La bomba y la plena	• La Universidad de Puerto Rico • Tu universidad • Guía para los visitantes

ENTRANDO AL TEMA

1. Approximately what percent of students at your school live in campus dormitories? What percent of students live at home? What are some of the reasons that students might live at home?

2. To fulfill your degree requirements, do you need to complete "general education" courses in fields that have little or no relationship to your major? Would you prefer a system in which you took only courses related to your major?

3. ¿Cierto o falso?

a. Puerto Ricans are United States citizens.	**Cierto**	**Falso**
b. There are as many Puerto Ricans living on the mainland United States as on the island of Puerto Rico.	**Cierto**	**Falso**
c. *Salsa* music originated in Puerto Rico.	**Cierto**	**Falso**

If you are not sure about the answers to these questions, you will find out in this chapter.

Así se dice

La vida universitaria

En el laboratorio

- la impresora
- imprimir
- el trabajo escrito
- el papel (una hoja de papel)
- la papelera

- los audífonos
- escuchar
- el disco compacto/el CD

- navegar por la red
- buscar información
- la página web, el sitio web
- el ratón

UNIVERSIDAD

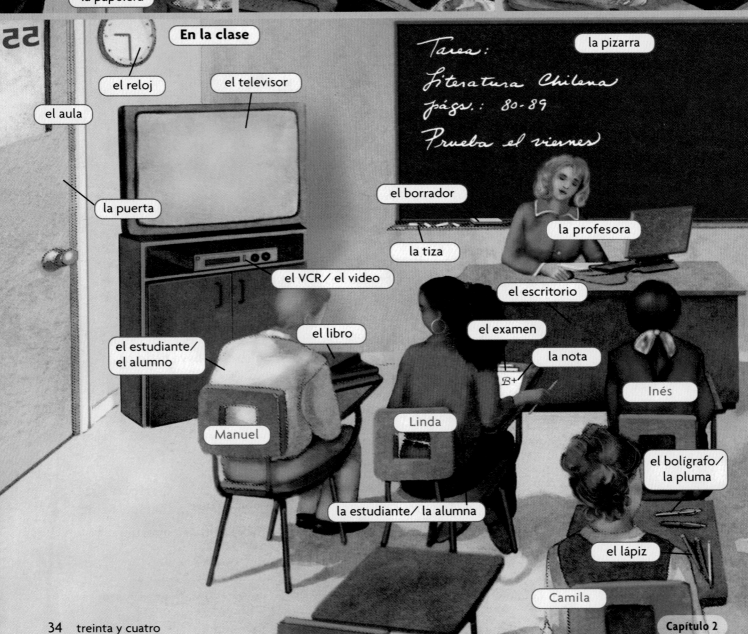

En la clase

- la pizarra

Tarea:
Literatura Chilena
págs.: 80-89

Prueba el viernes

- el reloj
- el televisor
- el aula
- la puerta
- el borrador
- la tiza
- la profesora
- el VCR/ el video
- el escritorio
- el examen
- el libro
- la nota
- el estudiante/ el alumno
- Inés
- Manuel
- Linda
- la estudiante/ la alumna
- el bolígrafo/ la pluma
- el lápiz
- Camila

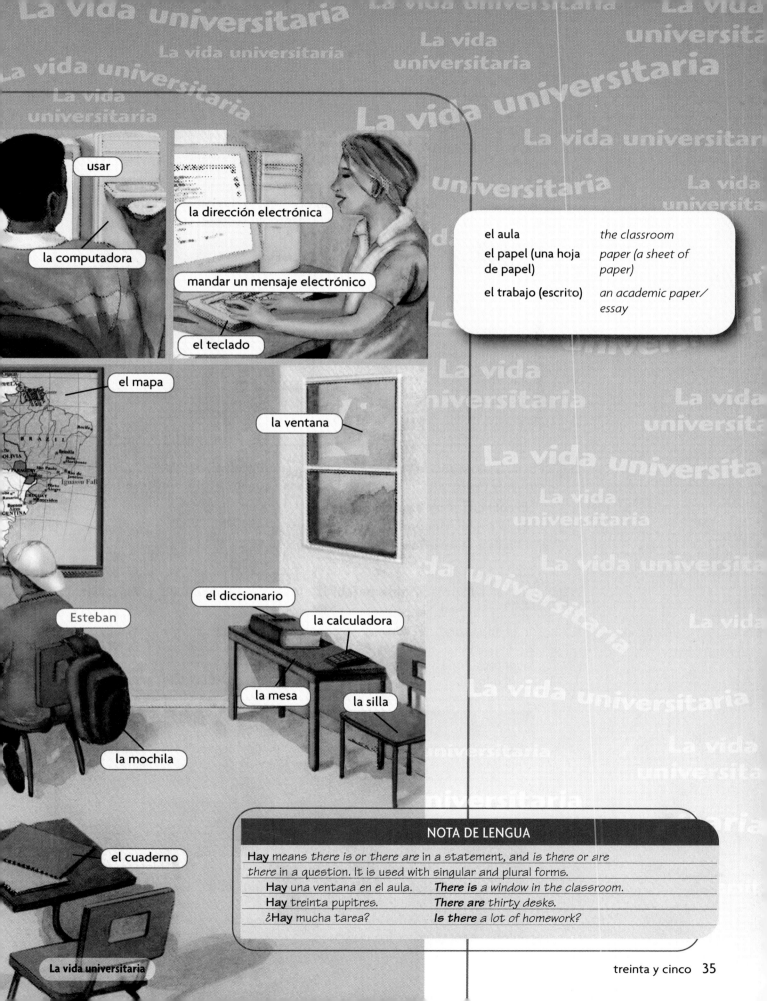

usar

la dirección electrónica

la computadora

mandar un mensaje electrónico

el teclado

el aula	the classroom
el papel (una hoja de papel)	paper (a sheet of paper)
el trabajo (escrito)	an academic paper/ essay

el mapa

la ventana

el diccionario

la calculadora

Esteban

la mesa

la silla

la mochila

el cuaderno

NOTA DE LENGUA

Hay means *there is* or *there are* in a statement, and *is there* or *are there* in a question. It is used with singular and plural forms.

Hay una ventana en el aula.	**There is** a window in the classroom.
Hay treinta pupitres.	**There are** thirty desks.
¿**Hay** mucha tarea?	**Is there** a lot of homework?

Así se dice

2-1 ¿Cuántos hay?

Paso 1. Work with a partner. Look at the following chart and fill in how many of each item there are (**hay**) in your classroom. Fill in the last line of the chart with an item that you feel is important for a classroom to have.

En el aula, hay...	(Número)
sillas	
ventanas	
televisores	
computadoras	
diccionarios	
pizarras	
_____	

Paso 2. Now decide how well-equipped (**equipada**) your classroom is. You can probably figure out the meanings of the cognates in the three options below.

El aula está **muy bien** equipada.

El aula está **adecuadamente** equipada.

El aula está **insuficientemente** equipada.

2-2 **Asociación de palabras.** Indicate which word does not fit with the others.

1. la impresora   el ratón   la computadora   la tiza   el CD
2. el examen   el lápiz   la pluma   el cuaderno   la calculadora
3. el teclado   la mesa   la ventana   la puerta   la silla
4. el reloj   el mapa   el borrador   la mochila   la pizarra

---

ESTRATEGIA PARA LEER

Scanning for cognates Anticipate information about the content of this ad by finding words that are cognates—words that are identical or similar in the two languages and have the same meaning. How many can you find?

2-3 **Internet para todos.**

Paso 1. Look at the advertisement on page 37 and circle the things you see:

dirección de una página web   libros   estudiantes   un ratón   una clase

Paso 2. Now scan the headings and text looking for cognates. How many can you find? Share them with a classmate.

Paso 3. Can you anticipate what is being advertised?

 Paso 4. Read the text and answer the questions with a classmate. Do not worry if you do not understand some of the words.

1. El servicio Internet de Telmex ofrece muchas ventajas (*advantages*). ¿Qué ventajas del servicio son importantes para (*for*) ustedes? Mencionen tres o cuatro.

2. ¿Qué tipo de información representan las imágenes del anuncio? Identifiquen estas categorías: **naturaleza, historia, tecnología y espacio, música, teatro, aviación** y **deportes** (*sports*).

3. ¿Qué tipo de sitios de Internet son interesantes para ustedes?

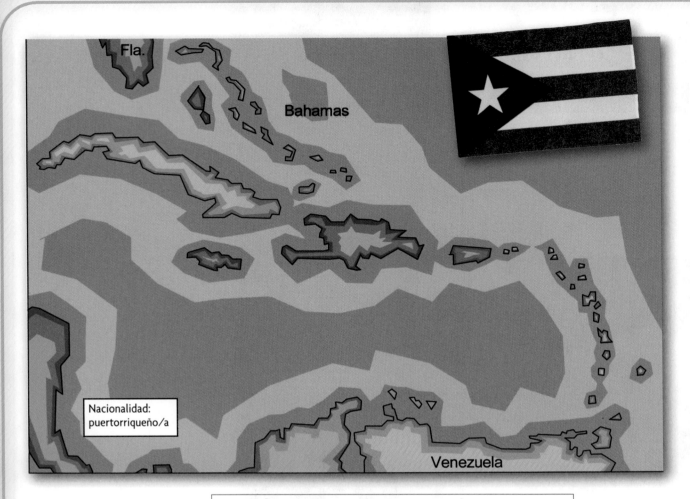

Bahamas

Fla.

Venezuela

Nacionalidad:
puertorriqueño/a

Antes de leer

Which of the islands on the map above is Puerto Rico?

UN TERRITORIO DIVERSO

Puerto Rico is a relatively small island—approximately 100 miles long and 40 miles wide—but it has a rich history. The original inhabitants, the Taíno Indians, called the island *Borinken*, or *Land of the great lords*. Today, the word **Boricua** is still popularly used to refer to the people of Puerto Rico.

A Taíno **bohío**,
or hut

LA HISTORIA

Columbus landed on Puerto Rico in 1493, on his second voyage from Spain, and the island became part of the Spanish empire. Although the Taíno population quickly diminished, many Taíno words made their way into the Spanish language. For instance:

hamaca	*hammock*		canoa	*canoe*
maracas	*maracas (musical instrument)*		barbacoa	*barbeque*

The Honorable Aníbal Acevedo-Vilá, Governor of the Commonwealth of Puerto Rico

Painting of the *Paseo Boricua* (*Puerto Rican Promenade*) in Chicago

In 1898, Puerto Rico was ceded to the United States as a result of the Spanish–American War, and in 1917, Puerto Ricans were granted United States citizenship. Since 1952, Puerto Rico has functioned as a self-governing territory of the United States, called a Commonwealth, and has its own governor. The 3.9 million residents of the island of Puerto Rico do not vote in United States elections, but the 3.8 million Puerto Rican residents living on the mainland are eligible to vote.

On the mainland United States, the Puerto Rican community represents the second largest national origin group among Hispanics after the Mexican origin population. Puerto Ricans on the mainland are predominantly concentrated in the eastern states of New York, Florida, New Jersey, Pennsylvania, and Massachusetts. During the last 30 years, there has also been a significant growth in the Puerto Rican communities located in Connecticut, Illinois, California, Ohio, and Texas.

Después de leer

1. Notice that there are two flags behind the Governor in the photo. In what year were Puerto Ricans granted United States citizenship? 1917

2. Why are Puerto Ricans often referred to as **Boricuas**?

Old San Juan (**El Viejo San Juan**), the capital of Puerto Rico

Así se forma

1. Identifying gender and number: Nouns; definite and indefinite articles

All nouns in Spanish have two important grammatical features: gender (masculine and feminine) and number (singular and plural). Note that, although gender may reflect a biological distinction in some nouns referring to persons and animals, it is merely a grammatical detail in nouns that refer to nonliving things.

The articles that accompany nouns must agree with respect to gender and number. Therefore, articles have masculine and feminine forms as well as singular and plural forms.

Los estudiantes están en clase. **Un** alumno escribe en **el** cuaderno. Dos alumnos escriben en **la** pizarra. **La** profesora conversa con **unas** alumnas.

Masculine and Feminine Nouns

Masculino	Femenino

• Most nouns referring to a male
  el estudiante **el** profesor **el** señor
	• Most nouns referring to a female
	  la estudiante **la** profesora **la** señora

• Most nouns that end in **-o**
  el escritori**o** **el** diccionari**o**
	• Most nouns that end in **-a**[1]
	  la impresora **la** puerta

• Most nouns that end in **-r** or **-l**
  el televiso**r** **el** borrado**r** **el** pape**l**
	• Almost all nouns ending in **-ión** and **-d**
	  la informac**ión** **la** orac**ión** **la** actitu**d**

• BUT some nouns that end in **-a** are masculine
  el mapa el día el problema
    el programa
	• BUT some nouns that end in **-o** are feminine
	  la mano la radio

Finally, some nouns ending in **-e** and **-ista** can be either masculine or feminine

  el estudiante   **el** turista

  la estudiante   **la** turista

la estudiante

el estudiante

Number

- Singular nouns ending in a vowel form the plural by adding **-s**
  un estudiante   dos estudiante**s**

- Nouns ending in a consonant add **-es**
  un reloj   dos reloj**es**

- But nouns ending in **-z** change to **-ces**
  un lápiz   dos lápi**ces**[2]

---

[1]**Aula** is feminine even though it uses the article **el**. The plural form is **las aulas**.
[2]Spanish-spelling rules disallow the combination z + e. Instead change the **z** to a **c**.

Definite and indefinite articles

The definite article or indefinite article that accompanies a noun must agree with the noun in gender and number. Therefore, articles have masculine, feminine, singular, and plural forms.

	Artículos definidos *the*		Artículos indefinidos *a/an; some*	
	singular	plural	singular	plural
masculino	**el** alumno	**los** alumnos	**un** alumno	**unos** alumnos
femenino	**la** alumna	**las** alumnas	**una** alumna	**unas** alumnas

NOTA DE LENGUA

Note that when talking about a group that includes both masculine and feminine nouns, we use the masculine plural.

dos chicos y tres chicas → un**os** chic**os**

2-4 Comparando (*Comparing*) mochilas.

Paso 1. Complete the description of the backpack contents of a student at the University of Puerto Rico by marking the correct option in each sentence. Then in the second column, indicate whether you have these same items in your backpack.

Modelo: hay un … ☒ cuaderno pluma

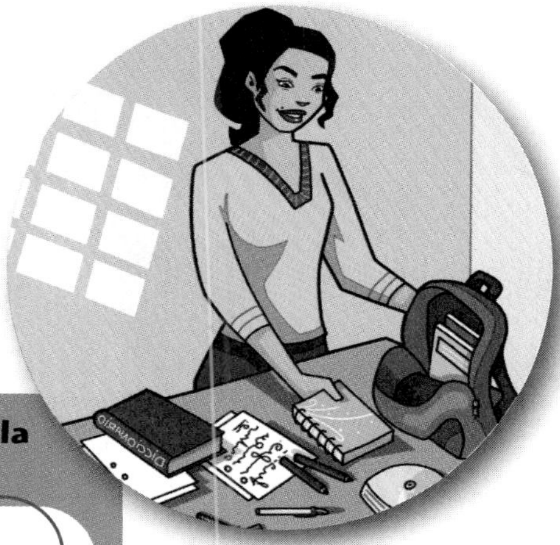

En la mochila del estudiante de la Universidad de Puerto Rico…			¿Hay en mi mochila también (*also*)?	
1. hay unos	☐ lápices	☐ diccionario	Sí	No
2. hay una	☐ cuaderno	☐ pluma	Sí	No
3. hay unas	☐ hojas de papel	☐ trabajos escritos	Sí	No
4. hay un	☐ calculadora	☐ disco compacto	Sí	No
5. hay una	☐ pluma	☐ bolígrafo	Sí	No
6. hay unos	☐ calculadoras	☐ libros	Sí	No

Así se forma

 Paso 2. Now work with a partner. Write down your guesses about the contents of your partner's backpack using the indefinite articles **un, unos, una, unas,** the vocabulary above, and some of the following words.

Modelo: **En la mochila de Karen, hay unos discos compactos, una pluma, unos libros y unos cuadernos.**

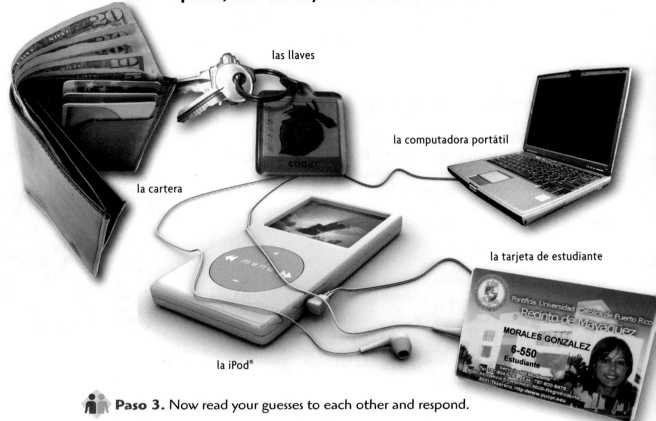

las llaves

la computadora portátil

la cartera

la tarjeta de estudiante

la iPod®

Pontificia Universidad Católica de Puerto Rico
Recinto de Mayagüez
MORALES GONZALEZ
6-550
Estudiante

 Paso 3. Now read your guesses to each other and respond.

Modelo: [Karen may respond to the example above]

Sí, en mi mochila hay una pluma y hay unos libros, pero no hay discos compactos o cuadernos.

NOTA CULTURAL

El coquí

There is a tiny tree frog in Puerto Rico called the **coquí**; its name imitates the sound that it makes at night. The sound of **coquíes**, often very loud in the countryside, is dearly missed by many Puerto Ricans who are away from the island. The **coquí** is a beloved symbol of Puerto Rico. **Coquíes** brought to the mainland United States usually do not survive, although they have flourished in the state of Hawaii due to the tropical climate.

2. The present tense and talking about going places: *Ir + a +* destination

¿No vas a la biblioteca esta noche?

No, voy a una fiesta.

To state where you are going, use the verb **ir** (*to go*) + **a** (*to*) + *destination*.

ir *to go*		
(yo)	**voy**	**Voy** <u>a la clase</u> todos los días (*every day*).
(tú)	**vas**	¿**Vas** <u>al teatro</u> con frecuencia?
(usted, él, ella)	**va**	Ella **va** <u>a la universidad</u>.
(nosotros/as)	**vamos**	**Vamos** <u>al restaurante</u>.
(vosotros/as)	**vais**	¿**Vais** <u>al café</u>?
(ustedes, ellos/as)	**van**	Ellas **van** <u>al gimnasio</u>.

Observe the uses of the present tense as illustrated with examples of **ir** + **a** + *destination*. The Spanish present tense can be used to:

- talk about actions that occur in the present.
  Voy al gimnasio ahora.   *I'm going* to the gym now.

- talk about recurring or habitual actions.
  Voy al gimnasio todos los días.   *I go* to the gym every day.
  ¿**Vas** con frecuencia?   *Do you go* frequently?

- talk about actions in the near future when accompanied by phrases indicating the future.
  María **va** a una fiesta   *María **will go/is going** to a party*
  esta noche.   *tonight.*

Así se dice

¿Adónde van? (*Where are you going?/ Where do you go?*)

Vamos a la clase de...

español, inglés
francés, alemán (*German*)
arte, música, literatura
religión, filosofía
historia, ciencias políticas
psicología/ sociología
biología/ física/ química (*chemistry*)
matemáticas/ álgebra/ cálculo
computación, informática (*computer science*)
contabilidad (*accounting*)
economía

Vamos a...

la universidad
la biblioteca (*library*)
la librería (*bookstore*)
la oficina del profesor/ de la profesora
el centro estudiantil
el restaurante, la cafetería
el gimnasio
la casa (*home*),[3] el apartamento
la residencia (estudiantil) (*dorm*)
el cuarto (*room*)
la fiesta

¿Cuándo (*When*) vamos?

ahora	*now*
más tarde	*later*
antes de/ después de (clase)	*before/ after (class)*
esta mañana/ tarde/ noche	*this morning/ this afternoon/ tonight*
(casi) siempre	*(almost) always*
(casi) todos los días	*(almost) every day*
con frecuencia	*frequently*
a veces	*sometimes*
casi nunca	*rarely*
nunca	*never*

NOTA DE LENGUA

a (*to*) + **el** (*the*) = **al**	Vamos **al** cuarto de Anita.
a + **la, los, las** = *no change*	Vamos **a la** biblioteca.
de (*from, about, of*) + **el** = **del**	Vamos a la oficina **del** profesor.
de + **la, los, las** = *no change*	Vamos a la oficina **de la** profesora.

---

[3]Note that the expression is **ir a casa**, without an article.

2-5 ¿Cuándo? Read the sentences below and indicate whether they are referring to a current moment present (**ahora**) action, to habitual/recurrent actions (**habitual**), or to an action in the near future (**futuro**) action.

	ahora	habitual	futuro
1. ¡Juan, espera (*wait*)! ¿Adónde vas?			
2. Voy al gimnasio los lunes y jueves.			
3. El sábado voy a una fiesta.			
4. Ahora voy a clase de inglés...			
5. ...y esta tarde voy a clase de historia.			
6. Ustedes siempre van tarde a clase.			

2-6 La vida universitaria.

Paso 1. Indicate how often you go to the following places.

	(casi) todos los días	con frecuencia	a veces	casi nunca
1. Voy a la biblioteca.			✔	
2. Voy al laboratorio de computadoras.		✔		
3. Voy a las horas de oficina de un profesor.				✔
4. Voy al centro estudiantil.				✔
5. Voy al gimnasio.				
6. Voy a la cafetería de la universidad.				
7. Voy a un restaurante.				
8. Voy a fiestas.				

Paso 2. Now work with a classmate. Take turns restating the statements above as questions, remembering to use the **tú** form. Listen and note your partner's answers.

Modelo: Estudiante A: **¿Cuándo vas a la biblioteca?**
Estudiante B: **Voy a la biblioteca a veces./ No voy casi nunca.**

Paso 3. Now tell your classmates what you and your partner have in common. Remember to use the **nosotros** form.

Modelo: Pablo y yo casi nunca vamos...

2-7 ¿Es lógico?

 Paso 1. Listen to the statements and indicate whether they are logical or illogical, based on what the following individuals have.

Modelo: You see: Carmen usa un libro de español.

You hear: Va a la clase de francés.

You choose: **Ilógico**

1. Marta y Alberto usan unos microscopios.	Lógico Ilógico
2. Alfonso usa un CD–Rom (cederóm) para la computadora.	Lógico Ilógico
3. Inés usa un violín.	Lógico Ilógico
4. Yo uso un tubo con ácido sulfúrico.	Lógico Ilógico
5. Tú usas un libro sobre Picasso.	Lógico Ilógico
6. Natalia y Linda usan una copia de *Hamlet*.	Lógico Ilógico

Paso 2. Now write sentences guessing where the following students are going.

Modelo: Manuel usa una calculadora.

      Va a la clase de matemáticas.

1. Camila y Linda usan un libro sobre (*about*) Abraham Lincoln.
2. Nosotros usamos libros sobre Sigmund Freud.
3. Ustedes usan un libro sobre la Biblia y el Corán.
4. Tú necesitas un libro sobre la política de los EE.UU. (Estados Unidos).
5. Yo necesito un libro sobre finanzas.
6. María, Jessica y yo necesitamos *Dicho y hecho*.

2-8 El horario (*Schedule*). Work with a classmate (write his/her name in the chart on page 47).

 Paso 1. Give your classmate a list of your classes. Then, take turns asking each other the days and times of your classes and write them in the chart (use the last row for any classes or labs after 5:00 P.M.).

> **REMEMBER**
>
> ¿Qué hora es? ≠ ¿A qué hora es?

Modelo: Estudiante A: **¿Cúando vas a la clase de química?**

Estudiante B: **Voy los martes y los jueves.**

Estudiante A: **¿A qué hora vas?**

      ...

El horario de _____					
	lunes	martes	miércoles	jueves	viernes
8:00 A.M.					
9:00 A.M.					
10:00 A.M.					
11:00 A.M.					
1:00 P.M.					
2:00 P.M.					
3:00 P.M.					
4:00 P.M.					
5:00 P.M.					

HINT

For additional course names, see **Apéndice 3**, p. A-17.

 Paso 2. Check the schedule your partner filled in about your daily routine. Let him/her know if there are any mistakes so that he/she can fix them.

Modelo: **No voy a clase de inglés los martes. Voy los miércoles.**

 Paso 3. Compare your schedules. Are they similar or different? Be prepared to report to the class.

Modelo: **Nuestros horarios son similares/ diferentes: yo voy... y/ pero Jason va...**

2-9 **¿Adónde vas después de las clases?**

Paso 1. In your notebook, complete the sentences below, indicating where you will be going today after class. You can write more than one place for each sentence.

Después de las clases voy a ...
Más tarde ...
Esta noche ...

 Paso 2. Now in small groups, compare your activities.

Modelo: Estudiante A: **Mike, ¿adónde vas después de las clases?**
Estudiante B: **Voy a la cafetería, ¿y ustedes?**
Estudiante C: **Yo voy a...**

NOTA CULTURAL

Phosphorescent bays
There is a small island off of Puerto Rico called Vieques, which contains a mangrove swamp with special inhabitants: Millions of tiny glowing organisms called *dinoflagellates* (measuring 1/500 of an inch) that react to the slightest disturbance in the water. A fish, boat, or a hand causes them to give off a blue-green light that traces the moving object. Tourists who take nighttime tours there are allowed to swim in the water. Few places in the world have such a high concentration of dinoflagellates. Go to www.biobay.com to see pictures of the phosphorescent bays in Vieques.

Escenas

Camila

Alfonso

small **Un pequeño° accidente**

va... in a hurry; collides *En un corredor de la universidad. Alfonso va muy de prisa° y choca°*
fall; to the floor *con Camila. Sus libros, cuadernos y otras cosas caen° al suelo°.*

> **Listening strategy**
> When you listen to someone, it is helpful to anticipate what you might hear, based on what you know about the person or your general knowledge of the topic.

Paso 1. Based on the title and introduction, try to anticipate whether the following statements may be true (**Cierto**) or false (**Falso**).

	Cierto	Falso
1. Alfonso va a casa.	☐	☐
2. Camila saluda (*greets*) a Alfonso.	☐	☐
3. Alfonso recoge (*picks up*) los libros de Camila.	☐	☐

> **Listening strategy**
> When you listen to a conversation or an audio text in Spanish, you will hear many words you do not know. Don't let that overwhelm you. Instead, ignore what you do not understand and focus on listening for words you do know, as well as other features of spoken language (i.e., tone) that will help you get the general meaning.

Paso 2. Listen to Alfonso and Camila and circle the appropriate answer.

1. Alfonso va...   **a.** al gimnasio.   **b.** al laboratorio.   **c.** a la biblioteca.
2. Camila necesita (*needs*)...   **a.** un libro.   **b.** un CD-rom.   **c.** una impresora.
3. Camila quiere (*wants to*) ir...   **a.** a clase.   **b.** al laboratorio.   **c.** a la cafetería.

Paso 3. Look at the questions below and listen again. Then answer the questions.

1. ¿Quién llega tarde a clase?
2. ¿Qué hora es?
3. ¿Qué trabajo necesita imprimir Camila?
4. ¿Cuántas impresoras hay en el laboratorio?
5. ¿Alfonso va con Camila a la cafetería?

Paso 4. Listen one more time as you read along. Then check your answers to the previous questions.

Alfonso
y Camila: ¡Ay!

Camila: ¡Hombre! ¡Qué rápido vas!°

¡Qué... ! You are going so fast!

Alfonso: Perdón, Camila. Es que voy tarde a clase.

Camila: No es tarde. Son las 9:20. ¿Adónde vas?

I have Alfonso: Voy al laboratorio. Tengo° una clase de computación a las 9:30.

Camila: Hum... Yo necesito imprimir un trabajo de historia del arte. ¿Hay una impresora en el laboratorio?

Alfonso: Sí, hay dos.

pick up (*Alfonso y Camila recogen° las cosas del suelo.*)

Camila: Estos son mis bolígrafos.

Alfonso: Aquí está el libro de matemáticas.

Camila: Gracias.

Alfonso: De nada. Bueno, vamos al laboratorio.

Camila: ¡Yo necesito un café! ¿Vamos a la cafetería un momento?

now Alfonso: ¡Ay, Camila! Lo siento, pero tengo la clase ahora°.

2-10 **La Universidad de Puerto Rico.** Imagine that you are studying abroad at the Río Piedras campus of the University of Puerto Rico (UPR). Using the campus map as a guide, answer the following questions.

PALABRAS ÚTILES

Facultad de...
School of . . .
estacionamiento
parking lot

1. ¿Adónde van los estudiantes para...

   comer (*to eat*)?   visitar al médico?   buscar libros?

   comprar (*to buy*) libros?   hablar con el decano (*dean*)?

   ver obras (*works*) de arte?   estacionar el auto?

   obtener una fotografía para su tarjeta de identificación (*ID*)?

   hacer un programa de radio?

2. ¿Cuántos estacionamientos hay? ¿Cuántas facultades?

3. ¿A qué facultad van los estudiantes para una clase de educación? ¿Y una clase de biología?

4. En la UPR, ¿hay departamentos, facultades, etc. que no hay en tu universidad? ¿Cuáles?

5. ¿Hay residencias estudiantiles en la UPR?

Mapa del Recinto de Río Piedras de la Universidad de Puerto Rico

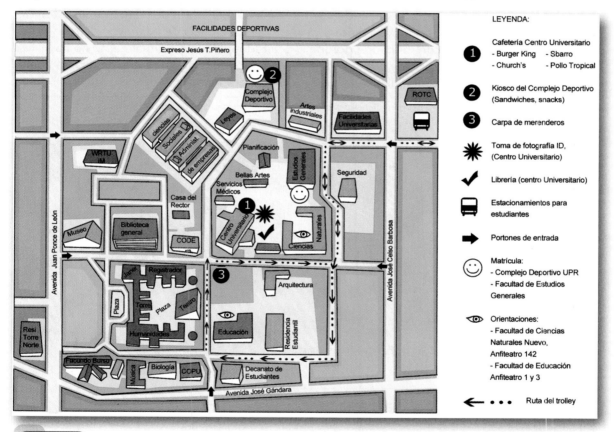

2-11 **Guía para los visitantes.** Using a map of your campus, begin a project to produce a *Guide for Spanish-Speaking Visitors* to your school. Select ten important or interesting places and write the corresponding Spanish names. Your professor can provide you with assistance. Be sure to keep your list for inclusion in the guide.

PALABRAS ÚTILES

edificio   *building*
estadio   *stadium*

Cultura: La vida universitaria en el mundo hispano

Antes de leer

What are some of your favorite aspects about college so far?

- Ability to take a wide range of courses
- Living in a dorm
- Sports
- Other: _____

While reading the following, take note of aspects that are similar and different from what you've noted above.

La mayoría de las universidades hispanas son instituciones públicas. En muchos países[1] hispanos, el gobierno[2] financia el costo de la educación en la universidad; los estudiantes sólo compran[3] los libros. Sin embargo[4], también existen universidades privadas. Los estudiantes universitarios normalmente viven con sus padres porque es más económico y porque, por lo general, no hay residencias estudiantiles.

Las clases son muy especializadas y los programas son muy rígidos. Un estudiante de medicina, por ejemplo[5], sólo toma cursos de medicina. No toma cursos en otras áreas. Por eso[6] los estudiantes hispanos seleccionan una carrera[7] antes de comenzar sus estudios.

A diferencia de las universidades estadounidenses, normalmente no hay equipos deportivos[8] ni organizaciones como las "fraternidades".

[1]countries [2]government [3]buy [4]However [5]for example [6]For this reason [7]major [8]sports teams

Investig@ en INTERNET

You really want to learn more Spanish and start looking into Spanish language programs in Puerto Rico for the summer. Find a program you are interested in and print out or write down all the important information (dates, price, what is included in the program). Be ready to explain why you chose that program.

Universidad de Puerto Rico en San Juan

Biblioteca de la Universidad del País Vasco, España

Después de leer

Are the following common in universities in Latin America?

1. Las residencias estudiantiles — ☐ Son comunes. ☐ No son comunes.
2. Los equipos deportivos — ☐ Son comunes. ☐ No son comunes.
3. Programas de estudio estructurados — ☐ Son comunes. ☐ No son comunes.

Conexiones y contrastes. Write two or three main differences between your college or university and Hispanic universities. Later you will add them to the *Guide for Spanish-Speaking Visitors* that the class will prepare.

Así se forma

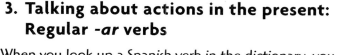

Alfonso, ¿estudias todas las noches?

¡Sí!

3. Talking about actions in the present: Regular -ar verbs

When you look up a Spanish verb in the dictionary, you will find the infinitive form, which in Spanish always ends in either **-ar**, **-er**, or **-ir**. It is important to notice which of these endings the infinitive has, because each type is conjugated in a different way.

In this section you will learn about regular **-ar** verbs.

Observe what happens when we use **hablar** to talk about the present (*I speak, he speaks, etc.*). Note that you drop the **-ar** from the infinitive and replace it with the endings indicated. The endings correspond to the subject of the verb.

hablar *to speak*
hablar → habl-

(yo)	habl**o**[4]
(tú)	habl**as**
(usted, él/ella)	habl**a**
(nosotros/as)	habl**amos**
(vosotros/as)	habl**áis**
(ustedes, ellos/as)	habl**an**

Read about what Natalia and her friend Camila do.

Camila

Natalia

Las actividades en la universidad

Natalia y Camila **llegan** a la universidad a las ocho de la mañana. Natalia **desayuna** en la cafetería de la universidad, pero Camila nunca desayuna, sólo° **compra** una Pepsi. Primero° van a la clase de psicología. Ahí° escuchan al profesor y **toman apuntes**. Luego van a la clase de español donde **practican, hablan** y **estudian** con los compañeros de clase. Por la tarde van a la biblioteca para estudiar y **preparar** sus lecciones. Son excelentes estudiantes. Generalmente **sacan** buenas notas en las pruebas y en los exámenes. Después de **cenar**, Camila **trabaja** tres horas en la librería de la universidad. Natalia **regresa** temprano a su casa, prepara su trabajo para la clase de historia, navega por la red y manda mensajes electrónicos a sus amigos.

only
First; There

cenar	*to have dinner*	**regresar**	*to return, go back*
comprar	*to buy*	**sacar... notas**	*to get ... grades*
desayunar	*to have breakfast*	**tomar apuntes**	*to take notes*
hablar	*to speak*	**trabajar**	*to work*
llegar	*to arrive*		

[4]Unlike nouns, Spanish verbs do not have gender: Both males and females say **hablo** (*I speak*).

2-12 Un día típico en la universidad.

 Paso 1. Read the following statements and indicate whether these activities are something you and most students at your school do (**Sí**) or don't do (**No**).

Yo	Sí/No	Los estudiantes en mi universidad	Sí/No
Desayuno en la cafetería casi todos los días.		Desayunan en la cafetería casi todos los días.	
Tomo apuntes en todas las clases.		Toman apuntes en todas las clases.	
Estudio en la biblioteca con frecuencia.		Estudian en la biblioteca con frecuencia.	
Practico español en el laboratorio.		Practican español en el laboratorio.	
Además de (*Besides*) estudiar, trabajo.		Además de estudiar, trabajan.	
Mando muchos mensajes electrónicos.		Mandan muchos mensajes electrónicos.	
Hablo con mi familia todas las noches.		Hablan con su familia todas las noches.	

 Paso 2. Compare your individual answers in small groups. Then answer the questions below.

Modelo: ¿Ustedes llegan a clase temprano?

¿Son sus actividades diarias similares o diferentes? ¿Son ustedes estudiantes "típicos"?

2-13 Imagina.

 Paso 1. In pairs, select one person to guess about. Write down five guesses about what you think that person does. Use verbs you have learned so far or from the box **Palabras útiles** on this page.

Modelo: Tina baila todas las noches.

Paso 2. Now, share some of your sentences with the class. The selected person will indicate whether your guesses are true (**Cierto**) or false (**Falso**).

PALABRAS ÚTILES	
bailar	*to dance*
mirar	*to watch*
cocinar	*to cook*
regresar	*to return*
descansar	*to rest*
viajar	*to travel*
limpiar	*to clean*
visitar	*to visit*

2-14 Las actividades de otras (*other*) personas.

 Paso 1. Describe some daily activities of the following people. Form sentences using verbs you have learned so far or from the box **Palabras útiles** on page 52.

1. Mi compañero/a de cuarto...
2. Mis amigos y yo...
3. Mi padre/madre...
4. Los estudiantes universitarios de Puerto Rico... (¡imagina!)

Paso 2. Share your descriptions in small groups. Are your descriptions of these peoples' daily activities mostly similar or different?

Así se dice

¿Cuándo... ?

La clase empieza a las nueve de la mañana.

Natalia llega **temprano**.

Pepita llega a **tiempo**.

Esteban llega **tarde**.

Por/ En	la mañana/ la tarde/ la noche...	*In the morning/afternoon/night . . .*
Toda	la mañana/ la tarde...	*All morning/afternoon . . .*
Todo	el día/ el fin de semana...	*All day/weekend . . .*
Todas	las mañanas/ las tardes...	*Every morning/afternoon . . .*
Todos	los días/ fines de semana...	*Every day/weekend . . .*

Así se dice

2-15 Cosas en común.

 Paso 1. Complete the first column with information that is true for you.

Paso 2. In the second column, write the questions that you will ask a classmate to find out if you have things in common.

¿Cuándo?	Preguntas
Modelo: Tomo __café__ **por** __las mañanas__.	¿Tomas café por la mañana?
Tomo _____ por _____.	
Casi siempre llego a mis clases (temprano, a tiempo... ?) _____.	
Voy a la cafetería _____.	
Voy a la biblioteca _____.	
Trabajo _____.	
Escucho música _____.	
Navego por la red _____.	
Mando mensajes electrónicos _____ _____.	
Voy a fiestas _____.	

Paso 3. In pairs, take turns asking each other about your routines. Answer with complete sentences and add details.

Modelo: Estudiante A: **¿Tomas café por la mañana?**

Estudiante B: **No, no tomo café. Tomo té todos los días, por la mañana y por la tarde.**

NOTA CULTURAL: LOS VEJIGANTES

The **vejigante** is a make-believe character, full of energy and color, which is part of Puerto Rican carnivals. Each main carnival in Puerto Rico has a unique **vejigante** character. For example, one of the most celebrated carnivals in the northern coastal town of Loiza uses masks made from coconut shells with bright colors and carefully crafted horns. The **vejigante** masks are a classical example of the fusion of African, Spanish, and Caribbean cultures in Puerto Rico.

Vejigante masks

Así se forma

Vivo para comer.

Como para vivir.

4. Talking about actions in the present: Regular -er and -ir verbs; hacer and salir

Regular -er and -ir verbs

Now observe the forms for **comer** and **vivir** in the present tense. Note that you drop the **-er/-ir** from the infinitive and replace it with endings to agree with the subject of the verb. Note, also, that **-er** and **-ir** verbs have identical endings except in the **nosotros** and **vosotros** forms.

	comer to eat comer → com-	**vivir** to live vivir → viv-
(yo)	com**o**	viv**o**
(tú)	com**es**	viv**es**
(usted, él/ella)	com**e**	viv**e**
(nosotros/as)	com**emos**	viv**imos**
(vosotros/as)	com**éis**	viv**ís**
(ustedes, ellos/ellas)	com**en**	viv**en**

Hacer and salir

The verbs **hacer** (to do, make) and **salir** (to leave, go out) are irregular only in the **yo** form.

> **hacer: hago,** haces, hace, hacemos, hacéis, hacen
> **salir: salgo,** sales, sale, salimos, salís, salen

Hago la tarea todas las noches.   **I do** homework every night.
Salgo con mis amigos los fines de semana.   **I go out** with my friends on weekends.

Read what Octavio has to say about his university life.

Más actividades en la universidad

Soy de Mendoza, Argentina, y **asisto** a la Universidad Politécnica de California. **Vivo** en la residencia estudiantil. Tomo cursos de informática, de ciencias políticas y de literatura latinoamericana. En mis clases de ciencias políticas y literatura **leemos** y **escribimos** mucho y yo participo con frecuencia en las discusiones. En la clase de informática analizamos sistemas de computadoras y **aprendemos** a usar *software*. A veces no comprendo todo, pero mis compañeros de clase me explican los conceptos difíciles. Me gustan° mucho mis clases. Al mediodía voy con mis compañeros al restaurante de la universidad. Ahí **comemos, bebemos** y conversamos de mil cosas°. La comida del restaurante no es excelente pero tampoco° es terrible. Los sábados por la mañana voy al gimnasio y por la noche **salgo** con mis amigos. No **hago** mucho los domingos.

Me... I like
mil... a thousand things
neither

aprender	to learn	**comprender**	to understand
asistir a	to attend	**escribir**	to write
beber	to drink	**leer**	to read

Así se forma

2-16 ¿En qué clase?

 Paso 1. Indicate what classes you have this semester and mark which statements are true for each.

En...	español			
1. aprendo cosas muy interesantes.				
2. hago mucha tarea.				
3. hablo y participo en clase.				
4. comprendo todo o casi todo.				
5. asisto a clase muchas horas por semana.				
6. miro películas (*films*).				
7. hago muchos exámenes.				
8. leo mucho.				
9. investigo° en Internet.				
10. escribo muchos trabajos.				

investigar *to research*

Paso 2. In small groups, share your responses and listen to your classmates.

 Paso 3. Of the classes you just heard about, which one would you like to take? Write briefly about why you would like to take that class.

Modelo: **Quiero (*I want to*) tomar la clase de _____ porque los estudiantes aprenden cosas interesantes...**

2-17 ¿Qué hacemos en... ?

 Paso 1. Write two or three activities that you do in the places below. Add one more place on campus you usually go to.

Modelo: En la biblioteca.

> **Voy a la biblioteca todos los días después de la clase de español; hago la tarea de cálculo y estudio filosofía. A veces leo o investigo para un trabajo escrito...**

1. En la biblioteca...
2. En mi cuarto...
3. En la residencia/ el laboratorio/ el centro estudiantil...

Paso 2. Interview a classmate about his/her activities in the places above. Take turns asking questions about the activities he/she does there, when he/she goes, etc.

Modelo: **¿Cuándo vas a la biblioteca?**

¿Estudias allí (*there*)?

¿Haces la tarea allí?

Now take a vote: Which is the class' favorite place (**el lugar favorito**)?

2-18 Sondeo (*Survey*): El tiempo libre (*Leisure time*).

Paso 1. Complete the first column in the chart below with what you like to do in your time off. Add one more activity of your choice at the end.

Paso 2. Walk around the classroom to find out who shares your preferences. Transform your statements into questions (see the example in parentheses) to ask your classmates. When someone answers affirmatively, write her/his name in the second column.

How many affirmative answers can you get in ten minutes? Your professor may ask you to share your results with the class.

PALABRAS ÚTILES

el bar	*bar*
el cine	*movie theater*
el teatro	*theatre*
la discoteca	*club*
un partido deportivo	
	sporting match, game

Actividades de tiempo libre	¿Quién?
Modelo: Asistir a... Asisto a los conciertos de rock. (¿Asistes a los conciertos de rock?)	Megan
1. Asistir a...	
2. Ir a...	
3. Salir a... con...	
4. Hablar con...	
5. Comer... en...	
6. Mirar...	
7. Leer...	
8. ¿ ... ?	

2-19 **El profesor.** You have talked a lot about what you and other students do. What do you think your teachers do? Write a short paragraph describing what you imagine is a typical day for your Spanish teacher. Try to add details and be creative!

SITUACIONES

You have a part-time job in the mornings and go to classes in the evenings. Your boss needs someone to cover for another employee on Thursday from 3:00 P.M. until 9:00 P.M. You are very busy on Thursday evenings and would rather not have to work. In pairs, tell your partner about what you do on Thursdays and negotiate who will work.

Así se pronuncia

Consonants

Below you will find general guidelines for pronouncing Spanish consonants. The symbol in brackets represents the sound, followed by a brief explanation of its pronunciation. In following chapters, you will continue practicing some of these sounds and learning about spelling rules.

Now listen carefully and repeat the examples. Before you know it, you will be surprised at how proficient you are.

Sound	Spelling	Position	Examples
[b] as in English *boy*	b, v	begins word	bote, vote
		after *m, n*	sombrero, enviar
[ß] a *b* with lips half-open	b, v	other positions	liberal, avaro
[s] as in English *son*	ce, ci	begins syllable	cero, gracias
	z[5]	all positions	pez, zapato, retazo
	s	all positions	seta, solo, susto, dos
[k] very similar to English	qu + e, i	begins syllable	queso, quiso
	c + a, o, u	begins syllable	saca, cosa, cuna
[d] as in English	d	begins word	doctor, dentista
		after *n, l*	banda, caldo, saldo
[d] as in *th* in *other*	d	other positions	ido, salud, nado
[h] but stronger than in English	j	all positions	jamás, reloj, ajo
	ge, gi	begins syllable	gente, gitano, agente

A. Read each sentence on your own. Focus on the highlighted consonants or consonant-vowel combinations. Then listen to the recorded pronunciation.

b/v   **V**endo **v**einte **v**acas y un **b**urro.

          Un a**v**e li**b**re **v**uela.

c/que, qui   **C**ompro **c**atorce **c**o**c**os y **qui**nce **que**sos.

c/ce, ci   **Ci**nco chimpan**cé**s **có**micos **c**elebran sus **c**umpleaños.

z/s   La **s**eñorita **s**irve **z**umo de **z**anahorias.

d/d   ¡**D**octor! ¡Me **d**uele el **d**e**d**o!

j/ge, gi   **J**erónimo es **j**oven, á**gi**l e inteli**ge**nte.

---

[5]In many regions of Spain, the letter *c* before *e* or *i*, and the letter *z* are pronounced like the English *th* in the words *thin, thanks.*

More consonants

Repeat the examples.

[y] as in English[6]	**ll, y** + *vowel*	begins syllable	**llanto, yeso, allí**
[g] as in English	**g + a, o, u**	begins syllable	**gato, gusto, gota**
	gu + e, i	begins syllable	**guitarra, guerra**
[gw] rare in English	**gu + a, o**	begins syllable	**agua, antiguo**
	gü + e, i	begins syllable	**pingüino, averigüe**
[r] as in Be*tt*y, E*dd*y	**r**	middle and end of a word	**aro, verdad, bar**
[rr] trilled, rolled sound	**r** + *vowel*	begins word	**rifle, rato**
	n, s, l + r		**enredo, alrededor**
	vowel + **rr** + *vowel*		**perro, corro**

Note that:

- The letter **h** is always silent:
  hotel   **hospital**   **deshonesto**

- The **ñ** is similar to the *ny* in the word *canyon*:
  montaña   **cañón**   **mañana**

- Double **cc** and **x** are pronounced [*ks*]:
  acción   **examen**

B. Read each sentence on your own. Focus on the highlighted consonants or consonant–vowel combinations. Then listen to the recorded pronunciation.

ll/y	Un mi**ll**ón de **ll**amas **y**acen en la **ll**anura.
g/gue, gui	El **g**urú, el **gue**rrero y el **guí**a son **g**olosos.
g/güe, güi	Ana es bilin**güe**. El pin**güi**no está en el a**g**ua.
g/ge, gi	El **gi**tano es **g**uapo y **ge**neroso.
r/rr	**R**ita co**rr**e por la ca**rr**etera. El pirata **r**inde el teso**r**o.
h	**H**éctor es un **h**otelero **h**olandés.
h/j	**H**ernán es **j**oven.
ñ	Ma**ñ**ana el ni**ñ**o va a las monta**ñ**as y al ca**ñ**ón.

---

[6]This sound varies in different regions of the Spanish-speaking world.

Dicho y hecho

¡A ESCUCHAR!

La Universidad de Puerto Rico

Paso 1. See if you know the following about your school:

In what year was it founded?   _____

How many students currently attend?   _____

Paso 2. Now listen to a student at the University of Puerto Rico talk about the university system. Then see if you can answer the questions. Use the list of helpful vocabulary and listen carefully for cognates that will help you understand what you hear.

1. La Universidad de Puerto Rico tiene...
   a. más de cien años.   **b.** aproximadamente diez años.
2. ¿Cuántos recintos hay en la isla?
   a. once   **b.** veinte
3. ¿Ofrece grados de Maestría esta Universidad?
4. Dos especialidades que ofrecen en la Universidad de Puerto Rico son...

   _____ y _____ .

PALABRAS ÚTILES	
beca	scholarship
cien	a hundred
inalámbrico	wireless
informática	computer systems
mil	thousand
recinto	campus
Bachillerato	Bachelor's degree*
Maestría	Master's degree

*Note that **Bachillerato** refers to secondary school in some other countries such as Spain.

CONVERSANDO

Tu universidad. Your class has been asked to produce a *Guide for Spanish-Speaking Visitors* for your school. In groups, talk about features of your campus that might be relevant to visitors and prospective students. Include the categories listed below. Take notes: You will need them later to complete the class project.

- lugares (*places*) interesantes o famosos
- restaurantes o cafés cerca de (*near*) la universidad
- el equipo de básquetbol/ fútbol americano, etc.
- clubes y organizaciones
- actividades: lo que (*what*) hacen los estudiantes

DE MI ESCRITORIO

Guía para los visitantes. Now it is time to write and compile the *Guide for Spanish-Speaking Visitors* for your college. Your professor will divide the class into five groups, assigning one of the categories listed below to each group. After completion of the assigned task, each group should type its section for incorporation into the total class project. Use your notes from Exercise 2—11 and *Conversando*.

> **HINT**
>
> Try to stick with structures and words you have studied. If you look up additional words in a dictionary, seek guidance from your instructor.

¡Bienvenidos a (*add the name of your university or institution*)!

Include a map of the campus with the names (in Spanish) of the main buildings. Include some differences between United States and Hispanic universities.

Lugares que usted debe (*should*) visitar

Describe things that are a "must" to visit—a gallery (**galería**) or museum (**museo**), the student union, gymnasium, bookstore, some good places to eat on campus or near campus, etc.

Los cursos académicos

Mention some of the more popular or interesting classes at your school. Talk about computer facilities, library, and where/when students generally study.

> **HINT**
>
> For additional course names, see **Apéndice 3**, p. A-17.

Clubes, organizaciones y equipos (*teams*) de la universidad

Mention some clubs, fraternities, sororities, and other important organizations on your campus. Highlight some of the school sports teams (**fútbol americano, básquetbol, béisbol,...**). Indicate if they win (**ganar**) frequently or are famous. Don't forget **la mascota de la universidad**.

La vida (*life*) universitaria y qué hacer en la universidad

Indicate where students live, where students go on campus, and what they frequently do in the mornings, afternoons, evenings, and on weekends.

Artes musicales: La bomba y la plena

Antes de leer

Are you familiar with any musical forms in the United States that originated in African or African-American communities? Which ones?

Puerto Rico and the other Caribbean islands developed unique musical traditions that often combined Spanish language and song forms with African-derived instrumentation and rhythms. **Bomba** is the oldest musical tradition in Puerto Rico, which comes directly from Africa. The musical form is a call and response between the leader and the chorus over multiple rhythmic patterns. The instruments used to play **bomba** are two barrel-shaped drums, a single maraca, and a pair of sticks called **cuá**. **Bomba** dances were performed outdoors. As people gathered to listen to the drums, the crowd grew. Soon the show started. Usually, a female began to sing, and the choir answered her back. Then the dancing began: one at a time, a dancer approached the drummers, giving cues with body movements and (for women) with a large skirt, which the drummers had to follow. Everybody took turns dancing and playing the drums.

A **bomba** dancer with drummers

Plena, on the other hand, surfaced in the early 1900's on the south coast. According to some historians, **plena** was born in the town of Ponce and later became popular throughout the island. A well-known verse from a **plena** song, roughly translated, indicates:

La plena que yo conozco
No es de la China ni del Japón
Porque la plena viene de Ponce
Viene del barrio de San Antón

The plena that I know
is not from China nor Japan
because the plena comes from Ponce
from the neighborhood of San Anton

Plena functions as a sort of singing newspaper in which residents recount events and scandals of the day. The main instruments of **plena** are the **panderetas** (tambourine-like hand-held drums) and the **güiro** (gourd scraper, pronounced "GWEE-ro"). As in **bomba**, **plena** follows a call-and-response between singer and chorus.

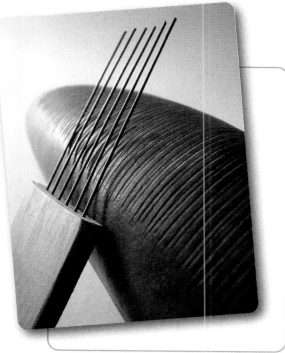

The **pandereta** and the **güiro**, used in **plena** music

Después de leer

1. What is one characteristic that **bomba** and **plena** have in common?

2. What is one characteristic that distinguishes **bomba** from **plena**?

Repaso de vocabulario activo

Adverbios y expresiones adverbiales

ahora/ más tarde
now/later

a tiempo/ temprano/ tarde *on time/ early/late*

a veces *sometimes*

antes de/ después de (clase) *before/after* (class)

casi nunca *rarely*

esta mañana/ tarde/ noche *this morning/ afternoon/evening*

el fin de semana
weekend

con frecuencia *frequently*

nunca *never*

por/ en la mañana/ tarde/ noche *in the morning/afternoon/ evening*

siempre *always*

toda(s) la(s) mañana(s)/ tarde(s)/ noche(s)
every morning/ afternoon/evening

todos los días *every day*

Sustantivos (Nouns)
En el aula

el alumno/ el estudiante *student (male)*

la alumna/ la estudiante *student (female)*

los apuntes *notes*

el bolígrafo/ la pluma *pen*

el borrador *eraser*

la calculadora *calculator*

el cuaderno *notebook*

el diccionario *dictionary*

el escritorio *desk*

el examen *exam*

la hoja de papel *sheet of paper*

el lápiz *pencil*

el libro *book*

el mapa *map*

la mesa *table*

la mochila *backpack*

la nota *grade*

la papelera *wastebasket*

la pizarra *blackboard*

el profesor *teacher/ professor (male)*

la profesora *teacher/ professor (female)*

la puerta *door*

el reloj *clock*

la silla *chair*

la tarea *homework*

la tiza *chalk*

el trabajo escrito *academic paper*

la ventana *window*

En el laboratorio

los audífonos *headphones*

la computadora *computer*

el mensaje electrónico *e-mail (message)*

la dirección electrónica *e-mail address*

el disco compacto/ el CD *compact disc*

la impresora *printer*

la página web *Web page*

el ratón *mouse*

el sitio web *website*

el teclado *keyboard*

el televisor *television set*

el VCR/ el video *VCR*

La clase de...

alemán *German*

álgebra *algebra*

arte *art*

biología *biology*

cálculo *calculus*

ciencias políticas *political science*

computación/ informática *computer science*

contabilidad *accounting*

economía *economy*

español *Spanish*

filosofía *philosophy*

física *physics*

francés *French*

historia *history*

inglés *English*

literatura *literature*

matemáticas *mathematics*

música *music*

psicología *psychology*

química *chemistry*

religión *religion*

sociología *sociology*

Lugares (Places)

la casa *home/house*

el apartamento *apartment*

la biblioteca *library*

la cafetería *cafeteria*

el centro estudiantil *student center*

el cuarto *room*

la fiesta *party*

el gimnasio *gymnasium*

la librería *bookstore*

la oficina *office*

la residencia estudiantil *student dorm*

el restaurante *restaurant*

la universidad *university*

Verbos y expresiones verbales

aprender *to learn*

asistir a *to attend*

beber *to drink*

buscar *to look for*

cenar *to have dinner*

comer *to eat, have lunch*

comprar *to buy*

desayunar *to have breakfast*

comprender *to understand*

escribir *to write*

escuchar *to listen to*

estudiar *to study*

hablar *to talk*

hacer *to do, make*

hay *there is, there are*

imprimir *to print*

ir *to go*

leer *to read*

llegar *to arrive*

mandar *to send*

navegar por la red *to surf the Web*

practicar *to practice*

preparar *to prepare*

regresar *to return*

salir *to go out*

ser *to be*

tomar (apuntes) *to take (notes)*

trabajar *to work*

usar *to use*

vivir *to live*

sacar una nota *to get a grade*

Palabras interrogativas

¿Cuándo? *When?*

¿Adónde? *Where to?*

Autoprueba y repaso WILEY PLUS ✓

I. Nouns and definite and indefinite articles.

A. Professor B is more demanding than Professor A, and she always gives more homework. Complete each professor's assignment with the appropriate definite article (**el, la, los, las**). Change nouns to the plural when necessary.

Modelo: Profesor A: Contesten __la__ pregunta n° 1.

Profesor B: Contesten __las preguntas__ 1 a 10.

1. Prof. A: Escriban _____ ejercicio A.
   Prof. B: Escriban _____ A y B.
2. Prof. A: Estudien _____ lección 1.
   Prof. B: Estudien _____ 1 y 2.
3. Prof. A: Lean _____ página 40.
   Prof. B: Lean _____ 40 y 41.
4. Prof. A: Completen _____ Capítulo 3.
   Prof. B: Completen _____ 3 y 4.

B. Describe your school by completing the sentences with **un, una, unos,** or **unas**.

En la universidad hay _____ centro estudiantil con _____ librería grande. Tenemos _____ laboratorio con _____ impresora y _____ computadoras nuevas. Hay _____ biblioteca grande con _____ libros muy antiguos e interesantes.

II. *Ir + a + destination.* Tell where the following people go to carry out the indicated activities. Avoid subject pronouns.

Modelo: Esteban / estudiar
Va a la biblioteca.

1. yo / desayunar
2. nosotros / trabajar en la computadora
3. mis amigos y yo / hacer ejercicio
4. los estudiantes / hablar con el profesor
5. tú / comprar libros y cuadernos
6. Susana / tomar una siesta

III. The present tense of regular *-ar* verbs.
Indicate or ask questions about what college students do. Change the verbs to correspond to the subjects given in parentheses. Avoid the use of subject pronouns.

Modelo: navegar por la red con frecuencia (yo)
Navego por la red con frecuencia.

1. comprar libros y cuadernos en la librería (yo)
2. llegar a clase a tiempo (todos los estudiantes)
3. ¿estudiar en la biblioteca por la tarde (tú)?
4. ¿trabajar por la noche (usted)?
5. usar el correo electrónico todos los días (nosotros)
6. escuchar música clásica por la noche (Ana)

IV. The present tense of regular *-er* and *-ir* verbs; *hacer* and *salir*. Indicate or ask questions about what college students do. Change the verbs to correspond to the subjects given in parentheses. Avoid the use of subject pronouns.

Modelo: hacer muchos exámenes y escribir muchas composiciones (ella)
Hace muchos exámenes y escribe muchas composiciones.

1. asistir a una universidad buena y aprender mucho (nosotros)
2. vivir en la residencia y estudiar en la biblioteca (yo)
3. comer en la cafetería y tomar café en el centro estudiantil (los estudiantes)
4. leer libros interesantes y escribir muchas composiciones (nosotros)
5. imprimir los trabajos y usar las computadoras en el laboratorio (tú)
6. hacer la tarea y después salir con mis amigos/as (yo)

V. General review.

1. ¿Vas a clase todos los días?
2. ¿A qué hora es tu primera (*your first*) clase?
3. ¿Cuántos estudiantes hay en la clase de español?
4. ¿Hay tarea todas las noches? (¿Mucha tarea?)
5. ¿Escriben ustedes en el Cuaderno de ejercicios todas las noches?
6. ¿Adónde vas para comprar libros interesantes? ¿Y para usar las computadoras?
7. ¿Adónde vas a conversar con tus amigos?
8. ¿A qué hora cenas?
9. ¿Dónde comes normalmente?

VI. *Cultura.*

1. What are some of the principal differences between universities in the Spanish-speaking world vs. the United States?
2. What is the **coquí**?
3. Briefly describe the origins of **bomba** and **plena** music.

Answers to the *Autoprueba y repaso* are found in **Apéndice 2.**

CAPÍTULO 3

Así es mi familia

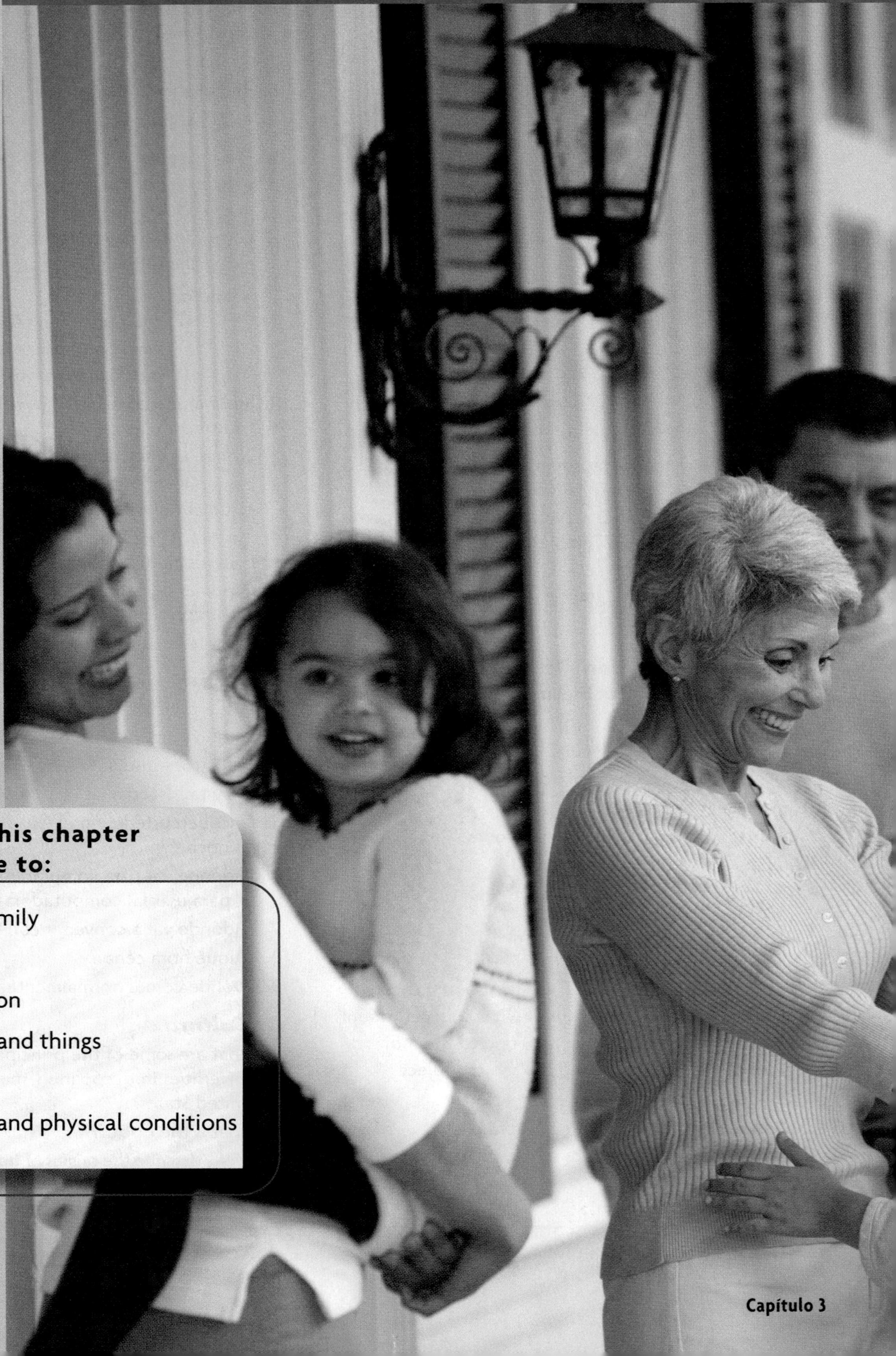

By the end of this chapter you will be able to:

- Talk about the family
- Tell age
- Indicate possession
- Describe people and things
- Indicate location
- Describe mental and physical conditions

Así se dice	Así se forma	Cultura	Dicho y hecho
• Así es mi familia • Adjetivos descriptivos • ¿Dónde están? ¿Cómo están?	**1. Tener** and **tener... años** **2.** Descriptive adjectives **3.** Possessive adjectives and possession with **de** **4. Estar** + location and condition	• Los hispanos en los Estados Unidos • La familia hispana • Artes populares: Los murales	• Linda conversa con su padre • Una persona muy especial • Así es mi familia

ENTRANDO AL TEMA

1. How many relatives are there in your family? How about your extended family?

2. How many people of Hispanic origin live in your town/city (or the place where you are from)? Do you know what their countries of origin are?

Andrés y Julia, novio y novia (1997)

Andrés y Julia, marido y mujer (2000)

Los niños: Juanito y Elena (2005)

Los nietos con el abuelo Noé (2007)

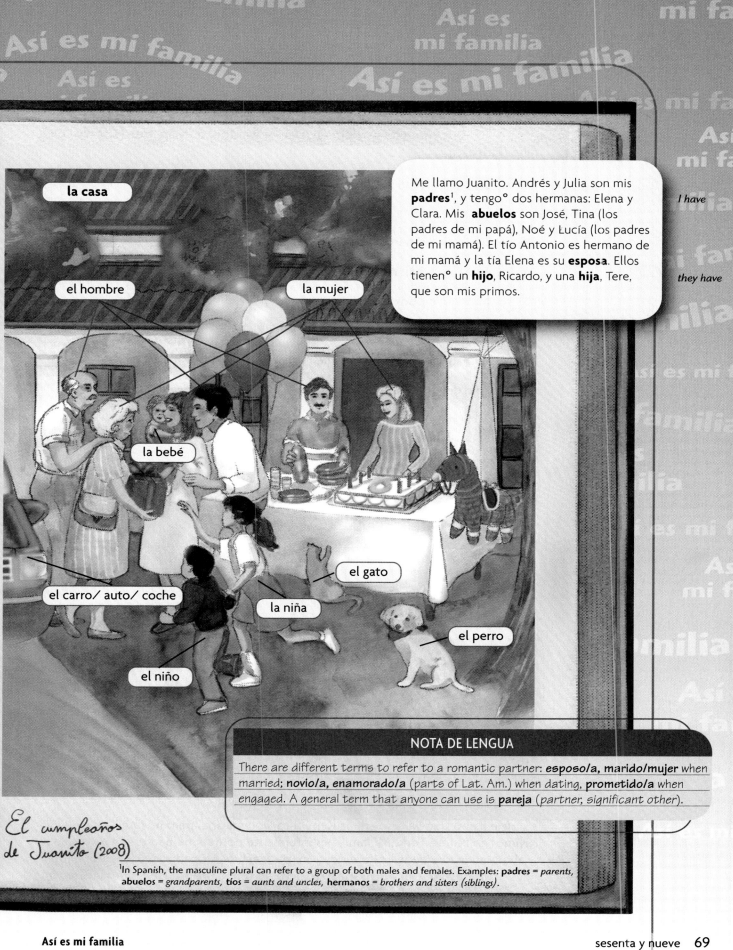

la casa

el hombre

la mujer

Me llamo Juanito. Andrés y Julia son mis **padres**[1], y tengo° dos hermanas: Elena y Clara. Mis **abuelos** son José, Tina (los padres de mi papá), Noé y Lucía (los padres de mi mamá). El tío Antonio es hermano de mi mamá y la tía Elena es su **esposa**. Ellos tienen° un **hijo**, Ricardo, y una **hija**, Tere, que son mis primos.

I have

they have

la bebé

el gato

el carro/ auto/ coche

la niña

el perro

el niño

El cumpleaños de Juanito (2008)

NOTA DE LENGUA

There are different terms to refer to a romantic partner: **esposo/a, marido/mujer** when married; **novio/a, enamorado/a** (parts of Lat. Am.) when dating, **prometido/a** when engaged. A general term that anyone can use is **pareja** (*partner, significant other*).

[1]In Spanish, the masculine plural can refer to a group of both males and females. Examples: **padres** = *parents*, **abuelos** = *grandparents*, **tíos** = *aunts and uncles*, **hermanos** = *brothers and sisters (siblings)*.

Así se dice

3-1 **¿La familia: cierto o falso?** Listen to the sentences below as your instructor reads them. Decide whether they are true (**Cierto**) or false (**Falso**).

Modelo: El hijo de mis padres es mi hermano. ☒ Cierto ☐ Falso

	Cierto	Falso
1. La abuela de mi hermana es mi abuela.	☐	☑
2. La hermana de mi madre es mi tía.	☐	☑
3. Los hijos de mis tíos son mis nietos.	☐	☑
4. El padre de mi madre es mi tío.	☐	☑
5. Mi hermana es la hija de mi padre y mi madre.	☐	☐
6. El padre de mi padre es el suegro de mi madre.	☐	☐
7. Yo soy el nieto/la nieta de mis primos.	☐	☐

3-2 **¿Quién es?** Explain who these family members are, as in the model.

Modelo: los primos: **Son los hijos del tío o la tía.**

el abuelo _____

el tío _____

la suegra _____

el nieto _____

NOTA DE LENGUA—DICHO (Saying)

stick; splinter

De tal palo°, tal astilla°.   **De tal padre, tal hijo.**

¿Cuál es el dicho equivalente en inglés? ¿Se aplica a su familia? ¿Es usted como (like) su madre o como su padre?

La familia, los parientes y los amigos

Camila tells us about her family, relatives, and friends.

Me llamo Camila, y soy de la República Dominicana, pero mi familia y yo vivimos en Nueva York. Mi familia es interesante porque mis padres son divorciados y ahora mi madre tiene° otro esposo: mi **padrastro**. Mi padrastro tiene dos hijos: *has* mi **hermanastro** y mi **hermanastra**, pero no tengo **medio hermanos**. El resto de mi familia, es decir°, un hermano **mayor**, la esposa de mi hermano (mi *es... that is* **cuñada**), las dos niñas de mi hermano (mis **sobrinas**) y mi hermana **menor** viven en Santo Domingo. También están allá mi padre, los cuatro abuelos y mi **bisabuela.** Mi **mejor amiga,** Pilar, es de Santo Domingo también. Sin embargo°, ya° tengo excelentes amigos aquí en los Estados Unidos. Bueno, así es mi familia.

However
already

¿**Cuántos** hermanastros tiene Camila? ¿**Cuántas** personas de su familia viven en la República Dominicana? ¿**Quién** es su mejor amiga? ¿**Dónde** vive?

el bisabuelo/la bisabuela	*great-grandfather/great-grandmother*
el hermanastro/la hermanastra	*stepbrother/stepsister*
el medio hermano/la medio hermana	*half-brother/half-sister*
mayor	*older*
el mejor amigo/la mejor amiga	*best friend (male/female)*
menor	*younger*
los parientes	*relatives*
¿Cuántos/Cuántas?	*How many?*
¿Quién/Quiénes?	*Who?*
¿Dónde?	*Where?*

  Las familias famosas. State the correct relationship among the following people.

Modelo: El rey (*King*) de España, Juan Carlos, la reina Sofía y el príncipe Felipe

Juan Carlos es el esposo de Sofía. Ellos son los padres de Felipe. Felipe es el hijo. (*etc.*)

Julio Iglesias con sus hijos: Chabeli, Julio Jr., y Enrique

1. Los actores Martin Sheen, Emilio Estévez y Charlie Sheen
2. Chelsea Clinton, los padres de Hillary Rodham Clinton y Bill Clinton
3. Julio Iglesias, Chabeli Iglesias, Julio Iglesias Jr. y Enrique Iglesias
4. La reina Isabel (*Queen Elizabeth*), el príncipe Carlos, Camila Parker y el príncipe Guillermo

Cultura: Los hispanos en los Estados Unidos

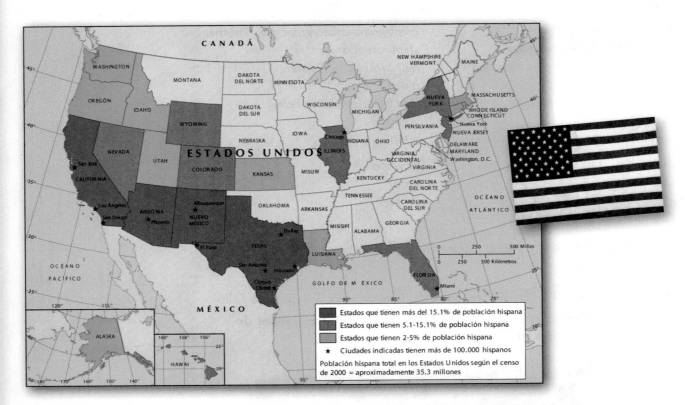

Estados que tienen más del 15.1% de población hispana

Estados que tienen 5.1-15.1% de población hispana

Estados que tienen 2-5% de población hispana

★ Ciudades indicadas tienen más de 100.000 hispanos

Población hispana total en los Estados Unidos según el censo de 2000 = aproximadamente 35.3 millones

Antes de leer

1. Do you know (or can you guess) what percentage of the U.S. population is Hispanic?

2. Looking at the map above, is there anything you did not expect?

¿CUÁNTOS HISPANOS HAY?

¿Sabes que los hispanos representan aproximadamente el 15% (por ciento) de la población de los Estados Unidos (EE.UU.)? La comunidad hispana es una de las más importantes del país. Aproximadamente el 70% de la población hispana se concentra en cuatro estados: California, Tejas, Nueva York y la Florida. Gran parte de esta población vive en ciudades como[1] Los Ángeles, Nueva York, Miami, Chicago, Washington, D.C. y San Antonio.

¿DE DÓNDE SON?

La mayoría de los hispanos en los EE.UU. son de México (60+ %), Puerto Rico (10+ %) y Cuba (5+ %). Gran parte de los nuevos inmigrantes hispanos de los últimos[2] treinta años son de Centroamérica —salvadoreños, nicaragüenses, hondureños y guatemaltecos— y también de la República Dominicana.

[1]like   [2]last

La amistad[3] entre México y los Estados Unidos se representa en la escultura *Torch of Friendship* en San Antonio, Tejas. El escultor es un famoso artista mexicano.

[3]friendship

A partir de 1959, como resultado de la revolución cubana, muchos cubanos inmigraron al sureste[4] de los EE.UU., especialmente a la Florida. Hoy, medio millón de cubanos y cubanoamericanos viven en Miami.

LA INFLUENCIA HISPANA

En algunas partes del país, como el suroeste y la Florida, la presencia de la población hispana es anterior a la llegada[5] de la población angloparlante[6]. Los **nombres** de varias ciudades y estados son la evidencia más notable de la presencia hispana en la historia del país. Por ejemplo, la ciudad más antigua en el territorio continental de los EE.UU. tiene un nombre hispano—San Agustín, FL.

La **vida diaria**[7] de los EE.UU. integra numerosos elementos de las artes, la comida[8] y el idioma de la cultura hispana. Por ejemplo, hay muchísimos restaurantes y tiendas con productos hispanos, y se puede escuchar el español en muchas partes.

Los hispanos también hacen contribuciones muy valiosas[9] a la **política, las ciencias y las artes** del país. Ellen Ochoa fue la primera mujer hispana astronauta en entrar al espacio[10]; Henry Cisneros sirvió en el gabinete del presidente Clinton; Ana Castillo es una escritora muy famosa. La **economía** de los hispanos también es notable—el mercado hispano se estima en[11] unos $200 billones de dólares.

Investig@ en INTERNET

Learn about a prominent U.S. Hispanic in the areas of politics, business, science, journalism, or the arts. Be prepared to share your findings with the class.

---

[4]*southeast* [5]*arrival* [6]*English-speaking* [7]*daily life* [8]*food* [9]*valuable* [10]*outerspace* [11]*the Hispanic market is estimated at*

Hoy hay más de un millón de puertorriqueños en Nueva York. La comunidad dominicana más grande del país también reside en esta ciudad.

Después de leer

Based on what you read, match these ideas.

1. El 60% de los hispanos en los EE.UU. son...
2. La mayoría de los hispanos en la Florida son...
3. Colorado, San Francisco, Nevada y Arizona son...
4. Hay muchos puertorriqueños y dominicanos en...
5. Las enchiladas, las empanadas, los tacos son...

a. comida hispana.
b. mexicanos.
c. Nueva York.
d. cubanos.
e. nombres hispanos.

Conexiones y contrastes

1. If you like Hispanic foods, which is your favorite? Is there a similar American dish?
2. Is there a Hispanic community or influence where you live?
3. Can you name any influential Hispanics in the U.S. such as actors/actresses, singers, politicians, or athletes?

Así se forma QUIA

> Abuelo, ¿cuántos años tienes?
>
> ¡Tengo ochenta y un años!

1. Indicating possession and telling age: The verb *tener* and *tener... años*

The verb *tener*

You have already informally used **tener** to express possession, as in **tengo dos hermanos**. Now observe the following forms (note that **tener** is irregular in the present).

	tener	*have*
(yo)	**tengo**	Tengo un hermano.
(tú)	**tienes**	¿Tienes bisabuelos?
(usted, él/ella)	**tiene**	Mi madre tiene cuatro hermanas.
(nosotros/as)	**tenemos**	Mi hermano y yo tenemos un perro.
(vosotros/as)	**tenéis**	¿Tenéis coche?
(ustedes, ellos/ellas)	**tienen**	Mis tíos tienen una casa nueva.

To be . . . years old   *Tener... años*

Whereas English uses *to be . . .* to tell age (*She is eighteen years old.*), Spanish uses **tener... años**. To inquire about age, the question **¿Cuántos años... ?** (*How many years . . . ?*) is used with **tener**.

— **¿Cuántos años tiene él?**   *How old is he?*
— **Tiene veintiún años.**   *He is twenty-one years old.*

3-4 **¿Cuántos años tienen?** Without looking back, try to recall the family drawing on page 69 and approximately how old each person (or animal) is.

1. La novia — Tiene veinticinco años. / Tiene cincuenta años.
2. El hijo — Tiene quince años. / Tiene siete años.
3. Los abuelos — Tienen treinta años. / Tienen sesenta años.
4. Los primos — Tienen diez años. / Tienen veinte años.
5. La bebé — Tiene trece años. / Tiene dos años.
6. El perro — Tiene tres años. / Tiene catorce años.

3-5 **¿Y nuestras (*our*) familias?**

Paso 1. Work with a partner and find out about his/her family members and how old they are. Ask the following questions and write down the answers.

1. ¿Cuántos años tienes tú?
2. ¿Tienes una hermana o un hermano mayor? ¿Cuántos años tiene?

3. ¿Tienes una hermana o un hermano menor? ¿Cuántos años tiene?

4. ¿Cuántos años tiene tu madre o tu padre?

5. ¿Tienes abuelos? ¿Cuántos años tienen?

6. ¿Tienes bisabuelos? ¿Cuántos años tiene tu bisabuelo o tu bisabuela?

7. ¿Cómo se llama tu tía o tu tío favorito, y cuántos años tiene?

Paso 2. Now write a short report, which you might be asked to share with the class. What do your families have in common, and what is different? Use the model to help you.

Modelo: **Ricardo y yo tenemos un hermano. Mi hermano tiene veinte años, pero el hermano de Ricardo tiene dieciocho años...**

3-6 **Mi árbol genealógico (_My family tree_).** This is the first step in the creation of a chapter project. First, draw your family tree in your notebook. Then write a description of your family with additional details. You may be asked to share it with a classmate.

Modelo: **Tengo una tía y dos tíos. Mi tía se llama... y tiene... años. Es divorciada, pero vive con su novio en...**

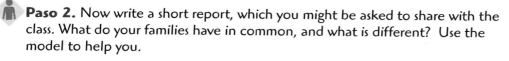

New York

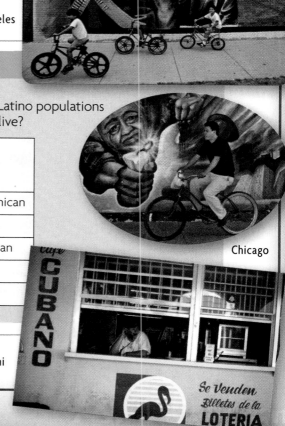

Los Angeles

Chicago

NOTA CULTURAL

Los hispanos en las grandes ciudades (_cities_)
Look at the following table with data from the 2000 Census about the Latino populations in some large U.S. cities. How large is the Latino community where you live?

	Number of Latinos	Percent of the city's population that is Latino	Majority Latino group(s)
New York	2,160,554	27%	Puerto Rican, Dominican
Los Angeles	1,719,073	47%	Mexican
Chicago	753,644	26%	Mexican, Puerto Rican
El Paso	431,875	77%	Mexican
Miami	238,351	66%	Cuban

Miami

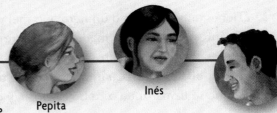
Pepita

Inés

Octavio

Escenas

Para... *That's what friends are for*

Para eso están los amigos°

En la cafetería de la universidad. Inés está sola en una mesa tomando un café. Llega Pepita con Octavio.

Paso 1. Listen to the conversation between Pepita, Inés, and Octavio and focus on the words and expressions that you know to get the general gist of the conversation. Then mark the statements that are correct according to what you heard.

1. Pepita presenta a Inés y Octavio.   Inés y Octavio son amigos.
2. Inés y Octavio hablan de sus clases.   Inés y Octavio hablan de sus familias.
3. Este fin de semana van a la biblioteca.   Este fin de semana van a una fiesta *(party)* de cumpleaños.

Paso 2. Look at the questions below and listen again. Then answer the questions.

1. ¿De dónde es Octavio?   5. ¿Cuándo es la fiesta?
2. ¿Quién tiene familia en España?   6. ¿Quiénes están invitados?
3. ¿Dónde vive el primo de Octavio?   7. ¿Acepta Inés la invitación de Pepita?
4. ¿Para quién es la fiesta de cumpleaños?   8. ¿Cómo van a la fiesta?

Paso 3. Listen one more time as you read along. Then check your answers to the previous questions.

Pepita:	¡Hola, Inés!
Inés:	Pepita, ¡qué sorpresa! *(Se dan un beso en la mejilla.)* ¿Cómo estás?
Pepita:	Muy bien. Quiero presentarte a Octavio. Es el compañero de cuarto° de Manuel.
Inés:	*(Inés y Octavio se dan la mano.)* Mucho gusto, Octavio. ¿Eres nuevo en la universidad?
Octavio:	Sí, soy de Mendoza, Argentina. ¿De dónde eres tú?
Inés:	Soy española, de León. La mayoría de mi familia todavía° vive allá, pero mi madre y mi padrastro viven aquí. Yo estudio economía, ¿y tú?
Octavio:	Estudio informática.
Inés:	¿Así que° eres el mejor amigo de Manuel?
Octavio:	En realidad no. Tengo un primo en Buenos Aires que es amigo de Manuel desde hace años°. Yo sólo conocí° a Manuel hace un mes°.
Inés:	¡Manuel y su familia tienen amigos en todo el mundo!
Pepita:	A propósito, Inés, ¿tienes planes para este fin de semana? Mi madre prepara una fiesta de cumpleaños para mi tía Rosita, es el sábado. ¿Puedes ir°?
Inés:	¡Por supuesto!° Gracias por la invitación.
Pepita:	¡Qué bueno! Manuel, su novia y Octavio también° están invitados.
Octavio:	Inés, tenemos espacio en el auto. ¿Por qué no vamos todos juntos° a la fiesta el sábado?
Inés:	¡Estupendo! Es un buen plan. Gracias, Octavio.
Octavio:	De nada. Para eso están los amigos.

Side glosses:
compañero... *roommate*
still
Así... *So*
desde... *for years; I met;*
hace... *a month ago*
Puedes... *Can you come/go?*
Por... *Of course*
also
together

Así se dice

Todas las mañanas Carmen besa y abraza a sus hijas.

Relaciones personales

See what an important role Carmen's family plays in her very busy lifestyle.

Carmen trabaja, estudia y es madre soltera°. Sus hijas gemelas°, Tina y Mari, tienen tres años. Carmen **ama a** sus hijas con todo el corazón°. Cuando va al trabajo o a la universidad, su tía o la niñera° **cuida a** las niñas. Todas las mañanas, al salir de la casa, Carmen **besa** y **abraza a** Tina y **a** Mari. Con frecuencia **llama a** sus padres y abuelos, que viven en Ponce, Puerto Rico. Ellos **visitan a** Carmen y **a** las nietas dos veces al año.

single; twins
heart
babysitter

abrazar	*to hug*	**cuidar**	*to take care of*
amar	*to love*	**llamar**	*to call*
besar	*to kiss*	**visitar**	*to visit*

NOTA DE LENGUA

a personal

Observe the use of the word **a** in the above description of Carmen's life. It precedes a direct object that is a specific person (or persons). It is called **a personal** and there is no equivalent in English. Note that **a + el → al**

— ¿**A** quién buscas?   Who(m) are you looking for?
— Busco **a** mi amigo/ **al** profesor.   I am looking for my friend/the professor.

Note that when the direct object is not a person, there is no **a**.

— ¿Qué buscas?   What are you looking for?
— Busco <u>su apartamento</u>.   I am looking for his apartment.

3-7 Tú y tu familia.

 Paso 1. In the table below, answer the questions about you and your family (both immediate and extended) in the column **Yo.**

 Paso 2. Then ask the questions to a classmate and write down his/her answers in the column **Mi compañero/a.** Can you find any similarities?

	Yo	Mi compañero/a
1. ¿A quién en tu familia amas mucho (*a lot*)?		
2. ¿A quién abrazas con frecuencia?		
3. ¿A quién besas?		
4. ¿A quién llamas por teléfono con frecuencia?		
5. ¿A qué parientes visitas con más frecuencia?		
6. ¿A quién admiras (*admire*) mucho?		
7. ¿A quién escuchas siempre (*always*)?		

Cultura: La familia hispana

Antes de leer

1. What family members live in a typical U.S. household? Do U.S. families tend to be nuclear or extended?

2. Think about events celebrated by many U.S. teenagers: Sweet 16, debutantes, bar/bat mitzvahs, etc. Describe who celebrates them and how.

LA FAMILIA HISPANA

Para la mayoría de los hispanos, la familia es una pequeña comunidad unida por la solidaridad y el cariño[1]. El concepto hispano de la familia incluye a los parientes más inmediatos (madre, padre, hijos, hermanos) y también a los abuelos, tíos, primos y numerosos otros parientes. En la familia tradicional, y especialmente en las zonas rurales, es común tener muchos hijos. Esta tabla demuestra[2] el tamaño promedio[3] de las familias de varios grupos en los Estados Unidos.

	Tamaño promedio de las familias (U.S. Census 2000)
Hispanos	3.87
Asiáticos	3.80
Afro-Americanos	3.00
Blancos	2.58

En los países hispanos, los padres, los hijos y los abuelos con frecuencia viven en la misma[4] casa. Los abuelos son muy importantes en la crianza[5] de sus nietos y normalmente los cuidan cuando los padres salen. Tradicionalmente, el padre trabaja y la madre cuida de la casa y de los niños. Los hijos solteros[6] generalmente viven en la casa de sus padres mientras[7] asisten a la universidad o trabajan.

Sin embargo[8], hoy en día el concepto de la familia hispana está cambiando[9]. Dos de los cambios más notables son que la familia es más pequeña y que muchas mujeres trabajan fuera de[10] casa.

Por lo general la familia, sea tradicional o moderna, es el núcleo de la vida social. Abuelos, nietos, padres, tíos, padrinos[11] y primos se reúnen con frecuencia para celebrar los cumpleaños, bautizos[12], Quince años, comuniones y otras fiestas. Las relaciones familiares ocupan un lugar[13] esencial en la sociedad hispana.

---

[1]affection [2]shows [3]average size [4]same [5]upbringing [6]single, unmarried [7]while [8]**Sin...** Nevertheless [9]changing [10]**fuera...** outside of [11]godparents [12]baptisms [13]place

Una celebración hispana es común en los Estados Unidos es la fiesta de los quince años. Aquí vemos a una quinceañera a la salida de la iglesia (*church*), rodeada de mariachis.

Después de leer

1. Fill in the diagram below with typical characteristics of Hispanic and U.S. families. Think about the following concepts:

   Number of children

   Who lives in the family household

   Roles of the family members

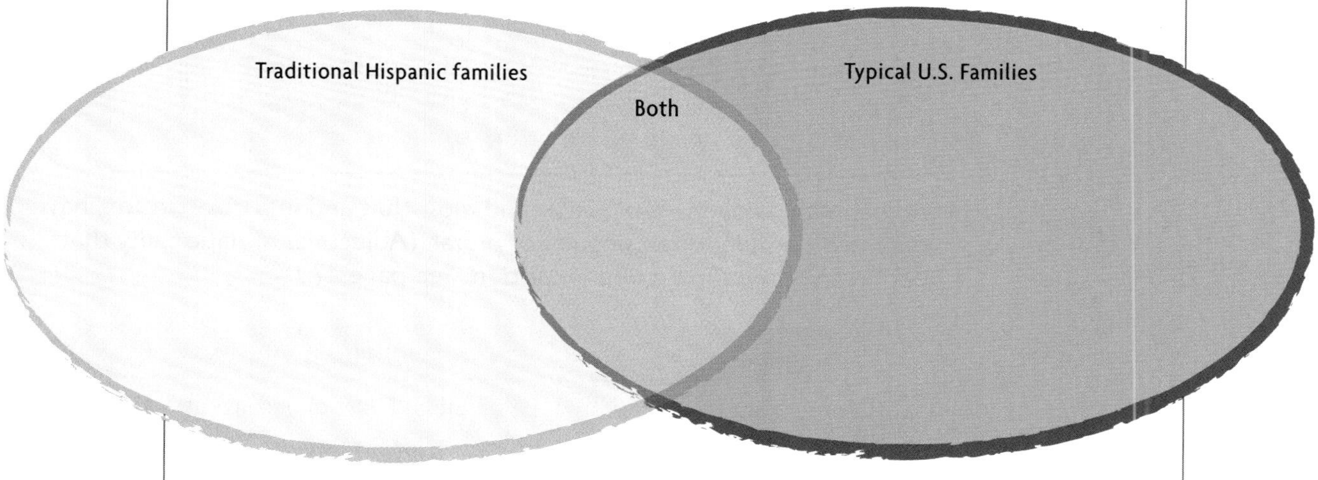

Traditional Hispanic families

Both

Typical U.S. Families

2. Read about the *15 años* celebrations and answer the questions below. Then, compare both celebrations. How are they similar or different?

   15 años: Chicas solamente. Se celebra en la iglesia. Después hay una comida y baile.

   Una celebración de adolescentes en los Estados Unidos: _____

   Características: _____

Some good movies about Hispanic families are *Mi familia* (1995) and *Real Women Have Curves* (2002).

es mi familia *Así es mi familia* *Así es mi fa*
mi familia *mi familia* *m*
es mi familia *Así es mi familia* *m*

Así se forma

Soy muy artística, ¿no?

2. Describing people and things: Descriptive adjectives

Adjectives are words that modify nouns. Descriptive adjectives describe and express characteristics of nouns (*tall, funny, interesting* . . .). You have already learned some adjectives of nationality (**mexicano/a**) and some that are cognates (**romántico/a**).

Formation of adjectives

Adjectives in Spanish agree in gender (masculine or feminine) and number (singular or plural) with the nouns or pronouns they modify.

- Adjectives that end in **–o** have four possible forms (masculine/feminine, singular/plural) to indicate agreement.

	Singular	Plural
masculine	Él es honest**o**.	Ellos son honest**os**.
feminine	Ella es honest**a**.	Ellas son honest**as**.

- Adjectives ending in **–e** or **–ista,** and most that end in a **consonant**, have only two possible forms: singular or plural. (Adjectives of nationality that end in a consonant are one exception. See page 27.)

Singular	Plural
Él/Ella es inteligent**e**.	Ellos/Ellas son inteligent**es**.
. . . ideal**ista**.	. . . ideal**istas**.
. . . sentiment**al**.	. . . sentiment**ales**.

- To make a singular adjective plural, add **–s** to the vowel or **–es** to the consonant, as is done with nouns.
  american**o** → american**os**   españo**l** → español**es**

Adjective position

- In contrast to English, Spanish descriptive adjectives usually <u>follow the noun</u> they describe.
  Marta es una **estudiante responsable.**   *Marta is a responsible student.*

- Adjectives of quantity (such as numbers) precede the noun, as in English.
  Tres estudiantes son de Nuevo México.
  Muchos estudiantes van al concierto.

Así se dice

Adjetivos descriptivos con *ser*

The following descriptive adjectives are most commonly used with the verb **ser** to indicate characteristics or qualities that are considered inherent or natural to the person or thing described. They indicate what the person or thing *is like*.

Observe the following pairs of opposites.

alto(a) → bajo(a)

fuerte → débil

joven² → mayor³

tonto(a) → inteligente

**perezoso(a)/irresponsable →
trabajador(a)/responsable/
serio(a)**

difícil → fácil

pobre → rico(a)

**bonito(a)/ hermoso(a)/
guapo(a) → feo(a)**

**flaco(a)/ delgado(a) →
gordo(a)**

malo(a) → bueno(a)

pequeño(a) → grande

viejo(a) →nuevo(a)

---

²The plural of **joven** is **jóvenes**.
³Although the most common Spanish word for *old* is **viejo**, it is not polite to use it to describe people. Use **mayor** instead.

Así se dice

Luis   Alberto

Opposites **Los opuestos°**

Observe how Pepita describes her cousins Luis and Alberto.

Tengo dos primos que son completamente diferentes. Luis es **moreno**, bajo, con unos kilos de más. Alberto es **rubio**, alto, delgado y guapo. Luis es **muy amable**; tiene un carácter agradable. Es **divertido** y **simpático**. Alberto no habla mucho; es serio, **un poco** egoísta y un poco **aburrido**. La verdad es que a veces es **antipático**. Los dos son mis primos, **pero** ¡qué contraste!

aburrido/a	boring	muy	very
amable	friendly, kind	pero	but
antipático	unpleasant, disagreeable	un poco	a bit, somewhat
divertido/a	amusing, fun, funny		
moreno/a	brunette, dark-skinned		
rubio/a	blonde		
simpático/a	nice, likeable		

NOTA DE LENGUA

Bueno/a and **malo/a** may be placed either before or after a noun. When placed before a masculine singular noun, **bueno** becomes **buen**, and **malo** becomes **mal**.

Es un estudiante **bueno/ malo**.	o	Es un **buen/ mal** estudiante.
Es una profesora **buena/ mala**.	o	Es una **buena/ mala** profesora.

Adjectives ending in **-dor** add **-a** to agree with a feminine singular noun:

    trabajador → trabajad**ora**   conservador → conservad**ora**

3-8 **¿Quién es?** Listen to Juanito talk about his family and decide whether each statement refers to his mother, father, sisters, or cousins. Note that some adjectives could refer to more than one category.

	la mamá	el papá	las hermanas	los primos
1.	✓			
2.				
3.				
4.				
5.				
6.				
7.				
8.				

(3-9) ¿Quién?

Paso 1. Answer the following questions with the names of famous people or fictional characters.

Modelo: ¿Quién es tonto?　　**Homer Simpson es tonto.**

1. ¿Quién es feo?
2. ¿Quién es muy mala?
3. ¿Quién es rico?
4. ¿Quién es joven?
5. ¿Quiénes son guapas?

6. ¿Quién es divertido?
7. ¿Quién es simpática?
8. ¿Quiénes son muy inteligentes?
9. ¿Quién es antipático?
10. ¿Quién es un poco aburrido?

Paso 2. Now work in small groups and read some of your names to your classmates, who will read the question they think is appropriate (as in the game *Jeopardy*).

Modelo:　Estudiante A: **Homer Simpson.**
　　　　　　Estudiante B: **¿Quién es tonto?**
　　　　　　Estudiante A: **Sí./ No.**

NOTA DE LENGUA

You often use more than one adjective when describing a person. In doing so, note the following:

y (*and*) becomes **e** before words beginning with **i** or **hi**.
　　　Mi madre es bonita **e** inteligente.
o (*or*) becomes **u** before words beginning with **o** or **ho**.
　　　¿El presidente es deshonesto **u** honesto?

PALABRAS ÚTILES

Tener pelo (*hair*) negro/ rubio/ castaño (*brown*)/ canoso (*grey*).
Ser pelirrojo (*redhead*).
Tener ojos (*eyes*) azules (*blue*)/ verdes (*green*)/ negros/ café.

(3-10) ¿Cómo soy?

Paso 1. Write a short paragraph on a card or a piece of paper listing the traits that best describe you, both physically and in terms of personality.

Soy...

Paso 2. In large groups, put all the pieces of paper in a bag and mix them up. Then each of you takes a piece of paper. If you take your own, put it back and get a different one. Read the description and write the name of the person you think is being described. Then read the descriptions and your guesses to the group. Did you guess correctly?

Así se dice

3-11 **Quiero ser...** Using adjectives from the previous **Así se dice** sections, first indicate characteristics that you do not wish to have. Then, using contrasting adjectives, indicate what you do wish to be. Begin with personality traits. You may be asked to share your ideas with the class.

No quiero (*I don't want*) ser...	Quiero ser...
No quiero ser antipático/a.	Quiero ser simpático/a.

3-12 **Similares y diferentes.** In most families there are some people that are similar in some ways but very different in other ways. Can you think of two people in your family like this (you and a sibling, your parents, two grandparents, etc.)?

_____ y _____

Paso 1. First, write three sentences describing the similarities between the two family members.

Modelo: **Mi mamá y mi hermana son...** *o*

Mi papá y yo somos...

1. _____
2. _____
3. _____

Now write three sentences describing their differences.

Modelo: **Mi mamá es... pero mi hermana es...** *o*

Mi papá es... pero yo soy...

1. _____
2. _____
3. _____

 Paso 2. Now, you and a classmate share what you've written. Ask each other additional questions.

3-13 **Adivinanza (*Guessing game*).** One student will assume the role of a well-known celebrity but will not divulge his/her identity. The other students will ask questions to discover his/her identity. Use the adjectives on page 81 and those from the box below. The mystery celebrity may respond only with **Sí** or **No**.

Possible categories:　　**político/a**　　**actor/actriz**　　**cantante (*singer*)**

Modelo: **¿Eres actor? ¿Eres joven/ mayor? ¿Eres cómico?**

PALABRAS ÚTILES	
amable → cruel	práctico → idealista
honesto/a → deshonesto/a	egoísta → modesto/a
ambicioso/a → perezoso/a	enérgico/a → tranquilo/a
moral → inmoral	serio/a → cómico/a
conservador/a → liberal	exótico/a → ordinario/a
optimista → pesimista	tolerante → intolerante
decente → grosero/a	

 3-14 **Amor y... menos amor (*Love and . . . less love*).** In pairs, take turns interviewing each other about each other's "favorite person" or "least favorite person." Below are some questions to help you, but try to ask other questions for details. Pay attention and/or take notes on your partner's answers, as you may need this information later.

1. ¿Quién es tu persona favorita/ menos favorita?
2. ¿Cómo es?
3. ¿Por qué (*Why*) es tu persona favorita/ menos favorita?

NOTA CULTURAL

Los hispanos "mixtos°"
Mixed Hispanics are increasingly common in Hispanic communities. Someone may have, for instance, a Mexican father and an Ecuadorian mother; a Dominican father and Haitian mother; or an African American father and a Cuban mother. In Chicago and New York, there are many "MexiRicans," who typically have features from both Mexico and Puerto Rican cultures.

mixed

La bandera puertorriqueña con la mexicana.

Así se dice

3-15 Los anuncios personales.

 Paso 1. Read the personal ads below. Decide who would make a good couple and draw lines connecting their ads.

Mujeres que buscan hombres:

1
> **Soy una señorita enérgica,** honesta y práctica. Tengo veintidós años y deseo conocer a un caballero romántico. En el futuro, quiero tener muchos hijos.

2
> **Soy una madre divorciada.** Tengo cuarenta años y tengo dos hijas. Quiero encontrar a un señor amable y responsable.

3
tatoos
> **Tengo veinte años** y trabajo en un estudio de tatuajes°. Busco a un hombre rico y guapo.

4
> **Señorita dominicana** de treinta años busca a un hombre inteligente y divetido. Soy muy religiosa.

Hombres que buscan mujeres:

A
> **Hombre ambiciosa busca** a mujer exótica y joven. Tengo venticinco años y soy muy trabajador.

B
Caribbean
> **Panameño guapo busca** a mujer caribeña° tradicional y seria.

C
> **Tengo treinta años** y busco a una mujer enérgica y liberal. Soy muy romántico y tengo una familia grande.

D
widower
> **Buscas a un hombre maduro y optimista?** Tengo cuarenta y dos años, soy viudo° y tengo una hija.

Paso 2. Share your matchmaking decisions with a partner. You might want to use these terms:

hacer buena... *make a good couple*

Modelo: **Creo que la mujer (...) hace/ no hace buena pareja° con el hombre (...) porque...**

Tienen mucho en común./ No tienen nada en común. Por ejemplo...

(3-16) Mi anuncio personal. Now, write your own personal ad, following the examples in the previous activity. Feel free to be either truthful or inventive.

Así se forma

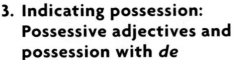

Ricardo y Tere son mis primos.

3. Indicating possession: Possessive adjectives and possession with *de*

A. Possessive adjectives

In addition to the verb **tener**, possession may also be expressed with possessive adjectives, which you have previously seen: ***Mis* abuelos viven en España**. Possessive adjectives also show ownership (*my house*) or a relationship between people (*my boyfriend*).

Los adjetivos posesivos		
Singular	**Plural**	
mi tío	**mis** tíos	*my*
tu[4] hermana	**tus** hermanas	*your (sing. informal)*
su abuelo	**sus** abuelos	*your (sing. formal), his, her, its*
nuestro/a amigo/a	**nuestros/as** amigos/as	*our*
vuestro/a primo/a	**vuestros/as** primos/as	*your (pl. informal, Spain)*
su abuelo	**sus** abuelos	*your (pl.), their*

- The choice of pronoun (**mi** vs. **tu**) depends on the possessor. Note that the possessive adjective agrees in number (**mi** vs. **mis**) and sometimes gender (**nuestro** vs. **nuestra**) with the thing possessed or person related (<u>not</u> with the possessor).

Susana tiene **nuestros libros**[5].	Susana has **our books**.
Mis padres y yo vivimos en **nuestra casa**[6].	**My parents and I** live in **our house**.

- If the ownership referred to by **su/sus** is not clear from the context, you may use an alternate form for clarity: **de** + *pronoun* or **de** + *person's name*.

Es **su carro**. *o* Es el carro **de él/ ella/ usted/ ellos/ ellas/ ustedes.**

Es el carro **de Elena.**

B. Possession with *de*

HINT

de + el = del

Whereas English uses *'s* (or *s'*) + noun to indicate possession, Spanish uses <u>**de** + noun</u>.

Es la casa **de** mi abuela.	It's my grandmother's house.
Es la casa **de** mis abuelos.	It's my grandparents' house.
Las hijas **de** Carmen son simpáticas.	Carmen's daughters are nice.
Las fotos **del** señor Soto son interesantes.	Mr. Soto's photos are interesting.

---

[4]**Tú** (with written accent) = *you*; **tu** (without written accent) = *your*. **Tú** tienes **tu** libro, ¿verdad? (*You have your book, right?*)
[5]**Susana**, is a feminine singular noun, but **nuestros** (masc. pl.) agrees with **libro**.
[6]**Mis padres y yo** is masculine plural, but **nuestra** (fem. sing.) agrees with **casa**.

To express the equivalent of the English *Whose?*, Spanish uses **¿De quién?**

— **¿De quién** es el álbum?   *Whose album is it?*

— **Es de** Susana.   *It's Susana's.*

3-17 **Tu álbum de fotos.** You were writing labels to put in your new family photo album. Now you are ready to print them, but the computer ruined your formatting. Can you fix it?

1. Esta foto es de mis *c*   **a.** coche.
2. Mi mamá y sus *f*   **b.** casa.
3. Aquí está mi hermana con su *e*   **c.** abuelos maternos.
4. Esta es nuestra *b*   **d.** gato.
5. Y este es nuestro *a*   **e.** novio.
6. El animal de la casa: nuestro *d*   **f.** hermanas (mis tías).

3-18 **Nuestras fotos.**

Paso 1. Write below what photos/posters you have in your room or on your computer. To get started, think about the following:

padres	hermano/a	coche	mejor amigo/a	perro/gato
parientes	casa	cantante/grupo favorito		lugar (*place*)

Modelo: **Tengo una foto/ fotos de mis padres.**
Tengo…

Paso 2. Now work in pairs and guess what photos your classmate has. Take notes and respond to him/her as well. Your instructor may ask you about your partner.

Modelo: Estudiante A: **Tienes una foto de tus padres.**

Estudiante B: **Sí, tengo una foto de mis padres en mi cuarto/ mi computadora.** *o* **No, no tengo fotos de mis padres.**

Estudiante A escribe: **Sandra tiene una foto de sus padres en…**

3-19 **Mis parientes favoritos.** Describe to your classmate three of your favorite relatives. Define the family relationship.

Modelo: **Mi abuelo favorito se llama…   Tiene… años.   Es de…**
Es muy inteligente…   Es el padre de mi madre.

You may be called upon to share information about your classmate with the class:

El abuelo favorito de (*classmate's name*) se llama…

Así se forma

3-20 **¿De quién es?** Close your eyes. Your instructor will "borrow" a few items from random students and will place them on her/his desk. One student will ask to whom an item on the desk belongs. Another will try to guess the owner.

Modelo: Estudiante A: **¿De quién es el libro de español?**
Estudiante B: **Es de Rita.**

4. Indicating location and describing conditions: The verb *estar*

A. Indicating location of people, places, and things

You have used the two Spanish verbs that mean *to be*: **ser** and **estar**. So far, you have used **ser** to tell origin, to indicate days of the week, dates, and time, and to describe inherent personality and physical characteristics. You have used **estar** with the expressions **¿Cómo está usted?** and **¿Cómo estás?** When **estar** is used with the preposition **en** (*in, at*), it indicates the location of people, places, or objects.

Study the forms of the present tense of the verb **estar** (*to be*), as well as the sample sentences.

estar to be		
(yo)	estoy	**Estoy** en la universidad.
(tú)	estás	**¿Estás** en casa?
(usted, él/ella)	está	Acapulco **está** en México.
(nosotros/as)	estamos	**Estamos** en clase.
(vosotros/as)	estáis	**¿Estáis** en el apartamento de Beatriz?
(ustedes, ellos/ellas)	están	Mis amigas **están** en clase.

Así se dice

¿Dónde están?

Fotos del álbum familiar

Mi hermano Ricardo está **en la escuela**.

en + *location*	*at + location*
el colegio	*school (high school)*
la escuela	*school (elementary school)*
la playa	*beach*
el trabajo	*work, workplace*

Así se dice

la ciudad	*city*
el campo	*country*
la montaña	*mountain*
allí	*there*
aquí	*here*

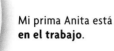

HINT

Note that **en** = *in* or *at*;
a = *to*. **Vamos *a* la playa.**
Están *en* la playa.

Mi prima Susana está **en el colegio**[7].

Mi prima Anita está
en el trabajo.

Mi primo y yo estamos **en la playa**.

Mis tíos están
en casa.

Aquí, estoy **en las
montañas** de Colorado.

Estamos **en el campo**.

Estamos **en la ciudad** de Los Ángeles.
¡Hay mucho tráfico **allí**!

---

[7]**El colegio, el liceo,** and **la preparatoria** (Mexico) are words to refer to primary or
secondary school (varies by region). Use **universidad** for university or college.

Así se dice

3-21 ¿Dónde están?

Paso 1. Guess where the following people are according to the information given.

Modelo: Juanito está en clase con su maestra. Tiene seis años.

Está en la escuela.

1. Sandra toma varias clases. Tiene muchos maestros. **Está...**
2. Tenemos varios profesores. Somos adultos. Las clases son difíciles. **Estamos...**
3. Trabajamos desde las 9:00 de la mañana hasta las 5:00 de la tarde. **Estamos...**
4. Tomo una siesta. Miro la televisión, hablo por teléfono. **Estoy...**
5. Estás de vacaciones. El océano es muy bonito. **Estás...**
6. Estás de vacaciones. Usas tus suéteres y tus esquís. **Estás...**
7. Los González dicen (*say*) que hay mucho tráfico allí. **Están...**
8. Los Martínez dicen que hay animales, flores y mucha tranquilidad allí. **Están...**

Paso 2. Now tell a classmate where some of the important people in your life are right now.

Modelo: **Mi pareja/ Mi mejor amigo/a...**

3-22 ¿Dónde estás?

Paso 1. Complete the column **Yo** in the table below indicating where you are at the times indicated.

Paso 2. Walking around the classroom, ask your classmates where they normally are on these days and times. When a classmate is at the same place as you, write his/her name in the column labeled **Mis compañeros**.

Modelo: **Normalmente, ¿dónde estás los lunes a las ocho de la mañana?**

	Yo	Mis compañeros
lunes – 8:00 A.M.		
martes – 9:30 A.M.		
miércoles – 10:45 A.M.		
jueves – 1:30 P.M.		
viernes – 3:00 P.M.		
sábado – 10:00 P.M.		
domingo – 8:00 A.M.		

Así se forma

B. Describing conditions

Estar can also be used with descriptive words to indicate the mental, emotional, or physical condition in which the subject is found at a given time.

Estoy cansado/a.	*I'm tired.* (physical)
¿**Estás** preocupado?	*Are you worried?* (mental/emotional)
¡Carlos **está** furioso!	*Carlos is furious!* (emotional).

Así se dice

¿Cómo están?

Rubén está **aburrido**.

Camila está **enojada**.

Octavio está muy **cansado**.

¡Pobre Alfonso!
Está **enfermo**.

Linda está **contenta** y **bien**.
Pero Manuel está **mal**, está **triste**.

Natalia está **ocupada**.

Carmen está **nerviosa**,
preocupada y **estresada**.

La puerta y el libro están
cerrados. La ventana y el
cuaderno están **abiertos**.

aburrido	*bored*	**mal**	*bad, badly, sick*
bien	*well*	**preocupado/a**	*worried*
contento/a	*happy*	**ocupado/a**	*busy*
enojado	*angry*	**triste**	*sad*

> **NOTA DE LENGUA**
>
> **Bien** and **mal** are adverbs and do not change in gender (masculine/feminine) or number (singular/plural) as adjectives do. **Bien** and **mal** are often used with estar.
> Estoy muy **bien**, gracias.

Así se dice

3-23 **Condiciones.** Read the descriptions below and indicate who they describe from the illustrations on page 93. Then decide on an adjective that accurately describes that person's current state.

Modelo: Está en una clase que no le gusta. No quiere poner atención.
Es Rubén. Está aburrido.

1. Está en la cama. Tiene una temperatura de 102 grados.
2. Está en la oficina, habla por teléfono y toma notas.
3. Está en el gimnasio, juega al básquetbol.
4. Está en la universidad. Tiene un examen muy difícil.
5. Está en su casa. ¡Su novio llega una hora tarde!

3-24 **¿Cómo estás?**

Paso 1. Choose three of the adjectives you just learned in this section and think of a situation in which you would feel each one.

Modelo: Enojado **Mi amigo no me llama en mi cumpleaños.**

Paso 2. Now, read your situations to a partner. Your partner will try to guess the appropriate adjective.

3-25 **Nuestro amigo Javier.** In small groups, describe what Javier is like (**ser** + *characteristics*) and/or imagine how he is feeling (**estar** + *condition*) according to the circumstances. Use the adjectives provided and others you think of.

cansado	contento	enfermo	estresado	fuerte
inteligente	ocupado	preocupado	trabajador	

Modelo: Javier juega al tenis toda la mañana.
No es perezoso, pero está muy cansado...

1. Saca buenas notas.
2. Va al gimnasio y levanta pesas.
3. Hoy está en la clínica.
4. Toma cinco clases, es voluntario y trabaja en el laboratorio por la noche.
5. Tiene dos exámenes mañana.
6. ¡Marlena, su mejor amiga, llega este fin de semana!

3-26 **La familia: ¿Cómo son? ¿Cómo están?** You and your classmate have just received a photo of the López family, with whom you will be staying during your upcoming trip to New York. Based on the picture, and using your imagination, describe the family: the number of children and what the mother, the father, the youngest/ oldest daughters, etc. are like (**ser** + *characteristics*). Talk about where they are now and how are they feeling (**estar** + *location/condition*).

Los López, Long Island,
Nueva York

Así se pronuncia

The pronunciation of *h* and *j*

h   Remember that the Spanish **h** is never pronounced.

   hermana   **h**ombre   **h**ermanastro   **h**ermoso

j   The Spanish **j** is pronounced like the *h* in the English word *help*.

   vie**j**o   **j**oven   mu**j**er de negocios

Repeat the following sentences to help perfect your pronunciation. Focus on the letters **h** and **j**.

h   **H**éctor y **H**elena tienen **h**ijos muy **h**onrados.

j   **J**osé y **J**uana tienen hi**j**os muy traba**j**adores.

Listen to your instructor and circle the spelling of the words he/she is going to pronounce. Note that the incorrect spellings do not correspond to any real words in Spanish.

1. hamón   (jamón)   4. paha   (paja) straw
2. mohado   (mojado) wet-soaked   5. (hueso)   jueso   bone
3. (zanahoria) zanajoria   6. trahe   (traje) suit
   carrot

Dicho y hecho

¡A ESCUCHAR!

Linda conversa con su padre. Linda comes from a very traditional Hispanic family. She is getting ready for her first date with Manuel, and of course her father wants to know all about Manuel's background. Listen to the conversation between father and daughter; then answer the first two questions.

1. ¿Quién hace la mayoría (*majority*) de las preguntas?
   el padre   Linda
2. ¿A quién describe Linda más (*more*)?
   a Manuel   a la familia de Manuel

Now listen to the conversation again, and then select the correct answers.

3. Linda dice (*says*) que Manuel es
   trabajador y un buen estudiante.   muy simpático y divertido.
4. La madre de Manuel es de
   San Francisco.   Los Ángeles.   Perú.
5. La madre es
   alta.   baja.   rubia.   morena.
6. El padre es
   alto.   bajo.   gordo.   delgado.
7. El padre es
   profesor de español.   hombre de negocios.

CONVERSANDO

Una persona muy especial. Bring to class a photo of a family member, your partner, or a friend. Describe the person in detail, including origin/nationality (see **Apéndice 3**, p. A–15), age, physical and personality traits, where he/she is right now, etc. Your classmates will ask you questions to elicit more information.

DE MI ESCRITORIO

Así es mi familia. Imagine that a student from México is going to spend a week with your family as part of a student exchange program. Write a letter to him describing your family. Include the family tree you did in Exercise 3–6 and complete the information you wrote with more details to describe your family: What are your grandparents, parents, siblings, and other relatives like? Include origin and nationality(ies), profession, age, physical and personality traits, and any other interesting details. Conclude by writing about yourself. You might want to add some family photos. Your professor will ask for volunteers to present their work to the class.

HINT

To describe deceased relatives, use: **era** (*he/she was*) or **eran** (*they were*). Refer to **Apéndice 3** for a listing of nationalities and professions.

Artes populares: Los murales

Antes de leer

1. Can you think of famous examples of public art?
2. Are there any murals where you live? Where are they? Do you know who painted them?

LOS MURALES

Los murales son creaciones que inspiran la imaginación y estimulan la conciencia. Los primeros[1] murales tienen miles[2] de años: están en las cuevas[3] de Lascaux (Francia) y Altamira (España). Históricamente, en los Estados Unidos, los murales son la autoexpresión y la autodefinición de muchas comunidades, especialmente en el oeste y el suroeste del país.

La creación de murales en las ciudades más importantes de California en los años 60 y 70 es labor de jóvenes chicanos[4]. Muchos murales presentan panoramas de la historia mexicano-americana. Los murales más recientes también manifiestan los intereses y preocupaciones de cada comunidad.

California es la capital del arte mural en los EE.UU. El sol[5] constante en la región, las numerosas paredes[6] de cemento y estuco, la influencia de la tradición muralista mexicana y la buena recepción que tiene el arte popular entre los californianos contribuyen a la preservación de la colección de arte público más impresionante de la nación. Examine los siguientes murales y conteste las preguntas.

[1]first [2]thousands [3]caves [4]Mexican-Americans [5]sun [6]walls

La ofrenda de Yreina Cervantes. Los Ángeles, California. En el centro está Dolores Huerta, fundadora del sindicato (*union*) United Farm Workers.

Mural *Siete punto uno* de John Pugh. Los Ángeles, California. Es un mural pintado en el exterior de un restaurante hispano. Muestra unas ruinas mayas.

Después de leer

1. Choose whether the following statements best describe the murals *La ofrenda, Siete punto uno,* or "Los Dos" (*both*).
   a. Celebra el activismo de la mujer hispana.
      ☐ *La ofrenda*   ☐ *Siete punto uno*   ☐ Los dos
   b. Hace referencia a una cultura precolombina.
      ☐ *La ofrenda*   ☐ *Siete punto uno*   ☐ Los dos
   c. Está en Los Ángeles.
      ☐ *La ofrenda*   ☐ *Siete punto uno*   ☐ Los dos
   d. Contiene referencias a los trabajadores del campo (*field workers*).
      ☐ *La ofrenda*   ☐ *Siete punto uno*   ☐ Los dos
   e. El título posiblemente se refiere a la escala Richter de temblores (*earthquakes*).
      ☐ *La ofrenda*   ☐ *Siete punto uno*   ☐ Los dos

2. Why are there so many murals in California? Add three reasons to the list below.
   a. Hay una población mexicana muy grande.
   b. _____
   c. _____
   d. _____

Repaso de vocabulario activo

Adjetivos

abierto/a   open
(estar) aburrido/a   to be bored
alto/a   tall
amable   friendly, kind
antipático/a   unpleasant
bajo/a   short
bonito/a   good looking, pretty/handsome
bueno/a   good
cansado/a   tired
cerrado/a   closed
contento/a   happy
débil   weak
delgado/a   thin
difícil   difficult
divertido/a   amusing, fun
enfermo/a   sick
enojado/a   angry
estresado/a   stressed
fácil   easy
feo/a   ugly
flaco/a   skinny
fuerte   strong
gordo/a   fat
grande   big
guapo/a   good looking, pretty/handsome
hermoso/a   good looking, pretty/ handsome
inteligente   intelligent
joven   young
malo/a   bad
mayor   old
menor   younger
moreno/a   dark skinned
nervioso/a   nervous
nuevo/a   new
ocupado/a   busy
pequeño/a   small
perezoso/a   lazy
pobre   poor

preocupado/a   worried
responsable   responsible
rico/a   rich
rubio/a   blonde
serio/a   serious, dependable
simpático/a   nice
tonto/a   dumb, silly
trabajador/a   hardworking
triste   sad
viejo/a   old

Adverbios

allí   there
aquí   here
bien   well
mal   badly
muy   very
un poco   a little

Conjunciones

o/u   or
pero   but
y/e   and

Sustantivos (Nouns)

La familia

el abuelo/ la abuela   grandfather/ grandmother
los abuelos   grandparents
el bisabuelo/ la bisabuela   great-grandfather/ great-grandmother
el cuñado/ la cuñada   brother-in-law/ sister-in-law
el esposo, el marido/ la esposa   husband/wife
el hermano/ la hermana   brother/sister
el hermanastro/ la hermanastra   stepbrother/stepsister

el hijo/ la hija   son/daughter
la madrastra   stepmother
la madre (mamá)   mother (mom)
el medio hermano/la media hermana   half-brother/half-sister
el nieto/ la nieta   grandson/grandaughter
el padrastro   stepfather
el padre (papá)   father (dad)
los padres   parents
el pariente   relative
el primo/ la prima   cousin (male/female)
el sobrino/ la sobrina   nephew/niece
el suegro/ la suegra   father/mother-in-law
el tío/ la tía   uncle/aunt

Otras personas

el amigo/ la amiga   friend (male/female)
mi mejor amigo/a   my best friend
el/ la bebé   baby
el chico/ la chica   boy/girl
el hombre   man
el muchacho/ la muchacha   boy/girl
la mujer   woman
el niño/ la niña   boy/girl
el novio/ la novia   boyfriend/girlfriend
mi pareja   my partner, significant other

Las mascotas (pets)

el gato   cat
el perro   dog

Las cosas (things) y los lugares (places)

el auto   car
el campo   countryside
el carro   car
la casa,   home, house
en casa   at home
la ciudad   city
el coche   car
el colegio   school
la escuela   school
las montañas   mountains
la playa   beach
el trabajo   work

Verbos y expresiones verbales

abrazar   to hug
amar   to love
besar   to kiss
cuidar   to take care of
estar   to be
llamar   to call
tener   to have
tener... años   to be ... years old
¿Cuántos años tienes?   How old are you?
visitar   to visit

Palabras interrogativas

¿Cuántos/as?   How many?
¿Dónde?   Where?
¿Quién/es?   Who?

Autoprueba y repaso PLUS ✓

I. The verb *tener*. Use the correct form of **tener**.

1. Yo _____ tres hermanos.
2. Mi hermano mayor _____ 21 años.
3. Mis padres _____ 55 años.
4. Mi hermano menor y yo _____ un perro.
5. ¿Cuántos años _____ tú?

II. Possessive adjectives. Use possessive adjectives to explain what each person has.

  Modelo: mi hermano/cuadernos
        Tiene sus cuadernos.

1. yo/fotos
2. ¿tú/libros?
3. José/diccionario
4. mi hermano y yo/televisor
5. ¿ustedes/calculadoras?

III. Possession with *de*. Indicate to whom each object belongs.

  Modelo: la mochila/Juan
        Es la mochila de Juan.

1. la foto/Marta
2. los cuadernos/José
3. los exámenes/los estudiantes

IV. Descriptive adjectives. Complete the first sentence in each item with the correct form of the verb **ser**. Then complete the second sentence with the correct form of **ser** and the adjective of opposite meaning.

  Modelo: Mi tío Paco __**es**__ un poco gordo. Al contrario, mi tía Lisa __**es delgada**__.

1. Yo _____ trabajador/a. Al contrario, algunos de mis amigos _____ _____.
2. Mis padres _____ muy altos. Al contrario, mi hermano _____ _____.
3. Nosotros no _____ antipáticos. Al contrario, _____ muy _____.
4. Nuestra clase de español _____ fácil. Al contrario, nuestras clases de ciencia _____ _____.

V. *Estar* to indicate location. Tell where on campus the students are located according to the activity.

  Modelo: Juana estudia mucho
        Está en la biblioteca.

1. Linda y Mónica compran lápices, bolígrafos y sus libros de texto.
2. Octavio y yo hacemos ejercicio.
3. Hablo con mis amigos y compro comida.
4. Mi amiga habla con la profesora Falcón. No están en el aula.

VI. *Estar* to indicate condition. React to the statements with forms of **estar** and appropriate adjectives.

  Modelo: Tenemos un problema.
        Estamos preocupados.

1. Tengo un examen mañana.
2. Mis amigos tienen mucha tarea.
3. Sancho tiene apendicitis.
4. ¡Tenemos un día sin (*without*) preocupaciones! ¡No hay clases!

VII. General review. Answer the following questions.

1. ¿Cuántos años tienes?
2. ¿Cómo es tu madre o padre?
3. ¿Cómo son tus amigos/as?
4. ¿Cómo están tus amigos/as?
5. ¿Están tú y tus amigos preocupados por sus notas? ¿En qué materias (*subjects*)?
6. ¿Qué días tienen ustedes clases?
7. ¿Cómo son sus clases?

VIII. *Cultura*.

1. ¿Cuáles son algunas características de la familia tradicional hispana?
2. ¿Qué porcentaje de la población en los Estados Unidos es de origen hispano? ¿En qué zonas viven la mayoría de ellos?
3. Describe algunos murales latinos en California.

Answers to the *Autoprueba y repaso* are found in **Apéndice 2.**

4

PLUS

¡A la mesa!

By the end of this chapter you will be able to:

- Buy and talk about food in a market, restaurant, etc.

- Express likes and dislikes

- Talk about actions, desires, and preferences in the present

- Express large quantities, prices, and dates

- Ask for specific information

ENTRANDO AL TEMA

1. Which factors do you think most strongly influence your eating habits in general: cost, time, flavor, health, family, etc?

2. What Hispanic foods or dishes have you tried? Have you heard of any that you would like to try?

¡A la mesa!

¡Así se dice

¡A la mesa!

arnes

el pollo

la salchicha/
el chorizo

el jamón

el ajo

Voy a preparar
arroz con pollo
esta noche.

el bistec

la carne de res

las chuletas de
cerdo/puerco

la carne de
cerdo/puerco

Legumbres
Verduras

el maíz

las cebollas

las papas/
patatas

los frijoles

las zanahorias

el bróculi

los tomates

el arroz

la lechuga

los guisantes

las judías verdes

los camarones	shrimp
la carne	meat
la chuleta	chop
el bistec	steak
costar (ue)	to cost
desear	to want, desire
los guisantes	peas
las judías verdes	green beans
la langosta	lobster
las legumbres	vegetables (in pods), legumes
el marisco	seafood, shellfish
necesitar	to need
el pescado	fish
el puerco/cerdo	pork
la res	beef
las verduras	vegetables
vender	to sell

NOTA DE LENGUA

There are many dialects and varieties of Spanish, and many words vary from one dialect to another. This variety is obvious, for instance, in the different words used for foods in different parts of the Hispanic world. Some examples from the vocabulary on the left are: **patatas** (Spain, except Canary Islands), **papas** (Latin America, Canary Islands), and **plátano** (Spain), **banana** (Latin America) but there are many more. Here are some of the names for green beans: **judías verdes** (Spain), **ejotes** (Mexico), **habichuelas** (Colombia), **chauchas** (Argentina and Chile), **porotos verdes** (parts of South America).

Así se dice

4-1 **¿Vegetariano o no?** Listen to the following food items and decide whether a vegetarian person would eat them or not. Write the names of the foods in the appropriate column.

	Sí, una persona vegetariana come esto.		No, una persona vegetariana no come esto.	
1.	Si papas	☐		☐
2.	Si manzanas	☐		☐
3.		☐	no cheltus de chezo	☐
4.	Si aho	☐		☐
5.		☐	no pollo	☐
6.		☐	no colecho	☐
7.	Si	☐		☐
8.	Si piscado	☐		☐

Did you all agree on your answers?

4-2 **La lista de compras.** Look at the following shopping lists and check off which ingredients you would need to prepare the following dishes. Add any items that you feel are missing.

Una ensalada de frutas

zanahorias
fresas
lechuga
uvas
pescado

Una sopa de pollo

duraznos
judías verdes
pollo
cebolla
zanahorias
peras

Un estofado° de carne de res   stew

cerezas
frijoles
zanahorias
carne de res
papas

NOTA CULTURAL

El vegetarianismo
While somewhere between 4–7% of people in the United States are vegetarians with increasing access to animal-free products, such diets are not as common in Spanish-speaking countries.

4-3 **Vamos al mercado.** Work in pairs.

Estudiante A:
You own a little grocery store. First, make a list of ten foods you carry in your store. Then help your customer with the things he/she needs.

HINT

When two Spanish verbs are used consecutively, the first is conjugated and the second is used in its infinitive form, just as in English.
¿Desea usted **cenar**? *Do you **want to have dinner**?*
Necesito comprar más tomates. *I **need to buy** more tomatoes.*

Estudiante B:
You are going to prepare a dish of your choice. First, prepare a list of four or more ingredients you will need. Then go to the store, inquire about and purchase what you need.

Modelo: Vendedor/a: **Buenos días, ¿qué desea?**
Cliente: **Pues, necesito...**
¿Tiene usted... ?

NOTA CULTURAL

El mercado
While supermarkets are very common in Latin America and in Spain, many people still prefer to shop at small markets, or **mercados**.

Así se dice

4-4 Chef Merito

ESTRATEGIA PARA LEER

Visual information Pay attention to the format, photos, graphs, or other visuals to anticipate what kind of text you are going to read. You may also anticipate some of the topics or ideas you might read about.

 Paso 1. Look at the image on the following page.

1. Based on its format and visuals, it probably is . . .

    a. a scientific article   **b.** a brochure   **c.** an ad   **d.** an excerpt from a novel

2. It probably advertises . . .

    a. a restaurant   **b.** healthy eating   **c.** a brand of spices   **d.** a supermarket

PALABRAS ÚTILES

sal — *salt*
pimienta — *pepper*
hierbas — *herbs*

ESTRATEGIA PARA LEER

Skimming for general content Read the ad quickly to get a general idea of its content. Do not attempt to translate it word for word.

 Paso 2. Skim for general content and write a phrase to summarize the main idea in this ad.

 Paso 3. Look at the tasks below and read the ad again. Then write your answers where appropriate.

1. Identifica las carnes y las legumbres en el anuncio.
2. Identifica en la fotografía los dos ingredientes típicamente mexicanos. Pregunta a tu profesor/a los nombres de estos ingredientes.
3. Indica las cualidades de los productos Chef Merito, según el anuncio (*according to the ad*).

    son baratos (*cheap*)   son fáciles (*easy*) de usar   tienen garantía de calidad
    son variados   son orgánicos   son auténticos

 Paso 4. ¿Y ustedes?

1. ¿Usan ustedes salsa picante? ¿En qué comidas?
2. ¿Qué sazonadores (*seasonings*) usan ustedes para preparar sus comidas favoritas? ¿Qué sazonadores del Chef Merito desean comprar?

Investig@ en INTERNET

Busca en Internet el sitio de Chef Merito, ¿cuánto cuesta la Salsa Picante? ¿y el Sazonador para Fajitas? ¿Qué producto es nuevo para ti (*for you*)?

HINT

Remember a previous strategy: Look for cognates.

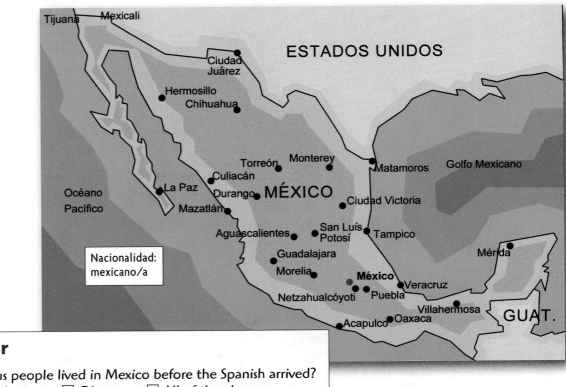

Tijuana Mexicali

ESTADOS UNIDOS

Ciudad Juárez

Hermosillo
Chihuahua

Torreón Monterey Matamoros Golfo Mexicano

Culiacán

Océano Pacífico La Paz Durango MÉXICO Ciudad Victoria

Mazatlán

Aguascalientes San Luís Potosí Tampico

Nacionalidad: mexicano/a

Guadalajara Mérida

Morelia México Veracruz

Netzahualcóyoti Puebla

Acapulco Oaxaca Villahermosa GUAT.

Antes de leer

1. Which indigenous people lived in Mexico before the Spanish arrived?
   ☐ Mayans ☐ Aztecs ☐ Olmecs ☐ All of the above

2. How many languages are spoken in Mexico today?
   ☐ One ☐ Approximately 20 ☐ Approximately 60

3. True or false: Mexico's climate is very hot all year round.
   ☐ True ☐ False

UN TERRITORIO DIVERSO

ESTRATEGIA PARA LEER

Reading Titles
When a reading has several sections, first read all of the heading titles to get a sense of their content. You may also wish to pause and summarize what you have read in one section before continuing with the next.

Where you see a place name in red text, quickly look back at the map to locate it.

México es un país[1] muy diverso. En el **norte** del país, incluyendo **Monterrey**, **Chihuahua** y **Hermosillo**, el clima es frío[2] en invierno. El **centro** del país, que incluye **Aguascalientes**, **San Luís Potosí**,

Puebla y **la ciudad de México**, es una vasta región de valles, donde el clima no es muy frío ni muy caluroso[3]. La región centro-oeste, incluyendo **Guadalajara** y **Mazatlán**, es una zona muy fértil con mucha agricultura y ganadería[4]. En el sureste, por ejemplo Cancún, hay mucho turismo.

[1]*country* [2]*cold* [3]*warm* [4]*catle-raising*

Ciudad	Enero		Abril		Julio		Octubre	
	Máx	Min	Máx	Min	Máx	Min	Máx	Min
Acapulco	87	72	87	73	89	77	89	77
Mexico City	66	42	77	51	73	53	70	50

Máx. = temperatura máxima; Min. = temperatura mínima.

LA HISTORIA

México tiene una de las poblaciones de indígenas más numerosas de Latinoamérica. En el pasado, existían muchos grupos diversos como los Olmecas, los Totonacos, los Maya y los Aztecas. Cada grupo hablaba un idioma diferente. Hoy, todavía[5] existen unos 60 de estos idiomas en el territorio mexicano.

Antes de llegar los conquistadores españoles, los aztecas eran[6] el grupo dominante. Controlaban 371 tribus en 33 provincias, y todos hablaban la lengua Náhuatl. La capital, Tenochtitlán, era una ciudad flotante[7] con unos 250.000 habitantes. Hernán Cortés conquistó Tenocthitlán y a su emperador, Moctezuma, en 1519.

[5]*still* [6]*were* [7]*floating*

¿Puedes identificar a Hernán Cortés y al emperador Moctezuma?

En la bandera[8] mexicana, hay un águila[9] con una serpiente[10] en la boca encima de un nopal[11].

[8]*flag* [9]*eagle* [10]*snake* [11]*prickly pear cactus*

La "Riviera maya"

LA CAPITAL

Hoy, el antiguo Tenochtitlán sigue[12] como la capital del país, pero se llama "la Ciudad de México", "el Distrito Federal", "el D.F", o simplemente "México". Actualmente[13] el D.F. tiene una población de casi 20.000.000 de habitantes—¡es la ciudad más grande del mundo! La cultura indígena es visible en los murales que decoran la capital y en las caras de muchos habitantes.

En las avenidas del centro de la ciudad hay tiendas[14], restaurantes, teatros y hoteles elegantes. La impresionante arquitectura es tradicional y futurista. El Ángel de la Independencia domina el Paseo de la Reforma, una de las avenidas principales de la ciudad capital.

[12]continues [13]currently (NOT actually) [14]stores

Antes: Tenochtitlán

¿Qué aspectos de la vida azteca ilustra el mural del famoso pintor mexicano, Diego Rivera?

Un complicado sistema de puentes[15] y canales unía la ciudad flotante de Tenochtitlán

[15]bridges

Ahora: La Ciudad de México

México es una ciudad fascinante donde coexisten la tradición y la modernidad. La Plaza de las Tres Culturas simboliza esta fusión; combina ruinas arqueológicas aztecas, una iglesia[16] colonial y edificios[17] modernos.

[16]church [17]buildings

¿Hay una avenida en tu ciudad similar al Paseo de la Reforma?

EL PRESENTE Y EL FUTURO

El petróleo es la industria principal de México, el turismo es la segunda industria del país y la tercera fuente de ingresos[18] son las *remesas*: el dinero que envían[19] a México los mexicanos y mexicano-americanos que viven y trabajan en los Estados Unidos. En el año 2004, el total de las remesas fueron unos 15.000 millones[20] de dólares.

Con el Tratado de Libre Comercio entre los Estados Unidos, México y Canadá (NAFTA, 1994), la frontera entre **Tijuana** y **Matamoros** es una región cada vez más[21] fundamental para el comercio y la industria. Muchas fábricas maquiladoras[22] en las ciudades fronterizas con México emplean a un millón de mexicanos, y millones de individuos vienen a buscar empleo en los Estados Unidos. Mexicanos y norteamericanos cruzan los puentes fronterizos constantemente para ir de compras[23].

---

[18]*income* [19]*send* [20]*This is how to say* **"15 billion"** *in Spanish-speaking countries:* "15 million" [21]**cada...** *increasingly* [22]*assembly plants* [23]**ir...** *shopping*

Mira la foto del puente entre Nuevo Laredo, México y Laredo, Tejas. Imagina cuántas personas cruzan este puente cada día.

Después de leer

1. Go back to the questions in **Antes de leer**. Do you want to change any of your answers?

2. Based on the photos on page 110, what do you find most impressive about Ciudad de México?

3. Looking at the Spanish words below, which ones do you think come from Nahuatl?

   ☐ Tenochtitlán   ☐ chocolate   ☐ tomate   ☐ elote (*sweet corn*)

¿Te gustan los champiñones?

Sí, me gustan mucho.

Inés

Octavio

1. Expressing likes and dislikes: The verb *gustar*

Read the following dialog between Octavio and Inés. Pay attention to the forms of **gustar**.

food

Do you like; food	Inés: ¿**Te gusta**° la comida° de la cafetería de la universidad?
I like it	Octavio: Sí, **me gusta**° mucho.
	Inés: ¿De veras? A mí **no me gusta** para nada y a mi compañera de
does not like it; either	cuarto **no le gusta**° tampoco°.
	Octavio: ¿Por qué no **les gusta**?
tasty	Inés: No **nos gusta** porque no es nutritiva ni muy sabrosa°.
mushrooms	Octavio: Pero esta sopa de champiñones° está deliciosa. **Me gusta** muchísimo.
	Inés: Sí, está deliciosa, pero el problema es que no tiene champiñones.
	Octavio: ¡Qué horror! ¿Qué son?
	Inés: ¿Quién sabe?

Spanish expresses likes and dislikes with the verb **gustar**, which literally means *to be pleasing (to someone)*.

		Literal Translation
Me gusta el helado.	*I like ice cream.*	*Ice cream is pleasing to me.*
¿Te gustan las fresas?	*Do you like strawberries?*	*Are strawberries pleasing to you?*
No le gusta tomar vino.	*He doesn't like to drink wine.*	*Drinking wine isn't pleasing to him.*

As you can see in the examples, the subject pronouns (**yo, tú, él,...**) are *not* used with **gustar**. To express who is doing the liking (or literally, to whom something is pleasing), the forms **me, te, le, nos, os, les**[1] are used. The verb takes the singular form **gusta** when the thing that is pleasing is a single item and the plural form **gustan** when the thing liked is plural.

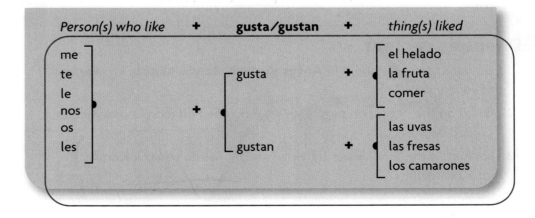

Person(s) who like	+	gusta/gustan	+	thing(s) liked
me te le nos os les	+	gusta	+	el helado la fruta comer
		gustan	+	las uvas las fresas los camarones

[1]The indirect-object pronouns, meaning *to me, to you, to you/him/her, to us, to you, to you/them*, will be studied in detail in **Capítulo 7**.

- The definite article is used with the thing(s) liked:

  Me gusta **el** helado.
  Me gustan **las** fresas.

- If what is pleasing is an activity, use singular form **gusta** with the infinitive (**-ar, -er, -ir** form) of the appropriate verb:

  Nos **gust<u>a</u> <u>comer</u>**.   We **like to eat.**
  Les **gust<u>a</u> <u>cenar</u>** en restaurantes   They **like to have dinner** in
      y **<u>asistir</u>** a conciertos.   restaurants and **attend** concerts.

- To clarify the meaning of **le** and **les**, add **a** + *person*: **a Pedro, a ella,** etc.:

  Pedro y Ana toman el desayuno   Pedro and Ana have breakfast
      juntos. **A Pedro** <u>le</u> gusta tomar   together. **Pedro** likes to drink
      café, pero **a ella** <u>le</u> gusta el té.   coffee, but **she** likes tea.

- For emphasis, add **a mí, a ti, a usted, a nosotros,** etc.:

  A mí no me gustan los camarones.   **I** don't like shrimp.
  A ti te gustan, ¿verdad?   **You** like them, right?

- To ask a follow-up question, use:

  ¿Y a ti?, ¿Y a usted?, ¿Y a él?, etc.

(4-5) **¡Me gusta!** Listen to the following series of statements. Decide which food item is being talked about in each one.

Modelo: You hear: Me gusta.
            You choose: ☐ los limones   ☒ el ajo

1. ☒ las zanahorias   ☐ el pescado
2. ☐ la lechuga   ☐ las fresas
3. ☐ las cerezas   ☒ el jamón
4. ☒ el bistec   ☐ las naranjas
5. ☐ las peras   ☐ la langosta
6. ☒ el pollo   ☐ los camarones.

(4-6) **¿A quién?** Read the following statements or questions and decide who is being referred to.

Modelo: Le gusta la langosta.   ☐ A ellos   ☒ A ella

1. Te gustan los tomates.   ☒ A ti   ☐ A él
2. El pescado les gusta mucho.   ☒ A Carmen y a Ana ☐ A nosotros
3. Le gustan los plátanos.   ☐ A ustedes   ☒ A Jorge
4. La piña nos gusta.   ☒ A nosotros   ☐ A ellos
5. ¿Le gusta el ajo?   ☒ A usted   ☐ A ti
6. El maíz me gusta.   ☐ A Elena   ☒ A mí

Así se forma

4-7 ¿Te gusta?

 Paso 1. First, answer the questions about yourself in the column **A mí** in the table below. Fill in the last two questions about additional food items that you choose.

	A mí		A mi compañero/a	
1. ¿Te gusta el bróculi?	☑ Sí	☐ No	☐ Sí	☑ No
2. ¿Te gustan las fresas?	☑ Sí	☐ No	☑ Sí	☐ No
3. ¿Te gustan los camarones?	☑ Sí	☐ No	☑ Sí	☐ No
4. ¿Te gustan los frijoles?	☑ Sí	☐ No	☑ Sí	☐ No
5. ¿Te gusta el maíz?	☑ Sí	☐ No	☑ Sí	☐ No
6. ¿Te gusta el ajo?	☑ Sí	☐ No	☑ Sí	☐ No
7. ¿ _Te gustan piña_ ?	☑ Sí	☐ No	☑ Sí	☐ No
8. ¿ _Te gusta café_ ?	☑ Sí	☐ No	☑ Sí	☐ No

Paso 2. Now, ask a classmate (**compañero/a**) the same questions about his/her likes and dislikes. Write his/her name in the header of the right column and mark his/her answers.

Modelo: ¿Te gusta el bróculi?

Paso 3. How much do you have in common? Write a short paragraph comparing and contrasting your likes and dislikes. Don't forget the **a** where needed.

Modelo:  **A nosotros <u>nos</u> gusta el ajo y el maíz. Pero <u>a</u> mí no <u>me</u> gustan** 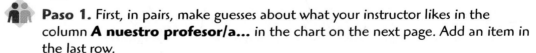 **los frijoles, y <u>a</u> Cristina sí <u>le</u> gustan... (etc.)**

4-8 Preguntas para tu profesor/a.

Paso 1. First, in pairs, make guesses about what your instructor likes in the column **A nuestro profesor/a...** in the chart on the next page. Add an item in the last row.

A nuestro profesor/a...	Detalles (*Details*)
1. Le gusta / No le gusta leer novelas.	¿Qué tipo? ¿Qué novela es su favorita?
2. Le gusta / No le gusta cenar en restaurantes.	¿Qué tipo de comida? ¿Cómo se llama su restaurante favorito?
3. Le gusta / No le gusta mirar la televisión.	¿Qué tipos de programas mira? ¿Qué programa no le gusta?
4. Le gusta / No le gusta asistir a conciertos.	¿Qué tipo de música? ¿Qué cantantes o grupos musicales son sus favoritos?
5. Le gusta / No le gusta usar Internet.	¿Con mucha frecuencia? ¿Envía mensajes electrónicos, navega por la red... ?
6. Le gusta / No le gusta _____.	¿_____?

 Paso 2. Now, take turns asking your instructor whether he/she likes those things, and follow up with the questions in the column **Detalles** or others of your own. Be sure to note his/her answers.

Modelo: **¿Le gusta leer novelas? ¿Qué tipo?**

How well do you know your instructor? Did you guess correctly?

 Paso 3. In small groups, discuss how your professor's likes and dislikes compare with your own.

Escenas

Camila

Esteban

Natalia

¿Qué hay para cenar?

Frente a la cafetería de la universidad. Es hora de cenar y Natalia lee el menú en la entrada. Llegan Camila y Esteban.

Paso 1. Based on the title and introduction, try to anticipate what types of foods Camila, Esteban, and Natalia may find on the menu.

sopa de verduras	pescado	ensalada de fruta	crema de espárragos
bistec de res	flan	papas	pollo frito (*fried*)

Escenas

Paso 2. Listen to the conversation focusing on the main ideas and indicate which of the following statements are true (**Cierto**) or false (**Falso**).

	Cierto	Falso
1. A Camila, Esteban y Natalia les gusta el menú del restaurante.	☐	☐
2. La comida del restaurante es saludable y nutritiva.	☐	☐
3. Van a cenar en el restaurante La Isla.	☐	☐
4. Deciden preparar la cena en casa.	☐	☐

Paso 3. Look at the questions below and listen again. This time focus on the specific information you need to answer the questions. You may take notes as you listen.

1. ¿Qué hay en el menú de hoy?
2. ¿Por qué no quiere Camila comer la ensalada de papa y zanahoria?
3. ¿Qué desea comer Esteban? ¿Y Camila?
4. ¿Van a un restaurante? ¿Por qué?
5. ¿Dónde van a cenar?
6. ¿Qué va a preparar cada persona?

Paso 4. Listen one more time as you read along. Then check your answers to the previous questions.

Camila y
Esteban: ¡Hola, Natalia! ¿Cómo te va?

Natalia: Bastante bien. ¿Qué hay de nuevo?

something   Esteban: Pues no mucho. Vamos a comer. ¿Hay algo° bueno en el menú de hoy?

Natalia: Depende. ¿Te gusta el arroz con guisantes y pollo frito?

healthy   Camila: ¿Pollo frito otra vez? ¡No es un plato muy saludable°! ¿Hay ensalada?

Natalia: Claro que sí, es tu favorita: ensalada de papa y zanahoria con mayonesa.

Camila: ¡Ugh! Esa ensalada tiene muchas calorías y yo estoy a dieta. Pero hay sopa de verduras, ¿verdad?

Natalia: Vamos a ver... Pues, no. Sólo hay sopa de pescado.

Esteban: Yo quiero comer algo diferente. Quiero unas chuletas de cerdo con

puré... *mashed potatoes*   puré de papas°, frijoles y arroz...

olives   Camila: Y una ensalada de lechuga fresca, con tomates, cebolla y aceitunas°...

caramel custard; dessert   Natalia: ¡Y flan° y café para el postre°!

Todos... *They all sigh*   (*Todos suspiran°*.)

Esteban: Bueno, ¿y por qué no vamos al restaurante La Isla?

expensive   Camila: Esteban, La Isla es un restaurante caro° y yo sólo tengo diez dólares.

Natalia: Es verdad. ¿Por qué no hacemos la cena en mi casa? Las chuletas de cerdo son mi especialidad y son muy fáciles de preparar.

cook   Esteban: Yo no cocino° bien, pero mi especialidad es el flan instantáne... Camila, tú puedes preparar la ensalada.

also   Camila: ¡Sí! Y también° puedo preparar las papas.

Natalia: ¡Fantástico! Vamos al supermercado. Mi coche está en el estacionamiento norte.

Así se forma

Rubén, ¿quieres cenar en un restaurante con nosotras esta noche?

Prefiero cenar solo, gracias.

¡Ay de mí!

2. Talking about actions, desires, and preferences in the present: Stem-changing verbs

Stem-changing (irregular) verbs have the same endings as regular **-ar, -er,** and **-ir** verbs. They differ from regular verbs in that a change occurs in the stem (**e → ie, o → ue,** or **e → i**) in all persons except **nosotros** and **vosotros**. The stem is the part of the verb that remains after the **-ar, -er,** or **-ir** ending is removed.

Study the pattern of change in the following model verbs.

e → ie

querer *to want, to love*
quer- → **quier-**

qu**ie**ro	queremos
qu**ie**res	queréis
qu**ie**re	qu**ie**ren

querer (ie)	*to want, to love*	No **quiero** comer ahora.
preferir (ie)	*to prefer*	**Prefiero** comer más tarde.
entender (ie)	*to understand*	¿**Entienden** el problema?
pensar[2] (ie)	*to think*	¿**Piensas** que hay un problema?

o → ~~ou~~ ue

dormir *to sleep*
dorm- → **duerm-**

d**ue**rmo	dormimos
d**ue**rmes	dormís
d**ue**rme	d**ue**rmen

 return to a place.

dormir (ue)	*to sleep*	¿**Duermes** bien?
almorzar (ue)	*to have lunch*	¿A qué hora **almuerzas**?
poder (ue)	*to be able, can*	¿**Puedes** cenar a las 7:00?
volver (ue)	*to return, go back*	¿A qué hora **vuelves** a la residencia?

e → i

pedir *to ask for*
ped- → **pid-**

p**i**do	pedimos
p**i**des	pedís
p**i**de	p**i**den

pedir (i)	*to ask for, request, order*	Ella siempre **pide** pizza.
servir (i)	*to serve, to be good (for something)*	¿**Sirven** langosta aquí? Esta cebolla **sirve** para la sopa.

DICHOS

Querer es poder
¿Puedes explicar este dicho en español?

---

[2]When seeking an opinion, ask **¿Qué piensas de... ?** *(What do you think about . . . ?).* When giving your opinion, say **Pienso que...** *(I think that . . .).*

Así se forma

 4-9 La confesión de Esteban.

 Paso 1. La confesión de Esteban. Read the following paragraph, paying special attention to the stem–changing verbs.

Sí, es verdad. Soy un poco glotón—bueno, muy glotón. Muchos estudiantes toman cereal por la mañana, pero yo pref**ie**ro tomar un desayuno más... tradicional, con huevos° y tocino°. Por la tarde alm**ue**rzo una hamburguesa con papas y Coca-Cola en McDonald's, v**ue**lvo a mi cuarto y d**ue**rmo la siesta. Antes de hacer la tarea, tomo café para estar alerta y como unas galletas°. No p**ue**do estudiar cuando no tomo un café; p**ie**nso que necesito la cafeína. Generalmente, ceno en la cafetería de la universidad; la comida no es muy variada pero siempre s**i**rven pizza, pollo frito y p**ue**do comer todo lo que qu**ie**ro. Verdaderamente p**ie**nso que no está mal. No ent**ie**ndo a esas personas que siempre hacen dietas y p**ie**nsan en la nutrición todo el día y ¡no qu**ie**ren comer estas cosas tan buenas!

eggs; bacon

cookies

 Paso 2. ¿Cierto o falso? Cover the paragraph above and decide whether the following statements are true or false.

	Cierto	Falso
1. Esteban pref**ie**re un desayuno ligero (*light*).	☐	☐
2. Esteban alm**ue**rza comida rápida (*fast food*).	☐	☐
3. Después de almorzar, v**ue**lve a la universidad.	☐	☐
4. Esteban nunca d**ue**rme la siesta.	☐	☐
5. P**ie**nsa que la cafeína es buena para él.	☐	☐
6. En la cafetería de la universidad s**i**rven comida nutritiva.	☐	☐

¿Prefieren ustedes la comida de la universidad o la comida rápida? ¿Por qué?

Paso 3. ¿Eres muy similar o muy diferente a Esteban? Write a short paragraph comparing yourself to Esteban. Be careful to make the stem changes in the **yo** and **él** (Esteban) forms, but to keep the original vowel in the **nosotros** forms.

Modelo: Esteban y yo somos (muy) similares/ diferentes. Nosotros preferimos tomar un desayuno... / El almuerza comida rápida y yo almuerzo en mi casa...

NOTA CULTURAL

La comida rápida en el mundo hispano

There are several popular fast-food chains in the Spanish-speaking world, including:

Pollo Campero	Guatemala, Costa Rica, Honduras, Nicaragua, Ecuador, Mexico, El Salvador, the United States
El Pollo Loco	Mexico, the United States
Pans & Company	Spain

In addition, United States fast-food chains that open in other countries often adopt local customs. For example, in Puerto Rico, McDonald's serves **tostones** (*fried plantains*) and in Spain, they serve beer. Even several McDonald's locations in Miami serve classic Cuban sandwiches (ham, pork, Swiss cheese, pickles, and mustard on toasted Cuban-style bread) and the *Dulce de Leche* McFlurry with caramelized, sweetened condensed milk.

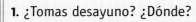

4-10 Sondeo alimentario.

 Paso 1. Answer the questions below about yourself.

SONDEO DE LAS COSTUMBRES ALIMENTARIAS

1. ¿Tomas desayuno? ¿Dónde?

2. ¿Dónde almuerzas?

3. ¿Dónde prefieres cenar durante la semana?

4. ¿Qué piensas de las cafeterías y restaurantes universitarios?

      a. son buenos **b.** son malos   **c.** son mediocres

5. En general, ¿qué piensas de la "comida rápida" en campus?

      a. es mala   **b.** es buena   **c.** es mediocre

6. ¿Qué restaurante prefieres para una comida rápida en campus?

7. ¿Puedes cocinar (*cook*) en tu cuarto/ apartamento?

8. ¿Qué platillos (*dishes*) puedes preparar?

9. Cuando vuelves a casa para visitar a tu familia, ¿qué comida pides?

Paso 2. Now, in groups of four, share your answers and take notes of the group's answers as well. Be ready to report back to the class.

4-11 La comida de la universidad.
A student from México is coming to your university next semester and he e-mails you asking about the university's food. Answer his questions.

Asunto : Recomendaciones para comer en campus

¡Hola!

Voy a estudiar en tu universidad el próximo semestre y me gustaría saber un poco sobre la comida. Por lo general, ¿cómo es la comida que sirven en la universidad? ¿Sirven carnes, pescados o mariscos con frecuencia? ¿Qué tipo de platillos? ¿Sirven ensalada y/o sopa todos los días? ¿Qué tipo? ¿Qué frutas sirven? ¿Hay frutas todos los días?

¿Qué otras opciones hay para comer? ¿Prefieren ustedes la comida de la universidad o la comida rápida?

Muchas gracias. Un saludo atento,

Pablo Morales

Así se forma

4-12 **Las preferencias y necesidades estudiantiles.** Pablo e-mails you with some more questions about students' study and rest habits.

Paso 1. In pairs, talk about some of the issues Pablo is raising. Each one of you will bring up one topic. Use the cues and the interrogative words provided below to ask follow-up questions.

Modelo: necesitar dormir más

        Estudiante A: **¿Necesitas dormir más?**

        Estudiante B: **Sí, necesito dormir más. ¡No duermo mucho!**

        Estudiante A: **¿Cuántas horas duermes normalmente?**

        Estudiante B: **Cinco horas.**

        Estudiante A: **Yo duermo seis horas aproximadamente.**

Estudiante A: Hábitos de estudio
- preferir la biblioteca o el cuarto para estudiar
- pedir ayuda (*help*) a los profesores en horas de oficina
- estudiar solo/a o con amigos

Estudiante B: Hábitos de descanso
- actividades para relajarse (*relax*)
- dormir la siesta
- poder descansar (*rest*)

¿Cuántos/as... ?	¿Dónde... ?	¿Qué... ?
¿Cuándo... ?	¿A qué hora... ?	¿Por qué... ?

Paso 2. Think about your partner's responses, what you know about other friends, and your own experience. Then reply to Pablo.

Asunto : Re: Hábitos

Hola Pablo,

Pues, por lo general los estudiantes...

Así se dice

Las comidas y las bebidas

- la leche
- la pimienta
- la sal
- CEREALES
- el cereal
- el pan (tostado)
- la mermelada
- los huevos
- la mantequilla
- el tocino, la tocineta

- el jugo, el zumo (Esp.)
- la crema
- el azúcar
- el café
- el té

- el refresco
- el sándwich, el bocadillo (Esp.)
- las papas fritas
- la hamburguesa

- el vinagre
- la aceituna
- el aceite
- la sopa
- la ensalada

- el vino
- la cerveza
- el agua
- el hielo

- el queso
- el pastel
- la torta
- las galletas
- el helado

el aceite	*oil*	**la mermelada**	*jam*
la aceituna	*olive*	**el refresco**	*soft drink*

Así se dice

¿Cuál es tu preferencia? Imagine that you are studying abroad in Mexico and staying with a Spanish-speaking family. Shortly after your arrival, your host mother (a great cook) has many questions for you. She aims to please!

Puedes tomar tres **comidas** en casa con nosotros: tomamos el **desayuno** a las 8 de la mañana, el **almuerzo** a las dos de la tarde y la **cena** a las ocho. En la mañana, ¿prefieres **tomar** una **bebida fría** (jugo) o una bebida **caliente**, (café o té)? ¿Prefieres jugo de naranja o jugo de piña? ¿Tomas el café **con** azúcar o **sin** azúcar? ¿Prefieres los huevos **fritos** o **revueltos**? Esta noche voy a preparar sopa, ensalada y pollo con papas fritas. ¿Prefieres el pollo **a la parrilla**, frito o **al horno**? ¿Comes **mucha** o **poca** carne? ¿Cuál es tu **postre** favorito? ¿Te gusta el pastel de Tres Leches? Como ves, ¡me gusta **cocinar**!

al horno	*baked*	**mucho/a/os/as**	*much, a lot, many*
a la parrilla	*grilled*	**poco/a/os/as**	*little (quantity), few*
cocinar	*to cook*		
la comida	*food, meal, main meal*	**con**	*with*
la bebida	*drink, beverage*	**sin**	*without*
frito/a	*fried*		
postre	*dessert*		
revuelto/a	*scrambled*		

NOTA DE LENGUA

- **Mucho** and **poco** do not change in gender and number when they modify verbs.
  Comemos **mucho/poco.**   We eat a lot/little.
  When they modify nouns, **mucho** and **poco** do change in gender and number to agree with the noun.
  Comemos **muchas** verduras y **poca** carne.
- Spanish uses the preposition **de** (*of*) to join two nouns for the purpose of description.
  helado **de** vainilla   vanilla ice cream
  jugo **de** naranja   orange juice
  How many combinations can you come up with?

DICHOS

king; middle-class person
beggar

Desayuna como un rey°, almuerza como un burgués° y cena como un mendigo°.
¿Cómo puedes explicar este dicho?

4-13 **Asociaciones.** With what do you associate the following foods? Write the foods listed into the appropriate box.

El desayuno	El almuerzo	La merienda[3]	La cena	El postre
breakfast	*lunch*	*snack*	*dinner*	*dessert*

1. pan tostado con mantequilla y mermelada
2. sopa y ensalada
3. pastel de manzana con helado de vainilla
4. un cóctel de camarones
5. huevos revueltos con tocino
6. jugo/ zumo de naranja
7. unas galletas y leche
8. un sándwich/ bocadillo de jamón y queso
9. arroz con pollo, pan y vino
10. café caliente con crema y azúcar
11. una hamburguesa con papas fritas
12. bistec a la parrilla con papas al horno y ensalada mixta

4-14 **¿Comes mucho o poco?**

Paso 1. Read the following list of food items. Pay attention to whether they are masculine or feminine and singular or plural. Then check off whether you eat a lot or a little of each one, filling in the correct ending.

Modelo: El pastel ☐ Como much___. ☒ Como poc_o_.

1. Las aceitunas ☐ Como much___. ☐ Como poc___.
2. Las galletas ☐ Como much___. ☐ Como poc___.
3. El cereal ☐ Como much___. ☐ Como poc___.
4. Los huevos ☐ Como much___. ☐ Como poc___.
5. El vino ☐ Tomo[4] much___. ☐ Tomo poc___.
6. El agua ☐ Tomo much___. ☐ Tomo poc___.
7. El queso ☐ Como much___. ☐ Como poc___.
8. La sopa ☐ Como much___. ☐ Como poc___.
9. El helado ☐ Como much___. ☐ Como poc___.
10. La leche ☐ Tomo much___. ☐ Tomo poc___.

Paso 2. Now compare your answers in small groups. How much do you have in common?

---

[3]A late afternoon snack, usually consisting of a sandwich or pastries.
[4]Note that you can say **tomar** or **beber** for *to drink*.

¡A la mesa! ciento veintitrés **123**

Así se dice

4-15 **Consejos (_Advice_) de los nutricionistas.** Medical studies show that certain foods are beneficial and reduce the risk of cancer and other diseases. In pairs, compile two lists of foods for incoming first-year students: those they should consume a lot of and those they should consume less of to maintain optimum health.

Deben comer/ tomar...	
mucho(a)/muchos(as)	**poco(a)/pocos(as)**

¡Tengo hambre!

Pepita jogs every morning and leads a very active life. She also has a big appetite! Read the conversation between Pepita and the waiter at a local café.

Mesero: ¿Qué desea usted, señorita?
Pepita: **¡Tengo mucha hambre! Quisiera** comer un sándwich de jamón y queso y **también** una ensalada.
Mesero: ¿Y para tomar?
Pepita: Una limonada grande, por favor. **Tengo** mucha **sed**.
Mesero: A la orden*, señorita.

(Pepita se lo come todo y decide que **todavía** tiene hambre. Pide **más** comida.)
Mesero: ¿Desea usted algo más?
Pepita: Sí, **otro** sándwich, por favor, y otra limonada, pero con **menos** hielo.
Mesero: Con mucho gusto, señorita.

tener (mucha) hambre	_to be (very) hungry_	**otro**	_another_
tener (mucha) sed	_to be (very) thirsty_	**también**	_also_
más/ menos	_more/less, fewer_	**todavía**	_still, yet_
quisiera	_I would like (polite)_		

*A... _At your service_

NOTA DE LENGUA

In Spanish, the verb **tener** has many uses. In **Capítulo 3** you learned the expression **tener... años** (_to be . . . years old_). **Tener hambre** and **tener sed** follow the same pattern.

¡Tengo mucha hambre!
I am very hungry.
Also note that **otro/a** does not use the indefinite article **un/una.**

Quisiera **otra** limonada, por favor.   _I would like **another** lemonade, please._

4-16 **¡Qué hambre tenemos!** Work in groups of three. Two of you have just run a marathon and you are famished and extremely thirsty. You are now at a restaurant where the third student is the waiter. Work together on a dialogue using the words and expressions in the box below. Be ready to act it out for the class.

tener hambre	tener sed	otro/a	más	menos	quisiera

Cultura: Las comidas en el mundo hispano

Antes de leer

1. What time are breakfast, lunch, and dinner typically eaten in the United States? Which is usually the heaviest meal of the day?

2. Are you familiar with any dishes consisting of a flour crust and meat filling, which are fried or baked?

¿Deseas un pan dulce (*sweet*) de esta pastelería mexicana?

El desayuno hispano es normalmente entre las 6 y las 9 de la mañana. Comparado con el desayuno tradicional estadounidense, el desayuno hispano es muy ligero[1]. Muchos españoles e hispanoamericanos desayunan una taza de café (expreso) con leche, y pan con mantequilla o mermelada. En las regiones costeras[2] de hispanoamérica, también es común desayunar café y plátanos verdes[3] o tortillas de maíz.

El almuerzo, generalmente es entre la 1 y las 2 de la tarde y es la comida más fuerte[4] del día. Muchos negocios[5], particularmente en los pueblos pequeños, cierran para esta comida. El almuerzo puede incluir una ensalada, sopa, arroz o verduras, carne o pescado y postre. En algunos países, a las 5 o a las 6 de la tarde es común comer la merienda, que consiste en café o té, leche, galletas, pastel o un bocadillo.

Generalmente los hispanos cenan más tarde que los estadounidenses, pero es una comida más ligera. La cena hispana típicamente es entre las 8 y las 9 de la noche, y en España puede ser más tarde, entre las 10 y las 12 de la noche.

Una parte importante de la comida es "la sobremesa". Este término define la charla[6] después de la comida. Es cuando se toma el café, a veces seguido[7] de un aperitivo de alcohol y se conversa de asuntos[8] serios o triviales.

---

[1]*light*   [2]*coastal*   [3]*green plantains*   [4]**más...** *largest*   [5]*businesses*   [6]*chat, conversation*   [7]*followed by*   [8]*issues*

Conexiones y contrastes

1. Name two differences between when people eat in Hispanic countries and in the U.S.

2. What dishes mentioned in the text would you like to try? Why?

Cultura: Las comidas en el mundo hispano

ALGUNOS PLATOS (*DISHES*) TÍPICOS DEL MUNDO HISPANO

La **empanada**: masa de harina rellena generalmente con carne, cebollas, huevos y aceitunas, frita o al horno.

La **paella** (España): plato de arroz con pollo, mariscos y guisantes, sazonado con azafrán (*saffron*).

La **tortilla** (España): contiene huevos, patatas y cebollas. Se sirve con frecuencia a la hora de la merienda en los bares de España. También se come en casa para la cena.

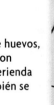

Las **quesadillas** (México): tortillas de maíz, fritas, con queso, pollo, champiñones y otros ingredientes al gusto. En el desayuno típico de la foto se sirven con frijoles, papaya, jugo de naranja y café con leche.

El **flan**: un postre de huevos, leche, azúcar y vainilla, cocido en un molde al horno con almíbar (*syrup*) de caramelo.

SITUACIONES

Uno de ustedes (Estudiante A) vive con una familia hispana por un semestre. Es la hora de tu primera (*first*) cena con la familia. La madre/El padre (Estudiante B) sirve su especialidad—lengua de ternera (*beef tongue*). Al Estudiante A no le gusta y definitivamente no puede comerla. El Estudiante B dice (*says*): **¡Buen provecho!** (*Bon appétit*), pero unos minutos más tarde observa que el Estudiante A no come y pregunta: **¿No te gusta la comida?**

Después de leer

Based on the text you have just read, determine if the following meals are typical of the U.S., a Hispanic country, or both.

1. desayuno con pan y café con leche
2. almuerzo con sopa, carne, arroz y postre
3. desayuno con cereal, huevos y tocino
4. cena a la medianoche
5. cena con una pizza y Coca-Cola
6. merienda con leche y galletas
7. almuerzo con un sándwich

Los **churros**: masa de harina cilíndrica frita. Frecuentemente se sirven (*are served*) con café con leche o con chocolate caliente.

Así se forma

ochocientos
noventa y uno, ...

3. Counting from 100 and indicating the year

In Hispanic countries, prices of meals and of everyday items are often expressed in thousands of **pesos, colones,** and so on. Therefore, it is important to become accustomed to understanding and using numbers over 100.

cien	100	**ochocientos/as**	800
ciento uno/a	101	**novecientos/as**	900
doscientos/as	200	**mil**	1000
trescientos/as	300	**dos mil**	2000
cuatrocientos/as	400	**cien mil**	100.000
quinientos/as	500	**doscientos mil**	200.000
seiscientos/as	600	**un millón (de + *noun*)**[5]	1.000.000
setecientos/as	700	**dos millones (de + *noun*)**	2.000.000

- **Cien** is used before a noun or as the number 100 when counting. **Ciento** is used with numbers 101 to 199.

   Hay **cien** estudiantes en la clase.   **Cien, ciento uno, ...**

   Sólo tengo **cien** pesos.   La torta cuesta **ciento un** pesos.

- In Spanish, there is no **y** between hundreds and a smaller number, although *and* is often used in English.

   205 (*two hundred and five*) = **doscientos cinco**
   ~~doscientos y cinco~~

- When the numbers 200–900 modify a noun, they agree in gender.

   trescient**os** alumnos y quinient**as** alumnas

- Years above 1000 are not broken into two-digit groups as they are in English.

   1971 (*nineteen seventy one*) = **mil novecientos setenta y uno**
   ~~diecinueve setenta y uno~~

- In writing numbers, Spanish commonly uses a period where English uses a comma, and vice-versa.

   English: $121,250.50 = Spanish: $121.250,50

---

[5] When **millón/millones** is immediately followed by a noun, the word **de** must be used: **un millón *de* pesos, dos millones *de* euros;** but **un millón doscientos mil quetzales.**

Así se forma

4-17 **Vamos a cambiar (*exchange*) dólares.** In pairs, take turns as the teller (**cajero/a**) at a money exchange booth at the Miami International Airport and a client going to a Hispanic country. The client will ask to exchange dollars for the currency of the country he/she is traveling to and the teller must calculate the amount according to the exchange rates listed in the chart below.

Modelo: Destino: Guatemala/$100 (EE.UU.)

Turista: **Quiero cambiar cien dólares a quetzales, por favor.**

Cajero/a: **Muy bien, señor/señorita.** (*He/She counts the money.*) **Aquí tiene 800 (ochocientos) quetzales. Buen viaje.**

Turista: **Muchas gracias.**

Cambio	Moneda	Dólar EE.UU.
España	euro	1,25
Guatemala	quetzal	8
Colombia	peso	3
Costa Rica	colón	350
México	peso	10

Destino

1. Guatemala/$175 (EE.UU.)

2. Colombia/$550

3. España/$2.000

4. Costa Rica/$700

5. México/$900

4-18 **¿Qué vamos a pedir?** You are in a restaurant in Taxco, Mexico, trying to decide what to order. Study the menu below. Prices are in **pesos** (1 dollar = 10 **pesos** approximately).

El Rincón

DESAYUNO (7 A.M.–10 A.M.)		ALMUERZO (11 A.M.–2 P.M.)		CENA (5 P.M.–10 P.M.)	
Huevos con tocino	50	Tacos de carne	70	Puerco en salsa verde	80
Huevos revueltos	75	Enchiladas suizas	80	Carne de res en salsa	80
Pan tostado	40	Ensalada el Rincón	70	Pollo a la parrilla	80
Cereal	50	Tamales	60	Pollo al horno	80

PLATO DEL DÍA: Pescado al mojo de ajo 90

SOPAS		BEBIDAS		POSTRES	
Caldo de verduras	60	Aguas frescas	40	Helados	70
Sopa de pollo	80	Refrescos	20	Flan	60

Bar y Restaurante El Rincón, Calle Guadalupe 15, Taxco, Tel. 417 817-1993

Now, in small groups, discuss your decisions.

Modelo: Estudiante A: **Pienso pedir... Cuesta... Y tú ¿qué vas a pedir?**

Estudiante B: **No voy a pedir... porque no me gusta...**
Voy a pedir...

4-19 **¿En qué año?** Here is a list of some well-known restaurants with a long history. Listen and fill in the last column with the date that each one opened.

Nombre del restaurante	Año
1. La Diligencia (Tarragona, España)	
2. El Faro (Nueva York, NY)	
3. Delmonico's (Nueva York, NY)	
4. Venta de Aires (Toledo, España)	
5. Richmond (Buenos Aires, Argentina)	
6. Casa Botín (Madrid, España)	
7. Restaurante El Quijote (Nueva York, NY)	

¿Cuál es el restaurante más antiguo (*oldest*) de esta lista? ¿Sabes (*Do you know*) cuál es el restaurante más antiguo de tu ciudad?

Así se forma

(4-20) El precio justo. Today you are playing *The Price Is Right!* In small groups, guess the price of each of the following items and write it down. A secretary will list your answers on the chalkboard to compare them with the "correct" price he/she has previously determined. The group that comes closest to the "correct" price for the most items without going over, wins. Remember: In this activity, the teacher is always right!

1. una cena elegante para dos en un restaurante de ★★★★★ en Nueva York
2. una mansión en Beverly Hills, California
3. un televisor plasma de 37 pulgadas (*inches*)
4. una computadora de último (*latest*) modelo con monitor y teclado
5. una cámara digital de 10 píxeles
6. un billete de avión de ida y vuelta (*round-trip plane ticket*) a México D.F.
7. la matrícula de un año en su universidad
8. un *Rolls Royce* nuevo

NOTA CULTURAL

La comida mexicana vs. la comida Tex-Mex

"Tex-Mex" is a term given to food, music, and other cultural items based on the combined cultures of Texas and Mexico. Many ingredients of Tex-Mex cooking are common in Mexican cuisine, although other ingredients are unknown in Mexico. Tex-Mex food encompasses a wide variety of dishes such as *burritos, chimichangas, nachos, fajitas,* tortilla chips with *salsa,* and *chili con carne,* all of which are usually not found in Mexico.

---

4. Asking for specific information: Interrogative words (A summary)

Vi a Octavio con una chica muy...

¿Con quién? ¿Cuándo? ¿Dónde?

You have used some interrogative words to ask questions: *¿Cómo estás? ¿Qué pasa? ¿De dónde eres? ¿Adónde vas después de la clase? ¿Cuántos años tienes? ¿Cuánto cuesta?* Following are the most commonly used interrogative words in Spanish.

¿Qué?	*What?*	¿**Qué** frutas tienen hoy?
		¿**Qué** quiere usted?
¿Cómo?	*How?*	¿**Cómo** están las fresas hoy?
¿Cuándo?	*When?*	¿**Cuándo** llegan las piñas?

¿Por qué?	*Why?*	**¿Por qué** no hay cerezas?
¿Quién/ Quiénes?	*Who?*	**¿Quién** vende mariscos?
¿De quién?	*Whose?*	**¿De quién** es?
¿Cuál/ Cuáles?	*Which (one/ones)?*	**¿Cuál/Cuáles** prefieres?
¿Cuánto?	*How much?*	**¿Cuánto** es en total?
¿Cuántos/ Cuántas?	*How many?*	**¿Cuántos** tomates/**Cuántas** peras quiere?
¿Dónde?	*Where?*	**¿Dónde** está el vendedor?
¿Adónde?	*(To) where?*	**¿Adónde** va?
¿De dónde?	*From where?*	**¿De dónde** es?

- Note the difference between **¿qué?** and **¿cuál?**:

¿Qué + *noun***?** When followed by a noun, always use interrogative **qué**.

> **¿Qué** postre deseas?   *What (Which) dessert do you want?*

¿Qué/ Cuál + **ser?** When followed by the verb **ser**, use interrogative **qué** to ask for a definition or explanation; use interrogative **cuál** to ask for specific data or piece of information.

> **¿Qué es** la dirección? (definition)   *What is the "address"? An appropriate answer would be: It is the information about where a place is located or where somebody lives . . .*

> **¿Cuál es** tu dirección? (specific information)   *What is your address? An appropriate answer would be: It is 34 Longwood Avenue.*

¿Qué/ Cuál + *verb***?** When followed by a verb different than **ser**, use interrogative **qué** to ask about a general choice; use interrogative **cuál** to ask about a choice among given options.

> **¿Qué** quieres comprar?   *What do you want to buy?*

> **¿Cuál** quieres, el rojo o el azul?   *Which one do you want to buy, the red one or the blue one?*

- Note that all the interrogative words above have written accents. When they appear without it, they connect two separate thoughts within a statement rather than ask a question.

que	*that, which, who*	En el mercado **que** está en la plaza venden mariscos.
lo que	*what, that which*	Compro **lo que** necesito.
cuando	*when*	**Cuando** tengo hambre, voy a la cafetería.
porque	*because*	Quiero una pizza grande **porque** tengo mucha hambre.

Así se forma

4-21 **¿Qué palabra interrogativa?** Imagine that one classmate interviewed another for a class assignment. Match the questions with the appropriate answers.

1. ¿Cómo estás?
2. ¿A qué hora es tu primera clase?
3. ¿Dónde prefieres estudiar?
4. ¿Cuándo vas a dormir?
5. ¿Cuál es tu clase favorita?
6. ¿Qué clases tienes?
7. ¿Cuánto cuestan tus libros?
8. ¿A quién pides ayuda con los problemas?
9. ¿Cuántas horas estudias cada día?
10. ¿Cómo es la comida en la cafetería?
11. ¿Qué haces después de las clases?

a. ____ Tres o cuatro.
b. ____ Voy al gimnasio o a la biblioteca.
c. ____ Quinientos dólares más o menos.
d. _1_ Muy bien, gracias.
e. ____ Español, historia y biología.
f. ____ A las 9 de la mañana.
g. ____ Buena... a mí me gusta.
h. ____ Normalmente, a medianoche.
i. ____ ¡Español, claro!
j. ____ A mi consejero (advisor).
k. ____ En mi cuarto.

4-22 **¿Qué o cuál?** Mark the correct interrogative word keeping in mind the given answers.

1. — ¿☐ Qué ☐ Cuál es tu dirección de correo electrónico?
   — Es *mar2@mail.com*.
2. — ¿☐ Qué ☐ Cuál es una manzana?
   — Es una fruta.
3. — ¿☐ Qué ☐ Cuál estudias?
   — Estudio economía y finanzas.
4. — ¿☐ Qué ☐ Cuál postre desea usted?
   — Querría un helado.
5. — ¿☐ Qué ☐ Cuál prefiere, el helado de chocolate o el de vainilla?
   — El de chocolate.

4-23 **Vamos a ser honestos.** You and your classmate have been friends for a while, but have not always been honest with each other. Finally you decide to come clean. Take turns telling each other about your lies and ask for the truth. Add one more "lie" of your own.

truth **Modelo:** Estudiante A: La verdad° es que mi plato favorito no son los raviolis.

Estudiante B: **¿No? ¿Cuál es tu plato favorito?**

Estudiante A: Los tamales.

Estudiante A:

1. No me llamo...
2. No tengo... años.
3. No estudio...
4. Mi cantante (*singer*) favorito no es...
5. ...

Estudiante B:

1. No soy de...
2. No vivo en una residencia estudiantil.
3. Después de las clases no voy a la biblioteca.
4. Mi comida favorita no es...
5. ...

 4-24 **El personaje misterioso.** In groups, each student will take on the identity of a famous celebrity. Each student will answer questions from the rest of the group until someone guesses correctly. There are two rules:

- the questions must start with an interrogative word
- each student can only guess once about each celebrity

PALABRAS ÚTILES			
cantante	*singer*	político	*politician*
actor/actriz	*actor/actress*	cómico	*comedian*
deportista	*athlete*	escritor	*writer*
científico	*scientist*		
presentador de televisión	*TV anchor/host*		
hombre/mujer de negocios	*businessman/woman*		

 4-25 **Una cena especial.** In groups of four, plan a special dinner together. Use interrogative words such as those in parentheses.

- el lugar, la fecha y la hora de la cena (¿Cuándo?)
- la lista de invitados (¿Cuántos/as? ¿Quién(es)?)
- lo que van a servir para cenar y para tomar (¿Qué?)
- los ingredientes que van a comprar y las cantidades (*quantities*) (¿Qué?) (¿Cuántos/as?)
- otros detalles (por ejemplo, música) (¿Qué?)
- las responsabilidades de cada persona (¿Quién?)

Investig@ en INTERNET

Do you know who Frida Kahlo is? Find information about her on the Internet, including some images of her and her work. Be prepared to share this information in class.

Así se pronuncia

The pronunciation of *gue/gui* and *que/qui*

Remember that **g** before **a, o,** and **u** has the same sound as the English g in *gold*.

    lan**g**osta   **g**alleta   **g**ustar   ju**g**o

But **g** before **e** or **i** has the same sound as **j** (as the English h in *help*).

    ar**g**entino   cole**g**io   **g**imnasio   jen**g**ibre (*ginger*)

In the combinations **gue, gui, que,** and **qui,** remember that the **u** is silent.

    hambur**gue**sa   **gui**santes   **que**so   mante**qui**lla

Repeat the following sentences:

g   A mucha **g**ente le **g**usta tomar ju**g**o y **g**alletas para desayunar.

gue/gui   Al señor **Gue**rra le gustan los **gui**santes y las fresas con meren**gue**.

que/qui   Ra**que**l **Qui**ntana **qui**ere comprar **que**so y mante**qui**lla.

Now listen and identify the correct spelling of the following words. The incorrect spellings do not correspond to any real words in Spanish.

1. ☐ gitarra   ☐ guitarra

2. ☐ congelar   ☐ conguelar

3. ☐ girar   ☐ guirar

4. ☐ gapa   ☐ guapa

5. ☐ gotera   ☐ guotera

6. ☐ geranio   ☐ gueranio

7. ☐ gardia   ☐ guardia

8. ☐ gerra   ☐ guerra

Dicho y hecho

¡A ESCUCHAR!

Un mensaje telefónico. The telephone rings. Nobody is home and the answering machine picks up.

Listen to the message and then answer the first two questions.

1. ¿Quién deja el mensaje?
   ☐ la esposa de Pablo   ☐ la madre de Pablo

2. ¿Quién va a preparar la comida?
   ☐ Pablo   ☐ ella

Listen to the message again and then complete the following sentences.

3. Puede preparar un sándwich con _____, _____, lechuga y _____.

4. Para tomar hay _____.

5. Para el postre hay _____ y _____.

SOPAS / SOUPS	
Sopa del día	$3.75
Soup of the day	
Sopa de pollo	$3.50
chicken soup	
Sopa de frijoles negros	$3.50
Black bean soup	

TORTILLAS / OMELETTES	
Tortilla española con arroz y plátanos	$6.75
Spanish omelette, rice & plantains	
Tortilla de plátano con arroz y frijoles negros	$5.95
Plantain omelette with rice & beans	

ENSALADAS / SALAD	
Ensalada mixta	$4.75
House salad	
Ensalada de sardinas	$6.95
sardine salad	
Ensalada de tomate	$3.50
Tomato salad	
Serrucho en escabeche	$8.25
Pickled kingfish	
Plato de frutas	$4.95
Fruit platter	

CARNES / MEATS	
Bistec de palomilla	$8.95
Cuban steak	
Lomo de puerco	$9.75
Roast pork lon-cuban style	
Masa de puerco	$9.95
Fried pork chunks	
Chuletas de puerco	$8.50
Pork chops	
Carne al pincho	$12.95
Shish kabob	
Picadillo a la cubana	$6.25
Cuban ground beef creole	

AVES / CHICKEN	
Pechuga de pollo a la plancha	$8.25
Boneless grilled chicken breast	
Pollo asado	$7.95
Roasted chicken	
Chicharrones de pollo	$7.95
deep fried chicken chunks	
Pechuga de pollo rellena con camarones	$8.95
Chicken breast stuffed with shrimp	

PESCADOS / FISH	
Pescado empanizado	$9.95
Breaded fish	
Pescado a la plancha	$9.75
Grilled fish	
Brocheta de camarones	$11.75
Shrimp kabob	
Camarones empanizados	$12.25
Breaded shrimp	
Camarones al ajillo	$12.25
Shrimp in garlic	
Langosta enchilada	$20.25
Lobster creole	

POSTRES / DESSERTS	
Pudín de pan	$3.75
Bread pudding	
Flan de leche	$3.75
Custard	
Arroz con leche	$3.75
Rice pudding	
Coco rallado	$3.25
Shredded coconut	

HELADOS / ICE CREAM	
Coco	$2.95
Mango	$2.95
Chocolate	$2.95
Vainilla	$2.95

EXPRESIONES ÚTILES

el mesero/la mesera
¿Qué desean ustedes? ¿Y para ustedes? ¿Qué desean tomar? Les recomiendo (comidas/bebidas)... Nuestros postres son exquisitos.

el/la cliente
Quisiera... ¿Cuál es la sopa del día? ¿Qué nos recomienda? ¿Sirven arroz y plátanos fritos con todos los platos? Muchas gracias. ¡La cuenta (check) por favor!

Dicho y hecho

 CONVERSANDO

Una cena especial. Larios' restaurant in Miami Beach serves typical Cuban food. Imagine that one of you is a waiter at the restaurant and the other three are customers. First, read the menu and discuss the dishes. The waiter offers several suggestions. Then decide what you are going to order, and order it.

DE MI ESCRITORIO

Eres guionista (*screenwriter*). You have been asked to complete the following TV script for a romantic soap opera scene featuring Linda and Manuel celebrating at a restaurant. Use your imagination to write the middle section of the scene.

Estamos en El Madrileño, un elegante restaurante español.
Es el cumpleaños de Linda, y Manuel quiere celebrarlo con su novia.

Anfitrión:	Buenas noches, ¿tienen reservaciones?
Manuel:	Sí, señor, a nombre de Manuel Cervantes.
Linda:	¡Ay, Manuel, qué restaurante tan elegante!
Manuel:	Lo mejor para ti en tu día, mi cielo°. Te quiero°.
Linda:	Yo también te quiero mucho.

darling; **Te...** *I love you*

(Your section goes here: Linda and Manuel review the menu together, talking about their likes, dislikes, and preferences. Then they place their order and enjoy the meal.)

Manuel:	La cuenta, por favor.
Mesero:	Aquí tiene, señor.
Manuel:	¡Dios mío, Linda, se me perdió la billetera°!
Linda:	No te preocupes°, mi amor. Te ayudo° a lavar° los platos. ¡Ja! ¡Ja!

se... *I lost my wallet!;*
No... *Don't worry;*
Te... *I'll help you; wash*

Artes culinarias:

Las tortillas de maíz

Antes de leer

What types of foods are consumed on a daily basis in your family or community? Are there any ingredients that are used very frequently?

ESTRATEGIA PARA LEER

Linking language and visuals The introductory paragraph and diagram come from a website about Mexican cuisine. Skim the passage quickly to find general information about the preparation of tortillas. Then refer to the diagram to help you determine the steps involved in making homemade tortillas.

El consumo diario de tortillas en México es de aproximadamente 300 millones. Desde luego[1], para satisfacer una demanda de esta magnitud, hay máquinas que las elaboran[2] en grandes cantidades. Pero en muchas partes del país, especialmente en zonas rurales, hacer las tortillas es el deber cotidiano[3] de las mujeres. La única[4] concesión a los tiempos modernos es el empleo[5] de la pequeña prensa[6] metálica para extender la masa[7]: un instrumento elemental, que se vende en todos los mercados de México y que ha ahorrado[8] millones de horas de trabajo a millones de manos[9]. Si quieres hacer tus propias[10] tortillas en casa, pon los siguientes pasos[11] en el orden correcto.

En México, la tortilla es la base de la comida típica y forma parte de muchos sabrosos (*tasty*) platos.

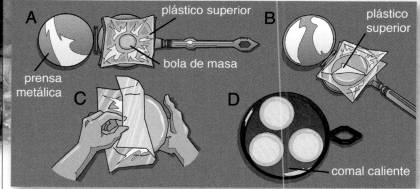

plástico superior

bola de masa

prensa metálica

plástico superior

comal caliente

Después de leer

1. How are *tortillas* produced in order to meet the huge demand?

2. Who makes *tortillas* in rural areas?

3. Do you know of any Mexican dishes that use *tortillas*?

Instrucciones:

_____ cerrar la prensa, presionar y luego abrir la prensa

_____ tomar la masa necesaria y hacer una bolita

_____ cocinar cada lado de la tortilla unos momentos

_____ poner la bolita en el centro de una prensa metálica, entre dos pedazos de plástico transparente

_____ extender la tortilla sobre el comal caliente

_____ separar la tortilla del plástico superior y luego del otro plástico

[1]**Desde...** *Of course* [2]*make them* [3]**deber...** *daily task* [4]*only* [5]*use* [6]*press* [7]*dough* [8]**ha...** *has saved* [9]*hands* [10]*own* [11]*steps*

Repaso de vocabulario activo

Adjetivos y expresiones adjetivales

al horno   *baked*

a la parrilla   *grilled*

caliente   *hot*

frío/a   *cold*

frito/a   *fried*

mucho/a/os/as   *much, a lot, many*

otro/a/os/as   *another/other*

poco/a/os/as   *little (quantity), few*

Adverbios

más/ menos   *more/less*

mucho/ poco   *a lot/a little*

también   *also*

todavía   *still*

Conjunciones

cuando   *when*

lo que   *what (that which)*

porque   *because*

que   *that, which, who*

Palabras interrogativas

¿Adónde?   *(To) where?*

¿Cómo?   *How?*

¿Cuál?/ ¿Cuáles?   *Which (one)/(ones)?*

¿Cuándo?   *When?*

¿Cuánto/a/os/as?   *How much?/How many?*

¿De dónde?   *From where?*

¿De quién?   *Whose?*

¿Dónde?   *Where?*

¿Por qué?   *Why?*

¿Qué?   *What? Which?*

¿Quién/es?   *Who?*

Preposiciones

con   *with*

sin   ~~sin~~ *without*

Sustantivos

Las comidas del día *Day's meals*

el almuerzo   *lunch*

la cena   *dinner*

el desayuno   *breakfast*

Las legumbres y verduras   *Vegetables*

el bróculi   *broccoli*

la cebolla   *onion*

los frijoles   *beans*

los guisantes   *peas*

las judías verdes   *green beans*

la lechuga   *lettuce*

el maíz   *corn*

la papa/ la patata   *potato*

las papas fritas   *French potatoes*

el tomate   *tomato*

la zanahoria   *carrot*

Las frutas   *Fruits*

la banana/ el plátano   *banana*

la cereza   *cherry*

la fresa   *strawberry*

el limón   *lemon*

la manzana   *apple*

el melocotón/ el durazno   *peach*

la naranja   *orange*

la pera   *pear*

la piña   *pineapple*

la sandía   *watermelon*

la uva   *grape*

Las carnes, los pescados y mariscos   *Meat, fish, and shellfish*

el bistec   *steak*

el camarón   *shrimp*

la carne de cerdo/ puerco   *pork*

la carne de res   *beef*

la chuleta de cerdo/ puerco   *pork chop*

la hamburguesa   *hamburger*

el jamón   *ham*

la langosta   *lobster*

el pescado   *fish*

el pollo   *chicken*

la salchicha/ el chorizo   *sausage*

la tocineta/ el tocino   *bacon*

Las bebidas *Beverages*

el agua   *water*

el café   *coffee*

la cerveza   *beer*

el jugo/ el zumo   *juice*

la leche   *milk*

el refresco   *soda drink*

el té   *tea*

el vino   *wine*

Los postres   *Desserts*

la galleta   *cookie*

el helado   *ice cream*

el pastel   *pie, pastry*

la torta   *cake*

Otras comidas y condimentos   *Other foods and condiments*

el aceite   *oil*

la aceituna   *olive*

el ajo   *garlic*

el arroz   *rice*

el azúcar   *sugar*

el cereal   *cereal*

la crema   *cream*

la ensalada   *salad*

el hielo   *ice*

el huevo   *egg*

los huevos revueltos/ fritos   *scrambled/ fried eggs*

la mantequilla   *butter*

la mermelada   *jam*

el pan   *bread*

el pan tostado   *toast*

la pimienta   *pepper*

el queso   *cheese*

la sal   *salt*

el sándwich/ el bocadillo   *sandwich*

la sopa   *soup*

el vinagre   *vinegar*

Verbos y expresiones verbales

almorzar (ue)   *to have lunch*

cocinar   *to cook*

costar (ue)   *to cost*

desear   *to want, to wish*

dormir (ue)   *to sleep*

entender (ie)   *to understand*

gustar   *to like*

necesitar   *to need*

pedir (i)   *to ask for, to order*

pensar (ie)   *to think*

poder (ue)   *to be able, can*

preferir (ie)   *to prefer*

preparar   *to prepare*

querer (ie)   *to want, to love*

servir (i)   *to serve*

tomar   *to take, to drink*

vender   *to sell*

volver (ue)   *to return, to go back*

quisiera   *I would like*

tener (mucha) hambre   *to be (very) hungry*

tener (mucha) sed   *to be (very) thirsty*

Autoprueba y repaso WILEY PLUS ✓

I. The verb _gustar_. Write questions according to the model and then answer them. Use the correct form of **gustar** and the appropriate corresponding pronoun.

Modelo: ¿A tu hermano / las legumbres?
¿A tu hermano le gustan las legumbres?
Sí, le gustan las legumbres.   _o_
No, no le gustan...

1. ¿A tus padres / tomar café?
2. ¿A ustedes / la comida italiana?
3. ¿A ustedes / desayunar temprano?
4. ¿A tu abuela / los postres?
5. ¿A ti / los frijoles negros?

II. Stem-changing verbs. Write questions to your friends using the **ustedes** form of the verb. Then write answers to the questions using the **nosotros** form.

Modelo: entender el ejercicio
¿Entienden el ejercicio?
Sí, entendemos el ejercicio.   _o_
No, no entendemos el ejercicio.

1. poder cocinar
2. querer ir al supermercado
3. almorzar a las doce todos los días
4. preferir cenar en un restaurante o en la cafetería
5. normalmente pedir postres en los restaurantes

III. Counting from 100 and indicating the year.

A. Mr. Trompa, a very wealthy man, is going to buy everything his two daughters need to start college. How much money does he need to buy two of each of the following items? Follow the model and write out the numbers.

Modelo: Un libro de psicología cuesta $90.
Dos cuestan ciento ochenta dólares.

1. Un libro de arte cuesta $125.
2. Una calculadora excelente cuesta $170.
3. Una impresora cuesta $450.
4. Una computadora con teclado y monitor cuesta $1400.
5. Un televisor para el cuarto cuesta $750.
6. Un coche nuevo cuesta $25.000.

B. Write out the following famous years.
1. Colón llega al Nuevo Mundo: 1492
2. La destrucción de la Armada Invencible de España: 1588
3. La Declaración de Independencia de EE.UU.: 1776
4. La caída (_fall_) del Muro de Berlín: 1989
5. La caída de las Torres Gemelas: 2001

IV. Interrogative words. Use various interrogative words to obtain more information.

Modelo: Ana no come en la cafetería.
¿Dónde come?   _o_   **¿Por qué no come en la cafetería?**

1. Ana no bebe vino.
2. La sandía no es su fruta favorita.
3. No trabaja por la mañana.
4. No es de Buenos Aires.
5. No tiene veinte años.
6. No vive en la residencia estudiantil.
7. No va a la librería ahora.
8. No está enferma hoy

V. General review. Answer the following questions about yourself and your friends. Use complete sentences.

1. ¿Qué comes en el desayuno?
2. ¿Cuál es tu postre favorito?
3. ¿Qué frutas te gustan más?
4. ¿Dónde quieres cenar esta noche?
5. ¿Cuántas horas duermes (generalmente) por la noche?
6. Tú y tus amigos, ¿pueden estudiar toda la noche sin dormir?

VI. _Cultura._

1. Name two or three differences between Hispanic culture and your culture with regard to diet and eating habits.
2. Describe the difference between a "tortilla" in México and a "tortilla" in Spain.
3. What are some of the largest contributors to México's economy?

Answers to the _Autoprueba y repaso_ are found in **Apéndice 2.**

CAPÍTULO 5

Recreaciones y pasatiempos

By the end of this chapter you will be able to:

- Talk about hobbies, pastimes, and activities
- Talk about the weather and the seasons
- Express future actions
- Describe an action in progress

Así se dice	Así se forma	Cultura	Dicho y hecho
• Recreaciones y pasatiempos • Los colores • El clima y las estaciones	1. Additional **yo**-irregular verbs 2. **Ir** + **a** + *infinitive* 3. The present progressive 4. **Ser** and **estar** (A summary)	• Cuba y la República Dominicana • El fútbol: rey de los deportes • Artes literarias: Nicolás Guillén	• ¡Todo sobre el fútbol! • Un día sin clases • Una excursión

ENTRANDO AL TEMA

1. What is the most popular sport in the Spanish-speaking world—that is, the one with the greatest number of players and fans?

2. Can you name three countries located in the Caribbean?

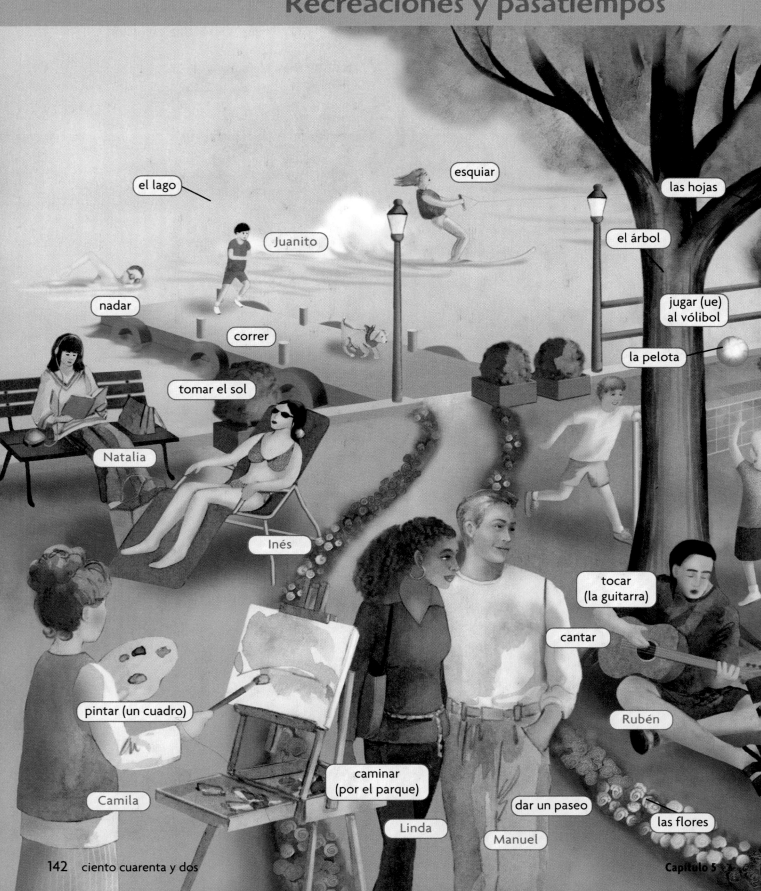

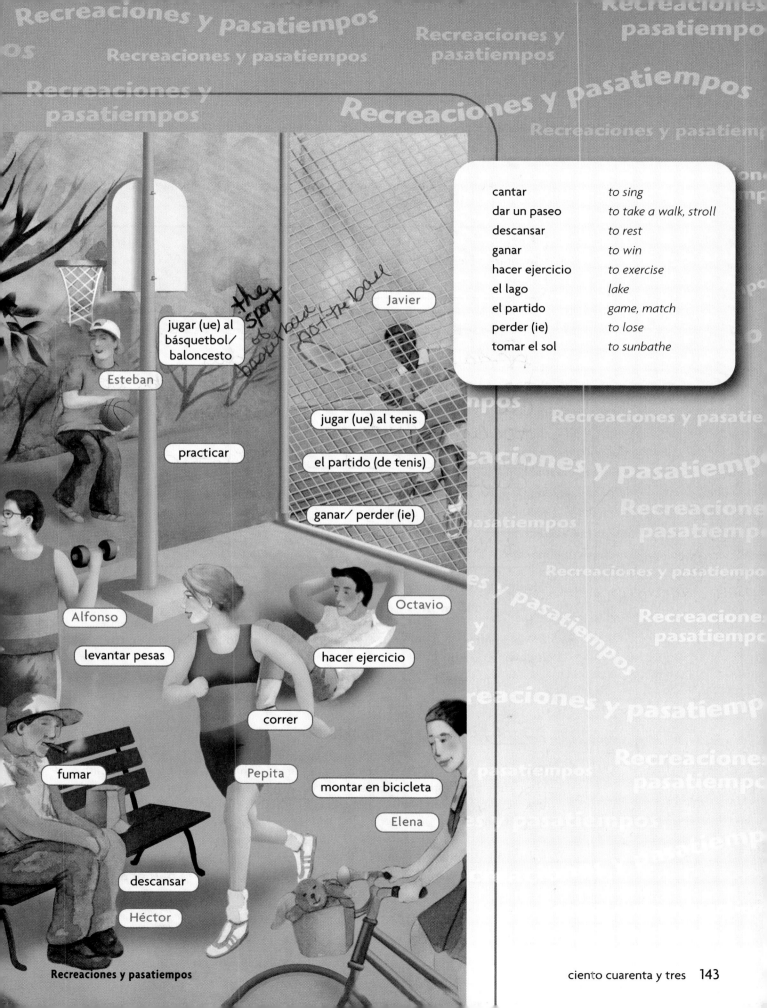

cantar	to sing
dar un paseo	to take a walk, stroll
descansar	to rest
ganar	to win
hacer ejercicio	to exercise
el lago	lake
el partido	game, match
perder (ie)	to lose
tomar el sol	to sunbathe

Esteban

jugar (ue) al básquetbol/ baloncesto

the sport of basketball not the ball

Javier

practicar

jugar (ue) al tenis

el partido (de tenis)

ganar/ perder (ie)

Alfonso

Octavio

levantar pesas

hacer ejercicio

correr

fumar

Pepita

montar en bicicleta

Elena

descansar

Héctor

Recreaciones y pasatiempos

Así se dice

Recreaciones y pasatiempos
Recreaciones y pasatiempos
pasatiempos
recreaciones y pasatiempos
pasatiempos

5-1 ¿Somos sedentarios o activos?

Paso 1. Put the following activities into the correct column based on whether they are sedentary or active.

nadar	tomar el sol	jugar al vólibol	levantar pesas
montar en bicicleta	cantar	pintar un cuadro	descansar
fumar	tocar la guitarra	esquiar	jugar al tenis

Actividades sedentarias	Actividades físicas
nadar fumar	nadar
tomar el sol	montar en bicicleta
canter	jugar al vólibol
tocar la guitarra	esquiar
pintar un cuadro	levantar pesas
descansar	jugar al tenis

Paso 2. Now write sentences that say how often you do each activity, using the following terms of frequency.

frequently	sometimes	rarely	never
frecuentemente	a veces	casi nunca	nunca

Modelos: Nado muy frecuentemente.

No monto en bicicleta nunca.

Paso 3. Now, share your answers in small groups and together discuss the following question:

En general, ¿son ustedes sedentarios o activos?

5-2 ¿Qué me recomiendas?

Paso 1. In pairs, take turns telling your partner what you want to accomplish and suggesting appropriate actitivities to each other. Can you recommend more than one activity? Be prepared to tell the class whether you agree with your partner's suggestions.

Modelo: Estudiante A says: "Me gustan las actividades rápidas".

Estudiante B suggests: **Te recomiendo jugar al baloncesto y correr.**

Estudiante A:

1. "Quiero expresarme artísticamente".

2. "Quiero jugar un deporte de dos personas".

3. "Quiero moverme por toda la ciudad, pero no puedo correr".

Estudiante B:

4. "Quiero ser más fuerte".

5. "Quiero reducir el estrés".

6. "Quiero hacer actividades con mi perro".

(5-3) ¿Qué te gusta hacer?

 Paso 1. You and a classmate will interview each other in depth about activities that you engage in frequently. Be sure to ask follow-up questions to get more details.

Modelo: Estudiante A: **¿Qué te gusta hacer en tu tiempo libre (*leisure time*)?**

Estudiante B: **Me gusta nadar.**

Estudiante A: **¿Nadas con frecuencia? ¿Prefieres nadar en un lago, una piscina (*pool*) o en el océano?** (etc.)

Paso 2. Write a short paragraph describing your classmate's activity.

Modelo: **A Ana le gusta nadar. Ella nada cuatro veces a la semana. Prefiere nadar en una piscina.** (etc.)

Los colores

Camila enjoys painting in the park. Observe the colors on her palette.

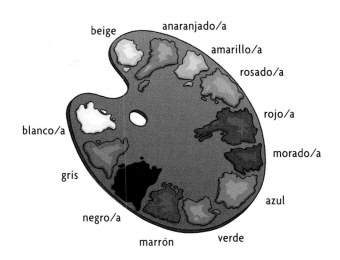

beige
anaranjado/a
amarillo/a
rosado/a
rojo/a
morado/a
blanco/a
azul
gris
negro/a
verde
marrón

NOTA DE LENGUA

All of the colors shown are adjectives. Those that end in **-o** change to reflect both gender and number: **blanco, blanca, blancos, blancas**. Those that end in **-e (verde)** or a consonant (**gris, marrón, azul**) have two forms: singular and plural (**verde, verdes**). Las flores son **azules** y **amarillas**.

Así se dice

5-4 **¿Cuáles son tus colores?** Sports teams' uniforms and their colors are important symbols for a team. Sports commentators even refer to teams by the colors of their jerseys: "**los blancos ganan el partido**" (the white team wins the game).

Paso 1. Listen to the descriptions of the jerseys of five popular soccer teams. Identify the jersey that corresponds to the description and write its number by the team name.

NOTA CULTURAL

Soccer, called **fútbol** in Spanish*, is by far the most popular sport in the Spanish-speaking world. You will read more about **el fútbol** in this chapter. However, baseball is the preferred sport in several Caribbean countries, including Puerto Rico, the Dominican Republic, Venezuela, and Cuba. Can you name famous baseball players from these places?

*What is called *football* in the United States is **fútbol americano** in Spanish.

PALABRAS ÚTILES

camiseta	t-shirt, jersey
raya	stripe

___ Real Betis   ___ Peñarol   ___ Club América

___ Boca Juniors   ___ River Plate

Paso 2. Now in small groups, describe the colors of a well-known sports team to your classmates. If they have trouble guessing, help by telling them which sport they play.

Modelo: Su camiseta es... Juegan baloncesto/ béisbol...

Investig@ en INTERNET

Find out what cities and countries are home to the teams mentioned in Exercise 5–4. Then choose one of those teams (or a different one you have heard about) and learn more about it. Your instructor may ask you to share your findings in class.

Más actividades y deportes

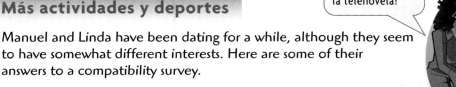

¡Pues yo prefiero la telenovela!

¡Quiero ver el fútbol!

Manuel and Linda have been dating for a while, although they seem to have somewhat different interests. Here are some of their answers to a compatibility survey.

Cuestionario de compatibilidad

1. ¿Qué le gusta hacer en su tiempo libre°?
(Manuel) *Me gusta ir a fiestas o a la discoteca y* **bailar** *con Linda.*
(Linda) *Me encanta pasear y salir con mis amigos, y me encanta° bailar merengue.*

leisure time
me... I love to

2. ¿Le gusta ver la televisión? ¿Qué tipo de programas ve?
(M) *Me gusta* **ver la tele,** *especialmente deportes:* **fútbol, béisbol,** *torneos de* **golf...**
(L) *Sí, veo partidos de tenis; también me gustan las telenovelas°.*

soap operas

3. ¿Qué hace los fines de semana?
(M) *Me encanta* **manejar¹** *mi carro nuevo, y casi siempre llevo a Linda cuando va de compras.*
(L) *Pues, generalmente limpio mi cuarto y voy de compras. A veces cocino para mis amigos.*

4. ¿Practica algún **deporte** con regularidad?
(M) *Sí, juego al baloncesto. Mi deporte favorito es el fútbol, pero en los Estados Unidos no es muy popular...*
(L) *Mi deporte favorito es el fútbol americano, pero juego al tenis.*

5. ¿Cuál es su **equipo** favorito?
(M) *Mi equipo favorito son los Padres.*
(L) *Pues, mi equipo son los Celtas.*

6. ¿Escucha música? ¿De qué tipo?
(M) *Sí, siempre escucho música en casa, en el carro, con mi iPod. Me gusta el rock latino: Maná, Los Jaguares y Café Tacuba.*
(L) *Sí, en casa casi siempre escucho música, y me gusta toda la música.*

7. ¿Qué hace para relajarse?
(M) *¿Relajarme? No tengo tiempo para eso.*
(L) *Casi siempre doy un paseo y, a veces, leo un libro.*

8. ¿Le gusta **viajar**? ¿Adónde?
(M) *No, nunca viajo si no es necesario. En las vacaciones prefiero descansar en casa.*
(L) *Me encantan los viajes a lugares exóticos, pero casi nunca hago viajes porque no tengo dinero.*

bailar	to dance	**manejar**	to drive
equipo	team	**ver la tele**	to watch TV
ir de compras	to go shopping	**viajar**	to travel
limpiar	to clean		

¹manejar = **conducir** in Spain. Present tense: **conduzco, conduces, conduce, conducimos, conducís, conducen.**

Así se dice

Frecuencia

Note the following expressions to express frequency, from the most (+) to the least (–) frequent.

+ siempre casi siempre	generalmente	a veces	casi nunca	nunca –
always →	→	→	→	*never*

5-5 Compatibilidad.

 Paso 1. Listen to the following statements and decide whether they refer to Linda, Manuel, or both (in which case, mark both columns).

	Manuel	Linda
1.		
2.		
3.		
4.		
5.		
6.		
7.		
8.		

 **Paso 2.** Now work in small groups to answer the following questions.

¿Tienen Linda y Manuel muchos intereses y hábitos en común? ¿Son muy similares o diferentes? ¿Piensas que son compatibles?

5-6 Mis hábitos.

 Paso 1. In pairs, talk about how often you do the following activities, using the terms of frequency **siempre**, **casi siempre**, **generalmente**, **a veces**, **casi nunca**, and **nunca**. Elaborate on your answers for a more interesting conversation.

Modelo: Estudiante A: **Nunca manejo para ir a clase.**

Estudiante B: **Yo tampoco, pero a veces monto en bicicleta para ir a clase.**

1. Manejar para ir a clase.

2. Bailar en fiestas o una discoteca (*club*).

3. Ver telenovelas o programas reality[2] como "Gran Hermano" (*Big Brother*) o "Sobrevivientes" (*Survivor*).

4. Ver partidos de fútbol/ básquetbol/ tenis/ béisbol en la tele.

5. Hacer ejercicio por la mañana/ tarde/ noche.

6. Ir de compras los fines de semana.

7. Limpiar mi cuarto/ apartamento.

8. Escuchar música rock/ pop/ country... a un volumen alto en mi cuarto.

9. Fumar.

 Paso 2. With your partner, discuss whether you could be compatible as roommates (you may not agree!). Be ready to explain your decision to the class.

Modelo: **Cristina y yo (no) somos compatibles como compañeros de cuarto porque...**

 Mis pasatiempos favoritos.

 Paso 1. Individually, make a list of your favorite pastimes, adding details such as how often you do each activity, when, where, etc.

 Paso 2. In groups, share your lists, and ask for more details regarding pastimes you find interesting. Take notes.

Paso 3. Select a pastime from your classmates' lists that you want to try or you think is interesting. Be prepared to report back to the class.

Modelo: **Quiero tocar la guitarra, como (*like*) Roberto, porque...**

 o **Roberto toca la guitarra. Es interesante porque...**

---

[2]In Spain and other Hispanic countries, the term *reality (show)* has been adopted from English for this new type of televised program.

Cultura: Cuba y la República Dominicana

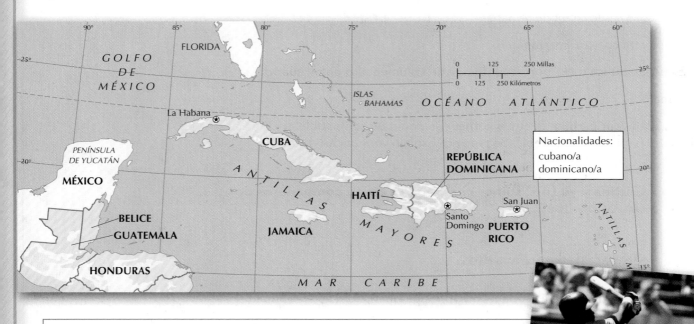

Nacionalidades:
cubano/a
dominicano/a

Antes de leer

1. Which island in the Greater Antilles is closest to Florida?

2. Who are the current leaders in Cuba and the Dominican Republic?

Las Antillas Mayores, situadas entre el océano Atlántico y el mar Caribe, incluyen tres países de habla hispana: Cuba, Puerto Rico y la República Dominicana. La República Dominicana ocupa gran parte de la isla "La Española", nombrada así por Cristóbal Colón en su primera visita a América. Las Antillas son territorios muy importantes por su posición como "puerta" al continente americano.

La caña de azúcar, el tabaco, las frutas tropicales y el ron[1] han sido[2] las principales industrias de estas islas durante siglos[3]. Hoy, por su clima y belleza natural, las Antillas Mayores atraen un gran número de turistas.

La música y las danzas de estas islas son una expresión cultural importante de sus habitantes. Los bailes como la salsa, el mambo, el bolero y el merengue tienen influencia española en sus melodías, pero en los ritmos es evidente la influencia africana. De hecho, la herencia de los esclavos africanos está muy presente hoy en los rasgos[4] físicos de los habitantes del Caribe.

El deporte nacional de Cuba, Puerto Rico y la República Dominicana es el béisbol. Hay muchos beisbolistas talentosos en estos países y ¡algunos juegan en equipos de Estados Unidos! ¿Sabes quién es el famoso jugador dominicano en la foto?

---

[1]rum [2]have been [3]for centuries [4]features

CUBA

Cuba fue una colonia de España desde 1511 hasta 1898. Después de la guerra entre los Estados Unidos y España, Cuba pasó a ser un "protectorado" de los EE.UU. Cuba se independizó en 1902, pero su economía continuó dependiendo de los EE.UU. La revolución de 1959 instituyó una dictadura marxista, y bajo[5] Fidel Castro, Cuba empezó a depender económicamente de la Unión Soviética.

Playa Varadero

El embargo de los Estados Unidos (1963) y la disolución de la Unión Soviética (1992) contribuyeron a la crisis económica en Cuba. Parte del plan de recuperación económica de Castro consiste en la construcción y restauración de hoteles y lugares de veraneo[6] para atraer el turismo, industria principal de la isla. Varadero (vea la foto) es un ejemplo, ofreciendo playas magníficas y otras atracciones naturales.

[5]under [6]summer vacation
[7]gold awards

Celia Cruz (1924–2003) fue la cantante cubana más famosa del mundo. Más de 20 de sus discos ganaron premios de oro[7] con canciones de rumba, salsa, boleros y otros géneros. Su frase famosa, que decía frecuentemente en sus canciones, era "¡Azúcar (Sugar)!"

LA REPÚBLICA DOMINICANA

En 1496, los españoles fundaron Santo Domingo, la primera ciudad de origen europeo en América. Los franceses establecieron una colonia, Haití, al oeste de la colonia española, en la misma isla. Después de años de guerra —¡contra los españoles, los franceses y los haitianos!— la República Dominicana se independizó en 1865.

En 1927, después de una ocupación estadounidense, el general Rafael Trujillo tomó el poder. Su dictadura fue totalitaria y terminó con su asesinato en 1965. Hoy la República Dominicana es una democracia.

La República Dominicana tiene las construcciones coloniales más antiguas del continente, como la catedral de Santo Domingo, la primera del Nuevo Mundo. También tiene 300 millas de playas que atraen el turismo.

Juan Luis Guerra es un famoso dominicano de cantante merengue, un tipo de música muy popular para bailar. Él y su grupo, que se llaman "los 440" ("cuatro cuarenta"), han ganado muchos premios musicales. Una canción famosa de este grupo se titula "Ojalá que llueva café en el campo" (*May it rain coffee in the countryside*).

Después de leer

To which country of the Greater Antilles does each of the following statements pertain?

1. Comparte "La Española" con otra nación. _____ _____
2. Es la isla más grande de las Antillas. _____ _____
3. Su gobierno no es democrático. _____ _____
4. La primera catedral del Nuevo Mundo está situada en su ciudad capital. _____ _____

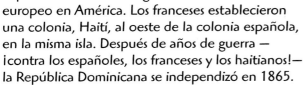

Así se forma

Conozco a María, el amor de mi vida, pero ella ni sabe mi nombre...

1. Talking about activities in the present: Additional *yo*-irregular verbs

A. *Saber* and *conocer*

These verbs both mean *to know*, but have very different uses. First, observe their forms and note the irregular **yo** form in their conjugations.

saber	
sé	sabemos
sabes	sabéis
sabe	saben

conocer	
conozco	conocemos
conoces	conocéis
conoce	conocen

> ### NOTA DE LENGUA
>
> When **saber** means *to know how to* it is followed by an infinitive.
> **Sé bailar salsa.**
> When **conocer** means *to know a person*, it is followed by "*a personal*".
> **Conozco a la profesora Ruiz.**

- **Saber** means *to know facts, information,* and *to know how to do things (skills)*. That is, it describes the kind of knowledge that one learns, such as a piece of information, and skills that can be demonstrated.

  Sé dónde vive Inés.
  Ella **sabe** tocar el piano.

- **Conocer** means *to know in the sense of being acquainted or familiar with persons, places, or things*. It also means *to meet for the first time*.

  Conozco a Carmen. Ella **conoce** bien la ciudad de Ponce.
  Quiero **conocer** a Marta Uribe. Creo que es dominicana.
  ¿**Conoce** usted la poesía de Nicolás Guillén?

5-8 **¿Qué sabemos hacer?** Moving about the classroom, find out who knows how to do each of the following things. Write down the name of the person by the activity. If he/she says "yes," ask him/her a follow-up question. Be prepared to report back to the class.

> ### PALABRAS ÚTILES
>
> **instrumentos musicales:**
> el piano, el violín, la guitarra, la trompeta, el saxofón, el clarinete
> **lenguas:** italiano, francés, ruso, japonés, alemán

Modelo: Estudiante A: **¿Sabes esquiar?**
Estudiante B: **Sí, sé esquiar.**
Estudiante A: **¿Esquías con frecuencia? ¿Dónde esquías?**

Estudiante A: **¿Sabes tocar un instrumento musical?**
Estudiante B: **No, no sé tocar un instrumento musical.**

	Nombre	Detalles
1. esquiar		
2. jugar un deporte		
3. montar en bicicleta		
4. cocinar		
5. tocar un instrumento musical		
6. hablar otra lengua		

  5-9 **Deportistas famosos.** Ask each other if you know who these athletes are. Use the categories in the box.

PALABRAS ÚTILES

jugador de básquetbol/
béisbol/golf
ciclista
futbolista
tenista

Modelo: Mia Hamm

Estudiante A: **¿Sabes quién es Mia Hamm?**
Estudiante B: **Sí, sé quién es. Es una futbolista.**
o **No, no sé quién es.**

¿Sabes quién es... ?

1. Tiger Woods
2. David Ortiz
3. Rafael Nadal
4. David Beckham
5. Pau Gasol
6. Lance Armstrong

David Ortiz

Rafa Nadal

Pau Gasol

Así se forma

NOTA CULTURAL

Julia Álvarez

Julia Álvarez is a famous author from the Dominican Republic. Her book *In the Time of the Butterflies* (**En el tiempo de las mariposas**) portrays a family during the dictatorship of Rafael Trujillo, which lasted from 1927–1965.

What do you think the title of this book refers to?

☐ Butterflies that regularly migrate to the Dominican Republic

☐ Three sisters who organized a resistance to Trujillo's dictatorship.

5-10 **¿Quieres conocerlo/la?** In pairs, ask each other whether you want to meet the following famous people and justify your answer. Use the pronouns **lo** (to refer to males, like *him*) and **la** (to refer to females, like *her*) as in the **Modelo** (you will learn more about these pronouns in **Capítulo 6**). If you don't know who the person is, just say: **No sé quién es.**

Modelo: Estudiante A: **¿Quieres conocer a Jennifer López?**
Estudiante B: **Sí, la quiero conocer./ No, no la quiero conocer.**
Estudiante A: **¿Por qué sí/ no?**

Estudiante A covers Estudiante B's list and vice versa.

Estudiante A:

1. Salma Hayek

2. Oprah Winfrey

3. el Presidente

Estudiante B:

1. Bill Gates

2. Antonio Banderas

3. Jon Stewart del *Daily Show*

5-11 Lugares (*Places*) interesantes.

Paso 1. In groups, share what interesting places you are acquainted with for each of the categories listed. Be sure to ask follow-up questions. Who has visited the most interesting places?

Modelo: parques nacionales

Conozco el parque Yosemite en California...

1. parques nacionales

2. ciudades

3. playas o montañas extraordinarias

4. otros lugares interesantes

Paso 2. Individually, write a paragraph telling which place(s) mentioned by your classmates you would like to visit, and briefly explain your reasons.

5-12 ¿Lo/La conoces bien?

Paso 1. Individually, fill in the blanks in the conversation on the next page with **sabes** or **conoces**, as appropriate.

Paso 2. In pairs, interview your partner about one of your other classmates using the conversation below as a guide. Then reverse roles to ask about a different classmate.

Estudiante A:

¿ _____ a (*classmate's name*)?

¿ _____ dónde vive?

¿ _____ su número de teléfono o su dirección electrónica?

¿ _____ cuántos años tiene?

¿ _____ si tiene novio/a?

¿ _____ a los amigos de él/ella?

Estudiante B:

Sí, lo/la _____.

...

...

...

...

...

¡Pienso que (no) lo/la _____ muy bien!

Siempre traigo mis libros, mi cuaderno, mi diccionario y mis bolígrafos a clase. ¿Y tú?

Siempre traigo mi lápiz.

B. Additional verbs with an irregular *yo* form

In **Capítulo 2** you learned two verbs with an irregular **yo** form: **salir** and **hacer**. Review them, and then observe the verbs that follow.

salir (de) to leave, go out	hacer to do, make	traer to bring	poner to put, place	oír to hear	ver to see	dar to give
salgo	**hago**	**traigo**	**pongo**	**oigo**	**veo**	**doy**
sales	haces	traes	pones	**oyes**	ves	das
sale	hace	trae	pone	**oye**	ve	da
salimos	hacemos	traemos	ponemos	oímos	vemos	damos
salís	hacéis	traéis	ponéis	oís	veis[3]	dais[3]
salen	hacen	traen	ponen	**oyen**	ven	dan

- **Salir** is followed by **de** when the subject is leaving a stated place.

  Salen del gimnasio.   *vs.*   **Salen** con sus amigos.

- When **hacer** is used in a question, it does not necessarily require a form of **hacer** in the answer. This is also true in English.

  — ¿Qué **haces** normalmente por la tarde?

  — **Voy** a la biblioteca, **hago** la tarea y después, **trabajo** en la librería.

---

[3]Note there is no accent on *veis* or *dais*.

Así se forma

HINT

Think of the following verbs as the "**yo-go** verbs"—verbs whose **yo** forms end in **go**: **salir, hacer, traer, poner, oír, tener, venir,** and **decir.**

Like **tener**, which you learned in **Capítulo 3**, the verbs **venir** and **decir** have irregular **yo** forms in addition to stem changes.

tener (ie) *to have*	venir (ie) *to come*	decir (i) *to say, tell*
tengo	**vengo**	**digo**
tienes	**vienes**	**dices**
tiene	**viene**	**dice**
tenemos	venimos	decimos
tenéis	venís	decís
tienen	**vienen**	**dicen**

5-13 **¿Qué hace tu instructor/a?** Read the following sentences about what your instructor does and decide whether they are true (**Cierto**) or false (**Falso**).

	Cierto	Falso
1. Salgo de mi casa a las 6 de la mañana.	_____	_____
2. Oigo las noticias (*news*) en el carro.	_____	_____
3. Traigo comida a la clase de español.	_____	_____
4. Digo "Buenos días" cuando entro a la clase.	_____	_____
5. Doy mucha tarea de español los viernes.	_____	_____
6. Veo a mis amigos frecuentemente.	_____	_____
7. Tengo cinco hijos.	_____	_____
8. Hago tortillas de maíz con frecuencia.	_____	_____

Ahora, pregunten a su profesor/a. ¿Quién tiene más respuestas correctas? ¿Quién conoce mejor (*best*) al profesor/a la profesora?

5-14 **¿Lo hago o no?**

Paso 1. Create six sentences about yourself using the verbs below. Three sentences should be true and three should be false.

poner	ver	oír	hacer	decir	dar

to put place   *to hear*   *to do*   *to say*   *to give*

Paso 2. In groups of three, read each statement to your partners, who will guess whether it is true or not.

5-15 ¿Qué hace Pepita?

 Paso 1. Look at what Pepita does on a typical weekday. Can you put the illustrations in order chronologically, numbering them from 1–8?

_____

_____

_____

_____

_____

_____

_____

_____

 Paso 2. Now, use the verbs below to write about what Pepita does, comparing her actions with yours.

| decir | hacer | llegar | llevar | oír | ver | salir |

Modelo: **Por las mañanas, Pepita oye el despertador a las siete y media, pero yo...** _o_

Por las mañanas, Pepita y yo oímos el despertador...

5-16 ¿Qué haces los sábados? Answer the question truthfully, writing down as many activities as possible. Your instructor will set a time limit. The student with the longest list wins.

Modelo: ¿Qué haces los sábados?

Tomo el desayuno.

Llamo a mis padres...

DICHOS

Decir y hacer son dos cosas, y la segunda es la dificultosa.
¿Puedes explicar este dicho?

Pepita

Esteban

Un deportista muy serio

grass El sábado por la mañana en el parque cerca de la universidad. Esteban duerme en la hierba°. Llega Pepita.

Paso 1. In pairs, answer the following question and justify your answer: Based on what you know about Esteban, do you think he is very committed to playing sports?

Paso 2. Listen to the conversation between Pepita and Esteban and indicate whether the following statements are true (**Cierto**) or false (**Falso**).

	Cierto	Falso
1. Esteban está tomando el sol en la hierba.	☐	☐
2. Pepita invita a Esteban a jugar al vólibol.	☐	☐
3. Esteban se cansa mucho (*gets very tired*) cuando hace deporte.	☐	☐
4. Esteban es un deportista muy dedicado.	☐	☐

Paso 3. Look at the questions below and listen again. Then answer the questions.

1. ¿Dónde está Esteban? ¿Qué hace?
2. ¿Con quién va a jugar Pepita al vólibol?
3. ¿Cuál es el deporte favorito de Esteban?
4. ¿Hace Esteban ejercicio? ¿Piensas que es mucho o poco ejercicio?
5. ¿Por qué está Esteban descansando?
6. ¿Cuál es el otro deporte favorito de Esteban?

Paso 4. Listen one more time, and this time you can read along. Then check your answers to the previous questions.

sleeping
Pepita: Esteban, ¿qué haces? ¿Durmiendo° tan temprano?
Esteban: Uhmm, Pepita... ¿Qué tal? Estoy... tomando el sol.
Pepita: ¿Con suéter y jeans?
Esteban: Bueno, estoy descansando antes de tomar el sol. ¿Qué haces aquí?
Pepita: Estoy buscando a Octavio. Vamos a jugar al vólibol. ¿Quieres jugar con nosotros?
Esteban: Mi deporte favorito es ver la televisión.

Laughing
Pepita: (*Riéndose°*) ¡Eres incorregible! ¿Nunca haces ejercicio?
Esteban: ¡Claro que sí! A veces juego al baloncesto o al fútbol con Manuel y Javier.
Pepita: ¡Qué bien!
Esteban: Pero con esos partidos me canso mucho.
Pepita: ¡Ah! Ahora comprendo. Por eso estás descansando hoy.

next
Esteban: Bueno... sí. Necesito recuperar energía para el próximo° partido.

Tienes... *You are right;*
ice-cream parlor
Pepita: Tienes razón°. Más tarde Octavio y yo vamos a la heladería°. ¿Quieres acompañarnos?
Esteban: ¿A la heladería? Sí, voy con ustedes. Comer helados es otro de mis deportes favoritos... ¡y soy un deportista muy dedicado!

Así se dice

Esteban · Alfonso

Preferencias, obligaciones e intenciones

Read the conversation between Esteban and Alfonso to find out about their preferences, obligations, and intentions.

Esteban: ¿Qué **piensas hacer** esta noche? ¿Tienes planes?
Alfonso: **Tengo que estudiar** para el examen de química.
Esteban: ¡Qué aburrido! ¿No **tienes ganas de salir** conmigo?
Alfonso: Tú sabes que **debo estudiar** hoy. Además, ¡a mí no me gusta la cerveza!

Now, identify the expressions that fall into each category. Add any other expressions you remember that belong to these categories.

Preferencia	Obligación	Intención

NOTA DE LENGUA

The expression *to need to* is often used to express obligation in English, but in Spanish, **necesitar** is generally not used with this meaning. The preferred forms to express obligation are **tener que** or **deber**.

I need to study tonight.
Tengo que/ Debo estudiar esta noche.

5-17 ¿Preferencias u obligaciones? Tell whether the characters *have to do* or *feel like doing* the activities depicted in the drawings.

Modelo: Esteban **Creo que Esteban tiene ganas de/tiene que...**

1. Esteban

2. Inés

3. Javier

4. Camila

5. Natalia

6. Rubén

7. Carmen

8. Pepita

9. Octavio

10. Linda

Así se dice

5-18 Obligaciones, preferencias y planes.

Paso 1. In groups of four, read the statements and decide on two activities that you have to do, feel like doing, or plan/intend to do in response to each circumstance. Appoint a secretary to record the information. For item 4, the group should invent a new circumstance.

EXPRESIONES ÚTILES

(Verás), es que...
   (You see/Well,) the thing is . . .
¿Sabes?   *You know, . . . ?*
¡Vamos!   *Come on!*

---

tener que...	deber...	tener ganas de...	pensar...

Modelo: Estamos muy preocupados/as hoy porque tenemos examen mañana.

Tenemos que estudiar mucho esta noche; no debemos ver la tele...

1. Estamos muy ocupados/as esta semana.
2. Estamos aburridos/as con la vida social de la universidad.
3. Estamos un poco estresados/as porque tenemos una presentación mañana.
4. _____

Paso 2. The group secretary reads two activities aloud to the entire class, who must decide which of the threee circumstances it corresponds to—or guess what the new, invented circumstance is.

The following expressions are useful to talk about the future.

Así se forma

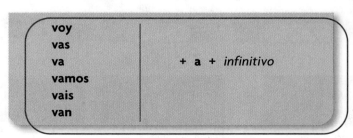

Voy a impresionar a Pepita con mis músculos.

2. Making future plans: *Ir + a + infinitive*

To talk about plans *and actions yet to occur,* use **ir** + **a** + *infinitive*

voy	
vas	
va	+ **a** + *infinitivo*
vamos	
vais	
van	

Vamos a jugar al básquetbol.   ***We are going to play*** basketball.
Inés **va a tocar** el piano esta noche.   *Ines **is going to play*** the piano tonight.
Y tú, ¿qué **vas a hacer** mañana   *And you, what **are you going to do***
   por la tarde?   *tomorrow afternoon?*

En el futuro

| el mes/ año/ verano . . . que viene | next month/year/summer |
| el próximo mes/ año/ verano . . . | next month/year/summer |

5-19 ¿Qué voy a hacer?

Paso 1. Read the statements below and decide which option best describes the circumstances when you would say them.

1. "Voy a dormir".   **a.** Tengo hambre.   **b.** Tengo sueño*.
2. "Voy a correr en el parque".   **a.** Tengo mucha energía.   **b.** Tengo sed.
3. "Voy a llamar a mi mamá".   **a.** Es su cumpleaños.   **b.** Tengo hambre.
4. "Voy a comer un sándwich".   **a.** Tengo sueño.   **b.** Tengo hambre.
5. "Voy a ver la tele".   **a.** Tengo mucha tarea.   **b.** Estoy aburrido/a.
6. "Voy a tomar un vaso . de agua"   **a.** Tengo muchos amigos.   **b.** Tengo sed.
7. "Voy a comprar tortillas".   **a.** Quiero hacer tacos.   **b.** Quiero hacer ensalada.
8. "Voy a ir a la biblioteca".   **a.** Necesito dinero.   **b.** Necesito escribir un reporte.

__tener sueño__   to be sleepy

Paso 2. In the column **Yo**, write what you are going to do in response to the following situations. When you finish writing, ask a classmate and fill in his/her answers in the column **Mi compañero/a**. Are they similar or different? Be ready to share with the class.

	Yo	Mi compañero/a
"¡Tengo un billete de lotería premiado (*a winning lottery ticket*)"!	Voy a…	Va a…
"Mis padres vienen de visita este fin de semana".		
"Tenemos un mes de vacaciones".		
"Necesito dinero".		

SITUACIONES

Estudiante A: Tu compañero/a de cuarto te invita a una fiesta con sus amigos, pero sus amigos no te gustan mucho y no tienes ganas de ir con ellos. Inventa excusas.

Estudiante B: Vas a ir a una fiesta con tus amigos. Invitas a tu compañero/a de cuarto pero es tímido/a y piensas que no acepta porque tiene vergüenza (*is embarrased*). Insiste.

Así se forma

5-20 **El grupo de estudio.** You have formed a study group with three or four classmates to prepare for a Spanish test.

 Paso 1. Fill in the agenda schedule pages below with your activities for today (**Hoy**) and tomorrow (**Mañana**).

Hoy	Mañana
8:00 A.M.	8:00 A.M.
9:00 A.M.	9:00 A.M.
10:00 A.M.	10:00 A.M.
11:00 A.M.	11:00 A.M.
12:00 P.M.	12:00 P.M.
1:00 P.M.	1:00 P.M.
2:00 P.M.	2:00 P.M.
3:00 P.M.	3:00 P.M.
4:00 P.M.	4:00 P.M.
5:00 P.M.	5:00 P.M.
6:00 P.M.	6:00 P.M.
7:00 P.M.	7:00 P.M.
8:00 P.M.	8:00 P.M.

 Paso 2. Now, talk with your classmates and try to find a 1–2 hour slot when you can meet at the library. Use the model below to structure your answers about what you will be doing.

Modelo: Estudiante A: **¿Pueden ir a la biblioteca esta tarde a las 2?**

Estudiante B: **No, voy a estar en mi clase de química.**

Estudiante C: **Y yo voy a jugar al fútbol de 1:30 a 3.**

Así se dice

El clima y las estaciones (*The weather and the seasons*)

There are several ways to ask what the weather is like: **¿Qué tiempo hace?**
¿Cómo está el clima? ¿Qué tal el clima?

Hace buen tiempo. Hace fresco
y está nublado (hay **nubes**).
Es **primavera**.

Llueve todas las tardes. Ahora
también **está lloviendo.** Dicen que
después de la **lluvia** sale el sol.

Hace sol y **hace (mucho) calor.**
Octavio **tiene calor.** Es **verano.**

Hace mal tiempo. Hace viento.
Es **otoño.**

Hace frío. Esteban **tiene frío.**
Es **invierno.**

Aquí, en el invierno, **nieva** casi
todos los días. **Está nevando** ahora.
¡Me encanta[4] la nieve!

El tiempo (clima)		Las estaciones	Las personas
hace	(muy) buen/ mal tiempo	primavera	tener calor/ frío
	sol	verano	
	fresco	otoño	
	(mucho) calor	invierno	
	(mucho) frío		
	(mucho) viento		
llover (ue) → la lluvia			
nevar (ie) → la nieve			

fresco	*cool*	**el sol**	*sun*
la nube	*cloud*	**el viento**	*wind*
nublado	*cloudy*		

---

[4]The verb **encantar** functions like **gustar** (see p.112): **Me encantan las rosas amarillas.**

Así se dice

5-21 **Por el mundo hispano.** In pairs and taking turns, one of you will select one of the photos below, describe what the weather is like and identify the season of the year. The other identifies the location being described.

Modelo: Estudiante A: **Hace frío y hay mucha nieve. Es invierno[5].**

Estudiante B: **Es el Parque Nacional Los Glaciares, Argentina.**

Parque Nacional
Los Glaciares, Argentina

Huracán Luis, Puerto Rico

Playa Manuel Antonio,
Costa Rica

Maestrazgo, España

Tres Piedras, Nuevo México

Refugio, Nevado de Ruiz, Colombia

[5]The seasons of the year are reversed in the northern and southern hemispheres; for example, when it is winter in Argentina, it is summer in the United States and Canada.

5-22 El clima y las estaciones.

 Paso 1. A prospective student from the Dominican Republic wants to come to the United States for a semester and she wants to know a bit more about the weather in the places she is considering and what people do in different seasons. Read her e-mail and talk about her questions with a classmate.

Asunto : Clima en los EE.UU.

Hola,
   Quiero estudiar en los Estados Unidos por un semestre, y tengo algunas preguntas. ¿Pueden ayudarme?
   Primero, ¿cuáles son los meses de invierno en su país? ¿y cuándo empieza la primavera? (¿Es igual o diferente que en la República Dominicana?)
   Pienso ir en el semestre de primavera, pero no sé dónde exactamente... ¿Qué tiempo hace en febrero en San Francisco? ¿en Miami? ¿en Chicago? ¿en Seattle? ¿y en Dallas? ¿y en su ciudad?
   ¿Cuál es su estación favorita? Donde Uds. viven, ¿qué deportes y actividades pueden hacer en el invierno? ¿y en la primavera? ¿Qué tipo de actividades hacen ustedes cuando llueve?
Muchas gracias por su ayuda°.

 Paso 2. Now, reply to her message.

Investig@ en INTERNET

¿Cuándo empieza (*begin*) y termina (*end*) la Liga de Fútbol en España? ¿y en Argentina? ¿Sabes por qué?

 DICHOS

A mal tiempo... buena cara°. *face*
¿Qué significa el dicho?

help

NOTA CULTURAL:

Grados Fahrenheit *vs.* grados centígrados
La mayoría de los países hispanos usan la escala de centígrados para hablar del tiempo.

Para convertir de °F a °C → _____ °C = (_____ °F − 32) ÷ 1,8
Para convertir de °C a °F → _____ °F = 1,8 x (_____ °C) + 32

El termómetro indica que la temperatura está a 50º (grados) Fahrenheit.
¿Cuál es la temperatura en centígrados? _____

Si la temperatura está a 40° Celsius, ¿hace mucho frío o hace mucho calor? _____

Cultura: El fútbol: rey de los deportes

Muchos jóvenes aspiran a ser famosos futbolistas.

Antes de leer

1. Are you a sports fan? Of which sport(s)?

2. What do "average" and "extreme" fans do to support their teams?

3. Do you know where the latest World Cup soccer event took place?

¡Los argentinos son muy aficionados al fútbol! (Buenos Aires)

Para los dominicanos, los puertorriqueños, los cubanos y los venezolanos, el béisbol es el deporte más importante. Pero para gran parte del mundo hispano —y la mayor parte de la gente del planeta— el fútbol es el rey de los deportes. En muchos países hispanos, el fútbol es más que un deporte—¡es una forma de vida!

Los fanáticos hacen de este deporte casi una religión. Ver un partido importante, en el estadio o por televisión, es una obligación. El fútbol no respeta horarios[1] ni lugares: en muchos países los empleados ponen televisores en sus lugares de trabajo para ver jugar a sus equipos favoritos.

La pasión por el fútbol aumenta al máximo cada cuatro años con la celebración de la Copa Mundial. Durante la Copa, los fanáticos no se pierden[2] ningún partido. Los futbolistas talentosos son auténticos héroes nacionales y mundiales.

[1]schedules [2]se... miss

Hugo Sánchez (México)

Maradona (Argentina)

Carlos "El Pibe" Valderrama (Colombia)

Pelé (Brasil)

En 2006, Italia ganó la Copa Mundial en Alemania.

Conexiones y contrastes

In your opinion, does football in the U.S. have as strong a following as soccer does in Latin America?

Así se forma

¿Qué estás pintando, Camila?

¿No es obvio?

3. Emphasizing that an action is in progress: The present progressive

To indicate that an action is in progress (*present progressive*), Spanish uses **estar** + *present participle* (**–ndo**). The present participle always ends in **–ndo**: It does not change to agree with the subject. **Estar**, however, always changes to agree with the subject.

estar (*to be*)		+ present participle		
(yo)	estoy			
(tú)	estás			
(Ud., él/ella)	está	estudia**ndo**	comie**ndo**	escribie**ndo**
(nosotros/as)	estamos			
(vosotros/as)	estáis			
(Uds., ellos/as)	están			

Elena **está estudiando** para un examen.   Elena **is studying** for an exam.

Nosotros **estamos comiendo**[6] galletas.   We **are eating** cookies.

Note how the present participle is formed.

	stem	+ ending	= present participle
-ar *verbs*	**estudi**ar	**-ando**	**estudiando**
-er *verbs*	**com**er	**-iendo**	**comiendo**
-ir *verbs*	**escrib**ir	**-iendo**	**escribiendo**

> ### NOTA DE LENGUA
>
> Some verbs have stem changes in the present participle, for instance:
>
> | decir (i) | diciendo |
> |---|---|
> | dormir (u) | durmiendo |
> | pedir (i) | pidiendo |
> | leer | leyendo |

As for the use of the Spanish present progressive, it emphasizes that an *action is in progress at a particular time.*

Estoy trabajando ahora.   **I am working** (*right*) *now.* (*act in progress*)

¿Ustedes todavía **están comiendo**?   **Are you** still **eating**? (*act in progress*)

Unlike English, the present progressive is generally <u>not</u> used to talk about habitual and repeated actions, nor is it used to talk about the future.

English

*He **is working** with his father (every day).*
*I **am leaving** in an hour.*

Spanish

Trabaja con su padre.
Salgo en una hora.
~~Estoy saliendo en una hora.~~

---

[6]English present progressive has a similar structure: *to be* + present participle (*–ing*).

Así se forma

 5-23 ¿Qué están haciendo?

Paso 1. Listen as your instructor reads each statement. Write the number of the sentence underneath its corresponding drawing.

Javier _____

Inés _____

Manuel / Linda _____

Esteban _____

Alfonso _____

Octavio _____

Manuel _____

Paso 2. With a partner, add two additional activities that each of these people is doing at the same time. Then share your ideas with the whole class.

Modelo: Javier está estudiando.

Está leyendo un libro de química, y está pensando en su examen de mañana.

Paso 3. The whole class should decide which of the seven activities pictured is the most physical, which is the most sedentary, and which the most fun.

La actividad más física es _____.

La actividad más sedentaria es _____.

La actividad más divertida es _____.

 5-24 **Probablemente.** Based on where these people are, invent two activities that they are probably doing. Finally, indicate which of the six situations you prefer.

Modelo: Linda y Manuel están en la discoteca.
Están bailando y tomando cerveza.

1. Pepita está en una clase de economía.
2. Javier está en el agua de un lago.
3. Octavio está en un laboratorio de computadoras.
4. Esteban y sus amigos están en un estadio (*stadium*) deportivo.
5. Inés y Camila están en un restaurante cubano.
6. Manuel está en su cuarto.

De estas actividades, mi favorita es: _____

5-25 **Actores y actrices.** Eight volunteers dramatize an activity in front of the class. The rest of the class indicates what each actor is *doing*. Close your textbooks!

Modelo: Profesor/a: ¿Qué está haciendo José?
Estudiantes: **Está caminando por el aula.**

4. Describing people, places, and things: *Ser* and *estar* (A summary)

> Lisa, ¿quieres conocer a Martín?
>
> Pues, ¿cómo es? ¿De dónde es?

Use *ser*	Use *estar*
• to identify *who or what the subject is* (vocation, profession, religion, etc.) Alex **es estudiante** de la Universidad de Texas. Quiere **ser biólogo**. **Es católico** (*Catholic*). • to indicate *origin* (where the subject is from) and *nationality* **Es de Puerto Rico. Es puertorriqueño.** • to indicate *what the subject is like*—descriptive characteristics or qualities, physical or personality traits inherent to the person, place, or thing described **Es alto, moreno, simpático y muy inteligente. Es un chico muy bueno.** Puerto Rico, su país natal, **es una isla muy bella** (*beautiful*).	• to indicate the physical or emotional *condition* of the subject at a given time (how the subject feels, appears)—often indicates a change from the usual Ahora **está un poco estresado** porque su carro **está en malas condiciones** y necesita un motor nuevo. • to tell *where the subject is* (indicate the physical location of the person, place, or thing) Su familia **está en Puerto Rico** y Alex los visita en las vacaciones.

HINT

Before beginning this section, review the information and exercises on **ser/ estar** in **Capítulo 3**, pp. 81–84 and 90–95.

Other uses of *ser*	Other uses of *estar*
• to express *day, date, season* **Es el ocho de abril. Es lunes.** **Es primavera.** • to tell *time* **Son las nueve de la mañana.** • to indicate possession — ¿**Es de Susana** la raqueta? — No, **es mi** raqueta.	• estar + -ando/-iendo to indicate an action in progress **Está jugando** al tenis **ahora**.

NOTA DE LENGUA

Note how the use of **ser** and **estar** with the same adjective can change or slightly alter the meaning of that adjective.

Roberto **es aburrido/ está aburrido.**	Roberto *is boring/is bored.*
Ana es muy **bonita/ está** muy **bonita** hoy.	Ana *is* very **pretty/looks** very **pretty** today.

Watch out for these nuances when speaking about your blind date or a friend!

Así se forma

Recreaciones y pasatiempos
Recreaciones y Recreaciones y pasatie
pasatiempos

5-26 **¿Quieres salir con él/ella?** Work with a classmate. One of you wants to arrange a blind date for the other. Complete the conversation with forms of **ser** or **estar**.

Estudiante A: ¿Cómo se llama tu amigo/a?

Estudiante B: _____. _____ de la ciudad de Nueva York.

Estudiante A: ¿_____ estudiante?

Estudiante B: Sí, de esta (*this*) universidad. Y también _____ atleta. Le gusta jugar al tenis y al básquetbol, montar en bicicleta, levantar pesas...

Estudiante A: Pues, ¿cómo _____? Descríbemelo/la.

Estudiante B: _____ una persona muy buena, muy amable.

Estudiante A: ¿_____ guapo/a?

Estudiante B: Sí, _____ muy guapo/a, rubio/a y delgado/a. ¿Quieres conocerlo/la?

Estudiante A: Sí, ¡por supuesto (*of course*)! ¿Dónde _____ ahora?

Estudiante B: Pienso que _____ en el laboratorio de biología. Probablemente _____ trabajando ahora porque _____ asistente del profesor.

Estudiante A: No importa. ¡Vamos al laboratorio!

5-27 **¿Por qué?** In the chart below, fill in the names of people that you know. In the second column, write what each person is *normally* like. In the third column, indicate a *change* in his/her disposition. Your partner will ask the reason for the change. Take turns.

PALABRAS ÚTILES

aburrido	animado
cansado	triste
enojado	estresado
nervioso	preocupado

Modelo: Estudiante A: **Mi hermano *normalmente* es muy enérgico, pero *ahora* está cansado.**

Estudiante B: **¿Por qué?**

Estudiante A: **Porque está en el equipo de fútbol y practica todos los días.**

Persona	Normalmente es...	Ahora está...

5-28 Una cita a ciegas (*blind date*). Now you will try to set up a blind date for a friend of yours, who is not in your Spanish class, with one of your classmates.

 Paso 1. First, think about what you would like to tell your classmates about your friend. Write a few sentences to describe him/her, talk about the activities he/she enjoys, etc.

Modelo: **Mi amigo/a se llama... Es...**

 Paso 2. Walk around the class telling your classmates about your friend. Also listen to the descriptions of their friends. Continue until you find three potential matches for your friend. Be sure to take notes about these three candidates in the chart below.

Modelo: Estudiante A: **Mi amigo/a se llama _____.**

Estudiante B: **Mi amigo/a se llama _____. ¿Cómo es tu amigo/a?**

	Se llama...	Es...	Qué hace/ Qué le gusta...	Dónde está ahora
Candidato 1				
Candidato 2				
Candidato 3				

 Paso 3. Study the profiles of your three candidates and select the best match for your friend. Share your conclusions with a classmate, explaining the reasons for your choice.

Así se pronuncia

The pronunciation of the consonants *ll* and *v*

ll Remember that double **l** approximates the English *y* sound as in *yes*.

llueve   **ll**oviendo   **ll**uvia   **ll**over

v/b Both are pronounced similarly. In initial position, **v/b** is pronounced like the English *b* in *boy*. Between vowels, the lips are barely touching.

vólibol   **v**iento   **v**iolín   **v**iernes

ll**ue**ve   ll**o**viendo   ll**u**via   ll**o**ver

Repeat the sentences to practice the pronunciation of **ll** and **v**.

ll En las noches de luna **ll**ena° las estrellas° brillan°.

v El **v**iento mueve la **v**ela° suavemente°.

luna... full moon; stars; shine brightly; sail; softly

Dicho y hecho

¡A ESCUCHAR!

¡Todo sobre el fútbol! Listen to the comments of the radio announcer and the commentator Andrés Mauricio. Then answer the first two questions.

1. ¿De dónde son los dos equipos rivales?   **a.** de España   **b.** de México

2. ¿Se decide el campeón de la liga hoy?   **a.** sí   **b.** no

Listen to the broadcast again and choose the correct answers to the following questions.

3. ¿Para qué equipo juega Sergio Flores?   **a.** Madrid   **b.** Barcelona

4. ¿Cuál es el número de Miguel?   **a.** 9   **b.** 45

5. ¿Quién marca el gol?   **a.** Miguel   **b.** Sergio

6. ¿Quién gana?   **a.** Barcelona   **b.** Madrid.

CONVERSANDO

Un día sin clases. Imagine that it is early in the morning on a day with no classes. You are going to spend your free day with a classmate. Plan a day outing or day trip. Talk about:

- el clima (para determinar las actividades y posibles destinos)
- lo que tienen ganas de hacer y adónde tienen ganas de ir
- lo que pueden/ van a hacer hoy
- lo que piensan comer y dónde
- si (*if*) salen de la universidad, cuándo piensan volver

Share some of your plans with the class.

DE MI ESCRITORIO

Una excursión. Write a paragraph to present to the class about the outing that you and your friend want to make.

- Pensamos ir a... Es un lugar... (*describe the place*)
- Queremos/ Podemos... (*mention activities, pastimes, etc.*)
- Vamos a...
- De comer vamos a llevar (*take*)...
- Regresamos...

Artes literarias: Nicolás Guillén

Antes de leer

1. Do you like poetry? Why?
2. You already know African heritage is central to Cuba's music and dance. What other aspects of Cuban life are influenced by African cultures and traditions?

Nicolás Guillén (1902–1989), poeta cubano, es conocido por su poesía afrocubana. Su estilo es rítmico, con temas derivados de la mitología del pueblo afroantillano. La poesía de Guillén adopta un nuevo estilo literario que revela la magnitud de la contribución africana a la cultura cubana y latinoamericana.

ESTRATEGIA PARA LEER

Using Title and Format to Understand Content
1. Read the poem's title: It will give you a clue about how to read it.
2. First, skim the poem, paying attention to the repetition of both verses and words.
3. On your second reading, focus on the rhythm created by the stress on certain syllables and the description of the snake.
4. Read the lines straight through and, while reading, tap out the rhythm as if you were playing bongo drums.

Sensemayá* (Canto para matar una culebra[1])
de Nicolás Guillén

¡Mayombe-bombe-mayombé!**
¡Mayombe-bombe-mayombé!
¡Mayombe-bombe-mayombé!
La culebra tiene los ojos de vidrio[2];
la culebra viene y se enreda[3] en un palo[4];
con sus ojos de vidrio, en un palo;
con sus ojos de vidrio.
¡Mayombe-bombe-mayombé!
Tú le das con el hacha[5] y se muere[6].

¡Dale[7] ya!
¡No le des con el pie[8], que te muerde[9];
no le des con el pie, que se va!
La culebra muerta no puede comer;
la culebra muerta no puede silbar[10];
no puede caminar,
no puede correr.
La culebra muerta no puede mirar[11];
la culebra muerta no puede beber;

no puede respirar,
no puede morder[12].
¡Mayombe-bombe-mayombé!
Sensemayá, la culebra...
¡Mayombe-bombe-mayombé!
Sensemayá, no se mueve[13]...
¡Mayombe-bombe-mayombé!
Sensemayá, la culebra...
¡Mayombe-bombe-mayombé!
¡Sensemayá, se murió[14]!

*Sensemayá: A goddess represented by a snake in some Afrocuban religions.
**The Mayombé: An African (Yoruba) religious act.
[1]**Canto...** *Incantation to kill a snake* [2]**ojos...** *eyes of glass* [3]**se...** *entwines itself* [4]*stick* [5]**Tú...** *Hit it with an ax* [6]**se...** *it dies* [7]*Hit it!* [8]**No...** *Don't kick it*
[9]**te...** *it will bite you* [10]*to whistle* [11]*look, see* [12]*to bite* [13]**no...** *it doesn't move* [14]**se...** *died*

Después de leer

1. Why is the snake in this poem dangerous for humans?
2. What is the only way to kill the snake?
3. In your opinion, what might the snake represent?

Repaso de vocabulario activo

Adjetivos

amarillo/a   *yellow*
anaranjado/a   *orange*
azul   *blue*
beige   *beige*
blanco/a   *white*
gris   *grey*
marrón   *brown*
morado/a   *purple*
negro/a   *black*
rojo/a   *red*
rosado/a   *pink*
verde   *green*

Adverbios y expresiones adverbiales

el mes/ año/ verano que viene
   next month/year/summer
el próximo mes/ año/ verano
   next month/year/summer

Las estaciones
The seasons

el invierno   *winter*
el otoño   *fall*
la primavera   *spring*
el verano   *summer*

El clima   *Weather*

¿Qué tiempo hace?/ ¿Cómo está
   el clima?/ ¿Qué tal el clima?
   What's the weather like?

Hace buen/ mal tiempo.
   The weather is nice/bad.
Hace (mucho) frío.   *It's (very) cold.*
Hace (mucho) calor.   *It's (very) hot.*
Hace fresco.   *It's cool.*
   Hace sol.
Hace viento.   *It's windy.*
Llueve./ Está lloviendo.
   It's raining.
   la lluvia   *rain*
Nieva./ Está nevando.   *It's snowing.*
   la nieve   *snow*
Está (muy) nublado.
   It's (very) cloudy.
   las nubes   *clouds*

Sustantivos
Los deportes   *Sports*

el baloncesto/ el básquetbol
   basketball
el béisbol   *baseball*
el fútbol   *soccer*
el fútbol americano   *football*
el golf   *golf*
el tenis   *tennis*
el vólibol   *volleyball*
el ejercicio   *exercise*
el equipo   *team*
el partido   *game*
la pelota   *ball*

En el parque
At the park

el árbol   *tree*
la flor   *flower*
la hoja   *leaf*
el lago   *lake*

Verbos y expresiones verbales

bailar   *to dance*
caminar   *to walk*
cantar   *to sing*
conocer   *to meet/know*
correr   *to run*
dar   *to give*
dar un paseo   *to take a walk*
deber + *infinitivo*   *should + verb*
decir (i)   *to say*
descansar   *to rest*
esquiar   *to ski*
fumar   *to smoke*
ganar   *to win*
hacer   *to do/make*
hacer ejercicio   *to exercise*
ir de compras   *to go shopping*
jugar (ue)   *to play*
   jugar al + *sport*
limpiar   *to clean*
llover (ue)   *to rain*
manejar   *to drive*
nadar   *to swim*
nevar (ie)   *to snow*

oír   *to hear*
pensar (ie) + infinitivo   *to think
   about doing something*
perder (ie)   *to lose*
pintar   *to paint*
poner   *to put*
practicar   *to practice*
saber   *to know*
salir (de)   *to leave*
tocar   *to touch*
   tocar + *musical instrument*
   to play
traer   *to bring*
venir (ie)   *to come*
ver   *to see*
   ver la tele(visión)   *to watch TV*
viajar   *to travel*

levantar pesas   *to lift weights*
me encanta(n)   *I really like it (them)*
montar en bicicleta
   to ride a bicycle
tener calor   *to be hot*
tener frío   *to be cold*
tener ganas de + *infinitivo*   *to feel
   like + infinitive*
tener que + *infinitivo*   *to have to +
   infinitive*
tomar el sol   *to sunbathe*

Autoprueba y repaso WILEY PLUS ✓

I. *Saber* and *conocer*. Complete the dialog with the correct form of the appropriate verb.

Marta: ¿_____ (tú) tocar la guitarra? Necesito encontrar un guitarrista para nuestra fiesta.

Pablo: No _____ tocar la guitarra, pero (yo) _____ a una persona que sabe tocarla muy bien.

Marta: ¿_____ (tú) dónde vive?

Pablo: No _____ . Pero podemos buscar su dirección (*address*) y número de teléfono en la guía telefónica y llamarlo/la. Podemos ir en mi coche a su casa. (Yo) _____ bien la ciudad y puedo acompañarte.

Marta: ¡Gracias!

II. *Additional yo-irregular verbs.* What do perfect students do?.

Modelo: tener interés en la clase (Juan, yo)
Juan tiene interés en la clase.
Yo tengo interés en la clase también.

1. venir a clase todos los días (tú, yo)
2. decir "hola" a los estudiantes al entrar en la clase (nosotros, yo)
3. traer la tarea a clase (ellas, yo)
4. poner la tarea en el escritorio del profesor (Ana, yo)
5. saber todo el vocabulario (nosotros, yo)
6. hacer preguntas en clase (ustedes, yo)
7. no salir de clase temprano (ella, yo)

III. *Ir + a + infinitive.* What is happening tomorrow?

Modelo: Lisa / estudiar
Lisa va a estudiar.

1. Marta / jugar al tenis
2. Luisa y Alberto / montar en bicicleta
3. (yo) / ver un partido de fútbol
4. (tú) / preparar una paella
5. nosotros / ir a la playa

IV. The present progressive. What is happening right now?

Modelo: Llueve.
Está lloviendo.

1. Nieva.
2. El niño duerme.
3. Leo una novela.
4. Vemos la tele.
5. Mis hermanos preparan la cena

V. *Ser* and *estar.* Use the correct form of **ser** or **estar**.

Luisa Pereira _____ mexicana. _____ de la Ciudad de México pero ahora _____ en Guadalajara. _____ abogada y _____ una mujer inteligente y dinámica. Hoy _____ preocupada porque tiene un caso importante en la corte municipal.

VI. General review. Answer with complete sentences.

1. ¿Qué estás haciendo en este momento?
2. ¿Qué vas a hacer esta noche?
3. ¿Qué haces los fines de semana?
4. ¿Qué tienes que hacer mañana?
5. ¿Qué tienes ganas de hacer ahora?
6. ¿A quién conoces muy bien en la clase de español?
7. ¿Qué traes a la clase?
8. ¿Cuál es tu estación favorita? ¿Por qué?
9. ¿Qué tiempo hace hoy?

VII. *Cultura.*

1. Regarding sports, in what way are the Spanish-speaking nations of the Caribbean different from other Hispanic nations?
2. What is the novel *In the Time of the Butterflies* about?
3. How is the African influence in the Dominican Republic and Cuba present today?

Answers to the *Autoprueba y repaso* are found in **Apéndice 2.**

WILEY
PLUS

La rutina diaria

By the end of this chapter you will be able to:

- Talk about daily routines
- Describe how actions take place
- Talk about actions in the past
- Talk about job-related issues

Así se dice	Así se forma	Cultura	Dicho y hecho
• La rutina diaria • El trabajo	**1.** Reflexive verbs **2.** Adverbs **3.** The preterit of regular verbs and **ser/ir** **4.** Direct-object pronouns	• España contemporánea: Herencia y modernidad • Los días festivos • Artes ornamentales: Los azulejos de España	• ¿La hora del examen ya pasó? • Mi rutina ideal • Un día muy interesante en mi vida

ENTRANDO AL TEMA

1. Do you know the name of the currency used in Spain? *Hint:* It is the same as the rest of the ECC (European Economic Community).

2. Which group lived in Spain for almost 800 years and exerted tremendous cultural influence?

☐ Moors (Arabs)　　☐ Germans　　☐ Chinese

Así se dice

La rutina diaria

Por la mañana

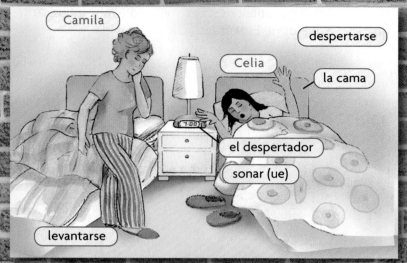

Camila

despertarse

Celia

la cama

el despertador

sonar (ue)

levantarse

vestirse

Tomás

Alex

ponerse (los zapatos, la ropa, etc.)

lavarse (la cara, las manos, etc.)

Cristina

Rósa

bañarse

secarse

el secador de pelo

cortarse (el pelo, las uñas, el dedo, etc.)

Natalia

las tijeras

Sonia

maquillarse

cepillarse el pelo

el cepillo

Lupe

el peine

el maquillaje

peinarse

Inés

Pepita

Alfonso

Pedro

la crema de afeitar

Felipe

el champú

la navaja

la toalla

gel

ducharse

el desodorante

José

Octavio

cepillarse los dientes

el papel higiénico

afeitarse

el jabón

la máquina de afeitar

el cepillo de dientes

la pasta de dientes

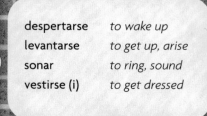

despertarse	*to wake up*
levantarse	*to get up, arise*
sonar	*to ring, sound*
vestirse (i)	*to get dressed*

La rutina diaria La rutina diaria La rutina diaria La rut
La rutina diaria La rutina diaria rutina La ru
La rutina diaria La rutina diaria
diaria

Por la noche

dormirse (ue)

Pepe

Esteban

CALCULO II

tener sueño

Alicia

Luisa

la compañera de cuarto

acostarse (ue)

quitarse (la ropa, etc.)

Leo

Ariel

Carmen

el profe Marín-Vivar

divertirse (ie)

Linda

Manuel

Marlena

Javier

Rubén

acostarse (ue)	*to go to bed*
el compañero/ la compañera de cuarto	*roommate*
divertirse (ie)	*to have a good time*
dormirse	*to fall asleep, to go to sleep*
quitarse (la ropa)	*to take off (one's clothes, etc.)*
tener sueño	*to be sleepy*

Así se dice

6-1 **Nuestras actividades diarias.** Which activities do you associate with the following items? Try to come up with as many as possible.

Modelo: el despertador   *despertarse, levantarse, sonar*

1. la ropa
2. el champú
3. el pelo
4. las tijeras
5. el peine
6. la pasta de dientes
7. el maquillaje
8. el jabón
9. el desodorante
10. la cama
11. la toalla
12. el cepillo

6-2 **La rutina diaria.**

Paso 1. Place the following activities in chronological order according to your personal daily routine. Number them 1–15.

_____ acostarse
_____ bañarse/ ducharse
_____ cenar
_____ cepillarse los dientes
_____ desayunar
_____ despertarse
_____ dormirse
_____ ir a clase

_____ estudiar
_____ levantarse
_____ peinarse
_____ quitarse la ropa
_____ secarse
_____ vestirse/ ponerse la ropa
_____ ver la tele

Paso 2. Now compare your list with that of a classmate. Are your routines similar or different?

6-3 **¡Adivina (*Guess*)!** Play with a partner. One of you will read descriptions 1–5 while the other listens (keeping the book closed!) and tries to guess the activities or things described. Then reverse roles: Estudiante B reads descriptions 6–10 for Estudiante A to guess. Who can identify the largest number of items? Keep score.

Estudiante A:

1. Un líquido para lavarse en la ducha.
2. Un objeto para cepillarse los dientes. Pones la pasta en él.
3. Una máquina para despertarse por la mañana, suena mucho.
4. La acción de cortarse el pelo con una navaja o una máquina.
5. Después de la ducha o después de lavarse, con una toalla.

Estudiante B:

6. Un objeto para cortarse el pelo o las uñas, para cortar papel, etc.
7. Un producto para lavarse la cara, las manos.
8. Ir a la cama para dormir.
9. Las chicas usan esto para estar guapas.
10. Un producto para lavarse el pelo.

NOTA DE LENGUA

Note that many **-se** verbs (reflexives) have different meanings than similar verbs that are not reflexive. For instance:

dormir = to sleep
dormirse = to fall asleep
poner = to put
ponerse = to put on one's clothes

You will find out more about them later in this chapter.

6-4 Colgate Total.

 Paso 1. Look at the ad below. What is it advertising?

    a. un cepillo de dientes   **b.** un desodorante   **c.** una pasta de dientes

Protege tu boca aún cuando no te estás cepillando.

¡La nueva COLGATE TOTAL, con su avanzada fórmula de acción prolongada sigue trabajando después de cepillarte y te ayuda a proteger tu boca contra las caries, el sarro, la placa, la gingivitis y el mal aliento, hasta por doce horas! Colgate Total es una pasta tan avanzada que sigue trabajando entre cepilladas mientras te diviertes, mientras trabajas y hasta cuando duermes. ¡Hora tras hora tras hora!

Visite nuestro website http://www.colgate.com

NEW **Colgate** Total
HELPS PREVENT CAVITIES • GINGIVITIS • PLAQUE
ANTICAVITY FLUORIDE AND   ANTIGINGIVITIS TOOTHPASTE
LONG LASTING FRESH BREATH PROTECTION • FIGHTS TARTAR

La cepillada tan avanzada que trabaja entre cepilladas.

PALABRAS ÚTILES

las caries	*cavities*
el sarro	*tartar*
el mal aliento	*bad breath*

NOTA DE LENGUA

Many name brands in Hispanic countries are the same as in the United Status, but with a Spanish pronunciation. How do you think Spanish-speakers pronounce these brands?

   Colgate
   Palmolive
   Vicks VapoRub
   Avon
   Oral-B

 Paso 2. Read the questions below. Then read the ad again and answer the questions.

   1. ¿Contra qué protege Colgate?

   2. ¿Cuándo sigue (*does it continue*) trabajando?

Paso 3. In small groups, discuss the following questions about your preferences regarding personal hygiene products.

   1. ¿Qué marca (*brand*) de pasta de dientes usas?

   2. En cuanto a productos de higiene personal, ¿tienes marcas preferidas? ¿Hay marcas que no te gustan para nada (*at all*)?

   3. ¿Qué factor es más importante cuando compras estos productos? ¿Cuánto cuestan? ¿El olor (*scent*) o sabor (*taste*)? ¿Prefieres productos "clásicos" o nuevos?

Cultura: España contemporánea: Herencia° y modernidad

Heritage

Antes de leer

1. Which of these people are from Spain?
   ☐ Penélope Cruz, actress
   ☐ Antonio Banderas, actor
   ☐ Miguel de Cervantes, author of the book *Don Quijote de la Mancha*
   ☐ Pedro Almodóvar, film director
   ☐ Pablo Picasso, painter
2. Which of the following are found in Spain?
   ☐ olive oil
   ☐ Flamenco music and dance
   ☐ A Guggenheim museum

When you see a placename in **red**, look back to the map to locate it.

LA HERENCIA

Por toda España se observa la herencia de varias culturas y civilizaciones, una de las cuales es la árabe. Los árabes vivieron en España durante casi 800 años (711–1492). La Alhambra, gran palacio y fortaleza situada en **Granada**, es exquisito ejemplo de la belleza arquitectónica de esta cultura. Una de las múltiples atracciones de su decoración interior es el uso de diseños geométricos y también azulejos[1] de colores vivos. ¿Qué contraste ves entre el interior y el exterior de la Alhambra?

[1]ceramic tiles

El Rey Juan Carlos de España y su esposa la Reina doña Sofía

El príncipe Felipe y su esposa, doña Letizia

LA FAMILIA REAL

¡En España hay reyes, príncipes y princesas! Sí, la familia real es muy querida por los españoles. El Rey Don Juan Carlos de Borbón tuvo un importante papel en la transición que llevó la democracia a España después de 40 años de la dictadura militar del General Franco. Ahora su papel es simbólico.

- Lope de Vega, un escritor español del siglo XVII, escribió más de 1.500 obras de teatro.

- Miguel de Cervantes, el autor del famoso libro *Don Quijote de la Mancha*, murió exactamente el mismo día que William Shakespeare—el 23 de abril de 1616.

Investig@ en INTERNET

What can you find out about the Spanish royal family? Look for the names of the king and queen, their children and grandchildren, and at least one more piece of information you find interesting about them. Also, find out who will be the next king.

España tiene la cuarta universidad más antigua de Europa, en **Salamanca**. Fue fundada en el año 1218.

Cultura: España contemporánea: Herencia y modernidad

LA MODERNIDAD

En España podemos visitar el pasado y vivir las innovaciones del presente al mismo tiempo. España es parte de la Unión Europea, un conjunto[2] de organizaciones creadas entre[3] la mayoría de los países de la Europa Occidental.

La unión tiene el objetivo de articular cooperación económica, política y social entre los países participantes. En el año 2002 entró en circulación en España el euro, sustituyendo la moneda[4] nacional, la peseta.

[2]grouping   [3]among   [4]currency

La Unión Europea

El euro

Las playas, montañas y los numerosos lugares históricos hacen de España uno de los destinos turísticos más populares de Europa. Por ejemplo, se puede esquiar en **los Pirineos**, y las playas de **las Islas Baleares** son muy famosas. **Madrid**, la capital del país, ofrece muchos museos internacionalmente famosos, y **Barcelona** fue la sede[5] de los Juegos Olímpicos en 1992.

[5]venue

Madrid

Barcelona

Pedro Almodóvar es un famoso director de cine español. ¿Has visto alguna de sus películas?

Volver (2006)
Mala educación (2004)
Hable con ella (2002)
Todo sobre mi madre (1999)
Átame (1990)
Mujeres al borde de un ataque de nervios (1989)

Las varias regiones de España constituyen diferentes zonas culturales con sus propios bailes, comidas, vestidos[6] típicos, música, etc. El baile flamenco es típico de Andalucía, región en el sur de España donde se encuentra **Sevilla**. ¿Hay bailes típicos en la región donde vives tú?

[6]*attire*

España tiene cuatro idiomas oficiales: el castellano (variedad del español hablado en el centro de la península ibérica), el catalán, el gallego y el vasco. Mira las diferencias entre estos cuatro idiomas.

inglés	Madrid castellano (español)	Barcelona catalán	La Coruña gallego	Bilbao vasco
dog	perro	gos	can	txakurra
water	agua	aigua	auga	ur
sister	hermana	germana	irma	arreba

El Museo Guggenheim, Bilbao

En la España contemporánea, se crea una vigorosa cultura que combina la herencia de un pasado brillante con las nuevas posibilidades del futuro. La arquitectura futurista del Museo Guggenheim en Bilbao, refleja la vitalidad de la vida cultural de España.

Las aceitunas, el aceite de oliva y las naranjas de **Valencia** son famosos en todo el mundo.

Después de leer

1. What might be good symbols of Spain—both its heritage and its modernity?

2. Assuming that 1 euro = 1.3 dollars, calculate the cost of the following items:

A *paella* for 4 people in Valencia	€ 35	_____ dollars
A bottle of olive oil in **Málaga**	€ _____	7 dollars
A ticket to the Guggenheim Museum in Bilbao	€ 10	_____ dollars

Así se forma

> Pero mamá, no quiero bañarme. Quiero jugar.

NOTA DE LENGUA

With reflexive verbs, the definite article (not possessive adjectives) is normally used to refer to parts of the body or articles of clothing.

Voy a cepillarme **los** dientes.

~~Voy a cepillarme **mis** dientes.~~

—I am going to brush **my** teeth.

¿Vas a ponerte **el** suéter?

~~¿Vas a ponerte **tu** suéter?~~

—Are you going to put on **your** sweater?

1. Reflexive verbs: Talking about daily routines

These verbs combine with reflexive pronouns (**me, te, se, nos, os, se**) to show that the person is doing the action to herself/himself.

Note the differences in form and meaning in the following examples.

Carlos **baña** a su hermanito.　Carlos **bathes** his little brother. (nonreflexive)

Carlos **se baña**.　Carlos **bathes** himself. (reflexive)

Vamos a **vestir** a los niños.　We're going **to dress** the children. (nonreflexive)

Vamos a **vestirnos**.　We're going **to get dressed**. (reflexive)

Note, however, that some verbs have a reflexive form but do not have a reflexive meaning:

Nunca **me duermo** en clase.　I never **fall asleep** in class.

Mis amigos **se divierten**.　My friends **have fun**.

Formation of reflexive verbs

Two important things to consider:

1. Which reflexive pronoun to chose? The reflexive pronoun and the subject of the verb refer to the same person, so they agree with each other.

vestirse			
(yo)	**me** vist**o**	(nosotros/as)	**nos** vest**imos**
(tú)	**te** vist**es**	(vosotros/as)	**os** vest**ís**
(Ud., él/ella)	**se** vist**e**	(Uds., ellos/ellas)	**se** vist**en**

2. Where to place the reflexive pronoun? This depends on the sentence structure:

- Immediately before a conjugated verb.
  Me despierto a las seis.　I wake up at six.
  No **nos** acostamos tarde.　We don't go to bed late.

- If a conjugated verb is followed by an infinitive or present participle (**-ando/-iendo** form), place the reflexive pronoun either *immediately before the conjugated verb or after and attached to the infinitive or present participle.*

  Me tengo que levantar temprano.
  Tengo que levantar**me** temprano.
  I have to get up early.

  Linda **se** está divirtiendo.
  Linda está divirtiéndo**se**.
  Linda is having a good time.

Note that some reflexive verbs have a stem change in the present participle:

e → i: v**e**stirse → v**i**stiéndose　　div**e**rtirse → div**i**rtiéndose

o → u: d**o**rmirse → d**u**rmiéndose

6-5 La rutina de Camila e Inés.

Paso 1. Listen to the following statements describing Camila and Ines' morning routine and write the appropriate number under each illustration.

Camila   **Inés**

 _____    _____

 _____    _____

 _____    _____

 _____    _____

 _____    _____

 _____    _____

La rutina diaria   ciento ochenta y siete **187**

Así se forma

 Paso 2. Now, indicate who you think does each of the following activities. For number 8, add an activity you think both women do.

	Camila	Inés
1. Se quita la ropa y la pone en el piso (*on the floor*).	☐	☐
2. Se acuesta a las 2:00 de la mañana.	☐	☐
3. Se corta el pelo[1] en un salón de belleza (*beauty shop*) muy elegante.	☐	☐
4. Nunca se pone camisas o pantalones de vestir (*dressy*).	☐	☐
5. Se divierte en un restaurante elegante.	☐	☐
6. Se divierte viendo una película extranjera (*foreign movie*).	☐	☐
7. Se duerme mientras estudia.	☐	☐
8. ...	☑	☑

6-6 **La rutina de Pepe.** Pepe, a Spanish student, is going to tell us about his routine at the **Colegio Mayor** (*the equivalent of student dorms in Spain*). He thinks it is quite ordinary.

 Paso 1. Look at Pepe's activities in the chart below. With a partner, try to anticipate whether he might do these activities in the morning, in the evening, or both (**los dos**).

Modelo: Estudiante A: **Pienso que Pepe se peina por la mañana.**
Estudiante B: **Sí, pero yo pienso que se peina por la noche también.**

	Por la mañana	Por la noche	Los dos
• peinarse			
• cepillarse los dientes			
• ducharse			
• afeitarse			
• ponerse ropa de casa (*loungewear*)			
• divertirse			
• quitarse los zapatos			
• lavarse la cara			

Paso 2. Now, listen to Pepe talk about his routine and check your answers in the chart. Also, try to answer the following question:
¿Qué hace Pepe después de llegar a su cuarto por la noche?

---

[1]**Cortarse el pelo** is a peculiar reflexive verb in that it does not necessarily mean than one cuts his/her own hair. Often, it means: *to get/have a haircut.*

Paso 3. With a partner, comment on Pepe's routine and whether it is common or not.

Modelo: Estudiante A: **Pepe se cepilla los dientes...**

Estudiante B: **Pienso que es/ no es común.**

6-7 Y ¿cuál es tu rutina diaria?

Paso 1. Read the following sentences about daily activities. In the column labeled "**Tú**," decide if the sentences are true (**Sí**) or false (**No**) for you.

	Tú		Tu compañero/a	
Por las mañanas...	Sí	No	Sí	No
¿te despiertas con un despertador?	☐	☐	☐	☐
¿te levantas antes de las 8 de la mañana?	☐	☐	☐	☐
¿te duchas en 5 minutos o menos (less)?	☐	☐	☐	☐
¿te cepillas los dientes antes de desayunar?	☐	☐	☐	☐
¿te afeitas o te maquillas?	☐	☐	☐	☐

	Tú		Tu compañero/a	
Por las noches...	Sí	No	Sí	No
¿te diviertes con tus amigos?	☐	☐	☐	☐
¿te duermes cuando ves la televisión?	☐	☐	☐	☐
¿te bañas para relajarte (relax)?	☐	☐	☐	☐
¿te peinas o cepillas el pelo?	☐	☐	☐	☐
¿te acuestas después de las 12 de la noche?	☐	☐	☐	☐

Paso 2. Now work with a partner. Take turns asking each other the questions from **Paso 1** and note your partner's responses in the second column. You can ask for and offer more details about your routines.

Modelo: Estudiante A: **Por las mañanas, ¿te despiertas con un despertador?**

Estudiante B: **No, no necesito un despertador porque mi compañero de cuarto siempre pone la televisión.**

Así se forma

6-8 **¿Qué prefieres?** Now you will find out some details about your classmate's daily routine.

 Paso 1. Looking at the options below, write what you prefer. Then, write sentences guessing what your partner prefers. Invent a new activity for number 5.

Modelo: **Yo me ducho pero pienso que Pedro se baña.**

Yo me ducho y pienso que Pedro se ducha también.

1. Ducharse vs. bañarse
2. Ducharse/ Bañarse por la mañana vs. por la noche
3. Usar gel (de ducha) vs. jabón
4. Secarse el pelo con secador vs. con toalla
5. ¿ ... ?

Paso 2. Take turns talking about your preferences and what you guessed in **Paso 1.** You should also share additional details where possible.

Modelo: Estudiante A: **Yo me ducho, pero creo que tú te bañas.**

Estudiante B: **No, yo me ducho también.**

Estudiante A: **¿Usas gel o jabón?/ ¿Qué marca de champú usas? ...**

6-9 **¿Nosotros en general?**

 Paso 1. Decide which of the following sentences are probably true for most university students. Invent three additional sentences.

	Cierto	Falso
1. Nos levantamos muy temprano.	☐	☐
2. Desayunamos todos los días.	☐	☐
3. Nos vestimos de manera muy informal.	☐	☐
4. No siempre nos cepillamos los dientes.	☐	☐
5. Nos quitamos el pijama para ir a clase.	☐	☐
6. Nos divertimos mucho en la clase de español.	☐	☐
7. Nos acostamos después de las 12:00 de la noche.	☐	☐
8. ...	☐	☐
9. ...	☐	☐
10. ...	☐	☐

Paso 2. In groups, share your answers. Do you agree on most sentences? On only some of them? Be prepared to report back to the class.

6-10 Los instructores.

Paso 1. Now think about your instructors. Select the option that you think completes the sentence accurately for the majority of your university instructors. Invent two additional sentences.

1. Se levantan ☐ antes de las 7 de la mañana. ☐ entre las 7 y las 8 de
   ☐ después de las 8 de la mañana. la mañana.

2. Se afeitan (ellos) o se maquillan (ellas)
   ☐ todos los días. ☐ frecuentemente. ☐ a veces.

3. Se visten de manera ☐ informal. ☐ formal. ☐ muy formal.

4. Van a la universidad
   ☐ a pie (by foot). ☐ en coche. ☐ en autobús. ☐ en bicicleta.

5. Se duermen ☐ viendo la televisión. ☐ leyendo.
   (grading). ☐ leyendo tareas

6. Se acuestan ☐ antes de las 12 de la mañana. ☐ entre las 12 y 1 de
   ☐ después de la 1 de la mañana. la mañana.

7. ...

8. ...

Paso 2. In pairs, share your answers. Afterwards, ask your instructor about a few of the activities.

Modelo: ¿A qué hora se levanta usted?

NOTA CULTURAL

In Spain, the form **usted** is generally used less than in Latin America, but it is very common to use **usted** for teachers. Does your Spanish instructor prefer that students use **tú** or **usted** when addressing him/her?

6-11 En la escuela secundaria y en la universidad. Is university life very different from life during high school?

Paso 1. With a classmate, write two activities that are common for university students, two that are common for high school students, and three that are common for both groups of students.

Los estudiantes **universitarios** vivimos en residencias, no nos levantamos tarde...

Los dos grupos de estudiantes nos acostamos tarde

Los estudiantes de **secundaria** tienen que levantarse temprano todos los días

Paso 2. In small groups, share your ideas and decide:

¿Qué prefieren, la rutina de la escuela secundaria o la rutina de la vida universitaria?

Así se forma

6-12 **Hábitos diarios.** Many college students complain about feeling tired and getting sick frequently. The Health Department of your university wants to research the cause of this problem. You are going to collaborate in the study.

Paso 1. Individually, answer questions 1–7. Afterwards, invent another relevant question for this study and answer it.

DEPARTAMENTO DE SALUD: Estudio *Hábitos de vida*

1. ¿Tienes sueño ahora? ☐ Sí ☐ Un poco ☐ No

2. ¿A qué hora te levantas los días de clase? _____

3. ¿A qué hora te acuestas normalmente? _____

4. ¿Te duermes cuando estudias o ves la televisión? ☐ Siempre ☐ A veces ☐ Nunca

5. ¿Necesitas un despertador para despertarte? ☐ Siempre ☐ A veces ☐ Nunca

6. ¿Cuántas tazas de café o té tomas cada día? _____

7. ¿Desayunas antes de ir a clase? ☐ Siempre ☐ A veces ☐ Nunca

8. ¿_____? _____

Paso 2. In groups of three to four students, share your answers. Write down your classmates' answers in order to share them with the class.

Paso 3. Share your group's answers with the rest of the class. Can you make any generalizations about the daily habits of the group?

Modelo: **Dos de nosotros tenemos sueño ahora... Todos nosotros nos acostamos tarde...**

6-13 **Consejos (*Advice*).** You and your partner want to help other students adopt a healthier lifestyle, so you volunteer for the Health Services campaign. As part of your training, you have to participate in some role-plays.

 Paso 1. In turns, indicate what kind of problem you have and listen to your partner's advice.

Modelo: Estudiante A: **Siempre tengo sueño.**

Estudiante B: **Debes acostarte/tomar una siesta** (*take a nap*).
o…

Be sure not to look at your partner's problems!

Estudiante A:

1. Siempre llego tarde a clase.

2. Siempre estoy débil.

3. Estoy estresado porque trabajo y estudio mucho todos los días.

Estudiante B:

1. Me canso mucho (*I get very tired*) cuando camino a mis clases.

2. No puedo levantarme por la mañana.

3. Me duermo en la clase de contabilidad.

Paso 2. You and your partner want to collaborate with the brochure Health Services is putting together. Decide on and write down the three most important pieces of advice you have for today's college students.

Investig@ en INTERNET

One of the oldest universities in Spain (and the world!) is the Universidad de Alcalá de Henares. Imagine that you want to study there next year. Go to their website www.uah.es, find one course that you want to take (**Departamentos → Asignaturas**), and write down any details you can find (**Profesorado, Bibliografía, Evaluación**, etc.).

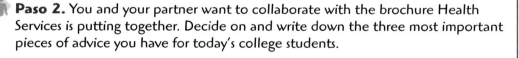

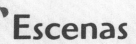

Javier

Clara

 war **La guerra° del baño**

Paso 1. Based on the title, anticipate what Javier and his sister Clara may be talking about.

    a. Javier se afeita y Clara se seca el pelo mientras conversan sobre sus clases.

    b. Javier está esperando para usar el baño pero su hermana Clara está allí.

    c. Clara pide a Javier una toalla y Javier la trae para ella.

Paso 2. Now listen to their conversation; did you guess correctly in **Paso 1**?

Paso 3. Read the following questions. Try to answer them as you listen to the conversation again.

  1. ¿Por qué está enojado Javier?
    ☐ Clara no quiere darle una toalla.   ☐ Clara no permite a Javier usar el baño.

  2. ¿Qué necesita hacer Javier en el baño?
    ☐ Peinarse.   ☐ Ducharse.

  3. ¿Qué más tiene que hacer Clara?
    ☐ Tiene que secarse el pelo solamente.   ☐ Tiene que hacer muchas cosas.

  4. ¿Por qué no puede esperar Javier?
    ☐ Tiene que ir a la universidad.   ☐ Tiene que ir al trabajo.

  5. ¿Qué tiene que hacer Javier en el futuro para solucionar este problema?
    ☐ Levantarse más temprano.   ☐ Peinarse en su cuarto.

Paso 4. ¡Ahora tú! Listen once more as you read their conversation and check your answers to the previous questions.

Javier: (*¡Pum!, ¡pum!, ¡pum!, dando con la mano en la puerta.*) ¿Qué estás haciendo, Clara?
shouting   Necesito usar el baño. (*Silencio.*) ¿No me oyes? (*Gritando°.*) ¿Puedes salir del baño y escucharme, por favor?

Clara: ¿Qué pasa? ¿Quieres ducharte?

Javier: No. Quiero peinarme.

mirror   Clara: ¡Peinarte! ¿No tienes espejo° en tu cuarto?

the right Javier: Sí, pero también vivo en esta casa y tengo derecho° a usar el baño.

Clara: Voy a salir en un minuto. Solamente tengo que secarme el pelo, cepillarme los dientes, peinarme, maquillarme, ponerme la ropa...

Enough! Javier: ¡Basta!° ¡Ya no puedo esperar más! Tengo que salir ahora para no llegar tarde a la universidad.

Clara: Lo siento. Vas a tener que levantarte más temprano si quieres entrar al baño antes que yo.

Así se dice

¿Qué acabas de hacer (*What have you just done*)?

Use the expression **acabar de** + *infinitive* to talk about things that have been just done.

acabar de + *infinitive*	*to have just (completed an action.)*
Acabo de vestirme.	*I have just gotten dressed.*

6-14 ¿Qué acaban de hacer?

Paso 1. Look at the timelines describing what Javier and Ricardo do on a typical day. Then, write what each person *has just finished doing* at the time indicated. The first one is done for you.

Javier

8:00 A.M.	9:00 A.M.	13:00 A.M.
Llega al hospital.	Examina a un paciente.	Escribe una receta médica (*prescription*).

1. A las 8:15 de la mañana, Javier acaba de llegar al hospital.
2. A las 9:15 de la mañana...
3. A las 1:15 de la tarde...

Ricardo

8:00 P.M.	9:00 P.M.	10:00 P.M.
Llega al discoteca.	Organiza todos sus discos compactos (CDs).	Ajusta el volumen de la música.

4. A las 8:15 de la noche...
5. A las 9:15 de la noche...
6. A las 10:15 de la noche...

Paso 2. Ahora adivina: ¿Cuáles son las profesiones de Javier y Ricardo?

Javier es: ☐ doctor ☐ profesor
Ricardo es: ☐ arqueólogo ☐ tocadiscos

6-15 **Una persona famosa.** In groups of three, decide on a famous person (actor, politician, singer, etc.). Then, write a brief paragraph about things they have just done at different times of the day. You will read your sentences to the rest of the class, who must guess who the famous person is.

Modelo: **A las 7:00 de la mañana, esta persona acaba de cantar "Material Girl" mientras se baña. A las 9:00, acaba de llevar a sus hijos Lourdes, Rocco y David a la escuela. A las 11:00, acaba de dar un paseo en bicicleta por Londres.**

Así se forma

Tengo que estudiar constantemente si quiero mejorar mis notas.

2. Adverbs: Describing how actions take place

An adverb tells *how, how much, how often, when, why,* or *where* an action takes place. Some adverbs you already know are: **ahora, hoy, mañana, tarde, aquí, allí, bien, mal, muy, a veces, nunca,** and **siempre.**

How?	Estoy **bien**, gracias.	*When?*	**A veces** desayuno en la cafetería.
Where?	Mi coche está **allí**.	*How much?*	Está **muy** enfermo.

Other adverbs are formed by adding **–mente** (equivalent to the English *–ly*) to an adjective.

- Add **–mente** to adjectives *ending in –e or a consonant.*
  posible → **posiblemente**
  personal → **personalmente**

- Add **–mente** to the feminine singular form of adjectives *ending in –o/–a.*
  rápido → rápida → **rápidamente**
  tranquilo → tranquila → **tranquilamente**

- Adjectives *with written accents* maintain the accent in the adverbial form.
  rápido → **rápidamente**   fácil → **fácilmente**

Some common adverbs

constantemente	*constantly*	**normalmente**	*normally*
desafortunadamente	*unfortunately*	**personalmente**	*personally*
fácilmente	*easily*	**posiblemente**	*possibly*
frecuentemente	*frequently*	**probablemente**	*probably*
generalmente	*generally*	**rápidamente**	*rapidly*
inmediatamente	*immediately*	**recientemente**	*recently*
lentamente	*slowly*	**tranquilamente**	*peacefully*

6-16 **¿Cómo o cuándo?** Complete the sentences with an adverb from the box and an appropriate activity (be creative!). Be prepared to report back to the class.

> fácilmente   rápidamente   frecuentemente   generalmente   tranquilamente
> lentamente   constantemente   inmediatamente   posiblemente   probablemente

Modelo: Cuando vuelvo a casa...
Cuando vuelvo a casa, llamo a mis amigos *inmediatamente*.

1. Cuando me levanto tarde, tengo que _____.
2. Cuando hablo con mi mamá, _____.
3. Cuando estoy muy cansado/a, _____.

4. Cuando estoy con mis amigos/as, _____.

5. Antes de acostarme, _____.

6. Este fin de semana, yo _____.

7. Mi profesor/a de español _____.

 **Lo que hacen normalmente.**

 Paso 1. Individually, select two people from the following list. Then choose appropriate adjectives and change them to adverbs to indicate *how, when, how often,* etc., they do certain activities.

Modelo: los profesores

Los profesores *generalmente* dan clases, hablan con los estudiantes, van a conferencias *frecuentemente*...

Personas	Adjetivos
los profesores	constante
mi profe de español	desafortunado
mi madre/ padre	fácil
mis padres	frecuente
mi hermano/a	general
mis hermanos/as	normal
mi compañero/a de cuarto	posible
mi mejor amigo/a	probable
mis amigos/as	rápido
mi novio/a	reciente
mi esposo/a	tranquilo

Paso 2. In small groups, take turns sharing one of your descriptions but do not mention who you are talking about. Your classmates will try to guess who it is.

Modelo: **Estas personas generalmente dan clases, hablan con los estudiantes, van a conferencias frecuentemente...**

Así se dice

Algunas profesiones

el señor Vega

el **abogado**/la **abogada**

la señora Vega

la **mujer de negocios**/
el **hombre de negocios**

el Dr. López

el **médica**/la **médica**/
el **doctor**/la **doctora**

la señorita Rojas

la **enfermera**/
el **enfermero**

la señora Ruiz

la **programadora**/
el **programador**

el señor Gómez

el **contador**/
la **contadora**

la señorita Cortés

la **maestra**/el **maestro**

la señora Casona

el **ama de casa**/
el **amo de casa**

El trabajo

El **trabajo** es otra de las rutinas en nuestra vida. Muchos adultos tienen un trabajo **de tiempo completo** y trabajan todo el día pero otros, por ejemplo muchos estudiantes, tienen trabajos **de tiempo parcial** y trabajan menos horas. No todos los trabajos compensan igual; los doctores, abogados y otros generalmente **ganan** mucho **dinero**, pero los maestros y las secretarias normalmente ganan poco. Algunas personas prefieren trabajar para una **compañía** grande como una multinacional; otras personas prefieren **empresas** pequeñas o familiares. Hay personas que trabajan en una oficina, otras en una escuela o universidad, en una **tienda** o en un centro comercial, o por toda la ciudad, como los policías. Otros son **empleados** de una **fábrica**, de un restaurante o de un supermercado. ¿Qué tipo de trabajo prefieres tú?

Carmen es **secretaria** y **recepcionista**. ¿Para qué compañía trabaja?

Linda es **dependienta** en esta tienda. ¿Qué vende?

Alfonso es **mesero** en un restaurante y Natalia es **cajera**. ¿Qué tipo de restaurante es?

Esteban es **repartidor** de pizzas. Reparte muchas pizzas a los estudiantes de la universidad. ¿Cómo se llama la pizzería?

el/la cajero/a	*cashier*	**la empresa**	*firm*
el/la dependiente/a	*salesclerk*	**la fábrica**	*factory*
la compañía	*company*	**ganar**	*to earn (money); to win*
el dinero	*money*	**a tiempo completo/ parcial**	*full-time/part-time*
el/la empleado/a	*employee*	**la tienda**	*store*

NOTA DE LENGUA

Many feminine nouns that start with a stressed **a** require the article **el** in the singular. It is easier to link **el** to the noun than **la**. However, in the plural, **las** is used rather than **los**.

> el **a**ma de casa BUT   **las** amas de casa   el **a**ula BUT   **las** aulas

When stating a person's profession or vocation without further qualifiers or description, the indefinite article **un** or **una** is not used. When an adjective is added, the indefinite article is used.

> Mi madre es **abogada**.   BUT   Mi madre es **una abogada** excelente.
> ~~Mi madres es **una** abogada.~~

6-18 ¿Sí o no? Listen to the following statements and decide whether they are logical (**Sí**) or illogical (**No**).

1. ☐ Sí ☐ No	3. ☐ Sí ☐ No	5. ☐ Sí ☐ No
2. ☐ Sí ☐ No	4. ☐ Sí ☐ No	6. ☐ Sí ☐ No

Así se dice

6-19 **¿Quién es? ¿Y cuál es su profesión?** Identify each person and their profession on pages 198–199. In the last column, if you know someone who has this profession, write his/her name.

Actividad	Persona	Profesión	También tiene esta profesión
Modelo: Trabaja con computadoras.	**Es la señora Ruiz.**	**Es programadora.**	**Mi tío Ernesto es programador.**
1. Trabaja en un hospital y cuida a los pacientes día y noche.			
2. Escribe informes sobre la situación económica de una compañía.			
3. Vende ropa y complementos en el centro comercial.			
4. Trabaja para una compañía grande, recibe visitas, contesta el teléfono, etc.			
5. Defiende a los "inocentes".			
6. Pasa el día en la sala de clase de una escuela primaria. Tiene muchos alumnos.			
7. Trabaja en una clínica o en el hospital. Diagnostica y cura a muchos pacientes.			
8. Sirve comida en un restaurante.			
9. Trabaja en casa.			
10. Lleva (*Takes*) comida a los clientes en su carro.			

NOTA DE LENGUA

Some countries, like Spain, use the word **camarero(a)** to refer to a waiter, while Mexico and other countries use **mesero(a)** (which is related to the word **mesa**).

6-20 La vida profesional.

 Paso 1. Choose one of the professions mentioned above and write a short paragraph about a day in the life of a person in that profession.

Modelo: Cada mañana esta persona se levanta a las...

Paso 2. In groups, share your descriptions and guess what profession each description refers to.

SITUACIONES

One of you will play the role of a career advisor and the other will be himself/herself seeking advice to plan for a professional career. Decide now who is going to play each role.

Career advisor:
1. You are going to interview the student, asking the questions below and two more questions that you think will be relevant. (Write them now.) Listen and take notes.
2. Based on your partner's answers, suggest a profession that would be good for him/her and explain why he/she would like it.

Student: Close your book for this part. In this conversation you are going to:
1. Listen to the questions the career advisor is going to ask you and respond truthfully and with as many details as you can.
2. Listen to the suggestion of the career advisor, tell him/her whether you agree with his/her choice or not, explaining why.

Cuestionario de orientación profesional. Nombre: _____

1. ¿Trabajas? (Si respondes "**No**", salta (*skip*) al número 5.) _____

2. ¿Qué tipo de trabajo tienes? _____

3. ¿Qué aspectos de tu trabajo te gustan? _____

4. ¿Qué aspectos no te gustan? _____

5. ¿Qué estudias? _____

6. ¿Cuáles son tus clases favoritas? _____

7. ¿Dónde quieres trabajar? En una oficina, en un hospital... _____

8. ¿Es importante para ti ganar mucho dinero? _____

9. ¿ ... ? _____

10. ¿ ... ? _____

Así se forma

¿Saliste con José anoche?

Sí, fuimos al cine.

¿A qué hora regresaron?

3. The preterit of regular verbs and *ser/ir*: Talking about actions in the past

The preterit tense is used to talk about *actions in the past we view/perceive as complete,*

Me levanté a las ocho y **desayuné**.	I **got up** at eight and **had breakfast**.
—¿Cuándo **volviste**?	When **did** you **return**?
—**Volví** a la una.	I **returned** at one.

or *past actions with a specific beginning, an end, or both.*

Estudié en la biblioteca por dos horas.	I **studied** at the library for two hours.
Comencé a estudiar a las tres.	I **began** to study at three.
Terminé a las cinco.	I **finished** at five.

Preterit form of regular verbs

	estudiar (*to study*)	volver (*to return*)	salir (*to leave*)
(yo)	estudié	volví	salí
(tú)	estudiaste	volviste	saliste
(Ud., él/ella)	estudió	volvió	salió
(nosotros/as)	estudiamos²	volvimos	salimos²
(vosotros/as)	estudiasteis	volvisteis	salisteis
(Uds., ellos/ellas)	estudiaron	volvieron	salieron

- Note that **-er/-ir** preterit verb endings are identical.

- In the preterit tense, **-ar** and **-er** verbs never change their stems. (See **volver** above.)

Other preterit forms

- **Ser** and **ir** have identical irregular preterit endings; the context clarifies which verb is used.

ser/ir	**fui, fuiste, fue, fuimos, fuisteis, fueron**
(ir) **Fueron** a la playa ayer.	*They went to the beach yesterday.*
(ser) **Fue** un día extraordinario.	*It was an extraordinary day.*

- The verbs **leer** (*to read*) and **oír** (*to hear*) change the **i** of the third-person singular and plural endings to **y** (**-ió → -yo; -ieron → -yeron**).
  - **leer**   leí, leíste, **leyó**, leímos, leísteis, **leyeron**
  - **oír**   oí, oíste, **oyó**, oímos, oísteis, **oyeron**

---

²The **nosotros** form of -ar and -ir verbs in the preterit are the same as their respective present-tense forms.

Así se dice

¿Qué pasó?

		(anteayer)	(ayer)	(hoy)			
12 lunes	**13 martes**	**14 miércoles**	**15 jueves**	**16 viernes**	**17 sábado**	**18 domingo**
	Un desastre ☹	Levantarme. Correr. Asistir a clases. Almorzar...	Escribir a Beatriz			

		En Égypte!		
🔁 **Répondre**	📑 **Faire suivre**	🗑 **Supprimer**	🖨 **Imprimer**	

De :	Chris Bailey <chris@voyageur.com>
Date :	le 21 mars
Pour :	Ben_et_Martha@canada.com
Asunto :	

¡Hola, hermanita! **Anteayer** fue un desastre—¿fue porque era el martes 13, el día de la mala suerte? No sé, pero al menos **ayer** fue un día bastante ordinario. **Primero** me levanté temprano y corrí tres millas. **Luego**, me bañé. Desayuné a eso de las siete de la mañana y **después** asistí a mis clases. Llegué temprano a mi primera clase porque nunca me gusta llegar tarde. A las doce almorcé y **entonces** fui al Centro Estudiantil para encontrarme con mis amigos. Más tarde mandé unos e-mails, oí las noticias en la radio y regresé al restaurante de la U. para cenar. **Anoche** estudié antes de acostarme. Ustedes **ya** saben que soy una magnífica estudiante. Bueno, muy estudiosa al menos. ¿Quieres saber lo que me pasó **el fin de semana pasado**? ¿Y la semana pasada? Eso es para otro episodio.

anoche	*last night*	**entonces**	*then*
el fin de semana pasado[3]	*last weekend*	**primero**	*first*
Luego	*then, later*	**ya**	*already*
después	*afterwards*		

[3]También **el año/ mes/ verano,** etc. **pasado.**

Así se dice

6-21 ¿Cómo fue tu día ayer?

Paso 1. Read the following sentences, and if they are true for you, write **Sí**. Otherwise rewrite them so that they are true for you.

1. Me levanté temprano.
2. Fui al gimnasio.
3. Desayuné en la cafetería de la universidad.
4. Llegué temprano a mis clases.
5. Vi noticias en la televisión.
6. Estudié en la biblioteca
7. Fui a cenar a un restaurante.
8. Leí una novela en mi cuarto.
9. Me acosté a las 11 de la noche.

Paso 2. Now, use the corrected sentences above and add more details to write about what you did yesterday. Use at least three of the expressions below.

primero	después	entonces	luego

6-22 Mi compañero y *yo*.

Paso 1. Write five sentences about what you did last weekend. Three should be true (**cierto**) and two should be false (**falso**).

Paso 2. Now, in small groups, read your sentences to your classmates, who will try to identify which sentences are true and which are false.

Modelo: El sábado jugué al tenis.

_____

_____

_____

_____

_____

6-23 **La semana de la Profesora Rodríguez.** Your friend is talking about her Spanish instructor, Professor Rodriguez. Some of the statements refer to things she always does and others to things she specifically did last week. Can you tell them apart? You will hear each statement twice.

PALABRAS ÚTILES	
enseñar	*to teach*
ayudar	*to help*

siempre	la semana pasada
1.	
2.	
3.	
4.	
5.	
6.	
7.	
8.	
9.	
10.	

6-24 **Nuestro instructor.** In small groups, imagine and write the story of what your instructor did yesterday after classes finished. It does not have to be realistic; imagine a very interesting, crazy or fun evening. Be prepared to share your story with the class.

Después de las clases, la Profesora Rodríguez fue a...

6-25 **El sábado pasado.** Listen as your instructor reads sentences about what Javier and his younger brother, Samuel, did last Saturday and write the number of each sentence under the appropriate drawing.

_____ _____ _____

_____ _____ _____

Así se dice

6-26 Un fin de semana interesante.

Paso 1. Write a brief paragraph narrating what you did last Saturday in some detail. Do not write your name on the piece of paper.

Paso 2. When the whole class has finished, the instructor will redistribute all the stories. Read your story and guess which one of your classmates wrote it.

6-27 El año pasado.

Paso 1. Write eight questions in the left-hand column for your classmates about whether they did the following things last year or not, and then add one more of your own.

Modelo: comprar un coche nuevo

You write and ask: **¿Compraste un coche nuevo?**

El año pasado	Firma (signature)
1. viajar a un lugar exótico ¿_____? ¿Dónde?	
2. ver una película extranjera (*foreign*) ¿_____? ¿Cuál?	
3. hablar con alguien famoso ¿_____? ¿Quién?	
4. probar (*to try*) una comida nueva ¿_____? ¿Cuál?	
5. ir con tus amigos a un sitio peligroso (*dangerous*) ¿_____? ¿Dónde?	
6. leer un libro escandaloso ¿_____? ¿Cuál?	
7. estudiar algo nuevo ¿_____? ¿Qué?	
8. ¿_____? ¿_____?	

Paso 2. Now, circulate around the room and ask your questions to your classmates. When you find someone who answers "**Sí,**" have him/her sign in the right-hand column and ask the follow-up question for that item or come up with a different one.

Paso 3. Everyone reports back to the class. Who had the most interesting year last year?

Antes de leer

Are there any famous celebrations where you live that are not necessarily celebrated around the entire U.S.? How are they celebrated?

Los días festivos marcan un cambio en la rutina diaria hispana. Son de dos tipos: religiosos o cívicos. Las fiestas religiosas celebran las tradiciones de la religión católica, y las cívicas, los hechos[1] históricos. Cada país tiene sus propias[2] fiestas, pero hay muchas que todos los hispanos conmemoran.

[1]*events, facts* [2]**sus...** *their own*

Semana Santa en Sevilla, España

Otras festividades religiosas honran al santo patrón de una ciudad o de un país. Durante la fiesta de San Fermín en Pamplona (España) ¡sueltan[4] toros por las calles[5]! Los habitantes de la ciudad y enorme cantidad de turistas se visten de blanco con pañuelos[6] y cinturones[7] rojos y corren detrás[8] o delante[9] de los toros. La fiesta atrae 1.5 millones de turistas cada año.

[4]*set free* [5]*streets* [6]*neck scarves*
[7]*sashes* [8]*behind* [9]*in front*

La fiesta religiosa hispana más popular es la Semana Santa. Muchos participan en procesiones por las calles, llevando imágenes de Cristo o de la Virgen María. Hay música y representaciones de escenas bíblicas. La celebración termina con bailes y fuegos artificiales[3].

[3]**fuegos...** *fireworks*

Las festividades cívicas son especialmente populares en Latinoamérica. El Día de la Independencia es una de las fechas más importantes. Generalmente, esta celebración consiste en grandes desfiles[10]. En algunas comunidades participan la armada nacional y los estudiantes de las escuelas. Numerosas banderas decoran las ciudades, y la gente se divierte hasta muy tarde en las ferias y bailes.

[10]*parades*

Conexiones y contrastes

Are there any celebrations in the U.S. that are considered dangerous, as are the San Fermines in Pamplona?

Así se forma

Felipe, mi amiga Rosa
quiere conocerte.

La conozco. ¡Es
muy simpática!

¿Rosa? La vi ayer
en la cafetería.

4. Direct-object pronouns

A **direct object** is the person or thing
that directly receives the action of the verb.
It answers the question *Who/Whom?* or *What?*

(Who/Whom?) Vi **a Laurie**.　　　　　　　*I saw **Laurie**.*
　　　　　　　La vi en el gimnasio.　　　　*I saw **her** in the gym.*
Laurie is the <u>direct-object noun</u>;　　*her* is the <u>direct-object pronoun</u>.

Important! When the direct-object noun is a person, it requires the personal **a**
(observe the contrast in the examples above).

(What?)　Laurie compró **el champú**.　　*Laurie bought **the shampoo**.*
　　　　　Lo compró ayer.　　　　　　*She bought **it** yesterday.*
Shampoo is the <u>direct-object noun</u>;　*it* is the <u>direct-object pronoun</u>.

Pronombres de objeto directo

me	Carlos no **me** llamó.	*Carlos did not call **me**.*
te	¿**Te** llamó Carlos?	*Did Carlos call **you**?*
lo	No **lo** conozco. (a Juan/ a Ud., *m.*) No **lo** tengo. (el libro)	*I don't know **him/you** (m.).* *I don't have **it** (m.).*
la	Juan **la** conoce. (a Lola/ a Ud., *f.*) Juan **la** come. (la fruta)	*Juan knows **her/you** (f.).* *Juan eats **it** (f.).*
nos	Laurie **nos** visitó anoche.	*Laurie visited **us** last night.*
os	¿Quién **os** visitó?	*Who visited **you** (pl.)?*
los	Voy a llamar**los**. (a ellos/ a Uds., *m.*) Voy a preparar**los**. (los cafés)	*I am going to call **them/you** (m.).* *I am going to prepare **them** (m.).*
las	Pedro **las** admira. (a ellas/ a Uds., *f.*) Pedro **las** va a preparar. (las bebidas)	*Pedro admires **them/you** (f.).* *Carlos is going to prepare **them** (f.).*

- Direct-object pronouns must agree with the nouns they replace or refer to.
  —¿Compraste **la pasta de dientes**?　　*Did you buy **the toothpaste**?*
  —Sí, **la** compré.　　　　　　　　　*Yes, I bought **it**.*
  —¿Usaste **el nuevo jabón**?　　　　*Did you use **the new soap**?*
  —Sí, **lo** usé.　　　　　　　　　　*Yes, I used **it**.*

Posición de los pronombres de objeto directo

- The direct-object pronoun is placed immediately before a conjugated verb.
  Lo compré.　　　　　　　　　　*I bought **it**.*

- If a conjugated verb is followed by an infinitive or present participle
  (**-ando**/**-iendo** form), place the direct-object pronoun either
  immediately before the conjugated verb or after and attached to the
  infinitive or present participle[4]. It cannot be placed between both forms.
  Voy a invitar**la**.　　*o*　　**La** voy a invitar.　　*I am going to invite **her**.*
  Estoy llamándo**la**.　*o*　　**La** estoy llamando.　*I am calling **her**.*

---

[4]In other instances, you must attach the pronoun to the infinitive or the **-ando**/**-iendo** form.
　　Voy al laboratorio para <u>ver**lo**</u>.　　Aprendo los verbos <u>practicándo**los**</u>.

Note that the pronoun *it* can only be translated as **lo/la** when it functions as a direct object. The English *it* subject pronoun is usually omitted in Spanish.

	I ate it.	→ **Lo comí.**
	We didn't write it.	→ **No lo escribimos.**
BUT	*It is expensive.*	→ **Es caro.**
	It opens at 8 A.M.	→ **Abre a las 8 de la mañana.**

6-28 **Compras en la farmacia.** You are in the drugstore to buy some things you and your roommate need. You are a bit absent-minded, so your friend calls you on your cellphone to make sure you do not forget anything. Listen and choose the correct response.

1.	☐ Sí, lo voy a comprar.	☐ Sí, la voy a comprar.	☐ Sí, los voy a comprar.	☐ Sí, las voy a comprar.
2.	☐ Sí, lo tengo.	☐ Sí, la tengo.	☐ Sí, los tengo.	☐ Sí, las tengo.
3.	☐ Sí, lo busqué.	☐ Sí, la busqué.	☐ Sí, los busqué.	☐ Sí, las busqué.
4.	☐ No, no lo tengo.	☐ No, no la tengo.	☐ No, no los tengo.	☐ No, no las tengo.
5.	☐ No, no lo tengo.	☐ No, no la tengo.	☐ No, no los tengo.	☐ No, no las tengo.
6.	☐ No, no lo puedo comprar.	☐ No, no los puedo comprar.	☐ No, no la puedo comprar.	☐ No, no las puedo comprar.

6-29 **¿Quién tiene mis tijeras?** Students tend to freely borrow each other's things. In pairs, imagine that you live in the dorm on pages 178–179 and you are missing some items.

First, Estudiante A asks Estudiante B about his/her "missing" items (1–5) and Estudiante B explains *who* has each item and *for what* it is being used. Then Estudiante B asks about his/her items (6–10) and Estudiante A replies.

Modelo: tijeras

Estudiante A: —**¿Quién tiene mis tijeras?**

Estudiante B: —**Natalia *las* tiene. *Las* está usándo para cortarse el pelo.**

Cosas del Estudiante A:

1. secador de pelo
2. peine
3. cepillo
4. maquillaje
5. champú

Cosas del Estudiante B:

6. máquina de afeitar
7. pasta de dientes
8. despertador
9. desodorante
10. guitarra

Así se forma

6-30 **Cosas (*Things*) para vender.** In small groups, imagine that you are students at a Spanish university. You need money and wish to sell some things that you no longer need.

Paso 1. Individually, select four items from the list that you want to sell. Decide in what condition each item is (**nuevo, casi nuevo, usado, muy usado**) and write the price you want for it in euros. (*Do not let your partners see!*)

Modelo: ☒ un refrigerador pequeño _____casi nuevo_____ € __39__

Investig@ en INTERNET

Since Spain is a member of the European Union (EU), it has adopted the euro (€) in replacement of its traditional currency, **la peseta**. Can you find out the currencies of three other Hispanic countries?

☐ una máquina de afeitar	_____	€ _____
☐ un radio-despertador	_____	€ _____
☐ un teléfono celular	_____	€ _____
☐ un libro de psicología	_____	€ _____
☐ una impresora a color	_____	€ _____
☐ un sofá	_____	€ _____
☐ un televisor muy grande	_____	€ _____
☐ una computadora IBM	_____	€ _____
☐ unos CDs de música clásica	_____	€ _____

Paso 2. Take turns trying to sell your items—you might have to negotiate the price. Keep track of the money you make. When you reject something, think of an excuse. When someone is not interested in one of your items, try to sell it to someone else.

Modelo: Estudiante A: **Tengo un refrigerador pequeño para vender. Está casi nuevo.**
Estudiante B: **¿Cuánto cuesta?**
Estudiante A: **Cuesta treinta y nueve euros. ¿Quieres comprarlo?**
Estudiante B: **Sí, lo compro./ No lo quiero, gracias. Es un poco caro (*expensive*)...**

Paso 3. Now add up your earnings. Which student made the most money?

Modelo: Gané...

6-31 **La telenovela *Un día de la vida*.** You are auditioning for the roles of Aurora and Anselmo, famous characters from a cheesy soap opera: *Un día de la vida*. First, complete the dialog filling in the blanks with the direct-object pronouns **me, te,** or **lo**. Then read it dramatically. You really want the parts!

Anselmo: Mi amor, estás muy triste. ¿Qué pasa?... _____ amas, ¿verdad?

Aurora: _____ amo con todo mi corazón, pero tengo que ser muy franca. También adoro a Rafael, y sé que él _____ adora a mí.

Anselmo: Pero yo también _____ adoro. Eres el amor de mi vida. _____ necesitas, ¿verdad?

Aurora: Claro que _____ necesito, pero no puedo imaginar mi vida sin Rafael. También _____ necesito a él. _____ extraño° mucho.   *miss*

Anselmo: Mi cielo, tú sabes muy bien que no va a volver, y tú sabes que yo estoy aquí y que _____ quiero.

Aurora: (*Ella solloza°.*) Pero él es único. Yo no _____ quiero a ti como _____ quiero a él.   *sobs*

Anselmo: (*También solloza.*) Tengo que reconocer° que también _____ quiero. Yo también _____ extraño.   *admit*

Aurora: Nunca vamos a encontrar otro perro como él.

Así se pronuncia

The pronunciation of *r* and *rr*

r (except in word-initial position) approximates the sound of *tt* as in *Betty* or *dd* as in *Eddy*.

desodorante   quedarse   tijeras   muro

word-initial *r* and *rr* have a trilled sound as in mimicking a motorcycle.

rápidamente   **r**estaurante   cerrar   **R**oma

Listen to the following verse and repeat:

Erre con erre cigarro,
Erre con erre barril.
Rápido corren los carros,
Carros del ferrocarril°.   *railroad*

¿Qué palabra es? Now you are going to work with a partner to practice the pronunciation of *r*. Exaggerating the pronunciation when you first practice new sounds will help you figure out how it's done, so don't be shy!

Paso 1. Look at the pairs of words below (all real Spanish words!) and note there is only one difference to set them apart, what is it? Obviously, making that difference in pronunciation is essential to avoid misunderstandings.

Work in pairs, Estudiante A will underline one word in each pair for numbers 1–3 and Estudiante B will do the same for numbers 4–6. Don't show your partner your work!

Estudiante A:
1. caro   carro
2. pero   perro
3. coro   corro

Estudiante B:
4. para   parra
5. moro   morro
6. ahora   ahorra

Paso 2. Each of you will read the words you <u>underlined</u> for your partner, who will listen and select the word he/she hears from each pair. After you finish, check your answers.

Dicho y hecho

¡A ESCUCHAR!

¿La hora del examen ya pasó? Esteban's phone has been ringing for a long time. Finally he answers. It is his friend Manuel calling. Listen to the conversation. Then answer the first three questions.

1. ¿Qué está haciendo Esteban cuando el teléfono suena?
   - ☐ Está estudiando.   ☐ Está durmiendo.
2. ¿Se canceló el examen de sociología?
   - ☐ Sí.   ☐ No.
3. ¿Estudió Esteban mucho para el examen?
   - ☐ Sí.   ☐ No.

Now listen to the conversation again and then answer the following questions.

4. ¿A qué hora se acostó Esteban? **A las...**
5. ¿A qué hora llamó Manuel?
6. ¿Cómo fue el examen?

CONVERSANDO

Mi rutina ideal. Pretend that your life is a bit boring. Share ideas on what you consider to be the ideal routine for a perfect day, from the time you get up until you go to bed.

- Me levanto a las...
- Luego,....

DE MI ESCRITORIO

Un día muy interesante en mi vida. Write a description of an interesting day in your life that occurred some time *in the past*. Write about yourself or pretend that you are another university student, a university professor, or a housewife/mother who also happens to be a businesswoman. Your instructor will ask several students to read their compositions aloud, and the class will decide who had the most interesting day.

Artes ornamentales:
Los azulejos[1] de España

La rutina diaria La rutina diaria La rutina di la rutina diaria rutina diaria la rutina la rutina

Antes de leer

Are there tiles in the building where you live? Are they decorative or simply practical?

Desde hace muchos siglos los azulejos de cerámica adornan los castillos y palacios de España. La palabra *azulejo* viene de *al zuleiq,* que en árabe quiere decir "pequeña piedra pulida"[2]. Con la presencia musulmana[3] (de origen árabe) comenzó la tradición de los azulejos en España.

Ya que[4] la religión musulmana no permite la representación de figuras humanas o de animales, los azulejos árabes utilizan sólo formas geométricas. El palacio de la Alhambra en Granada y la Gran Mezquita[5] en Córdoba contienen los ejemplos más espectaculares de este arte decorativo. Los diseños más recientes también contienen imágenes religiosas, describen una historia o imitan tapices[6] y pinturas.

Los azulejos tienen colores vivos y se utilizan para decorar exteriores e interiores de iglesias, restaurantes y hasta[7] estaciones de metro. España produce azulejos para uso doméstico y para exportación. Hoy todavía existen muchos artesanos que hacen azulejos tradicionales a mano, pero gran parte de la producción de azulejos en España utiliza técnicas industriales.

Plaza de España. Sevilla, España

Azulejo decorativo en el palacio de la Alhambra, Granada, España

---

[1]*ceramic tiles* [2]*polished* [3]*Muslim* [4]**Ya...** *Since* [5]*Mosque* [6]*tapestries* [7]*even*

Después de leer

1. Look at the two photos and decide which one is being referred to in each sentence.

   It represents an Arabic tradition. ☐ Plaza de España ☐ la Alhambra
   It contains a more recent design. ☐ Plaza de España ☐ la Alhambra
   It depicts religious images. ☐ Plaza de España ☐ la Alhambra

2. Are there buildings or public places where you live that have decorative tile? Describe one.

Repaso de vocabulario activo

Adverbios y expresiones adverbiales

constantemente *constantly*

desafortunadamente *unfortunately*

fácilmente *easily*

generalmente *generally*

inmediatamente *immediately*

lentamente *slowly*

normalmente *normally*

personalmente *personally*

posiblemente *possibly*

probablemente *probably*

rápidamente *quickly*

recientemente *recently*

tranquilamente *calmly*

anoche *last night*

anteayer *the day before yesterday*

ayer *yesterday*

el fin de semana pasado *last weekend*

el... pasado (año/ mes/ verano, etc.) *last (year/month/ summer)*

la semana pasada *last week*

ya *already*

entonces *then*

después *later*

luego *later, then*

más tarde *later*

primero *first*

Sustantivos

La rutina diaria *Daily routine*

la cama *bed*

el cepillo *brush*

  el cepillo de dientes *toothbrush*

el champú *shampoo*

la crema de afeitar *shaving cream*

el desodorante *deodorant*

el despertador *alarm clock*

el jabón *soap*

el maquillaje *makeup*

la máquina de afeitar *electric shaver*

la navaja *razor*

el papel higiénico *toilet paper*

la pasta de dientes *toothpaste*

el peine *comb*

el secador de pelo *hair dryer*

las tijeras *scissors*

la toalla *towel*

El trabajo *Work*

la compañía *company*

el dinero *money*

la empresa *a business, company*

la fábrica *factory*

la tienda *store, shop*

  de ropa *clothing store*

el trabajo *work*

  de tiempo completo/ parcial *full-time/part-time*

Más personas y profesiones

el/ la abogado/a *lawyer (m./f.)*

el/ la amo/ a de casa *homemaker (m./f.)*

el/ la cajero/a *cashier (m./f.)*

el/ a compañero/ a de cuarto *roommate (m./f.)*

el/ la contador/a *accountant (m./f.)*

el/ la dependiente/ a *salesclerk (m./f.)*

el/ la enfermero/ a *nurse (m./f.)*

el/ la empleado/a *employee (m./f.)*

el hombre/ la mujer de negocios *businessperson (m./f.)*

el/ la maestro/a *teacher (m./f.)*

el/ la médico/a *doctor (m./f.)*

el/ la mesero/a *waiter/waitress*

el/ la programador/a *computer programmer (m./f.)*

el/ la recepcionista *receptionist (m./f.)*

el/ la repartidor/a *delivery person (m./f.)*

el/ la secretario/a *secretary (m./f.)*

Verbos y expresiones verbales

acostarse (ue) *to go to bed*

afeitarse *to shave*

bañarse *to take a bath*

cepillarse los dientes/ el pelo *to brush one's teeth/hair*

cortarse el pelo/ las uñas/ el dedo *to cut one's hair/nails/a finger*

stem

despertarse (ie) *to wake up*

divertirse (ie) *to have fun*

dormirse (ue) *to sleep*

ducharse *to take a shower*

ganar *to earn, make (money)*

lavarse las manos/ la cara, etc. *to wash one's hands/face, etc.*

levantarse *to get up*

maquillarse *to put on makeup*

peinarse *to comb one's hair*

ponerse los zapatos/ la ropa, etc. *to put on one's shoes/ clothes, etc.*

quitarse *to take off*

  la ropa *one's clothes*

secarse *to dry (oneself)*

sonar (ue) *to ring, sound*

vestirse (i) *to get dressed*

acabar de + *infinitivo* *to have just (completed an action)*

tener sueño *to be sleepy, tired*

trabajar para... *to work for*

Autoprueba y repaso WILEY PLUS ✓

I. Reflexive verbs. It is 8:00 A.M. in the dorm. Indicate what happens.

Modelo: Alfonso / levantarse **Alfonso se levanta.**

1. mi compañero / a de cuarto / despertarse.
2. yo / levantarse.
3. tú / bañarse.
4. Pepita / cepillarse los dientes
5. nosotros / ponerse suéteres porque hace frío
6. Octavio y Manuel / vestirse.

II. Adverbs. Express each idea in a different way by using an appropriate adverb.

Modelo: Mi abuela no camina muy rápido.
Camina... **lentamente.**

1. Carmen llama a sus abuelos con mucha frecuencia. Los llama...
2. Sofía habla español con facilidad. Lo habla...
3. Tomás acaba de llegar. Llegó...
4. Felipe responde a mis mensajes electrónicos el momento en que los recibe. Me responde...

III. The preterit of regular verbs and *ser/ir*.

A. Indicate what happened this morning before work.

Modelo: yo / levantarse temprano
Me levanté temprano.

1. yo / ducharse
2. Pepita / peinarse
3. tú / lavarse la cara
4. nosotros / afeitarse
5. ellos / cepillarse los dientes

B. Indicate what happened during the workday.

Modelo: yo / desayunar en Starbucks
Desayuné en Starbucks.

1. yo / llegar al trabajo a las nueve
2. dos colegas / leer las noticias (*news*) del día
3. mi colega y yo / mandar un mensaje electrónico al presidente de la compañía
4. tú / escribir un memo muy importante
5. nosotros / ir a un restaurante chino para almorzar
6. en la tarde, mi colega / llamar a varios de nuestros clientes
7. ella / resolver un problema serio
8. nosotros / salir del trabajo a las cinco de la tarde

IV. Direct-object pronouns.

A. Camila is going to invite to her party everyone who wants to come.

Modelo: Elena quiere ir a la fiesta.
Pues, Camila va a invitarla.

1. Yo quiero ir.
2. Nosotros queremos ir.
3. Ustedes quieren ir.
4. Mis hermanas quieren ir.
5. Mis hermanos quieren ir.
6. Pepita quiere ir.
7. Tú quieres ir.

B. Answer the questions with the appropriate direct-object pronoun.

Modelo: ¿Quieres conocer al presidente de la universidad?
Sí, quiero conocerlo. / Sí, lo quiero conocer.
o **No, no quiero conocerlo. / No, no lo quiero conocer.**

1. ¿Quieres ver a tus amigos/as hoy?
2. ¿Vas a llamar a tus padres esta noche?
3. ¿Estás haciendo la tarea para la clase de español ahora?
4. ¿Completaste todos los ejercicios del Capítulo 6?
5. ¿Vas a estudiar todo el vocabulario?

V. General review. Answer each question with as many activities as possible.

1. ¿Qué haces por la mañana después de levantarte?
2. ¿Qué haces antes de acostarte?
3. ¿Adónde fuiste ayer? ¿Qué más ocurrió ayer?
4. ¿Qué pasó el fin de semana pasado?
5. ¿Llamaste a tu mejor amigo/a la semana pasada? ¿De qué hablaron?

VI. Cultura.

1. Name two things you have learned about Spain's history.
2. Name two things you have learned about modern-day Spain.
3. Explain what **azulejos** are and how they got to Spain.

Answers to the *Autoprueba y repaso* are found in **Apéndice 2.**

WILEY
PLUS

Por la ciudad

By the end of this chapter you will be able to:

- Talk about places and things in the city
- Carry out transactions at the post office and the bank
- Talk about actions in the past
- Express negation

Así se dice

- En el centro de la ciudad
- En la oficina de correos
- El dinero y los bancos

Así se forma

1. Prepositions: pronouns with prepositions
2. Demonstrative adjectives and pronouns
3. The preterit of **hacer** and stem-changing verbs
4. Indefinite and negative words

Cultura

- Argentina y Chile
- La plaza en el pueblo hispano
- Artes literarias: Pablo Neruda

Dicho y hecho

- Unas vacaciones fabulosas en Buenos Aires, Argentina
- Un día en el centro
- Un folleto turístico

ENTRANDO AL TEMA

1. La ciudad de esta foto está en Sudamérica. ¿Sabes cuál es?
2. ¿Sabes cuál es la ciudad más al sur (*southernmost*) del planeta?
3. Chile y Argentina forman parte de:

☐ Sudamérica. ☐ Cono Sur. ☐ los dos

Así se dice

Por la ciudad

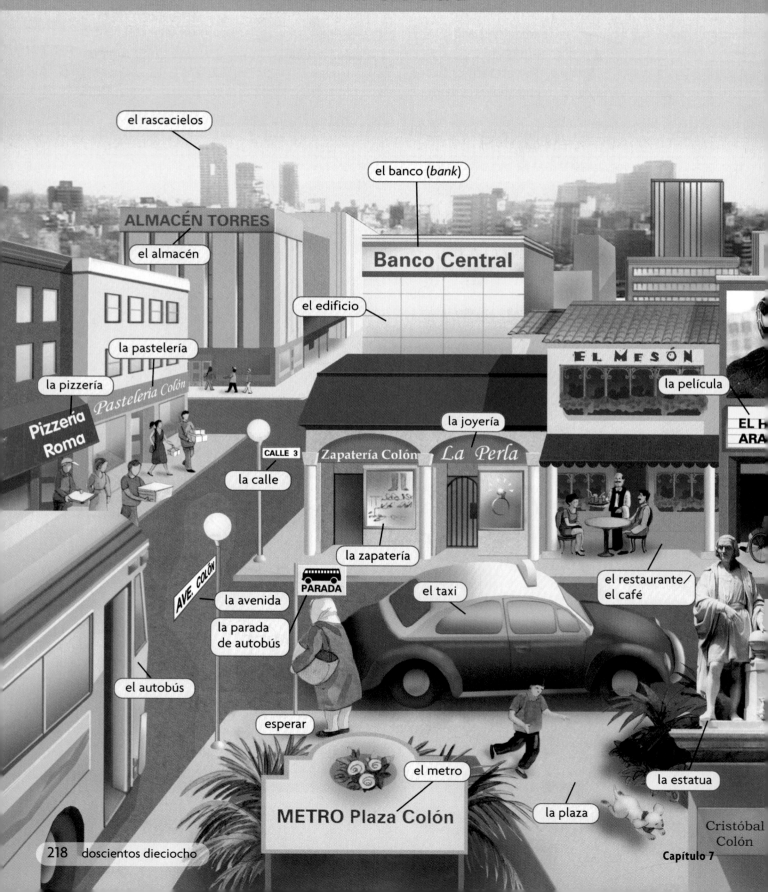

el rascacielos

el banco (*bank*)

ALMACÉN TORRES

el almacén

Banco Central

el edificio

EL MESÓN

la pastelería

la película

la pizzería

Pastelería Colón

la joyería

Pizzería Roma

La Perla

EL H ARA

CALLE 3

Zapatería Colón

la calle

la zapatería

AVE. COLÓN

el taxi

el restaurante/ el café

la avenida

PARADA

la parada de autobús

el autobús

esperar

el metro

la estatua

METRO Plaza Colón

la plaza

Cristóbal Colón

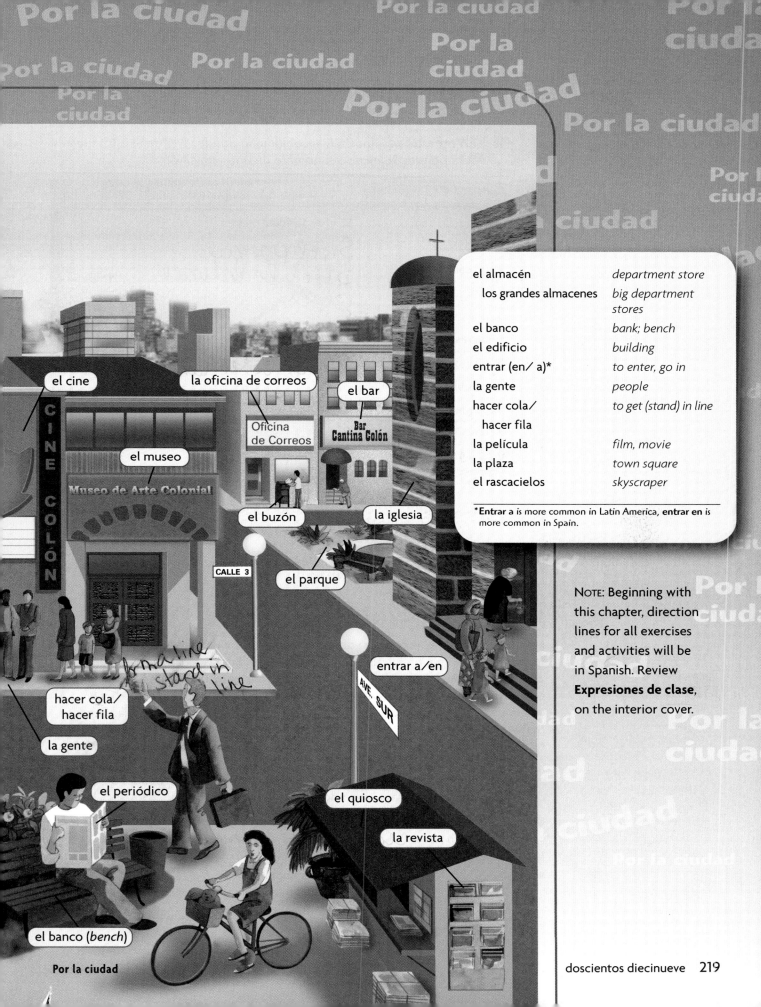

el cine

la oficina de correos

el bar

el museo

Oficina de Correos

Bar Cantina Colón

el buzón

la iglesia

CALLE 3

el parque

entrar a/en

AVE. SUR

el periódico

el quiosco

la revista

hacer cola/ hacer fila

la gente

el banco (bench)

el almacén	department store
los grandes almacenes	big department stores
el banco	bank; bench
el edificio	building
entrar (en/ a)*	to enter, go in
la gente	people
hacer cola/ hacer fila	to get (stand) in line
la película	film, movie
la plaza	town square
el rascacielos	skyscraper

*Entrar a is more common in Latin America, entrar en is more common in Spain.

NOTE: Beginning with this chapter, direction lines for all exercises and activities will be in Spanish. Review **Expresiones de clase**, on the interior cover.

Por la ciudad

Así se dice

7-1 **En mi ciudad.** Indica si la comunidad donde vives tiene estos lugares. Si respondes **Sí**, escribe el nombre de uno específico.

	Sí, (escribe el nombre de uno)	No
Modelo: un banco	**Sí, el American Trust**	
1. un parque	Si, el parque	
2. un café	Si, el Boardwalk	
3. una zapatería	Si, el	
4. una estatua	Si,	
5. un rascacielos		.
6. una avenida	Si, la wheatland	
7. un quiosco		
8. una iglesia	Si,	
9. un cine	Si,	
10. una parada de metro		

7-2 **¿Adónde?** Escucha las actividades que lee tu instructor. ¿Adónde vas para cada actividad?

Modelo: Oyes:　　Quieres comprar una pizza.
Escribes: **Voy a una pizzería.**

En el centro de la ciudad

Mi amigo y yo vamos a **pasar** el día en el centro porque allí encontramos los **lugares** más interesantes de la ciudad. Primero tenemos que saber a qué hora **se abren** las tiendas y los museos, y a qué hora **se cierran.** También queremos preguntar dónde comprar **entradas** para una **obra de teatro**, y a qué hora **empieza** la representación. Por la mañana queremos ir de compras en las tiendas pequeñas y también en el **centro comercial.** Después podemos visitar los museos, tomar algo y luego pasar la tarde en un parque o dar un paseo en un jardín botánico o el zoológico. El **mejor** restaurante también está en el centro y quiero **invitar**[1] a mi amigo a cenar allí. Después de ir al **teatro** y **terminar** las actividades de un largo día, podemos regresar a casa tomando el metro o un taxi.

abrir	to open	**el/ la mejor**	the best
cerrar (ie)	to close	**la obra (de teatro)**	play
la entrada	ticket	**pasar**	to spend (time)
el lugar	place	**terminar**	to finish

(handwritten note: cerro-it closed)

NOTA DE LENGUA

The structure **se** + a verb in the third-person singular or plural often indicates that the subject (the doer of the action) is unknown or unimportant. The emphasis is on the action instead.

El banco **se abre** a las nueve.
　The bank opens at nine.
Las tiendas **se abren** a las diez.
　The stores open at ten.

---

[1]**Invitar** requires the preposition a when followed by the infinitive: **Me invitó** *a* cenar.

7-3 ¿Qué pueden hacer?

Paso 1. En parejas (dos personas), el Estudiante A explica sus problemas al Estudiante B, que ofrece sugerencias, y viceversa. Toma nota de las sugerencias de tu compañero/a.

Modelo: Estudiante A lee: Quiero ver una película, pero no quiero ir al cine.
Estudiante B: **Puedes rentar una película en Blockbuster.**

Estudiante A:

1. "Tenemos hambre, pero no queremos salir de casa para ir a un restaurante".
2. "Mis tíos quieren ir al museo, pero se cierra a las 6:00 de la tarde".
3. "Mi novia quiere leer un periódico o una revista, pero no encuentra un quiosco".
4. "Jesús va a la joyería para comprar un regalo a su novia Ana, pero no tiene mucho dinero".
5. "Mis amigos/as y yo queremos ir a un bar en el centro de la ciudad, pero hay mucho tráfico".

Estudiante B:

1. "Necesito enviar esta carta, pero no hay ninguna oficina de correos cerca".
2. "Quiero ir de compras y ver muchas tiendas, pero hace frío para pasear en la calle".
3. "Queremos asistir al concierto, pero empieza en quince minutos y no tenemos entradas".
4. "Mis padres quieren ir al mejor restaurante de la ciudad para celebrar su aniversario".
5. "Queremos ver el edificio más bonito, el museo más interesante y la iglesia más vieja de la ciudad".

Paso 2. En grupos (Estudiantes A o Estudiantes B solamente), compartan las sugerencias de sus compañeros/as y respondan a las siguientes preguntas:

¿Fueron similares las sugerencias? ¿Cuáles fueron más interesantes u originales?

7-4 Nuestras actividades comunes.

Paso 1. ¿Con qué frecuencia haces estas actividades? Indícalo en la columna "Yo".

	Yo			Mi compañero/a		
	Mucho	**A veces**	**Nunca**	**Mucho**	**A veces**	**Nunca**
1. ir al cine *Vas*		✓		✓		
2. ver una obra de teatro *Vas*			✓		✓	
3. ir al centro comercial *Vas*	✓				✓	
4. tomar el autobús *Tomas*		✓				✓
5. ver una exposición de arte en un museo		✓				✓
6. leer el periódico *leo*	✓			✓		
7. ir a la oficina de correos *Vas*		✓			✓	
8. comprar algo en una pastelería *compro compro*		✓				✓

Paso 2. Ahora pregunta a un/a compañero/a con qué frecuencia hace estas actividades; indícalo en la columna "Mi compañero/a."

Modelo: Estudiante A: **¿Con qué frecuencia vas al cine?**
Estudiante B: **Voy al cine mucho./ No voy al cine nunca. (etc.)**

Cultura: Argentina y Chile

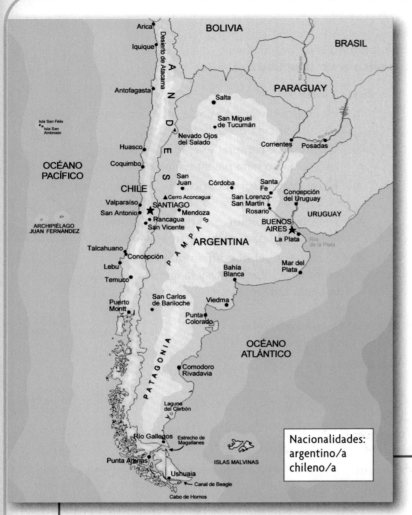

Nacionalidades:
argentino/a
chileno/a

Antes de leer

1. ¿Cuál es la capital de Argentina? ¿Con qué países tiene frontera[1] Argentina? Localiza La Pampa y la Patagonia en el mapa.

2. ¿Cuál es la capital de Chile, y cómo se llama el desierto que está en el norte de Chile?

3. ¿Cómo se llama la cordillera[2] que pasa por Chile y Argentina?

[1]boundary, border   [2]mountain range

Investig@ en INTERNET

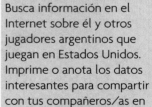

Manu Ginóbili es un jugador de básquetbol argentino. Busca información en el Internet sobre él y otros jugadores argentinos que juegan en Estados Unidos. Imprime o anota los datos interesantes para compartir con tus compañeros/as en clase.

DOS COLOSOS DEL CONO SUR

Chile y Argentina son los dos países con mayor influencia europea en Latinoamérica. Esta influencia es aparente en su cultura y en su población.

Cuando veas un nombre **en rojo**, localízalo en el mapa.

UN ESCRITOR EXCEPCIONAL

Jorge Luis Borges (1899–1986), autor argentino y gigante de la literatura latinoamericana, terminó sus días ciego[3], dictando sus creaciones literarias a una secretaria.

[3]blind

La avenida 9 de Julio, una de las más anchas[4] del mundo, y el obelisco, que conmemora la fundación de la ciudad, son símbolos famosos de Buenos Aires. ¿Cuántos carriles[5] tiene esta avenida?

_____
[4]*wide* [5]*lanes*

ARGENTINA

Argentina es el país hispano más grande del mundo. Tiene varias regiones distintas. Al noreste encontramos las planicies[6] del **río Paraná**, donde está la jungla; al sur está **La Patagonia**, una llanura[7] rica en petróleo. A pesar de la gran extensión de su territorio, la

vida argentina se centra en su capital, **Buenos Aires**, llamada "el París de las Américas". Un poco más del 30% de la población argentina es bonaerense, es decir, vive en el área de Buenos Aires.

_____
[6]*flatlands* [7]*plain*

¡Evita, Evita!

¿Conoces la obra musical *Evita* y la canción "No llores por mí, Argentina"? Pues, el tema de este musical es Eva Perón, esposa del dictador Juan Perón (1895–1974). Perón fue presidente hasta 1955, cuando los militares lo obligaron a abandonar el poder. Después de una serie de dictaduras militares, Argentina volvió a un sistema democrático.

El espectacular Teatro Colón de la capital presenta conciertos, óperas, recitales y *shows*. Atrae músicos y artistas del mundo entero. ¿Cuántas gradas[8] hay en el teatro?

_____
[8]*tiers*

En esta ciudad fascinante de tiendas elegantes, restaurantes y una intensa vida nocturna, las artes son muy importantes. En Buenos Aires nació el tango, el baile sofisticado que todo el mundo asocia con Argentina. ¿Sabes bailar el tango?

Cultura: Argentina y Chile

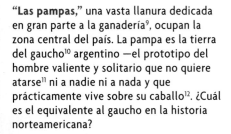

"**Las pampas,**" una vasta llanura dedicada en gran parte a la ganadería[9], ocupan la zona central del país. La pampa es la tierra del gaucho[10] argentino —el prototipo del hombre valiente y solitario que no quiere atarse[11] ni a nadie ni a nada y que prácticamente vive sobre su caballo[12]. ¿Cuál es el equivalente al gaucho en la historia norteamericana?

[9]*cattle-raising;* [10]*cowboy;* [11]*tie himself;* [12]*horse*

Los Andes están al oeste del país y es aquí donde está el pico más alto de Sudamérica: **el Aconcagua**, de 22.835 pies de altura[13]. ¿Te gustaría (*Would you like*) escalar[14] esta montaña?

[13]**pies...** *feet high*   [14]*to climb*

CHILE

Chile tiene una configuración geográfica única: es una larga faja[15] de tierra que va desde los Andes en el este hasta el océano Pacífico en el oeste. El país tiene 2.880 millas de largo y solamente 265 millas de ancho. Es el país más largo del mundo. En Chile, es posible hacer esquí acuático en el mar por la mañana y esquiar en la nieve por la tarde.

En 1970 los chilenos eligieron[16] al primer presidente socialista del continente, Salvador Allende; pero en 1973 Augusto Pinochet dio un golpe de estado[17] y estableció una dictadura militar. En 1989 Chile tuvo elecciones libres; hoy en día continúa siendo un país democrático. En 2006, Michelle Bachelet se convirtió en la primera mujer presidente de Chile.

[15]*strip;* [16]*elected;* [17]**golpe...** *coup d'etat*

Al norte de Chile está el desierto de **Atacama**, ¡el lugar más seco del mundo! En esta región hay muchas minas de cobre[18], un metal que Chile exporta a varias partes del mundo. ¿Te gustaría pasar unos días explorando este desierto? ¿Por qué?

[18]*copper*

¿Te gusta esquiar?

La superficie esquiable más grande del hemisferio sur está al este de Santiago. "Los Tres Valles de los Andes" tiene un total de 10.000 hectáreas y montañas que sobrepasan los 5.000 metros (16.400 pies) de altura.

Los 1.100 km de la Carretera Austral cruzan los lugares más atractivos del sur de Chile, con sus montañas, parques nacionales, fiordos, termas[19], ríos y lagos, ideales para la pesca[20] deportiva. El Parque Nacional Torres del Paine (en la foto de la izquierda) es uno de los más espectaculares del país. ¿Te gustaría visitar esta región? ¿Hay glaciares en alguna región de tu país? ¿Dónde?

El centro de Chile es una zona fértil de clima moderado donde vive la mayoría de la población, y en la que se producen muchas frutas y legumbres. En esta zona está la capital, **Santiago**, una ciudad cosmopolita, moderna y con aspecto europeo.

[19]*hot–water springs;* [20]*fishing*

¡PRIMER PREMIO NOBEL LATINOAMERICANO!

En 1945, la poeta chilena Gabriela Mistral (1889–1957) ganó el primer Premio Nobel de Literatura, para un autor de Hispanoamérica.

¿Sabías que muchas de las uvas que compramos son importadas de Chile? Los vinos chilenos también son famosos.

Después de leer

En parejas, identifiquen cada una de las siguientes referencias:

Santiago	Evita Perón	Jorge Luis Borges	Buenos Aires
Salvador Allende	Gabriela Mistral	la pampa	Juan Perón
Atacama	los gauchos		

Luego, su profesor/a le va a asignar a cada pareja una de las referencias. Escriban una descripción de la referencia y entréguensela (*turn it in*) al profesor/a la profesora.

Investig@ en INTERNET

Imagina que vas a pasar unas cortas vacaciones en Santiago de Chile, y quieres organizar todo antes de (*before*) llegar. Busca un hotel cerca del (*near*) centro y planea actividades para cinco días, incluyendo detalles sobre el transporte, lugares que quieres visitar, algunos restaurantes donde te gustaría comer... Calcula cuánto dinero vas a necesitar aproximadamente.

Así se forma

¿Sabes dónde está el apartamento de Carmen?

1. Indicating relationships: prepositions

A. Prepositions of location and other useful prepositions

Prepositions are words that express a relationship between nouns (or pronouns) and other words in a sentence. You have already learned some prepositions such as: **a** (*to, at*), **en** (*in, on, at*), **de** (*from, of, about*), **con** (*with*), and **sin** (*without*). Below are some additional prepositions to describe location and movement through a place.

Sí. Está en la avenida Sur, cerca del museo y frente al parque.

Preposiciones de lugar		Otras preposiciones útiles	
cerca de	*near*	antes de	*before*
lejos de	*far from*	después de	*after*
dentro de	*inside*	en vez de	*instead of*
fuera de	*outside*		
debajo de	*beneath, under*	para + *infinitive*	*in order to*
encima de	*on top of, above*		*(do something)*
detrás de	*behind*	al + *infinitive*	*upon +*
delante de	*in front of*		*(doing something)*
enfrente de, frente a	*opposite, facing*		
al lado de	*beside, next to*		
sobre, en	*on*		
entre	*between, among*		
por	*by, through, alongside, around*		

¡Importante! In Spanish a verb following a preposition is always in the infinitive (**-ar, -er, -ir**) form. In contrast, English uses the *–ing* form.

Antes de ir al teatro, vamos a cenar.
~~Antes de yendo al teatro...~~

Before going to the theater, we're going to have dinner.

7-5 **¿Cierto o falso?** Tu amigo/a dice que conoce esta ciudad (en la páginas 218-219) perfectamente, pero en realidad está un poco confundido/a. Lee sus comentarios, decide si son ciertos o falsos y, si son falsos, corrígelos (*correct them*).

Modelo: La pizzería está al lado de la joyería.
No, la pizzería está al lado de la pastelería.

1. El buzón está detrás de la oficina de correos, ¿verdad?
2. Y el cine Colón está entre el restaurante El Mesón y el Museo de Arte Colonial.

3. El autobús pasa por la Avenida Sur, junto a la plaza Colón, ¿no?
4. Creo que el Museo de Arte Colonial está cerca del Almacén Torres.
5. El Banco Central está delante de la zapatería y de la joyería.
6. En la Plaza Colón, hay un banco al lado del quiosco, ¿verdad?
7. Todas las mesas de El Mesón están dentro del restaurante, ¿verdad?
8. No hay ningún rascacielos cerca de la plaza Colón, ¿verdad?
9. Y hay un parque enfrente de la iglesia, ¿no?
10. En la Plaza Colón hay una estatua de Hernán Cortés muy bonita, ¿verdad?

PALABRAS ÚTILES

Spanish speakers use the following question tags to seek agreement:
After an affirmative statement, use either **¿verdad?** or **¿no?** After a negative statement, use **¿verdad?**

Tienes tiempo, ¿verdad/ no? **No tienes tiempo, ¿verdad?**

7-6 **Nuestros lugares interesantes.** Un estudiante de Chile acaba de llegar para estudiar en tu universidad. ¿Qué lugares interesantes de la ciudad puedes recomendar?

Paso 1. Escribe una lista de cinco lugares y explica dónde están con el mayor detalle posible (*with as much detail as possible*). Usa las preposiciones de lugar.

Paso 2. En grupos pequeños, comparen sus listas y escojan (*choose*) los diez lugares más interesantes. Guarda (*Save*) la información para usarla más tarde en la sección **De mi escritorio**.

7-7 **¿Qué o quién es?**

Paso 1. Escoge (*Choose*) cuatro objetos o personas que ves en la clase y escribe oraciones describiendo donde están.

Modelo: **Esta persona/ cosa está entre la puerta y Sara.**
Está detrás de Tom y al lado de...

Paso 2. En parejas, lee tus oraciones a tu compañero/a. El/Ella va a intentar (*try*) deidentificar la cosa o persona a la que te refieres.

(7-8) **Tus hábitos.**

Paso 1. Completa estas oraciones pensando en tus hábitos y preferencias; incluye unos típicos y otros menos habituales.

Modelo: Casi nunca llevo ___ropa formal___ para ___ir a clase___ .

1. Casi siempre voy _____ para _____ .
2. Siempre necesito _____ para _____ .
3. No me gusta _____ sin _____ .
4. Me gusta _____ antes de _____ .
5. A veces _____ en vez de _____ .
6. Nunca, nunca _____ después de _____ .

Paso 2. Ahora, en grupos pequeños, comparte esta información con tus compañeros/as y pregunta si ellos/as también lo hacen.

Modelo: Estudiante A: **Casi nunca llevo ropa formal para ir a clase, ¿y ustedes?**
Estudiante B: **Yo llevo ropa formal a veces, por ejemplo, cuando hago una presentación.**
Estudiante C: **No, yo tampoco llevo ropa formal casi nunca.**

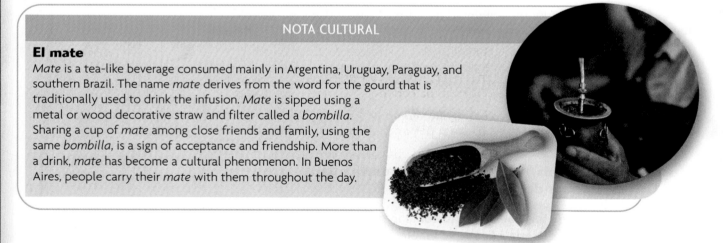

NOTA CULTURAL

El mate

Mate is a tea-like beverage consumed mainly in Argentina, Uruguay, Paraguay, and southern Brazil. The name *mate* derives from the word for the gourd that is traditionally used to drink the infusion. *Mate* is sipped using a metal or wood decorative straw and filter called a *bombilla*. Sharing a cup of *mate* among close friends and family, using the same *bombilla*, is a sign of acceptance and friendship. More than a drink, *mate* has become a cultural phenomenon. In Buenos Aires, people carry their *mate* with them throughout the day.

B. Pronouns with prepositions

The pronouns that follow prepositions (**pronombres de objeto de preposición**) are the same as subject pronouns except for **yo** and **tú**, which become **mí** and **ti**.

—¿Es este cuadro para **mí**?   *Is this painting for **me**?*
—Sí, es para **ti**.   *Yes, it's for **you**.*

The combination of **con** + **mí** or **ti** becomes **conmigo** (*with me*) or **contigo** (*with you*).

—¿Quieres ir **conmigo**?   *Do you want to go **with me**?*
—¡Sí! Voy **contigo**.   *Yes! I'll go **with you**.*

NOTA DE LENGUA

Note the accent on **mí** (*me*) to differentiate from mi (*my*) and avoid ambiguity.

Mi hijo hizo un dibujo para **mí**.

Pronombres de objeto de preposición (*a, de, para, por, sin*, etc.)	
para **mí**	para **nosotros/as**
para **ti**	para **vosotros/as**
para **usted**	para **ustedes**
para **él/ella**	para **ellos/ellas**

7-9 ¿Te gusta o no?

Paso 1. Si tu pareja (novio/a, esposo/a) te dice estas cosas, ¿te gusta o no?

		Sí, a mí me gusta.	No, a mí no me gusta.
1.	"Quiero ir de compras **contigo**".		
2.	"Quiero estar siempre **cerca de ti**".		
3.	"Estas flores son **para ti**".		
4.	"No puedo vivir **sin ti**".		
5.	"¿Quieres viajar a Hawaii **conmigo**?"		
6.	"Nunca hablo **de ti** con mis **amigos/as**".		
7.	"No puedo estudiar **contigo**".		
8.	"Nunca tienes tiempo **para mí**".		
9.	"Tengo un regalo **para ti**".		

Paso 2. En grupos, comparen y expliquen sus respuestas.

7-10 **Linda y Manuel.** En parejas, lean la conversación dramáticamente, completándola con los pronombres apropiados.

Linda está sentada en un sillón grande en la sala de su casa.
Habla por teléfono con su amor, Manuel.

Manuel: Linda, ¿quieres salir con_____ esta noche? Me muero por verte.
Linda: Sí, mi amor. Voy con_____ adonde quieras.
Manuel: Pues, te voy a llevar a un lugar muy especial, y... ¡tengo una sorpresa maravillosa para _____!
Linda: ¿Para _____? ¡Eres un ángel, Manuel! A _____ me encantan las sorpresas. Yo también tengo una sorpresa para _____.
Manuel: ¿Ah, sí? ¿Cuál es?
Linda: Pues, no vamos a estar solos esta noche porque mi hermanito menor tiene que venir con _____.
Manuel: ¿Con _____? ¿No pueden quedarse° tus padres con _____?
Linda: Manuelito, sé° flexible. ¿No quieres hacerlo por _____?
Manuel: Bueno, está bien.
Linda: ¡Gracias, mi amor! Por cierto, ¿qué sorpresa tienes para _____?

° stay
° be (command)

> **HINT**
>
> Remember that with verbs like **gustar, a** + *prepositional pronoun* is sometimes used for emphasis or clarification.
>
> **A él** no **le** gustó la película.
> ***He** didn't like the movie.*
> **A mí** tampoco **me** gustó.
> ***I** didn't like it either.*

Escenas

Inés

Linda

Manuel

Una ciudad fascinante

Inés, Manuel y Linda van a un café en la plaza después de ir al cine. Inés acaba de regresar de unas vacaciones en Buenos Aires.

Paso 1. Lee el título y la introducción y, basándote en éstos, anticipa si las siguientes declaraciones son ciertas or falsas.

a. Los tres amigos están planeando unas vacaciones a Argentina.

b. Inés ya fue a Buenos Aires y explica que no hay muchas cosas que hacer.

c. Inés fue a muchos lugares interesantes en Buenos Aires.

Paso 2. Ahora escucha la conversación, concentrándote en las ideas principales y las palabras que ya conoces.

Paso 3. Lee las preguntas mientras escuchas por segunda vez. Después de escuchar, trata de contestarlas.

1. ¿Le gustó Buenos Aires a Inés?
2. ¿Dónde pasea la gente en Buenos Aires?
3. ¿Qué transporte público menciona Inés?
4. ¿Dónde se puede ir de compras?
5. ¿Bailó Inés en Buenos Aires?

Paso 4. Escucha otra vez mientras lees la conversación y comprueba tus respuestas para las preguntas del Paso 3.

Manuel: Chicas, ¿les gustó la película?

Linda: ¡A mí me gustó mucho! Las películas filmadas en Latinoamérica siempre me fascinan.

Inés: Es verdad, Buenos Aires es una ciudad única.

Manuel: Inés, tú visitaste Buenos Aires el mes pasado, ¿verdad? ¿Te gustó?

Inés: Claro, es una ciudad fascinante, pero muy diferente.

Linda: ¿Por qué?

Inés: Bueno, en las calles de Buenos Aires hay tanta vida... hay muchas plazas donde la gente pasea, va a un café para tomar algo, o incluso protesta, como las Madres de la Plaza de Mayo. También es una ciudad muy sofisticada. Hay muchos barrios° diferentes y muy interesantes como San Telmo, Puerto Madero, Retiro, Palermo...

neighborhoods

Linda: ¿Hay barrios étnicos, como en algunas ciudades de Estados Unidos?

Inés: No, pero la ciudad tiene influencias muy variadas por los grupos inmigrantes que viven allí: españoles, italianos, alemanes, armenios... es una cultura de muchas culturas. Y hay restaurantes excelentes de todas las nacionalidades.

Linda: ¿Cómo es el centro de la ciudad?

besides

Inés: Hay grandes calles y avenidas; es muy fácil encontrar cualquier lugar. Además° el subterráneo y colectivo, que es como llaman al metro y al autobús, son muy accesibles.

Manuel: ¿Fuiste al teatro o a algún museo?

Inés: ¡Claro! Dicen que Buenos Aires es la capital cultural de Sudamérica. Vi una obra en el Teatro Colón y visité el Centro Cultural Recoleta, un centro de arte visual y arte escénico° muy vanguardista. Organizan muchas exposiciones y actividades culturales. Pero, para mí, la arquitectura de la ciudad es lo más impresionante; es como una gran ciudad europea. Y ¿saben que tienen una réplica de la Estatua de la Libertad? Es igual que la de Nueva York, pero más pequeña.

arte... performing arts

Linda: ¿Y las tiendas? ¿Fuiste de compras?

Manuel: ¿Fuiste a alguna discoteca?

Inés: ¡Es imposible no ir de compras! Hay tantas tiendas y centros comerciales... No fui a ninguna discoteca, pero aprendí a bailar tango, bueno, un poco...

Linda: ¿Te divertiste? ¿Conociste a alguien interesante?

Inés: Sí, muchísimo, los argentinos son muy interesantes y simpáticos y les encanta hablar y contar cosas de su país.

Así se forma

¿Quién es ese muchacho que está con Inés?

¿Ése? Es su amigo de Madrid.

2. Demonstrative adjectives and pronouns

Demonstrative adjectives

Demonstrative adjectives point out the location of nouns (such as objects and people) with respect to the speaker. Like all adjectives, demonstratives agree in gender and number with the noun they refer to. The demonstrative adjective to use depends upon how close the speaker is to the item being pointed out.

Me gusta **este** parque.
*I like **this** park.*

Vamos a visitar **esos** museos.
*We are going to visit **those** museums.*

Aquella tienda tiene cuadernos.
That store (over there) has notebooks.

Adjetivos demostrativos		
close to speaker	*at a short distance*	*at a great distance*
este bar **esta** calle	**ese** bar **esa** calle	**aquel** bar **aquella** calle
estos bares **estas** calles	**esos** bares **esas** calles	**aquellos** bares aquellas calles

Demonstrative pronouns

Demonstrative pronouns are pronounced and spelled like demonstrative adjectives, but they have a written accent on the stressed vowel. Also, remember that while adjectives go together with the noun, pronouns replace the noun to avoid repetition and redundancy. Observe in the following examples the use of both demonstrative adjectives and pronouns.

Compramos en **esta** tienda y en **aquélla**.
        adjective   *pronoun*
*We shop in **this** store and **that one**.*

— ¿Te gustan **estos** zapatos?
        adjective
*Do you like **these** shoes?*

— No. Prefiero **ésos**.
        pronoun
*No. I prefer **those**.*

NOTA DE LENGUA

The demonstratives **esto** (this) and **eso** (that) are neutral in gender (neither masculine nor feminine) because they refer to an idea, situation or statement, or to an object that has not yet been identified. Since they cannot be confused with demonstrative adjectives, no written accent is needed.

— ¿Qué es **esto**?	What is this?
— ¡No sé!	I don't know!
— No quiere pagar la cuenta.	He doesn't want to pay the bill.
— ¡**Eso** es ridículo!	That's ridiculous!

Así se forma

7-11 **¿Dónde está?** Estás paseando por la ciudad con una amiga. Escucha las oraciones que dice y decide si los lugares que menciona están cerca, están un poco lejos o están muy lejos. ¡Presta atención al adjetivo demostrativo que menciona tu amigo!

Modelo: Me gusta este parque.   ☒ **Está cerca.**
Vamos a comer en aquella pizzería.   ☒ **Está muy lejos.**

1. ☐ Está cerca. ☑ Está un poco lejos. ☐ Está muy lejos.
2. ☑ Está cerca. ☐ Está un poco lejos. ☐ Está muy lejos.
3. ☐ Está cerca. ☐ Está un poco lejos. ☑ Está muy lejos.
4. ☐ Está cerca. ☑ Está un poco lejos. ☐ Está muy lejos.
5. ☐ Está cerca. ☐ Está un poco lejos. ☑ Está muy lejos.

7-12 **Soy guía turístico.** Imagina que trabajas para una agencia de turismo en Buenos Aires y le muestras (*show*) la ciudad a un grupo de visitantes. Usa adjetivos demostrativos para simplificar las oraciones.

Modelo: La iglesia que (*that*) está un poco lejos es del período colonial.
Esa iglesia es del período colonial.

1. El rascacielos que está muy lejos es el más moderno de la ciudad.
2. La estatua que está un poco lejos es del presidente.
3. La estación del metro que está cerca fue la primera (*the first*) de la ciudad.
4. El parque que está un poco lejos es muy famoso.
5. Las ceremonias importantes se celebran en la iglesia que está muy lejos.
6. Los almacenes que están cerca venden de todo.
7. El restaurante que está un poco lejos sirve churrasco (*barbecue*) y otros platos argentinos.

NOTA CULTURAL

Benito Quinquela Martín

Benito Quinquela Martín is an Argentine painter famous for depicting the port of Buenos Aires and the nearby area known as La Boca. La Boca is known for its numerous brightly painted houses.

7-13 ¡Tengo hambre! ¿Cuánto cuestan? Todos tienen hambre, así que llevas al grupo de turistas a la Pastelería Río de la Plata. Trabaja con un compañero/a, que va a ser el/la dependiente/a. El/La cliente/a pregunta los precios de los productos, el dependiente contesta consultando los precios de la lista.

PALABRAS ÚTILES

medialuna   *croissant*
empanada   *turnover/pie*

Modelo: Cliente/a: **¿Cuánto cuesta este pastel de limón?**
Dependiente/a: **Ése cuesta dos pesos, cincuenta y cinco centavos.**

Al final, decide qué vas a comprar y completen la transacción.

Cliente/a: **Voy a comprar este/ ese/ estos...**
Dependiente/a: **Muy bien, son... pesos.**

Río de la Plata

galletas de chocolate	– $4.75 la docena
de azúcar	– $4.00 la docena
pastel de manzana (ración)	– $2.50
de limón (ración)	– $2.75
torta de chocolate	– $12.95
de fresa	– $13.25
pan de queso	– $2.25
de aceitunas	– $2.60
empanadas de carne	– $1.60 cada una
vegetarianas	– $1.15 cada una
medialunas de jamón y queso	– $1.90 cada una
de chocolate	– $1.80 cada una

Así se dice

En la oficina de correos

Quiero mandarle/ **enviar**le esta **tarjeta postal** a mi amigo.

Recibí una **carta** de mi amiga.

Quiero **contestarle** inmediatamente. Escribo la **dirección** en el **sobre**.

Necesito comprar una **estampilla**/ un **sello**.

¿Para quién es este **paquete**?

enviar *to send*   **recibir** *to receive*   **contestar** *to answer*

7-14 La historia de una carta.

 Paso 1. En parejas, determinen el orden cronológico de estos eventos. ¿Qué pasó primero? ¿Y después?

5/6 ___ buscar el buzón

9 ___ mi amigo / contestarme inmediatamente

6/8 ___ enviar la carta

2 ___ escribir la dirección en el sobre

3 ___ ir a la oficina de correos

8 ___ mi amigo / abrirla y leerla

4 ___ comprar un sello de 80 centavos

7 ___ mi amigo / recibir la carta

1 ___ escribir la carta

 Paso 2. Ahora narren la historia cronológicamente, cambiando los verbos al pretérito.

Modelo: **Primero, escribí la carta.**

7-15 ¿Correo tradicional o correo electrónico?

 Paso 1. Trabajen con un/a compañero/a. Ustedes son defensores del correo electrónico o el correo tradicional (su instructor les asignará uno). Escriban una lista de razones para justificar su preferencia.

Paso 2. Ahora, formen un grupo con una pareja que prefiere el otro tipo de correo

Modelo: Pareja A: **El correo electrónico es muy rápido.**

Pareja B: **Sí, pero con el correo tradicional no necesitas tener una computadora.**

Antes de leer

¿Cuál es el lugar público más importante de tu ciudad o pueblo? ¿Qué pasa allí?

La plaza es el corazón[1] de las ciudades y los pueblos hispanos. Normalmente ocupa la parte más vieja de la ciudad o del pueblo, y es el centro político, religioso, social y comercial de una población. En la plaza se instalan[2] mercados al aire libre y se celebran festivales y ceremonias importantes.

Una plaza típica tiene a su alrededor[3] una iglesia, edificios públicos, cafés, tiendas y bares. Generalmente en el centro hay una estatua o un monumento, y en muchas ocasiones también hay fuentes[4] y jardines. Las plazas aún[5] tienen mucha importancia para los habitantes de una comunidad. Durante el día la gente camina, conversa, toma refrescos, lee o juega cartas[6] o dominó. Por la noche los jóvenes se reúnen para charlar y para hacer planes para ir al cine o a bailar.

La Plaza de Mayo en Buenos Aires es un sitio de reunión y protesta para los argentinos. Está rodeada por la catedral, el cabildo[7] y la Casa Rosada, el equivalente de la Casa Blanca en Washington, D. C. Otras plazas famosas son la Plaza Mayor en Madrid, la Plaza del Zócalo en México, D.F. y la Plaza de Armas en Chile.

[1]*heart* [2]*se... are set up* [3]*surrounding it* [4]*fountains* [5]*still* [6]*cards* [7]*city (town) hall*

Después de leer

Nombra tres cosas que frecuentemente se encuentran en las plazas hispanas.

Conexiones y contrastes

¿Es la función social de las plazas latinoamericanas comparable a la de los centros comerciales en los EE.UU.? Menciona similitudes y diferencias.

Plaza de Mayo, Buenos Aires, Argentina

Plaza de Armas, Santiago, Chile

3. Talking about actions in the past: The preterit of *hacer* and stem-changing verbs

A. *Hacer*

The verb **hacer** is irregular in the preterit. Note that the stem (**hic–**) is constant and that **c → z** before **o**. Also observe the special preterit endings **–e** and **–o**.

hice	**hic**imos
hiciste	**hic**isteis
hizo	**hic**ieron

—¿Qué **hiciste** anoche?   *What **did** you **do** last night?*

—Fui al gimnasio e **hice ejercicio**.   *I went to the gym and **worked out**.*

Remember that you do not always use **hacer** to answer **hacer** questions.

—¿Qué **hicieron** ustedes ayer?   *What **did** you **do** yesterday?*

—**Fuimos** al centro y **vimos** una película.   *We **went** downtown and **saw** a movie.*

7-16 **Los sábados de Javier.** Escucha las siguientes oraciones e indica si Javier se refiere a los sábados en general (verbo en presente) o el sábado pasado (verbo en pasado).

Modelo: Oyes: Juan hizo una fiesta.
            Escribes: "X" debajo de "El sábado pasado"

	Los sábados	El sábado pasado
1.		
2.		
3.		
4.		
5.		
6.		

> **HINT**
>
> Before doing Exercise 7–17, review the preterit of regular verbs and of **ser** and **ir** (pp. 202–203).

 7-17 **El sábado pasado.**

Paso 1. Lee la descripción que hace Javier de sus sábados. Basándote en esto, ¿qué hizo Javier *el sábado pasado*? Cambia los verbos en **negrilla** (*boldface*) al pretérito.

¿Qué **hago** los sábados? Pues, **me levanto** un poco tarde y **desayuno** en casa. A las diez de la mañana **juego** al tenis con mi hermanito Samuel y luego **hacemos** una visita a los abuelos. Me gusta mucho visitarlos y mi abuela siempre **hace** chocolate caliente para merendar. Por la tarde **hago** algunas compras en el centro con mi amiga Nidia. Y más tarde, **salimos** con nuestros amigos, **cenamos** en algún restaurante y **vamos** al cine. **Volvemos** a casa bastante tarde. Claro, después, **llego** a casa tan cansado... que los domingos ¡no hago nada!

Modelo: ¿Qué **hice** el sábado pasado? Pues...

Paso 2. Ahora escribe un párrafo comparando to sábado pasado con el de Javier.

Modelo: Javier se levantó tarde pero yo me levanté a las 6:00 de la mañana...

¿Quién pidió los espaguetis?

B. Stem-changing verbs

- Note that **–ir** verbs with a stem change in the present tense (**o → ue, e → ie, e → i**) also change in the preterit[2].

- The change in the preterit (**o → u** and **e → i**) occurs only in the third-person singular (**usted/ él/ella**) and third-person plural (**ustedes/ ellos/ellas**) forms.

HINT

First, review the present tense stem-changing verbs on page 117. Then practice the preterit tense of the verbs presented in this section.

dormir (o → u)	
dormí	dormimos
dormiste	dormisteis
durmió	durmieron

pedir (e → i)	
pedí	pedimos
pediste	pedisteis
pidió	pidieron

The same change also occurs in the present participle (**–ando/–iendo** form) of these verbs.　　　　d**u**rmiendo　　　　p**i**diendo

Note the pattern of change in the following model verbs.

o → ue; u	**morir** (ue, u)	*to die*	El perro **murió** en un accidente.
e → ie; i	**preferir** (ie, i)	*to prefer*	Las chicas **prefirieron** no hablar del incidente.
	divertirse (ie, i)	*to have a good time*	¿**Se divirtieron** en el restaurante anoche?
e → i; i	**pedir** (i, i)	*to ask for, request*	Tina **pidió** una paella de mariscos.
	servir (i, i)	*to serve*	¿Qué más **sirvieron**?
	repetir (i, i)	*to repeat*	El mesero **repitió** la lista de postres.
	vestirse (i, i)	*to get dressed*	Más tarde **se vistieron** y fueron a un baile.

[2]Note that -ar and -er stem-changing verbs in the present tense never change their stems in the preterit.

NOTA DE LENGUA

Note that when a verb shows two stem changes in parentheses, for example (**ue, u**), the first (**ue**) refers to a stem change in the present tense, and the second (**u**) refers to a stem change in the preterit tense and in the -ndo form. Note the pattern of change in *dormir*.

dormir (ue, u)

present:	duermo, duermes, duerme...
preterit:	dormí, dormiste, durmió...
-ndo form:	durmiendo

Así se forma

7-18 **Las actividades de Alicia.** ¿Qué hizo Alicia ayer? Relaciona las actividades de A con las actividades correspondientes de B.

A

_e_ 1. Por la tarde hizo su tarea de francés, y escuchó el CD del Capítulo 7.

_d_ 2. Luego, para descansar un poco, buscó un periódico.

_b_ 3. A las siete de la tarde, ella y dos de sus amigas cenaron en un restaurante.

_a_ 4. El mesero les sirvió tres postres diferentes.

_c_ 5. Después de cenar, estudió casi toda la noche en la biblioteca.

B

a. Las chicas prefirieron la torta de chocolate.

b. Todas pidieron pasta con camarones y ensalada.

c. No durmió mucho.

d. Leyó que tres personas murieron en un accidente. ¡Qué triste!

e. Repitió las palabras del vocabulario.

7-19 **El día de Jaime.** Primero, determina el orden cronológico de las actividades de Jaime. Luego, escribe lo que hizo, usando el pretérito.

Modelo: Se levantó a las siete de la mañana. Luego,...

se fue _6_ irse al trabajo

se bañó _2_ bañarse

desayunó _4_ desayunar en un café

salió _9_ salir con sus amigos _salió_

se levantó _1_ levantarse a las siete

se vistió _3_ vestirse

_5_ pedir café con leche y pan _pidió_

_11_ acostarse a medianoche _el acostó_

_12_ dormirse _durmió_

_8_ cenar en casa _cenó_

_10_ divertirse mucho _se divirtió_

_7_ regresar a casa después del trabajo _regresó_

7-20 **¿Y tú, ¿qué hiciste?**

Paso 1. Piensa en lo que hiciste ayer y completa la columna **Yo** con tus actividades.

	Yo	Mi compañero/a _____
Por la mañana temprano		
a media mañana (*midmorning*)		
a mediodía (*midday*)		
por la tarde		
por la noche		

Paso 2. Ahora entrevista a un/a compañero/a. Haz preguntas sobre los detalles: ¿Dónde?, ¿Con quién?, ¿Qué? (¿Qué película viste?, ¿Qué comiste?) y anota sus respuestas. Túrnense.

Modelo: Estudiante A: **¿Qué hiciste ayer por la mañana temprano?**
Estudiante B: **Bueno, me levanté a las ocho de la mañana, me duché y tomé el desayuno.**
Estudiante A: **¿Sí? ¿Qué tomaste? (¿Dónde? ¿Fuiste con alguien? ...)**

EXPRESIONES ÚTILES	
¿Sí?/ ¿De verdad?	These expressions look for confirmation (similar to "*Really?*").
No me digas.	This expresses disbelief/surprise and encouragement to continue (as in "*No way!*").
Yo también/ tampoco.	This expresses agreement (equivalent to "*Me too/neither.*").

7-21 ¿Qué hizo el/la profesor/a?

Paso 1. En grupos pequeños, imaginen qué hizo su profesor/a de español ayer, incluyendo algunos detalles. ¡Sean creativos!

Modelo: **El profesor Redondo se levantó a las siete de la mañana, se duchó, se afeitó y preparó el desayuno para la familia...**

	El/La profesor/a _____
Por la mañana temprano	
a media mañana	
a mediodía	
por la tarde	
por la noche	

Paso 2. Hagan preguntas a su profesor/a para confirmar sus ideas.

Modelo: **¿Se levantó a las siete de la mañana?**

Así se forma

(7-22) El fin de semana.

Paso 1. Escribe oraciones sobre tus actividades el fin de semana pasado en la columna **Yo**. Añade otras dos actividades que hiciste.

Modelo: leer

Leí una novela muy interesante en mi cuarto.

	Yo	Mis compañeros/as
1. leer (¿Qué?, ¿Dónde?)		
2. hacer ejercicio/ jugar a un deporte (¿Dónde?, ¿Con quién?)		
3. estudiar (¿Qué?, ¿Dónde?)		
4. comer (¿Qué?, ¿Dónde?)		
5. ir de compras (¿Dónde?, ¿Con quién?, ¿Qué compraron?)		
6. ver la tele/ una película... (¿Cuál?, ¿Dónde?)		
7. comprar (¿Qué?, ¿Dónde?)		
8. ir a...		
9. ¿...?		
10. ¿...?		

Paso 2. En grupos, hablen de las cosas que hicieron y tomen apuntes en la columna **Mis compañeros/as**.

Modelo: Estudiante A: **Yo leí un libro de poesía de Borges, y ustedes ¿leyeron algo?**

Estudiante B: **Sí, yo leí unos artículos de *Newsweek* en la biblioteca.**

Estudiante C: **Pues yo leí mis libros de texto y una revista.**

Paso 3. Ahora comenten las cosas que averiguaron (*you found out*).

Modelo: Todos leímos algo, pero leímos cosas diferentes...

Así se dice

El dinero y los bancos

Nicolás **cuenta** su dinero.

Cuando tiene suficiente dinero, lo **gasta** en una tienda.

Nicolás también **gana** dinero vendiendo periódicos.

Por fin decide **abrir una cuenta** en un banco para **ahorrar** su dinero.

¿Qué más podemos hacer con el dinero?

cambiar	to change, exchange	**pagar (la cuenta)**	to pay (for) (the bill, check)
contar (ue)	to count	**retirar**	to withdraw
depositar	to deposit		
invertir (ie, i)	to invest		
encontrar (ue)	to find		
perder (ie)	to lose		

> ### NOTA DE LENGUA
> Note the difference between the use of **gastar** (dinero/ energía) vs. **pasar** (tiempo)
>
> **Gastamos** mucho **dinero** en libros.
>
> Jorge **pasa** bastante **tiempo** estudiando.

¿Cómo pagamos? ¿Cómo recibimos dinero?

el cajero automático	ATM machine	**el efectivo**	cash
el cambio	change, small change, exchange	**firmar (un cheque)**	to sign (a check)
el cheque	check	**la moneda**	currency, money, coin
el cheque de viajero	traveler's check	**la tarjeta de crédito/ débito**	credit/debit card
cobrar	to cash; to charge		

NOTA CULTURAL

Los mapuches de Chile

The Mapuche indigenous group successfully resisted attempts by the Spaniards to conquer them. Once Chile won its independence from Spain in 1817, the new government negotiated with the Mapuche and granted them land. But once European immigration began, the Mapuche began to lose a lot of land. Today, the Mapuche still grow wheat, maize (type of corn), and other grains. The Mapuche also herd vicuña, guanaco, alpaca, and the llama, which are all American camels and are used as beasts of burden. Mapuche children are monolingual in Mapudungun for the first six to nine years, when they begin to learn Spanish in school.

Unos mapuches

Así se dice

7-23 **Hay que ser organizado.** En parejas, imaginen que están de vacaciones en Santiago, Chile. Háganse las preguntas para saber si ya hicieron ciertas cosas. Usen pronombres en sus respuestas.

Modelo: ¿Encontraste el cajero automático?
Sí, ya lo encontré. *o* **No, no lo encontré.**

1. ¿Contaste el dinero que retiraste del cajero automático?
2. ¿Cambiaste los cheques de viajero?
3. ¿Pagaste la cuenta del hotel?
4. ¿Usaste la tarjeta de crédito?
5. ¿Encontraste la oficina de correos?
6. ¿Enviaste las tarjetas postales con fotos de los mapuches a tu familia?
7. ¿Compraste las entradas para el concierto?
8. ¿Hiciste las reservaciones en el restaurante?

7-24 **Tus finanzas.**

Paso 1. Marca tus respuestas a esta encuesta (*survey*) sobre tus hábitos financieros.

Usted y el dinero

¿Va usted a hacerse rico o tendrá problemas económicos?

1. Casi siempre pago…
   a. con efectivo   **b.** con tarjeta de débito   **c.** con tarjeta de crédito

2. Intento ahorrar…
   a. un 10% de mi salario   **b.** un 25% de mi salario   **c.** no ahorro nada

3. Cuando tengo monedas pequeñas…
   a. las uso   **b.** no las quiero   **c.** las ahorro, luego las llevo al banco

4. Reviso mis gastos…   **a.** cada semana   **b.** cada mes   **c.** nunca

5. Cuando viajo…   **a.** uso cheques de viaje   **b.** uso la tarjeta de crédito

6. Mis tarjetas de crédito…
   a. tienen un saldo (*balance*) pequeño   **b.** tienen un saldo grande
   c. ¿qué tarjetas de crédito?

7. Invierto…   **a.** en la bolsa (*stock market*)   **b.** no invierto en nada
   c. en productos seguros (*safe*)

8. Pago mis cuentas a tiempo…
   a. siempre   **b.** a veces   **c.** casi nunca

Paso 2. Ahora, compara tus respuestas con las de un/a compañero/a y respondan a las siguientes preguntas:

- ¿Tienen hábitos similares o diferentes?
- ¿Piensan que sus hábitos son típicos entre estudiantes?
- ¿Qué hábitos les gustaría cambiar?

 Paso 3. En grupos, escriban una pequeña **Guía de consejos financieros para estudiantes.**

 7-25 **Una visita al banco.** En grupos pequeños, tienen cinco minutos para describir la escena según el dibujo. Mencionen lo que está pasando, lo que pasó y/o lo que va a pasar. Un/a estudiante sirve de secretario/a y apunta las ideas. ¡Usen la imaginación! ¿Qué grupo puede escribir la descripción más completa?

PALABRAS ÚTILES

se escapa	*escapes*
recoger	*to pick up*
suelo	*floor*

SITUACIONES

Estás en el aeropuerto y decides tomar un taxi con una persona a quien no conoces, compartiendo el precio del viaje para llegar al centro. Cuando llegas a tu destino, ¡descubres que no tienes tu billetera (*wallet*)! ¿Qué dices? ¿Cómo reacciona el otro viajero? Intenten llegar a una solución.

EXPRESIONES ÚTILES

¡Ay, Dios mío!	*Oh, my God!*
¡Lo siento muchísimo!	*I am very sorry!*
¿Qué le parece si...?	*What do you think about...?*
(No) Me parece bien/ mal...	*I (do not) think it's OK/not OK...*

Así se forma

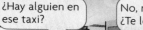

¿Hay alguien en ese taxi?

No, no hay nadie. ¿Te lo llamo?

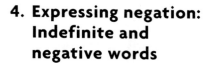

4. Expressing negation: Indefinite and negative words

You have previously used some indefinite and negative Spanish words, such as **siempre**, **a veces**, and **nunca**. Here are some additional indefinite and negative words.

PALABRAS INDEFINIDAS Y NEGATIVAS			
algo	something, anything (interrogative) →	**nada**	nothing, (not) anything
alguien	someone, anyone (interrogative) →	**nadie**	no one, nobody
también	also	→ **tampoco**	neither, not either

- Note that, in Spanish, negation must be expressed before the verb. We may use the negative expressions above preceding the verb.

> negative word + verb

—**Nunca** uso el metro.   I **never** use the metro.
—Yo **tampoco** lo uso.   I don't use it **either**.

If we use the negative expression after the verb, "no" must precede the verb in a "double negative" construction.

> **no** + verb + negative word

—¿Compraste **algo** en la tienda?   Did you buy **something/anything** at the store?

—Hoy **no** compré **nada**.   I did**n't** buy **anything** today.

—¿Hay **alguien** en el taxi?   Is there **anyone/someone** in the taxi?

—**No**, **no** hay **nadie**.   **No**, there is **no one**/there is**n't anyone**.

- When **alguien** and **nadie** are direct objects, they are preceded by the "personal **a**" (review in **Capítulo 3**, page 77).

—¿Viste **a alguien** corriendo por el parque?
—No, no vi **a nadie**.

7-26 **¿Cierto o falso?** Refiéranse al dibujo de la ciudad, páginas 218–219. ¿Son las siguientes declaraciones ciertas o falsas? Si son falsas, corríjanlas, usando palabras indefinidas y negativas.

Modelo: En este momento, nadie espera el autobús.   **Falso**
Alguien espera el autobús —una mujer.

1. Alguien está entrando en la iglesia.
2. Hay algo en la mesa que está delante del restaurante.
3. Nadie entra en el cine.
4. El hombre que está delante de la oficina de correos pone algo en el buzón.
5. El hombre en el quiosco no vende periódicos. Tampoco vende revistas.
6. El autobús nunca para (stops) en la avenida Colón.
7. Hay alguien paseando en bicicleta en la plaza.

7-27 **¿Eres un buen testigo (witness)?**

Paso 1. Mira los tres dibujos de abajo durante un minuto y después cúbrelos (cover them) con la mano o un papel. Después, pasa la página (turn the page).

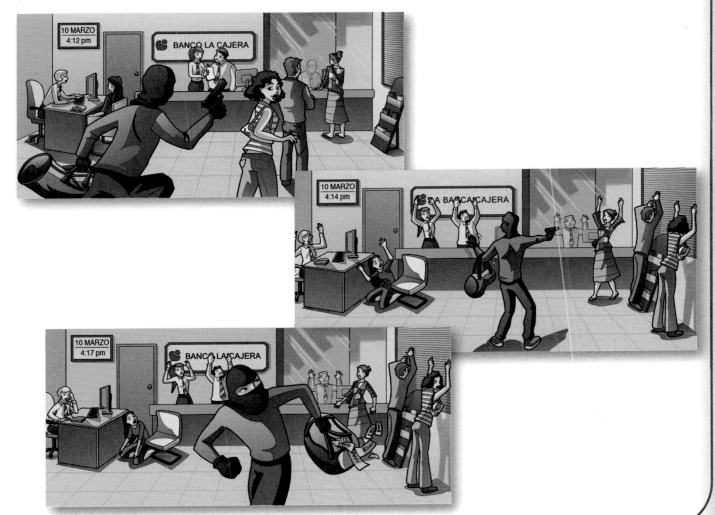

Paso 2. Ayer fuiste testigo de un atraco a un banco (*a bank robbery*) y ahora la policía te interroga sobre el ladrón (*robber*) y la situación. Lee las instrucciones y preguntas de la policía y anota tus respuestas en una hoja.

> ### Informe policial
>
> Imagina que estás viendo todo en este momento y contesta:
>
> 1. Cuando llega el ladrón, ¿hay alguien en el banco? ¿Cuántos empleados hay? ¿Y clientes? ¿Dónde están?
> 2. ¿El ladrón entra solo o con alguien?
> 3. Describe al ladrón: ¿Cómo es? ¿Qué ropa lleva? ¿Tiene algo cubriéndole la cara?
> 4. ¿Lleva (*Does he carry*) algo en la mano?
> 5. ¿Habla con alguien? ¿Dice algo?
> 6. ¿Qué hace el empleado? ¿Qué hacen los demás (*the rest*)?
> 7. Cuando el ladrón sale, ¿hay algo en su bolsa (*bag*)? ¿Qué?
> 8. ¿Llamó alguien a la policía?

Paso 3. Compara tus respuestas con las de un/a compañero/a que también fue testigo del atraco. ¿Quién recuerda más detalles?

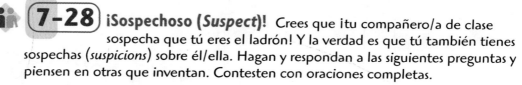

7-28 ¡**Sospechoso (***Suspect***)!** Crees que ¡tu compañero/a de clase sospecha que tú eres el ladrón! Y la verdad es que tú también tienes sospechas (*suspicions*) sobre él/ella. Hagan y respondan a las siguientes preguntas y piensen en otras que inventan. Contesten con oraciones completas.

1. ¿Estudiaste con alguien ayer por la tarde? (¿Con quién? ¿Desde qué hora hasta qué hora?)
2. ¿Hablaste con alguien por teléfono? (¿Con quién? ¿Cuánto tiempo?)
3. ¿Fuiste a clases después de almorzar? (¿Qué clases? ¿Quién es el profesor?)
4. ¿Fuiste a la biblioteca o al laboratorio? (¿A qué hora? ¿Solo/a o con alguien?)
5. ¿A qué hora fuiste a tu cuarto? ¿Viste a tu compañero/a de cuarto?
6. ¿...?

Así se pronuncia

The pronunciation of the consonants g and z and ce/ci

g   Before **e** or **i**, **g** has the English *h* sound as in *help*.

      gente   **gen**eralmente   **gi**mnasio   pá**gi**na

but it sounds like English before **a, o, u**.

      gato   **gor**ra   **gu**apo

Remember that in the combinations **gue** and **gui** the **u** is *not pronounced* so we pronounce **g** as in English + **e/i**.

      guerra   **gui**tarra

z   In Spanish America, **z** is pronounced the same as **s**. (In Spain it is commonly pronounced with a *th* sound.) The English z sound is never used in Spanish.

      bu**z**ón   pi**z**arra   pla**z**a   **z**apatería

Remember that the combination **z + e/i** is rarely used in Spanish. Instead **ce** and **ci** are used.

      cereal   **ci**ne

That is why there are spelling changes (**z → c**) in some verb forms.

      empie**z**o   empe**c**é

Repeat the poem line by line.

Zapatero°, zapatero, zapatero remendón°	*Shoemaker/cobbler*
Cuando haces los zapatos pones vida y corazón°...	***pones...** you put your heart and soul into it*
Analizas tu trabajo, su pureza y perfección,	
zapatillas° o sandalias, zapatito° o zapatón°.	*slippers/little shoe/big shoe*

Dictado. Escucha las siguientes palabras y escríbelas.

1.
2.
3.
4.
5.
6.
7.
8.

[handwritten note: z's in spanish always sound like (s) English]

¡A ESCUCHAR!

Unas vacaciones fabulosas en Buenos Aires, Argentina. Marta habla con su amiga Inés. Es la primera visita de Inés a Buenos Aires. Las dos se sientan en un café en la calle Corrientes. Escucha la conversación. Luego, contesta las dos primeras preguntas.

1. ¿Cómo fue el día de Inés? ☐ muy activo ☐ muy tranquilo

2. ¿Visita ella la ciudad de Buenos Aires con su amiga Marta? ☐ sí ☐ no

Ahora, escucha la conversación otra vez y completa las oraciones.

3. La calle Florida y la calle Corrientes están en _____.

4. Una atracción del barrio (*neighborhood*) La Boca es _____.

5. En el barrio La Recoleta ellas pueden visitar _____.

6. En Buenos Aires el subte es el _____.

7. La sorpresa (*surprise*) de Marta es que Inés _____ dos _____ para la ópera en el Teatro Colón.

8. Además de las entradas, ¿qué quiere Inés? _____.

CONVERSANDO

Un día en el centro. Un grupo de estudiantes y profesores de Argentina vienen a visitar su universidad y ustedes forman parte del comité organizador de actividades de fin de semana (*weekend*) para estos visitantes. En grupos de cuatro o cinco personas, organicen una serie de actividades para su fin de semana en la ciudad donde estudian ustedes. Consideren el tipo de actividades que van a ofrecer y lugares que van a visitar. Después, escriban un programa con los detalles para distribuir al grupo.

DE MI ESCRITORIO

Un folleto (*brochure*) turístico. Puesto que tienen ahora un poco de experiencia como guías turísticos para estudiantes extranjeros (*foreign*), la oficina del Decano les pide que elaboren un folleto turístico de la ciudad donde está su universidad para los estudiantes y visitantes hispanohablantes.

El folleto debe describir:

- la ciudad (incluso la población)
- cuatro atracciones interesantes de la ciudad y dónde están (refiéranse al Ejercicio 7–6)
- los mejores restaurantes, cines, museos, etc.
- los mejores lugares para ir de compras (almacenes, tiendas, centros comerciales)

Si quieren mejorar su folleto, incluyan fotos.

Artes literarias: Pablo Neruda

Antes de leer

1. Estudia la ilustración de la derecha. ¿Puedes adivinar el significado de las palabras **vuela** y **pájaro**?

2. ¿Tienes preguntas profundas o filosóficas sobre la vida?

¿Cómo se llama una flor que vuela de pájaro en pájaro?

Pablo Neruda acepta el Premio Nobel del Rey de Suecia.

Pablo Neruda (1904–1973) es de origen chileno, pero pasó gran parte de su vida adulta en varios países de Asia y Europa. Es una de las figuras más distinguidas de la poesía latinoamericana del siglo XX. Su producción literaria es extensa y excepcional, y le ganó el Premio Nobel de Literatura en 1971. Dejó[1] al morir ocho libros inéditos[2]. Las siguientes selecciones vienen de una de esas obras: *Libro de las preguntas*.

[1]He left behind [2]unpublished

¿Y por qué el sol es tan mal amigo del caminante en el desierto?

¿Y por qué el sol es tan simpático en el jardín del hospital?

¿Qué cuentan[3] de nuevo las hojas de la reciente primavera?

¿Hay algo más triste en el mundo que un tren inmóvil en la lluvia?

¿Dónde está el niño que yo fui, sigue adentro de mí o se fue?

¿Conversa el humo[4] con las nubes?

[3]tell [4]smoke

DICHOS

Una película sobre los años que Neruda pasó en exilio en Italia se titula *Il postino (The postman)*. Intenta verla y haz un informe para la clase.

Después de leer

1. Hagan dibujos (*drawings*) de tres de las preguntas. Luego, compártanlas con otra pareja. ¿Pueden identificar sus compañeros/as las preguntas que corresponden a las ilustraciones? Cambien de papel (*Change roles*).

2. Escriban dos preguntas originales al estilo de Pablo Neruda. Luego, compártanlas con la clase.

Repaso de vocabulario activo

Adjetivo

el mejor   *the best*

Palabras indefinidas y negativas

algo   *something*

alguien   *someone*

nada   *nothing*

nadie   *no one, nobody*

también   *also*

tampoco   *neither, not either*

Preposiciones

al lado de   *beside, next to*

antes de   *before*

cerca de   *near, close to*

debajo de   *beneath, under*

delante de   *in front of*

dentro de   *inside*

después de   *after*

detrás de   *behind*

en   *in, on*

encima de   *on top of, above*

enfrente de   *opposite, facing*

entre   *between, among*

en vez de   *instead of*

frente a   *opposite, facing*

fuera de   *outside*

lejos de   *far from*

para + *infinitivo*   *in order to + do something*

por   *by, through, alongside, around*

sobre   *on*

Sustantivos

En el banco   *In the bank*

el cajero automático   *ATM machine*

el cambio   *change, small change, exchange*

el cheque   *check*

el cheque de viajero   *traveler's check*

la cuenta   *account*

el efectivo   *cash*

la moneda   *currency, money, coin*

la tarjeta de crédito/ débito   *credit/debit card*

En la ciudad   *In the city*

el almacén   *department store*

el autobús   *bus*

la avenida   *avenue*

el banco   *bank; bench*

el bar   *bar*

el café   *coffee place*

la calle   *street*

la catedral   *cathedral*

el centro comercial   *shopping mall*

el cine   *movie theatre, cinema*

el edificio   *building*

la entrada   *entrance; ticket*

la estatua   *statue*

la gente   *people*

la iglesia   *church*

la joyería   *jewelry store*

el lugar   *place*

el metro   *metro, subway*

el museo   *museum*

las noticias   *news*

la obra de teatro   *play (theater)*

la parada de autobús   *bus stop*

el parque   *park*

la pastelería   *pastry shop, bakery*

la película   *film, movie*

el periódico   *newspaper*

la pizzería   *pizzeria*

la plaza   *plaza, town square*

el quiosco   *kiosk, newsstand*

el rascacielos   *skyscraper*

el restaurante   *restaurant*

la revista   *magazine*

el taxi   *taxi*

el teatro   *theater*

la zapatería   *shoe store*

En la oficina de correos   *In the post office*

el buzón   *mailbox*

la carta   *letter*

la dirección   *address*

la estampilla/ el sello   *stamp*

el paquete   *package*

el sobre   *envelope*

la tarjeta postal   *postcard*

Verbos y expresiones verbales

abrir   *to open*

ahorrar   *to save*

cambiar   *to change, exchange*

cerrar (ie)   *to close*

cobrar   *to cash; to charge*

contar (ue)   *to count*

contestar   *to answer, reply*

depositar   *to deposit*

empezar (ie) (a)   *to start*

encontrar (ue)   *to find*

entrar (en/ a)   *to enter, go in*

enviar   *to send*

esperar   *to wait (for)*

firmar   *to sign*

gastar   *to spend (money)*

hacer cola/ fila   *to be in line*

invertir (ie, i)   *to invest*

invitar (a)   *to invite*

morir (ue, u)   *to die*

pagar   *to pay (for...)*

pasar   *to pass, go by; to spend (time)*

perder (ie)   *to lose*

recibir   *to receive*

repetir (i, i)   *to repeat*

retirar   *to withdraw (money)*

terminar   *to finish*

Autoprueba y repaso

 WILEY PLUS ✓

I. Prepositions of location. Todas las oraciones siguientes son falsas. Para corregirlas, cambia las preposiciones.

Modelo: El buzón está detrás de la oficina de correos.

El buzón está *delante de* la oficina de correos.

1. La gente está fuera del cine.
2. La iglesia está enfrente del banco.
3. La estatua está lejos del centro de la ciudad.
4. En el quiosco, las revistas están debajo de los periódicos.

II. Pronouns with prepositions. Termina las oraciones con los pronombres de preposición correctos.

1. ¿Quieres ir con _____ (me)?
2. Lo siento; no puedo ir con _____ (you, fam., s.).
3. El pastel es para _____ (them).
4. Y, ¿qué tienes para _____ (us)?

III. Demonstrative adjectives and pronouns.

A. Indica qué lugares vas a visitar. Usa adjetivos demostrativos según las indicaciones.

Modelo: Voy a visitar el museo. (cerca)

Voy a visitar este museo.

1. Voy a visitar la iglesia. (un poco lejos)
2. Voy a visitar el museo. (cerca)
3. Quiero ver las obras de arte. (cerca)
4. Queremos ver los rascacielos. (muy lejos)

B. Contesta con un pronombre demostrativo.

Modelo: ¿Te gusta este almacén?

No, prefiero ése.

1. ¿Te gustan estas tiendas?
2. ¿Te gustan estos zapatos?
3. ¿Te gusta este restaurante?
4. ¿Te gusta esta pizzería?

IV. The preterit of *hacer* and stem-changing verbs. Hoy tú eres el/la profesor/a. Usando el pretérito, hazles preguntas a las personas indicadas. Imagina que ellos responden. Escribe las preguntas y las respuestas.

Modelo: repetir los ejercicios/ Ana

Profesor/a: **Ana, ¿repetiste los ejercicios?**

Ana: **Sí, los repetí.**

1. pedir ayuda a un tutor / Carlos y Felipe
2. dormir bien después de volver del centro / Alberto
3. hacer algo interesante en el centro / Linda y Celia
4. divertirse / Linda y Celia
5. preferir la ópera o el ballet / el director de la escuela (Sr. Sancho)

V. Indefinite and negative words. Contesta con oraciones negativas.

Modelo: ¿Compraste algo en el almacén ayer?

No, no compré nada.

1. ¿Alguien fue contigo a Nueva York?
2. ¿Hiciste algo interesante en el centro?
3. Yo no visité la Zona Cero (*Ground Zero*). ¿Y tú?

VI. *Repaso general.* Contesta con oraciones completas.

1. ¿A qué hora abren los bancos en tu ciudad? ¿Y los almacenes?
2. ¿Gastaste mucho dinero en restaurantes el mes pasado? (¿Qué pediste?)
3. Ayer fuiste a un café con tus amigos/as. ¿Qué pidieron ustedes?
4. ¿Fueron tú y tus amigos/as al centro el sábado por la noche? (¿Para qué?)
5. ¿Cuántas horas dormiste anoche?
6. ¿Duermes ocho horas casi siempre o casi nunca? (¿Por qué?)
7. ¿Qué hiciste anoche?
8. ¿Qué hicieron tú y tus amigos/as el fin de semana pasado?

VII. *Cultura.*

1. ¿Cuáles son los dos países más grandes del Cono Sur?
2. ¿Cuáles fueron los grupos de europeos más numerosos que inmigraron a Buenos Aires?
3. Explica quiénes son **tres** de las siguientes personas o grupos: Salvador Allende, Augusto Pinochet, Juan Perón, los mapuches, Benito Quinquela Martín, los gauchos, Jorge Luis Borges, Gabriela Mistral.

Respuestas a *Autoprueba y repaso* se pueden encontrar en el **Apéndice 2.**

De compras

By the end of this chapter you will be able to:

- Talk about and purchase clothing
- Indicate and emphasize possession
- Talk about actions in the past
- Indicate to or for whom something is done

Así se dice	Así se forma	Cultura	Dicho y hecho
• De compras	1. Possessive adjectives and pronouns 2. The preterit of irregular verbs 3. Indirect-object pronouns 4. Direct- and indirect-object pronouns combined	• Perú, Ecuador y Bolivia • La ropa tradicional • Artes ornamentales: El oro de los lambayeque	• Desfile de modas • El equipaje perdido • Mi ropero

ENTRANDO AL TEMA

1. ¿Sabes cuál es la moneda oficial de Ecuador?

☐ El peso   ☐ El sucre   ☐ El dólar

2. En los Estados Unidos, ¿en qué compras se puede regatear (negociar) el precio? Y, ¿con qué cosas o en qué lugares no se puede regatear?

Así se dice

De compras

La Única ROPA PARA DAMAS

- las joyas
- el collar
- el suéter (de lana)
- el vestido
- la cadena
- la pulsera
- los aretes/ los pendientes
- la blusa (de algodón)
- el anillo
- el sombrero
- la ropa interior
- las medias
- la falda
- llevar
- la bolsa/el bolso
- las botas
- las sandalias
- el traje de baño
- los zapatos
- el regalo
- el paraguas
- el impermeable

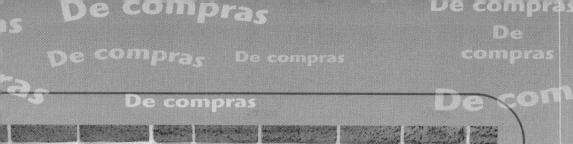

Y CABALLEROS

el algodón	*cotton*
el cuero	*leather*
la lana	*wool*
la seda	*silk*
llevar	*to wear*
las joyas	*jewelry*

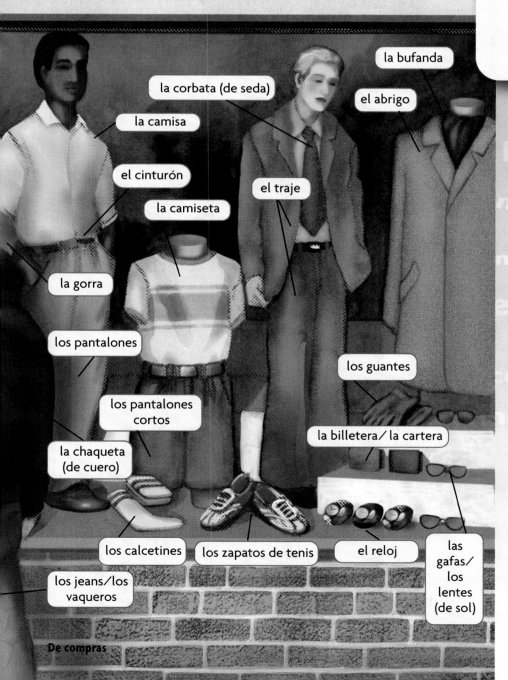

la bufanda

la corbata (de seda)

el abrigo

la camisa

el cinturón

el traje

la camiseta

la gorra

los guantes

los pantalones

la billetera/ la cartera

los pantalones cortos

la chaqueta (de cuero)

los calcetines

los zapatos de tenis

el reloj

las gafas/ los lentes (de sol)

los jeans/los vaqueros

NOTA DE LENGUA

There is much regional variation in clothing vocabulary. Watch out for differences when you travel.

la chaqueta → el saco (México/ Argentina)

el suéter → el jersey (España); el pulóver (Argentina)

la falda → la pollera (Argentina)

el abrigo → el tapado Argentina); el sobretodo (Colombia)

Así se dice

 8-1 **¿Para damas o caballeros?** Escucha los artículos de ropa que lee tu instructor/a. Decide si cada uno normalmente se asocia con las damas, los caballeros o los dos.

	las damas	los caballeros	los dos
1.			
2.			
3.			
4.			
5.			
6.			
7.			
8.			
9.			
10.			

8-2 **¿De quién es?** Tus amigos/as olvidaron (*forgot*) algunas cosas en tu cuarto.

Paso 1. Lee las siguientes oraciones y completa el cuadro para deducir de quién es cada prenda (*article of clothing*).

1. La bolsa es negra.
2. Sandra no tiene prendas o complementos de cuero.
3. La gorra es de algodón.
4. Una prenda es de seda, otra es blanca y roja.
5. Raquel no olvidó una gorra.
6. La corbata es azul con lunares blancos.
7. Óscar olvidó una prenda de algodón.
8. Una chica olvidó su bolsa de cuero.
9. La bufanda es de rayas verdes y blancas.
10. La prenda de Sandra es de lana.

PALABRAS ÚTILES

de/ a rayas	*striped*
lunares	*dots*

Amigo/a	Prenda (*article of clothing*)	Material	Color
Óscar	corbata lunares	algodón	blanca y roja
Sandra	gorra	la lana	rayas verdes y blancas
Raquel	una bolsa	de cuero	
Alberto	corbata	de seda	azul lunares blancos

[handwritten margin notes]
canasta - woven basket w/o lid
cesto - woven basket w/ lid

Paso 2. Ahora escribe oraciones para describir las prendas que tus amigos/as olvidaron.

Modelo: Andrea olvidó una blusa de algodón amarilla.

8-3 **¿Qué combina mejor?**

Paso 1. Empareja (*Match*) los artículos de ropa de la columna A y la columna B, especificando un color para la ropa de la columna B.

A	B
1. Una chaqueta gris	**a.** con una camiseta _____
2. Unos vaqueros	**b.** con unos zapatos _____
3. Un vestido blanco	**c.** con una corbata _____
4. Un traje azul	**d.** con una falda/ unos pantalones cortos _____
5. Un abrigo marrón	**e.** con unas botas _____
6. Un impermeable rosado	**f.** con unas sandalias _____
7. Una blusa/ camisa blanca	**g.** con unos pantalones _____

Paso 2. Compara tus respuestas con las de un/a compañero/a, y después con la clase.

8-4 **¿Qué ropa es apropiada?** Escucha las siguientes descripciones e indica en qué ocasión es apropiado llevar esta ropa. (Algunas opciones pueden ser apropiadas para más de una ocasión.)

_____   para ir a la playa

_____   para ir a una entrevista de trabajo (*job interview*)

_____   para correr en el parque

_____   para ir a clase

_____   para ir a una cena formal

_____   para ir a la discoteca

compras De compras compras De De con
De compras De compras
compras De con
De compras

Así se dice

8-5 El color perfecto para cada ocasión.

 Paso 1. Antes de leer.

¿Cuál es tu color favorito? ¿Qué características asocias con ese color?

ppp purple morado - Creativity -

 Paso 2. Lee el texto siguiente.

el color perfecto para cada ocasión

• ROJO. Ideal para buscar trabajo. Se relaciona con el éxito; refleja energía, excitación y pasión. • NARANJA. Para comunicar mensajes. Te dota de vibras positivas, vitalidad y buen humor. • AMARILLO. Para un evento alegre (una boda). Es el color del sol y sugiere calidez y optimismo. • VERDE. Es el color del dinero, llévalo cuando estés en una campaña para reunir fondos. • AZUL. Ideal para viajar en auto con los niños porque transmite serenidad y calma. • MORADO. Para fiestas: sugiere que eres misteriosa y creativa.

 Paso 3. Después de leer.

1. ¿Qué color representa energía? ¿Calma? ¿Misterio?
2. ¿Qué colores se¹ llevan con frecuencia cuando hace mucho calor? ¿Y cuando hace frío?
3. ¿Qué colores asocias con una persona que frecuentemente está contenta? ¿Y con una persona que está triste?
4. Según (*According to*) el texto, ¿qué es lo que se asocia con tu color favorito? ¿Crees que estas características describen tu personalidad correctamente?

---

¹The word **se** placed before the verb slightly alters the meaning of the verb. Here, **se llevan** = *are worn*; **llevan** = *they, you (pl.) wear.*

Paso 4. Basándote en el texto *El color perfecto para cada ocasión*, ayuda a estas personas a escoger ropa apropiada para las siguientes ocasiones.

Modelo: Rosa quiere pedir un aumento (*raise*) en el trabajo.
Puede llevar un traje negro porque es elegante y profesional, y una blusa verde para atraer (*attract*) el dinero.

1. El Sr. Donoso va a comer con un cliente importante.
2. Pedro va a trabajar cuidando a niños esta noche.
3. Bernardo tiene una cita (*a date*) esta noche.
4. Andrea va a hacer una presentación en la clase de historia mañana.
5. Leo va a visitar a su abuela en el hospital.

La transformación de Carmen

Carmen nos habla de su pequeña transformación.

Para empezar, fui a visitar al oftalmólogo y como resultado de la visita cambié mis **gafas** por **lentes de contacto** —algo que cambió mi vida radicalmente porque ahora me siento° más joven, más **a la moda.** Luego, organicé mi **ropero**; eliminé varias **cosas** y lavé toda la ropa **sucia**, y ahora todo está **limpio** y ordenado. Por supuesto, mi amiga Irene y yo tenemos que ir de compras. Primero, voy a pensar en lo que necesito: voy a comprar unos aretes, un collar y tal vez unos anillos de fantasía° porque las joyas de **oro** o **plata** son muy **caras** y yo no tengo mucho dinero ¡El **precio** siempre es importante para una madre de gemelas! También necesito una falda **corta** para salir, una falda **larga** para el trabajo, unos pantalones negros, una blusa **de manga corta** y otra **de manga larga.** No sé cuánto va a **costar** todo esto, pero Irene me dice que en el **centro comercial** hay unas tiendas donde venden ropa de moda y **barata** porque tienen **rebajas.** Además, primero vamos a **mirar** en varias tiendas y a comparar precios. ¡Ah! y en cuanto a° la **talla**, debo olvidarme° de ese problemita; me voy a poner a dieta y todo va a estar perfecto.

Antes

me... *I feel*

Después

costume

en... *as for, concerning; forget about*

la moda[2]	*fashion, style*	**talla**	*size*
plata	*silver*	**oro**	*gold*
la cosa	*thing*	**corto/a**	*short*
el ropero	*closet*	**largo/a**	*long*
costar (ue)	*cost*	**limpio/a**	*clean*
las rebajas	*sales*	**sucio/a**	*dirty*
de manga (corta)	*(short-)sleeved*		

gemelas - twins

dice - to say or to feel

---

[2]While **ir/estar a la moda** is used to refer to people (to dress with style), **estar de moda** is used to talk about a particular article of clothing, color, etc. that is in fashion: **El negro está de moda.**

Así se dice

8-6 ¿Qué puedes llevar?

Paso 1. Indica qué prendas y complementos son apropiados para estos lugares y situaciones.

	clases	una cena formal	la oficina	el cine	el centro comercial	una fiesta
joyas de oro						
una camiseta vieja						
una bolsa elegante						
una corbata						
una gorra						
sandalias						
jeans						
pantalones cortos						
zapatos de tenis						
una falda corta						
un vestido largo						

 Paso 2. En grupos pequeños, comparen sus respuestas. ¿Tienen opiniones similares?

 Paso 3. En sus grupos, escriban una lista de ropa o complementos que consideran inapropiados para cada ocasión.

NOTA CULTURAL

La formalidad de la ropa

In most United States universities, it is acceptable for students to attend class in informal clothing such as sweatpants and baseball caps. However, in many Spanish-speaking countries, such attire would be viewed as inappropriate. People tend to dress a bit more formally for school and for going out in general.

Esteban   Octavio

8-7 **Un gran contraste.** En parejas, tomen turnos para describir el aspecto y la ropa de Esteban y Octavio. Un estudiante dice una oración y el otro adivina (*guesses*) si se refiere a Esteban o a Octavio.

Modelo: Estudiante A: **Lleva una camiseta limpia.**

Estudiante B: **Es Octavio.**

¿Qué impresiones tienen sobre la personalidad de Esteban y Octavio según su estilo?

NOTA DE LENGUA

While shopping, one usually looks for, looks at, and sees various items. Observe the differences between the verbs **buscar** (*to look for*), **mirar** (*to look at*), and **ver** (*to see*).

Natalia y Camila...	**buscan** un regalo,	**are looking for** a gift,
	miran varias gafas de sol	**look at** various sunglasses,
	y **ven** las que quieren comprar.	and **see** the ones they want to buy.

8-8 **¿Qué prefieres?**

Paso 1. Indica tus preferencias respecto a la ropa y las compras y responde a las preguntas de abajo.

1. los suéteres   ☐ de lana   ☐ de algodón   ☐ de seda
2. las faldas   ☐ largas   ☐ cortas
3. las camisas   ☐ de manga larga   ☐ de manga corta
4. los pantalones   ☐ cortos   ☐ largos   ☐ los jeans
5. calzado   ☐ los zapatos   ☐ las sandalias   ☐ las botas
6. para los ojos   ☐ gafas   ☐ lentes de contacto
7. la ropa   ☐ elegante   ☐ de calidad   ☐ de moda
   ☐ cómoda (*comfortable*)
8. comprar en   ☐ el almacén   ☐ el centro comercial
   ☐ el Internet
9. ¿Vas de compras frecuentemente? ¿Vas sólo cuando buscas algo específico o para mirar?
10. ¿Cuáles son tus marcas favoritas? ¿Qué tiendas o almacenes prefieres para comprar ropa?
11. ¿Qué tipo de artículo de ropa o complemento te gusta especialmente?

 Paso 2. En grupos, comparen sus preferencias: ¿son similares o diferentes?

NOTA CULTURAL

Los mercados y el regateo (*bargaining*)

It is common to see various types of merchants in Spanish-speaking countries, including street vendors, merchants in open-air markets, modern indoor shopping malls, specialty stores, etc. Normally a degree of bargaining is expected with street vendors and in markets, particularly for handicrafts, clothing, and jewelry. When bargaining, never insult the quality of the item or the vendor. Simply suggest a lower price than the one that is offered, and be prepared to meet somewhere in the middle. Bargain only for items that you intend to purchase. Shopping malls and stores almost always have fixed prices, so bargaining is inappropriate there.

Así se dice

8-9 **El precio correcto.** Trabajan en el Almacén Galerías de la Moda y deben poner las etiquetas de precios en estos artículos, pero ¿dónde está la lista de precios? En parejas, decidan qué precio corresponde a cada artículo.

Modelo: Estudiante A: **Yo creo que el reloj cuesta $370.**

Estudiante B: **¿Tú crees? Me parece un precio barato.**

Estudiante A: **Pero no es de oro, ¿verdad?...**

$3.450
$2.500
$25
$6
$10
$175
$125
$36
$65

EXPRESIONES ÚTILES

¿Tú crees?
  Do you think so?
¿Estás seguro/a?
  Are you sure?
¿Qué te parece?
  What do you think?
Me parece (caro...)
  It seems (expensive . . .)

NOTA DE LENGUA

The prepositions **por** and **para** can be problematic for English speakers because they both can be equivalent to *for*. Which one is used depends on the meaning we want to convey. You have already studied some uses of **por** and **para** (**Capítulo 7**, p. 226). Additional uses are:

Para + *person/thing* = *for* + *the recipient/beneficiary of something*

| Esta blusa es **para** mi novia. | *This blouse is **for** my girlfriend.* |
| Necesita una silla **para** su oficina. | *He needs a chair **for** his office.* |

Por + *an amount* = *for; in exchange for*

| Pagué $200 **por** el collar. | *I paid $200 **for** the necklace.* |
| ~~Pagué $200 **para** el collar.~~ | |

8-10 **Regalos para todos.** El Almacén Galerías de la Moda tiene rebajas y ustedes compran muchos regalos para su familia y sus amigos/as. Habla con tu compañero/a y dile qué compraste, para quién es cada regalo y cuánto dinero gastaste. Haz preguntas y comentarios sobre sus compras. Túrnense.

EXPRESIONES ÚTILES

¡Qué (barato/ caro)!
How cheap/expensive!
¡No me digas!
Really? Seriously?

Modelo: Estudiante A: **Estos guantes son para mi hermana. Los compré por $4.**

Estudiante B: **¡Qué baratos! Pero ahora no hace mucho frío.**

Estudiante A: **Sí, pero mi hermana siempre tiene frío.**

8-11 ¿Qué necesitamos?

Paso 1. El año próximo vas a estudiar en Ecuador y estás planeando tu equipaje. ¿Qué ropa y accesorios piensas que necesitas para ir a los lugares indicados? En la sección de cultura sobre Ecuador, en la página 266–267, vas a encontrar información interesante sobre su clima.

Las playas de Guayaquil (agosto)	Selva Amazónica (septiembre)	Cena en la Embajada de los EE.UU., Quito (octubre)	Volcán Chimborazo (noviembre)

Paso 2. ¡Qué casualidad! Tu compañero/a también va a ir a Ecuador. Comparen sus listas y expliquen por qué van a llevar estas cosas. ¿Quieres sacar, añadir (*add*) o cambiar algo en tu lista?

Cultura: Perú, Ecuador y Bolivia, los países andinos de un antiguo imperio

Antes de leer

1. ¿Cuáles son las capitales de estos tres países? ¿Qué país tiene dos capitales?

2. ¿Qué tienen Ecuador y Perú que no tiene Bolivia?

   ☑ costa (*coast*)   ☐ frontera con otro país   ☐ montañas

3. ¿Sabes por qué es famoso Machu Picchu?   *famos anchor*

4. ¿Cómo se llama el lago que está en la frontera entre Perú y Bolivia?   *Pacific ocean*

Donde veas un nombre **en rojo**, vuelve a mirar el mapa y localiza el lugar.

EL GRAN IMPERIO INCA

Ecuador, Perú y Bolivia, situados en el corazón[1] de los Andes, formaron el antiguo imperio inca llamado *Tahuantinsuyo*. Con una extensión de 3.000 millas de norte a sur, la zona contiene espectaculares picos nevados, impresionantes volcanes y el inmenso **lago Titicaca**. Los emperadores incas gobernaron durante casi 400 años y fueron bastante benevolentes: bajo su gobierno, nadie tuvo hambre o estuvo sin ropa, y después de conquistar a otras tribus, los incas incorporaban a los líderes conquistados en su gobierno. El último emperador inca se llamaba Atahualpa. Fue capturado por Francisco Pizarro cuando los españoles conquistaron la región en 1560. En este período Lima, Perú, se convirtió en el centro colonial más importante de Sudamérica.

[1]*heart*

En la frontera entre Bolivia y Perú, a 12.506 pies de altura, está el lago Titicaca. En la parte boliviana del lago se encuentra la Isla del Sol. Una leyenda dice que el primer inca salió de esta isla para fundar Cuzco, la capital del imperio Tahuantinsuyo. El Titicaca es el lago más grande de Sudamérica (122 millas cuadradas) y el lago navegable más alto del mundo. En esta foto, se cruza el lago en una canoa de totora[2].

[2]*cattail plant*

En 1999, en las afueras de Lima, Perú, se descubrió un cementerio inca con una extensión aproximada de 20 acres. Esta zona se conoce con el nombre de Puruchuco-Huaquerones. Hasta el momento más de 2.200 momias en bultos de tela[3] han sido exhumadas de este sitio arqueológico. Dichos bultos pueden llegar a pesar[4] hasta 500 libras y contienen cuerpos[5] y los artefactos que los difuntos[6] usaron en vida.

[3]**bultos...** *bundles of cloth* [4]*weigh* [5]*bodies* [6]*dead*

Los incas eran ingenieros brillantes. Sus fortalezas[7] utilizaron piedras cortadas tan perfectamente que no requerían mortero, y hasta hoy siguen en condiciones excelentes. Además de sus adelantos[8] en la ingeniería, la arquitectura y la medicina, los incas perfeccionaron el cultivo de la patata y el cuidado del ganado[9] de los Andes, como las llamas y las alpacas. Muchos indígenas continúan llevando el traje típico de los indios andinos: sarapes, ponchos y sombreros hechos de lana de alpaca.

[7]*forts* [8]*advances* [9]*livestock*

Cultura: Perú, Ecuador y Bolivia, los países andinos de un antiguo imperio

PERÚ

Perú es el tercer país más grande de Sudamérica. La costa árida del Pacífico (donde están **Lima** y el puerto principal, **El Callao**) es la región más dinámica del país. Pero el área andina, con montañas muy elevadas, domina la geografía del país. La influencia indígena en Perú es muy marcada. En la foto, la calle de **Cuzco** muestra la fusión de la cultura indígena y la española: Los incas construyeron el muro de piedra[10], y los españoles construyeron la parte superior del edificio. Las lenguas oficiales de Perú son el español y el quechua.

Cerca de Cuzco, Perú, a más de 8.000 pies de altura, los incas construyeron la ciudad de **Machu Picchu**. Esta ciudad refleja el alto nivel de tecnología del imperio inca. Los españoles no sabían de la existencia de Machu Picchu y, después de la conquista, el sitio se perdió durante siglos. ¡No fue redescubierta hasta 1911!

[10]**muro...** *stone wall*

ECUADOR

La línea ecuatorial que pasa por el norte de **Quito** le dio su nombre al país. Ecuador es un país pequeño pero de grandes contrastes geográficos. En sus costas cálidas y secas hay playas excelentes. En la región oriental está la zona amazónica, donde el clima es caliente y húmedo y existe una gran variedad de vegetación y fauna. El área andina, con impresionantes volcanes, tiene un clima frío y seco.

Mario Vargas Llosa es un famoso autor peruano. Fue parte del boom literario latinoamericano. Sus libros *La ciudad y los perros* (1963) y *La casa verde* (1966) son muy famosos. En 1990, Vargas Llosa se presentó para la presidencia de Perú, pero perdió frente a Alberto Fujimori.

Quito, la capital de Ecuador, tiene una zona antigua de gran belleza con numerosos ejemplos de arte y de arquitectura coloniales. Por eso, muchas personas la llaman «la cara de Dios». En la foto se ve la Plaza de la Independencia. El 10 de agosto de 1809 se dio en Quito el primer grito[11] de independencia de América Latina. En 1822, Ecuador se independizó de España y se incorporó a la Gran Colombia. En 1830 se convirtió en república independiente.

[11]*call*

Hoy en día, muchas de las flores y plantas que se venden en las florerías en los EE.UU. y en Europa vienen de Ecuador. En el año 2000, Ecuador adoptó el dólar de los Estados Unidos como moneda nacional.

Las Islas Galápagos, donde formó Darwin muchas de sus teorías, son un verdadero tesoro ecológico a 960 millas de la costa ecuatoriana. Coexisten especies de reptiles, aves[12] y plantas únicas en el mundo. Las tortugas[13] de las Galápagos, Ecuador, pueden vivir un año sin comer y pueden pesar 500 libras y vivir por 100 años.

---

[12]birds [13]turtles

BOLIVIA

El nombre de este país es un homenaje a Simón Bolívar, el héroe sudamericano de las guerras de independencia. Bolivia fue parte de Perú durante casi toda la época colonial. Las minas de plata de Potosí fueron la atracción principal para los españoles. ¡En tiempos coloniales Potosí fue la ciudad más poblada de América! Bolivia se independizó en 1825, pero poco después tuvo varias guerras con países vecinos[14]. En una guerra con Chile perdió su única salida al mar.

Sucre es la capital constitucional de Bolivia. La Paz, la capital administrativa, es la sede del gobierno. A 12.725 pies de altura, es famosa por ser la ciudad más alta del mundo. De hecho, debido a la altura y al poco oxígeno, es muy difícil encender[15] y mantener un fuego en La Paz; por eso hay muy pocos incendios[16].

Igual que en Perú y en Ecuador, la presencia indígena es muy visible in Bolivia. Sólo la mitad de los bolivianos hablan español como primera lengua. Las otras lenguas del país son el quechua y el aymara. El carnaval de la ciudad de Oruro es uno de los eventos folclóricos más famosos de Sudamérica, especialmente la "Danza del diablo".

---

[14]neighboring [15]start
[16]fires

Después de leer

1. ¿Dónde se encuentra el Lago Titicaca, y por qué es famoso?

2. ¿Qué hacían los Incas después de conquistar a otra tribu?

3. ¿A qué país pertenecen (belong to) las Islas Galápagos?

   ☐ Perú   ☐ Bolivia   ☐ Ecuador

4. Adivina cuáles de las palabras siguientes vienen del quechua:

   ☐ cóndor   ☐ puma   ☐ gaucho

La Danza del diablo

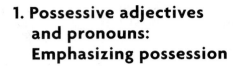

¡No es tuya!
¡Es mía!

¡Niñas!

¡Esta pelota es mía!

1. Possessive adjectives and pronouns: Emphasizing possession

You have already learned one form of possessive adjectives (**mi, tu, su, nuestro, vuestro, su**). These have a corresponding form that is used for emphasis.

Es **mi** bolsa.   *It's **my** purse.*
Esa bolsa es **mía**.   *That purse is **mine**.*

These emphatic possessive forms are also adjectives and therefore agree in gender (masculine/feminine) and number (singular/plural) with the thing possessed.

Los posesivos enfáticos		
mío/a, míos/as	*mine*	Esa chaqueta es **mía**.
tuyo/a, tuyos/as	*yours*	¿Los guantes azules son **tuyos**?
suyo/a, suyos/as[3]	*his*	Pepe dice que esa gorra es **suya**.
	hers	Ana dice que esas botas son **suyas**.
	yours	¿El bolso de cuero es **suyo**?
nuestro/a, nuestros/as	*ours*	Esa casa es **nuestra**.
		Esos dos gatos son **nuestros**.
vuestro/a, vuestros/as	*yours*	¿Es **vuestro** ese carro?
		¿Son **vuestras** las bicicletas?
suyo/a, suyos/as	*theirs*	Ana y Tere dicen que esas cosas son **suyas**.

They follow either a form of the verb **ser** to indicate *mine, yours* . . .

Esas botas son **mías**.   *Those boots are **mine**.*

or a noun to indicate *of mine, of yours,* etc.

Pero un amigo **mío** dice que son **suyas**.   *But a friend of **mine** says that they are **his**.*

Possessive pronouns are used when the possessed object has been mentioned before, to avoid repetition. Their form is similar to that of emphatic pronouns but they require the use of definite articles (**el, la, los, las**).

—Tengo mi suéter. ¿Tienes **el tuyo**?   *I have my sweater. Do you have **yours**?*
—Sí, tengo **el mío**.   *Yes, I have **mine**.*

---

[3]As with su/sus (see p. 88), if the context does not clearly indicate who **suyo/a/os/as** refers to, you may use an alternate form for clarity.

Es su ropa.   o   Es la ropa **de...** él/ella/ usted.
Esa ropa es **suya**.   o   Esa ropa es **de... ellos/ellas /ustedes.**

8-12 En la lavandería (*Laundromat*). Alfonso y Rubén están en la lavandería y usan la misma (*same*) secadora. Ahora cada uno busca su ropa.

Alfonso   Rubén

Paso 1. Presta atención a lo que dicen e indica a qué prendas se refieren.

Rubén dice:

1. Ésta es mía.   **a.** la chaqueta   **b.** los pantalones   **c.** el suéter
2. Éste es mío.   **a.** los calcetines   **b.** el suéter   **c.** la camiseta

Alfonso dice:

3. Éstos son míos.   **a.** la chaqueta   **b.** la camisa   **c.** los pantalones cortos
4. Éstas son mías.   **a.** las camisas   **b.** los jeans   **c.** el impermeable

Paso 2. Ahora, completa estas oraciones indicando de quién es cada prenda.

5. Rubén dice que la **chaqueta es...**
6. Alfonso dice que las...
7. Rubén dice que el...
8. Alfonso dice que los...

8-13 ¡Un ladrón o una ladrona (*thief*) en la clase! ¡Cierren los ojos! (El profesor/La profesora camina por la clase "robando" algunos de los artículos de los estudiantes. Los pone sobre su escritorio.) Ahora, abran los ojos y contesten las preguntas del profesor/de la profesora.

Modelo: Profesor/a: Señor/Señorita, ¿es suyo este reloj?
               Estudiante: **No, no es mío.**
               Profesor/a a la clase: Pues, ¿de quién es?
               Un/a estudiante indica: **Es suyo.** o **Es de Lisa.**

 # Escenas

Camila   Natalia

En el Almacén Torres

Natalia y Camila van de compras. Están buscando un regalo para Rubén.

Paso 1. Basándote en el título y la breve descripción de arriba, ¿qué artículos piensas que van a comprar Camila y Natalia?

	es probable	no es probable
1. un cinturón	_____	_____
2. un libro	_____	_____
3. un collar	_____	_____
4. una billetera	_____	_____
5. un CD	_____	_____
6. unas gafas de sol	_____	_____

Escenas

Paso 2. Escucha la conversación y contesta las siguientes preguntas sobre las ideas principales.

1. ¿Qué hacen Natalia y Camila?
2. ¿Encuentran algo apropiado para Rubén?

Paso 3. Escucha la conversación otra vez y completa las siguientes oraciones.

1. Camila y Natalia entran en un _____.
2. Camila tiene una idea para el regalo de Rubén: _____ y
   _____.
3. Natalia piensa que Rubén no va a querer una camisa y una corbata porque
   _____.
4. Camila y Natalia deciden que van a comprar _____.
5. El dependiente dice que tienen suerte porque _____.

Paso 4. Escucha una vez más y lee el texto. Después, revisa tus respuestas.

	Camila:	¡Mira, Natalia, un almacén nuevo! ¿Por qué no entramos? Allí podemos comprar el regalo de cumpleaños para Rubén.
	Natalia:	Está bien, vamos. Pero yo no sé qué comprar. ¿Tienes alguna idea?
	Camila:	No sé... ¿qué tal un suéter y una gorra de lana?
ni... *not even*	Natalia:	No, a Rubén no le gustan los suéteres; prefiere las camisetas negras. Además él nunca lleva gorras. Dice que dan mucho calor. ¿Sabes que ni siquiera° en invierno lleva calcetines?
	Camila:	Es verdad, él adora sus sandalias. ¡Ya sé! Podemos comprarle una camisa de algodón y una corbata.
	Natalia:	¡Camila, por favor! No me puedo imaginar a Rubén con corbata. Él siempre lleva camisetas y dice que detesta las corbatas porque no tienen ninguna función práctica.
	Camila:	Esto es difícil. Vamos a ver... Necesitamos algo práctico, algo que corresponda a la personalidad de Rubén... ¡Ya! ¡Tengo la solución!
A... *Let's see*	Natalia:	A ver°, ¿qué?
¿Qué... *What do you think?*	Camila:	Pues, ¡unas gafas de sol! ¿Qué te parece?°
	Natalia:	Es una excelente idea. Rubén perdió sus gafas favoritas en la playa la semana pasada.
	Camila:	Sí, vamos al departamento de ropa para caballeros.
	(Van hasta la sección "Caballeros".)	
	Dependiente:	Buenos días. ¿En qué puedo servirles?
	Camila:	Buenos días. Necesitamos unas gafas de sol de buena calidad.
luck	Dependiente:	Tienen suerte°. Tenemos una gran selección y a muy buen precio.
display case	*(Van hasta un mostrador° lleno de gafas.)*	
	Natalia:	Mira, Camila. Esas gafas son muy similares a las de Rubén.
en... *on sale*		(Al dependiente.) Señor, ¿están en oferta° esas gafas?
	Dependiente:	Sí. (Saca las gafas del mostrador.) Estas gafas están hechas de plástico reciclado y el precio es excelente. ¡Ah!, y además traen esta camiseta de regalo.
	Camila:	A ver, ¿y qué dice la camiseta?
	Dependiente:	"Plasti–gafas: reciclamos para ver mejor el futuro".
	Camila y Natalia:	¡Es el regalo perfecto! ¿Dónde pagamos?

2. The preterit of irregular verbs: Expressing actions in the past

In **Capítulo 7**, you learned the irregular preterit forms of the verb **hacer**. The following verbs also have one consistent preterit stem and the same endings as **hacer**.

estar estuv-	tener tuv-	poder pud-	poner pus-	saber sup-	venir vin-	querer quis-	traer traj-	decir dij-
estuve	tuve	pude	puse	supe	vine	quise	traje	dije
estuviste	tuviste	pudiste	pusiste	supiste	viniste	quisiste	trajiste	dijiste
estuvo	tuvo	pudo	puso	supo	vino	quiso	trajo	dijo
estuvimos	tuvimos	pudimos	pusimos	supimos	vinimos	quisimos	trajimos	dijimos
estuvisteis	tuvisteis	pudisteis	pusisteis	supisteis	vinisteis	quisisteis	trajisteis	dijisteis
estuvieron	tuvieron	pudieron	pusieron	supieron	vinieron	quisieron	trajeron	dijeron

- Notice the difference in the **ellos, ellas, ustedes** endings (**-ieron** and **-eron**) between the two groups of verbs above. Verbs whose stems end in **j** add **-eron** instead of **-ieron**.

- Observe the use of the irregular preterit forms in the sample sentences.
  No **tuve** que trabajar anoche.   I **did**n't **have** to work last night.
  Algunos amigos **vinieron** a visitarme.   Some friends **came** to visit me.
  Rubén **trajo** su guitarra.   Rubén **brought** his guitar.

- The verbs **saber, querer,** and **poder** convey a slightly different meaning in the preterit than in the present.

saber	**Supe** hacerlo.	I **found out/figured out** how to do it.
querer	**Quise** hablar con ella.	I **tried** to speak with her.
no querer	Ella **no quiso** hablar conmigo.	She **refused** to speak with me.
poder	**Pude** terminar el proyecto.	I **succeeded** (after much effort) in finishing the project.
no poder	**No pude** encontrar al profesor.	I **failed** (after trying) to find the professor.

Así se forma

8-14 ¿Qué hicieron el último fin de semana?

Paso 1. Indica qué oraciones de la columna **"El fin de semana yo..."** son ciertas para ti. Añade una oración original al final.

El fin de semana yo...	El fin de semana mi compañero/a...
☐ hice ejercicio.	☐ hizo ejercicio.
☐ tuve que estudiar mucho.	☐ tuvo que estudiar mucho.
☐ estuve en el centro comercial.	☐ estuvo en el centro comercial.
☐ traje comida a mi cuarto/ apartamento.	☐ trajo comida a su cuarto/ apartamento.
☐ fui al cine.	☐ fue al cine.
☐ dormí mucho.	☐ durmió mucho.
☐ me divertí en una fiesta.	☐ se divirtió en una fiesta.
☐ dije una mentira (*lie*).	☐ dijo una mentira.
☐ _____	☐ _____

Paso 2. Ahora, comparte tus respuestas con un/a compañero/a y anota sus respuestas en la columna **"Ayer mi compañero/a..."**. Túrnense.

Modelo: Estudiante A: **El fin de semana hice ejercicio.**
Estudiante B: **Pues yo no, este fin de semana no hice ejercicio.**

8-15 **La fiesta de cumpleaños.** Este fin de semana fue el cumpleaños de Carmen y todos fueron a su fiesta.

Paso 1. Escucha las siguientes descripciones y escribe el número correspondiente debajo del dibujo que describe la actividad.

Actividad número ___.

Actividad número ___.

Actividad número ___.

Actividad número ___.

Actividad número ___.

Actividad número ___.

 Paso 2. Ahora, en parejas, organicen las actividades en orden cronológico y escriban una descripción de cada actividad. Pueden inventar más detalles. Si no recuerdan (*remember*) las palabras exactas que oyeron, usen su creatividad.

 8-16 **Excusas.** Tu compañero/a y tú iban a (*were going to*) cenar juntos ayer, pero ¡los dos lo olvidaron (*forgot*)! Siguiendo el modelo, inventen excusas para explicar su ausencia y pregunten a su compañero/a sobre las suyas. Túrnense.

EXPRESIONES ÚTILES

¿De verdad?
Ah, ¿sí?   } ● *Oh, really?*
¡No me digas!

Modelo: Estudiante A: **Lo siento, Pete, pero ayer tuve un laboratorio de química.**
Estudiante B: **¿De verdad? ¿A qué hora fue? ¿Dónde?...**

Estudiante A:
1. no poder salir del cuarto/ apartamento
2. tener que ayudar a un/a amigo/a
3. hacer una sustitución en el trabajo
4. ...

Estudiante B:
1. no saber llegar al cine
2. querer llamar por teléfono y no poder
3. estar enfermo/a
4. ...

8-17 **Mi aventura.**

 Paso 1. Escribe un párrafo (cinco o seis oraciones) describiendo una aventura (real o imaginaria). ¿Adónde fuiste? ¿Cuánto tiempo estuviste allí? ¿Tuviste alguna experiencia interesante? ¿Qué hiciste? ¿Hay algo que quisiste hacer pero no pudiste?

 Paso 2. En grupos de cuatro, cada estudiante lee su aventura a los otros, y éstos hacen preguntas sobre los detalles —si tu aventura es imaginaria, ¡invéntalos! El resto del grupo intenta adivinar si las aventuras de sus compañeros/as son reales o imaginarias.

Cultura: La ropa tradicional

Antes de leer

¿Se lleva ropa tradicional hoy en algunas regiones de tu país?
¿Dónde? ¿Puedes describir un ejemplo?

La ropa tradicional de España y de Hispanoamérica es muy variada. En las ciudades, sólo se usa la ropa tradicional en los días de fiesta nacional. En los desfiles[1] cívicos, los niños, jóvenes y adultos se visten con la ropa típica de las diversas regiones de su país y bailan música tradicional. Las compañías nacionales de danza también usan ropa típica. Todo el mundo conoce los trajes típicos del sur de España, gracias a los bailarines de flamenco.

Sin embargo, los indígenas de las zonas rurales de muchos países, por ejemplo, Bolivia, Ecuador, Guatemala y México, usan ropa típica todos los días. En la península de Yucatán en México, las mujeres usan el **huipil**, un vestido blanco (o blusa) de origen maya con un bordado[2] de flores de colores vivos[3]. Se distingue la región donde vive la mujer por el diseño del huipil.

[1]*parades*   [2]*embroidery*   [3]*bright*

La pollera panameña

Las **polleras** de las panameñas son verdaderos tesoros: estas prendas están decoradas con finos encajes[4] y bordadas con hilos[5] de oro. En las regiones costeras, sobre todo en el Caribe, es común ver hombres con **guayaberas**: camisas de telas livianas[6] y bordadas en colores claros que son perfectas para el clima caliente de la zona.

[4]*lace*   [5]*threads*   [6]**telas...** *light fabrics*

Una guayabera

En el pueblo de Otavalo, en la región andina de Ecuador, las mujeres llevan una falda negra con bordados de colores, una blusa blanca bordada de encajes, muchos collares y pulseras de cuentas[7] rojas y doradas[8] y un turbante en la cabeza. Generalmente, los hombres de esta región llevan un poncho de lana sobre una camisa y pantalones blancos con alpargatas[9] blancas y un sombrero negro.

[7]*beads*   [8]*golden*   [9]*rope-soled sandals*

Después de leer

Empareja (*Match*) estos artículos de ropa con las regiones donde se usan:

a. los huipiles   __ Panamá
b. la pollera   __ el Caribe
c. el poncho de lana   __ Ecuador
d. la guayabera   __ Yucatán, México

¿Cuál te gusta más?

Así se forma

¿Quién te regaló ese suéter tan bonito?

3. Indirect-object pronouns: Indicating to whom or for whom something is done

An indirect object identifies the person **to whom** or **for whom** something is done. Thus, this person receives the action of the verb indirectly.

To whom?   *I gave the ring **to her**./I gave **her** the ring.*
For whom?   *I bought a necklace **for her**./I bought **her** a necklace.*

In contrast, remember that the direct object indicates **who** or **what** directly receives the action of the verb.

Who(m)?   *I saw **her** yesterday.*   What?   *Did you buy **the ring**?*

Indirect objects are always preceded by **a**.

Dimos <u>una sorpresa</u> **a Juan**.
     (OD)   (OI)

HINT

Review the direct object pronouns in **Capítulo 6**, pages 208–209. Remember to ask the questions *Who(m)?* or *What?* to identify the direct object.

Pronombres de objeto indirecto (OI)

You already know the indirect-object pronouns: they are the forms used with the verb **gustar** to indicate *to whom* something is pleasing.

A Carlos **le** gustó mucho el regalo.   *Carlos liked the gift very much.*
    (OI)   (S)

me	me (to/for me)	José **me** dio un reloj.
te	you	¿**Te** dio un anillo?
le	you (formal)	Él quiere dar**le** un regalo a usted.
	him	Yo quiero dar**le** un regalo a él.
	her	Quiero dar**le** un regalo a ella también.
nos	us	Nuestros amigos **nos** compraron chocolates.
os	you	¿**Os** trajeron algo?
les	you/them	¿Ellos **les** mandaron tarjetas postales **a ustedes**?

- **Position.** The indirect-object pronoun, like the direct object pronoun and reflexive pronoun, is placed immediately before a conjugated verb. However, it may also be attached to the infinitive and to the present participle.

  Me dijeron que esa tienda es muy buena. ¿Quieres entrar?
  ¿Vas a comprar**me** esa cartera? / ¿**Me** vas a comprar esa cartera?
  Estoy preguntándo**le** el precio. / **Le** estoy preguntando el precio.

- **Redundancy**. Even though it may sound redundant, third-person indirect-object pronouns (**le/ les**) are generally used *in conjunction with* the indirect-object noun.

Les escribí **a mis primos.**	*I wrote **to my cousins**.*
También **le** escribí **a Mónica.**	*I wrote **to Monica**, too.*

- **Le** and **les** are often clarified with the preposition **a** + *pronoun*.

Le escribí **a ella** anoche.	*I wrote **to her** last night.*

It is also common to use the forms **a mí, a ti, a usted, a él, a ella, a nosotros/as, a vosotros/as, a ustedes, a ellos, a ellas** with the indirect-object pronoun for emphasis.

Sancho **me** mandó el paquete **a mí**.	*Sancho sent the package **to me**. (not to someone else)*

Dar and other verbs that frequently require indirect-object pronouns

The verb **dar** (*to give*) is almost always used with indirect objects. Review its present tense conjugation and study the preterit.

dar *to give*	
Presente	**Pretérito**
doy	di[4]
das	diste
da	dio
damos	dimos
dais	disteis
dan	dieron

- Some verbs that frequently have indirect objects are **contestar**, **decir**, **enviar**, **escribir**, **mandar**, and **pedir**, because one generally tells, sends, asks for something (OD) *to someone* (OI).

Here are some new verbs that frequently have indirect objects:

contar (ue)	*to tell, narrate (a story or incident)*	**preguntar**	*to ask*
		prestar	*to lend*
devolver (ue)	*to return (something)*	**regalar**	*to give (as a gift)*
explicar	*to explain*		
mostrar (ue)	*to show*		

---

[4]Note that in the preterit **dar** uses -**er**/-**ir** endings but with no written accent.

8-18 **¿Qué hice o qué voy a hacer?** Relaciona las declaraciones de la columna A con las actividades correspondientes de la columna B. Lee las oraciones relacionadas.

A

f **1.** Mis abuelos siempre quieren saber lo que estoy haciendo en la universidad.

g **2.** Es el cumpleaños de mi madre.

e **3.** Fui de compras ayer y compré unos pantalones, una chaqueta y zapatos.

a **4.** Mi amiga Natalia no tiene transporte y necesita ir al centro.

c **5.** Quiero ir al restaurante Cuba-Cuba esta noche. Tú sabes dónde está, ¿verdad?

d **6.** Mi hermana quiso saber lo que pasó anoche.

i **7.** ¿No entendiste los pronombres?

b **8.** Camila tiene problemas con las matemáticas.

h **9.** Rubén y Oscar van a tocar en un concierto este fin de semana.

B

a. Voy a prestarle mi carro.

b. Le di una de mis calculadoras.

c. Voy a pedirte la dirección.

d. Le conté toda la historia (*story*).

e. Les mostré las cosas nuevas a mis amigas.

f. Voy a escribirles una carta.

g. Le mandé un regalo. *I sent her a gift*

h. Voy a ir para darles apoyo (*support*).

i. Te voy a explicar las ideas más importantes.

Así se forma

8-19 **Sondeo: Las relaciones.** Casi todos tenemos buenas relaciones con nuestros padres, hermanos, nuestros mejores amigos/as... pero ¿hasta qué punto?

Paso 1. Marca las respuestas a las siguientes preguntas.

	padre	madre	hermanos /as	mejor amigo/a	pareja	otros
¿A quién...						
...le pides consejo?						
...le cuentas todo?						
...le cuentas secretos?						
...le pides dinero?						
...le dices tus notas?						
...le prestas tus apuntes de clase?						
...le prestas libros, CDs, etc.?						
¿Quién...						
...te pide consejo?						
...te cuenta todo?						
...te cuenta secretos?						
...te pide dinero?						
...te dice sus notas?						
...te presta sus apuntes de clase?						
...te presta libros, CDs, etc.?						

Paso 2. Ahora, en grupos, hablen sobre sus respuestas y comenten las posibles diferencias personales.

Modelo: **Yo les pido consejo a mi madre y a mi padre porque... pero no les pido consejo a mis hermanos porque...**

NOTA CULTURAL

Friendship expectations

In Hispanic countries, good camaraderie and helping out your fellow students is an important value. Class notes are often shared, homework done in study groups, exams and grades are discussed, etc. In fact, reluctance to share one's work may be considered arrogant and selfish.

8-20 **El regalo de cumpleaños de Linda.** Completen las oraciones. Usen el pronombre **lo** (directo) o **le** (indirecto) según la situación.

Manuel _____ dio un regalo a Linda para su cumpleaños. _____ compró un suéter muy bonito. Me dijo que _____ compró en una tienda muy elegante. Linda _____ abrió inmediatamente y _____ dio las gracias a Manuel con una gran sonrisa (*smile*). ¡Es evidente que el suéter _____ gustó mucho porque _____ lleva frecuentemente.

8-21 **¿Y para tu cumpleaños?**

Paso 1. Dile a un/a compañero/a lo que hicieron tu familia y tus amigos/as para ti en tu mejor cumpleaños. Tienes algunas ideas en el cuadro de abajo.

Modelo: **Mi mejor amigo/a me...**

organizar una fiesta	llamar por teléfono	comprar/ hacer un pastel
escribir una carta	enviar/ dar una tarjeta	hacer un regalo
cocinar algo especial	cantar *Cumpleaños Feliz*	invitar a un restaurante

Paso 2. ¿Cuál fue tu mejor (*best*) regalo de cumpleaños? ¿Y el peor (*worst*)? Cuéntaselo a tu compañero/a y explica por qué uno te gustó y el otro no.

NOTA CULTURAL

Los cumpleaños. Many Hispanic countries have special birthday customs. In Mexico, for instance, family and friends of the birthday person will sing **"Las mañanitas."** In Spain, people pull the birthday persons' ears the same number of times as the number of years old they have become. People usually end up with very red earlobes!

...diecinueve y veinte. ¡Feliz cumpleaños!

SITUACIONES

Tu novio/a te da un regalo. Lo abres y descubres que es... ¡una camisa/ blusa rosada que detestas (*hate*)! ¿Qué le dices?
Mi amor,...

EXPRESIONES ÚTILES

Sí que (me gusta/ es bonito...), pero...
I do like it/It really is pretty, but . . .
La verdad es que...
The truth is . .

Investig@ en INTERNET

Quieres hacer regalos originales a tu familia y amigos/as. ¿Por qué no compras productos y artesanía de Perú, Bolivia o Ecuador? Busca los regalos en el Internet y escribe qué vas a comprar para cada persona. (¡Puedes comprar algo para ti también!)
www.artourperu.com
www.boliviamall.com
www.thebestofecuador.com/crafts.htm
www.camari.org

Así se forma

Speech bubbles (from illustration):
¿Quién nos mandó las flores?
¡Manuel me las mandó!
¿Pepe? ¿Octavio? ¿Rubén?

4. Direct- and indirect-object pronouns combined

- When both the indirect and direct object are replaced with pronouns, the indirect-object pronoun is always placed first: OI + OD.

  La profesora **me lo** prestó.   The professor lent **it**
        (OI)(OD)   **to me.**

- Placement rules stay the same: before conjugated verbs and attached to infinitives and the **–ndo** form. In a negative statement, **no** precedes both objects.

  ¿Pedro no **te lo** explicó?   *Didn't Pedro explain **it to you**?*

  No, Carlos va a explicár**melo**⁵ *o*   *No, Carlos is going to explain **it to me.***
  Carlos **me lo** va a explicar.

- When both the indirect- and direct object pronouns refer to the third person and they are used together, the indirect-object pronoun **le** or **les** changes to **se**.

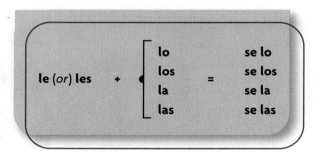

le (*or*) les	+	lo los la las	=	se lo se los se la se las

Se lo expliqué a ellas.   *I explained **it to them.***

Estoy explicándo**selo**. *o*   *I am explaining **it to him/her/you.***
Se lo estoy explicando.

—¿**Le** diste **la foto** a Linda?   —*Did you give the photo to Linda?*
—Sí, **se la** di.   —*Yes, I gave **it to her.***

---

⁵Note that when two pronouns are added to the infinitive or present participle, a written accent is added to preserve the original stress pattern: **Va a mostrármelo. Está mostrándoselo.**

8-22 **¡Nos encantan los regalos!** Octavio fue a Ecuador y les trajo varios regalos a sus amigas. Observa los dibujos para ver qué regalos trajo y para quién.

Natalia / la camiseta

Pepita / el póster

Carmen e Inés / las toallas para la playa

Camila y Linda / los collares y los pendientes

 Paso 1. Éstas son las reacciones de las chicas. Identifica el dibujo correspondiente y responde a estas preguntas.

		¿Quién lo dice?	¿De qué regalo habla/n?
_____	**a.** ¡Impresionante! Octavio me lo regaló.	_____	_____
_____	**b.** ¡Nos encantan! Octavio nos las regaló.	_____	_____
_____	**c.** ¡Qué bonitos son! Octavio nos los regaló.	_____	_____
_____	**d.** ¡Me encanta! Octavio me la regaló.	_____	_____

Paso 2. En parejas, una persona explica qué regalo le dio Octavio a una de sus amigas. El/La compañero/a tiene que confirmar o negar la información sustituyendo los objetos por pronombres.

Modelo: Estudiante A: **Octavio le dio la camiseta a Natalia.**

Estudiante B: **Sí, *se la* dio a Natalia.** *o* **No, se la dio a...**

Así se forma

8-23 ¿Son generosos o no?

Paso 1. Pregúntale a tu compañero/a si te puede prestar, explicar, dar y mostrar las cosas siguientes. Anota si él/ella responde "sí" o "no". Túrnense.

Modelo: Estudiante A: Prestarme... un lápiz
¿Puedes prestarme un lápiz? / ¿Me puedes prestar un lápiz?

Estudiante B: **Sí, puedo prestártelo. / Sí, te lo puedo prestar.
No, prefiero no prestártelo. / No, no te lo puedo prestar.**

	Estudiante A			Estudiante B		
Prestarme...	...tu tarjeta de crédito	☐ sí	☐ no	...tu paraguas	☐ sí	☐ no
	...tu bicicleta	☐ sí	☐ no	...tu coche	☐ sí	☐ no
Explicarme...	...la tarea	☐ sí	☐ no	...la gramática	☐ sí	☐ no
	...los verbos irregulares	☐ sí	☐ no	...las palabras que no entiendo	☐ sí	☐ no
Darme...	...ese reloj/ ese anillo	☐ sí	☐ no	...cien dólares	☐ sí	☐ no
	...cincuenta centavos	☐ sí	☐ no	...una pluma	☐ sí	☐ no
Mostrarme...	...las fotos en tu cartera	☐ sí	☐ no	...tu reloj	☐ sí	☐ no
	...tu ombligo (belly button)	☐ sí	☐ no	...tu examen	☐ sí	☐ no

Paso 2. Basado en sus respuestas, decide si tu compañero/a es generoso/a.

☐ Sí, mi compañero/a es generoso/a.   ☐ No, mi compañero/a no es generoso/a.

8-24 **¿Quién te lo dio?** Cada estudiante le da a un/a compañero/a de clase un artículo (reloj, tarjeta de crédito, gorra, pluma, etc.). Los estudiantes caminan por la clase, haciéndoles preguntas a cinco o seis compañeros diferentes.

Modelo: Estudiante A: **Melvin, ¿quién te dio ese reloj?**
Estudiante B: **Carla me lo dio. Y ¿quién te dio esas plumas?**
Estudiante A: **Cliff me las dio.**

¡No te olvides de devolverle el artículo a tu compañero/a de clase!

8-25 **El/La amigo/a invisible.** Van a hacer un/a "amigo/a invisible"[6] en su clase. Lean las instrucciones con atención.

Paso 1.

a. Escribe tu nombre en un pedazo de papel y dáselo al profesor.
b. Ahora, toma un papelito y mira el nombre.
c. Piensa en un regalo perfecto para esta persona y escríbelo en la parte de atrás (*back*) del papel. Dale el papel al profesor otra vez.
d. El profesor va a leer los nombres y distribuir los "regalos".

Paso 2. Cada estudiante cuenta a la clase qué le regalaron, si el regalo le gusta o no, y por qué. Después pregunta quién le hizo este regalo. El estudiante responsable responde y explica sus razones.

Modelo: Estudiante A: **Me regalaron un/a..., (no) me gusta porque...**
Profesor (a la clase): ¿Quién se lo regaló?
Estudiante B: **Yo se lo regalé porque...**

---

[6]This is the Spanish version of "Secret Santa."

Así se pronuncia

Accents and stress

You have probably noticed that some words have written accent marks (**acentos**) and that they indicate where to stress the word when we pronounce it. Even though not every word has a stress mark, knowing the Spanish stress rules will allow you to predict where the oral stress is in every word, whether it has a written stress mark or not.

- Words with **predictable stress patterns** (below) **do not need** a written accent mark.
  - → Words ending in a vowel, -n, or -s are stressed on the next-to-last syllable:

    mapa   **lu**nes   **co**sas

  - → Words ending in a consonant, except -n or -s, are stressed on the last syllable:

    a**zul**   profe**sor**   co**mer**

A. Applying the principles above, find and underline the syllable that should be stressed in the following words. Then, pronounce them, stressing the correct syllable. Listen for confirmation.

1. profesor
2. dentista
3. presidente
4. Marta
5. tormenta
6. españo
7. ciudad
8. Carmen
9. flores

- Words with a **different stress pattern need** an accent mark. (Compare with the two cases above—these are the opposite!)
  - → Words ending in a consonant, except -n or -s, with the oral stress on the next-to-last syllable:

    lápiz   **fá**cil

  - → Words ending in a vowel, -n, or -s with stress on the last syllable:

    alma**cén**   ca**fé**   in**glés**

  - → Words with stress in the third- (or fourth-) to-last syllable:

    lápices   **miér**coles   **pá**jaro

B. Look at the words below; they all have written stress marks. Explain why as in the model.

Modelo: París: **It needs an accent mark because it is stressed on the last syllable and the word ends in -s.**

1. Perú
2. difícil
3. exámenes
4. dinámico
5. ratón
6. Inés
7. líder
8. cómico

C. All of the following words need written accent marks. Listen to them and write the accent mark where needed.

1. mecanico
2. cortes
3. bebe
4. debil
5. poster
6. rapido
7. pulmon
8. politica
9. arbol

- When a strong vowel (**a, e, o**) and weak vowel (**i, u**) combine, the predictable stress pattern is that the oral stress is on the strong vowel.

  nieta   baile   feo

  Therefore, if we have such a combination and the oral stress is on the weak vowel, we need an **accent mark** (regardless of what syllable it is).

  día   tío   biología

D. Listen to the following words and underline the vowel where you hear the oral stress. Then, decide whether the words need an accent mark or not.

1. mia   2. viaje   3. lio   4. dios   5. pausa   6. baúl

Other important things:

- All interrogative and exclamatory words need a stress mark.

  ¿Cuándo vienes?   ¿Por qué no?   ¡Qué sorpresa!

- Stress marks are also used to differentiate between words that have the same spelling:

  tú → *you*   **tu** → *your*
  él → *he*   **el** → *the (m.)*
  sí → *yes*   **si** → *if*

Dicho y hecho

¡A ESCUCHAR!

Desfile de modas. Temporada otoño–invierno. Escucha la descripción del desfile de modas. Presta atención a los tres tipos de ropa que se presentan y a los colores que predominan. Luego, contesta las tres primeras preguntas.

1. ¿Qué tipo de ropa presentan primero? ☐ ropa para la mujer profesional
   ☐ ropa informal   ☐ ropa para reuniones de cóctel

2. ¿Qué tipo de colores son populares en la ropa de Ana Sastre? Hay más de una opción.   ☐ blanco, negro y gris   ☐ rojo, amarillo y azul   ☐ verde pistacho

3. ¿Llevan las modelos muchas joyas?   ☐ sí   ☐ no

Escucha otra vez. Apunta el nombre de la prenda o accesorio que combine bien con la ropa o los accesorios indicados.

4. Los pantalones de cuero negro combinan con _____.
5. Las chaquetas de lana de cachemir combinan con _____.
6. Los zapatos de la colección Sastre combinan con _____.
7. Los vestidos cortos de seda (*silk*) combinan con _____.

CONVERSANDO

El equipaje perdido (*Lost luggage*). Imaginen que están en el aeropuerto Mariscal Sucre en Quito, Ecuador. Los empleados de la línea aérea les dicen que el equipaje del grupo no llegó, y que probablemente ¡está perdido! Ustedes van a estar en Ecuador por una semana, visitando las zonas montañosas y la costa. Ahora necesitan ir de compras para poder continuar su viaje (*trip*). La línea aérea es muy generosa y les da $175 a cada uno/a. (El dólar es la moneda de Ecuador.)

Vayan de compras a las siguientes tiendas. Cada tienda tiene dos dependientes/dependientas (estudiantes de la clase).

- Mi Comisariato (venden productos de higiene personal)
- Zapatería Cotopaxi
- Beatriz (ropa para mujeres)
- El Ecuatoriano (ropa para hombres)
- La Esmeralda (tienda unisex)

Hagan una lista de sus compras y lo que pagan. No deben gastar más de $175. ¡Es buena idea regatear (*bargain*)! Al final, compartan su lista con un/a compañero/a de clase. ¿Quién tuvo más éxito (*success*) en sus compras?

DE MI ESCRITORIO

Mi ropero. Escribe una descripción de tu ropa. Incluye:

- cuál es tu ropa favorita y cómo expresa tu personalidad
- dónde compras generalmente tu ropa
- tus accesorios favoritos y por qué te gustan
- la ropa o los accesorios que alguien te regaló

El oro de los lambayeque

Antes de leer

¿Conoces una cultura que enterraba a sus líderes importantes con objetos para "la otra vida"?

La cultura lambayeque se desarrolló[1] en la costa norte de Perú entre los años 900 y 1100–1200 d. c. Se cree[2] que los lambayeque convivieron[3] con los chimús e incas. Hacia los años 1940[4] se encontraron grandes entierros[5] de esta cultura en Batán Grande, su capital.

Los lambayeque creían en otra vida después de la muerte[6]. Por eso, cuando enterraban a los caciques[7] (la máxima autoridad de esa época), incluían con ellos todas sus posesiones, para llevarlas a la otra vida. En los entierros de los caciques se encontraron grandes piezas[8]

de oro y ornamentos que cubrían[9] al muerto. Las piezas en las fotos son de esos entierros.

La máscara funeraria se utilizaba en ritos ceremoniales y también cubría la cara del muerto en los entierros. Los collares hechos de oro y de crisocola (una turquesa de Perú) del monarca lo acompañaban también en su entierro. El *tumi* —un cuchillo ceremonial de oro y crisocola— era utilizado en ritos ceremoniales para cortar o para hacer sacrificios rituales.

[1]*se... developed* [2]**Se...** *It is believed* [3]*coexisted* [4]**Hacia...** *around the 1940s* [5]*burial sites*
[6]*death* [7]*chiefs* [8]*pieces* [9]*covered*

El tumi o cuchillo ceremonial de oro y crisocola fue utilizado en ritos ceremoniales. Los tunis de cobre[10] con filo[11] se utilizaron para cortar o para hacer sacrificios rituales.
Créditos: Museo Oro del Perú, Fundación Miguel Mujica Gallo. Lima, Perú.

[10]*copper* [11]**con...** *sharp edge*

Los collares de oro y crisocola (turquesa peruana) del monarca lo acompañaban también en su entierro.
Créditos: Museo Oro del Perú, Fundación Miguel Mujica Gallo. LIma, Perú.

La máscara funeraria fue utilizada en ritos ceremoniales y también cubría la cara del muerto en los entierros.
Créditos: Museo Oro del Perú, Fundación Miguel Mujica Gallo. Lima, Perú.

Después de leer

1. ¿Dónde se encuentran las ruinas de la ciudad precolombina Batán Grande?

2. ¿Qué objetos se encuentran en los entierros de los caciques?

3. ¿Tienes algún objeto de oro muy valioso? ¿Qué es?

Repaso de vocabulario activo

De compras

Adjetivos

barato/a   *cheap, inexpensive*
caro/a   *expensive*
corto/a   *short*
largo/a   *long*
limpio/a   *clean*
sucio/a   *dirty*

Sustantivos

La ropa   *Clothes, Clothing*

el abrigo   *coat*
la blusa   *blouse*
   de manga corta/ larga
      short/long sleeve
las botas   *boots*
la bufanda   *scarf*
los calcetines   *socks*
la camisa   *shirt*
la camiseta   *T-shirt*
la chaqueta   *jacket*
el cinturón   *belt*
la corbata   *tie*
la falda   *skirt*
la gorra   *cap*
los guantes   *gloves*
el impermeable   *raincoat*
los jeans/ los vaqueros   *jeans*
las medias   *stockings, hose*
los pantalones   *pants*
los pantalones cortos   *shorts*
la ropa interior   *underwear*
las sandalias   *sandals*
el sombrero   *hat*
el suéter   *sweater*

el traje   *suit*
el traje de baño   *bathing suit*
el vestido   *dress*
los zapatos   *shoes*
los zapatos de tenis   *tennis shoes*
el algodón   *cotton*
el cuero   *leather*
la lana   *wool*
la seda   *silk*

Las joyas   *Jewelry*

de oro/ plata   *gold/silver*
el anillo   *ring*
los aretes/ los pendientes
      earrings
la cadena   *chain*
el collar   *necklace*
la pulsera   *bracelet*
el reloj   *watch*

Otras palabras útiles

la billetera/ la cartera   *wallet*
el bolso/ la bolsa   *purse, bag*
el centro comercial   *shopping mall*
la cosa   *thing*
las gafas/ los lentes   (de sol)
      glasses/sunglasses
los/ las lentes de contacto
      contact lenses
la moda   *fashion*
el paraguas   *umbrella*
el precio   *price*
las rebajas   *sales*
el regalo   *gift*
el ropero/ el clóset   *closet*
la talla   *size*

Verbos

contar (ue)   *tell*
dar   *give*
devolver (ue)   *return (something)*
explicar   *explain*
llevar   *wear, carry, take*
mirar   *look at*
mostrar (ue)   *show*
preguntar   *ask*
prestar   *lend*
regalar   *give (a gift)*

Autoprueba y repaso

I. Possessive adjectives and pronouns.

A. Tú y tus amigos/as tienen su ropa en la residencia estudiantil. Indique de quién es la ropa.

Modelo: yo: calcetines, impermeable, chaqueta
Los calcetines son míos.
El impermeable es mío.
La chaqueta es mía.

1. yo: abrigo, botas, guantes, gorra
2. nosotros: ropa interior, jeans, corbatas
3. tú: blusa, vestido, camiseta, medias
4 Ana y Elena: ropa de verano, faldas, trajes de baño

B. Indica con quienes van las personas a la fiesta. Sigue el modelo.

Modelo: yo / un amigo
Voy con un amigo mío.

1. mi primo / unos amigos
2. Viviana / un amigo
3. mi hermana y yo / un amigo
4. yo / unos amigos

II. The preterit of irregular verbs. Di quién hizo las siguientes cosas.

Modelo: hacer la torta para la fiesta (yo)
Hice la torta para la fiesta.

1. traer las decoraciones (Natalia y Linda)
2. poner las flores en la mesa (nosotros)
3. querer venir pero no poder (Javier)
4. venir (casi todos los estudiantes)
5. estar en la fiesta por cuatro horas (tú)
6. tener que salir temprano (yo)

III. Indirect-object pronouns. ¿Qué hizo el generoso tío Pedro?

Modelo: a mí / comprar / una chaqueta nueva
Me compró una chaqueta nueva.

1. a mí / dar / su reloj
2. a mi hermana / regalar / un bolso de cuero
3. a mis hermanos / comprar / una computadora nueva
4. a nosotros / mandar / tarjetas postales del Perú
5. a ti / prestar / su cámara

IV. Direct- and indirect-object pronouns combined. Forma oraciones en el pasado usando el verbo **regalar** y pronombres de objeto directo e indirecto.

Modelo: yo / unas gafas de sol / a Luisa
Se las regalé.

1. nosotros / un televisor pequeño / a los abuelos
2. mi hermano / una mochila nueva / a su prima
3. mis hermanas / joyas / a mamá
4. yo / una chaqueta de cuero / a mi hermano
5. mi madre / un perrito / a nosotras

V. *Repaso general.* Contesta con oraciones completas.

1. ¿Qué ropa llevan las mujeres a un restaurante elegante? ¿Y los hombres?
2. ¿Qué ropa debes llevar a Alaska? ¿Y a la Florida?
3. ¿Fue usted de compras el fin de semana pasado? (¿Adónde?) (¿Qué compró?)
4. ¿Dónde estuviste anoche? ¿Y qué hiciste? (Menciona varias cosas.)
5. ¿Qué trajiste a clase hoy/ ayer/ anteayer?
6. ¿Le diste la tarea para hoy a la profesora/al profesor?

VI. *Cultura.*

1. Identifica los siguientes lugares: Quito, Cuzco, La Paz, Machu Picchu, el lago Titicaca, las Islas Galápagos.
2. Nombra y describe tres artículos de ropa tradicional usada en Latinoamérica.
3. Describe la cultura lambayeque.

Respuestas a *Autoprueba y repaso* se pueden encontrar en el **Apéndice 2.**

La salud

By the end of this chapter you will be able to:

- Talk about health and related ailments
- Identify parts of the body
- Use commands in formal situations
- Talk about and describe persons, places, and actions in the past
- Indicate how long an action has been going on, or how long ago it happened

Así se dice	Así se forma	Cultura	Dicho y hecho
• La salud • El cuerpo humano	1. **Ud./Uds.** commands 2. The imperfect 3. The preterit vs. the imperfect 4. **Hacer** in time constructions	• Colombia y Venezuela • Remedios caseros del mundo hispano • Artes literarias: Miguel Fernando Caro	• En la Facultad de Medicina • En la sala de emergencias • Cuando era niño/a...

ENTRANDO AL TEMA

1. ¿Conoces alguna expresión en inglés que use una parte del cuerpo? Por ejemplo: *Putting your foot in your mouth* o *Gut feeling*.

2. ¿Usas algún remedio casero (*home remedy*)? ¿Cuál?

Así se dice

La salud

el pulmón

tomar la temperatura

el corazón

el termómetro

2

el estómago

tomar la presión arterial/ el pulso

poner una inyección/ una vacuna

¿Te duele?

3

HORAS DE VISITA
10:00 A.M.-12:00 P.M.
4:00 P.M.-7:00 P.M.

sacar sangre/ hacer un análisis de sangre

la habitación

la infección

quedarse

Usted tiene una infección grave.

preocuparse (por)

estar de pie

enfermarse

sentarse

estar sentado/a

el hueso

1

examinar

la sala de espera

← Radiología

la recepción

hacer una cita

sacar una radiografía

lastimarse (el brazo)

estar embarazada

el consultorio de la médica

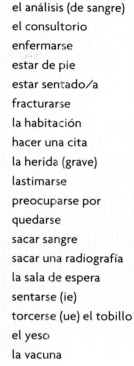

el análisis (de sangre)	a (blood) test
el consultorio	doctor's office
enfermarse	to get/become sick
estar de pie	to stand
estar sentado/a	to be seated
fracturarse	to break (a bone)
la habitación	room
hacer una cita	to make an appointment
la herida (grave)	(serious) wound
lastimarse	to hurt oneself
preocuparse por	to worry about
quedarse	to stay
sacar sangre	to draw blood
sacar una radiografía	to X-ray
la sala de espera	waiting room
sentarse (ie)	to sit down
torcerse (ue) el tobillo	to sprain one's ankle
el yeso	cast
la vacuna	vaccine

el hospital

Hospital San Rafael

(la sala de) emergencias

Emergencias

AMBULANCIA

los paramédicos

la ambulancia

una herida grave (en la cabeza)

el/la paciente

la venda

el yeso

fracturarse el brazo/ la pierna

las muletas

la silla de ruedas

torcerse el tobillo

Así se dice

9-1 Pobre Octavio.

Paso 1. Determina el orden cronológico de lo que le pasó a Octavio.

_4_ la médica/ ponerle un yeso

_2_ salir del hospital en una silla de ruedas

_10_ ir a la sala de emergencias

_1_ fracturarse la pierna esquiando

_7_ empezar a caminar con muletas

_5_ la médica/ examinarle la pierna

_9_ varias semanas más tarde, la médica/ quitarle el yeso

_6_ la médica/ sacarle una radiografía

_8_ empezar un programa de fisioterapia

_3_ la médica/ darle medicamentos para el dolor (pain)

Paso 2. Ahora, narra (narrate) lo que pasó en orden cronológico, cambiando los verbos al pretérito y usando conectores (**primero, luego, después, por fin**).

Modelo: Primero, Octavio se fracturó la pierna esquiando;...

El cuerpo humano

la cabeza

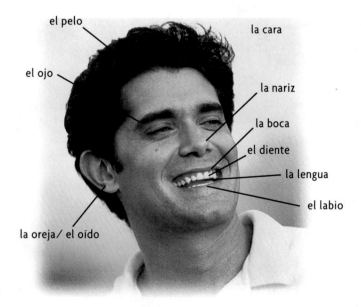

el pelo

la cara

el ojo

la nariz

la boca

el diente

la lengua

el labio

la oreja/ el oído

el cuerpo

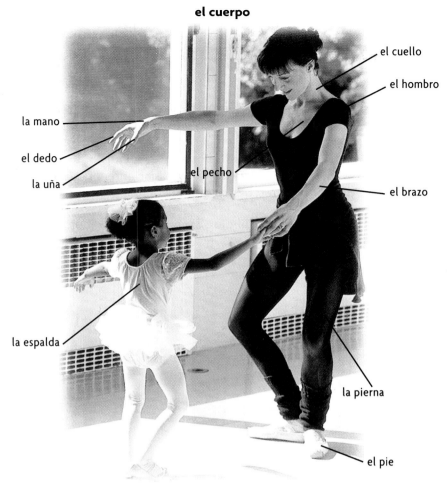

- el cuello
- el hombro
- la mano
- el dedo
- la uña
- el pecho
- el brazo
- la espalda
- la pierna
- el pie

9-2 ¿Qué partes del cuerpo?

Paso 1. En parejas, describe para tu compañero/a en qué actividades se usan las siguientes partes del cuerpo. Tu compañero/a va a intentar identificar la parte del cuerpo.

Modelo: cabeza
    La usamos para pensar, para peinarnos...

Cubre (*Cover*) con un papel o con la mano la lista de tu compañero/a.

Estudiante A:

1. los dedos
2. la boca
3. la nariz

Estudiante B:

1. los ojos
2. las piernas
3. el oído

Paso 2. Ahora, juntos (*together*) indiquen qué partes del cuerpo se usan para cada una de las siguientes actividades.

Modelo: esquiar **Para esquiar se usan los brazos, los hombros y las piernas.**

1. manejar
2. leer
3. tocar el piano
4. nadar
5. comer
6. besar

Así se dice

9-3 ¡Los extraterrestres (*aliens*)! Un grupo de extraterrestres de varias galaxias están visitando la ciudad y ¡tú viste a uno ayer!

 Paso 1. Inventa cómo es el extraterrestre que viste y dibújalo. Después, descríbeselo a un/a compañero/a, que lo va a dibujar, ¡sin mirar tu dibujo! Después, tú vas a dibujar al extraterrestre que tu compañero/a te describe.

 Paso 2. En parejas, comparen los dibujos. ¿Son similares el dibujo original y el dibujo del/de la compañero/a?

NOTA CULTURAL

The word "Hispanic" is often used in the U.S. to refer to race or ethnicity and is usually identified with such traits as having dark hair and eyes and an olive complexion. However, Hispanics have many different faces and ethnic makeups: Caucasian, African, Native American, and other origins. Most Latin American people are of mixed ethnicity, such as **mestizos** (European and Native American) and **mulatos** (European and African). The ethnic makeup of different regions varies. There are many unmixed Caucasians in Argentina, Chile, and Uruguay. There are also unmixed Native Americans in the Andes and parts of Central America, and a great range of mixed populations in the Caribbean region. Here are some statistics about Colombia and Venezuela.

Colombia: 58% mestizo, 20% Caucasian, 14% mulato, 4% African, 3% African and Native American, 1% Native American

Venezuela: 67% mestizo and mulato, 21 % Caucasian, 10 % African, 2% Native American

Cultura: Colombia y Venezuela

Antes de leer

1. ¿En qué país es posible visitar las playas del Pacífico y también las del mar Caribe?

2. ¿Con qué países tiene frontera Colombia?

3. ¿Cuál es la capital de Colombia? ¿Cuáles son dos ciudades importantes en la costa?

4. ¿Cuál es el río principal que pasa por Venezuela y Colombia?

5. ¿Cuál es la capital de Venezuela?

Cuando veas un lugar **en rojo**, vuelve al mapa y búscalo.

Esmeraldas

COLOMBIA

Los españoles llegaron a Colombia en 1500, buscando "El Dorado". Según esta leyenda, en esta región existía muchísimo oro. Durante la época colonial, Colombia era parte de la "Nueva Granada" con los territorios que hoy son Panamá, Ecuador y Venezuela. Pero la Nueva Granada se independizó de España en 1810, y el líder Simón Bolívar creó la Federación de la Gran Colombia. Después, Ecuador, Venezuela y Panamá se separaron de esta Federación.

Hoy, Colombia es el principal productor de esmeraldas del mundo y el primer productor de oro de Sudamérica. **Bogotá**, la capital de Colombia, está en un valle central. Tiene más de seis millones de habitantes y es una ciudad moderna, llena de rascacielos, tiendas de moda y grandes avenidas. Pero en esta ciudad también existen barrios[1] muy pobres que contrastan con el lujo[2] de muchas áreas.

---

[1]neighborhoods [2]luxury

El espíritu del pueblo colombiano se ve en su música, sus bailes y en sus diversiones populares. La cumbia y el vallenato son ritmos bailables de origen colombiano muy famosos en todo el mundo.

Bogotá

Colombia es el segundo productor de café del mundo, después de Brasil. Según el "diccionario cafetómano", ¿qué tipos de café son populares en Colombia? ¿Cuál es tu café favorito?

Breve diccionario cafetómano latinoamericano

- **AMERICANO (México, Miami):** café aguado, en taza grande.
- **CAFÉ (todos los países):** cualquier cosa, pida más información.
- **CAFÉ-CAFÉ (Chile):** café de grano, normalmente en taza chica.
- **CAFÉ COMÚN (Argentina):** café aguado, en taza grande.
- **CAFÉ CON LECHE (todos los países):** autoexplicativo, pero la proporción leche/café es variable.
- **CAFÉ DOBLE (Argentina):** café cargado, en taza grande.
- **CAPUCHINO (todos los países):** un tercio de café, un tercio de leche, un tercio de espuma de leche. En Chile lleva además crema batida.
- **CAPUCCINO (Argentina, Colombia):** capuchino.
- **CARIOCA (Brasil):** café aguado, en taza chica.
- **CORTADO (Chile, Argentina):** café cargado con un toque de leche.
- **CORTADITO (Miami):** ídem.
- **CUBANO (Miami):** café muy cargado, muy dulce y muy "tacaño": menos de la mitad de una taza chica.
- **CURTO (Brasil):** café cargado en taza chica.
- **EXPRESO (varios países):** café concentrado especial en taza chica.
- **ESPRESSO (Miami):** expreso.
- **EXPRESS (Chile):** expreso.
- **GRANIZADO (Colombia):** café helado, con hielo picado, en vaso.
- **GUAYOYO (Venezuela):** café negro suave, hecho en colador de tela.
- **MARRÓN (Venezuela):** café cargado con un toque de leche.
- **NEGRITO (Venezuela):** café sin leche en taza chica.
- **NEGRO (varios países):** café sin leche ni azúcar.
- **PERICO (Colombia):** café cargado con un toque de leche.
- **PINGADO (Brasil):** café con leche en taza grande.
- **TETERO (Venezuela):** leche caliente con un poco de café.
- **TINTO (Colombia):** café relativamente suave, en taza chica.

Investig@ en INTERNET

¿Sabes quién es Shakira? Ella es de **Barranquilla**, Colombia. Busca información sobre Shakira en el Internet y compártela con tus compañeros/as de clase.

VENEZUELA

En Venezuela, los españoles encontraron riquezas fabulosas de oro, plata y perlas. El nombre del país significa "Pequeña Venecia[3]". ¿Por qué? Porque en 1500, los españoles encontraron unos habitantes, los indios guajiros, que vivían en chozas[4] suspendidas sobre unas islas muy pequeñas en el **Lago Maracaibo**.

[3]*Venice* [4]*huts*

Caracas, la capital, está cerca de la costa y es una de las ciudades más cosmopolitas del continente. Los caraqueños son amantes del arte y tienen un admirable Museo de Bellas Artes y una magnífica Orquesta Sinfónica. Caracas también cuenta con uno de los servicios de metro más sofisticados del mundo.

Caracas

El "oro negro" o petróleo es la mayor riqueza del país. La explotación de los grandes depósitos petrolíferos en el Lago Maracaibo comenzó a principios del siglo XX. La industria petrolera generó mucha prosperidad en el país y su población se cuadruplicó.

En Venezuela está el Salto Ángel, ¡la cascada más alta del mundo (3.281 pies/ 979 metros)!

Después de leer

¿A qué país se refiere cada oración?

1. Es el primer productor de esmeraldas del mundo.
   ☐ Colombia   ☐ Venezuela
2. Los indios guajiros vivían en chozas suspendidas en un lago.
   ☐ Colombia   ☐ Venezuela
3. La cumbia y el vallenato son dos ritmos típicos.
   ☐ Colombia   ☐ Venezuela
4. La capital cuenta con un sofisticado sistema de transporte metropolitano.
   ☐ Colombia   ☐ Venezuela

> Por favor, no se levante hoy. Descanse todo el día.

1. Ud./Uds. Commands: Giving direct orders and instructions to others

Spanish has different command forms, depending on who is being addressed. In this chapter, you will learn about formal commands to use with a person that you would address formally (**usted**) and with more than one person (**ustedes**). You have already seen **ustedes** commands when instructions were given to more than one student (**cierren el libro, lean la oración**).

Regular forms

All **Ud./Uds.** regular **-ar** verb commands end in **-e(n)**; all regular **-er/-ir** verb commands end in **-a(n)**. The appropriate ending is attached to the verb stem.

	esperar	**beb**er	**escrib**ir
usted	(no) esper**e**	(no) beb**a**	(no) escrib**a**
ustedes	(no) esper**en**	(no) beb**an**	(no) escrib**an**

Object and reflexive pronouns *are attached* to the end of all *affirmative* commands. Note that a written accent is often added[1].

| Béba**lo**. | *Drink it.* |
| Siénte**se**, por favor. | *Please, sit down.* |

But they *precede* the verb in all *negative* commands.

| **No lo** beba. | *Don't drink it.* |
| **No se** siente todavía, por favor. | *Do not sit down yet, please.* |

Stem-changing and yo-irregular forms

Stem-changing and **yo**-irregular verbs delete the final **-o** from the **yo** form of the present tense and add the indicated endings. The verb **ir** has an irregular command form (not based on the present tense **yo**).

Infinitivo	Presente (yo)	Mandato (*Command*)
decir	digø	**diga/ digan**
hacer	hagø	**haga/ hagan**
repetir	repitø	**repita/ repitan**
encontrar	encuentrø	**encuentre/ encuentren**
dormir	duermø	**duerma/ duerman**
ir	voy	**vaya/ vayan**

[1]The emphasis in command forms with more than one syllable is in the second-to-last syllable (<u>to</u>me, <u>be</u>ba), so it does not need an accent mark. When adding an extra syllable, that syllable becomes third-to-last; therefore it needs a stress mark.

Así se dice

¿Qué nos dice la médica?

Nos da instrucciones para hacer un examen físico.

Saque la lengua.

Diga ¡ah!

Abra la boca.

Respire profundamente

respirar *to breathe*

Después de examinarnos, nos da consejos.

Descanse.

Vaya a la farmacia con esta receta.

la receta *prescription*

Tome líquidos.

Tome aspirinas (las pastillas/ las cápsulas).

Así se dice

9-4 **¿Usted o ustedes?** Escucha estas instrucciones. Decide si le habla "**usted**" o a "**ustedes**".

	Usted	Ustedes
1.		
2.		
3.		
4.		
5.		

NOTA CULTURAL

La forma "usted" en Colombia

In Colombia, the form "**usted**" is taking over where the "**tú**" form is used in many other countries. It is common to hear friends, sisters and brothers, and wives and husbands use "**usted**" with each other. A similar phenomenon happened in English over 500 years ago, when the informal "thou" was eventually replaced by the formal "you."

9-5 **¿Qué dice un buen doctor?** Decide si un buen doctor le dice las frases siguientes a su paciente.

	Sí	No
1. Coma muchas frutas y verduras.		
2. No haga ejercicio nunca.		
3. Duerma ocho horas cada noche.		
4. Tome vitaminas.		
5. No fume.		
6. Si tiene náuseas, corra cinco millas.		

9-6 **¿Puede pedirlo?** Eres dietista y estás en un restaurante cubano de Miami con un paciente. Tu paciente te va a hacer preguntas sobre los platos del restaurante (vean el menú en la siguiente página). Contesta con formas de mandatos y pronombres de objeto directo. Después, cambien los papeles (*reverse roles*).

Modelo: Paciente: **Para empezar, ¿puedo pedir la sopa de pollo?**
Dietista: **Sí, pídala.**
Paciente: **¿Y los plátanos fritos?**
Dietista: **No, no los pida.**

Paciente A: Tienes el colesterol alto.
Paciente B: Estás un poquito obeso/a.

Larios

SOPAS
SOUPS

SOPA DEL DÍA
SOUP OF THE DAY — $3.75

SOPA DE POLLO
CHICKEN SOUP — $3.50

SOPA DE FRIJOLES NEGROS
BLACK BEAN SOUP — $3.50

TORTILLAS
OMELETTES

TORTILLA ESPAÑOLA
CON ARROZ Y PLÁTANOS — $6.75
SPANISH OMELETTE, RICE & PLANTAINS

TORTILLA DE PLÁTANO
CON ARROZ Y FRIJOLES NEGROS — $5.95
PLANTAIN OMELETTE WITH RICE & BEANS

ENSALADAS
SALADS

ENSALADA MIXTA
HOUSE SALAD — $4.75

ENSALADA DE SARDINAS
SARDINE SALAD — $6.95

ENSALADA DE TOMATE
TOMATO SALAD — $3.50

SERRUCHO EN ESCABECHE
PICKLED KINGFISH — $8.25

PLATO DE FRUTAS
FRUIT PLATTER — $4.95

AVES
CHICKEN

PECHUGA DE POLLO A LA PLANCHA
BONELESS GRILLED CHICKEN BREAST — $8.25

POLLO ASADO
ROASTED CHICKEN — $7.95

CHICHARRONES DE POLLO
DEEP FRIED CHICKEN CHUNKS — $7.95

ARROZ CON POLLO
CHICKEN AND YELLOW RICE — $6.95

PECHUGA DE POLLO RELLENA
CON CAMARONES — $8.95
CHICKEN BREAST STUFFED WITH SHRIMP

PESCADOS
FISH

PESCADO EMPANIZADO
BREADED FISH — $9.95

PESCADO A LA PLANCHA
GRILLED FISH — $9.75

BROCHETA DE CAMARONES
SHRIMP KABOB — $11.75

CAMARONES EMPANIZADOS
BREADED SHRIMP — $12.25

CAMARONES AL AJILLO
SHRIMP IN GARLIC — $12.25

LANGOSTA ENCHILADA
LOBSTER CREOLE — $20.50

**TODOS ESTOS PLATOS SE SIRVEN
CON ARROZ Y PLÁTANOS FRITOS**

CARNES
MEATS

BISTEC DE PALOMILLA
CUBAN STEAK — $8.95

LOMO DE PUERCO
ROAST PORK LOIN-CUBAN STYLE — $9.75

MASAS DE PUERCO
FRIED PORK CHUNKS — $9.25

CHULETAS DE PUERCO
PORK CHOPS — $8.50

CARNE AL PINCHO
SHISH KABOB — $12.95

PICADILLO A LA CUBANA
CUBAN GROUND BEEF CREOLE — $6.25

POSTRES
DESSERTS

PUDÍN DE PAN
BREAD PUDDING — $3.75

FLAN DE LECHE
CUSTARD — $3.75

ARROZ CON LECHE
RICE PUDDING — $3.75

COCO RALLADO
SHREDDED COCONUT — $3.25

HELADOS
ICE CREAM

COCO	$2.95
MANGO	$2.95
GUANÁBANA SORBET	$2.95
CHOCOLATE	$2.95
VAINILLA	$2.95

Para regular el colesterol

EVITE alimentos con mucha grasa y colesterol.

NO FUME.

BAJE de peso (si lo necesita).

HAGA ejercicio con regularidad.

COMA más frutas y vegetales.

COMA más pan integral, cereales, frijoles y arroz.

SIGA las instrucciones de su médico.

¿Qué instrucciones nos dan para regular el colesterol? En tu opinión,
¿cuáles son las más importantes?

Así se dice

9-7 **¿El/La doctor/a o los padres?** Lee los mandatos siguientes y decide si estas instrucciones son de un/a doctor/a a sus pacientes o de unos padres a sus hijos.

DICHOS

Ajo, cebolla y limón, y déjate de° inyección.
¿Qué significa el dicho?
¿Es verdad?

°stop having

	Doctor	Padres
1. Saquen la lengua.	✓	
2. Péinense.		✓
3. Respiren profundamente.	✓	
4. Digan ¡ah!	✓	
5. Lávense las manos.	✓	✓
6. Hagan gárgaras (*gargle*) con sal.	✓	✓
7. Quítense los zapatos en la casa.		✓
8. Tomen la pastilla cada dos horas.	✓	

9-8 **¿Qué manda el/la profesor/a?** En grupos, escriban una lista de mandatos —positivos y negativos— que da el profesor/a de español a los estudiantes. Tienen dos minutos. ¡El grupo con más mandatos gana!

Modelo: **Hagan su tarea.**
...

Tu salud

To express aches, pains, and how you feel, use the following verbs and expressions:
doler (like **gustar**): indirect object + **doler (ue)** + **el/la/los/las** + *body part*

> **Me duelen las piernas.**   **¿Te duele el estómago?**
> *My legs **hurt**.*   *Do you have a stomach**ache**?*

tener dolor de + *body part*

> **Tengo dolor de espalda.**
> *I have a backache.*

sentirse (ie, i) + *adjective*

> **Se sintió/ Se siente bien, mal, enfermo/a, triste, cansado/a, etc.**
> *She/He felt/feels . . .*

Estás *muy* enfermo/a. Antes de ver al médico necesitas completar el siguiente cuestionario para pacientes.

Su salud		
1. **¿Le duele la cabeza** con frecuencia?	Sí	No
2. **¿Tiene dolor de estómago**?	Sí	No
3. ¿Tiene mucha **tos/ Tose** mucho?	Sí	No
4. ¿Tiene **fiebre**?	Sí	No
5. ¿Tiene **diarrea**?	Sí	No
6. ¿Tiene **resfriados** o **gripe** con frecuencia?	Sí	No
7. ¿Tiene **alergias**?	Sí	No
8. ¿Tiene **congestión nasal**? **¿Estornuda** mucho?	Sí	No
9. **¿Le duele la garganta** con frecuencia?	Sí	No
10. **¿Tiene vómitos/ Vomita**?	Sí	No
11. ¿Tiene **náuseas**?	Sí	No
12. ¿Tiene **escalofríos**?	Sí	No
13. **¿Se cansa** con frecuencia?	Sí	No
14. ¿Duerme bien?	Sí	No
15. **¿Se siente deprimido/a**?	Sí	No

Otros síntomas _____

cansarse	*to get tired*	**la gripe**	*flu*
el resfriado	*cold*	**la salud**	*health*
el escalofrío	*chill*	**sentirse (ie, i)**	*to feel*
estornudar	*to sneeze*	**la tos**	*cough*
la garganta	*throat*	**toser**	*to cough*

NOTA CULTURAL

Ayuda médica
There are different resources for medicine and healing in Latin America. Public health systems are the main providers of health care, with many well-equipped hospitals and highly trained doctors. For minor health issues, many people rely on their pharmacist, with whom a personal relationship is often developed. The pharmacist offers advice and provides over-the-counter medication. *Herbolarios*, where plants and homeopathic remedies are sold, are also common. Spiritual healers such as *curanderos* and *shamans* heal through the use of medicinal plants and religious rituals.

Así se dice

9-9 **¿De quién es el diagnóstico y el tratamiento?** Mientras estudias en Venezuela, tus amigos **Jorge, Pedro, Alberto** y **Daniel** se enferman y van al médico. Escúchales describir sus síntomas e indica a quién pertenece cada diagnóstico y tratamiento.

DIAGNÓSTICO: Otitis (infección de oído)
TRATAMIENTO: Tome antibióticos cada (*every*) 6 horas. Debe aplicar calor seco (*dry*) para aliviar el dolor.

1. Es de: ☑ Jorge ☐ Pedro ☐ Alberto ☐ Daniel

DIAGNÓSTICO: Alergia al polen
TRATAMIENTO: Cierre las ventanas. Si sale a la calle, tome Alegra por la mañana.

2. Es de: ☐ Jorge ☑ Pedro ☐ Alberto ☐ Daniel

DIAGNÓSTICO: Gastroenteritis
TRATAMIENTO: No necesita medicina, tome líquidos para evitar (*avoid*) la deshidratación y descanse mucho.

3. Es de: ☐ Jorge ☑ Pedro ☐ Alberto ☐ Daniel

DIAGNÓSTICO: Gripe
TRATAMIENTO: Tome aspirinas, líquidos y descanse.

4. Es de: ☐ Jorge ☐ Pedro ☐ Alberto ☑ Daniel

NOTA CULTURAL

Gabriel García Márquez

Gabriel García Márquez is a Colombian author and journalist. He first won international fame in 1967 with his masterpiece, *One Hundred Years of Solitude*, a defining classic of twentieth century literature. He was awarded the Nobel Prize for Literature in 1982. His journalistic work includes 1996's *News of a Kidnapping*, which details the atrocities of the Colombian drug trade. A film adaptation of his novel *Love in the time of cholera* was released in 2007.

9-10 **¿Qué me pasa, doctor?** Ahora tú te sientes enfermo/a también y vas al consultorio. Túrnate con tu compañero/a en los papeles de paciente y médico/a.

 Paso 1. El/La paciente describe sus síntomas y responde a las preguntas del/de la doctor/a.

 Paso 2. El/La doctor/a debe hacer un diagnóstico y recomendar un tratamiento, según el cuadro (*chart*). El/La paciente debe hacer preguntas sobre otras cosas que puede/ no puede hacer.

DIAGNÓSTICO	TRATAMIENTO
gripe	tomar aspirinas, líquidos, descansar
mononucleosis	tomar Tylenol®, líquidos, descansar mucho
acidez de estómago	tomar un líquido anti-acidez
infección de...	tomar antibióticos
resfriado	tomar muchos líquidos, descansar
bronquitis	tomar jarabe para la tos y un expectorante
depresión	ir a ver al psicólogo

DICHOS

El amor y la tos no pueden ocultarse°.
¿Por qué no pueden ocultarse ni el amor ni la tos?

°*be hidden*

Modelo: Paciente: **Buenas tardes, doctor/a... Tengo muchos problemas. Estoy.../ Me siento...**

Médico/a: **A ver, ¿le duele(n)... ?**
¿Tiene usted... ?
Tengo varias recomendaciones: Primero.../ Tome...

Paciente: **¿Puedo... ?/ ¿Tengo que... ?**

Escenas

Octavio va a la clínica

Octavio

Hace ya tres días que Octavio está enfermo. Aunque° no le gustan mucho los doctores, hoy está en la clínica de la universidad. Son las dos de la tarde y tiene cita a las dos y cuarto. La enfermera ya le tomó la temperatura, la presión arterial y el pulso.

Although

(Entra la doctora Ruiz con el expediente médico° en mano.)

expediente... *medical record*

Paso 1. En parejas, escriban una lista de las tres enfermedades más frecuentes entre estudiantes universitarios. Piensen juntos en dos síntomas comunes que presentan estas enfermedades y den recomendaciones típicas de los doctores en cada caso.

Escenas

Paso 2. Escucha la conversación e indica si Octavio tiene una enfermedad de la lista (*Paso 1*). En caso afirmativo, ¿tiene Octavio los síntomas que Uds. anticiparon? ¿Hizo el doctor algunas recomendaciones similares a las que Uds. dieron?

Paso 3. Lee las siguientes preguntas. Después, escucha la conversación otra vez y escribe las respuestas.

1. ¿Cuál es la temperatura de Octavio?
2. ¿Qué síntomas menciona Octavio?

escalofríos	diarrea	fiebre	dolor de garganta	náuseas
congestión	vómitos	tos	se siente cansado	dolor de estómago

3. ¿Qué tipo de medicamento quiere Octavio?
4. ¿Qué le recomienda la doctora?

Paso 4. Escucha una vez más y lee el texto. Después, revisa tus respuestas.

Doctora: Buenas tardes. A ver, ¿qué le pasa, Sr. Bermúdez? Según veo en su expediente, usted tiene una fiebre de 39[2] grados.

hace... *three days ago*

Octavio: Buenas, doctora. Todo comenzó hace tres días°. Al principio me dolía un poco la cabeza. Ahora me duele todo el cuerpo y tengo escalofríos. Me tomé la temperatura y descubrí que tenía una fiebre de 38 grados.

Doctora: ¿Le duele la garganta también?

Octavio: Bastante. Además, tengo tos y congestión nasal.

Doctora: Bien, permítame examinarlo. Respire profundamente, por favor. Otra vez. Abra la boca y diga ¡ah!, por favor. (*Lo examina.*) Bueno, usted tiene gripe. Por esta época del año es muy común.

Octavio: Necesito sentirme bien pronto. Tengo un examen en mi clase de ciencias políticas mañana. Por favor recéteme un antibiótico que me quite esta gripe.

Doctora: Lo siento, los antibióticos no resultan efectivos contra las infecciones virales. Para recuperarse debe descansar y tomar muchos líquidos. Y no se preocupe por los exámenes en este momento; el estrés contribuye a debilitar las defensas inmunológicas.

Octavio: Entonces, ¿no me va a recetar nada?

Doctora: Sí, un expectorante para la congestión nasal y la tos. ¿Es usted alérgico a la aspirina?

Octavio: No, doctora.

Doctora: Muy bien. La aspirina le puede ayudar a bajar la fiebre.

Octavio: Muchas gracias, doctora. Me voy a quedar en la cama descansando y viendo televisión. A veces, como dice el dicho, "No hay mal que por bien no venga".

---

[2]39° Celsius = 102.2° Farenheit

Así se forma

Era medianoche y hacía mucho viento. Los niños caminaban por la calle desierta...

2. The imperfect: Describing in the past

Spanish has two simple past tenses: the preterit and the imperfect. You have already learned to use the preterit to talk about past actions perceived as complete and past actions within a specific time frame (*yesterday, last night, etc.*).

Use of the imperfect

As the preterit, the imperfect tense also expresses actions or events that took place in the past, but the imperfect does not focus on the completion of the action. It does not express beginning and/or end; it just views an action as something that was in place or in progress. It is used primarily:

- to describe in the past (background, weather, ongoing conditions, persons, places, things).

Hacía sol.	It **was** sunny.
La playa **era** hermosa.	The beach **was** beautiful.
El mar **estaba** muy tranquilo.	The sea **was** very tranquil.
Los niños **llevaban** trajes de baño y camisetas.	The children **were wearing** bathing suits and T-shirts.
Estaban muy contentos.	They **were** very happy.

- to indicate that past actions were in progress, ongoing, or habitual.

Un niño **jugaba** en el agua.	One child **was playing** in the water.
Otro **construía** un castillo.	Another **was building** a castle.
A otros siempre **les gustaba** jugar a pelota.	Others always **liked** to play ball.

Note that, although most of these actions and conditions surely started and finished at some point, we do not "perceive" a beginning or end in the examples above.

The imperfect tense can be translated with the English forms below, depending on the actual meaning expressed:

Mientras **esperaba** al médico, leyó un artículo en una revista.
*While she **was waiting/waited** for the doctor, she read an article in a magazine.*

El doctor le **examinaba** el colesterol una vez al año.
*The doctor **used to/would check** her cholesterol once a year.*

Así se forma

Forms of the imperfect

To form the imperfect in regular verbs, delete the **-ar**, **-er**, or **-ir** from the infinitive and add the endings indicated below. Note that the imperfect **-er/-ir** endings are identical.

	examin**ar** *to examine*	tos**er** *to cough*	sal**ir** *to leave, go out*
(yo)	examin**aba**	tos**ía**	sal**ía**
(tú)	examin**abas**	tos**ías**	sal**ías**
(Ud., él/ella)	examin**aba**	tos**ía**	sal**ía**
(nosotros/as)	examin**ábamos**	tos**íamos**	sal**íamos**
(vosotros/as)	examin**abais**	tos**íais**	sal**íais**
(Uds., ellos/ellas)	examin**aban**	tos**ían**	sal**ían**

Irregular verbs

Only three verbs are irregular in the imperfect:

ser *to be*		**ir** *to go*		**ver** *to see*	
era	éramos	iba	íbamos	veía	veíamos
eras	erais	ibas	ibais	veías	veíais
era	eran	iba	iban	veía	veían

9-11 En la época de nuestros abuelos.

Paso 1. El mundo era diferente cuando nuestros abuelos eran jóvenes, por ejemplo, en asuntos de salud. Indica si estas afirmaciones son ciertas o falsas y escribe una afirmación más para el número 10.

Cuando mis abuelos eran jóvenes...	Cierto	Falso
1. Los doctores recetaban muchos antibióticos.		✓
2. Muchas personas consumían comida rápida.		✓
3. Casi todos consumían comida muy saludable (*healthy*).	✓	
4. El SIDA (*AIDS*) era una enfermedad peligrosa.		✓
5. Todos conocían los efectos negativos de fumar.		✓
6. Las personas no tenían mucho estrés.	✓	
7. Los jóvenes no eran activos; pasaban muchas horas sentados.		✓
8. Había muchos problemas con las drogas.		✓
9. Muchas personas usaban remedios caseros (*home remedies*).	✓	
10. ... Los doctores recetaban muchos aspirians		✓

Paso 2. En parejas, contrasten **antes** y **ahora**. Incluyan sus afirmaciones originales.

Modelo: Los doctores recetaban muchos antibióticos.
Antes los doctores no recetaban muchos antibióticos, pero ahora sí lo hacen.

NOTA DE LENGUA

Había, like **hay**, denotes existence, but in the past.
Había tres pacientes en la sala de espera. **There were** three patients in the waiting room.

9-12 ¿Mejorando la salud?

Paso 1. Esta persona está intentando mejorar su salud y te pide tu opinión. Primero quieres saber más sobre sus hábitos pasados y actuales (*current*). Escucha sus descripciones e indica si habla de antes o ahora.

	Antes	Ahora
1. tomar mucha cerveza los fines de semana	_____	_____
2. comer pocas ensaladas y fruta	_____	_____
3. ver la televisión dos o tres horas por la noche	_____	_____
4. no tomar desayuno	_____	_____
5. dormir menos de seis horas	_____	_____
6. fumar bastante	_____	_____
7. tomar mucho café todos los días	_____	_____
8. ser poco activo	_____	_____
9. ir al gimnasio una vez por semana	_____	_____

Paso 2. Tu amigo/a todavía tiene algunos hábitos poco saludables. Tú también hacías cosas similares antes, pero ahora tienes costumbres más sanas y ¡te sientes mucho mejor! Explícaselo en una breve carta.

Modelo: Hola Andrés,
Ya veo que tienes algunos buenos hábitos, pero todavía puedes mejorar otras cosas. ¡Merece la pena!° Antes yo no tomaba desayuno tampoco, pero ahora tomo cereal todas las mañanas y tengo mucha energía…

It's worth it!

9-13 Cuando teníamos diez años.

Paso 1. Escribe oraciones describiendo cómo eras y qué hacías cuando tenías diez años.

1. ser (tímido/a; perezoso/a; trabajador/a...)	
2. estudiar (¿Cuánto?, ¿Dónde?...)	
3. hacer (deporte/ actividades extraescolares)	
4. ver la tele (¿Cuánto?, ¿Qué programas?...)	
5. leer (¿Qué revistas/ libros?...)	
6. escuchar música (¿Qué tipo/ cantante/ grupo?...)	
7. hablar mucho por teléfono (¿Con quién?...)	
8. salir mucho con mis amigos/as (¿Adónde?....)	
9. trabajar (¿Dónde?...)	
10. querer tener o hacer... (¿Qué?...)	

Así se forma

 Paso 2. Ahora, en parejas, haz preguntas a tu compañero/a sobre varios aspectos de su infancia (*childhood*). ¿Eran ustedes similares o diferentes cuando tenían diez años?

Modelo: **¿Cuánto estudiabas? ¿Dónde preferías estudiar? ¿Qué materia te gustaba estudiar?**

9-14 Los hábitos diarios.

 Paso 1. Escribe párrafos breves comparando tus hábitos respecto a las siguientes actividades cuando tenías quince años y ahora.

Modelo: dormir

Me acostaba a las diez de la noche y me levantaba a las siete de la mañana entre semana (*on weekdays*). Los fines de semana me acostaba tarde pero no me levantaba hasta las once... ¡dormía mucho! Ahora me acuesto...

1. dormir
2. comer
3. beber
4. ejercicio/ deporte
5. tiempo libre

Paso 2. En grupos pequeños, compartan y comparen sus ideas. ¿Eran sus hábitos más saludables antes o lo son ahora?

SITUACIONES

Estudiante A: Eres estudiante de primer año. Estás cansado/a, te enfermas con frecuencia, además engordaste 5 kilos y estás estresado porque los exámenes son la semana próxima... pero te encanta tu nueva "libertad" (*freedom*) y quieres disfrutarla (*enjoy it*).

Estudiante B: Tu amigo/a está cometiendo muchos errores típicos del primer año: no come bien, no hace ejercicio, sale con los amigos/as durante la semana y duerme poco. Tu tienes ya más experiencia; habla con él/ella y ofrécele algunos consejos (*advice*).

Cultura: Remedios caseros[1] del mundo hispano

[1]**Remedios...** *Home remedies*

Antes de leer

1. ¿Usan remedios caseros en tu familia? ¿Cuáles? ¿Son efectivos?

2. ¿Prefieres usar remedios caseros o farmacéuticos?

La flor del naranjo, los azahares

Un té de tilo es bueno para calmar el estrés.

Desde[2] que el ser humano se dio cuenta[3] de que podía aliviar sus padecimientos[4] con la ayuda de hierbas[5] y plantas medicinales, hay toda una tradición de remedios que se transmite de generación a generación. Cada cultura, cada país, cada región tiene sus propias curas[6]. A continuación vas a encontrar algunas de las tradiciones médicas populares del mundo hispano. Recuerda que no debes tomar remedios caseros ni farmacéuticos sin consultar con tu médico/a.

[2]*Since*   [3]**se...** *realized*   [4]*pains*   [5]*herbs*   [6]*cures*

RESFRIADOS/ GRIPE

Todos los remedios comienzan con una limonada caliente. Lo que cambia de receta a receta son los ingredientes que se agregan[7]. Algunos ponen miel[8] en la limonada, otros ron o whisky.

[7]**se...** *are added*   [8]*honey*

ORZUELOS[14]

Se recomienda hervir[15] unos clavos de olor[16] en agua y cuando está tibia[17] aplicarla al orzuelo. Según los costarricenses es un remedio seguro. Otros afirman que lo mejor es aplicar miel. En realidad los orzuelos son infecciones y si persisten deben ser tratadas con antibióticos.

[14]*Sties*   [15]*boil*   [16]**clavos...** *cloves*   [17]*lukewarm*

DOLOR DE OÍDO

Se recomienda dorar[19] un ajo al fuego, ponerlo en un algodón y colocarlo a la entrada del oído.

[19]*roast*

HIPO[9]

Otra vez los consejos son múltiples. Se recomienda poner jugo de limón en la lengua o tomar sorbos[10] de agua. Otros piensan que se debe asustar[11] al paciente. En México, las abuelitas les ponen un hilo[12] rojo en la frente[13] a los bebés para detener el hipo.

[9]*Hiccup*   [10]*sips*   [11]*to scare*   [12]*a piece of thread*   [13]*forehead*

NERVIOSISMO/ ESTRÉS

Las flores del naranjo, los azahares, hervidas en agua tienen propiedades sedantes. También un té de tilo, otra hierba medicinal, ayuda a calmar la ansiedad.

La próxima vez que le preguntes a un hispanoparlante sobre remedios caseros, prepárate; vas a recibir muchos consejos[18] y respuestas.

[18]*advice*

DOLOR DE PIES

Para relajar los pies y aliviar el cansancio no hay como ponerlos en agua de sal tibia. También un masaje con una crema hidratante hace maravillas.

Después de leer

Empareja los siguientes remedios con los problemas que curan.

_____ limonada caliente   **a.** el estrés

_____ los azahares   **b.** el resfriado

_____ el ajo   **c.** el dolor de oído

Así se forma

Los niños caminaban por la calle desierta cuando de repente ¡vieron un fantasma!

3. The imperfect vs. the preterit: Talking about and describing persons, things, and actions in the past

Although both the preterit and the imperfect tenses refer to the past, they convey different meanings. The difference is not one of time (when the event took place) but aspect (how the event is perceived or what parts of it the focus is on). The main contrast is that, while the preterit presents the event as a complete one from beginning to end, or expresses its beginning or end points, the imperfect presents an action or event in the past with no reference to its beginning and/or end. All the different uses of the preterit and imperfect convey this general contrast.

Because it is sometimes difficult to make concrete decisions based on this general concept, here are more specific guidelines to help you decide which tense to use.

> **HINT**
>
> Review the preterit tense of regular, stem-changing, and irregular verbs in **Capítulos 6, 7,** and **8**.

The imperfect . . .	The preterit . . .
1. Describes the *middle* of a past action, state, or condition; indicates that it was *in progress*, with no emphasis on the beginning or end. **No quería** comer. Sólo **dormía** y **veía** la tele. Juan **estaba enfermo**.	1. Focuses on a past action or condition with an evident *beginning, end,* or *time frame*. Anita **se enfermó el sábado**. **Estuvo enferma toda la semana**. **Salió** del hospital **ayer**. **Pasó tres días** allí. **Se recuperó** completamente.
2. Describes a past action that was *repeated* or *habitual* over an indefinite period of time. La enfermera **visitaba** a sus pacientes **todas las noches**. **Siempre** les **llevaba** jugo de naranja.	2. Indicates a *single past action*, generally quickly completed, or a *series of actions* in the past. El paciente **entró** en el consultorio. El enfermero le **tomó** la temperatura, le **explicó** el problema y le **puso** una inyección.

In addition, *when narrating* an incident or telling a story we use . . .

The imperfect . . .	The preterit . . .

1. To set the stage, give background information:
• The date, the season
    Era el 12 de diciembre. **Era** invierno.
• What time it was
    Era medianoche.
• The weather
    Hacía frío y **nevaba**.
• A description of the setting
    La casa era muy vieja y **tenía** un árbol muy grande enfrente.
• A description of the people involved, both their physical and personality traits, and also their age
    La abuela **era** bonita y muy amable.
    Tenía ochenta años.
	1. To express an event that interrupts an ongoing (imperfect) action.
	    Mientras ella leía el libro, **sonó** el teléfono.
	
	2. To narrate sequential events; moves the story forward, telling what happened
	    Se levantó, contestó el teléfono y **salió** de la casa inmediatamente.

2. To indicate people's emotional/physical state or condition. **Estaba** tranquila./ **Tenía** frío.	
3. Describe ongoing actions. Ella **leía** un libro.	

Time references will often help to determine which past tense to use. The following words or expressions serve as a general guideline.

IMPERFECTO		PRETÉRITO	
muchas veces	*many times, often*	una vez	*once, one time*
todos los días	*every day*	ayer, anoche	*yesterday, last night*
mientras	*while*	el verano pasado	*last summer*
con frecuencia	*frequently*	hace diez años	*ten years ago*
siempre/ generalmente	*always/generally*	de repente	*suddenly*

<u>Todos los veranos</u> **íbamos** a la playa, pero <u>el verano pasado</u> **fuimos** a las montañas.

9-15 Nuestro gato Rodolfo.

 Paso 1. Lean esta historia sobre lo que le pasó al gato.

Ayer, nuestro gato Rodolfo **se enfermó**. No **quería** comer y **tenía** diarrea. ¡Pobrecito! Por supuesto, todos **estábamos** muy preocupados. Elena y yo lo **llevamos** al veterinario y **nos sentamos** en la sala de espera, donde **había** muchos animales. Rodolfo **estaba** en una caja de cartón° y, por supuesto, no **estaba** nada contento. ¡**Tuvimos** que esperar por una hora! Por fin, el veterinario lo **examinó, descubrió** que el pobre Rodolfo **tenía** una infección intestinal y le **recetó** un antibiótico. **Volvimos** a casa e inmediatamente le **dimos** su medicamento. En poco tiempo, **se recuperó**. ¡Qué suerte!°

caja... *cardboard box*

Qué... *What luck!*

Paso 2. Para cada verbo, indica si expresa una **acción** (A), o una **descripción** o **estado** (*state*) (D/E).

1. **se enfermó**
2. no **quería** comer
3. **tenía** diarrea
4. **estábamos** preocupados
5. lo **llevamos** al veterinario
6. **nos sentamos** en la sala de espera
7. **había** muchos animales
8. Rodolfo **estaba** en una caja
9. no **estaba** nada contento
10. el veterinario lo **examinó**
11. **descubrió**
12. Rodolfo **tenía** una infección
13. le **recetó** un antibiótico
14. **volvimos** a casa
15. le **dimos** su medicamento
16. **se recuperó**

Así se forma

9-16 **¡Pobre Rodolfo!** La familia llevó a Rodolfo al veterinario porque notaron varios cambios en el pobre gato. En parejas, escriban oraciones sobre lo que Rodolfo hacía *casi todos los días* y lo que hizo *ayer*. ¡Usen la imaginación!

Modelo: pasear por el jardín por las noches
Siempre paseaba por el jardín por las noches, pero ayer no salió de la casa.

Casi todos los días...   **pero ayer...**
1. comer toda la comida de su tazón   ...
2. descansar junto a la chimenea   ...
3. pelear con Teo, el perro   ...
4. jugar con Elena y Juanito   ...
5. dormir una siesta por la tarde   ...
6. ¿...?   ...

9-17 **Más sobre nuestro famoso gato Rodolfo.** Describan al gato Rodolfo y algunas de sus aventuras juveniles. Usen el pretérito o el imperfecto según el caso.

unique Es verdad que Rodolfo es un gato único°. Cuando _____ (tener) dos años y _____ (llegar) a nuestra casa, _____ (ser) gordo y bonito. _____ (Poder) correr muy rápido
birds y aún subir a los árboles, donde le _____ (encantar) "mirar" los pájaros°. Año
after tras° año nos _____ (dar) sorpresas. Por ejemplo, normalmente _____ (tomar)
toilet agua de su tazón, pero un día la _____ (tomar) ¡del inodoro°! Casi siempre _____ (dormir) en el sótano, en el sofá, pero una noche _____ (dormir) afuera, en el
Gypsy jardín. Allí _____ (conocer) a Gitana°, su gata favorita. Unos días más tarde, nos _____ (dar) otra sorpresa: ¡_____ (Comer) el jamón de mi sándwich! Cuando yo _____ (entrar) en la cocina y lo _____ (descubrir), el "delincuente" ¡_____ (salir) corriendo de la casa! Allí _____ (ver) a Gitana, y los dos _____ (escaparse). _____ (Regresar) a casa ¡tres días más tarde! Ahora tenemos una pareja gatuna durmiendo junto a la chimenea y probablemente una familia por venir.

9-18 **Martes y trece.** No eres supersticioso/a, pero ayer fue martes, día 13, y ¡todo fue mal!

Paso 1. Decide qué acciones de la primera columna hacías cuando sucedieron los eventos de la segunda columna. Escribe el número de la primera frase al lado de la segunda frase.

Mientras...		
1. ducharse	_____	encontrar un pelo en la sopa
2. desayunar	_____	empezar a llover
3. hacer un examen	_____	congelarse (*freeze*) la computadora
4. comer en la cafetería	_____	acabarse (*run out*) el agua caliente
5. escribir un trabajo	_____	sonar mi teléfono celular
6. volver a mi cuarto	_____	derramar (*spill*) café en mi camisa

Paso 2. Usando las ideas del *Paso 1*, explica qué hacías y qué pasó. Luego, continúa la historia contando dos cosas que pasaron por la noche.

Modelo: **Por la mañana, mientras me duchaba, se terminó el agua caliente...**

9-19 **El accidente de Martín un martes trece.** Narra la historia en el pasado. Cambia los verbos al pretérito o al imperfecto según el caso. Explica tus razones.

Martín **maneja** muy contento. No **ve** el alto° y **choca°** con otro coche que *stop sign; collides*
viene en la dirección opuesta. Al otro conductor no le **pasa** nada, pero el pobre
Martín **se lastima**. **Llega** la policía y una ambulancia que lo **lleva** al hospital. La
pierna le **duele** mucho. El médico lo **examina** y lo **manda** a radiología. **Es** un
mal día para Martín. **Se fractura** la pierna y **sale** del hospital en muletas. **Es** un
martes trece y ya lo dice bien el dicho: "Martes, ni te cases ni te embarques, ni de
tu casa te apartes".

9-20 **Un evento memorable en mi vida.**

Paso 1. En grupos, cada estudiante piensa en un evento <u>verdadero o ficticio</u> del pasado. Debe pensar en los detalles también. Luego va a narrárselo al grupo.

Paso 2. Cada estudiante va a contar su historia. El resto del grupo puede hacer seis preguntas sobre los detalles. Después, el grupo decide si el evento es verdadero o no.

9-21 **¡Una noche increíble!** En grupos, inventen la historia de una noche increíble. Pueden usar una de las ideas de abajo o una diferente. Un/a secretario/a escribe la historia para leérsela a la clase más tarde. Presten atención al uso del pretérito y del imperfecto.

Temas posibles:
1. una noche en la ciudad de Nueva York
2. una noche en la sala de emergencias de un hospital
3. un sábado por la noche en una fiesta en la universidad
4. una noche viajando en autobús en Colombia o Venezuela
6. una noche en casa de los Simpson

Incluyan:
- referencia a la fecha, el día, la hora y el lugar donde estaban
- descripción del tiempo, del lugar, de las personas
- descripción de lo que pasaba en ese lugar (acciones en progreso, etc.)
- lo que pasó
- final de la historia

Así se forma

Speech bubbles:
¿Cuánto tiempo hace que se siente mal?

Mmm...

4. *Hacer* in time constructions: Indicating that an action has been going on for a period of time

A. *Hacer* to express an action that has been going on for a period of time

Spanish uses a special construction to indicate that an action or condition started in the past is still going on.

> **hace**[3] + *time* + **que** + *present tense*

Hace dos días **que está** enfermo.	*He has been sick for two days.*
Hace veinte minutos **que estamos** aquí.	*We have been here for twenty minutes.*

To ask how long an action or condition has been going on, use the question **¿Cuánto tiempo hace que... ?**

—**¿Cuánto tiempo hace que** Carmen espera a la doctora?	*How long has Carmen been waiting for the doctor?*
—**Hace diez minutos que la espera.**	*She has been waiting for her for ten minutes.*

9-22 **¿Hace mucho o poco tiempo?** Lee las siguientes oraciones e indica cuánto tiempo es más lógico.

1. La familia Rivera quiere comprar una casa...	☐ hace tres meses.	☐ hace tres minutos.
2. Silvia espera a su amigo...	☐ hace media hora.	☐ hace dos semanas.
3. Carlos tiene un resfriado...	☐ hace dos años.	☐ hace dos días.
4. Natalia estudia francés...	☐ hace un año.	☐ hace diez minutos.
5. Miguel espera en el tráfico...	☐ hace un mes.	☐ hace cuarenta y cinco minutos.
6. Margarita navega en la red...	☐ hace quince minutos.	☐ hace quince días.

---

[3]In this construction, the word **hace** never changes.

9-23 **¿Cuánto tiempo hace?** ¿Cuánto tiempo hace que estas personas participan en las actividades?

Modelo: **Hace dos horas que Javier trabaja en su proyecto de química.**

¿En cuál de las situaciones te gustaría estar (*would you like to be*)?

Javier / dos horas

Inés / quince minutos

Linda y Manuel / media hora

Esteban / dos horas

Alfonso / una hora

Octavio / cuarenta minutos

Manuel / veinte minutos

9-24 **Entrevista.** En parejas, háganse las preguntas de abajo. Cubre las preguntas de tu compañero/a con un papel o con la mano.

Modelo: Estudiante A: **¿Cuánto tiempo hace que estudias en la universidad?**

Estudiante B: **Hace tres años que estudio en la universidad, ¿y tú?**

Estudiante A: **Yo estudio en esta universidad hace dos años, pero antes estudiaba en otra universidad...**

Estudiante A:

1. ¿Cuánto tiempo hace que estudias en la universidad?
2. ¿Dónde vives ahora?¿Cuánto tiempo hace que vives allí?
3. ¿Tienes novio/a? ¿Cuánto tiempo hace que lo/la conoces?
4. ¿Tocas un instrumento musical? ¿Cuánto tiempo hace que lo tocas?

Estudiante B:

1. ¿Cuánto tiempo hace que estudias español?
2. ¿Quién es tu mejor amigo/a? ¿Cuánto tiempo hace que lo/la conoces?
3. ¿Cuánto tiempo hace que no hablas con tus padres? ¿Y con tus abuelos?
4. ¿Practicas algún deporte? ¿Cuánto tiempo hace que lo practicas?

Así se forma

¿Cuándo se lastimó el brazo?

Hace tres horas.

B. *Hacer* to express *ago*

We also use an expression with **hace** to indicate how long ago an action took place.

> *preterit tense of the verb* + **hace** + *the amount of time*

Salió **hace diez minutos**.	He left ten minutes ago.
Estuvo aquí **hace dos semanas**.	He was here two weeks ago.

- Statements about how long ago something took place have two possible word orders.

> *preterit* + **hace** + *time*   or   **Hace** + *time* + **que** + *preterit*

Lo **vi** hace una hora.	*o*	Hace una hora que lo **vi**.
I saw him an hour ago.		*I saw him an hour ago.*

- Note that in answering questions with the *ago* construction, we can omit the verb.

—¿Cuánto (tiempo) hace que te hiciste un examen médico?
—Hace dos meses (que me hice un examen médico).

How long ago did you have a physical examination?
(I had a medical exam) two months ago.

9-25 ¿Cómo es nuestra vida social?

Paso 1. Contesta las siguientes preguntas indicando en la columna **Yo** cuánto tiempo hace (horas, días, semanas, meses, años) que pasaron estas cosas. Añade (*Add*) otra pregunta y contéstala también.

Modelo: ¿Cuándo fue la última vez (*the last time*) que fuiste a un concierto?

> **Hace seis meses que fui a un concierto.**
>
> *o* **Fui a un concierto hace seis meses.**
>
> *o* **Hace seis meses.**

	Yo	Mi compañero/a
1. ¿Cuándo fue la última vez que fuiste a un concierto?		
2. ¿Cuándo fue la última vez que comiste algo fantástico?		
3. ¿Cuándo fue la última vez que fuiste al cine?		
4. ¿Cuándo fue la última vez que jugaste un partido deportivo?		
5. ¿Cuándo fue la última vez que viste a tu mejor amigo/a?		
6. ¿Cuándo fue la última vez que te divertiste mucho?		
7. ¿Cuándo estuviste en una reunión familiar especial?		
8. ¿Cuándo hiciste un viaje divertido?		
9. ¿...?		

 Paso 2. Ahora, en parejas, haz las preguntas a tu compañero/a y escribe sus respuestas en la columna de la derecha. Pregunta también sobre algunos detalles. Túrnense.

Modelo: Estudiante A: **¿Cuándo fue la última vez que fuiste a un concierto?**

Estudiante B: **Hace seis meses.**

Estudiante A: **¿De quién?/ ¿Te gustó?/ ¿Adónde fue?...**

9-26 Otras actividades memorables.

 Paso 1. Prepara una lista de tres cosas interesantes que hiciste hace un tiempo (*some time ago*).

Modelo: Visité Alaska.

 Paso 2. En grupos pequeños, compartan sus actividades y háganse preguntas para averiguar cuándo y otros detalles.

Modelo: Estudiante A: **¿Cuándo visitaste Alaska?**

Estudiante B: **Hace cinco años.**

Estudiante C: **¿Con quién fuiste?/ ¿Cómo fuiste?/ ¿Qué viste?...**

 9-27 **Guía para la comunidad médica.** La clase va a preparar una guía para la comunidad médica que debe atender a los hispanohablantes. La clase va a dividirse en tres grupos. Cada grupo, con un/a secretario/a, prepara una lista de preguntas, expresiones y mandatos útiles para las situaciones indicadas abajo. Incluyan preguntas y expresiones con *hace* (por ejemplo: **¿Cuánto hace que le duele... ?**). Al final, compartan sus listas con la clase.

Grupo 1: La recepcionista al hablar con un paciente

Grupo 2: El enfermero/La enfermera al hablar con un paciente

Grupo 3: Preguntas y mandatos que debe usar el doctor/la doctora con un paciente

Dicho y hecho

¡A ESCUCHAR!

En la Facultad de Medicina. Escucha lo que les dice la doctora Alvarado a los estudiantes. Luego, completa las dos primeras oraciones.

1. La doctora va a hablar sobre _____.

2. Muchos tienen interés en el tema porque ahora son los meses de _____, cuando se presenta la enfermedad.

   Escucha otra vez y completa las siguientes oraciones.

3. Aún cuando una persona contrae la gripe después de la vacuna, los síntomas son _____.

4. La vacuna es necesaria para personas mayores de _____ y para personas con enfermedades del _____ o del _____.

5. Para los que vivimos en el hemisferio norte, la vacuna generalmente se aplica entre los meses de _____ a _____.

6. Algunas personas son alérgicas a la vacuna porque también son alérgicas a _____.

CONVERSANDO

En la sala de emergencias. Imaginen que tres de ustedes están en la sala de emergencias de la clínica de la universidad. Cada uno/a le explica al/a la recepcionista por qué necesita ver a la doctora. El/La recepcionista les hace preguntas para determinar quién va primero.

Posibilidades:

- estabas corriendo, te caíste (*fell*) y ahora...
- comiste unos mariscos y ahora...
- crees que tienes la gripe
- tienes bronquitis

DE MI ESCRITORIO

Cuando era niño/a... Escribe una descripción de algo que te ocurrió cuando eras niño/a. Usa el imperfecto y el pretérito.

Incluye:

- cuándo (cuánto tiempo hace que) ocurrió
- cuántos años tenías cuando ocurrió
- dónde estabas y una descripción del lugar
- lo que pasó y si estabas triste/ contento(a)/ enojado(a), etc., al final.

Miguel Fernando Caro

Antes de leer

¿Sabes los nombres de algunos de tus vecinos? ¿Hay uno que saludas regularmente pero no sabes cómo se llama?

La siguiente narración del escritor colombiano **Miguel Fernando Caro** es un ejemplo del minicuento o minifición, un género literario entre el cuento y el poema. El objetivo del minicuento es establecer una historia interesante y revelar una sorpresa con muy pocas palabras. Por eso, su composición es difícil y algunas personas dicen que es similar al *haikú* japonés. El minicuento es muy popular, especialmente en Colombia y Venezuela en donde existen revistas especializadas y se han publicado varias colecciones.

EL AMIGO

de Miguel Fernando Caro

Todas las mañanas, cumpliendo[1] con la rutina de mi trabajo, paso por una casa en cuyo[2] balcón hay un viejo sentado en su silla de ruedas. Siempre, al pasar junto a la casa, el viejo y yo nos saludamos batiendo[3] nuestras manos.

No sé cómo se llama ni él sabe mi nombre. Tal vez el vernos todos los días casi obligatoriamente nos haya hecho amigos.

Hoy no nos vimos y al pasar por su balcón me he sentido muy triste al pensar en lo que pudo haberle ocurrido; ya a su edad, y con la mala salud que aparentaba[4], despertar a un nuevo día era una sorpresa.

Esta mañana me he sentido muy alegre, pues el viejo ha sido el primero en traer flores a mi tumba[5].

---

[1]*fulfilling* [2]*whose* [3]*waving* [4]*appeared to have* [5]*grave*

Después de leer

1. ¿Por dónde pasa el narrador cada día? ¿Quién está allí?

2. ¿Cómo se saludan los personajes de la historia?

3. ¿Por qué se siente triste el narrador? ¿Qué piensa el narrador que ha pasado? Y después, ¿por qué se siente contento?

4. Según la información de la última línea, ¿quién muere primero?

5. ¿Qué demuestra la acción del viejo?

6. ¿Tienes una amistad como la de esta historia? ¿Qué sabes de esa persona?

ESTRATEGIA PARA LEER

Noticing verb tenses
Focus on the verb endings and note the variety of verb tenses that the author uses throughout the story.
- How many different tenses can you identify?
- Are similar verb tenses grouped together? Interwoven?
- Is the tense at the beginning and the end of the story the same?

Repaso de vocabulario activo

Adjetivos

deprimido/a   *depressed*
embarazada   *pregnant*

Adverbios

cada   *each*
de repente   *all of a sudden, suddenly*
mientras   *(mean)while*
por fin   *finally*
una vez/ muchas veces
   once/many times

Expresiones sobre la salud

dolerle el/la/los/las (cabeza...)
   to have a (head)ache
hacer un análisis de sangre/ sacar
   sangre   *to do a blood test/to draw
   blood*
hacer una cita   *to make an
   appointment*
poner una inyección/ una vacuna
   to give a shot/vaccination
sacar una radiografía   *to X-ray*
tener dolor de (cabeza...)   *to have
   a (head)ache*
tener náuseas/ escalofríos/
   vómitos   *to have nausea/chills/to
   be vomiting*
tomar la temperatura/ la presión
   arterial/ el pulso   *to take one's
   temperature/blood pressure/pulse*

Órdenes que nos da un doctor/ una doctora   *Things the doctor tells us to do*

Abra la boca.   *Open your mouth.*
Descanse.   *Rest.*
Diga ¡ah!   *Say ¡ah!*
Lleve la receta a la farmacia.
   Take the prescription to the pharmacy.
Respire profundamente.   *Take a
   deep breath.*
Saque la lengua.   *Stick out your
   tongue.*
Tome aspirinas/ las pastillas/ las
   cápsulas.   *Take aspirin/the
   pills/the capsules.*

Tome líquidos.   *Take liquids.*
Vaya a la farmacia.   *Go to the
   pharmacy.*

Sustantivos

Algunos problemas de salud

la alergia   *allergy*
la congestión nasal   *nasal
   congestion*
la diarrea   *diarrhea*
la fiebre   *fever*
la gripe   *flu*
la herida (grave)   *wound (serious)*
la infección   *infection*
el resfriado   *cold (illness)*
la tos   *cough*

El cuerpo humano

la boca   *mouth*
el brazo   *arm*
la cabeza   *head*
la cara   *face*
el corazón   *heart*
el cuello   *neck*
el dedo   *finger*
el diente   *tooth*
la espalda   *back*
el estómago   *stomach*
la garganta   *throat*
el hombro   *shoulder*
el hueso   *bone*
el labio   *lip*
la lengua   *tongue*
la mano   *hand*
la nariz   *nose*
el oído   *ear (inner)*
el ojo   *eye*
la oreja   *ear (outer)*
el pecho   *chest*
el pelo   *hair*
el pie   *foot*
la pierna   *leg*
el pulmón   *lung*
el tobillo   *ankle*
la uña   *nail*

En el hospital

la ambulancia   *ambulance*
la camilla   *gurney*
el consultorio del médico/de la
   médica   *doctor's office*
(la sala de) emergencias
   emergency room
la habitación   *room*
el hospital   *hospital*
la inyección   *shot, injection*
las muletas   *crutches*
el/la paciente   *patient*
el/la paramédico   *paramedic*
la recepción   *reception desk*
el/la recepcionista   *receptionist*
la receta   *prescription*
la sala de espera   *waiting room*
la silla de ruedas   *wheelchair*
el termómetro   *thermometer*
la vacuna   *vaccine*
la venda   *bandage*
el yeso   *cast*

Verbos

cansarse   *to get tired*
enfermarse   *to get sick*
estornudar   *to sneeze*
examinar   *to examine*
fracturar(se)   *to break (one's arm)*
lastimarse   *to hurt oneself*
preocuparse   *to worry*
quedarse   *to stay*
sentarse (ie) estar sentado/ de pie
   to seat to be seated/to be standing
sentirse (ie, i)   *to feel*
torcer(se) (ue)   *to sprain (one's ankle)*
toser   *to cough*
vomitar   *to vomit*

Autoprueba y repaso 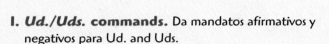 ✓

I. Ud./Uds. commands. Da mandatos afirmativos y negativos para Ud. and Uds.

Modelo: traerlo
> **Tráigalo. / No lo traiga.**
> **Tráiganlo. / No lo traigan.**

1. traérmelos
2. examinarla
3. descansar más
4. estudiar las palabras
5. leer el libro

II. The imperfect. Di cómo eran estas personas y lo que hacían cuando eran niños/as.

Modelo: yo / ser muy obediente
> **Era muy obediente.**

1. mis hermanos y yo / ser niños muy buenos
2. nosotros / ir a una escuela pequeña
3. yo / escuchar a mis maestras
4. José / jugar al voli durante el recreo
5. Ana y Tere / ver la tele por la tarde
6. tú / comer galletas todos los días

III. The imperfect and the preterit. Lee la historia y luego decide si los verbos en paréntesis deben estar en el imperfecto o el pretérito.

Modelo: Roberto no **se sentía** (sentirse) nada bien.

1. Por eso _____ (llamar) al consultorio de su doctor y _____ (hablar) con la recepcionista.
2. Roberto le _____ (explicar) que _____ (estar) enfermo.
3. La recepcionista le _____ (preguntar) qué _____ (tener).
4. Él le _____ (explicar) que le _____ (doler) todo el cuerpo y que _____ (tener) fiebre, dolor de cabeza y escalofríos.
5. Ella también _____ (querer) saber si _____ (estar) muy congestionado.
6. Roberto _____ (contestar) afirmativamente.
7. La recepcionista le _____ (decir) que le _____ (poder) dar una cita para las dos de la tarde.
8. Roberto la _____ (aceptar) y le _____ (dar) las gracias.
9. Como era temprano y _____ (sentirse) mal, _____ (dormirse) otra vez.

IV. Hacer in time expressions.

A. Di cuánto tiempo hace que...

Modelo: estudiar en esta universidad.
> **Hace un año que estudio en esta universidad.**

1. estar en clase
2. estudiar español
3. conocer al/a la profesor/a de español
4. vivir en la misma casa o en el mismo apartamento
5. tener permiso de conducir un auto

B. Di cuánto tiempo hace que pasó lo siguiente.

1. hablar con su familia
2. comprar un regalo para alguien
3. hacerse un examen médico
4. visitar un museo
5. llegar a la universidad

V. Repaso general. Contesta con oraciones completas.

1. ¿Qué síntomas tenías la última vez que fue al médico?
2. ¿Hace cuánto tiempo que estudias en la universidad?
3. ¿Hace cuánto tiempo que conociste a tu mejor amigo/a?
4. ¿Quién y cómo era tu maestro/a preferido/a en la escuela primaria?
5. ¿Dónde estabas cuando ocurrió el ataque terrorista del 11 de septiembre?
6. ¿Cómo te sentiste al oír las noticias? ¿Qué hiciste después?

VI. Cultura.

1. Nombra por lo menos un país que tiene frontera con Colombia y otro que tiene frontera con Venezuela.
2. ¿De dónde vino el nombre de Venezuela?
3. Describe por lo menos un remedio casero (*home remedy*) que es común en Latinoamérica.
4. ¿Quién es Gabriel García Márquez?

Answers to the *Autoprueba y repaso* are found in **Apéndice 2**.

Así es mi casa

By the end of this chapter you will be able to:

- Describe a house or an apartment and its contents
- Talk about household chores
- Use commands in informal situations
- Talk about what has or had happened
- Make comparisons

Así se dice	Así se forma	Cultura	Dicho y hecho
• Así es mi casa • Los quehaceres domésticos	**1. Tú** commands **2.** The present perfect **3.** The past perfect **4.** Comparisons of equality and inequality; the superlative	• Paraguay y Uruguay • El patio de las casas hispanas • Artes pictóricas: Pedro Figari	• El nuevo apartamento de Susana • Bienes raíces • Una casa muy especial

ENTRANDO AL TEMA

1. ¿Cuántas horas por semana pasas haciendo quehaceres (*chores*) en tu casa?

2. Piensa en las características de tu casa ideal. Al final del capítulo, la vas a describir.

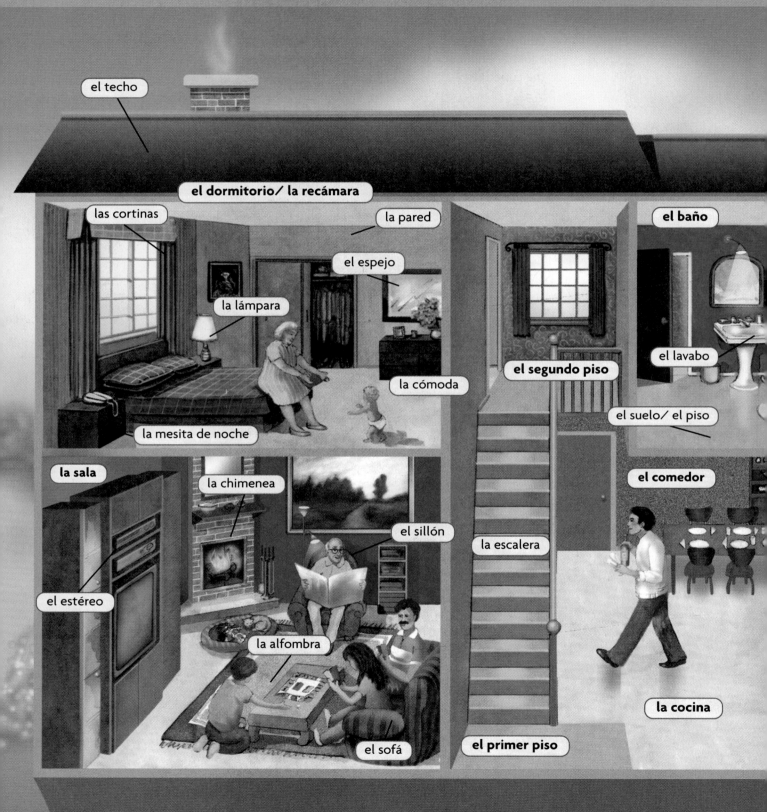

el techo

el dormitorio/ la recámara

las cortinas

la pared

el espejo

la lámpara

el baño

la cómoda

el lavabo

la mesita de noche

el segundo piso

el suelo/ el piso

la sala

la chimenea

el comedor

el sillón

la escalera

el estéreo

la alfombra

la cocina

el sofá

el primer piso

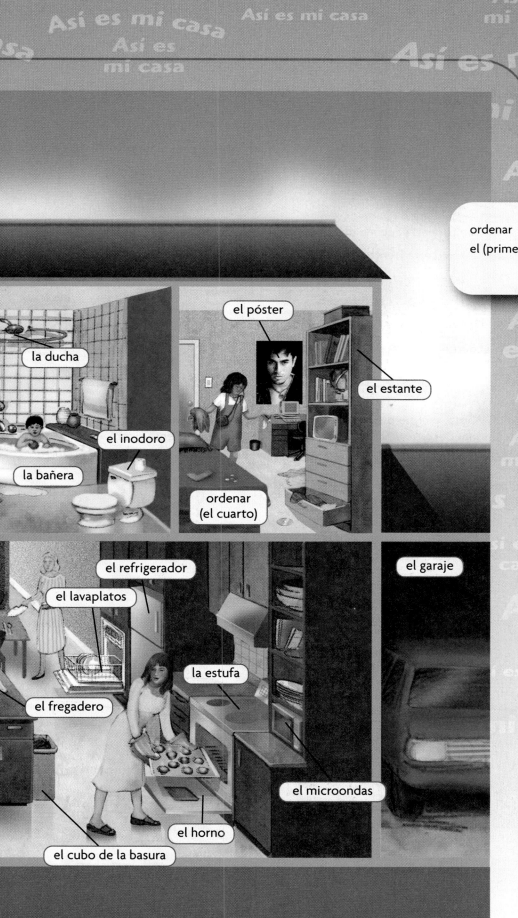

| ordenar | to tidy |
| el (primer) piso | (first) floor |

la ducha

el inodoro

la bañera

el póster

el estante

ordenar
(el cuarto)

el refrigerador

el garaje

el lavaplatos

la estufa

el fregadero

el microondas

el horno

el cubo de la basura

10-1 ¿Dónde están?

 Paso 1. Decide si las siguientes descripciones son ciertas o falsas, según los dibujos de las páginas 328–329.

	Cierto	Falso
1. La lámpara está **encima de** la mesita de noche.	✓	
2. El estéreo está **frente al** sofá.		✓
3. El cubo de basura está **lejos del** fregadero.		✓
4. El garaje está **al lado de** la casa.	✓	
5. El lavabo está **cerca del** horno.		✓
6. El dormitorio está **debajo del** techo.	✓	
7. El baño está **al lado del** dormitorio de Elena.	✓	

Paso 2. Ahora, escribe tres descripciones sobre otras habitaciones y cosas de la casa como las del *Paso 1*. Después, en grupos pequeños, túrnense para leer sus descripciones y adivinar las habitaciones y cosas que sus compañeros/as describen.

Modelo: Estudiante A: **Está entre la sala y la cocina.**

Estudiante B: **Es la escalera.**

Una mesa elegante

10-2 ¿Para qué sirve?

Paso 1. Escoge tres objetos de la mesa y otras dos cosas de la casa (por ejemplo: la cómoda, el estante, el espejo, etc.) y escribe breves definiciones indicando para qué sirve cada objeto o lugar.

Modelo: (el vaso) Sirve para beber agua,...

Paso 2. En parejas, lee tus definiciones a tu compañero/a. Él/Ella identifica la palabra. Túrnense.

En el hogar

Vivo en una casa grande de dos pisos que pertenece° a mi familia; no tenemos que **alquilar**la. Me encanta esta casa y no tengo deseos de **mudarme** a otra. Mi cuarto preferido en el invierno es la **sala familiar**. ¿Saben por qué? Pues muy sencillo: cuando hace frío, me acuesto junto a la chimenea y no quiero **moverme** de allí. No me molesta cuando los otros miembros de la familia **prenden** o **apagan** la **luz**, el radio o el televisor. Si suena el teléfono, lo ignoro. En el verano prefiero **bajar** al **sótano** porque es más fresco. Aunque° en la sala hay un sofá, un sillón y otros **muebles** cómodos, mi mueble favorito, un viejo sofá, está en el sótano. Además, los **ruidos** de la **lavadora** y de la **secadora** me **ayudan**[1] a dormirme. Pero no crean que soy perezoso. **Guardo** mis energías para los paseos de noche por el **jardín**, para **subir** al techo de la casa y para las visitas a los **vecinos** de las casas cercanas; son todos muy amables y simpáticos conmigo. También **ayudo** a mantener la casa libre de ratones°. ¿Saben quién soy?

belongs

Although

libre... free of mice

alquilar	*to rent*	**el mueble**	*piece of furniture*
apagar	*to turn off*	**mudarse**	*to move (to new house, city, etc.)*
apague			
ayudar	*to help*	**prender**	*to turn on*
bajar	*to go down*	**el ruido**	*noise*
guardar	*to keep, to put away*	**la secadora**	*dryer*
la lavadora	*washer*	**subir**	*to go up*
la luz	*light*	**el/la vecino/a**	*neighbor*
mover	*to move (something)*		
moverse	*to move (oneself)*		

---

[1]**Ayudar** requires the preposition a when followed by an infinitive.

10-3 **Asociaciones.** En parejas, un/a estudiante lee una palabra de su lista a su compañero/a. El/La compañero/a dice dos o tres palabras asociadas con esta palabra. El/La primer/a estudiante las escribe. Túrnense.

Modelo: Estudiante A: **prender**

Estudiante B: **la luz, la televisión, la lavadora**

(el Estudiante A escribe estas palabras junto a **prender**)

¡Atención! El Estudiante A debe cubrir con la mano la columna de Estudiante B y viceversa.

Estudiante A:

bajar _____

sótano _____

secadora _____

vecino _____

Estudiante B:

alquilar _____

jardín _____

ruido _____

mueble _____

10-4 **La casa familiar.** En grupos pequeños, hablen de su casa familiar.

Modelo: Estudiante A: **¿Dónde vive tu familia?**

Estudiante B: **En Denver, Colorado.**

Estudiante C: **¿Cuánto tiempo hace que viven en esa casa?**

Estudiante B: **Hace ocho años. Y ¿cómo es la casa?...**

10-5 **Tu apartamento o cuarto actual (*current*).**

Paso 1. En una hoja de papel, dibuja un plano de tu apartamento o cuarto actual. Incluye elementos arquitectónicos (puertas, ventanas) así como muebles y accesorios (televisor, estéreo, pósters...).

Paso 2. En parejas, describe tu plano a tu compañero/a, que lo va a dibujar. Luego revisa el dibujo de tu compañero/a e indica que diferencias hay entre el dibujo y tu apartamento o cuarto. Túrnense.

10-6 **¿Cómo viven los estudiantes?**

Paso 1. Hagan estas preguntas a tres compañeros/as de clase. Escriban sus nombres en las columnas y anoten sus respuestas.

	Estudiante 1: _____	Estudiante 2: _____	Estudiante 3: _____
1. ¿Es mejor vivir en una residencia universitaria o en un apartamento/ una casa? ¿Por qué?	☐ Residencia ☐ Apartamento/ casa Porque...	☐ Residencia ☐ Apartamento/ casa Porque...	☐ Residencia ☐ Apartamento/ casa Porque...
2. ¿Es mejor vivir solo/a o con compañeros/as de cuarto? ¿Por qué?	☐ Solo/a ☐ Con compañeros/as Porque...	☐ Solo/a ☐ Con compañeros/as Porque...	☐ Solo/a ☐ Concompañeros/as Porque...
3. ¿Qué te gusta, y qué no te gusta, del lugar donde vives ahora? ¿Por qué?	Me gusta... No me gusta...	Me gusta... No me gusta...	Me gusta... No me gusta...

 Paso 2. Compartan lo que aprendieron con la clase. ¿Tienen ustedes preferencias similares?

Los quehaceres domésticos°

Housekeeping chores

El verano pasado los estudiantes alquilaron una casa en el campo° para pasar unas semanas. Todos colaboraron en los quehaceres domésticos. Alfonso y Javier ordenaron los cuartos en el segundo piso. Alfonso tiene alergia al polvo°; por eso prefirió **hacer las camas** mientras Javier **pasaba la aspiradora.** Todos los días, antes de comer, Carmen **ponía la mesa.** Después de comer Natalia **quitaba la mesa** y llevaba los platos a la cocina. Allí Linda y Manuel estaban muy bien organizados para terminar pronto: Linda **lavaba los platos** y Manuel los **secaba.** También había un poco de trabajo que hacer fuera de la casa. Como siempre, Esteban no tenía muchas ganas de trabajar duro y sólo quería **sacar la basura.** ¡Qué suerte que Pepita no es perezosa y no le molestaba **cortar el césped**!

countryside

dust

Así se dice

10-7 Los quehaceres domésticos.

 Paso 1. Completa la tabla escribiendo quién hacía estos quehaceres en tu casa familiar y si tú los haces ahora. Añade dos quehaceres más.

	En tu casa familiar, ¿quién lo hacía?	Ahora, ¿lo haces?
1. hacer mi cama	**Modelo: Mi mamá lo hacía.**	**Sí, lo hago./ No, no lo hago.**
2. poner la mesa		
3. lavar los platos		
4. sacar la basura		
5. pasar la aspiradora		
6. cortar el césped		
7.		
8.		

 Paso 2. Ahora, en grupos pequeños, compartan la información de sus tablas.

Modelo: De niño, yo hacía mi cama, y ahora también la hago.
  o **pero ahora no la hago.**

Paso 3. Basándose en sus respuestas anteriores, contesten las siguientes preguntas.

1. ¿Ayudaban mucho en su familia cuando eran niños? ¿Qué quehaceres les gustaban más/menos? ¿Recibían alguna compensación por su ayuda?
2. ¿Cómo era la división de los quehaceres en su familia entre adultos y niños? ¿Y entre hombres y mujeres?
3. ¿Qué quehaceres hacen ahora? ¿Con qué frecuencia? Si viven con otras personas, ¿cómo comparten los quehaceres?

NOTA CULTURAL

Los quehaceres y las criadas (maids)
Due to the relatively low wages in Latin America, many middle class families can afford to hire maids who take care of most of the household chores. In other families, it is often (but not always) the case that girls are expected to take care of cooking and cleaning tasks.

PALABRAS ÚTILES

darle comida (al perro)	*feed (the dog)*
lavar/ planchar (la ropa)	*to wash/iron (clothes)*
limpiar (el baño, el garaje...)	*to clean (the bathroom, garage)*
preparar (la comida)	*to prepare (the meal)*
sacudir los muebles	*to dust*

Nacionalidades:
paraguayo/a
uruguayo/a

Antes de leer

1. ¿Cómo se llama el río que conecta Paraguay con Uruguay?

2. ¿Cuál es la capital de Paraguay?

3. ¿Dónde está situada la capital de Uruguay?

4. Paraguay tiene el mismo tamaño que (*same size as*), ¿qué estado?
   ☐ Illinois
   ☐ Rhode Island
   ☐ California

Uruguay y Paraguay, junto con Brasil y Argentina, crearon en 1991 el Mercosur, una zona económica que corresponde a un área cuatro veces más grande que la de la Unión Europea. Durante el período colonial estos dos países tuvieron una historia muy similar. Sin embargo, su situación geográfica y su destino político generaron diferencias regionales que resultaron en dos naciones con identidades muy distintas.

PARAGUAY

Paraguay es del tamaño del estado de California. Como Bolivia, Paraguay está en el corazón de Sudamérica y no tiene salida al océano. El Río Paraguay cruza el país de norte a sur y lo divide en dos partes. Casi el 95% de la población vive al este del río.

Existen en Paraguay dos lenguas oficiales, el español y el guaraní. El 94% de los paraguayos hablan, escriben, cantan y expresan sus emociones en las dos lenguas. La constitución federal y los libros de texto son escritos en las dos lenguas. Las palabras *jaguar* y *piraña* vienen del guaraní, y también el nombre del país: **pará** = *océano*; **gua** = *a o de*; **y** = *agua*; es decir, *agua que va al océano*.

La dictadura militar de Alfredo Stroessner duró treinta y cinco años, hasta el año 1989, y ahora Paraguay es un país democrático.

La gente de Paraguay es muy diversa. La población incluye inmigrantes europeos y aproximadamente veinticinco tribus indígenas. El 95% de la población es de origen mestizo y la mayoría vive de la agricultura.

Cultura: Paraguay y Uruguay

La capital, Asunción, está a orillas[1] del río Paraguay. Es la ciudad más moderna del país y es el puerto más importante. La ciudad conserva muchos ejemplos de arquitectura colonial. Los tranvías[2] amarillos de Asunción se consideran una antigüedad. ¿Qué otras ciudades famosas tienen tranvías?

[1]a... on the banks [2]trolleys

Paraguay es el único país de Latinoamérica en el cual la biosfera no está contaminada. Las espectaculares cataratas del Iguazú están en la frontera entre Argentina, Brasil y Paraguay.

A partir de 1609 los jesuitas establecieron comunidades autosuficientes que agrupaban a cientos de indígenas guaraníes y los protegían de los traficantes de esclavos[3] portugueses y españoles. Mira la foto de las ruinas de las misiones en Trinidad, Paraguay. ¿Conoces otras misiones como éstas? ¿Dónde están?

[3]slaves

URUGUAY

Uruguay es la república sudamericana más pequeña. La geografía uruguaya es uniforme: al norte están las llanuras[4] y al sur está la Banda Oriental, una región muy plana donde está situada la capital.

La exportación de la agricultura y la ganadería[5] son la base de la economía del país, que es una de las más fuertes de Latinoamérica. La industria pesquera y la manufactura de productos derivados del ganado (lana, cuero, carne) son otra parte importante del sector comercial. El turismo también genera muchos beneficios y representa casi el 30% de la actividad económica.

[4]flatlands [5]livestock

En Uruguay la población es uniforme —casi un 90% de los uruguayos descienden de inmigrantes europeos, sobre todo de España e Italia. El nivel de alfabetismo[6] es 97%, el más alto de Latinoamérica, y la vida cultural en Uruguay es muy intensa. La legislación social de Uruguay es una de las más innovadoras de Hispanoamérica. Todas las personas que han trabajado treinta años tienen derecho a jubilarse[7] con pensión.

[6]literacy [7]to retire

Montevideo, la bella capital, está situada a orillas del Río de la Plata y el Atlántico; posee el mejor puerto natural de Sudamérica. En esta ciudad vive la mitad[8] de la población del país.

[8]half

Punta del Este, centro vacacional de fama mundial, es sinónimo de playas. Ofrece kilómetros de variada costa, desde las tranquilas aguas de sus bahías hasta el mar abierto y las olas[9] fuertes del lado del Atlántico.

[9]waves

Cristina Peri Rossi (12 noviembre 1941) nació en Montevideo, donde completó sus estudios universitarios. Es considerada una de los líderes de la novela latinoamericana de la época pos–1960. Ha escrito más de treinta y siete obras, incluyendo novelas, poemas y cuentos cortos. Vive en España desde 1975.

Después de leer

Existen varios contrastes importantes entre Paraguay y Uruguay. ¿A qué país hace referencia cada oración?

1. No tiene costas.
   ☐ Paraguay   ☐ Uruguay
2. Su capital tiene costas sobre el Atlántico.
   ☐ Paraguay   ☐ Uruguay
3. El español es la única lengua oficial.
   ☐ Paraguay   ☐ Uruguay
4. El nivel de alfabetización es muy alto.
   ☐ Paraguay   ☐ Uruguay
5. Su población es diversa; existe una gran variedad de tribus indígenas.
   ☐ Paraguay   ☐ Uruguay
6. Su población es uniforme; casi todos descienden de inmigrantes.
   ☐ Paraguay   ☐ Uruguay

Los uruguayos son fanáticos del fútbol. Han conquistado dos títulos olímpicos, dos campeonatos mundiales, catorce americanos y la Copa de Oro en 1980. El estadio Centenario en Montevideo es un monumento histórico del fútbol mundial y el sitio del primer mundial de fútbol en 1930. Capacidad: 80.000 personas.

Así se forma   QUIA

> Ven, mi amor.
> No te desanimes.
> Camina hacia tu
> abuelita.

1. Giving orders and advice to family and friends: *Tú* commands

Informal **tú** commands are used to give orders or advice to persons whom you address informally as **tú** (friends, children, etc.). Note that affirmative and negative **tú** command forms differ from each other.

A. Affirmative *tú* commands

Regular affirmative **tú** command forms have the same form as the third-person singular of the present tense.

¡Mira!	*Look!*
¡Espera!	*Wait!*
¡Vuelve!	*Come back!*

Some affirmative **tú** command forms are irregular:

decir	**di**	**Di**me la verdad.
hacer	**haz**	**Haz** la cama, por favor.
ir	**ve**	**Ve** al garaje para buscar los refrescos.
poner	**pon**	**Pon** la ropa en el ropero.
salir	**sal**	**Sal** de mi cuarto, por favor.
ser	**sé**	**Sé** bueno, por favor.
tener	**ten**	**Ten** paciencia. Vamos a cenar muy pronto.
venir	**ven**	**Ven** a la cocina para ayudarme.

Note that, like affirmative **Ud.** commands, object and reflexive pronouns follow and are attached to affirmative **tú** commands. A written accent is added in combinations of more than two syllables[2].

Muéstramelo. *Show it to me.*   **Hazlo**. *Do it.*   **Póntelo.** *Put it on.*

10-8 **Los quehaceres domésticos.** Lee los siguientes infinitivos; después, escucha los mandatos. Escribe cada mandato debajo del dibujo correcto.

lavar	regar (ie)	barrer	hacer	sacudir	sacar
ordenar	poner	dar	cortar	secar	pasar

---

[2]The oral stress in affirmative **tú** command forms is on the second-to-last syllable: mira, **com**pra (unless, of course, the verb form only has one syllable: h<u>a</u>z). The oral stress does not change, but adding pronouns means adding syllables: **mí**rame, **cóm**pralo, **haz**lo.

1. _____

2. _____

3. _____

4. _____

5. _____

6. _____

7. _____

8. _____

9. _____

10. _____

11. _____

12. _____

10-9 **¿Los niños pueden hacerlo?** Mira otra vez los dibujos de la actividad 10–8. ¿Qué quehaceres son apropiados para un niño de siete años? ¿Cuáles debe hacer un adulto? Escribe mandatos afirmativos de **tú** para cada actividad en la columna apropiada. Después, comparte tus respuestas con un/a compañero/a.

Mandatos para un niño de siete años.	Mandatos para un adulto solamente

10-10 ¡Hazlo, por favor! En parejas, imaginen que Uds. son compañeros/as de cuarto. Estudiante A: Hay muchas cosas que te molestan de los hábitos de tu compañero/a y hoy, por fin, decides resolver esta situación. Usa mandatos de **tú** afirmativos para pedirle a tu compañero/a lo que quieres. Estudiante B: Responde a tu compañero/a con una excusa o justificación. Túrnense.

Modelo: salir del cuarto

Estudiante A: **Si quieres fumar, ¡sal del cuarto!**

Estudiante B: **Pero hace mucho frío afuera.**

¡Atención! Cubran la lista de su compañero/a con la mano.

Estudiante A:

1. lavar...
2. poner la ropa...
3. ayudarme a...
4. traerme...
5. apagar...
6. venir a...

Estudiante B:

1. sentarte en...
2. quitarte...
3. ponerte...
4. decirme...
5. ir a...
6. ser...

B. Negative *tú* commands

To make a negative **tú** command, simply add **-s** to the **Ud.** command form.

Ud. command	Negative *tú* command	
Espere en la sala.	No **esperes** en la sala.	*Don't wait in the living room.*
Ponga los libros allí.	No **pongas** los libros allí.	*Don't put the books there.*
Cierre la ventana.	No **cierres** la ventana.	*Don't close the window.*

Object and reflexive pronouns are placed before the verb in all negative commands. Observe the placement of the pronouns in the following negative commands and compare them with the corresponding affirmative commands.

Negative	Affirmative
¡No **lo** comas!	¡Cóme**lo**!
¡No **los** compres!	¡Cómpra**los**!
¡No **lo** hagas!	¡Haz**lo**!
¡No **te** vayas!	¡Ve**te**!

DICHOS

No digas en secreto lo que no quieres oír en público.
¿Qué puede pasar si le dices algo en secreto a otra persona?
No dejes para mañana lo que puedes hacer hoy.
¿Estás de acuerdo? ¿Hay un dicho equivalente en inglés?

10-11 El diablito y el ángel. Hay un conflicto en tu conciencia entre lo que dice el diablito y lo que dice el ángel. Decide si estos mandatos vienen del diablito o del ángel. Inventa dos mandatos adicionales.

	El diablito	El ángel
1. No bebas muchas cervezas.		
2. Come las verduras.		
3. Gasta todo tu dinero en ropa y fiestas.		
4. No salgas todas las noches.		
5. No llames a tus padres todos los días.		
6. No duermas todo el día.		
7. ¡Fuma cigarrillos! Son buenos para la salud.		
8. ¿...?		
9. ¿...?		

¡Hazlo! ¡No lo hagas!

 10-12 **Nuestro amigo Esteban.** Esteban es "un poco" desordenado. En grupos pequeños, estudien el dibujo y díganle lo que debe o no debe hacer. Usen tres mandatos de **tú** afirmativos y tres mandatos de **tú** negativos. Un/a secretario/a escribe los mandatos y luego se los presenta a la clase.

 10-13 **¡No, no, no!** Tu compañero/a de cuarto todavía hace algunas cosas que te molestan. ¿Qué le dices? Justifica o explica intentando ser creativo/a. Responde también a las peticiones de tu compañero/a y ofrece una solución.

Modelo: prender el televisor

Estudiante A: **No prendas el televisor ahora, por favor; necesito silencio para hacer yoga.**

Estudiante B: **¡Pero empieza mi programa favorito! Si quieres, puedo bajar el volumen.**

PALABRAS ÚTILES

cajón	*drawer (bureau)*
recoger	*to gather, pick up*

¡Atención! Cubran la parte de su compañero/a con la mano.

Estudiante A:

1. tocar mis objetos personales
2. usar mi computadora
3. traer a tus amigos/as al cuarto a las...
4. ponerse mi ropa
5. ¿...?

Estudiante B:

1. comer mi comida
2. hablar por teléfono todo el tiempo
3. hacer ruido
4. poner tu ropa en el suelo
5. ¿...?

Escenas

Inés

Linda

Manuel

Buscando el apartamento ideal

Inés y Linda van a compartir un apartamento el próximo año académico. Después de buscar un apartamento durante todo el día, las chicas se encuentran con Manuel en un café.

Paso 1. Indica si los siguientes aspectos son importantes para estudiantes que buscan un apartamento.

	Muy importante	Importante	Poco importante	No importa
precio del alquiler				
número de dormitorios				
número de baños				
tamaño (*size*) de habitaciones				
una sala grande				
una cocina bien equipada				
amueblado (*furnished*)				
garaje				
espacio exterior (jardín, patio)				
piscina (*swimming pool*), gimnasio				
distancia de escuelas y parques				
distancia de tiendas/ mercados				
distancia de la universidad				

Paso 2. Escucha la conversación e indica si las siguientes afirmaciones son ciertas o falsas.

1. Linda e Inés encontraron un apartamento perfecto.
2. Es difícil encontrar un apartamento porque hay pocos.
3. Las chicas son flexibles pero los apartamentos son muy malos.
4. Manuel piensa que van a encontrar un apartamento ideal rápidamente.

Paso 3. Lee las siguientes preguntas. Después, escucha la conversación otra vez y escribe las respuestas.

1. ¿Cuántos apartamentos vieron Inés y Linda hoy?
2. ¿Cuántos dormitorios y baños quieren?
3. ¿Qué otras características quieren?
4. ¿Cuánto quieren pagar Inés y Linda?

Paso 4. Escucha una vez más y lee el texto. Después, revisa tus respuestas.

Manuel:	¿Qué tal? ¿Encontraron un apartamento apropiado?
Linda:	Bueno, vimos seis apartamentos, pero no encontramos exactamente lo que buscábamos.
Manuel:	¿Y cómo eran los apartamentos que vieron?
Inés:	Uno tenía dos dormitorios, pero sólo un baño; otro tenía una cocina muy pequeña...
Linda:	Y no encontramos nada cerca de la universidad.
Inés:	Uno que vimos cerca del parque tenía sala y comedor, pero tenía muy pocas ventanas; no había suficiente luz.
Linda:	¡Ay, Manuel! ¡Nunca vamos a encontrar nuestro apartamento ideal!
Manuel:	Pues, ¿qué es lo que buscan?
Inés:	El apartamento que queremos debe tener dos dormitorios grandes, dos baños completos, una sala y un comedor alfombrados, ¡y muchas ventanas!
Linda:	Sí, y también una cocina equipada con microondas y lavaplatos. Y una piscina°.
Inés:	¡Ah! Y el alquiler debe ser barato. Sólo queremos pagar 700 dólares mensuales.
Manuel:	Supongo° que también quieren aire acondicionado, ¿no?
Inés y Linda:	¡Claro que sí!
Manuel:	Pues... ¡buena suerte°! Van a necesitarla.

swimming pool

I suppose

buena... *good luck!*

Paso 5. Imagina que vas a buscar tu primera casa o tu primer apartamento. ¿Cómo es la casa/ el apartamento de tus sueños? ¿Qué aspectos van a ser más importantes? Díselo a un/a compañero/a de clase.

Así se forma

¡Mira! ¡Por fin he aprendido a esquiar!

2. The present perfect: Saying what has happened

The Spanish present perfect corresponds closely to the English one, both in its use and in how it is formed. The present perfect describes actions that began in the past but are still connected to the present in that the event still continues or its consequences are still felt in the present.

Juan **ha viajado** mucho y siempre cuenta historias interesantes.
*Juan **has traveled** a lot and he always tells interesting stories.*

He perdido mi libro de español y ahora tengo que comprar otro.
*I **have lost** my Spanish book and now I have to buy another one.*

The time period that frames the action is not over yet. When the action is completed in a period of time that is over, *the preterit*, not the present perfect, *is* used. Compare:

He estudiado mucho hoy; por eso ahora voy a jugar al tenis.
*I **have studied** a lot today; so now I am going to play tennis.*

El semestre pasado estudié mucho.
*Last semester **I studied** very hard.*

The present perfect is formed by combining the present tense of **haber** (*to have*) and the past participle of a verb.

- To form the past participle of most Spanish verbs, add **-ado** to the stem of **-ar** verbs and **-ido** to the stem of **-er** and **-ir** verbs.

- When used with **haber**, the past participle does not change; it always ends in **-o**.

llamar	llam	+	**-ado**	=	**llamado**
comer	com	+	**-ido**	=	**comido**
vivir	viv	+	**-ido**	=	**vivido**

presente de *haber* + participio pasado		
(yo)	**he llamado**	*(I have called)*
(tú)	**has llamado**	*(you have called)*
(Ud., él/ella)	**ha llamado**	*(you have called, he/she has called)*
(nosotros/as)	**hemos llamado**	*(we have called)*
(vosotros/as)	**habéis llamado**	*(you have called)*
(Uds., ellos/ellas)	**han llamado**	*(you/they have called)*

The following **-er** and **-ir** verbs have irregular past participles.

abrir	**abierto**	opened, open
decir	**dicho**	said, told
escribir	**escrito**	written
hacer	**hecho**	done, made
morir	**muerto**	died, dead
romper (to break)	**roto**	broken
poner	**puesto**	put, placed
ver	**visto**	seen
volver	**vuelto**	returned
devolver	**devuelto**	returned
resolver (to resolve)	**resuelto**	resolved

Object and reflexive pronouns immediately precede the conjugated form of **haber**.

Todavía no **lo** he terminado.	I haven't finished **it** yet.
Le he escrito varias veces.	I have written **(to) him** several times.
Nos hemos preocupado por él.	We have worried about **him**.

10-14 **Una visita especial.** Tus amigos Max y Nicolás acaban de mudarse a su nuevo apartamento y hacen una fiesta para celebrarlo. Estás muy impresionado/a porque ¡todo está perfecto! Escucha a Max, anota todo lo que han hecho e indica la persona que hizo cada cosa.

Modelo: Oyes: **He pasado la aspiradora.**
Marcas: **Max (Yo)**

	Max (yo)	Nicolás (él)	Los dos (nosotros)
1.			
2.			
3.			
4.			
5.			
6.			
7.			
8.			

NOTA DE LENGUA

The past participle may also be used as an adjective with **estar** and with nouns to show a condition. As an adjective, it agrees in gender and number with the noun it describes. You have used this construction in previous chapters.
La puerta está **cerrada**.
　The door is **closed**.
Duermo con las ventanas **abiertas**.
　I sleep with the windows **open**.
Mis amigos/as están **sentados/as** en el sofá.
　My friends are **seated** on the sofa.

DICHOS

Sobre gustos no hay nada escrito.

Del dicho al hecho hay largo trecho°. distance
Dicho y hecho.
¿Cuál de estos refranes es el título de tu libro de español? ¿Cuál se refiere a las personas que hablan mucho pero no hacen nada? ¿Cuál se refiere a las preferencias individuales?

10-15 **¿Qué hay de nuevo?** Este fin de semana han ocurrido muchas cosas. Usando verbos del cuadro, escribe oraciones para describir estos cambios.

fracturarse	aprender a	sacar	afeitarse
pintar	ganar	cortarse	

Modelo: **Octavio se ha fracturado una pierna.**

Octavio

Esteban

Rubén

el profesor
Marín-Vivar

Javier

Linda

Camila

10-16 **Experiencias.**

Paso 1. Completa la columna **Yo** con información verdadera sobre tus experiencias especificando dónde has ido, qué has ganado, etc. Añade otra experiencia interesante en la última línea.

HINT

* = irregular past participle

Modelo: **1. He viajado a China.**

	Yo	Un/a compañero/a
1. viajar a otro país	✓	
2. conocer a alguien famoso	.	
3. ganar una competición	-	
4. visitar un lugar fascinante	✓	
5. practicar deportes de aventura	.	✓
6. hacer* algo peligroso	✓	
7. comer algo exótico	✓	
8. ver* un concierto/ obra de teatro muy especial	✓	
9. participar en un evento especial/ importante		`
10. ¿...?		

Paso 2. Caminando por la clase, haz preguntas a tus compañeros/as para averiguar si alguien ha hecho algo similar. Si un estudiante responde afirmativamente, anota su nombre en la columna Un/a compañero/a en la tabla de arriba. Todos los nombres deben ser de personas diferentes. Responde también a las preguntas de tus compañeros/as, hablando de tus experiencias.

Modelo: —¿Has viajado a China?
—Sí, he viajado a China./ No, no he viajado a otros países./ No, pero he viajado a Polonia.

Paso 3. ¿Quién tiene el mayor número de compañeros/as en la lista? ¿Qué experiencias compartes con otros/as estudiantes de la clase?

Modelo: **Abel y yo hemos viajado a China.**

10-17 ¡Qué mentiroso (*What a liar*)!

Paso 1. Escribe en un papel tres oraciones describiendo cosas que has hecho (o no has hecho). Piensa en actividades poco frecuentes o atípicas. Dos deben ser ciertas y una falsa.

Modelo: **He montado en elefante.**

He jugado tenis con Venus Williams.

Nunca he visto el océano.

Paso 2. En grupos de cuatro personas, tomen turnos: una persona lee sus oraciones; después de cada afirmación, los/las compañeros/as le hacen preguntas. La persona que contesta tiene que inventar los detalles de la experiencia falsa para hacerla creíble.

Paso 3. El grupo vota para decidir qué experiencia es falsa y la persona que hizo la afirmación explica si lo era o no.

SITUACIONES

Son hermanos. Sus padres salieron el fin de semana y los dejaron a ustedes encargados (*in charge*) de la casa. Ustedes decidieron tener una pequeña fiesta. Sus padres regresan un día antes, y la casa está hecha un desastre. Ellos les preguntan enojados: **¿Qué ha pasado aquí?** Intenten culparse uno a otro diciendo lo su hermano/a ha hecho o no ha hecho.

Antes de leer

¿Tiene tu casa un patio o un "deck"?
¿Qué haces allí?

Un patio tradicional hispano, en
Colombia. ¿Qué actividades son
posibles en esta parte de la casa?

Antes de leer

¿Tiene tu casa un patio o un "deck"?
¿Qué haces allí?

Uno de los elementos más representativos de muchas viviendas hispanas es el patio. Muchas casas —incluso las más pequeñas— tienen algún tipo de patio. El diseño tradicional del patio hispano, rodeado de[1] paredes altas, es una mezcla[2] de influencias romanas y árabes. En estas dos culturas la vida privada era muy importante y las casas estaban separadas de la calle por paredes y muros. La luz y el aire entraban en los cuartos por las ventanas, puertas y balcones que rodeaban el patio central.

Hoy, las casas hispanas de estilo colonial tienen este tipo de patio central, con una fuente[3] y plantas; pero en las casas más modernas, el patio generalmente está detrás de la casa. A diferencia de los "decks" tan populares en los EE.UU., los patios hispanos no tienen pisos de madera[4]; frecuentemente el suelo está cubierto de cerámica o piedra[5].

El patio, un lugar privado al aire libre[6], es un espacio fundamental en la vivienda hispana porque tiene varias funciones importantes. Es un sitio cómodo[7] para tomar un poco de sol, recibir visitas o dar una pequeña fiesta.

---

[1]rodeado... *surrounded by* [2]*mixture* [3]*fountain* [4]*wood* [5]*stone* [6]**al...** *open air* [7]*comfortable*

Después de leer

Nombra dos diferencias entre los patios/ decks en los Estados Unidos
y el patio latinoamericano.

Así se forma

...pero, Juanito, me dijiste que ya habías ordenado tu cuarto.

3. The past perfect: Saying what had happened

The past perfect describes an action that had already occurred prior to another event or given time in the past.

> Cuando llegaron los abuelos, ya **habíamos limpiado** la casa.
> *When our grandparents arrived, we **had** already **cleaned** the house.*

> A las diez de la noche aún no **habían cenado**.
> *At 10 p.m. they **had** not **eaten** dinner yet.*

The past perfect is formed with the imperfect tense of **haber** and the past participle of the verb. It corresponds to the English *had eaten, had spoken,* etc.

imperfecto de *haber* + participio pasado		
(yo)	**había llamado**	*(I had called)*
(tú)	**habías llamado**	*(you had called)*
(Ud., él/ella)	**había llamado**	*(you/he/she had called)*
(nosotros/as)	**habíamos llamado**	*(we had called)*
(vosotros/as)	**habíais llamado**	*(you had called)*
(Uds., ellos/ellas)	**habían llamado**	*(you/they had called)*

10-18 **¿Qué ocurrió primero?** Decide para cada oración qué acción ocurrió primero (márcalo con un "1") y cuál sucedió después (márcalo con un "2"). Luego decide si cada oración es lógica o ilógica.

Modelo: Esteban <u>llegó</u> a su casa cansado porque ya <u>había estudiado</u> más
de tres horas.   **2**   **1**

☐ Lógico.   ☐ Ilógico.

1. Alfonso ya había hecho la cama cuando se despertó.

   ☐ Lógico.   ☐ Ilógico

2. Pepita sacó la basura. Ya había cortado el césped.

   ☐ Lógico.   ☐ Ilógico

3. Natalia lavó los platos. Ya había quitado la mesa.

   ☐ Lógico.   ☐ Ilógico

4. Esteban había secado los platos y los lavó.

   ☐ Lógico.   ☐ Ilógico

5. Manuel ordenó su cuarto cuando ya había barrido el patio.

   ☐ Lógico.   ☐ Ilógico

Así se forma

10-19 ¡Qué hijos tan malos! Los padres salieron de casa. ¿Qué descubrieron al regresar? ¿Qué habían y no habían hecho los hijos?

Modelo: ordenar la sala familiar
Probablemente no habían ordenado la sala familiar.

1. pasar la aspiradora

2. hacer las camas

3. invitar a amigos/as a la casa

4. comer toda la comida en el refrigerador

5. sacar la basura

6. lavar los platos

7. ver muchas películas

8. romper una ventana

10-20 Las experiencias de la vida.

Paso 1. Escribe tres oraciones describiendo algunas cosas interesantes que ya habías hecho antes de los dieciocho años, y tres cosas que todavía no habías hecho.

Modelo: Ya **había jugado** muchos torneos de tenis.
Todavía **no había aprendido** a nadar.

Cosas que ya había hecho antes de los dieciocho años	Cosas que todavía no había hecho antes de los dieciocho años.
1.	1.
2.	2.
3.	3.

Paso 2. En grupos pequeños, compartan sus experiencias y pidan más detalles sobre las experiencias de sus compañeros/as.

Paso 3. Ahora, en sus grupos, van a elegir una persona famosa. Escriban tres oraciones describiendo lo que la persona ya había hecho antes de los dieciocho años y tres cosas que no había hecho todavía pero que iba a hacer (*was going to do*) después. Cuando terminen, lean sus oraciones a la clase sin decir el nombre de la persona. La clase va a intentar adivinar quién es.

Modelo: Cuando tenía deiciocho años, José Luis Chilavert ya **había jugado** muchos partidos de fútbol en Paraguay. Todavía **no había ganado** la Copa Intercontinental.

4. Comparisons of equality and inequality: Making comparisons

A. Comparisons of equality

We can compare adjectives (**guapo/a, inteligente**), adverbs (**bien, mal, tarde**), nouns (**dinero, amigos, problemas**) and verbs (**estudiar, comer**).

Es tan guapo como Antonio Banderas, ¿no?

= (Equality)	
Adjective (**guapo**)	Ana es **tan** guapa **como** Elena.
Adverb (**tarde**)	Llegué **tan** tarde **como** tú.
Noun (**dinero...**)	No tengo **tanto** dinero **como** mis padres.
	Rita no hace **tanta** tarea **como** nosotros.
	Nadie tiene **tantos** tíos **como** yo.
	Tienes **tantas** clases **como** Roberto.
Verb (**leer**)	Leo **tanto como** tú.

- Note that the adjective in a comparison (**guapa**) agrees with the noun it refers to (**Ana**).

- Note also the word order *verb + comparison expression* (**tanto como**) when comparing actions.

Así se forma

 10-21 **¿Son parecidos (Are they alike)?** Mira los dibujos y decide si las oraciones son ciertas o falsas.

1. Octavio es tan inteligente como Javier.

2. Javier es tan atlético como Manuel.

3. Camila es tan alta como su hermana.

4. El ogro está tan gordo como su amigo.

5. Alfonso tiene tanto dinero como su profesor.

6. Linda tiene tantas flores como Inés.

7. Natalia estudia tanto como Rubén.

8. Pepita come tanto como Esteban.

 10-22 **Otras personas y yo.** Escribe comparaciones de igualdad entre algunos/as compañeros/as de clase, o entre algún/alguna compañero/a de clase y tú. Tienes cinco minutos. Algunos/as estudiantes van a leer sus comparaciones a la clase. Incluye:

1. características personales	**Soy tan... como...**
2. cosas que tienen	**... tiene tanto/a/os/as... como...**
3. actividades en que participan	**... estudia tanto como...**

B. Comparisons of inequality

Teo, ¡corres más rápido que yo! ¡No te escapes!

	+	−	=
Adjective (**guapo**)	Ana es **más** guapa **que** yo.	...**menos** guapa **que**...	...**tan** guapa **como**...
Adverb (**tarde**)	Luis llegó **más** tarde **que** tú.	...**menos** tarde **que**...	...**tan** tarde **como**...
Noun (**dinero...**)	Tienes **más** dinero **que** él	...**menos** dinero **que**...	...**tanto** dinero **como**... ...**tanta** tarea **como**... ...**tantos** tíos **como**... ...**tantas** tías **como**...
Verb (**leer**)	Leo **más que** tú.	Leo **menos que** tú.	Leo **tanto como** tú.

- Otros ejemplos:

  Este apartamento es **más/ menos** caro **que** el otro.
  *This apartment is **more/less** expensive **than** the other one.*

  Ella limpia su apartamento **más/ menos** frecuentemente que yo.
  *She cleans her apartment **more/less** frequently **than** I.*

  Esta casa tiene **más/ menos** ventanas que la otra.
  *This house has **more/fewer** windows **than** the other one.*

  Ella paga **más/ menos** que tú.
  *She pays **more/less than** you.*

- Use **de** instead of **que** before a number.

  El sillón costó **más/ menos** de $625.
  *The armchair cost **more/less** than $625.*

Some Spanish adjectives and adverbs have irregular comparative forms. These forms do not use **más** or **menos**.

Adjetivo		Adverbio		Comparativo	
bueno/a	good	bien	well	mejor	better
malo/a	bad	mal	badly	peor	worse
joven	young			menor	younger
viejo/a	old			mayor	older (referring to age of a person)

Esta película es **buena**.	*This movie is **good**.*
Ésa es **mejor que** ésta.	*That one is **better than** this one.*
Ese restaurante es **malo**.	*That restaurant is **bad**.*
Aquél es aún **peor**.	*That one is even **worse**.*

Así se forma

 10-23 ¿De acuerdo (*Do you agree*)? En grupos de tres personas, digan si ustedes están de acuerdo con las siguientes generalizaciones. Si no están de acuerdo, indiquen su opinión. Túrnense.

Modelo: El español es más difícil que el inglés.
Sí, el español es... o **No, el español no es... Es más fácil.** o
El español es tan difícil/ fácil como el inglés.

1. La clase de español es más divertida que la clase de matemáticas.
2. Las mujeres de esta clase son más inteligentes que los hombres.
3. Los hombres de esta clase estudian más que las mujeres.
4. Las mujeres, en general, gastan menos dinero que los hombres.
5. Los hombres hispanos bailan mejor que los hombres estadounidenses.
6. Los coches estadounidenses son mejores que los japoneses.
7. El dinero es más importante que el amor.
8. Vivir en la ciudad es mejor que vivir en el campo.
9. El alcohol es peor que los cigarrillos.

10-24 Entre nosotros.

Paso 1. Formen grupos de tres personas. Primero, escriban los nombres de las personas en cada columna de la tabla. Luego, háganse preguntas para completar el cuadro y apunten la cantidad (*quantity*). Después, hagan comparaciones usando la información del cuadro.

Modelo: **Tengo más/ menos clases que Juan.** o
Tengo tantas clases como Juan.

	_____	_____	_____
1. Número de clases este semestre			
2. Horas de estudio por día			
3. Horas de trabajo por semana			
4. Tiempo para deportes/ actividades extra-curriculares cada semana			
5. Horas de descanso (televisión, amigos/as) por día			
6. Horas para mensajes electrónicos/ el Internet personal por día			
7. Horas que duermes cada noche			

Capítulo 10

Paso 2. Ahora, basándose en la información anterior, comparen sus estilos de vida. Aquí tienen algunas preguntas para empezar la conversación:

- ¿Quién está más ocupado? ¿Quién tiene más tiempo para relajarse?
- ¿Quién es más activo? ¿Quién es más tranquilo?
- ¿Quién tiene una vida más equilibrada? ¿Quién está estresado?
- ¿Quién está más concentrado en sus estudios? ¿Quién tiene más variedad en sus actividades?

10-25 **Necesito alquilar un apartamento.** Decides alquilar un apartamento en Asunción, Paraguay. Lee los tres anuncios y escribe cuatro oraciones comparando los tres apartamentos. ¿Cuál prefieres y por qué? Usa comparaciones para explicar tu preferencia.

1.

ENCANTADOR PENTHOUSE
en Manorá,
G 5.200.000, 3 habs.,
2 baños con terraza,
jacuzzi, bar. BUENA VISTA
565-2132

2.

ESTUDIO AMUEBLADO.
C/ Igatimí. G 4,000,000.
Bello, 1 hab., baño, sala,
comedor, cocina. Totalmente
equipado. Muebles nuevos.
Inversor. NUEVOS
HORIZONTES 592-2100

3.

PENTHOUSE AMUEBLADO.
Avda. Carlos Antonio
López. 4 habs., 4.5 baños, 3
balcones, 2 terrazas
techadas, amplias áreas de
servicio. Vista panorámica,
2 parqueos techados,
planta full, ascensor. G
10.250.000. Lucía. 541-1987

10-26 Las fotos de mi amiga.

 **Paso 1.** En grupos de tres personas, comparen los siguientes grupos de fotos. Hagan varias comparaciones en cada caso basadas en las fotografías.

Grupo 1: Familias

1.

Una familia indígena en México

2.

La familia de Gustavo y Elvira, San Juan, Puerto Rico

3.

Un padre con sus hijos

Grupo 2: Casas

4.

Casa en la ciudad, Mérida, Yucatán, México

5.

Casa (choza) en el campo, Yucatán, México

6.

Apartamento en San Juan, Puerto Rico

Grupo 3: Comidas

7.

Preparando un plato maya

8.
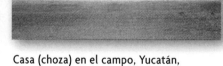

Desayuno en México D.F.

9.

Desayuno en Madrid, España

 Paso 2. Imaginen que cada uno de ustedes es miembro de una de las familias de las fotos anteriores (1–3). En sus grupos, expliquen a los otros los aspectos positivos de sus vidas, comparándolas con las de las otras fotos. Usen su imaginación.

C. The superlative

The superlative form of the adjective is used when persons or things are singled out as being *the most . . . , least . . . , best . . . , worst . . . , tallest . . . ,* etc. To form the superlative use:

> el/la/los/las + (noun) + más/ menos + (adjective) + de...

La cocina es **el cuarto más popular de** nuestra casa.

The kitchen is the most popular room in our house.

To form the superlative of **bueno/a**, **malo/a**, we use the same irregular forms as in the comparative.

> el/la/los/las + mejor(es)/ peor(es) + (noun) + de...

Los mejores restaurantes **de** la ciudad están en el centro.

The best restaurants in the city are downtown.

Investig@ en INTERNET

¿Cuál es el río más caudaloso (*largest*) del mundo?

¿Cuál es la ciudad más poblada del continente americano?

¿Qué región española tiene clima tropical?

¿Cuáles son las cataratas más altas del mundo?

¿Cuál es la ciudad más meridional (*southernmost*) del mundo?

Mendoza, Argentina. Según la tienda, ¿cuáles son los mejores productos de Argentina? ¿Puedes identificar tres?

10-27 **Premios "Superlativo"** (*"Superlative" prizes*). Cada año se conceden en tu universidad los premios "Superlativo". Este año tu clase de español forma el jurado (*jury*).

Paso 1. En grupos pequeños, piensen en cuatro nominados para la(s) categoría(s) que va a asignar su instructor/a. Escriban los nombres en las columnas **"Nominado"**. Añadan una categoría más en la última línea y las nominaciones correspondientes.

	Nominado	votos	Nominado	votos	Nominado	votos	Nominado	votos
1. la clase más fácil								
2. la clase más aburrida								
3. el mejor lugar para estudiar								
4. la peor comida de la cafetería								
5. el edificio más feo								
6. el lugar más romántico								
7. el evento (o fiesta) más popular								
8. la mejor residencia								
9. ¿...?								

Paso 2. Compartan sus nominaciones y su nueva categoría con la clase. Un/a representante de cada grupo las escribe en la pizarra. Después, realicen la votación para decidir los ganadores de estos premios.

10-28 **¿Cuál es el mejor?**

Paso 1. Primero, escoge (*choose*) tres de las siguientes categorías. Luego, para cada categoría, usa superlativos para escribir tu opinión sobre tres aspectos.

Modelo: actores: **Jim Carrey es el menos guapo de todos.**
Morgan Freeman es el mejor de todos.
Robin Williams es el más divertido.

1. películas recientes
2. programas de televisión
3. revistas
4. actores/actrices
5. cantantes/ grupos musicales
6. restaurantes en la ciudad
7. equipos deportivos
8. ciudades de los Estados Unidos

Paso 2. En grupos, lean sus opiniones a sus compañeros/as y escuchen las de ellos/as. ¿Están de acuerdo?

10-29 **Un anuncio comercial.** En grupos, escriban un anuncio comercial de treinta segundos para la televisión. Comparen tres productos similares (hamburguesas de tres restaurantes populares, por ejemplo) usando comparativos y superlativos. Después, van a presentar sus anuncios a la clase.

¡A ESCUCHAR!

PALABRA ÚTIL

el rincón *corner*

El nuevo apartamento de Susana. Tu amiga Susana alquiló un apartamento y ahora necesita tu ayuda para colocar (*place*) los muebles y otras cosas. Escucha las instrucciones de ella y escribe el número de cada cosa en el lugar correspondiente. Opcional: Dibuja las cosas en el lugar correspondiente.

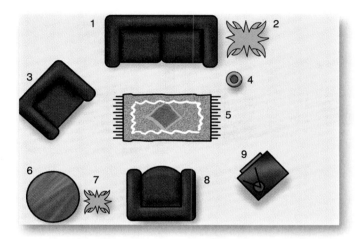

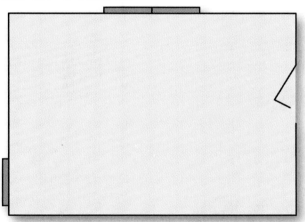

CONVERSANDO

Bienes raíces (*Real estate*). Uno/a de ustedes es agente de bienes raíces con propiedades en Latinoamérica. Dos de ustedes quieren comprar propiedad en Costa Rica, Ecuador o Uruguay. Comparen las opciones presentadas (en la página 360).

Hablen de:

- ubicación (*location*)
- precio
- tipo de vivienda
- ventajas (*advantages*) y desventajas de cada una
- su decisión

Una nueva forma de vivir...

Entrega Inmediata

Envueltos por la verde naturaleza

80% vendido Primera Etapa. ¡LLAME YA!

CONDOMINIO BALCONES DE SANTA ANA

BALCONES DE SANTA ANA está compuesto por 16 condominios independientes de 248 a 293 mts² cada uno.
Situado en Santa Ana, la zona de más plusvalía en San José, cuenta con piscina, casa club, zona de juegos, generosos jardines y hermosas vistas sobre los cerros de Escazú. Localizado a sólo 5 minutos de Multiplaza, 700 mts. de Santa Ana y fácil acceso a la pista San José - Caldera.

Cada casa cuenta con:
- Habitación principal con balcón, walk-in closet, baño y jacuzzi
- 2 y 3 habitaciones con closet
- 3 ½ - 4 ½ baños
- Amplio ático para múltiples usos*
- Sala de T.V.
- Sala con prevista para bar
- Comedor
- Cuarto de servicio o estudio
- Cocina de Euromobilia
- Lavandería y pilas
- Amplio jardín privado
- Terraza techada
- Cochera cubierta para dos carros

San José, Costa Rica

En la bella playa de Atacames, Ecuador.

Suites Playa Atacames

Usted merece un espacio propio para disfrutar de sus vacaciones.
- Frente al mar
- Departamentos de dos dormitorios, sala, cocina, comedor y balcón
- Pisos de cerámica
- Áreas comunales
- Tres piscinas
- Micromercado
- Áreas de estacionamiento

TODO ESTO POR: $36.000US

Playa de Atacanes, Ecuador

En la más exclusiva ciudad vacacional de Latinoamérica, Punta del Este, Uruguay.

Condominios Península

Propiedades en venta. Amplios y luminosos ambientes, frente al mar y próximo a todo.
- Living-Comedor
- Terraza
- Dos dormitorios, dos baños
- Cocina
- Lavadero
- Dormitorio y baño de servicio
- Garage
- Muebles

$98.000US

Punta del Este, Uruguay

 DE MI ESCRITORIO

Una casa muy especial. Escribe una descripción de la casa en la que vivías cuando eras niño/a. (Usa formas del imperfecto y del pretérito.)

Menciona:

- cuántos pisos tenía
- los colores
- si tenía jardín
- las diferentes habitaciones
- los muebles de la casa
- recuerdos especiales vividos allí

Después compárala con tu casa ideal, la casa de tus sueños. (Usa formas de presente.)

Artes pictóricas: Pedro Figari

Antes de leer

Observa el cuadro. ¿Están las personas dentro o fuera de la casa? ¿Cómo lo sabes?

El pintor uruguayo Pedro Figari nació en Montevideo, Uruguay, en 1861 y murió en 1938. Pasó una gran parte de su infancia en una granja[1] y allí vivió la cultura uruguaya que luego pintó en sus cuadros. Además de pintor fue un distinguido abogado, educador, periodista, político, filósofo y escritor.

En la pintura[2] *Baile criollo*, nos presenta una escena de danzas típicas. Figari pensaba que las culturas europeas habían alterado[3] la armonía de la vida en el Nuevo Mundo y que le correspondía al latinoamericano reestablecer ese orden o armonía. Le interesaban los temas nativos como este baile con gauchos. Observa atentamente la pintura antes de continuar.

[1]*farm*

[2]*painting* [3]**habían...** *had altered*

Pedro Figari, *Baile Criollo*; 61x82 cm, óleo sobre lienzo.
Photo courtesy Museo Virtual de Artes El País.
©1997 País.

Después de leer

1. ¿Por qué se viste de manera diferente la mujer del vestido rojo?
2. ¿Por qué tienen ventanas con rejas (*bars*)? ¿Tienen rejas las ventanas en tu ciudad?
3. ¿De qué maneras son similares los trajes de los gauchos y los trajes del vaquero (*cowboy*) de los Estados Unidos?

Repaso de vocabulario activo

Adverbio

peor   *worse*

Sustantivos

En el baño
In the bathroom

la bañera   *bathtub*

la ducha   *shower*

el espejo   *mirror*

el inodoro   *toilet*

el lavabo
    bathroom sink

En la cocina
In the kitchen

la estufa   *stove*

el fregadero   *kitchen sink*

el horno   *oven*

el lavaplatos   *dishwasher*

el microondas   *microwave*

el refrigerador   *refrigerator*

En la mesa
On the table

la copa   *goblet*

la cuchara   *spoon*

la cucharita   *teaspoon*

el cuchillo   *knife*

el plato   *plate*

la servilleta   *napkin*

la taza   *cup*

el tenedor   *fork*

el vaso   *glass*

Las partes de la casa
The parts of the house

el baño   *bathroom*

la chimenea   *fireplace*

la cocina   *kitchen*

el comedor   *dining room*

el dormitorio   *bedroom*

la escalera   *stairs*

el garaje   *garage*

el jardín   *garden/backyard*

la pared   *wall*

el (primer) piso   *(first) floor*

la sala   *living room*

la sala familiar   *family room*

el sótano   *basement*

el suelo/ el piso   *floor*

el techo   *roof/ceiling*

Las cosas en la casa/ el
apartamento   *The things*
in the house/apartment

la alfombra   *carpet*

la cómoda   *bureau, dresser*

las cortinas   *curtains*

el cubo de la basura   *garbage can*

el estante   *shelf*

el estéreo   *stereo*

la lámpara   *lamp*

la lavadora   *washing machine*

la luz   *light*

la mesita (de noche)   *nightstand*

los muebles   *furniture*

el póster   *poster*

la secadora   *clothes dryer*

el sillón   *armchair*

el sofá   *sofa*

Otras palabras útiles
Other useful words

el ruido   *noise*

el vecino/la vecina   *neighbor*

Verbos y expresiones
verbales   *Verbs and*
verbal expressions

alquilar   *to rent*

apagar   *to turn off*

ayudar   *to help*

bajar   *to go down*

guardar   *to put away*

mover(se) (ue)   *to move (oneself)*

mudarse   *to move (from one*
    residence to another)

prender   *to turn on*

resolver (ue)   *to solve*

romper   *to break*

subir   *to go up*

cortar el césped   *to mow*
    the lawn

hacer la cama   *to make the bed*

lavar/ secar los platos   *to wash/*
    dry dishes

ordenar el cuarto   *to tidy up*
    the room

pasar la aspiradora   *to vacuum*

poner/ quitar la mesa
    to set/clear the table

sacar la basura   *to take out*
    the trash

Autoprueba y repaso PLUS ✓

I. Affirmative *tú* commands. ¿Qué le dice la mamá a los diferentes miembros de la familia?

Modelo: Irma / ir al mercado
Irma, ¡ve al mercado!

1. Beatriz / hacer la cama
2. María / pasar la aspiradora
3. Luis / devolver los libros al estante
4. Laila / poner la mesa
5. Miguel / limpiar el baño
6. Juanito / sacar la basura

II. Negative *tú* commands. ¿Qué le dice el hermano mayor al menor?

Modelo: no ponerte mi ropa
No te pongas mi ropa, por favor.

1. no prender el estéreo
2. no usar mi computadora
3. no tocar mis cosas
4. no salir ahora
5. no decirme mentiras (*lies*)
6. no preocuparte

III. The present perfect. ¿Qué han hecho las siguientes personas esta semana?

Modelo: yo / dormir mucho
He dormido mucho.

1. la abuela / trabajar en el jardín
2. todos nosotros / lavar y secar la ropa
3. papá / limpiar el garaje
4. mi hermana / salir dos veces a bailar
5. tú / no hacer nada

IV. The past perfect. Una noche hubo una tormenta y un apagón (*blackout*). ¿Qué habíamos hecho antes del incidente?

Modelo: nosotros / terminar nuestro proyecto
Habíamos terminado nuestro proyecto.

1. yo / apagar la computadora
2. tú / imprimir tu trabajo escrito
3. mi compañero/a de cuarto / cerrar las ventanas
4. nosotros / hacer la tarea para la clase de español
5. Linda y Teresa / leer la novela para la clase de inglés

V. Equal comparisons. Haz comparaciones de igualdad.

Modelo: Teresa tiene dos clases por la tarde. Yo tengo dos clases también.
Tengo tantas clases por la tarde como Teresa. *o* **Teresa tiene tantas clases por la tarde como yo.**

1. Los estudiantes son simpáticos. Los profesores también son simpáticos.
2. El francés es difícil. El tailandés también es difícil.

3. Ana tiene mucha paciencia. Susana también tiene mucha paciencia.
4. Alberto compró dos libros. Su hermano también compró dos.

VI. Unequal comparisons and the superlative.

A. Di qué elemento de la serie es más grande, mejor, etc., que el otro.

Modelo: grande: Nueva York, Toronto
Nueva York es más grande que Toronto.

1. caro: el reloj Rolex, el reloj Timex
2. económico: comprar una casa, alquilar un apartamento
3. mejor: ir de vacaciones a la playa, ir de vacaciones a las montañas
4. divertido: limpiar la casa, ver la tele

B. Di qué elemento de la serie es el mejor, el más interesante, etc., de los tres.

Modelo: vieja: Roma, Boston, Calgary
Roma es la más vieja de las tres.

1. fría: Duluth, Minnesota; Santa Fe, New Mexico; Atlanta, Georgia
2. rico: Bill Gates, su profesor/a, George W. Bush
3. mejor: el Ford, el Subaru, el Honda
4. interesante: las revistas *National Geographic, Newsweek, Movie Line*

VII. *Repaso general.* Contesta con oraciones completas.

1. ¿Eres tan generoso/a como tu mejor amigo/a?
2. ¿Tienes tantos amigos/as como él/ella?
3. ¿Estudias más o menos que él/ella?
4. ¿Cuál es la clase más interesante de la universidad? ¿Por qué?
5. ¿Quién es el/la mejor profesor/a de esta universidad? ¿Por qué?
6. Viste el apartamento perfecto ayer. ¿Cómo era? (Usa la imaginación.)
7. ¿Qué cosas importantes has hecho este año?
8. ¿Qué cosas interesantes habías hecho antes de empezar tu carrera universitaria?

VIII. *Cultura.*

1. ¿Cuál es la diferencia principal en la composición étnica entre Paraguay y Uruguay?
2. ¿Quién es Cristina Peri Rossi?
3. ¿Por qué es tan importante el patio en las casas hispanas?
4. ¿Quién fue Pedro Figari?

Answers to the *Autoprueba y repaso* are found in **Apéndice 2.**

Amigos y algo más

By the end of this chapter you will be able to:

- Talk about human relationships and the stages of life

- Express wishes and requests related to other people's actions

- Express emotional reactions and feelings about other people's actions

Así se dice	Así se forma	Cultura	Dicho y hecho
• Amigos y algo más • Hablando del amor... • Las llamadas telefónicas	**1.** Reciprocal constructions **2.** The subjunctive mood; the present subjunctive **3.** The subjunctive with expressions of influence **4.** The subjunctive with expressions of emotion	• Panamá • Los cibercafés • Artes populares: Las molas	• La radionovela "Amalia" • Problemas matrimoniales • Cartas a los "desesperados"

ENTRANDO AL TEMA

1. ¿Conoces algo acerca del Canal de Panamá?

2. Tienes amigos/as o familiares que han conocido a su novio/a por Internet?

la amistad

juntos/as

llevarse bien

Pepita

Natalia

Pepita y Natalia tienen una gran **amistad**. Son amigas porque **se llevan** muy **bien**: se divierten **juntas** y tienen intereses similares.

el amor

Manuel

enamorarse (de)

Linda

estar enamorado/a (de)

Linda y Manuel **se enamoraron** a primera vista hace dos años y todavía **están** tan **enamorados** como el primer día.

Marlena

Javier

Esteban

Rubén

reunirse (con)

Esteban y sus amigos **se reúnen** frecuentemente para charlar y tomar algo.

Carmen

Alfonso

encontrarse (ue) con

A veces Carmen **se encuentra** con Alfonso cuando va a clase.

la cita

Inés

Octavio

salir con

Inés **sale con** Octavio hace ya unos meses. Esta noche tienen **una cita** para una cena romántica.

Camila

llorar

pensar (ie) en

extrañar

romper con

Camila **rompió con** su novio recientemente pero todavía **piensa en** él. A veces **llora** porque lo **extraña**.

LAS ETAPAS DE LA VIDA

el nacimiento

la infancia

nacer

la niñez

los niños

la juventud/ la adolescencia

los jóvenes/ los adolescentes

la madurez

los adultos

NOTA DE LENGUA

una cita	a date	Inés y Octavio tienen una cita esta noche.
		Van al cine y a un restaurante romántico.
	an appointment	El jueves tengo cita para el dentista.

comprometerse (con)

Manuel

Linda

estar prometido/a

El día de San Valentín Manuel y Linda **se comprometieron**. Ahora que **están prometidos** viven **juntos**.

la boda

la profesora Falcón

Juan

casarse (con)

estar casado/a (con)

La profesora Falcón y su esposo, Juan, **se casaron** hace diez años. Fue **una boda** pequeña pero muy elegante.

encontrarse con	to run into
extrañar	to miss
llevarse bien/ mal	to get along/not get along
la luna de miel	honeymoon
juntos/as	together
reunirse (con)	to get together (with)
romper con	to break up with

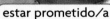
los recién casados

¡Felicidades!

irse de luna de miel

Después de la boda, **los recién casados se fueron de luna de miel**.

dar a luz

HOSPITAL

Nancy

el profesor Marin-Vivar

Nancy, la esposa del profesor Marín-Vivar, **está embarazada**. Van al hospital porque Nancy va a **dar a luz** muy pronto.

la vejez

los ancianos

la muerte

Así se dice

Amigos y algo más Amigos y algo más Amigos y algo más Amigos y algo más Amigos y algo más

HINT

Pienso en... *I think about (something or someone).*

¿Qué piensas de... ? *What do you think about . . . ? (opinion)*

Pienso/ Creo que... *I think/believe that . . .*

11-1 Amistad o algo más...

Paso 1. En parejas, tienen cinco minutos para hacer listas de palabras asociadas a los siguientes conceptos. Tienen que estar preparados para justificar la relación entre las palabras de su lista y el concepto al que se asocian. No pueden repetir ninguna palabra.

> la amistad   la cita   casarse   el amor

Paso 2. Cuenten el número de palabras que escribieron. ¿Qué pareja tiene más palabras? Compartan sus listas con la clase.

11-2 Las etapas de la vida.

Paso 1. Escoge tres de las siguientes etapas de la vida y escribe una breve descripción de cada una.

> la infancia   la niñez   la juventud   la madurez   la vejez

Modelo: **En esta etapa la gente no trabaja; van a pasear, ven la televisión o hacen viajes. Pero a veces están enfermos y pasan mucho tiempo en casa.**

Paso 2. Lee una de tus descripciones a tu compañero/a, que va a intentar identificarla. Túrnense hasta leer todas las descripciones.

11-3 Preguntas personales. En parejas, van a entrevistarse sobre los temas de la amistad y el amor. Primero el Estudiante B cierra el libro, y el Estudiante A le hace las preguntas de abajo y toma apuntes. Después, el Estudiante A cierra el libro y el Estudiante B lo entrevista.

Estudiante A: Vas a hacer una entrevista a tu compañero/a sobre la amistad.

1. ¿Con quiénes te reúnes[1] en tu tiempo libre? ¿Tienes buenos/as amigos/as en la universidad?
2. ¿Te llevas bien o mal con tu compañero/a de cuarto (o de apartamento)? ¿Lo/La consideras un/a amigo/a?
3. ¿Quién es tu mejor amigo/amiga? ¿Por qué piensas en esta persona como tu mejor amigo/a?

---

[1]The present tense of **reunirse** is: **me reúno, te reúnes, se reúne, nos reunimos, os reunís, se reúnen.** Note the accents.

4. ¿Tienes muchos amigos/as fuera de la ciudad? ¿Los/Las extrañas? ¿Estás en contacto con ellos/as por teléfono, correo electrónico... ?

5. En tu opinión, ¿qué características debe tener un/a amigo/a?

Estudiante B: Vas a hacer una entrevista a tu compañero/a sobre las relaciones amorosas.

1. ¿Sales con alguien ahora? (¿Cuánto tiempo hace que lo/la conoces?) (¿Estás enamorado/a? ¿Cuántas veces has estado enamorado/a?)

2. ¿Tienes amigos que están comprometidos? ¿Estás comprometido/a? ¿Es importante para ti regalar o recibir un anillo?

3. ¿Qué piensas del matrimonio? ¿Piensas casarte, o estás casado/a? (¿Qué tipo de boda quieres? Si ya estás casado/a, ¿cómo fue tu boda?)

4. ¿Quieres tener hijos, o ya los tienes? ¿Cuántos tienes o cuántos quieres tener? ¿Prefieres tener una familia grande o pequeña?

11-4 Pensamientos sobre la amistad.

 Paso 1. En grupos de tres, lean los pensamientos siguientes y luego indiquen la idea central de cada uno. Apunten sus ideas para luego compartirlas con la clase.

Modelo: "La amistad supone sacrificios y sólo el que está dispuesto a hacerlos sin molestia comprende la amistad." (Noel Clarasó, escritor español)

Es necesario hacer sacrificios por los amigos.

1. "Al amigo no lo busques perfecto. Búscalo amigo." (José Narosky, escritor argentino)

2. "Un buen amigo es un hombre para el cual° no tenemos secretos y que, a pesar de° todo, nos aprecia." (León Daudí, escritor español)

   para... *for whom*
   a... *in spite of*

3. "La amistad no se compra, aunque muchos la venden, que los amigos comprados no lo son y valen° poco." (Baltasar Gracián, jesuita y escritor español)

   are worth

4. "A los amigos, como a los dientes, los vamos perdiendo con los años, no siempre sin dolor." (Santiago Ramón y Cajal, médico español)

Paso 2. Ahora hablen de sus mejores amigos/as: quiénes son y por qué son buenos/as amigos/as.

Así se dice

Hablando del amor...

Es difícil definir el amor, esa química misteriosa que nos transforma. Sin embargo, todos lo sentimos tarde o temprano; y cuando llega ese "alguien especial" hay una magnífica explosión interna y la vida cambia de color. Lee los siguientes anuncios personales y aprende las nuevas expresiones para poder hablar del amor y de las relaciones.

Amigos y algo más

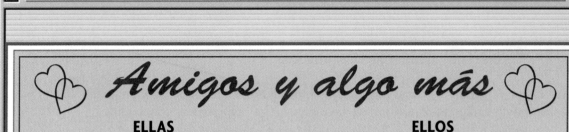

ELLAS

Liliana Matamoros. Viuda, 50 años, **sincera, cariñosa;** con mucha personalidad e independencia. Soy arquitecta, me encanta leer buenos libros y viajar. Mi media naranja° puede ser **soltero,** viudo o **divorciado.** Mi único requisito es que pueda **comunicarse** bien. Busco solamente un compañero. ¡No me quiero casar! Si usted **está listo** para una relación como la que deseo, escríbame al Apartado Postal 555, San Jacinto, Honduras.

Irma Murillo. Soltera, 28 años, abogada. Busco un príncipe de buen carácter, divertido y **comprensivo. Creo** en el amor a primera vista°; no creo en el **divorcio** ni en la separación. Soy optimista y romántica de pies a cabeza. Nos vamos a cuidar y estar juntos para toda la vida. Dirección: Apartamentos Los Pinos, Apto. C, 125 metros oeste Catedral. Moravia, Costa Rica.

Genoveva Vásquez. Programadora informática, casada, 33 años. Mi signo es Sagitario, soy amistosa, expresiva, atractiva e inteligente. Estoy atrapada en un matrimonio sin amor y necesito **separarme** o **divorciarme. He tratado de resolver** nuestros problemas, pero ¡mi marido es imposible! ¡Busco un caballero valiente que me libere de esta prisión! Dirección: 18 Av. A, 119, Zona 1, Guatemala, Guatemala.

ELLOS

Arturo Flores. Estoy divorciado, tengo 45 años y soy administrador de negocios y estudiante de artes plásticas. Creo que **me he olvidado** un poco del amor; no **recuerdo** cuándo fue la última vez que salí a divertirme. Nací en Perú, pero ahora soy ciudadano de EE.UU. Signo Leo, romántico y deportista. Serio, responsable, católico. No bebo ni fumo. Busco amistades. Enviar foto. Dirección: 375 Forest Ave., Des Plaines, Illinois, EE.UU.

Roberto R. Mendoza. Soltero, 27 años, dibujante comercial. Apasionado y romántico. Busco la compañera de mi vida. Mi única condición es: "Ud. no debe ser **celosa.**" Mi experiencia es que los celos **matan** el amor. Dirección: Barrio Sta. Marta, Calle Atlántica No. 1180, San Salvador, El Salvador.

Gregorio José Ramírez. Soltero, 32 años, profesor universitario. Me gustaría recibir correo de chicas de 25 a 32 años con fines matrimoniales. Soy responsable, sin vicios, delgado y simpático. Siempre **me acuerdo de** los cumpleaños y otras fechas especiales. Nunca **tengo celos,** no **me quejo de** nada y solamente **me enojo** cuando alguien **miente**[2]. Busco a alguien que pueda **reírse de**[3] los problemas de la vida, alguien optimista y **fiel.** Dirección: Cerrado del Cóndor, 175 Bis. Acayucán, México, D.F.

Mi... *my soulmate, other half*

amor... *love at first sight*

---

[2]The present tense of **mentir** is: **miento, mientes, miente, mentimos, mentís, mienten.**
[3]The present tense of **reírse** is: **me río, te ríes, se ríe, nos reímos, os reís, se ríen.**

acordarse (ue) de…	to remember . . .	olvidarse de/	to forget
recordar (ue)	to remember	olvidar	

cariñoso/a	affectionate	creer	to believe
celoso/a	jealous	enojarse	to get/become angry
tener celos	to be jealous	estar listo/a	to be ready
fiel	faithful	matar	to kill
soltero/a	single	mentir	to lie
viudo/a	widower/widow	quejarse de	to complain about
reírse de	to laugh at		
tratar de + *infinitive*	to try to (do something)		

NOTA DE LENGUA

Remember that past participles used as adjectives agree with the noun they describe. (See page 345). This form is used throughout this chapter.
Linda y Manuel están **enamorados**.
Mi hermana está **soltera**.

11–5 ¿Qué dicen? Busca la declaración que mejor corresponda a cada circunstancia.

Circunstancias

1. Es muy cariñoso.
2. Tiene celos.
3. Extraña a su novia.
4. Rompió con su novio.
5. Se encuentra con su amigo.
6. Está enamorado.
7. ¡Dio a luz ayer!
8. Se olvidó del cumpleaños de su amiga.
9. Es muy comprensiva.
10. No miente.

Declaraciones

a. "Te amo con todo mi corazón".
b. "Quiero verte. Hace mucho tiempo que no te veo".
c. "¡Hola, Paco! ¿Qué hay de nuevo?"
d. "¡Estoy furioso! ¡Mi novia bailó con otro chico en la fiesta!"
e. "Lo siento, pero ya no te amo y no puedo salir más contigo".
f. "Me gustan los abrazos°".   *hugs*
g. "La verdad° es muy importante para mí".   *truth*
h. "¡Ay! Lo siento. Estaba tan ocupado que ni pensé en la fecha".
i. "Mira al bebé. ¡Qué precioso es!"
j. "Entiendo exactamente cómo te sientes".

11–6 **Anuncios personales.** En grupos, contesten las siguientes preguntas.

1. ¿Qué anuncio de los de la sección **Hablando del amor** (p. 370) es el más interesante en la categoría **ellas**? ¿Y en la categoría **ellos**? ¿Por qué?
2. Según los anuncios, ¿quién es (posiblemente) la mujer ideal para Roberto R. Mendoza? ¿Por qué?
3. ¿Quién va a tener la mayor dificultad para encontrar pareja? ¿Por qué?

Así se dice

11-7 Cita a ciegas (*Blind date*).

Paso 1. Piensa en un/a amigo/a (hermano/a, etc.) que no tiene pareja, pero quiere encontrar a su media naranja (*soulmate, other half*). Escribe su nombre aquí: ___Angela___

Paso 2. Quizá (*Maybe*) puedes encontrar una media naranja para tu amigo/a en la clase de español o, al menos, organizar una cita a ciegas. Escribe una descripción interesante y atractiva de tu amigo/a; describe algunas de sus características físicas, cualidades personales y también lo que él/ella busca en una pareja y en una relación.

Paso 3. Camina por la clase y entrevista a varias personas para encontrar **tres** candidatos/as para tu amigo/a. Haz preguntas sobre estos/as candidatos/as y toma notas. Describe también a tu amigo/a.

Modelo: Estudiante A: **Mi amigo se llama... ¿Tú tienes un amigo o una amiga?**

Estudiante B: **Tengo una amiga; se llama...**

Estudiante A: **Mi amigo es... y busca una chica...**

Estudiante B: **Mi amiga es... Dime, ¿qué tipo de música le gusta a tu amigo?...**

(Los dos estudiantes toman notas)

Paso 4. Ahora, comparte con la clase los resultados de tu búsqueda (*search*). ¿Encontraste a un candidato/a interesante para tu amigo/a? ¿Por qué te parecen compatibles?

11-8 Nuestras relaciones. En grupos de tres o cuatro, respondan a las siguientes preguntas. Un/a secretario/a apunta información interesante para luego compartirla con la clase.

- ¿Es posible el amor a primera vista?
- ¿Existe sólo una "media naranja" para cada persona o existen varias?
- ¿Cuáles son las ventajas (*advantages*) o desventajas de ser soltero/a?
- ¿Cuáles son las ventajas o desventajas de casarse joven?
- ¿Creen que es mejor vivir juntos antes de casarse? ¿Por qué sí/no?

11-9 Pensamientos sobre el amor.

Paso 1. En parejas, lean los siguientes pensamientos sobre el amor. Discutan si están de acuerdo o no y decidan cuáles son sus favoritos.

treasure

1. "El amor es el único tesoro° que se multiplica al dividirlo". (Anónimo)

root; pleasure

2. "La raíz° de todas las pasiones es el amor. De él nace la tristeza, el gozo°, la alegría y la desesperación". (Lope de Vega, España)

3. "Ama como puedas, ama a quien puedas, ama todo lo que puedas, pero ama siempre". (Amado Nervo, México)

4. "No hacemos el amor. El amor nos hace". (Mario Benedetti, Uruguay)

5. "Hombre invisible busca mujer transparente para hacer lo nunca visto". (Pintado en el metro de Madrid)

 Paso 2. Ahora, inventen su propio (*own*) "pensamiento" y compártanlo con sus compañeros/as de clase.

 11–10 **Una invitación a una boda hispana.** Examinen la siguiente invitación a una boda en Latinoamérica e indiquen los datos siguientes:

los nombres de los novios: _____

los nombres de los padres de los novios: _____

_____

_____

_____

la fecha de la boda: _____

la ciudad en que se celebra: _____

Luis Felipe Cabezas Burgos   *Víctor José Luna Castillo*

M.ª Teresa Hernández de Cabezas   *Gabriela Consuelo Valladares de Luna*   *M.ª = María*

Participan a usted(es) del próximo enlace de sus hijos

Mónica y Eduardo

y tienen el gusto de invitarle(s) a la ceremonia religiosa

que se celebrará (D.m.) el viernes 31 de agosto, a las 7 de la tarde,   *D.m. = Dios mediante*

en la Iglesia del Carmen, Avda. España con Avda. Federico Boyd   *(God permitting/willing)*

y a la cena que se servirá a continuación

en el Salón Las Tinajas,

Hotel Paitilla,

Avenida Balboa, Ciudad de Panamá

Se ruega confirmación

31 julio, 2007

C/ 13 Condado del Rey, 2824   *C/ 50 Torrijos Carter*

Apartado Postal: 87-3547   *Apartado Postal: 87-1751*

Tel. (507) 239-7100   *Tel. (507) 269-0205*

NOTA CULTURAL

Los padrinos

In many parts of Latin America, there is a tradition of adopting **padrinos**, or godparents, to assist with a wedding. The bride's family asks close relatives and friends to contribute a specific item to the event. This custom of sponsorship, in addition to deflecting some of the financial burden from the bride's family, establishes a strong social bond that serves to honor people on both sides of the relationship. Here are three examples of roles of wedding **padrinos**:

Padrinos de velación (vigil, watching over): A stable couple that serves as an example for the newlyweds, the **padrinos de velación** pay for the costs of the religious ceremony.

Padrinos de anillos (rings)   **Padrinos de pastel** (wedding cake)

Cultura: Panamá

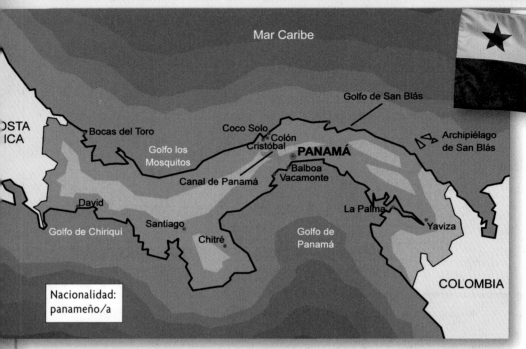

Mar Caribe

Golfo de San Blás

Bocas del Toro
Coco Solo
Colón
Cristóbal
Archipiélago
de San Blás

COSTA RICA

Golfo los Mosquitos

PANAMÁ

Canal de Panamá

Balboa
Vacamonte

David

La Palma

Santiago

Yaviza

Golfo de Chiriquí

Chitré

Golfo de Panamá

COLOMBIA

Nacionalidad:
panameño/a

Antes de leer

¿Qué océanos se conectan por el Canal de Panamá?

¿Cuál es la capital de Panamá?

Una niña kuna de las islas de San Blas

Cristóbal Colón llegó a Panamá en 1502. En el siglo XVI, llegaron otros españoles para explorar y abrir rutas comerciales entre el Viejo y el Nuevo Mundo. Todas las expediciones españolas a Sudamérica pasaron por Panamá, y esta función de conexión entre norte y sur ha traído al istmo una mezcla de personas que normalmente no se asocian con Latinoamérica. Con la construcción del Canal, llegaron inmigrantes del este y del sur de Asia, europeos, norteamericanos, africanos antillanos y del Medio Oriente para aprovechar las oportunidades comerciales.

Casi el 70% de los panameños son mestizos, y un 20% se divide entre los de ascendencia africana y española. Un 10% de la población pertenece a grupos indígenas, siendo los más famosos los Kuna de las islas San Blas. Los festivales del país reflejan la influencia de los diferentes grupos étnicos. En la zona de Colón, se observan las tradiciones africanas, como las congas y el festival del Cristo Negro. En la zona de Bocas del Toro, se baila el Palo de Mayo[1], de origen europeo.

---

[1]**Palo...** *Maypole dance*

Investig@ en INTERNET

Investiga sobre alguno de los grupos indígenas de Panamá y comparte la información con tus compañeros/as de clase después. Busca información sobre dónde viven, cómo es su cultura, que lengua hablan, etc. Si encuentras fotografías, imprímelas y tráelas a clase.

La *pollera* es el vestido tradicional de las mujeres panameñas. Se teje con hilo fino en colores fuertes, y pueden tardar hasta un año en completarlo.

La Ciudad de Panamá

La selva tropical

Por su clima tropical es posible practicar en Panamá deportes acuáticos todo el año —las costas del país cuentan con casi 1.500 islas. Panamá también tiene algunas de las más espectaculares selvas tropicales del mundo. Al igual que en su vecina Costa Rica, en Panamá se han establecido varios parques nacionales para proteger la diversidad ecológica. La capital del país, la Ciudad de Panamá, está en la parte del Canal que termina en el Pacífico. En su zona colonial, conocida como el Casco Antiguo, se conservan edificios de arquitectura francesa, italiana y española que contrastan con los rascacielos, centros comerciales, hoteles y bancos de la zona moderna.

En 1999, Mireya Moscoso, la primera mujer presidente de Panamá, fue elegida por el pueblo por su dedicación a combatir los enormes problemas del desempleo y de la pobreza. Fue la tercera presidente después de la dictadura problemática del General Manuel Noriega. En 2004, los panameños eligieron presidente a Martín Torrijos, hijo de Omar Torrijos, que fue dictador militar de Panamá de 1968 a 1981.

EL CANAL DE PANAMÁ

En 1902 los EE.UU. comenzaron la construcción del Canal de Panamá —que sería el mayor canal navegable del continente, con 82.6 kilómetros (50 millas) de largo. Es una de las mayores maravillas de la ingeniería moderna. Cuenta con tres esclusas[2] que levantan los barcos 15.24 metros (85 pies) sobre el nivel del mar. A cada lado del canal, hay selvas densas y montañas verdes. Cerca de la entrada del Canal al océano Pacífico, hay una vista impresionante: el arco de metal del Puente de las Américas, que atraviesa el canal y lleva vehículos por la Carretera[3] Panamericana hasta Alaska.

El 31 de diciembre de 1999 los EE.UU. les entregaron[4] el Canal a los panameños. Gracias al tránsito de barcos por el Canal —unos 15.000 cada año— Panamá es muy importante para el comercio mundial. La Zona del Canal, que es libre de impuestos[5], es otro atractivo del país. El dólar estadounidense y el balboa panameño son las monedas oficiales del país.

---

[2]locks [3]highway [4]handed over [5]taxes

¿NADAR EL CANAL?

En 1913, dos nadadores profesionales de Nueva York, un hombre y una mujer, obtuvieron permiso para nadar el Canal de Panamá. En 1914, los primeros en atravesar el Canal entero, de océano a océano, fueron dos empleados del Canal. Luego, en 1928, el autor-aventurero Richard Halliburton nadó a través del Canal en 10 días (el pasaje típico de un barco de carga tarda unas nueve horas). Se requiere la misma cantidad de trabajo para hacer pasar por el Canal a una persona a nado que para hacer pasar un barco enorme de muchas toneladas, y se cobra el pasaje según el peso en toneladas. El precio más alto pagado para cruzar el Canal de Panamá fue de $226,194.25 por el crucero Crown Princesa en 2003. El más bajo lo pagó el señor Halliburton: sólo pagó 36 centavos. El precio promedio es de $54,000.

Después de leer

1. ¿Por qué es la Zona del Canal muy atractiva para hacer compras?

2. ¿Cuál es la función de una esclusa?

3. ¿Por qué hay una mezcla tan interesante de grupos étnicos en Panamá?

Así se forma

Linda y yo nos entendemos y nos queremos mucho. Vamos a estar juntos para toda la vida.

1. Reciprocal constructions: Talking about each other

English uses the phrases *each other* and *one another* to express reciprocal actions: *They love each other/one another.* Spanish uses the pronouns **nos**, **os**, and **se**, accompanied by the corresponding verb forms, to express reciprocal or mutual actions.

Ana y yo **nos** queremos mucho.

Claudia, Juana y Bill **se** conocen muy bien.

Ana and I love **each other** very much.

Claudia, Juana, and Bill know **one another** very well.

11-11 **Una historia de amor triste.** Determinen la cronología de la "historia de amor" de él y ella, dándole un número a cada actividad.

__6__ encontrarse en el parque / la siguiente noche

__7__ una semana más tarde / comprometerse

__1__ conocerse en una fiesta

__5__ besarse

__3__ enamorarse

__4__ abrazarse

__10__ finalmente, desafortunadamente / divorciarse

__8__ dos meses más tarde / casarse

__2__ hablarse

__9__ ¡Cómo es la vida! Cuatro meses más tarde / separarse

Ahora, narren la historia para indicar lo que ocurrió: **Se conocieron en una fiesta...**

11-12 **Tu propia historia de amor.** Describe tu historia (verdadera o imaginaria) en cinco oraciones. ¿Qué cosas ocurrieron entre tu pareja y tú? Algunos voluntarios van a leer sus historias.

Modelo: **Nos vimos por primera vez en...**

11-13 **¿Un buen matrimonio o el divorcio?**

 **Paso 1.** Formen grupos de mujeres y grupos de hombres. En sus grupos, escriban dos listas con la información que se pide en el cuadro.

Las características de un matrimonio feliz	Las razones principales de los divorcios
1. Se comunican bien.	**1.** No tratan de resolver sus problemas.
2.	**2.**
3.	**3.**
4.	**4.**
5.	**5.**

 Paso 2. Ahora formen nuevos grupos con dos hombres y dos mujeres y presenten sus ideas. ¿Son diferentes las opiniones de las mujeres y las de los hombres?

Escenas

Fin del amor

Natalia   Rubén

Natalia y Rubén tienen una cita en el parque, cerca de la universidad. Natalia está sentada en un banco. Rubén llega.

Paso 1. En parejas, escriban una lista de razones posibles por las que puede terminar el amor.

Paso 2. Escucha la conversación entre Rubén y Natalia y escribe un resumen de su conversación en dos o tres oraciones.

Paso 3. Lee las siguientes oraciones y las opciones que las siguen (*follow*). Después, escucha la conversación otra vez y escoge la opción correcta.

1. Natalia quiere romper la relación con Rubén porque...
   - **a.** se llevan mal
   - **b.** su amistad es más importante
   - **c.** no piensan igual

2. Natalia y Rubén salen juntos hace...
   - **a.** unos días
   - **b.** algunas semanas
   - **c.** varios meses

3. Natalia ahora prefiere...
   - **a.** no tener novio
   - **b.** un novio serio para casarse
   - **c.** conocer a muchos chicos

4. Rubén...
   - **a.** insiste en continuar la relación
   - **b.** bromea con (*teases*) Natalia
   - **c.** está tan deprimido que decide irse a Costa Rica

5. Al final Natalia y Rubén...
   - **a.** deciden continuar su relación de novios; no pueden separarse
   - **b.** se despiden; no van a verse nunca más
   - **c.** mantienen su amistad pero no son novios

Escenas

Paso 4. Escucha una vez más mientras lees el texto y revisa tus respuestas del *Paso 3*.

Rubén: Hola, Natalia, tengo algo para ti. (*Le da una flor.*)

Natalia: Gracias. Rubén, tenemos que hablar.

Rubén: ¿Qué pasa? Te veo muy preocupada. (*Se sienta a su lado.*)

Natalia: Rubén... lo siento, pero tenemos que romper nuestra relación. Nuestra amistad es maravillosa, pero tenemos ideologías un poco diferentes...

Rubén: Pero, Natalia, yo te quiero... nos llevamos muy bien, y ¡hace apenas° una semana que estamos juntos!

barely

No... *It's no use* **Natalia:** No tiene caso° que digas nada. En este momento de mi vida prefiero estar sola.

Rubén: Está bien. Como tú quieras, Natalia.

Natalia: Perdóname.

Rubén: (*Con un tono híper-dramático.*) Te prometo que no te voy a molestar nunca más. Me voy a ir de voluntario a las junglas de Costa Rica y jamás° volveremos a vernos. Adiós, Natalia. (*Se levanta y comienza a irse.*)

never

Natalia: ¡Pero, Rubén!... ¿Todavía podemos escribirnos, no?

hope **Rubén:** ¿Cómo? ¿Es que aún tengo alguna esperanza°? (*Vuelve.*)

Natalia: No... pero estoy coleccionando sellos. (*Sonríe.*)

Rubén: (*Sonríe también.*) ¡No podemos separarnos! Me encantan las personas con sentido del humor... ¿Amigos?

Natalia: ¡Amigos! (*Se dan la mano.*)

Paso 5. En grupos, contesten estas preguntas:

1. Natalia piensa que tener ideologías diferentes es un problema en su relación con Rubén. ¿Qué aspectos son importantes para ustedes en una relación amorosa? Ideología, intereses similares, creencias religiosas, ...

2. En su opinión, ¿funcionan mejor las relaciones cuando las personas son muy similares o muy diferentes?

3. ¿Creen que es posible ser amigo/a de un ex-novio/a?

Así se dice

Para estar en contacto: Las llamadas telefónicas

Pepita y Natalia visitan la ciudad de Panamá y desean comunicarse con amigos/as y familiares. Lean la conversación y aprendan las nuevas expresiones.

Natalia: Vamos a buscar un teléfono público para llamar a mi amigo Carlos. Creo que vive en la ciudad de Colón, que está cerca de aquí.

Pepita: ¿Tienes su número de teléfono?

Natalia: No. A ver si° lo encuentro en esta **guía telefónica**. Necesito su **código de área** porque creo que es llamada **de larga distancia**.

Pepita: ¿No puedes usar tu **teléfono celular**?

Natalia: No, pero tengo una **tarjeta telefónica**. (*Natalia encuentra el número y llama a su amigo.*)

Natalia: ...Hay un **contestador automático**... pero no quiero **dejar un mensaje**.

Pepita: A propósito°, necesito hacer una llamada a mi familia, para decirles que estamos aquí y que todo va bien. (*Pepita marca° el número.*) ¡Ay! ¡**La línea está ocupada**!

Natalia: Podemos llamar otra vez más tarde. Ahora tengo hambre. ¿Quieres almorzar en ese restaurante?

A ver... *Let's see if*

A... *By the way*
dials

dejar	to leave	el mensaje	message
la llamada telefónica	telephone call	ocupado/a	busy
largo/a	long	la tarjeta	card

11-14) Las llamadas telefónicas. Escucha las siguientes descripciones e identifica el término al que se refieren.

a. el código de área ___ 5

b. el contestador automático ___ 2

c. el mensaje ___ 6

d. el teléfono celular ___ 3

e. la tarjeta ___ 1

f. la guía telefónica ___ 4

Así se dice

11-15) Los hábitos telefónicos. Primero, contesta las siguientes preguntas en la columna "Yo". Después, en parejas, háganse las preguntas y completen la columna **Mi compañero/a** con la información obtenida. ¿Tienes hábitos parecidos o diferentes?

	Yo	Mi compañero/a
1. ¿A quién llamas con mucha frecuencia?		
2. ¿Quién te llama mucho?		
3. ¿Haces muchas llamadas de larga distancia? ¿A quién?		
4. ¿Cómo prefieres comunicarte con tus amigos/as, por teléfono o por correo electrónico? ¿Por qué?		
5. ¿Tienes un teléfono en casa o usas solamente un teléfono celular?		
6. ¿Qué aspectos negativos tienen los teléfonos celulares?		

NOTA CULTURAL

Rubén Blades

Rubén Blades is a singer and songwriter from Panama City. His Cuban mother and Colombian father were both musicians. He is famous for salsa music with socially conscious lyrics that address urban problems and seek unification among all Latin Americans. Having earned a law degree from Harvard University, he ran for the presidency of Panama in 1994 as the head of a movement with a platform of social equity between cultural and social groups across all economic classes.

One of his most famous songs is *Pedro Navaja* (1978), a narrative about a mugging with a surprise ending. It topped all records for salsa songs, selling more than a million copies and earning gold and platinum records in Spanish-speaking countries as well as in the United States. See if you can listen to the song and locate the lyrics online.

Así se forma

Quiero que aprendan el subjuntivo.

¡¿El qué?!

2. The subjunctive mood—an introduction; the present subjunctive: Expressing subjunctive reactions to the actions of others

Most verb tenses that you have studied (such as the present, the preterit, and the imperfect) are part of what is called the indicative mood. The indicative is used for stating facts, communicating specific knowledge, or asking questions.

Quiero conocer a Jaime.	*I want to meet Jaime.*
¿Sabes dónde vive?	*Do you know where he lives?*

The subjunctive mood is another set of verb tenses. In contrast to the indicative, it often expresses subjectivity and conveys a speaker's wishes, attitudes, hopes, fears, doubts, uncertainties, and other personal reactions to events and to the actions of others[4].

Quiero que *conozcas* a Jaime.	*I want you to meet Jaime.*
Espero que *esté* en casa.	*I hope that he is at home.*

You have already used forms of the subjunctive in **Ud./Uds.** commands and in negative **tú** commands. In this and subsequent chapters you will be introduced to various uses of the subjunctive and to its four tenses (**present, present perfect, imperfect,** and **past perfect**).

You will first learn and practice the forms of the subjunctive and then review some of its uses later on in this chapter and following ones.

A. Regular and stem-changing verbs

The present subjunctive of regular **-ar, -er,** and **-ir** verbs is formed by deleting the final **-o** from the **yo** form of the present indicative and adding the endings indicated. Note that **-er** and **-ir** verbs have the same endings.

	bailar → bail∅	comer → com∅	vivir → viv∅
(yo)	bail**e**	com**a**	viv**a**
(tú)	bail**es**	com**as**	viv**as**
(Ud., él/ella)	bail**e**	com**a**	viv**a**
(nosotros/as)	bail**emos**	com**amos**	viv**amos**
(vosotros/as)	bail**éis**	com**áis**	viv**áis**
(Uds., ellos/ellas)	bail**en**	com**an**	viv**an**

> **HINT**
>
> To form the present subjunctive, always think "opposite endings:" **-ar** verbs have an **e** in every ending; **-er** and **-ir** verbs have an **a**.

---

[4] English has a subjunctive mood too, although it is not used as frequently as in Spanish. Note that the subjunctive forms are often mistaken for other forms of the indicative. Here are some examples:
   It is imperative that Mr. Brown *appear* before the judge.
   If I *were* you . . .
   The director insists that the report *be* sent through express mail.

Así se forma

- Note that many irregular verbs follow the same pattern in the present subjunctive as in the present indicative and show the irregularity in the other persons (*tú, él/ella, Ud., etc.*)

conocer	→	conozcø	→	**conozca, conozcas,...**

decir	digø	**diga, digas,...**
hacer	hagø	**haga, hagas,...**
poner	pongø	**ponga, pongas,...**
salir	salgø	**salga, salgas,...**
tener	tengø	**tenga, tengas,...**
traer	traigø	**traiga, traigas,...**
venir	vengø	**venga, vengas,...**

- Stem-changing **–ar** and **–er** verbs also follow the same pattern as in the present indicative—stem changes occur in all forms except **nosotros** and **vosotros**.

pensar (e → ie)		volver (o → ue)	
p**ie**nse	pensemos	v**ue**lva	volvamos
p**ie**nses	penséis	v**ue**lvas	volváis
p**ie**nse	p**ie**nsen	v**ue**lva	v**ue**lvan

- Stem-changing **–ir** verbs follow the pattern of the present indicative, but also have <u>an additional stem change</u> (**e → i** and **o → u**) in the **nosotros** and **vosotros** forms.

divertirse (e → ie, i)		pedir (e → i, i)		dormir (o → ue, u)	
me div**ie**rta	nos div**i**rtamos	p**i**da	p**i**damos	d**ue**rma	d**u**rmamos
te div**ie**rtas	os div**i**rtáis	p**i**das	p**i**dáis	d**ue**rmas	d**u**rmáis
se div**ie**rta	se div**ie**rtan	p**i**da	p**i**dan	d**ue**rma	d**ue**rman

- Verbs ending in **–gar**, **–car**, and **–zar** have spelling changes in all persons in the present subjunctive. They are the same spelling changes that occur in the **yo** form of the preterit (see page 203).

–gar (g → gu) lle**gar** → lle**gue**, lle**gues**,...

–car (c → qu) to**car** → to**que**, to**ques**,...

–zar (z → c) almor**zar** → almuer**ce**, almuer**ces**,...

11-16 **Amigos perezosos.** Tienes unos amigos con problemas académicos serios. ¿La causa? ¡Son muy perezosos! ¿Les recomiendas que hagan o que no hagan las siguientes cosas?

Modelo: estudiar más **Les recomiendo que estudien más.**

1. ☑ Les recomiendo que...	☐ Les recomiendo que no...	asistan a todas sus clases.
2. ☑ Les recomiendo que...	☐ Les recomiendo que no...	lleguen a las clases a tiempo.
3. ☐ Les recomiendo que...	☑ Les recomiendo que no...	salgan con amigos/as todas las noches.
4. ☑ Les recomiendo que...	☐ Les recomiendo que no...	hagan la tarea todos los días.
5. ☐ Les recomiendo que...	☑ Les recomiendo que no...	se duerman durante las clases.
6. ☑ Les recomiendo que...	☐ Les recomiendo que no...	desayunen antes de ir a clase.
7. ☐ Les recomiendo que...	☑ Les recomiendo que no...	vean la tele todas las noches.
8. ☐ Les recomiendo que...	☐ Les recomiendo que no...	_____

11-17 **¿Qué prefieres en un/a compañero/a de apartamento?**

Paso 1. Quieres encontrar un/a compañero/a de apartamento. Usando formas del presente del subjuntivo, escribe si quieres o no quieres que la persona haga las siguientes cosas.

Modelo: hacer la cama todos los días
> **Quiero que haga la cama todos los días.**
> **Quiero que... / No quiero que...**

1. fumar
2. hablar en su teléfono celular día y noche
3. escucharme cuando yo hablo
4. tener intereses similares a los míos
5. beber mucha cerveza
6. prender la tele a las dos de la mañana
7. pagar las cuentas a tiempo
8. comer toda la comida que yo compro
9. ayudarme a limpiar el apartamento
10. ¿_____?

Paso 2. Ahora, comparte tus preferencias con un/a compañero/a. ¿Serían (*Would be*) ustedes dos buenos/as compañeros/as de apartamento?

B. Irregular verbs in the present subjunctive

The following verbs are the only ones with irregular forms in the present subjunctive.

dar	dé	des	dé	demos	deis	den
estar	esté	estés	esté	estemos	estéis	estén
ir	vaya	vayas	vaya	vayamos	vayáis	vayan
saber	sepa	sepas	sepa	sepamos	sepáis	sepan
ser	sea	seas	sea	seamos	seáis	sean
haber	haya	hayas	haya	hayamos	hayáis	hayan

Haya is the subjunctive form of **hay** (*there is, there are*).

Espero que **haya** otras soluciones.   *I hope that **there are** other solutions.*

Así se forma

11–18 La agencia *Su Media Naranja.*

 Paso 1. En este momento, no tienes novio/a y por eso decides ir a la agencia *Su Media Naranja* para encontrar la persona de tus sueños. Completa el formulario.

Ficha personal *Su Media Naranja*

Nombre: _____

Edad: _____

Soltero/a ☐   Divorciado/a ☐

Fuma ☐   No fuma ☐

Describa brevemente su personalidad: _____

_____

Indique sus intereses y pasatiempos: _____

¿Qué busca en su media naranja? _____

¿Qué opina sobre los siguientes atributos? _____

Es indispensable que...	Es importante que...	No es importante que ...	
			...sea fiel
			...sea comprensivo/a
			...sea sincero/a
			...me dé regalos
			...sepa cocinar
			...tenga sentido del humor
			...esté conmigo mucho tiempo
			...se acuerde de mi cumpleaños
			...vaya a la iglesia/ templo, etc.

Ahora describa otras cosas que busca usted.

Es indispensable que...

Es importante que...

No es importante que...

 Paso 2. Ahora, uno/a de ustedes es el/la empleado/a de la agencia. El/La otro/a le dice sus preferencias según el cuestionario. Quizás (*Perhaps*) él/ella conozca la persona perfecta para ti. Después, cambien de papel.

Cultura: Los cibercafés: otro modo de consolidar amistades

Emoticones

:) sonriendo   : (triste

> : | enojado   : x un besito

¿Cómo hacen nuevas amistades los jóvenes hispanos? Los métodos son múltiples y las viejas tradiciones siguen en vigor. Es a menudo[1] por medio de otros amigos, en la universidad, en el trabajo, a la salida de la iglesia o en fiestas que comienzan la gran mayoría de las amistades. En los pueblos, las plazas también sirven de lugar de encuentro. Tampoco hay que excluir las discotecas y los cines donde los jóvenes van en grupos para pasar un buen rato.

Ahora, sin embargo, los hispanos tienen otro medio de conocer y estar en contacto con personas del mundo entero: el ciberespacio. Con tan sólo oprimir[2] unas teclas, están conectados. Nadie se escapa de ese fenómeno de la globalización.

¿Sabes lo que son los *cibercafés*? Si tu respuesta fue "café espacial" casi acertaste[3]. Son sitios que, además de ser acogedores[4], ofrecen una lista extensa de bebidas y comidas. Sin embargo, el verdadero atractivo es ofrecerle a la clientela un lugar donde puede ponerse en contacto con familiares y amigos vía la red. En cómodas[5] estaciones semiprivadas con computadoras, los cibernautas, o internautas, pasan el rato "chateando", estudiando o comprando en línea. Los españoles fueron pioneros del concepto y lo han estado disfrutando[6] desde el año 1994.

Los cibercafés, o los cafés Internet, se han puesto de moda en todo el mundo hispano. No es raro encontrarlos aun en los pueblecitos más remotos. La próxima vez que vayas de viaje a Latinoamérica o a España y sientas la necesidad de ponerte en contacto con algún ser querido, pregunta por el cibercafé más cercano. ¡Y no te olvides de usar la lengua del ciberespacio y de las emociones, los *Emoticones*!

Un cibercafé en Guatemala

---

[1]*often*   [2]*pressing*   [3]*were right*   [4]*inviting*   [5]*comfortable*   [6]*enjoying*

Después de leer

1. ¿Eres internauta? ¿Dónde "te conectas"? ¿Hay cibercafés donde vives?

2. ¿Tienes una página en Myspace o Facebook?

3. ¿Mandas tarjetas o invitaciones por la red? ¿Te gusta recibirlas o prefieres un método tradicional?

4. ¿Encuentras verdaderos/as amigos/as en la red o solamente conexiones de corta duración?

Así se forma

Juanito, quiero que ordenes tu cuarto ahora mismo.

3. Expressing wishes and requests related to other people's actions: The subjunctive with expressions of influence

You have learned how to express what someone wants or prefers to do by using verbs such as **querer/ preferir/ desear** + *infinitive*.

Quiero ir a la fiesta.	*I want to go to the party.*
Desean cantar una canción.	*They want to sing a song.*

Note that in the sentences above, the subject is the same in both clauses. However, to express someone's desire, preference, recommendation, request, or suggestion that *someone else* do something, use *a verb of preference* + **que** + *subjunctive form*.

Quiero que vayas a la fiesta.	*I want you to go to the party.*
Desean que Eva cante una canción.	*They want Eva to sing a song.*

Notice that the verb in the first clause, which expresses a desire, is in the indicative (**Quiero...**); the verb in the second clause, which expresses what the speaker wishes, is in the subjunctive (**que vayas a la fiesta**). There are *two* subjects involved: the person influencing and the person being influenced.

Subject 1		Subject 2
expression of wish to influence +	**que** +	*action influenced*
indicative		*subjunctive*

Here are some verbs that express the wish to influence and require the use of the subjunctive in the subordinate (dependent) clause when its subject is different:

querer (ie)	*to want*	Quiero que me **ayudes**.
preferir (ie, i)	*to prefer*	Prefieren que **salgamos** ahora.
insistir (en)	*to insist (on)*	Insisten en que **lleguemos** a tiempo.
recomendar (ie)	*to recommend*	Te recomienda que lo **llames**.
sugerir (ie, i)	*to suggest*	Te sugiero que lo **invites** a la fiesta.
pedir (i, i)	*to request*	Le pedimos que **traiga** pan.
decir (i)	*to say*	Te digo que no **esperes** más.
aconsejar	*to advise*	El profesor les aconseja que **estudien** más.

- The verbs **recomendar, sugerir, pedir,** and **decir** are commonly used with indirect-object pronouns (**me, te, le, nos, os, les**), as one recommends, suggests, etc., something *to someone else*. Place the indirect-object pronoun immediately before the main verb.

Te sugiero que vayas.	*I suggest that you go.*

- When clarification is needed, the clarifying noun or pronoun is usually placed after the verb.

Le recomiendo **a Leticia** que hable con el profesor.

I recommend that Leticia speak with the professor.

 11-19 Las mamás y los niños.

 Paso 1. ¿Quién pide estas cosas, Juanito a su mamá o la mamá a Juanito?

	El niño a la mamá.	La mamá al niño.
1. No quiero que veas tanta televisión.	☐	☑
2. Te digo que me compres un juguete.	☑	☐
3. Sugiero que hagas la tarea ahora.	☐	☑
4. Quiero que me des chocolate.	☑	☐
5. No quiero que me pongas el abrigo.	☑	☑
6. Te pido que hagas la cama inmediatamente.	☐	☐
7. Te aconsejo que no seas desobediente.	☐	☐

Paso 2. Ahora, indica lo que tiene que hacer Juanito (y el perro) según los deseos de la madre.

La madre quiere que

Modelo: La madre quiere que se acueste.

1. La madre quiere que...
2. La madre le pide que...
3. La madre le pide que...
4. La madre le sugiere que...
5. La madre insiste en que...
6. La madre le dice al perro que...

Así se forma

11-20 Todos piden algo.

Paso 1. Indica las recomendaciones, deseos y sugerencias que las siguientes personas tienen para ti. Completa cada oración con varias actividades.

1. La profesora/El profesor de español me recomienda que...
2. Mi mamá me pide que...
3. Mis amigos/as me dicen que...
4. Mi compañero/a de cuarto insiste en que yo...
5. Mis hermanos/as quieren que ...

Paso 2. Comparen sus oraciones en grupos. ¿Recibieron todos ustedes las mismas recomendaciones? ¿Qué indican estas recomendaciones sobre los hábitos o la personalidad de ustedes?

11-21 ¿Qué queremos?

Paso 1. Indica qué quieres de estas personas. Escribe al menos tres cosas que quieres de cada uno.

Modelo: **Quiero que mis padres sean pacientes, que no...**

Mis padres
Mi compañero/a de cuarto
Mi novio/a

Paso 2. En grupos de cuatro o cinco personas, compilen sus respuestas y escriban una lista con las cinco cosas más importantes que quieren de estas personas. Prepárense para compartir sus ideas con la clase.

Los padres	El/La compañero/a de cuarto	Un/a novio/a
Queremos que...	Queremos que...	Queremos que...
1.	1.	1.
2.	2.	2.
3.	3.	3.
4.	4.	4.
5.	5.	5.

11-22 **Consejos para todos.** Ustedes colaboran en una organización estudiantil de apoyo (*support*) a otros estudiantes. Muchos estudiantes les escriben correos electrónicos pidiendo consejo. En grupos, respondan a estos estudiantes. Usen verbos de la lista.

| recomendar | sugerir | decir | pedir | insistir en | querer |

Modelo: "Mi novio ha roto conmigo y lo extraño mucho. Estoy deprimida y no puedo concentrarme en los estudios".

Te sugerimos que salgas con tus amigos/as y que conozcas a otras personas. También...

1. "Estoy muy estresado y no duermo bien. ¡Ayuda, por favor!"

2. "Mi compañera de cuarto es muy desordenada y nuestro cuarto es un desastre. Además nunca encuentra sus libros y "toma prestados" los míos, que pierde también. ¿Qué puedo hacer?"

3. "¿Tienen algunas ideas sobre cómo puedo vivir bien y divertirme con poco dinero?"

NOTA CULTURAL

PANAMA HATS

What are called "Panama hats" are actually made in Ecuador. The hat became known as the Panama when workers involved in the construction of the Panama Canal used them as protection against the sun. Their popularity was enhanced in 1906 when President Theodore Roosevelt was photographed wearing one while viewing the construction of the Canal.

Panama hats are woven by hand from a plant called the *toquilla*. Coarser hats may take a few hours to weave, while the finer hats may take up to five months. Constantly dipping their fingers in water, the weavers split the fiber into thin pieces and braid ring after ring of palm into a fabric so soft and dense that it feels like silk. The hats are then pummeled, trimmed, and scrubbed.

The finest Panamas have a smooth texture in which the weave is barely perceptible, but if held up to the light, a spiral of rings is visible. These rings indicate where new strands were started in the weaving. It is the number of rings that determines the quality of the Panama. The cheaper hats may have up to ten rings, whereas the finer quality hats contain as many as forty rings. Prices range accordingly, from $20 up to several hundred dollars.

Espero que llame...

4. Expressing emotional reactions and feelings about other people's actions: The subjunctive with expressions of emotion

The subjunctive is also used when a speaker expresses emotional reactions and feelings (joy, hope, sorrow, etc.) about the actions or condition of another subject.

<u>Me alegro de</u> que mi amigo me **visite**.   *I'm glad that my friend is visiting me.*

<u>Esperamos</u> que **pueda** quedarse unos días.   *We hope that he can stay a few days.*

Así se forma

Note that the first and main clause, expressing the speaker's emotions/feelings, is in the indicative (**Me alegro de...**). The dependent clause, which expresses the actions or condition of another person or thing, is in the subjunctive (**que mi amigo me visite**).

> expression of emotion   +   **que**   +   action or condition of another subject
> indicative   subjunctive

Here are some verbs and expressions of emotion that require the use of the subjunctive in the subordinate clause when the subject is different:

alegrarse (de)	to be glad (about)	<u>Me alegro</u> de que **estén** comprometidos.
esperar	to hope, expect	<u>Espero</u> que **se casen** este verano.
sentir (ie, i)	to be sorry, regret	<u>Siento</u> que **vivan** tan lejos.
temer	to fear, be afraid	<u>Tememos</u> que **no puedan** visitarnos.
¡Ojalá que[5]...!	I hope	<u>¡Ojalá que</u> me **inviten** a la boda!

Remember that if there is no change of subject after the expression of emotion, the infinitive is used, not **que** + *subjunctive*.

One subject	Change of subject
Siento no **poder** ir a la reunión.	Siento que ellos no **puedan** ir a la reunión.
I regret not being able to go to the meeting.	*I regret that they cannot go to the meeting.*
Temo no **oír** el despertador.	Temo que no **oiga** el despertador.
I am afraid that I will not hear the alarm clock.	*I am afraid that he will not hear the alarm clock.*

 **¿Cuál es una emoción lógica?** Escucha lo que dice Natalia y decide si es lógico o no. Si no es lógico, corrígelo para que sí sea lógico.

Modelo: Oyes: Me alegro de que mi amiga esté enferma.
Marcas: ☐ Sí, es lógico. ☒ No, no es lógico.
Escribes: *Probablemente siente que su amiga esté enferma.*

1. ☐ Sí, es lógico.   ☐ No, no es lógico. _____
2. ☐ Sí, es lógico.   ☐ No, no es lógico. _____
3. ☐ Sí, es lógico.   ☐ No, no es lógico. _____
4. ☐ Sí, es lógico.   ☐ No, no es lógico. _____
5. ☐ Sí, es lógico.   ☐ No, no es lógico. _____
6. ☐ Sí, es lógico.   ☐ No, no es lógico. _____

---

[5]This expression comes from Arabic and it means literally "God grant" or "God willing." In modern Spanish it is synonymous with *I hope*. It is always followed by a verb in the subjunctive.

11-24 **Mis deseos.** En parejas, combinen cada declaración de A con la expresión de B que le corresponde. Luego hagan una oración usando **Espero que… / Ojalá que…** para expresar sus deseos. Túrnense.

Modelo: Jaime no estudió mucho para el examen. → pasar el examen
Ojalá que pase el examen.

A

1. Mi hermana se queja de que no tiene novio.
2. Inés va a dar una fiesta para celebrar el compromiso de Linda y Manuel.
3. No me acordé del cumpleaños de mi amiga.
4. Mañana cumplo veintiún años.
5. Pepita y su amiga quieren ir a Costa Rica.
6. Esteban estudió mucho, pero la clase es difícil.

B

a. pasar el examen
b. por fin encontrar su media naranja
c. nadie olvidarse de mi cumpleaños
d. invitarme
e. no enojarse conmigo
f. poder ir este verano

11-25 **Reacciones y emociones.** Describan las reacciones o emociones de las personas según las situaciones.

Modelo: Juanito, Elena y el perro sienten que… **llueva.**

NO HAY EXAMEN HOY

Waah!

¡Ánimo, Javier!

1. Juanito, Elena y el perro se alegran de que…
2. Nancy y su marido sienten que…
3. Esteban se alegra de que…
4. Linda y Manuel esperan que Javier…
5. Pepita siente que Natalia…
6. Camila espera que su ex-novio… pero teme que…

Así se forma

11-26 Reacciones. En parejas, túrnense para leer estas situaciones a su compañero/a, que debe reaccionar con una expresión de emoción del cuadro. Al final, cada estudiante debe pensar en una situación más.

> me alegro de que...   (no) me gusta que...
> siento que...   temo que...

Modelo: Hoy tenemos mucha tarea.

> **No me gusta que tengamos mucha tarea** o
> **Temo que no pueda ver mi programa favorito en la tele.**

Estudiante A:

1. No hay clase el viernes.
2. El examen final es difícil.
3. Estoy muy cansado/a hoy.
4. Mi novio/a y yo nos hemos comprometido.
5. ¿...?

Estudiante B:

1. Tengo mucho dolor de cabeza.
2. Mi familia viene de visita este fin de semana.
3. Mi novio/a ha roto conmigo.
4. ¡Voy a... para las vacaciones de primavera!
5. ¿...?

11-27 El valor de la amistad.

Paso 1. Lee el título del texto de la siguiente página y observa la fotografía. En parejas, respondan a estas preguntas:

- ¿Qué relación une a las personas de la foto?
- ¿Qué valores o cualidades tiene la amistad para ustedes?

el valor de la
AMISTAD

POR DORIS TORRES

bond
support

La amistad es una de las relaciones más importantes y hermosas de la vida. Somos afortunados cuando contamos con amigos verdaderos. Este vínculo° nos brinda confianza, solidaridad y apoyo°, tanto en los momentos buenos como en los malos, y nos hace sentir entendidos y aceptados incondicionalmente. Todos queremos tener y ser amigos excepcionales.

 Paso 2. Lean el párrafo acerca de la amistad y, en parejas, contesten las preguntas.

1. ¿Qué dice el artículo acerca de la amistad? ¿Estás de acuerdo?
2. ¿Qué nos dan nuestros amigos?
3. ¿Qué queremos todos?

Y tú, ¿tienes buenos amigos? ¿Eres tú un buen amigo?

 Paso 3. Ahora compartan con su compañero/a lo que ustedes aprecian (*appreciate*) de sus amigos, explicando sus razones y/o dando ejemplos. Usen expresiones de emoción del cuadro.

> Me alegro de que... Me gusta mucho que... Me encanta que... Es fenomenal que...

Modelo: **Me gusta mucho que mi amiga Alicia sea tan sincera porque siempre puedo confiar en ella. Por ejemplo...**

PALABRAS ÚTILES

apoyar	to support (morally)
cómico/a	funny
comprensivo/a	understanding
confiar	to trust
divertido/a	fun
leal	loyal

DICHOS

**Amigo en la adversidad, amigo de verdad.
En largos caminos° se conocen los amigos.**
¿Cómo explicas estos dichos?

roads

11-28 Generaciones.

 Paso 1. Piensa en las etapas diferentes de la vida y completa las oraciones. ¡Atención! En la primera oración de cada serie el sujeto no cambia (por lo tanto no se usa el subjuntivo), pero en la segunda, sí.

Modelo: Los bebés necesitan... **dormir mucho y tomar mucha leche.**

Los bebés necesitan que sus padres... **los bañen.**

1. Los niños quieren...
   Los niños quieren que sus padres...

2. Los jóvenes prefieren...
   Los jóvenes prefieren que los adultos...

3. Los adultos esperan...
   Los adultos esperan que los jóvenes...

4. Los ancianos temen... Los ancianos temen que los jóvenes...

Paso 2. Ahora, compartan sus ideas en grupos.

SITUACIONES

Tu amigo/a te llama por teléfono y te dice que está deprimido/a por una serie de incidentes o está enojado/a con su pareja/ un familiar. Escúchalo/la, muestra apoyo y dale consejos. Usa las siguientes expresiones.

Estudiante A: ¡Aló!

Estudiante B: Hola, Pedro, soy Ana. ¡Ay! Estoy deprimida.

Estudiante A: Cuéntame. ¿Qué pasa?

Estudiante B: Pues,...

Estudiante A: Siento mucho que...

Estudiante B: Y además...

Estudiante A: Te sugiero que...

PALABRAS ÚTILES

¿Cómo se contesta el teléfono?

¡Hola!	*Argentina*
¡Sí!/ ¡Diga!/ ¡Dígame!	*España*
¡Bueno!/ ¡Mande!	*México*
¡Aló!	*otros países*

Dicho y hecho

¡A ESCUCHAR!

La radionovela "Amalia". En este episodio de la radionovela "Amalia, el corazón nunca se olvida", Luisa Fernanda habla con José Ricardo, su marido. Escucha el episodio para determinar qué problema tienen. Luego, contesta las tres primeras preguntas.

1. ¿José Ricardo estaba en la oficina cuando su esposa lo buscó? ☐ sí ☐ no

2. ¿Es Amalia cliente de José Ricardo? ☐ sí ☐ no

3. ¿José Ricardo conocía a Amalia antes de casarse con Luisa Fernanda? ☐ sí ☐ no

Ahora escuche el episodio otra vez y conteste las tres preguntas siguientes.

4. ¿Dónde vio Luisa Fernanda a Amalia?

5. ¿Qué noticia tiene Luisa Fernanda para su marido?

6. Imagine que usted es escritor/a del próximo episodio. ¿Qué va a pasar?

CONVERSANDO

Problemas matrimoniales. Dos de ustedes visitan a un/a consejero/a matrimonial (*marriage counselor*) porque tienen problemas serios.

Ustedes hablan con el/la consejero/a acerca de:

- los problemas en su matrimonio
- por qué quieren separarse
- la custodia compartida (*joint*) de sus niños

Él/Ella habla con ustedes acerca de:

- lo que deben tratar de hacer para resolver los problemas
- lo que deben tratar de hacer para mantener la familia unida
- las decisiones que deben tomar

DE MI ESCRITORIO

Cartas a los "desesperados". Imagina que eres Victoria, periodista del periódico *El Investigador* y responsable de la columna "Problemas personales" (en página 396). Escríbeles una carta breve a dos de las siguientes tres personas, indicando tus reacciones y recomendaciones. Usa las siguientes expresiones.

> Le recomiendo que...   Le sugiero que...   Espero que...

Querida Victoria:

Tengo un novio magnífico. Se llama Luis y es el hombre más simpático y cariñoso del mundo. ¡Siempre me trae flores y chocolates! Hace dos años que salimos juntos. El problema es Ronaldo, un chico que conocí el fin de semana pasado. ¡Es tan guapo! ¡Y qué ojos! Salimos a cenar, pero todavía no le he dicho nada a Luis. ¿Qué debo hacer?

"Confundida en Caracas"

Querida Victoria:

A... *I like*
tattoo

A mí me cae bien° Leonardo, el nuevo amigo de nuestra hija Elsa, pero a mi esposo no le gusta para nada. Critica el tatuaje° de serpiente que tiene en el brazo, los aretes que lleva en la nariz y en la oreja, su pelo largo ¡y su motocicleta! Leonardo se siente muy incómodo en nuestra casa a causa de mi marido, y Elsa está desesperada. ¿Cómo puedo resolver esta situación?

"Madre preocupada en Valencia"

Querida Victoria:

Hace dos semanas me comprometí con mi novia y decidimos casarnos este verano. La semana pasada mi novia me dijo que su mejor amigo le había declarado amor eterno y rompió nuestro compromiso. Anteayer mi novia me llamó para pedirme que la perdone: quiere continuar con nuestra relación y los planes de matrimonio. Yo la quiero mucho pero no quiero más sorpresas. ¿Debo darle otra oportunidad?

"Un indeciso en Maracaibo"

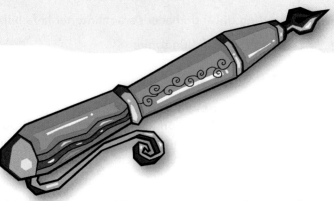

Artes populares: Las molas

Mola con las banderas de Panamá y los EE.UU.

Antes de leer

1. ¿Dónde están las islas de San Blas? Vuelve al mapa de la página 374 para localizarlas.

2. ¿Es común que la ropa exprese una opinión o una personalidad?

Mola con la imagen de un dragón.

Por lo general, todas las regiones de un país tienen artesanías típicas. Por ejemplo, las mujeres indígenas de la tribu kuna, que viven en las islas de San Blas, en Panamá, son famosas en todo el mundo por sus molas.

Las molas son una forma de arte textil[1]. Consisten en una base de tela[2] de algodón negro y varias capas[3] de tela de colores brillantes cosidas[4] una sobre la otra. Las capas de tela se cortan y se unen con puntadas[5] especiales para crear ilustraciones detalladas[6]. Hace muchos siglos los kunas pintaban diseños geométricos muy complejos en su piel[7], pero el comercio textil cambió la tradición: ahora el medio de expresión es la mola y no la piel.

Los diseños geométricos todavía son los más populares. La flora y la fauna de la región también son elementos comunes tanto como las escenas que ilustran tradiciones, supersticiones y la vida diaria de la tribu. Las imágenes más abstractas tienen origen en los sueños y la fantasía de los kuna. Hoy, las imágenes en revistas y anuncios publicitarios inspiran nuevas ideas para las molas.

Lo interesante es que no hay dos molas idénticas; por eso, muchos museos a nivel mundial incluyen molas en sus colecciones de arte. Observa cuidadosamente las fotografías de las dos molas y contesta las siguientes preguntas.

[1]textile [2]cloth [3]layers [4]sewn [5]stitches [6]detailed [7]skin

Después de leer

1. ¿Qué figuras aparecen en estas molas?

2. ¿Cuál de estas molas puede representar mejor la superstición? ¿Y la política?

3. En tu opinión, ¿por qué hay dos banderas en la mola? En el pasado, ¿qué relación existía entre Panamá y los EE.UU.?

4. ¿Cuál de las molas te gusta más? ¿La prefieres por sus colores o por el tema?

5. ¿Tienes ropa que expresa tu opinión o tu personalidad?

6. ¿Tienes ropa o accesorios que puedan considerarse arte? ¿Cuáles son?

Repaso de vocabulario activo

Adjetivos

cariñoso/a   *affectionate*

celoso/a   *jealous*

comprensivo/a   *understanding*

divorciado/a   *divorced*

fiel   *faithful*

juntos/as   *together*

sincero/a   *sincere, honest*

soltero/a   *single*

viudo/a   *widower/widow*

Expresiones útiles

el amor a primera vista   *love at first sight*

felicidades   *congratulations*

Ojalá que...   *I hope . . .*

Sustantivos

Las llamadas telefónicas
Telephone calls

el código de área   *area code*

el contestador automático   *answering machine*

la guía telefónica   *phone book*

la línea está ocupada   *the line is busy*

la llamada   *the phone call*

de larga distancia   *long distance*

la tarjeta telefónica   *phone card*

el teléfono celular   *cell phone*

Las relaciones y más
Relationships and more

el adulto   *adult*

la amistad   *friendship*

el amor   *love*

los ancianos   *the elderly*

la anciana   *old lady*

el anciano   *old man*

la boda   *wedding*

la cita   *date; appointment*

el divorcio   *divorce*

las etapas de la vida   *stages of life*

la infancia   *infancy*

los jóvenes/ los adolescentes   *young people; adolescents*

la juventud/ la adolescencia   *youth; adolescence*

la luna de miel   *honeymoon*

la madurez   *maturity*

el marido   *husband*

la muerte   *death*

el nacimiento   *birth*

la niñez   *childhood*

los niños   *children*

los recién casados   *newlyweds*

la vejez   *old age*

la vida   *life*

Verbos reflexivos

acordarse de (ue)   *to remember*

alegrarse (de)   *to be glad (about)*

casarse (con)   *to get married (to)*

comprometerse (con)   *to get engaged (to)*

comunicarse   *to communicate*

divorciarse   *to get divorced*

enamorarse (de)   *to fall in love (with)*

encontrarse (ue) (con)   *to meet up (with) (by chance)*

enojarse   *to get angry*

irse   *to leave, go away*

olvidarse (de)   *to forget (about)*

quejarse (de)   *to complain (about)*

reírse (de)   *to laugh (at)*

reunirse (con)   *to meet, get together (with)*

separarse (de)   *to separate (from)*

Otros verbos y expresiones verbales

aconsejar   *to advise*

creer   *to believe*

esperar   *to hope, expect*

extrañar   *to miss*

insistir (en)   *to insist (on)*

llorar   *to cry*

matar   *to kill*

mentir   *to lie*

nacer   *to be born*

olvidar   *to forget*

pensar (ie) (en)   *to think (about)*

recomendar (ie)   *to recommend*

recordar (ue)   *to remember*

resolver (ue)   *to resolve*

romper (con)   *to break up (with)*

salir (con)   *to go out (with)*

sentir (ie, i)   *to feel*

sugerir (ie, i)   *to suggest*

temer   *to fear*

dar a luz   *to give birth*

dejar un mensaje   *to leave a message*

estar casado/a (con)   *to be married (to)*

estar embarazada   *to be pregnant*

estar enamorado/a (de)   *to be in love (with)*

estar juntos/as   *to be together*

estar listo/a   *to be ready*

estar prometido/a   *to be engaged*

llevarse bien/ mal   *to get along well/poorly*

tener celos   *to be jealous*

tratar de + *infinitivo*   *to try to*

Autoprueba y repaso

I. Reciprocal constructions. Imagina que estás contándoles a tus amigos/as anécdotas de tus padres. Usa el pretérito o el presente según la situación.

Modelo: mis padres / conocerse en la universidad
Se conocieron en la universidad.

1. enamorarse inmediatamente
2. comprometerse seis meses más tarde
3. casarse en secreto dos meses más tarde
4. aún hoy, después de veinticinco años, amarse mucho

II. The present subjunctive (formation). Indica lo que quiere la profesora. Completa las oraciones con la forma correcta del verbo. Usa el presente del subjuntivo.

Modelo: traer la tarea a clase (yo, nosotros)
Quiere que traiga la tarea a clase.
Quiere que traigamos la tarea a clase.

1. estudiar más (nosotros, Ana y Linda)
2. hacer la tarea (Esteban, nosotros)
3. volver pronto (Juan, nosotros)
4. divertirse en clase (yo, nosotros)
5. ser puntual/es (los estudiantes, tú)
6. ir a la biblioteca (yo, todos los estudiantes)

III. The subjunctive with expressions of influence. Tus amigos se van a Puerto Rico. Indica lo que deseas o recomiendas que ellos hagan.

Modelo: querer / que pasar unas buenas vacaciones en Puerto Rico
Quiero que pasen unas buenas vacaciones en Puerto Rico.

1. sugerirles / que ir durante el invierno
2. preferir / que explorar las playas remotas
3. querer / que divertirse mucho durante su visita a San Juan
4. querer / que visitar el bosque lluvioso (*rain forest*)
5. recomendarles a mis amigos / que hablar en español todo el tiempo
6. pedirles a todos / que comprarme un regalo

IV. The subjunctive with expressions of emotion. Es tu primera cita con una persona muy especial. Expresa tus sentimientos.

Modelo: esperar / que ser muy sincero/a conmigo
Espero que sea muy sincero/a conmigo.

1. alegrarse de / que (nosotros) tener una cita esta noche
2. Ojalá / que (él/ella) llevarme a un buen restaurante
3. temer / que (él/ella) llegar un poco tarde
4. esperar / que (él/ella) no olvidarse de la cita
5. Ojalá / que (nosotros) poder comunicarnos bien

V. *Repaso general.* Contesta con oraciones completas.

1. Cuando sales con sus amigos/as, ¿adónde van? ¿Qué hacen ustedes normalmente?
2. ¿Con quién/es te llevas muy bien?
3. ¿Haces muchas llamadas de larga distancia? ¿A quién? ¿De qué hablan?
4. Imagina que fuiste a una fiesta y conociste a una persona muy interesante. ¿Qué pasó?
Nos conocimos, nos...
5. Es lunes por la noche. ¿Qué quieres que hagan o no hagan tus amigos/as?
6. ¿Qué prefieres que haga o no haga la persona con quien vives?
7. ¿Qué esperas que haga tu profesor/a de español?

VI. *Cultura*

1. ¿Cuáles son las dos monedas oficiales de Panamá?
2. Describe algo sobre el Canal de Panamá: su historia, su estructura, su impacto, etc.
3. ¿Dónde se fabrican los "sombreros de Panamá"?

Answers to the *Autoprueba y repaso* are found in **Apéndice 2.**

12

WILEY
PLUS

Aventuras al aire libre

Aventuras al aire libre
Amigos y algo más
Aventuras al aire libre

By the end of this chapter you will be able to:

- Talk about outdoor adventures and the environment
- Express likes, dislikes, and interests
- Express destination, purpose, and motive
- Express doubt and disbelief
- React to recent events

Así se dice	Así se forma	Cultura	Dicho y hecho
• Aventuras al aire libre • Más aventuras • La naturaleza y el medio ambiente	1. Verbs similar to **gustar** 2. **Para** and **por** (A summary) 3. The subjunctive with expressions of doubt or negation 4. The present perfect subjunctive	• Costa Rica • Los parques nacionales en el mundo hispano • Arte folklórico: Las carretas	• ¡Vamos a Costa Rica! • Una visita al Parque Arqueológico Xcaret • Mi aventura

ENTRANDO AL TEMA

¿Piensas en los problemas del medio ambiente (*environment*)?
¿Cuáles son los más serios?

Así se dice

Aventuras al aire libre

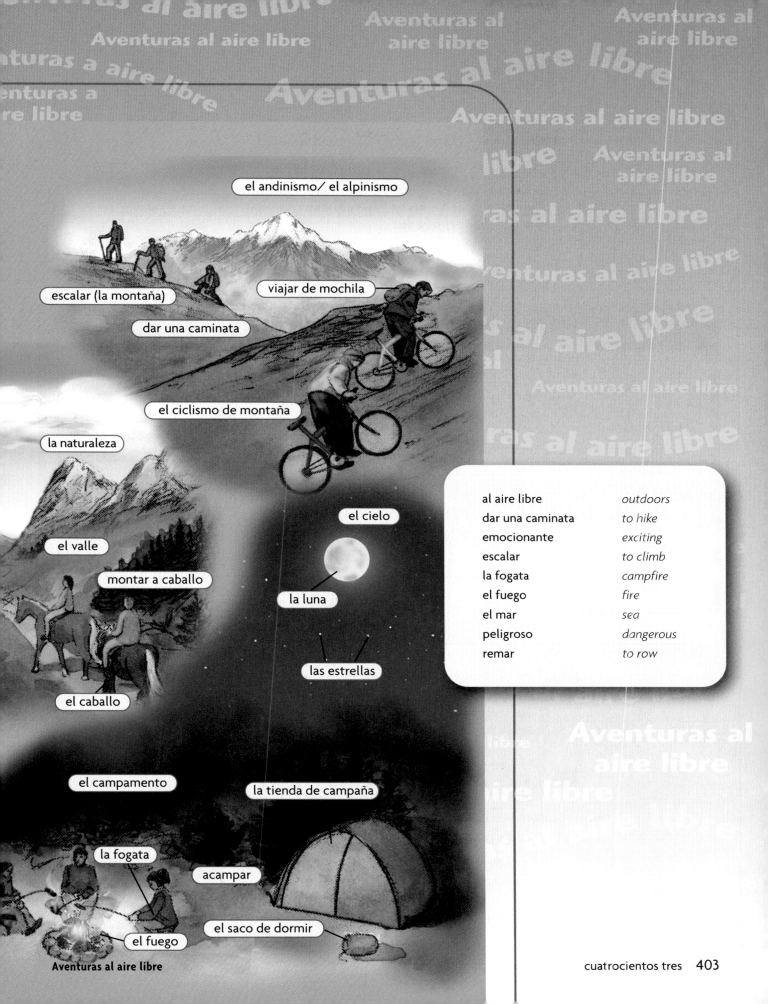

el andinismo/ el alpinismo

escalar (la montaña)

dar una caminata

viajar de mochila

el ciclismo de montaña

la naturaleza

el valle

montar a caballo

el cielo

la luna

el caballo

las estrellas

el campamento

la tienda de campaña

la fogata

acampar

el fuego

el saco de dormir

al aire libre	outdoors
dar una caminata	to hike
emocionante	exciting
escalar	to climb
la fogata	campfire
el fuego	fire
el mar	sea
peligroso	dangerous
remar	to row

Aventuras al aire libre

Así se dice

 Aventuras al aire libre

12-1 ¿Es peligroso? ¿Emocionante?

Paso 1. Indica si, en tu opinión, las siguientes actividades son peligrosas y emocionantes. Indica también cuáles has hecho, y si te gustaría hacerlas por primera vez/ otra vez.

¿A quién le gustaría saltar de un avión en paracaídas?

	¿Peligroso?			¿Emocionante?		¿Lo has hecho?		¿Quieres hacerlo (otra vez)?	
	Sí	Un poco	No	Sí	No	Sí	No	Sí	No
Pescar									
Nadar en el mar									
Construir castillos de arena									
Hacer *surf*									
Bucear									
Practicar el *parasail*									
Practicar el descenso de ríos									
Escalar montañas									
Montar a caballo									
Saltar en paracaídas (ver foto)									

Paso 2. Ahora, compartan sus respuestas en grupos de cuatro o cinco personas y respondan a las siguientes preguntas.

¿Qué miembros del grupo son los más aventureros? ¿Qué actividades del cuadro quieren hacer? ¿Cuáles no son tan interesantes para el grupo?

12-2 El descenso de ríos.
Tú y dos amigos/as buscan una aventura para hacer descenso de ríos juntos. Lean juntos la información y luego contesten las preguntas.

1. ¿Qué equipo se necesita para practicar el descenso de ríos?
2. ¿Cuáles son las cosas más importantes que debe ofrecer la compañía de *rafting*?
3. ¿Qué clasificación de ríos prefieren? ¿Por qué?
4. ¿Qué ríos prefieren navegar? ¿Por qué?

Rafting y algo más

El *rafting* en Latinoamérica permite explorar y conocer santuarios remotos y fascinantes de la naturaleza. Algunos ejemplos:

▶ **El río Savegre, en Costa Rica:** un paraíso con aguas cristalinas, fauna abundante y bella selva° tropical.

jungle

▲ **El río Usumacinta, en México:** revela remotos templos y pirámides mayas, selva densa y cascadas impresionantes.

◀ **El río Futaleufu, en Chile:** pasa por bosques de la Patagonia y por espectaculares paisajes° de roca, nieve y hielo.

landscapes

Equipo

los remos

el casco

el chaleco salvavidas

▲ **El río Colca, en Perú:** pasa por dramáticos cañones con cataratas altas y vistas de volcanes activos.

LA COMPAÑÍA DE *RAFTING* DEBE TENER:

- Equipo en buen estado
- Guías experimentados
- Guías capacitados en cursos de rescate° y primeros auxilios°
- Seguro° contra accidentes.

rescue

primeros... *first aid*

insurance

Clasificación de ríos

Clase 1: Corriente moderada, sin rápidos.

Clase 2: Rápidos suaves y algo de oleaje, apto para toda la familia.

Clase 3: Rápidos más fuertes, olas grandes y algunas pendientes escalonadas. Es apto para todas las edades, pero se debe tener más precaución.

Clase 4: Rápidos fuertes, olas grandes, rocas en el camino y, en algunas partes, pendientes muy pronunciadas. Sólo para mayores de dieciséis años.

Clase 5: Rápidos muy fuertes, sólo para personas experimentadas.

Clase 6: Río peligroso y no explorado. Cuando alguien logra navegar un río de clase 6, éste se convierte en categoría 5.

Así se dice

12-3 **¿Recuerdas las palabras?** Trabajen en parejas. Cada uno de ustedes lee una lista de definiciones relacionadas con la naturaleza o el deporte, mientras el otro escucha e identifica las palabras definidas.

Modelo: Estudiante A (lee):   Tierra rodeada por agua, como Cuba
Estudiante B (escucha e identifica):   **la isla**

Estudiante A:

1. Agua que cae desde lo alto de un río, como la del Niágara
2. Terreno plano (*flat*) entre montañas, como San Fernando en California
3. Gran extensión de agua, como el Pacífico
4. Un espacio con muchos árboles y plantas
5. Donde están el sol, la luna y las estrellas
6. Hacemos esto en los campamentos para poder cocinar
7. Cuando acampamos, lo usamos para dormir

Estudiante B:

1. Este deporte se practica en los ríos con una balsa
2. Capturar peces
3. Viajar en un barco grande, como un hotel
4. Actividad que sólo se puede practicar cuando hay olas
5. Subir montañas
6. Caminar por el campo, un bosque, etc.
7. Se practica bajo el agua y con equipo especial, para admirar la fauna marina

> **Más aventuras**

Es primavera y los estudiantes **están de vacaciones**. Van con sus amigos/as a lugares muy diferentes.

Linda e Inés dan un paseo por el campo, donde viven los abuelos de Linda.

la araña

el pájaro

el animal

la mariposa

los insectos

la mosca

el mosquito

Esteban está explorando la **selva** costarricense. **Tiene miedo** porque hay muchos **animales** e **insectos**.

la tormenta

el relámpago

la colina

la cámara

sacar/ tomar fotos

la serpiente

Natalia y Pepita dan una caminata por el **desierto** de Arizona. La familia de Natalia vive cerca de allí.

la colina	hill	**tener miedo**	to be afraid
la hierba	grass		
la tierra	earth, land		

12-4 La palabra diferente.

Paso 1. Lee las siguientes listas de palabras y subraya (*underline*) la palabra que es diferente.

1. **a.** el mosquito   **b.** el pájaro   **c.** el cerdo   **d.** la mosca   **e.** la mariposa
2. **a.** el valle   **b.** la colina   **c.** la tierra   **d.** la granja   **e.** el río
3. **a.** la serpiente   **b.** el cerdo   **c.** la vaca   **d.** la gallina   **e.** el caballo
4. **a.** tener miedo   **b.** acampar   **c.** escalar   **d.** bucear   **e.** hacer ciclismo
5. **a.** el relámpago   **b.** la luna   **c.** las estrellas   **d.** el sol   **e.** el cielo

Paso 2. Con un/a compañero/a, comparen sus palabras subrayadas. ¿Son las mismas? Si son diferentes, comparen sus criterios.

DICHOS

Más vale pájaro en mano que cien volando°.   *flying*
En boca cerrada no entran moscas.
¿Conoces el equivalente en inglés de estos dos dichos?

12-5 Aventureros/as.

Paso 1. Caminando por la clase, hazles preguntas a tus compañeros/as y anota sus nombres y sus respuestas en la tabla siguiente. Atención: no puedes poner el nombre del mismo estudiante en más de un espacio.

Modelo: bucear

Estudiante A: **¿Has buceado alguna vez?**

Estudiante B: **Sí, he buceado.**

Estudiante A: **¿Dónde? ¿Cuándo?**

Estudiante B: **En Cancún. El verano pasado./ Hace dos años.**

Estudiante A: **¿Con quién fuiste?/ ¿Viste peces?...**

(*El Estudiante A anota el nombre del estudiante y la información en el cuadro.*)

	Nombre	¿Cuándo?	¿Dónde?	Algo más...
hacer* esnórquel				
practicar el parasail				
viajar por un desierto				
dar una caminata por una selva				
vivir en/ visitar una granja con muchos animales				
descender un río en balsa, kayak o canoa				
ver* una catarata grande				
ver una serpiente (no en un zoo)				
hacer un viaje en crucero				
hacer surf				
escalar una montaña				
acampar				

 Paso 2. Ahora, dile a la clase algo de las aventuras de tus compañeros/as.

HINT

* = this verb has an irregular past participle

Investig@ en INTERNET

Averigua (*Find out*)...
...cuál es la montaña más alta de Sudamérica y cuántos metros mide.
...cuál es la cascada más alta del mundo, dónde está y cuántos metros mide.
...cuál es la selva más extensa del mundo y en qué países se encuentra.
...cuál es el lago navegable más alto del mundo y dónde está.

Ésta es la cascada más alta del mundo. Mide 979 metros (3.281 pies).

Cultura: Costa Rica

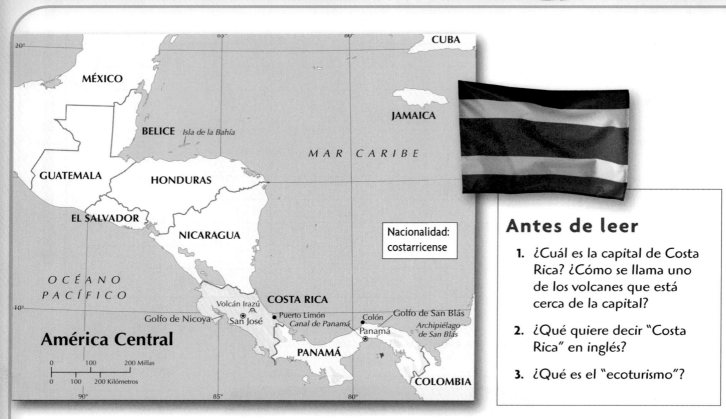

MÉXICO
BELICE · Isla de la Bahía
GUATEMALA
HONDURAS
EL SALVADOR
NICARAGUA
CUBA
JAMAICA
MAR CARIBE
OCÉANO PACÍFICO
Volcán Irazú
COSTA RICA
Golfo de Nicoya · San José
Puerto Limón
Canal de Panamá
Colón
Golfo de San Blás
Archipiélago de San Blás
Panamá
PANAMÁ
COLOMBIA
América Central
0   100   200 Millas
0   100   200 Kilómetros

Nacionalidad: costarricense

Antes de leer

1. ¿Cuál es la capital de Costa Rica? ¿Cómo se llama uno de los volcanes que está cerca de la capital?

2. ¿Qué quiere decir "Costa Rica" en inglés?

3. ¿Qué es el "ecoturismo"?

COSTA RICA

El primer explorador europeo que llegó a Costa Rica fue el mismo Cristóbal Colón, el 18 de septiembre de 1502. Colón hacía su cuarto y último viaje al Nuevo Mundo, y cuando se acercaba a la costa, un grupo de indígenas caribes salieron en canoas a saludarlo. Los caribes llevaban aros de oro en las narices y en las orejas, y por eso los españoles dieron el nombre "Costa Rica" a la región.

Había civilizaciones en Costa Rica miles de años antes de la llegada de Colón. Entre los misterios culturales de los habitantes precolombinos se encuentran miles de bolas, hechas de granito y en forma esférica perfecta, que se encontraron en la costa del oeste. Algunos sitios arqueológicos muestran evidencia de una influencia de los olmecas y los náhuatl —dos grupos indígenas de México. Cuando llegó Colón, había cuatro grupos principales de indígenas en Costa Rica, pero hoy en día, sólo un 1% de la población costarricense es de herencia indígena. Los españoles trajeron a esclavos africanos, y unos 70,000 de sus descendientes viven en el país hoy. El otro 98% del país es gente blanca, y los de ascendencia española se llaman *ticos*.

Cuando México se rebeló contra España en 1821, Costa Rica y el resto de Centroamérica se unieron. El primer presidente fue Juan Mora Fernández, elegido en 1824. Aunque sí ha habido dictadura militar en Costa Rica, nunca existió la violencia extrema que sufrieron otros países de Centroamérica. Hubo una guerra civil en 1948, y José María "Don Pepe" Figueres Ferrer ganó la presidencia en un mes. Don Pepe llegó a ser uno de los líderes más influyentes de Costa Rica. En 1987, el presidente Óscar Arias Sánchez ganó el Premio Nobel a causa de sus esfuerzos por acabar la guerra civil de Nicaragua. Hoy en día, Costa Rica tiene la reputación de ser uno de los países más estables y más prósperos de Latinoamérica —de hecho, el país no tiene ejército.

La capital de Costa Rica, San José, es una ciudad diversa, con parques hermosos y lugares históricos. Sin embargo, la verdadera atracción del país está en su geografía, su fauna y su flora. Costa Rica se distingue por sus playas, ríos, cascadas, volcanes y montañas con abundante vegetación. Los volcanes son característicos del país. A unos treinta kilómetros de San José y de Cartago (la capital original), hay cuatro volcanes. Dos de ellos, el Poás y el Irazú, a veces están activos. Desde el Irazú (con 3.432 m de altura) se puede ver las costas del Caribe y el Pacífico al mismo tiempo.

Costa Rica es uno de los países latinoamericanos con más conciencia ecológica —se protege más del 25% de su territorio. Existen más de quince reservas y parques nacionales que contienen una biodiversidad sorprendente: 14,000 especies de

El volcán Irazú

plantas y árboles, 1,000 especies de mariposas y 850 especies de pájaros. Costa Rica goza hoy de una imagen turística muy única, basada en intereses ecológicos y el "ecoturismo": los viajes a áreas naturales que conservan el medio ambiente a la vez que apoyan y respetan a los residentes locales.

Después de leer

1. ¿Te parece buena idea el ecoturismo? ¿Dónde se puede hacer ecoturismo en los Estados Unidos?
2. ¿Te gustaría vivir en un país sin ejército? ¿Por qué?

Monteverde, un "Bosque Nubloso"

Así se forma

Me fascina bucear.

1. Verbs similar to *gustar*: Expressing likes, dislikes, and interests

In **Capítulo 4** you learned to use **gustar** to express likes and dislikes.

gusta + *verb*	**Me gusta nadar.**
gusta + *singular noun*	**Me gusta el agua verde-azul del Caribe.**
gustan + *plural noun*	**Me gustan las playas de Costa Rica.**

Although the meaning of **gustar** is closest to the English *like*, its structure is similar to that of "to be pleasing (to someone)." That is, whatever is pleasing is the subject (and therefore agrees with the verb) and the person who is pleased by it is the indirect object.

<table>
<tr><td>A mi hermano</td><td>le</td><td>gust**an** los deportes.</td><td>*Sports*</td><td>*are pleasing*</td><td>*to my brother.*</td></tr>
<tr><td>(OI)</td><td>(OI)</td><td>(S)</td><td>(S)</td><td></td><td>(OI)</td></tr>
</table>

HINT

Review **gustar** on pp. 112–113.

The following verbs express additional degrees of likes, dislikes, and interests, and they function like **gustar**, that is, they are used with indirect-object pronouns (**me, te, le, nos, os, les**) and the verb is in the third-person singular or plural in agreement with the subject (what is delightful, fascinating, bothersome, etc.).

encantar	*to love, delight, enchant*	**Me encanta** esquiar en el lago.
fascinar	*to be fascinating to, fascinate*	**¿Te fascinan** las tormentas?
molestar	*to be annoying to, bother*	**Le molesta** el calor.
interesar	*to be interesting to, interest*	**Nos interesan** los reptiles.
importar	*to be important to, matter*	No **les importa** si llueve.

12-6 ¿Le encanta/n, le fascina/n, le interesa/n, le molesta/n... ?

Paso 1. Escucha a Camila, toma apuntes e indica a qué se refiere.

Modelo: (Escuchas) Me encanta.

(Indicas) ☒ esquiar   ☐ los peces

(Anotas) **Le encanta**

1.	☐ bucear	☐ los animales	_____
2.	☐ el campo	☐ las olas	_____
3.	☐ la naturaleza	☐ los insectos	_____
4.	☐ la arena	☐ las gallinas	_____
5.	☐ el alpinismo	☑ las serpientes	_____
6.	☐ el desierto	☑ las tormentas	_____
7.	☐ el desierto	☐ los pájaros	_____

Paso 2. Ahora, en parejas, decidan qué vacaciones le gustarían más a Camila y expliquen por qué.

☐ Explorar la selva.   ☐ Ir a las montañas.   ☐ Pasear por el campo.

(12-7) ¿Qué te importa?

Paso 1. Completa el siguiente sondeo individualmente.

Me importa...	Mucho	Un poco	Nada
1. sacar buenas notas	☐	☐	☐
2. practicar deportes	☐	☐	☐
3. ganar mucho dinero	☐	☐	☐
4. tener ropa de moda	☐	☐	☐
5. vivir cerca de mi familia	☐	☐	☐
6. viajar y conocer el mundo	☐	☐	☐
7. reciclar y cuidar la naturaleza	☐	☐	☐

Paso 2. Ahora, compartan sus respuestas en grupos de cuatro personas. ¿Tienen ustedes mucho en común? Prepárense para presentar algunas de sus conclusiones a la clase.

(12-8) Mis reacciones.

Paso 1. Escribe sobre cada uno de los siguientes temas y explica brevemente tus razones.

- los aspectos de la vida universitaria que **te encantan/ gustan**

- los aspectos de la vida universitaria que **no te gustan**

- una clase que **te ha fascinado**

- una clase que **no te ha gustado**

Paso 2. En grupos pequeños comenten y comparen sus reacciones.

NOTA CULTURAL

Los ticos
In Spanish, we can say that something is small or that we have an affection towards it by using **-ito** o **-ico** at the end of the word:

abuela → abuel**ita**
momento → moment**ito**, moment**ico** ("¡Espérame un moment**ico**!")

People from Costa Rica are called **ticos** (*masculine*) and **ticas** (*feminine*). It is said that this is because they are famous for using these diminutive endings very frequently.

Escenas

Javier

Natalia

Rubén

Pepita

Octavio

Aventuras en el parque ecológico

Nuestros amigos están acampando en el parque ecológico del Arenal en Costa Rica. Es de noche y Pepita y Natalia se están preparando para visitar el volcán.

Paso 1. Imagina la experiencia de nuestros amigos en el parque ecológico Arenal.

1. ¿Qué pueden hacer?

   ☐ acampar   ☐ ir al cine   ☐ bucear

   trails   ☐ caminar por senderos°   ☐ hacer surf   ☐ dormir en una tienda de campaña

   y también _____

2. ¿Qué pueden ver?

   ☐ peces tropicales   ☐ serpientes   ☐ árboles y plantas exóticos

   ☐ vacas y cerdos   ☐ insectos grandes   ☐ muchos turistas

   y también _____

3. ¿Cómo se sienten?

   ☐ están cansados   ☐ están relajados

   ☐ tienen miedo   ☐ están fascinados

Paso 2. Escucha la conversación e indica si las siguientes afirmaciones son ciertas o falsas.

	Cierto	Falso
1. El parque ecológico tiene problemas de contaminación.	☐	☐
2. Natalia y Pepita quieren caminar cerca del volcán.	☐	☐
3. Octavio y Javier quieren ir con las chicas.	☐	☐
4. Natalia y Pepita dicen que no tienen miedo de nada.	☐	☐

Paso 3. Lee las siguientes preguntas; después, escucha la conversación otra vez y escribe tus respuestas.

1. ¿Por qué quieren las chicas visitar el volcán por la noche?
2. ¿Qué animal les dio miedo a Octavio y Javier en su aventura nocturna?
3. ¿Por qué tienen miedo Natalia y Pepita?
4. ¿Quién es el "animal"?

El Arenal es el único volcán activo de Costa Rica.

Paso 4. Escucha una vez más y lee el texto. ¿Son correctas tus respuestas del *Paso 3*?

Nuestros amigos están acampando en el parque ecológico del Arenal en Costa Rica. Es de noche y Pepita y Natalia se están preparando para visitar el volcán.

Pepita: Este parque ecológico debe de ser el lugar más espectacular del planeta. Aquí no hay basura ni contaminación, sólo bosques y animales...

Natalia: *(Interrumpiéndola)...* y me encanta respirar aire puro.
(Llegan Octavio y Javier.)

Pepita: ¡Hola, chicos! ¿Dónde está Rubén?

Octavio: Está en el pueblo organizando la manifestación contra la deforestación.

Pepita: ...y se le olvidó que Natalia y yo vamos a dar una caminata por los senderos cerca del volcán. ¿Quieren venir con nosotras?

Javier: ¿Ahora? ¿De noche? ¡No!

Natalia: ¿Por qué no? La actividad volcánica es más impresionante de noche.

Javier: El año pasado Octavio y yo tuvimos una experiencia nocturna muy extraña...

Pepita: ¿De verdad? ¿Qué pasó?

Octavio: Una noche nosotros decidimos usar las linternas° y explorar los bosques cerca del campamento. De repente, comenzó una tormenta con relámpagos y una lluvia muy fuerte. Decidimos regresar y en el camino° oímos un ruido muy extraño. Vimos un animal muy grande y empezamos a correr.   *flashlights*

   en... *on the way*

Natalia: ¿Qué era? ¿Un puma? ¿Un oso°?   *bear*

Javier: No, una vaca.

Pepita: ¿Una vaca? ¡Qué miedosos!

Octavio: Bueno, entonces si ustedes no tienen miedo, pueden dar su caminata solas.

Natalia: Pues sí, no nos importa ir solas. Nosotras somos muy valientes; no tenemos miedo a nada.

Pepita: ¡Vámonos! *(Se escucha un ruido...)* ¿Qué fue eso?

(Aparece Rubén, totalmente cubierto de lodo°.)   *mud*

Natalia: ¡Miren! ¡Es un animal salvaje! ¡Es un Yeti°!   *Bigfoot*

Todos: ¡Qué horror! ¡Vámonos! ¡Socorro°!   *Help!*

(Se van corriendo, con miedo.)

Rubén: ¿Adónde van? Soy yo, Rubén. Tuve un pequeño accidente. Me caí° en el lodo... ¡Qué amigos tan extraños tengo!   **Me...** *I fell*

Así se forma

¡Qué emocionante! Vamos a pasar por estos rápidos para llegar al campamento.

2. *Para* and *por* (A summary): Stating purpose, destination, and motive

You have been using **para** and **por** since **Capítulo 2**. Both prepositions often translate as *for* in English, but convey very different meanings in Spanish. The following charts review some of their more frequent uses and meanings.

Para *indicates*:

1. Purpose/Goal	*in order to + infinitive*	Sonia fue a Costa Rica **para** ver los bosques tropicales.
	for; used for + noun	Llevó un impermeable **para** la lluvia.
2. Recipient	*for*	Sacó unas fotos del bosque **para** su madre.
3. Destination	*toward*	Sonia sale **para** Panamá el viernes.
4. Deadline	*by, for*	Tiene que estar allí **para** el lunes.
5. Employment	*for (in the employ of)*	Ella trabaja **para** una compañía hotelera.

Por *indicates*:

1. Cause, reason, motive	*because of*	Esteban no terminó su trabajo **por** estar un poco enfermo.
	on behalf of	Su amiga habló con el profesor **por** él.
	for (the sake of)	Es tímida, pero lo hizo **por** su amigo.
2. Duration of time	*for, during*	Después habló con Esteban **por** media hora.
	in, at	Esteban trabajó en el proyecto **por** la tarde.
3. Exchange, price	*for*	Compró un diccionario **por** diez dólares.
	for, *in exchange for*	Él le dio las gracias[1] **por** el diccionario.
4. General physical movement in and around a given place	*down, by, along, through*	Ahora camina **por** el campus con sus libros y su diccionario.

12-9 **El viaje de Carmen.** Carmen hizo un viaje de negocios a San José, Costa Rica. Lee las oraciones acerca de su viaje y escoge el significado que expresan **para** y **por** en cada oración.

---

[1]To thank someone for something, always use **gracias por**...

handwritten note in margin: if you can Day in order to — ya have to use Para

para		por	
a. purpose/goal **d.** deadline		**f.** cause, reason, motive	**h.** exchange, price
b. recipient **e.** employment		**g.** duration of time	**i.** movement in and around a place
c. destination			

Carmen trabaja para (1) AT&P. Hizo un pequeño viaje de negocios a San José y después tomó unas pequeñas vacaciones y viajó por (2) Costa Rica. Estuvo allí por (3) una semana.

Salió para (4) San José el 8 de abril. Su compañía pagó 375 dólares por (5) el boleto de avión por (6) ser de un viaje de negocios. Estuvo dos días en San José para (7) sus reuniones de trabajo. También paseó por (8) el centro de la ciudad y fue a la Avenida Central para (9) ir de compras. Compró un traje de baño y un sombrero para (10) la playa y regalos para (11) sus parientes y amigos. Después viajó por (12) el país visitando los parques nacionales y finalmente salió para (13) la playa. Ésta fue la parte más relajada del viaje: tomaba el sol en la playa por (14) la mañana y paseaba y leía por (15) la tarde.

Cuando Carmen regresó a casa, sus amigos la visitaron para (16) ver las fotos y le dieron las gracias por (17) los regalos. ¡Les gustaron mucho! Claro que después Carmen tuvo que trabajar mucho para (18) terminar su informe sobre su viaje a Costa el Rica para (19) el lunes siguiente.

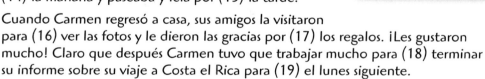

1. __e__   5. _____   9. _____   13. _____   17. _____

2. _____   6. _____   10. _____   14. _____   18. _____

3. _____   7. _____   11. _____   15. _____   19. _____

4. _____   8. _____   12. _____   16. _____

Así se forma

El Monte Chirripó

12-10 ¡A las montañas! Tú y unos/as amigos/as van a las montañas para escalar y acampar en el monte Chirripó en Talamanca, Costa Rica. Tú y otro/a amigo/a conversan sobre el viaje. Completen la conversación con **por** o **para**.

Tú: Salimos _____ el Chirripó el sábado a las seis de la mañana.

Amigo/a: ¿_____ cuántos días van?

Tú: _____ tres o cuatro días. Vamos _____ acampar y escalar el pico más alto de la región.

Amigo/a: ¡Qué emocionante! ¿Van a tomar la ruta que va _____ el río?

Tú: Sí, y luego vamos a dar una caminata _____ el bosque hasta encontrar un buen lugar _____ acampar.

Amigo/a: ¿Saben tus amigos armar la tienda de campaña?

firewood   Tú: Creo que no. Pero yo puedo hacerlo mientras ellos buscan leña° _____ la fogata.

Amigo/a: ¿Están ellos en buenas condiciones físicas para subir el monte?

summit   Tú: Pues, espero que sí. Vamos a salir muy temprano _____ la mañana y llegar a la cumbre° _____ el mediodía, antes de que empiece a llover.

A... *by the way*   Amigo/a: Es un buen plan. A propósito°, tu saco de dormir se ve muy nuevo. ¿Dónde lo compraste?

Tú: Lo compré en una tienda de descuento _____ $38.00.

Amigo/a: Buen precio... y antes de que se me olvide, tengo algo _____ ustedes: un mapa topográfico de la región para que no se pierdan.

Tú: Muchas gracias _____ el mapa. ¡Nos va a ser muy útil!

Amigo/a: Pues, ¡buen viaje!

12-11 Nuestra aventura. En grupos pequeños, imaginen que tienen una semana libre (*free, off*) y deciden organizar una aventura para sus próximas vacaciones. Usen las preguntas que siguen para formular su plan. Un/a secretario/a escribe el plan.

1. ¿Adónde van? ¿Cuándo van a salir para ese lugar?
2. ¿Por cuánto tiempo van a estar allí?
3. ¿Para qué van?
4. ¿Cómo van a viajar? ¿Cuánto piensan pagar por el viaje?
5. ¿Dónde van a alojarse? ¿En un hotel? ¿Van a acampar?
6. ¿Qué cosas necesitan llevar? ¿Para qué?
7. ¿Qué piensan hacer por la mañana/ tarde/ noche?
8. ¿Para qué fecha tienen que volver?

DICHOS

Más sabe el diablo por viejo que por diablo.

En tu opinión, ¿saben las personas mayores más que los jóvenes?

Así se dice

La naturaleza y el medio ambiente

A causa de los **problemas** ambientales que existen en el **mundo**, muchos científicos creen que nuestro **planeta** está en peligro.

¿Qué se puede hacer para **conservar** el planeta tierra?

Podemos: controlar la **contaminación** producida por las fábricas...

... y por los vehículos;

reducir la contaminación que **destruye**[2] la **capa de ozono** y **contribuye al calentamiento global**;

controlar la **deforestación** y plantar más árboles;

prevenir los **incendios forestales**;

evitar el uso excesivo de pesticidas;

proteger[3] los animales que están en peligro de extinción;

prevenir la contaminación de ríos y mares;

no **desperdiciar** los **recursos naturales**;

reducir el consumo de gasolina;

y **recoger** y **reciclar** basura.

a causa de	*because of*	**destruir (y)**	*to destroy*	**el mundo**	*world*
la capa	*layer*	**evitar**	*to avoid*	**recoger**[3]	*to pick up, gather*
contribuir (y)	*to contribute*	**el incendio forestal**	*forest fire*	**el recurso**	*resource*
desperdiciar	*to waste*	**el medio ambiente**	*environment*		

[2]**Destruir** changes the **i** to **y** in all forms of the present tense except **nosotros** and **vosotros**: destruyo, destruyes, destruye, destruimos, destruís, destruyen.
[3]**Proteger** and **recoger** change the **g** to **j** in the **yo** form of the present tense: protejo, proteges,... ; recojo, recoges...

Así se dice

12-12 Serios problemas ecológicos.

 Paso 1. ¿Cuánto afectan los siguientes problemas ecológicos tu vida diaria: mucho, bastante (*quite a bit*) o poco?

	Mucho	Bastante	Poco
la contaminación del agua			
la lluvia ácida			
el uso de pesticidas tóxicos			
la deforestación			
la destrucción de la capa de ozono			
los incendios forestales			
el calentamiento global			
la extinción de especies animales			
la escasez del agua			
la cantidad de basura generada			

PALABRAS ÚTILES

derretirse (i, i)	*to melt*
la escasez	*scarcity, shortage*
el petróleo	*crude oil*
la sequía	*drought*
respirar	*to breathe*

Paso 2. En parejas, comparen y expliquen sus opiniones.

Modelo: **A mí me afecta un poco la escasez del agua porque soy de Florida y a veces hay restricciones; entonces sólo podemos regar (*water*) el jardín una vez por semana.**

12-13 El medio ambiente. Consideren los problemas siguientes. En parejas, piensen en al menos (*at least*) una actividad —pequeña o grande— que puede contribuir a resolver ese problema. Luego, compartan sus ideas con el resto de la clase.

Problema	Para resolverlo
Se usan pesticidas tóxicos. (Es posible que exista una relación entre el uso de estos pesticidas y el cáncer.)	*Podemos comprar frutas y verduras orgánicas.*
Los incendios forestales y la tala (*cutting down of trees*) de árboles causan deforestación.	
Se desperdicia el agua. Muchas regiones sufren sequías.	
La producción de energía eléctrica es una de las causas más importantes de la contaminación medioambiental.	
Los Estados Unidos constituyen el 5% de la población del mundo, pero generan el 30% de la basura mundial.	

Problema	Para resolverlo
La combustión de gasolina y gasoil (*diesel*) produce mucha contaminación ambiental.	
El crecimiento de la población y la contaminación causan la extinción de muchas especies animales.	

Vista aérea de un vertido (*spill*) de crudo en la costa.

¿Un mundo ideal?

12-14 ¡Protege tu mundo!
En grupos de cuatro, imaginen que forman parte de un comité universitario para la protección del medio ambiente. Su objetivo es crear un folleto (*brochure*) con consejos sobre cómo proteger el medio ambiente en su vida diaria. Piensen en acciones apropiadas para los siguientes aspectos:

- el transporte
- el consumo de energía
- la reducción de la basura
- el consumo de agua
- ¿otros?

Modelo: **Ve a clase a pie o en bicicleta.**

¿Cuál es el tema del Día Mundial del Medio Ambiente este año?

EL DESHIELO - ¿UN TEMA CANDENTE?

pregúntaselo a...

un oso polar un campesino un isleño un asegurador un indígena ¡pregúntalo!

PNUMA DÍA MUNDIAL DEL MEDIO AMBIENTE • 5 de junio de 2007

Cultura: Los parques nacionales en el mundo hispano

Antes de leer

1. ¿Cuáles son algunos parques nacionales famosos en los Estados Unidos? ¿Has visitado algunos?

2. Cuando viajas, ¿prefieres visitar un parque nacional o prefieres conocer una ciudad?

El quetzal

La protección del medio ambiente no es una idea nueva en el mundo hispano: la creación de muchos parques nacionales y reservas en estos países ocurrió en la primera mitad[1] del siglo XX. España tiene muchos parques de belleza notable, pero los parques y reservas más conocidos están en Costa Rica: los "bosques nubosos" en la reserva de Monteverde protegen a los quetzales (pájaros sagrados[2] para los mayas), y cada verano miles de tortugas[3] ponen sus huevos en las playas del parque nacional Tortuguero.

[1]half [2]sacred [3]turtles

Otros países también tienen parques espectaculares. México combina las reservas naturales con monumentos arqueológicos: un ejemplo es Xcaret en Yucatán. Allí es posible admirar ruinas mayas entre la flora y fauna de la región. En las selvas del interior de Venezuela están los tepuyes, altas mesetas[4] rodeadas de nubes y vegetación tropical. En las Islas Galápagos de Ecuador podemos ver de cerca las aves y reptiles que inspiraron la teoría de la evolución de Darwin. Torres del Paine en el sur de Chile es famoso por sus montañas de granito, costas impresionantes y glaciares gigantescos. Este parque de 450.000 acres protege a los guanacos (animales parecidos a las llamas) y los ñandús (similares a las avestruces[5]).

Hoy, los países hispanos continúan creando parques y reservas para reflejar el aumento de la conciencia ecológica y el interés por el ecoturismo de sus habitantes.

[4]high plateaus [5]ostriches

Después de leer

1. De todos los parques y reservas que se mencionaron en la lectura, ¿cuáles te gustaría visitar más?

   Costa Rica: La reserva de Monteverde   El parque nacional Tortuguero
   México: Xcaret
   Ecuador: Las Islas Galápagos
   Chile: Torres del Paine

2. ¿Qué efectos negativos tiene el turismo en los parques nacionales? ¿Existen soluciones para este tipo de problemas?

Así se forma

Creo que podemos escalar este pico.

Sí, pero dudo que podamos escalarlo hoy.

3. The subjunctive with expressions of doubt or negation

When a speaker expresses doubt, uncertainty, or disbelief relevant to an action or condition, the subjunctive is used.

The verb of the first clause, which indicates the speaker's doubt, uncertainty, or disbelief, is in the indicative (**Dudo… / No puedo creer…**); the second clause is in the subjunctive.

> *expression indicating*
> *doubt/uncertainty/*
> *disbelief* → *indicative* + **que** + → *subjunctive*
>
> *action or condition that*
> *is doubted, uncertain, etc.*

Dudo que el guía **llegue** a tiempo.   *I doubt that the guide will arrive on time.*

No creo que las balsas **estén** listas.   *I don't think that the rafts are ready.*

Some verbs and expressions of doubt, uncertainty, or disbelief are:

dudar	to doubt	**Dudo** que <u>haya</u> rápidos de clase 5 en este río.
no estar		
seguro/a (de)	not to be sure	**No estamos seguros de** que <u>haya</u> guías.
no creer	not to believe	**No creen** que <u>podamos</u> descender el río hoy.
no pensar	not to think	**No pienso** que el rafting <u>sea</u> peligroso.

- When **creer, pensar** and **estar seguro/a** express certainty, they are followed by the indicative. If these words ask a question, then there's doubt. So the subjunctive is used in the dependent clause.

  El guía **está seguro de/ cree/ piensa**   *The guide is sure/believes/thinks*
  que <u>podemos</u> navegar los rápidos.   *that we can run the rapids.*

  ¿**Está seguro/ cree/ piensa** el guía   *Is the guide sure/Does the guide believe/*
  (de) que <u>podamos</u> navegar los rápidos?   *think that we can run the rapids?*

- Certainty can also be expressed with the verb **saber** and the expression **es seguro que**.

  Sé que <u>tenemos</u> sacos de dormir para todos.
  Es seguro que Octavio <u>quiere</u> llevar mucha comida.

turas al aire libre Aventuras al aire libre Aventuras al ai
Aventuras al Aventuras al aire libre Avent
aire Aventuras al aire libre aire

Así se forma

12-15 ¿Qué piensas tú?

Paso 1. Completa las siguientes opiniones subrayando la opción correcta. Después añade dos opiniones más.

1. Creo que mucha gente (ignora / ignore) la destrucción de la capa de ozono.
2. No creo que mucha gente (intenta / intente) reducir su consumo de gasolina.
3. No creo que (reciclamos / reciclemos) lo suficiente.
4. Creo que (debemos / debamos) proteger las especies animales en peligro de extinción.
5. No creo que (es / sea) fácil dejar de consumir productos derivados del petróleo.
6. Creo que a la gente no le (importa / importe) vivir en un mundo contaminado.
7. Creo que... _mucha gente intenta ⓭ per amable_
8. No creo que... _mucha gente quería el examen!_

Paso 2. En grupos pequeños, hablen sobre las opiniones anteriores. ¿Están de acuerdo con las oraciones 1 a 6?

Modelo: Estudiante A: **Estoy de acuerdo con el número 1; creo que mucha gente todavía ignora la destrucción de la capa de ozono.**

Estudiante B: **Yo no estoy de acuerdo; no creo que mucha gente ignore la destrucción de la capa de ozono, pero creo que los gobiernos sí lo ignoran y ése es el problema...**

Compartan también sus opiniones personales (7 y 8). ¿Qué opinan sobre las afirmaciones de sus compañeros/as?

12-16 **Deportes de aventura.** En parejas, expresen sus opiniones sobre los deportes de aventura.

Modelo: El ciclismo de montaña requiere mucha experiencia.
No estoy de acuerdo. Dudo que *requiera* mucha experiencia.
o **Sí, sé que el ciclismo de montaña *requiere* mucha experiencia porque...**

1. Escalar rocas (*Rock climbing*) requiere equipo especial.
2. Es peligroso navegar en un lago en canoa.
3. El buceo en aguas profundas requiere instrucción.
4. Es peligroso esquiar en pistas negras.
5. Es difícil viajar de mochila en las montañas por tres días.
6. El casco protege la cabeza en el descenso de ríos.
7. La balsa tiene más flexibilidad en el agua que el kayak.

👥 (12-17) **La compañía de *rafting*.** Tú y tu amigo/a van a descender ríos y tienen opiniones muy diferentes respecto a la compañía que van a usar. Indiquen sus reacciones.

Modelo: el equipo / estar en buen estado

Estudiante A: **Dudo que/ No estoy seguro(a) de que el equipo *esté* en buen estado.**

Estudiante B: **Estoy seguro de/ Creo que el equipo *está* en buen estado.**

1. la compañía / tener balsas nuevas
2. los guías / ser experimentados
3. los guías / saber qué hacer en caso de emergencia
4. la compañía / llevar a niños en los rápidos de clase 4
5. la compañía / evitar / los rápidos de clase 5

SITUACIONES

Estás en Costa Rica con tu amigo/a y deciden practicar el *rafting*. Piensan que van a descender un río de clase 3 pero al llegar al punto de partida, descubren que en realidad es ¡un río de clase 5! Como no sabes nadar, tienes miedo. Tu amigo/a es muy aventurero/a e insiste en descender el río. Ustedes hablan de la situación.

Tú: **¡Ay! ¿Un río de clase 5? ¡Ni pensarlo! ¡No sé nadar!**
Tu amigo/a: **¡No pasa nada! Tenemos todo el equipo necesario.**

EXPRESIONES ÚTILES

para negarse (*to refuse*)   **para animar** (*to encourage*)
¡Ni pensarlo!   ¡Vamos hombre/ mujer!
¡Ni hablar!   ¡No pasa nada!
¡De ninguna manera!   ¡Qué sí, hombre/ mujer!
¡Ni loco/a!   ¡Anímate!

Revisa también el vocabulario del ejercicio 12–3.

Así se forma

 12-18 **Las Cabañas Bataburo.** Ustedes piensan hacer un viaje por la selva del Ecuador. Están considerando ir a las Cabañas Bataburo. Para llegar, van a navegar por el río Tinguino en canoas con motor. Lean la siguiente información.

Cabañas Bataburo

¿Desean más información? Visiten:

http://www.kempery.com/ecuador_amazon_bataburolodge.htm

En el corazón místico y salvaje de la selva primaria del territorio Huaorani, se han construido las Cabañas Bataburo. El diseño de las cabañas sigue las técnicas y el estilo de la construcción huaorani y está totalmente en armonía con la selva. Al mismo tiempo, y sin perder el sentimiento de aventura de este paraíso lleno de misterio, les ofrecemos el mayor confort posible.

Tenemos alojamiento en habitaciones dobles o matrimoniales con baños privados o compartidos, mosquiteros, luz eléctrica y torre de observación de aproximadamente cuarenta metros. El comedor sirve excelente comida típica local como mandioca, frutas recogidas en granjas selváticas cercanas y pescado del río. También se ofrece carne de res, pollo y comida vegetariana.

Actividades:

- Caminatas de cinco a seis horas en las que el guía habla sobre la flora y fauna de la zona.
- Excursión para observar monos y otros mamíferos.
- Tour nocturno de observación de insectos (tierra) y caimanes (río).
- Pesca de pirañas; observación de anacondas en su hábitat.

POSIBLES REACCIONES

¡Qué bueno que... !
Dudo que...
Me fascina(n)/ encanta(n)...
No me gusta(n)...
Estamos seguros/as de que...

Ahora comenten y den sus reacciones respecto a:

1. la localización de las cabañas
2. su diseño (design)
3. el alojamiento (lodging)
4. la comida
5. las actividades

¿Van a ir a las Cabañas Bataburo o prefieren buscar una alternativa?

"La Negrita", Santa Patrona de Costa Rica

Basílica de los Ángeles, Cartago

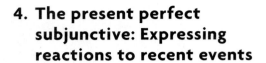

¿Crees que Octavio y Rubén aún estén en la montaña?

No lo sé, pero espero que hayan bajado.

Así se forma

4. The present perfect subjunctive: Expressing reactions to recent events

You have already learned that certain expressions of influence to others, emotion and uncertainty require the use of the subjunctive in the clause that expresses what is wanted, felt, or doubted.

When the actions or events we express in the subjunctive have occurred in the past but are closely tied to the present we use the present perfect subjunctive[4].

Espero que **hayan visto** las cataratas.   *I hope that they **have seen** the waterfalls.*
Dudo que **hayan cruzado** el río.   *I doubt that they **have crossed** the river.*
Me molesta que no **haya llamado**.   *It bothers me that he **has not called**.*

The present perfect subjunctive is formed with the present subjunctive of **haber** + *past participle*.

el presente del subjuntivo de haber + el participio pasado

Al guía le <u>molesta</u> que...	The guide is annoyed that . . .
(yo) **haya perdido** un remo.	*I have lost an oar.*
(tú) **hayas perdido** un remo.	*you have lost an oar.*
(Ud., él/ella) **haya perdido** un remo.	*you have/he/she has lost an oar.*
(nosotros/as) **hayamos perdido** un remo.	*we have lost an oar.*
(vosotros/as) **hayáis perdido** un remo.	*you have lost an oar.*
(Uds., ellos/ellas) **hayan perdido** un remo.	*you/they have lost an oar.*

12-19 **Alberto se va a Costa Rica.** Tu amigo Alberto te cuenta que va a pasar un semestre estudiando en San José, Costa Rica y menciona algunos detalles del viaje. Responde apropiadamente a cada detalle.

Alberto te dice:

1. No debo llevar dinero en efectivo.
2. Me gusta sacar fotos.
3. Voy a vivir con una familia costarricense.
4. La familia costarricense no habla inglés.
5. Mis abuelos siempre se preocupan cuando viajo a otro país.
6. Siempre espero hasta el último momento para organizarme.

Tú le respondes:

a. Me alegro de que hayas aceptado su invitación.
b. Espero que hayas conseguido una tarjeta de ATM.
c. Espero que te hayas comprado una cámara digital.
d. ¡Ojalá que hayas solicitado tu pasaporte!
e. ¡Ojalá que no les hayas dicho que te vas por un semestre!
f. Me alegro de que hayas estudiado español.

---

[4]Note that the choice between the indicative and the subjunctive mood is independent of tense. If it seems complicated at first, it may help to decide first whether the structure requires subjunctive, and then think about the appropriate tense.

No creo que...   →   requires subjunctive
No creo que sea fácil.   *I don't think it is/will be easy.*
No creo que haya sido fácil.   *I don't think it has been easy.*

12-20 **¿Es verdad o no?** Tu amigo Alberto, que ya está en Costa Rica, llamó cuando no estabas y tu compañero de cuarto Leo habló con él. Ahora tú llamas a Alberto y le preguntas sobre algunas cosas que te contó Leo, pero la conexión telefónica no es muy buena. Escucha a Alberto y selecciona la opción que completa cada oración.

Modelo: Leo me contó que has escalado el Monte Chirripó.
(Oyes:)   ... que haya escalado el Monte Chirripó.
(Seleccionas:) ☐ Sí, es verdad   ☒ No, no es verdad

1. Leo dice que has buceado en el océano.   ☐ Sí, es verdad...   ☐ No, no es verdad...

2. También dice que ha hecho sol todos los días.   ☐ Sí, es verdad...   ☐ No, no es verdad...

3. Y has conocido a muchos ticos, ¿no?   ☐ Sí, es cierto...   ☐ No, no es cierto...

4. Leo cree que me has comprado un regalo.   ☐ Sí, es verdad...   ☐ No, no es verdad...

5. Y también me dijo que has aprendido mucho español.   ☐ Sí, es cierto...   ☐ No, no es cierto...

12-21 **¿Cómo reaccionan ustedes?** En parejas, indiquen su reacción positiva o negativa a lo que ha ocurrido recientemente según los dibujos. Usen: **Nos alegramos de que...** o **Sentimos que....**

Modelo: **Nos alegramos de que Octavio haya ganado el campeonato de esquí.**

...Octavio...
el campeonato de esquí

1. ...Inés... cantar en un concierto.

2. ...Camila... sacar en su trabajo escrito.

3. ...Esteban... sacar en su trabajo escrito.

4. ...Javier... tener para su cumpleaños.

5. ...Alfonso... cocinar para nosotros.

6. ... morir el abuelo de Carmen.

12-22 ¿Qué han hecho ustedes?

Paso 1. Escribe tres cosas interesantes que has hecho en tu vida. Pueden ser reales o imaginarias.

1. _____

2. _____

3. _____

Paso 2. En grupos de cuatro personas, compartan lo que han escrito. Después de que una persona lea una oración, los/las compañeros/as reaccionan, usando una de las siguientes expresiones:

Expresiones que requieren subjuntivo:	Expresiones que requieren indicativo:
Dudo que...	Creo que...
No creo que...	Pienso que...
No pienso que...	Es seguro que...
Me alegro de que...	
Siento que...	

Modelo:

Tú: **He saltado de un avión en paracaídas.**

Compañero/a: **Creo que sí has saltado de un avión en paracaídas./ Me sorprende que hayas saltado de un avión en paracaídas.**

Dicho y hecho

¡A ESCUCHAR!

¡Vamos a Costa Rica!

El Instituto Costarricense de Turismo te invita a descubrir Costa Rica y a gozar de (*enjoy*) una experiencia fascinante.

Paso 1. Escucha el anuncio. Luego, identifica los tres lugares siguientes.

a. Manuel Antonio _____
b. Monteverde _____
c. Arenal _____

1. volcán
2. bosque nubloso
3. playa

Paso 2. Escucha el anuncio otra vez y contesta las preguntas para indicar sus preferencias.

1. ¿Qué quieres hacer en Manuel Antonio? _____

2. ¿Qué deseas ver en Monteverde? _____

3. ¿Qué puedes hacer en Arenal? _____

CONVERSANDO

Una visita al Parque Arqueológico Xcaret. En grupos de cuatro personas, imaginen que van a pasar dos días en este parque fabuloso, situado en la Riviera Maya de México. Estudien las opciones presentadas en la página 432 y decidan qué atracciones les interesan más. Luego formulen un plan de lo que van a hacer cada día. Un/a secretario/a apunta la información. Al final, algunos grupos presentan su plan a la clase.

Pueden encontrar más información en: http://www.xcaret.com.mx.

DE MI ESCRITORIO

Mi aventura. Escribe una descripción de una aventura al aire libre que hayas tenido en el pasado. ¡Puedes usar la imaginación! ¡Ojo! Atención al pretérito y al imperfecto.

Incluye:

- cuántos años tenías cuando ocurrió
- adónde fuiste y con quién
- cómo era el lugar
- lo que hiciste/ hicieron

Dicho y hecho

Aventuras al aire libre Aventuras al aire libre Aventuras al aire libre

PRINCIPALES ATRACTIVOS DEL INCREIBLE PARQUE ECO-ARQUEOLÓGICO XCARET

(VER MAPA DESPLEGABLE) 👉

B-2 / C-1 DELFINES I y II. Lo invitamos a retozar, nadar y convivir con estas inteligentes criaturas. Haga su reservación en el Museo; existe gran demanda y cupo limitado (actividad no incluida en su boleto de entrada).

B-2 LOS RIOS SUBTERRANEOS. Lo culminante de XCARET, son una maravilla natural única en el mundo. Disfrute de una experiencia que jamás olvidará, flotando río abajo en cristalinas aguas de cenote, a través de canales y túneles naturalmente iluminados.

D-1 SALIDA DE LOS RIOS SUBTERRANEOS. Al concluir, devuelva el chaleco salvavidas y con su llave contraseña le entregarán su bolsa con sus pertenencias

D-1 TOUR DE BUCEO Y ESNORQUEL. Centro de reservaciones para la excursión y renta de equipo (no incluido en su boleto de entrada).

C-1 CAMINANDO BAJO EL MAR. Disfrute de la fascinante experiencia de caminar bajo el mar de la manera más sencilla, segura y divertida. No se requiere saber nadar. (No incluido en su boleto de entrada).

C-1 LA CALETA. Ideal para aprender a esnorquelear y admirar peces de mil colores. Esta pequeña entrada de agua es de donde el Parque toma su nombre (XCARET significa "pequeña caleta" en maya).

C-1 / D-1 LAS PLAYAS Y POZAS DE MAR. De finas arenas blancas, son ideales para asolearse y nadar. Aquí, puede rentar equipo para una estancia más placentera.

B-3 LAS CABALLERIZAS. Admire la gracia y habilidad de caballos y jinetes que hablan por sí mismos de México y sus tradiciones. Aventúrese a cabalgar entre la selva hasta llegar a la playa y sentir la brisa del Mar Caribe (actividad no incluida en su boleto de entrada).

C-2 PUEBLO MAYA. Aventúrese a recorrer un pasaje subterráneo que lo conducirá al sorprendente nacimiento de un pequeño pueblo maya.

D-2 MARIPOSARIO. Considerado uno de los más grandes del mundo y único en su género por su reproducción autosuficiente de mariposas. Le sugerimos visitarlo antes del mediodía.

D-2 CAPILLA SAN FRANCISCO DE ASIS. Muestra arquitectónica, de la fusión de dos culturas con una fachada producto de la conquista española y la nave prehispánica de la cultura maya.

B-2 ACUARIO DE ARRECIFES DE CORAL. El más grande del mundo en su tipo, donde se puede admirar toda la belleza de este impresionante jardín submarino. Asómbrese con la riqueza de colores y formas de un hábitat natural con peces viviendo entre arrecifes.

C-2 TORTUGAS MARINAS. Conozca de cerca a estos legendarios y maravillosos animales en diferentes etapas de su desarrollo.

B-3 EL JARDIN BOTANICO Y VIVERO. Acceso junto al "Arbol Caído" (que se negó a morir en el huracán "Gilberto" en 1988). Gran variedad de plantas y árboles nativos en estado virgen, que se encuentran en una hondonada protegida, formando su propio microclima.

A-4 TORRE ESCENICA. La más bella vista del Caribe Mexicano y el punto más alto para disfrutar de Xcaret , la Riviera Maya y en el horizonte la isla de Cozumel.

A-3 ORQUIDEARIO. Aprecie nuestra colección de 52 especies nativas más 26 híbridos. La reproducción in-vitro nos permite rescatar las orquídeas en peligro de extinción repoblando y decorando Xcaret con sus sorprendentes flores.

A-3 CULTIVO DE HONGOS. La "Granja de Hongos" comestibles, donde estamos estudiando la posibilidad de desarrollo de una industria semicasera para las comunidades rurales de la región.

A-4 EL GRAN TLACHCO. (Lugar donde se juega la pelota). Majestuoso escenario en el que más de 250 artistas lo harán disfrutar de la inigualable aventura de Xcaret, Noche Espectacular.

C-3 JUEGO DE PELOTA. Es la representación en vivo del más importante evento religioso deportivo de la Cultura Maya.

B-2 VOLADORES DE PAPANTLA. Ceremonia dedicada al Dios del Sol, que representa una de las tradiciones prehispánicas que se conservan hasta nuestros días.

C-2 ISLAS DE FELINOS. Jaguares y pumas en un hábitat perfectamente integrado para lograr la reproducción en cautiverio de estas especies nativas en peligro de extinción.

C-3 EL MUSEO DE XCARET. Edificación proyectada para mimetizarse con el paisaje y el entorno natural que la rodea. Alberga escenificaciones en miniatura de los asentamientos mayas más importantes. Centro de información, cafetería, banos casilleros, tienda y centro fotográfico.

D-2 AVIARIO DE VUELO LIBRE. Localizado detras del Museo y muestra un fantastico mundo de aves del sureste de México, muchas de ellas en peligro de extinción.

C-2 LAGUNA DE LOS MANATIES. Contemple a los fabulosos Manaties en una laguna de agua cristalina, observe con que parsimonia se mueven estos tambien llamados elefantes marinos,

B-1 / B-2 / C-2 LAS ZONAS ARQUEOLOGICAS DE XCARET. Con más de mil años de historia, XCARET es uno de los sitios mayas más importantes de Quintana Roo, destacando principalmente en el postclásico tardío (1400 D.C.) hasta la llegada de los españoles en 1517.

B-3 PLAZA DEL VITRAL. Con un edificio de mejestuosa arquitectura disfrute de un vitral dedicado a las mariposas de México así como al colorido de la vegetación.

B-2 RINCON MEXICANO. Imagine estar en en el antiguo México, un domingo en la tarde, con la banda en el quiosco, vendedores de caramelos, aguas frescas, frutas picadas con chile.

C-2 PASEO POR EL CIELO. Vuele entre las nubes y contemple el maravilloso paisaje de Xcaret y la Riviera Maya, una experiencia inolvidable.

C-1 / D-1 HAMACAS. Le ofrececemos la oportunidad de descansar frente a la laguna y tambien en los estanques, una serie de hamacas para reponer fuerzas y retornar a la exploración de Xcaret.

¡Ah...y no olvide traer su camará y esnorquel!

Arte folklórico: Las carretas[1]

Antes de leer

Mira la foto de la carreta. ¿Te parece que es para usar en el campo para transporte o se parece más a una forma de arte?

Las carretas se usaban para transportar el café y otros productos durante los primeros días de la república de Costa Rica. Pueden pasar fácilmente por el lodo[2], las playas, las lomas[3] y los ríos. Se puede decir que la carreta es un símbolo de las tradiciones pacíficas, industriosas y optimistas (por sus colores y diseños vibrantes) de la gente del país. La carreta fue designada Símbolo Nacional del Trabajador en 1988.

Todavía se usan en algunos caminos rurales, pero más que nada las carretas aparecen en cada desfile[4] y festival, y muchos turistas compran modelos pequeños para llevar a casa como recuerdo.

La mayoría de las carretas son pintadas a mano. Esto se convirtió en una artesanía que pasa de generación a generación a principios del Siglo XX. No hay dos carretas iguales. El pueblo de Sarchí, a unos treinta kilómetros de Alajuela, es uno de los centros artesanales donde se puede admirar y comprar las carretas. En años recientes, los artesanos han incorporado imágenes de la flora y la fauna tropicales de Costa Rica, incluyendo la orquídea morada[5], la flor nacional.

Después de leer

1. Los turistas compran carretas en muchos tamaños diferentes, desde doce centímetros (unas cinco pulgadas) hasta un tamaño real de dos metros (casi siete pies). Si pudieras comprar una carreta de cualquier tamaño, ¿sería muy pequeña o muy grande?

2. Localiza el pueblo de Sarchí en un mapa de Costa Rica. ¿A cuántos kilómetros queda de San José?

---

[1]oxcarts [2]mud [3]hills [4]parade [5]purple orchid

Repaso de vocabulario activo

Adjetivos

emocionante   *exciting*
peligroso/a   *dangerous*

Palabras y expresiones útiles

a causa de   *because of*
para   *for, in order to, toward, by*
por   *for, because of, during, through, on behalf of, along*

Sustantivos

La naturaleza   *Nature*

el agua   *water*
la arena   *sand*
el bosque   *forest*
el castillo de arena   *sand castle*
la catarata/ la cascada   *waterfall*
el cielo   *sky*
la colina   *hill*
el desierto   *desert*
la estrella   *star*
la fogata   *campfire*
el fuego   *fire*
la granja   *farm*
la hierba   *grass*
la isla   *island*
la luna   *moon*
el mar   *sea*
el medio ambiente   *environment*
el océano   *ocean*
la ola   *wave*
el relámpago   *lightning*
el río   *river*
la selva   *jungle, rain forest*
el sol   *sun*
la tierra   *earth, land*
la tormenta   *storm*
el valle   *valley*

Los animales y los insectos
Animals and insects

la araña   *spider*
el caballo   *horse*
el cerdo   *pig*
la gallina   *hen, chicken*
la mariposa   *butterfly*
la mosca   *fly*

el mosquito   *mosquito*
el pájaro   *bird*
el pez (los peces)   *fish*
la serpiente   *snake*
la vaca   *cow*

Aventuras y otras palabras
Adventures and other words

al aire libre   *outdoors*
el alpinismo/ el andinismo   *mountain climbing*
la aventura   *adventure*
la balsa   *raft*
el barco   *ship*
el bote   *boat*
la cámara   *camera*
el campamento   *camp*
el ciclismo de montaña   *mountain biking*
el crucero   *cruise*
el kayak   *kayak*
el saco de dormir   *sleeping bag*
la tienda de campaña   *tent*

El medio ambiente
The environment

la basura   *garbage*
el calentamiento global   *global warming*
la capa de ozono   *ozone layer*
la contaminación   *pollution*
la deforestación   *deforestation*
la destrucción   *destruction*
la escasez   *scarcity, shortage*
la especie animal   *animal species*
la extinción   *extinction*
la gasolina   *gas*
el incendio forestal   *forest fire*
la lluvia ácida   *acid rain*
el mundo   *world*
el pesticida tóxico   *poisonous pesticide*
el planeta   *planet*
el problema   *problem*
el recurso natural   *natural resource*
la sequía   *drought*

Verbos y expresiones verbales

acampar   *to go camping*
bucear   *to scuba dive*
conservar   *to save, conserve*
contribuir (y)   *to contribute*
desperdiciar   *to waste*
destruir (y)   *to destroy*
dudar   *to doubt*
encantar   *to be very pleasing, delight, love, enchant*
evitar   *to avoid*
fascinar   *to be fascinating, fascinate*
importar   *to be important, matter*
interesar   *to be interesting, interest*
molestar   *to be annoying, bother*
nadar   *to swim*
pescar   *to fish*
prevenir   *to prevent*
proteger   *to protect*
reciclar   *to recycle*
recoger   *to pick up, gather*
reducir   *to reduce*
remar   *to row*
viajar   *to travel*

dar una caminata   *to hike*
escalar una montaña   *to climb a mountain*
estar de vacaciones   *to be on vacation*
estar seguro/a (de)   *to be sure of*
hacer *esnórquel*   *to snorkel*
hacer *surf*   *to surf*
hacer un viaje en barco/ crucero   *to go on a boat/cruise*
ir(se) de vacaciones   *to go on vacation*
montar a caballo   *to ride a horse*
practicar el descenso de ríos/ el *rafting*   *to go rafting*
practicar el parasail   *to parasail*
sacar/ tomar fotos   *to take photos*
saltar en paracaídas   *to go parachute jumping*
tener miedo   *to be afraid*
viajar de mochila   *to travel with a backpack*

Autoprueba y repaso  PLUS ✓

I. Verbs similar to *gustar*. Primero, determina quién habla; luego, escribe una oración usando el verbo en paréntesis.

> **Modelo:** Veo el océano. (encantar)
> **Me encanta el océano.**

1. Vemos los relámpagos. (fascinar)
2. Juan y José oyen los mosquitos. (molestar)
3. Tina está leyendo un libro de biología. (interesar)
4. Voy a pescar. (encantar)
5. Para Pablo, la familia es su prioridad. (importar)

II. *Para* and *por*. Indica lo que hiciste el verano pasado. Completa las oraciones con la forma **yo** (excepto "mi madre" en el número 7) del verbo en el pretérito y **por** o **para**. Sigue el modelo.

> **Modelo:** trabajar / el Banco Nacional
> **Trabajé para el Banco Nacional.**

1. trabajar / poder ir a Costa Rica
2. salir / Costa Rica el 6 de agosto
3. estar allí / un mes
4. viajar / todo el país
5. comprar un libro sobre los bosques nubosos / mi madre
6. comprarlo / tres mil colones
7. mi madre decirme, "Gracias / el libro"

III. The subjunctive with expressions of doubt or negation.

A. Escribe tus reacciones.

> **Modelo:** dudar / que la balsa / pasar por ese cañón
> **Dudo que la balsa pase por ese cañón.**

1. no creer / que ustedes / encontrar el remo
2. no estar seguro(a) de / que el guía / saber hablar español
3. dudar / que los kayaks / llegar a tiempo
4. no estar seguro(a) de / que (nosotros) / estar remando bien
5. no creer / que (tú) / poder ir con nosotros.

B. Contesta las preguntas. Usa el subjuntivo sólo (*only*) para expresar duda.

> **Modelo:** ¿Tiene Roberto la tienda de campaña?
> (creer) **Sí, creo que la tiene.**
> ¿Tiene el mapa? (no creer) **No, no creo que lo tenga.**

1. ¿Cuesta el viaje más de doscientos dólares? (creer)
2. ¿Hay un problema serio? (no creer)
3. ¿Es muy larga la caminata al río? (dudar)
4. ¿Son los guías buenos? (no estoy seguro/a de)
5. ¿Vienen con nosotros nuestros amigos? (estoy seguro/a de)

IV. The present perfect subjunctive. ¿Sientes que o te alegras de que las siguientes cosas hayan ocurrido?

> **Modelo:** mi mejor amiga / irse de la universidad
> **Siento que mi mejor amiga se haya ido de la universidad.**

1. mis amigos / llegar recientemente
2. mi mejor amiga / comprarme un regalo
3. tú / perder tu cámara
4. mis amigos / llamarme
5. ellos / tener un accidente

V. *Repaso general.* Contesta con oraciones completas.

1. ¿Qué animales/ insectos/ reptiles te fascinan o interesan más? ¿Cuáles te molestan?
2. ¿Qué aspectos de la naturaleza te encantan?
3. ¿Qué aventuras al aire libre te interesan más?
4. ¿Crees que sea muy bueno para la salud hacer ejercicio al aire libre?
5. ¿Dudas que hayamos hecho todo lo posible para proteger el medio ambiente? ¿Qué debemos hacer para protegerlo más?
6. ¿Has viajado mucho? ¿Te alegras de haber viajado mucho? ¿Sientes no haber viajado más?

VI. *Cultura.*

1. ¿Por qué se llaman "Ticos" las personas de Costa Rica?
2. ¿Qué tipo de turismo se practica mucho en Costa Rica? ¿Cómo se describe?
3. ¿Qué son las carretas?

Answers to the *Autoprueba y repaso* are found in **Apéndice 2**.

WILEY
PLUS

De viaje

De viaje De viaje De viaje
De viaje De viaje De viaje
De viaje
De viaje

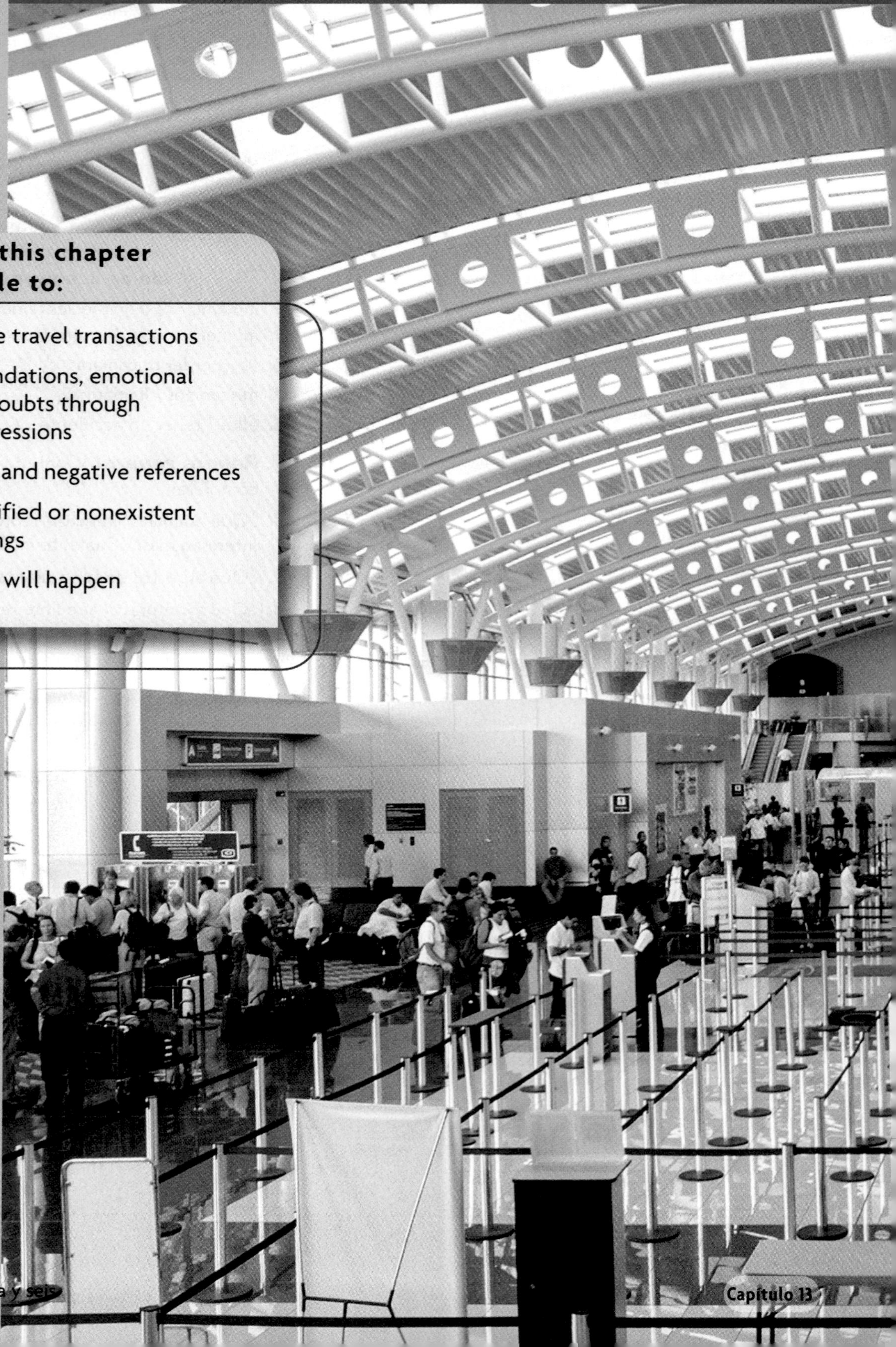

By the end of this chapter you will be able to:

- Carry out simple travel transactions

- State recommendations, emotional reactions, and doubts through impersonal expressions

- Make indefinite and negative references

- Refer to unspecified or nonexistent persons and things

- Talk about what will happen

Así se dice

- De viaje
- Se van de viaje
- En el hotel
- Los números ordinales

Así se forma

1. The subjunctive with impersonal expressions
2. More indefinite and negative words
3. The subjunctive with indefinite entities
4. The future tense

Cultura

- Guatemala y El Salvador
- El alojamiento en el mundo hispano
- Artes populares: Los textiles de Guatemala

Dicho y hecho

- La inversión del siglo
- ¡Problemas en el viaje!
- Unas vacaciones maravillosas

ENTRANDO AL TEMA

Cuando viajas, ¿prefieres un hotel de lujo o un hotel económico?

¿Sabes qué porcentaje de la población de Guatemala es de origen indígena maya?

el aeropuerto

la aerolínea

despegar

el vuelo

AeroSA

la llegada

VUELO	SALIDA	LLEGADA
901 Quito	8:15	
515 San Salvador	9:05	
782 Guatemala	DEMORA	
701 Lima		11:45

aterrizar

el horario

la demora

el boleto/ el billete

el avión

la salida

la puerta de salida

la tarjeta de embarque

1

2

despedirse (i, i) de

facturar

la maleta

el botones

el pasajero/ la pasajera

el maletín

el/la piloto

el equipaje

tener prisa

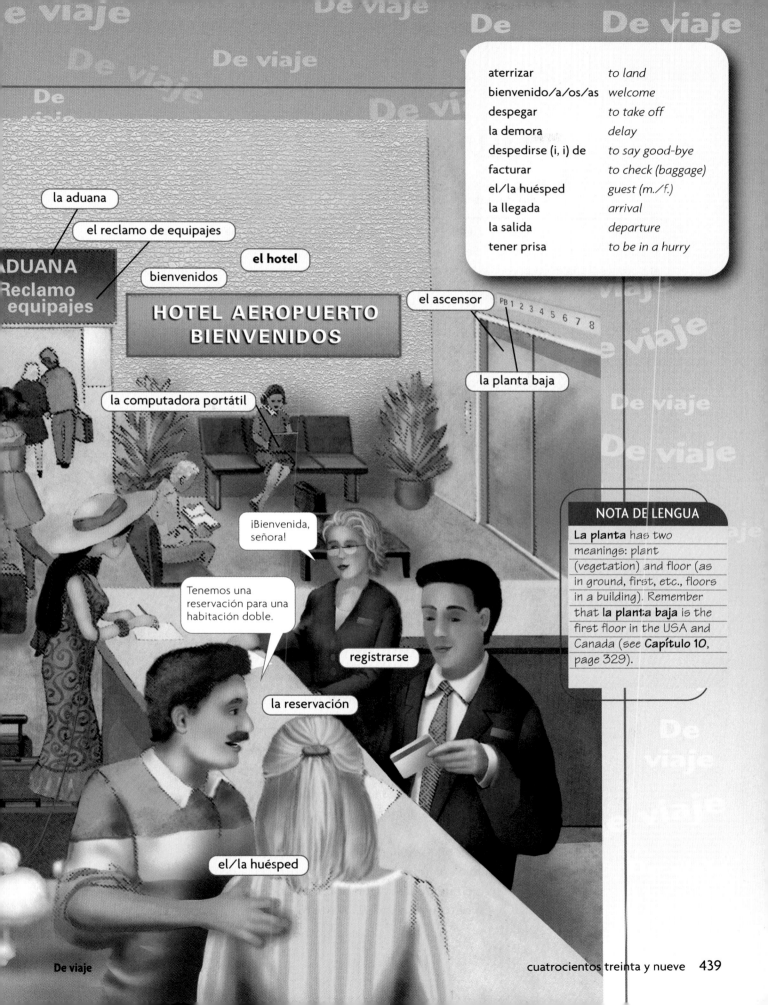

aterrizar — to land
bienvenido/a/os/as — welcome
despegar — to take off
la demora — delay
despedirse (i, i) de — to say good-bye
facturar — to check (baggage)
el/la huésped — guest (m./f.)
la llegada — arrival
la salida — departure
tener prisa — to be in a hurry

la aduana

el reclamo de equipajes

el hotel

ADUANA
Reclamo
equipajes

bienvenidos

el ascensor   PB 1 2 3 4 5 6 7 8

HOTEL AEROPUERTO
BIENVENIDOS

la planta baja

la computadora portátil

¡Bienvenida, señora!

Tenemos una reservación para una habitación doble.

registrarse

la reservación

el/la huésped

NOTA DE LENGUA

La planta has two meanings: plant (vegetation) and floor (as in ground, first, etc., floors in a building). Remember that **la planta baja** is the first floor in the USA and Canada (see **Capítulo 10**, page 329).

Así se dice

13-1 Conexiones.

Paso 1. Lee las palabras del cuadro y escribe parejas de palabras que, en tu opinión, estén asociadas.

aterrizar	el/la piloto	el boleto	la tarjeta de embarque	el hotel
el avión	el/la huésped	el/la pasajero/a	el equipaje	la computadora portátil
el botones	la maleta	despegar	el aeropuerto	el maletín
				el ascensor

Modelo: el boleto
la tarjeta de embarque

Paso 2. Ahora, compara tus asociaciones con un/a compañero/a. ¿Son similares o diferentes? Explica las asociaciones.

Modelo: **Para mí *el boleto y la tarjeta de embarque* están asociados porque los dos son de papel/ porque los necesitas para viajar en avión.**

13-2 Hablando de viajar. En parejas, tomen turnos entrevistándose.

Paso 1. Estudiante A: lee las preguntas a tu compañero/a y anota sus respuestas. **Estudiante B:** cierra tu libro. Pide más detalles (ejemplos, explicar por qué, etc.).

1. ¿Cuántas veces has viajado en avión? (¿A qué países/ ciudades?)
2. ¿Te gusta viajar en avión?
3. ¿Te da miedo volar?
4. ¿Cuál es tu parte favorita del viaje? ¿Qué no te gusta? ¿Te gusta despegar? ¿Y aterrizar?
5. ¿Qué aerolínea prefieres?
6. ¿Conoces varios aeropuertos? ¿Cuáles son? ¿Qué aeropuerto te gusta menos? ¿Por qué?

Paso 2. Estudiante B: lee las preguntas a tu compañero/a y anota sus respuestas. **Estudiante A:** cierra tu libro. Pide más detalles (ejemplos, explicar por qué, etc.).

1. ¿Has tenido problemas en algún viaje?
2. ¿Has tenido una demora en algún viaje? ¿Cuánto tiempo tuviste que esperar? ¿Qué hiciste?
3. ¿Ha perdido la aerolínea tu equipaje alguna vez?
4. ¿Ha habido algún pasajero problemático cerca de ti? ¿Qué hacía?
5. ¿Has sido huésped en algún hotel? ¿Dónde?
6. ¿Quién hizo las reservas? ¿Llevaste tu equipaje a la habitación o lo llevó un botones?

Se van de viaje

Antes del viaje, los estudiantes van a **sacar los pasaportes** en la oficina de correos...

... **conseguir** los boletos, **confirmar** los vuelos...

... **hacer las maletas/ empacar...**

... y llegar al aeropuerto **con** dos horas **de anticipación.**

el auxiliar de vuelo

la azafata

Camila, Pepita y Rubén son parte del grupo que se va a Guatemala. Ahora van a **subir** al avión. ¿Quiénes los saludan?

la ventanilla

el asiento

el pasillo

¿Prefiere Camila el asiento de la **ventanilla** o del **pasillo**? ¿Y Rubén? ¿Quién debe **abrocharse el cinturón**? ¿**Parece que** les gusta **volar**?

Carmen y sus amigos **se bajan del** avión. Van a **disfrutar de** su viaje, ¿verdad? ¿A qué **países** has viajado tú?

abrocharse	*to fasten*	**el país**	*country*
conseguir (i, i)	*to get, obtain*	**parecer (que)**	*to seem (that)*
disfrutar (de)	*to enjoy (something)*	**volar (ue)**	*to fly*

NOTA DE LENGUA

Many words take the prefix **des-** to indicate something is undone or reversed.
Some examples that apply to travel are:

desabrocharse (el cinturón)	*to unfasten one's seatbelt*
deshacer (el equipaje)	*to unpack*

13-3 **¿Antes, durante o después?** Decide si las actividades siguientes normalmente se hacen antes, durante o después de un vuelo.

	Antes del vuelo	Durante el vuelo	Después del vuelo
Llegar al aeropuerto			
Abrocharse el cinturón de seguridad			
Despedirse de la azafata			
Sacar el pasaporte			
Pedirle un refresco al auxiliar de vuelo			
Enviar una tarjeta postal			
Esperar porque hay una demora			
Facturar el equipaje			
Registrarse en el hotel			
Ir a la puerta de salida con la tarjeta de embarque			

13-4 Mis preferencias.

 Paso 1. Escribe un párrafo describiendo lo que te gusta más y lo que te gusta menos de hacer un viaje en avión.

Modelo: Lo que más me gusta es empacar las maletas porque...
Lo que menos me gustan son las demoras porque...

 Paso 2. Comparte tus respuestas con un/a compañero/a, y después con toda la clase. ¿Hay algunas cosas que mencionaron muchas personas?

Cultura: Guatemala y El Salvador

MÉXICO

Nacionalidades:
guatemalteco/a
salvadoreño/a

▲Tikal

BELICE

Mar Caribe

GUATEMALA

Antigua
◉ Guatemala

HONDURAS

Océano Pacífico

San Salvador
◉

EL SALVADOR

América Central

Antes de leer

Estudia el mapa para contestar las preguntas. Indica si la frase describe Guatemala, El Salvador o los dos.

	Guatemala	El Salvador	Los dos
Tiene cuatro países vecinos.			
Su capital tiene un nombre igual o muy similar al nombre del país.			
Es el país más pequeño de América Central.			
Tiene costa en el Océano Pacífico solamente.			
Las famosas ruinas de Tikal se encuentran aquí.			

GUATEMALA Y EL SALVADOR

Guatemala y El Salvador forman parte de Centroamérica, y tienen un clima y una geografía similares. Sus tierras son muy fértiles y fáciles de cultivar; y los dos países tienen volcanes.

El clima de la región es agradable, pero los huracanes y las tormentas son comunes. En 1998, el huracán Mitch causó grandes daños[1] en toda el área.

[1]damages

Cultura: **Guatemala y El Salvador**

GUATEMALA

La mitad de la población guatemalteca es de origen maya. Por eso, Guatemala tiene la cultura indígena más dinámica de todos los países centroamericanos. Las ruinas mayas más impresionantes están en Tikal, en la selva guatemalteca.

Originalmente, la capital del país era la ciudad de Antigua. Después de varios terremotos[2] catastróficos, la capital se transfirió a la ciudad de Guatemala. Hoy Antigua es un importante destino turístico por la belleza de su paisaje[3] y su arquitectura colonial.

---

[2]*earthquakes;* [3]*landscape*

Antigua, Guatemala

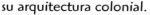

El quetzal

Las ruinas de Tikal

En 1964 empezó la lucha entre grupos revolucionarios y el ejército nacional. Rigoberta Menchú es una mujer maya que ganó el Premio Nobel de la Paz por contribuir a ponerle fin a los treinta años de guerra en Guatemala. En 1996 se puso en marcha un plan para alcanzar la reconciliación y finalmente la paz. Hoy en día, el país celebra elecciones democráticas.

Rigoberta Menchú

La moneda oficial de Guatemala se llama el quetzal, pájaro que también aparece en la bandera del país.

El novelista británico Aldous Huxley dijo sobre el lago Atitlán: "Es el lago más bello del mundo". Miles de turistas visitan este lago y el volcán del mismo nombre cada año. Junto al lago está la Reserva Natural de San Buenaventura.

El Lago Atitlán

EL SALVADOR

El Salvador tiene casi seis millones de habitantes. Es el país más poblado y más pequeño de Centroamérica, con volcanes impresionantes. El volcán Izalco permaneció activo desde 1770 hasta 1966.

De 1980 hasta 1992 el país sufrió una guerra civil terrible que costó unas 75.000 vidas. Durante ese tiempo, muchos salvadoreños salieron del país para vivir en los Estados Unidos. Hoy en día El Salvador tiene un gobierno democrático.

En el año 2001 sucedieron varios eventos importantes en El Salvador. En enero, una serie de terremotos destruyó casi el 20% de las viviendas[4] del país. Ese verano, una sequía[5] devastadora destruyó un 80% de la cosecha nacional, dejando a mucha gente con hambre. También ese año, el país adoptó el dólar estadounidense como moneda nacional. Muchos salvadoreños han emigrado a otros países; el dinero que enviaron a su país constituyó un 16% del Producto Interno Bruto en 2004.

El Lago de Coatepeque, al pie del volcán Santa Ana, se formó debido al hundimiento[6] de un grupo de volcanes hace miles de años. Actualmente el lago es un bello lugar natural, excelente para practicar la pesca y otros deportes acuáticos.

[4]*housing* [5]*drought*

[6]*sinking*

Después de leer

Decide a qué país le corresponde cada oración: El Salvador, Guatemala o los dos.

	El Salvador	Guatemala	Los dos
El 50% del país es de origen maya.			
Hoy en día tiene un gobierno democrático.			
La moneda oficial es el dólar estadounidense.			
Una mujer del país ganó el Premio Nobel.			
La bandera es azul y blanca.			
Tiene volcanes y lagos famosos.			

El Lago de Coatepeque

Así se forma

> Es fenomenal que podamos quedarnos en Guatemala por un mes, ¿verdad?

1. The subjunctive with impersonal expressions: Expressing recommendations, emotion, and doubt

Use the subjunctive in clauses that follow impersonal expressions formed with the verb **ser...**

> **Es** + *importante/ bueno/ necesario...* + **que** + subjuntivo

to express:

- the desire to influence the actions of someone else

es bueno	*it's good*
es mejor	*it's better*
es necesario/ es preciso	*it's necessary*
es importante	*it's important*
es urgente	*it's urgent*

Es importante que **hagas** la reservación.

It's important that **you make** the reservation.

- emotional reactions to the actions or conditions of another person or thing

es una lástima	*it's a shame*
es extraño	*it's strange*
es fenomenal	*it's wonderful*
es ridículo	*it's ridiculous*
es horrible	*it's horrible*
no es justo	*it's unfair*

Es una lástima que **tengas** que irte tan temprano.

It's a shame that **you have** to go so early.

- doubts and uncertainties

es posible	*it's possible*
es imposible	*it's impossible*
es probable	*it's likely*
es improbable	*it's improbable*

Es posible que **perdamos** la conexión en Miami.

It's possible that **we'll miss** the connection in Miami.

- If there is no specific subject after the impersonal expression, the infinitive is used instead of **que** + *subjunctive*.

Es necesario ir al aeropuerto temprano.

It's necessary to go to the airport early.

Es necesario **que vayamos** al aeropuerto temprano.

It's necessary **for us to go** to the airport early.

- Note that expressions such as **es verdad, es cierto,** and **es obvio** used affirmatively <u>require the indicative</u>, not the subjunctive, as they introduce factual vs. subjective statements.[1]

Es verdad/ cierto que **hace** calor en Madrid en el verano.	**It's true** that it **is** hot in Madrid in the summer.
Es obvio que Carmen **necesita** un ventilador.	**It's obvious** that Carmen **needs** a fan.

13-5 **Un vuelo en la aerolínea "Buena Suerte".** En parejas, imaginen que vuelan juntos en el vuelo 13 con destino a Antigua, Guatemala. Este vuelo tiene algunas "sorpresas".

Primero, el Estudiante A lee sus opiniones, y el Estudiante B escucha y reacciona con oraciones completas. Después, cambien papeles *(switch roles.)*

Modelo: Estudiante A: Es interesante que no haya asientos reservados.

Estudiante B: **Sí, sí, es interesante que no haya asientos reservados.** *o*
¿Interesante? ¡Es ridículo que no haya asientos reservados!

Estudiante A:

1. Es extraño que la azafata no dé instrucciones para emergencias.
2. Es posible que el auxiliar de vuelo sirva langosta.
3. Es bueno tener películas en español.
4. Es emocionante que haya mucha turbulencia.
5. Es obvio que este vuelo es un poco diferente.

Estudiante B:

6. Es mejor tener asientos pequeños.
7. Es posible fumar en el baño.
8. Es verdad que un bebé está llorando.
9. Es fenomenal que el piloto esté tomando un cóctel.
10. Es probable que no vuele con la "Aerolínea" en el futuro.

NOTA CULTURAL

Guatemalan cuisine
Guatemalan food is similar to Mexican food, with a lot of tortillas and tacos. But it also has influences from Spain, India, and France. Basic food items include rice and beans, coffee and meat. A regional specialty, called *pepián,* is a chicken and vegetable dish in a spicy sauce.

---

[1] Note that when the statement is negative, the subjunctive is used:
No es verdad/ cierto que **haga** calor en Madrid.
No es obvio que Carmen **necesite** un ventilador.

Así se forma

 13-6 **Los primeros días de Esteban en la Ciudad de Guatemala.** Basándote en los dibujos, sugiere a Esteban lo que debe hacer. ¡Atención! Algunas expresiones requieren el subjuntivo y otras no.

Modelo: Es obvio que... Es urgente que...
Es obvio que estás muy cansado porque anoche saliste con tus amigos, pero es urgente que te levantes para ir a clase.

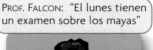
PROF. FALCON: "El lunes tienen un examen sobre los mayas"

1. Es verdad que...
Es necesario que...

2. Es obvio que...
Es mejor que...

3. Es probable que...
Es bueno que...

4. Es bueno que...
Es mejor que...

5. Es buena idea que...
Es obvio que...

6. Es...

 13-7 **¿Es posible?** En parejas, respondan a las siguientes preguntas indicando su opinión sobre lo que los estudiantes van a hacer durante su primera semana en Guatemala. Usen expresiones del cuadro y subjuntivo.

> es probable que...   es posible que...   es improbable que...   es imposible que...

Modelo: Estudiante A: ¿Crees que Esteban va a perder su pasaporte?

Estudiante B: **Sí, es probable que Esteban pierda su pasaporte porque es bastante desorganizado.**

1. ¿Piensas que Carmen va a perderse en la Ciudad de Guatemala?

2. ¿Crees que el grupo puede visitar el Museo Ixchel del Traje Indígena?

3. ¿Piensas que Esteban va a comer pepián?

4. ¿Piensas que la profesora Falcón va a bailar en una discoteca?

5. ¿Crees que Carmen puede aprender a bailar flamenco?

6. ¿Crees que todos van a comer chiles rellenos?

7. ¿Piensas que Esteban puede enamorarse de una chica guatemalteca?

8. ¿Piensas que Pepita va a comprar muchos recuerdos (*souvenirs*) para su familia?

9. ¿Crees que los estudiantes van a ir a Antigua?

El Museo Ixchel del Traje Indígena, Ciudad de Guatemala. (Puedes visitarlo en http://museoixchel.org.)

 13-8 **¡Qué situación!** Las vacaciones de primavera están cerca y el periódico de la universidad necesita una sección sobre cómo reaccionar en situaciones problemáticas. En grupos de cuatro, escriban sus reacciones y consejos para cada situación con expresiones de la lista.

Es posible/ imposible que...	Es urgente que...	Es importante/ necesario que...
Es una lástima que...	Es obvio que...	Es cierto/ verdad que...

1. Me voy de viaje mañana, ¡y no puedo encontrar mi pasaporte!
   Es obvio que... En primer lugar es importante que... Es urgente que...

2. Tengo que salir para el aeropuerto en veinte minutos, ¡y no estoy listo/a!

3. Estoy en el aeropuerto y anuncian que nuestro vuelo tiene una demora de cinco horas.

4. Estoy en el avión y el piloto anuncia que vamos a pasar por una zona de tormenta y que el avión tiene problemas mecánicos.

5. Estoy en la aduana y el inspector de aduanas sospecha que tengo algo ilegal en la maleta.

6. Estoy en un hotel y descubro que en el baño no hay agua caliente y que hay una araña en la cama.

Así se forma

13-9 **Un hotel terrible.** Durante tus últimas vacaciones, tu experiencia en el hotel fue terrible. Escribe una carta al director del hotel explicando lo que pasó y expresando tu indignación. Usa expresiones de la página 446

> Estimado Señor Director:
>
> Le escribo para expresar mi indignación por la terrible experiencia que tuve en su hotel durante mis últimas vacaciones...
>
> (Es ridículo que... / Es imposible que..., etc.)
>
> Deben ustedes mejorar su servicio. (Es necesario que... / Es importante que...)
>
> Atentamente,

Escenas

Carmen

Prof. Falcón

Esteban

A la llegada a Guatemala

La profesora Falcón viaja con sus estudiantes a Guatemala. Van a pasar el mes de julio en ese país. Después de un vuelo largo, aterrizan en el Aeropuerto La Aurora, en la Ciudad de Guatemala...

Paso 1. Considerando donde están en este momento, ¿qué piensas que van a hacer ahora la profesora y los estudiantes hagan?

	No	Sí
Van a dormir en el hotel.		
Van a pasar por el control de pasaportes.		
Van a recoger su tarjeta de embarque.		
Van a registrarse en el hotel.		
Van a pasar por el control de aduana.		
Van a tomar un taxi para ir al hotel.		
Van a facturar el equipaje.		
Van a llevar su equipaje a sus habitaciones.		
Van a despedirse de sus familias.		
Van al reclamo de equipajes para recoger sus maletas.		

Paso 2. Lee las siguientes preguntas; después, escucha la conversación otra vez y escribe tus respuestas.

1. ¿Cómo estuvo el vuelo? ¿Cuándo se puso nerviosa la profesora Falcón?
2. ¿Qué se le cae a Esteban?
3. ¿Adónde van cuando salen del aeropuerto?
4. ¿Cuántas habitaciones ha reservado la profesora Falcón?
5. ¿Qué le pide la profesora Falcón al recepcionista? ¿Adónde van esta tarde?
6. ¿Dónde está el restaurante del hotel?

Paso 3. Escucha una vez más y lee el texto. ¿Son correctas tus respuestas del *Paso 2*?

Carmen:	Bueno, por fin llegamos. Para un vuelo largo, no estuvo mal, ¿no le parece, profesora?
Prof. Falcón:	Siempre me pongo nerviosa cuando el avión despega y cuando aterriza, pero es verdad que los asientos eran relativamente cómodos° y las azafatas muy amables. Mira, allí llega nuestro equipaje.
Esteban:	Parece que todo está aquí. ¿Vamos a inmigración?
Prof. Falcón:	Sí. A ver si encuentro mi pasaporte.
Esteban:	Y a ver si encuentro el mío también. *(Busca en su mochila.)* Sí, aquí lo tengo. *(Se le cae° un papel al suelo.)*
Prof. Falcón:	Mira, se te cayó° ese papel.
Esteban:	¡Ah! Es mi tarjeta de embarque. Ya no la necesito, ¿verdad? Voy a tirarla a la basura.
Prof. Falcón:	Bueno, vamos a la aduana.

comfortable

falls/drops

se... *you dropped*

(Más tarde, en el Hotel Atitlán del Centro Histórico, donde van a pasar dos días antes de mudarse a la Casa del Estudiante.)

Recepcionista:	Buenas tardes. ¡Bienvenidos!
Prof. Falcón:	Buenas tardes. Tenemos reservaciones para seis habitaciones. Están a nombre de Ana María Falcón.
Recepcionista:	Vamos a ver. Sí, aquí están: son todas habitaciones sencillas°, con baño privado.
Prof. Falcón:	Correcto. Aquí están los pasaportes y mi tarjeta de crédito. También, si no es mucha molestia, ¿podría enviar nuestro equipaje a las habitaciones con el botones? Y ¿tiene usted un mapa de la ciudad? Nos esperan en la Universidad de San Carlos[2] esta tarde.
Recepcionista:	Sí, señora. Primero les voy a dar las llaves° de las habitaciones. Y aquí están sus pasaportes y el mapa.
Carmen:	¿En qué piso está el restaurante?
Recepcionista:	Tomen el ascensor hasta la planta doce. Allí encontrarán el restaurante y la cafetería. ¿Algo más?
Prof. Falcón:	No, creo que es todo. Gracias.

single

keys

---

[2]**La Universidad de San Carlos,** fundada en 1676, es la tercera universidad más antigua del Nuevo Mundo.

Así se dice

En el hotel

la habitación doble
el aire acondicionado
la piscina
el baño privado
la calefacción
la camarera
las llaves
la propina
el servicio de habitación
la cama doble
la almohada
la sábana
la manta/ la cobija

Los huéspedes ya se han ido. **Dejaron** una nota y una propina para la camarera, y **se dejaron** algunas cosas. ¿Qué se dejaron?

(cama/ habitación)	**sencilla**	*single (bed/room)*
(cama/ habitación)	**doble**	*double (bed/room)*
	dejar	*to leave, to leave behind*

13-10 Buscando hotel. Imagina que tú y tu amigo/a van a ir a Antigua, Guatemala, para hacer un curso intensivo de español y necesitan hacer reservaciones en un hotel.

 Paso 1. Indica la importancia que los siguientes servicios y características de un hotel tienen para ti.

> ### NOTA DE LENGUA
>
> Note the difference between **salir** (*to leave, go out*) and **dejar** (*to leave an object behind*): Camila **salió** de su habitación y **dejó** la chaqueta.

	Indispensable	Importante	Conveniente	No me importa
baño privado				
cambio diario de toallas y sábanas				
servicio de habitación				
servicio diario de camarera				
servicio de lavandería				
teléfono privado				
aire acondicionado				
televisión con cable				
mini refrigerador				
acceso al Internet				
piscina				

 Paso 2. Compara tus respuestas con tu compañero/a y, juntos, decidan qué tres características debe tener su hotel y qué tres características les gustarían.

Así se dice

13-11 **¿Hotel Best Eastern u Hostal Las Flores?** Tú y tu amigo/a buscan un hotel para alojarse durante su estancia en Guatemala. Cada uno tiene información sobre un hotel diferente, así que hablan por teléfono para compartir sus datos y tomar una decisión.

Paso 1.

Estudiante A: Lee la información sobre el *Hotel Best Eastern* y marca las características más interesantes.

El **Hotel Best Eastern** está ubicado en el centro de la ciudad y le ofrece un ambiente agradable y las comodidades necesarias para hacer su estancia placentera. Nuestras habitaciones están completamente equipadas y decoradas con elegancia, y nuestros profesionales le ofrecen servicio personalizado:

- 152 habitaciones dobles
- Servicio de camarera (diario)
- Baños privados con ducha
- Servicio de habitación 24 horas
- Aire acondicionado
- Piscina y gimnasio

- Teléfono e Internet en la habitación
- Restaurante: *Eastern Grill*
- Televisión
- Parqueo ($15/ día)

Precio: $125/ día

Estudiante B: Lee la información sobre el *Hostal Las Flores* y marca las características más interesantes.

Precios:

Suite: $95/ día
Habitación sencilla: $70/ día

El **Hostal Las Flores** se encuentra en una casa colonial en una tranquila área residencial de Antigua, a 15 minutos a pie del centro. Este pequeño hotel familiar se caracteriza por la atención personalizada, para que usted se sienta como en casa. Comience el día con el desayuno casero y café de Guatemala. Descanse en su habitación, disfrute del jardín o del living común donde puede ver la televisión o navegar por el Internet.

- 4 suites dobles con baños privados
- 6 habitaciones sencillas con baños compartidos
- Servicio de camarera (dos veces/ semana)

- Aire acondicionado en suites.
- Sala común con televisión, teléfono, Internet
- Desayuno incluido; café disponible todo el día

Paso 2. Compartan la información más relevante sobre sus hoteles y háganse preguntas sobre otros detalles que les interesan; comparen las ventajas y desventajas de cada uno y decidan a qué hotel van a ir.

13-12 **¿Cómo se dice?** Llamas al hotel y hablas con el/la recepcionista sobre los servicios que deseas. El problema es que te has olvidado de algunas palabras... Explica a el/la recepcionista lo que deseas *sin usar las palabras en paréntesis*; el/la recepcionista identifica la palabra y confirma contigo, el cliente. Túrnense. ¡Atención! Cubran la parte de su compañero/a.

Modelo: una habitación (doble)
Estudiante A: **Deseo una habitación para dos personas.**
Estudiante B: **¿Quiere decir Ud. que desea una habitación doble?**
Estudiante A: **Sí, sí, una habitación doble.**

Estudiante A:
1. una habitación (sencilla)
2. un baño (privado)
3. (la llave)
4. otra (almohada)

Estudiante B:
1. otra (toalla)
2. otra (cobija)
3. el servicio (de habitación)
4. una (sábana) más

Los números ordinales

primer³, primero/a	*first*	**sexto/a**	*sixth*
segundo/a	*second*	**séptimo/a**	*seventh*
tercer³, tercero/a	*third*	**octavo/a**	*eighth*
cuarto/a	*fourth*	**noveno/a**	*ninth*
quinto/a	*fifth*	**décimo/a**	*tenth*

13-13 **Trivia.** ¿A cuántas preguntas puedes responder correctamente en dos minutos?

Preparados, listos... ¡ya! (*Ready, set . . . go!*)

1. ¿Cuál es el **cuarto** día de la semana (según los hispanos)?
2. Cuando estás muy contento/a y todo va bien estás en el **séptimo...**
3. ¿Cómo se llama el **noveno** mes?
4. ¿Sobre qué dos países aprendiste en el **décimo** capítulo de *Dicho y hecho*?
5. ¿De qué material es la **segunda** medalla en las Olimpiadas?
6. ¿Quién es el **tercer** estudiante más alto de la clase?
7. ¿Cuál es el **quinto** planeta desde el Sol?
8. ¿Quién fue el **sexto** presidente de los EE.UU.?
9. ¿Cuál fue el **primer** día de clase este semestre?
10. ¿Cómo se llama la **primera** y **octava** nota de la escala musical? (como en inglés)

³**Primero** and **tercero** become **primer** and **tercer** when they immediately precede a masculine, singular noun: El ascensor está en el *tercer* piso.

13-14 **Suba al quinto piso.** En parejas, uno de ustedes se aloja en el Hotel Plaza Libertad y el otro es el/la recepcionista. El huésped llama a la recepción para averiguar dónde puede encontrar algunos lugares o servicios. El/La recepcionista responde a las preguntas según la "Guía para huéspedes".

Modelo: Quieres cortarte el pelo.
   Huésped: **Buenas tardes. ¿Me podría decir dónde se encuentra la peluquería del hotel?**
   Recepcionista: **Suba/ Vaya al quinto piso. Allí está la peluquería.**

Hotel Plaza Libertad

GUÍA PARA HUÉSPEDES

	Piso
Recepción	Planta baja
Restaurante	2
Bar	2
Piscina	9
Gimnasio	9
Salas de conferencias	3, 7
Balcón	
—Vista panorámica	10
Peluquería	5
Boutique	1
Garaje	Sótano
Bebidas y hielo	2, 4, 6, 8

Estudiante A:

1. Deseas tomar una bebida y cenar.
2. Quieres hacer ejercicio.
3. Quieres comprar un regalo para tu novio/a.
4. Deseas asistir a una conferencia en este hotel.

Estudiante B:

1. Deseas unos refrescos y hielo para la habitación.
2. Quieres sacar fotos panorámicas de la Plaza Libertad.
3. Necesitas buscar algo que dejaste en el coche.
4. Te gustaría nadar un rato.

Así se forma

Lo siento, no hay ninguna habitación con vista al mar.

2. More indefinite and negative words: Making indefinite and negative references

In **Capítulo 7** you studied some indefinite words and their negative counterparts: **algo/ nada, alguien/ nadie, también/ tampoco**. Observe the additional words in the following chart.

Palabra indefinida		Palabra negativa	
alguno/a/os/as	any, some, someone	**ninguno/a**	no, none, no one
o	or	**ni**	nor, not even
o... o	either . . . or	**ni... ni**	neither . . . nor

- Just as **uno** shortens to **un**, the forms **alguno** and **ninguno** become **algún** and **ningún** before a masculine singular noun.

  ¿Vas a visitar San Salvador **algún** día?   Are you going to visit San Salvador **some** day?

- Notice that the words **ninguno/a** mean *not a single* and consequently do not have a plural form.

  —¿**Algunos** estudiantes van a Santa Ana?   ¿Are **some** students going to Santa Ana?

  —No, **ningún** estudiante va a Santa Ana.   No, **no** students are going to Santa Ana. (**Not a single** student is going to Santa Ana.)

  —**Ninguno/a** va a San Miguel tampoco.   **None** is going to San Miguel either.

Así se forma

(13-15) **Alojamiento estudiantil: el Hostal El Encanto.** Tú y tu amigo/a van a visitar El Salvador y quieren quedarse en el Hostal El Encanto. Tu amigo/a quiere saber si el hostal tiene ciertas comodidades (*comforts*). Lee la descripción del hostal. Después, escucha las preguntas y escoge la respuesta correcta.

HOSTAL EL ENCANTO

Le ofrecemos una atmósfera amigable donde puede descansar y convivir con otros viajeros como usted. Los baños, la cocina y la sala de televisión son de uso común. Tenemos dormitorios comunes de hasta seis personas y algunos cuartos privados con tres camas. La ropa de cama está incluida en el precio del hostal. Para su uso le ofrecemos lavadoras y secadoras que funcionan con monedas. Los usuarios° tienen llave para los dormitorios; además el hostal cuenta con cajas de seguridad°. La recepción está abierta de las 7:00 a las 22:30.

users
cajas... *safety deposit boxes*

---

1. ☐ Sí, hay alguna.	☐ Sí, hay alguno.	☐ No, no hay ninguna.	☐ No, no hay ninguno.
2. ☐ Sí, hay algunas.	☐ Sí, hay algunos.	☐ No, no hay ninguna.	☐ No, no hay ninguno.
3. ☐ Sí, hay algunas.	☐ Sí, hay algunos.	☐ No, no hay ninguna.	☐ No, no hay ninguno.
4. ☐ Sí, hay algunas.	☐ Sí, hay algunos.	☐ No, no hay ninguna.	☐ No, no hay ninguno.
5. ☐ Sí, hay alguna.	☐ Sí, hay algunos.	☐ No, no hay ninguna.	☐ No, no hay ninguno.
6. ☐ Sí, hay alguna.	☐ Sí, hay alguno.	☐ No, no hay ninguna.	☐ No, no hay ninguno.
7. ☐ Sí, hay algunas.	☐ Sí, hay algunos.	☐ No, no hay ninguna.	☐ No, no hay ninguno.

(13-16) **Una nueva experiencia para Inés.** Inés nunca se ha quedado en un hostal y tiene muchas preguntas para el recepcionista. Completen la conversación, usando palabras de la siguiente lista. Al final, lean el diálogo.

alguna	algunos/as	ningún	ninguna	ni... ni

Inés: Perdón, señor. ¿Hay _____ habitación que tenga televisor?

Recepcionista: Lo siento mucho, señorita. Aquí _____ habitación tiene televisor, pero sí hay una sala de televisión de uso común.

Inés: Bueno... ¿y tienen _____ cuartos con baño privado?

Recepcionista: Lo siento pero en este hostal no hay _____ cuarto con baño privado.

Inés: Pues, ¿hay piscina o gimnasio en el hostal? Me gusta hacer ejercicio.

Recepcionista: No hay _____ piscina _____ gimnasio aquí, pero en el Hotel Continental en el centro, sí hay. Señorita, ¿se ha quedado usted _____ vez en un hostal?

Inés: No, señor, pero el lugar me gusta y como dice el refrán: "La curiosidad mató al gato".

13-17 **Un día en la capital.** Alfonso va a un Café Internet en la Ciudad de Guatemala y te escribe un mensaje electrónico. Léelo.

De: Alfonso
Para: yo@uni.com
Cc:
Asunto: mis experiencias

Hola,…

Nuestro primer día en la capital fue fenomenal. Fuimos a la Universidad de San Carlos y **también** al centro. En la universidad conocimos a **algunos** estudiantes universitarios muy simpáticos pero **no** tuvimos la oportunidad de conocer a **ningún** profesor. Nuestros nuevos amigos nos mostraron una parte de esa antigua universidad. ¡Es la universidad más antigua de todo el continente americano! **Alguien** nos acompañó a la universidad pero después nos fuimos en autobús al centro, **sin** la ayuda de **nadie**. Visitamos **algunos** lugares interesantes como el impresionante Palacio Nacional y el Museo Nacional de Arqueología. ¡La colección de objetos mayas y oltecas nos encantó! Luego caminamos por el Mercado Central, donde hay muchas artesanías. Javier compró **algo** bonito para su amiga Marlena —un huipil, que es como una blusa— y los otros **también** compraron **algunas** artesanías. Yo no me compré **nada**. **También** fuimos a un restaurante donde pedimos algunos platos típicos guatemaltecos que nos gustaron mucho. No pedimos **ningún** plato norteamericano porque "Adonde fueres, haz como vieres"°. Por la noche decidimos **no** ir **ni** a la ópera **ni** al cine. **Tampoco** fuimos a un concierto. Pero sí vimos una obra de teatro en el Teatro Nacional, y claro, **también** nos reunimos con nuestros amigos guatemaltecos de la universidad y fuimos a una discoteca. Te escribo pronto.

Tu amigo,
Alfonso

"When in Rome, do as the Romans do."

Ahora, tú y tu amigo/a (que también recibió un mensaje de Alfonso) hablan sobre lo que les contó Alfonso. Usen las palabras de la lista y los verbos indicados a continuación. Túrnense.

algo	alguien	también	o... o	nada
algunos/as	ningún/ninguno/a	tampoco	ni... ni	nadie

Modelo: Estudiante A: **Esta mañana recibí un mensaje de Alfonso y contaba que él y sus amigos *fueron* a...**
Estudiante B: **Sí, a mí también me escribió y me contó que *conocieron*...**

Estudiante A: **1.** ir   **2.** acompañar   **3.** (no) comprar   **4.** decidir

Estudiante B: **5.** (no) conocer   **6.** visitar   **7.** (no) pedir   **8.** ir

---

Investig@ en INTERNET

La actual Guatemala fue el centro de la civilización maya. Elige uno de los siguientes aspectos de la civilización maya para investigar y compartir en la clase. Si encuentras imágenes que puedas imprimir, tráelas a clase también.

  la arquitectura
  la religión
  las matemáticas
  la escritura
  la astronomía
  el arte y la artesanía

Cultura: El alojamiento¹ en el mundo hispano

El Parador de Granada

Antes de leer

¿Qué tipo de viajero eres? ¿Prefieres un hotel de cinco estrellas, de dos estrellas o un hostal para jóvenes?

A todos los viajeros, el mundo hispano les ofrece el alojamiento ideal para hacer su visita memorable. Para los empresarios o los turistas exigentes², todas las ciudades importantes cuentan con hoteles de calibre excepcional y cadenas reconocidas mundialmente como los hoteles Meliá o Hilton. Para los trotamundos, los jóvenes con un presupuesto módico³ o los viajeros menos exigentes, hay hostales y pensiones (hoteles modestos a veces en casas privadas) que son más "caseros" y económicos. Estos establecimientos no tienen las comodidades y lujos de los grandes hoteles, pero en cambio⁴ ofrecen la oportunidad de conocer mejor a los nacionales y de hacer amigos en un ambiente⁵ amigable.

Entre los hospedajes más bellos y pintorescos del mundo hispano están los paradores* nacionales o históricos. En España, algunos son antiguos monasterios, castillos o palacios. En la opulencia de la Alhambra, con vista a los Jardines del Generalife**, se encuentra uno de los más bellos paradores de España: *El Parador de Granada*. El sitio fue un antiguo convento franciscano donde reposaron los restos6 de los Reyes Católicos hasta el año 1521, fecha en que fueron trasladados7 a la catedral de Granada.

---

¹*lodging* ²*demanding* ³**presupuesto...** *modest budget*
⁴**en...** *on the other hand* ⁵*atmosphere*

⁶*remains* ⁷*moved*

---

*Historical buildings transformed into luxurious hotels.
**The fourteenth-century summer palace of the Moorish kings of Granada.

Hacienda Gripiñas, Jayuya, Puerto Rico

Si dirigimos los ojos hacia Sudamérica, Venezuela nos ofrece *Los Frailes,* un parador de excepcional belleza enclavado en lo alto de los Andes. Se trata de un antiguo monasterio convertido en hospedaje para el viajero que exige lo mejor. En México, el *Hotel Parador San Javier* era una hacienda en Guanajuato, pero hoy es patrimonio cultural del país. Puerto Rico también tiene un sistema de paradores por toda la isla.

No importa cuáles sean tus intereses o gustos; el mundo hispano te espera con un lugar especial para satisfacer tus necesidades y exigencias.

Parador *Los Frailes,* Venezuela

Después de leer

1. ¿Qué ofrecen los paradores que no tienen los grandes hoteles?
2. ¿Qué era anteriormente el *Parador de Granada?*
3. ¿Te gustaría pasar unos días en uno de estos paradores? ¿En cuál? ¿Por qué?

Conexiones y contrastes

¿Hay alojamientos similares a los paradores en tu país? ¿Cómo son?

SITUACIONES

Estás en un vuelo internacional y quieres dormir porque estás muy cansado/a. El/La pasajero/a a tu lado quiere conversar contigo. Intenta evitar la conversación sin ser grosero/a (*rude*). Primero, él/ella se presenta (**Hola. Me llamo... ¿Y tú?...**).

Así se forma

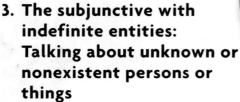

Prefiero una habitación que tenga una cama doble.

3. The subjunctive with indefinite entities: Talking about unknown or nonexistent persons or things

We use adjectives to describe or modify nouns, but often the description involves a complex idea that cannot be expressed with just one adjective, so we use an adjectival clause.

Vamos a un hotel **lujoso**.   Vamos a un hotel **que tiene piscina y gimnasio**.

Busco un hotel **barato**.   Busco un hotel **que no cueste más de $100 al día**.

We use the **subjunctive** in adjectival clauses following **que** when the person or thing we refer to is either (1) *nonspecific* (*unidentified, hypothetical, unknown*) or (2) *nonexistent* in the mind of the speaker.

Busco un <u>hotel</u> que **cueste** menos de $100 al día.   *I'm looking for a hotel that costs less than $100 per day.*

Queremos un <u>botones</u> que **pueda** ayudarnos.   *We want a bellhop who can help us.*

Necesitamos un <u>coche</u> que **tenga** aire acondicionado.   *We need a car that has air-conditioning.*

If the person or thing is *known, identified,* or *definitely exists* in the mind of the speaker, the **indicative** is used in the clause following **que**.

Me quedo en un <u>hotel</u> que **tiene** piscina y gimnasio.   *I am staying at a hotel that has a pool and a gym.*

Hay un <u>botones</u> que **puede** ayudarle.   *There is a bellhop who can help you.*

Alquilamos un <u>coche</u> que **tiene** aire acondicionado.   *We rented a car that has air-conditioning.*

If we are asking whether someone/something exists or if we say that someone/something does not exist, we also use the **subjunctive**.

¿Hay alguien aquí que **pueda** ayudarnos?   *Is there someone here who can help us?*

No hay **ningún hotel** aquí que **tenga** piscina.   *There isn't any hotel here that has a pool.*

DICHOS

No hay mal que por bien no venga.
¿Puedes explicar el significado de este dicho español?

13-18 **¿Hay o no hay?** Escucha las oraciones que lee el profesor/la profesora y decide si hay o no hay las cosas que se mencionan. Pon atención a la forma del verbo.

Modelo: (Oyes:) ...un pueblo en Guatemala que **tiene** ruinas mayas.
(Marcas:) **X** Sí hay...   ___ No hay...

(Oyes:) ...una ciudad en Guatemala que **sea** tan grande como Nueva York.
(Marcas:) ___ Sí hay.   **X** No hay.

1. ___ Sí hay...   ___ No hay...
2. ___ Sí hay...   ___ No hay...
3. ___ Sí hay...   ___ No hay...
4. ___ Sí hay...   ___ No hay...
5. ___ Sí hay...   ___ No hay...
6. ___ Sí hay...   ___ No hay...

13-19 **Un sondeo.**

Paso 1. En grupos de tres o cuatro personas, respondan a las preguntas del cuestionario y escriban el número de personas que contesten afirmativamente. Anoten también sus nombres y algún detalle interesante (por ejemplo: ¿qué otra lengua hablan?).

En su grupo, ¿hay alguien...	Número	Nombre(s)	Detalles
1. ...que hable otra lengua*?			
2. ...que sepa pilotear un avión?			
3. ...que sea vegetariano/a?			
4. ...que tenga más de cuatro hermanos?			
5. ...que tenga su cumpleaños este mes?			
6. ...que piense ir a un país hispano pronto?			
7. ...que se haya quedado en un hostal?			
8. ...que se haya comprometido o casado?			

*además de inglés y español

Paso 2. Compartan sus respuestas con la clase. Un secretario anota el número total de respuestas afirmativas en la pizarra.

Así se forma

13-20 **Preguntas personales.** En parejas, háganse las siguientes preguntas y anoten las respuestas. Escribe una pregunta más para hacer a tu compañero/a.

Modelo: ¿Hay alguien en tu familia que... saber / hablar español?

¿Hay alguien en tu familia que *sepa* hablar español?
Sí, mi tía *sabe*... o No, no hay nadie en mi familia que *sepa*...

Estudiante A: ¿Hay alguien en tu familia que...
tener / más de ochenta años? (¿Quién?)
saber / tocar un instrumento?
(¿Quién? ¿Qué instrumento?)
conocer / una persona famosa? (¿Quién? ¿A quién?)
haberse / graduado de esta universidad?
(¿Quién? ¿Qué carrera hizo?)
ser / muy interesante o especial? (¿Por qué?)

Estudiante B: ¿Conoces a algún/alguna estudiante que...
haber / sacado una "A" en todas sus clases? (¿Quién?)
tomar / una clase muy "original"? (¿Quién? ¿Qué clase?)
tener / más de cuarenta años?
jugar / en uno de los equipos de la universidad?
ser / muy interesante o especial? (¿Por qué?)

13-21 **El mundo real y el mundo ideal.** Trabajen en grupos de tres. Su instructor les va a asignar un tema y van a comparar la realidad y lo ideal con tres o cuatro posibilidades diferentes. En cada grupo, un/a secretario/a escribe las oraciones. Al concluir, él/ella las comparte con la clase.

Modelo: Nuestros empleos
Tenemos empleos que son bastante aburridos, no pagan mucho dinero...
Queremos/ Buscamos empleos que nos den un poquito más de dinero, que sean interesantes...

1. Nuestros profesores
2. Nuestras clases
3. Nuestros compañeros/as de cuarto
4. Nuestra residencia/ nuestro apartamento
5. Nuestra universidad
6. Nuestra comunidad/ ciudad

4. The future tense: Talking about what will happen

The future tense of all regular **-ar**, **-er**, or **-ir** verbs is formed by adding the same set of endings to the infinitive.

Viajarás por todo el mundo, te casarás con una persona fenomenal, encontrarás el trabajo de tus sueños,...

	llamar	volver	ir
(yo)	llamaré	volveré	iré
(tú)	llamarás	volverás	irás
(Ud., él/ella)	llamará	volverá	irá
(nosotros/as)	llamaremos	volveremos	iremos
(vosotros/as)	llamaréis	volveréis	iréis
(Uds., ellos/ellas)	llamarán	volverán	irán

—¿**Irás** a Guatemala con la profesora Falcón?   ***Will** you **go** to Guatemala with Prof. Falcón?*

—**Iré** si consigo bastante dinero.   *I'**ll go** if I get enough money.*

The following verbs add regular future endings to the irregular stems shown (not to the infinitive).

HINT

Remember: Add the future endings to the *entire infinitive*, not the stem.

Infinitivo	Raíz	Formas del futuro
hacer	**har-**	haré, harás, hará, haremos, haréis, harán
decir	**dir-**	diré, dirás,...
poder	**podr-**	podré, podrás,...
querer	**querr-**	querré, querrás,...
saber	**sabr-**	sabré, sabrás,...
poner	**pondr-**	pondré, pondrás,...
salir	**saldr-**	saldré, saldrás,...
tener	**tendr-**	tendré, tendrás,...
venir	**vendr-**	vendré, vendrás,...

Los estudiantes **harán** un viaje a Antigua.   *The students **will take** a trip to Antigua.*

The future of **hay** (*there is, there are*) is **habrá** (*there will be*).

Habrá varias conferencias en la universidad.   ***There will be** several lectures at the university.*

Note that in Spanish future actions and events may be expressed in three different ways:

- the present tense
  Ella **llega** esta noche.

  *She **arrives/is arriving** tonight. (immediate future)*

- **ir** + **a** + *infinitive*
  Voy a estudiar[4] en México **este verano**.

  ***I'm going to study** in Mexico this summer.*

---

[4]In spoken Spanish, the **ir** + **a** + *infinitive* construction (**voy a comer**) is used more frequently than the future tense (**comeré**).

Así se forma

- the future tense

Estudiaré en México este verano.	**I will study** in Mexico this summer.

Also note that the present progressive does *not* express future in Spanish.

Ahora estoy cenando con Alberto.	*I am having dinner with Alberto (right now).*
Mañana voy a cenar con Alberto.	*I am having dinner with Alberto (tomorrow).*
~~**Mañana estoy cenando** con Alberto~~.	

13-22 En el año 2050.

 Paso 1. En grupos de cuatro, indiquen si ustedes están de acuerdo o no con los siguientes pronósticos (*predictions*). Algunos grupos van a compartir sus ideas con la clase. Observen los usos del futuro y del subjuntivo en el modelo.

Modelo: El número de aeropuertos aumentará.
Creemos que el número de aeropuertos *aumentará.* o
No creemos que el número de aeropuertos *aumente.*

1. Los aviones tendrán capacidad para más de 700 pasajeros.
2. Habrá más contaminación del aire y de los ríos y mares.
3. En las ciudades grandes tendremos que llevar máscaras de oxígeno por la contaminación.
4. Para disminuir la congestión en las ciudades, muchas personas se mudarán al campo.
5. Habrá más pobreza en el mundo.
6. El uso de la tecnología y de las computadoras aumentará.
7. En las universidades, las máquinas reemplazarán a muchos de los profesores.
8. Encontraremos una cura para el SIDA y el cáncer.
9. Podremos hacer viajes interplanetarios.
10. También, dentro de cincuenta años...

Paso 2. En sus grupos, escojan uno de los siguientes temas y escriban cinco predicciones para 2050.

- El transporte (coche, avión, tren...)
- La medicina
- La educación
- El medio ambiente
- La tecnología

Modelo: Creemos que, en las ciudades, mucha gente irá en bicicleta para ahorrar dinero.

NOTA DE LENGUA

The subjunctive mood does not have a future tense, so when we need a subjunctive to talk about the future, we use the present subjunctive.

Creo que **lloverá** mañana.

No creo que **llueva** mañana.

13-23 **Quiromancia (*Palmistry*).** La quiromancia es el arte de pronosticar el futuro según las líneas de la mano.

 Paso 1. Observa la ilustración mientras examinas la mano de tu compañero/a de clase y dile cómo será su futuro. ¡Sé creativo/a! Túrnense.

> graduarte en...   ser... (profesión)   vivir en...   hacer un viaje a...
> casarte con...   tener... (hijos/ nietos)   ganar la lotería...

Modelo: Esta línea de tu mano me dice que... **tendrás cinco hijas**.

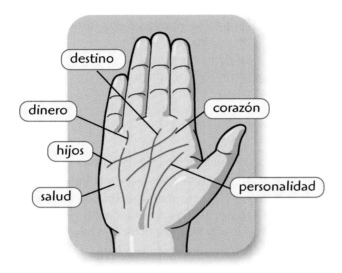

 Paso 2. ¿Qué te parecen las predicciones de tu compañero/a? Escribe cuatro o cinco oraciones describiendo sus predicciones y explica si estás de acuerdo o no.

Modelo: **Andrew dice que tendré muchos hijos y creo que tiene razón. ¡Tendré muchos hijos porque me encantan los niños!**

NOTA CULTURAL

La pupusa salvadoreña
The *pupusa* is the national dish of El Salvador. It is made with two corn tortillas filled with meat, beans, and sometimes cheese, and normally has tomato salsa, *curtido* (pickled cabbage relish, similar to coleslaw or sauerkraut), and a bit of spicy chile.

Dicho y hecho

♪ ¡A ESCUCHAR!

La inversión (*investment*) del siglo. Estamos en el vuelo 515 con destino a San Salvador cuando de repente se oye un anuncio. Habla la azafata. Escucha lo que dice y también los comentarios de la pasajera del asiento 23F. Luego, contesta las dos primeras preguntas.

1. ¿Por qué enciende el capitán la señal (*signal*) de emergencia?
   ☐ Hay problemas mecánicos.   ☐ Hay turbulencia.
2. ¿La pasajera del asiento 23F coopera inmediatamente con la azafata? ☐ Sí ☐ No

Ahora, escucha la conversación otra vez y completa las oraciones para indicar las instrucciones de la azafata y el problema de la pasajera.

3. La azafata dice que es urgente que los pasajeros regresen a...
4. Ella les dice: "Abróchense..., pongan..., terminen... y apaguen..."
5. La pasajera estaba mandando mensajes por...
6. Ella dice que ha perdido...

👥 CONVERSANDO

¡Problemas en el viaje! En grupos, seleccionen una de las siguientes situaciones y resuelvan el problema. Al final, dos grupos pueden representar las situaciones frente a la clase.

1. En la aduana: *Personajes:* Dos pasajeros y el inspector/la inspectora de aduanas.
   Situación: Dos pasajeros jóvenes llegan a la aduana del aeropuerto. El inspector/La inspectora de aduanas sospecha que hay un problema.

Modelo: Inspector/a: (*a los pasajeros*) **Abran las maletas, por favor... ¿Qué es esto?**
Pasajero/a 1: **...**
Inspector/a: **...**
Pasajero/a 2: **...**

2. En la recepción de un hotel:
   Personajes: Tú, tu amigo/a y el/la recepcionista
   Situación: Ustedes están un poco desilusionados con el hotel porque su habitación, las condiciones del baño, etc., no son buenas. Hablan con el/la recepcionista para tratar de resolver los problemas.

Modelo: Usted: **Perdón, señor/señorita, pero tenemos algunos problemas con nuestra habitación.**
Recepcionista: **¿Sí? ¿Qué tipo de problemas?**
Tú: **...**
Amigo/a: **...**

👤 DE MI ESCRITORIO

Unas vacaciones maravillosas. Imagina que estás organizando un viaje a una ciudad del mundo hispano para ir en grupo con otros estudiantes. Escribe un anuncio promoviéndolo. Busca información sobre el lugar en el Internet. Incluye:

- preparaciones que se debe hacer antes del viaje (**Es importante que..., Es preciso que...,** etc.)
- información sobre el transporte (avión, autobús, tren, coche)
- descripción del lugar
- alternativas para alojamiento (hoteles, paradores, hostales)
- sugerencias para actividades durante el día
- actividades para la noche (restaurantes, teatro, etc.)
- en conclusión, palabras que apoyen la idea de escoger este lugar para las vacaciones

Artes populares: Los textiles de Guatemala

Antes de leer

En tu país, ¿se utilizan símbolos en la ropa? Da algunos ejemplos.

Las telas[1] guatemaltecas son famosas en todo el mundo por sus colores brillantes y sobre todo por sus diseños, que indican la región de origen del textil. Esto ocurre porque hasta hace poco tiempo, la población guatemalteca vivía en regiones bastante aisladas[2] entre sí. La falta de comunicación contribuyó a la conservación de las tradiciones de origen maya, que han cambiado poco desde la época prehispánica.

En los textiles tradicionales de Guatemala se utilizan materiales, colores y técnicas que forman parte de la herencia cultural maya. La fibra favorita en esta zona desde tiempos prehispánicos es el algodón, y los guatemaltecos usan tintas y colorantes naturales hechos a base de plantas, insectos y minerales. Cientos de símbolos diferentes aparecen en los textiles mayas. Cada persona que fabrica una tela selecciona una combinación de símbolos para representar una historia o un episodio mitológico; por eso, es casi imposible encontrar dos piezas idénticas. Los siguientes son ejemplos de los símbolos más comunes:

[1]fabrics [2]isolated

1.　　**2.**　　**3.**　　**4.**　　**5.**

Detalle de los coloridos bordados de un huipil.

Los diamantes (1) representan el universo y el movimiento diario del sol: los diamantes más pequeños que están arriba y abajo representan el este y el oeste. El diamante del centro representa el sol al mediodía. La segunda figura (2) representa una deidad[3] suprema: el dios de la tierra. El siguiente símbolo (3) representa la cola[4] de un escorpión y a su lado (4) está la representación de una rana[5]. El último símbolo (5) representa un buitre[6]. Observa los ejemplos de textiles.

[3]deity [4]tail [5]frog [6]vulture

Una interesante combinación de figuras y motivos tradicionales decoran este tzute (manto para la cabeza).

Después de leer

1. ¿Cuáles son los símbolos que reconoces en los tejidos que aparecen en las fotos?
2. ¿Puedes encontrar un diseño nuevo en estas fotos? ¿Puedes describirlo?
3. ¿Qué tipo de textiles prefieres usar? ¿Algodón? ¿Lana? ¿Lino?

Repaso de vocabulario activo

Expresiones impersonales

es bueno   *it's good*

es cierto   *it's true*

es emocionante
it's exciting

es extraño   *it's strange*

es fenomenal
it's wonderful

es horrible   *it's horrible*

es importante
it's important

es imposible
it's impossible

es improbable
it's improbable

es interesante
it's interesting

es mejor   *it's better*

es necesario
it's necessary

es obvio   *it's obvious*

es posible   *it's possible*

es preciso   *it's necessary*

es probable   *it's probable*

es ridículo   *it's ridiculous*

es una lástima   *it's a pity*

es urgente   *it's urgent*

es verdad   *it's true*

no es justo   *it's not fair*

Números ordinales

primero/a   *first*

segundo/a   *second*

tercero/a   *third*

cuarto/a   *fourth*

quinto/a   *fifth*

sexto/a   *sixth*

séptimo/a   *seventh*

octavo/a   *eighth*

noveno/a   *ninth*

décimo/a   *tenth*

Otras palabras y expresiones útiles

bienvenido/a(s)
welcome

la computadora portátil
laptop computer

con ... de anticipación
...ahead of time

el país   *country*

Palabras indefinidas y negativas

alguno/a/os/as   *any, some, someone*

ninguno/a   *no, none, not even one*

ni   *nor, not even*

ni... ni   *neither . . . nor*

o   *or*

o... o   *either . . . or*

Sustantivos

En el aeropuerto/ En el avión
In the airport/ In the plane

la aduana   *customs*

la aerolínea   *airline*

el asiento   *seat*

el auxiliar de vuelo
flight attendant (m.)

el avión   *plane*

la azafata   *flight attendant (f.)*

el boleto/ el billete
ticket

la demora   *delay*

el equipaje   *luggage*

el horario   *schedule*

la llegada   *arrival*

la maleta   *suitcase*

el maletín   *briefcase*

el pasajero/la pasajera
passenger (m./f.)

el pasaporte   *passport*

el pasillo   *aisle*

el/la piloto   *pilot (m./f.)*

la puerta de salida
gate (at airport)

el reclamo de equipajes
baggage claim

la salida   *departure*

la tarjeta de embarque
boarding pass

la ventanilla   *window*

el vuelo   *flight*

En el hotel/ En la habitación
In the hotel/ In the room

el aire acondicionado
air conditioning

la almohada   *pillow*

el ascensor   *elevator*

el baño privado
private bath

la calefacción   *heating*

la cama doble
double bed

la cama sencilla
single bed

la cobija/ la manta
blanket

la habitación doble
double room

la habitación sencilla
single room

la llave   *key*

la piscina   *pool*

la planta (baja)
(main) floor

la propina   *tip*

la reservación
reservation

la sábana   *sheet*

el servicio de habitación
room service

Las personas en el hotel

el botones   *bellhop*

la camarera   *maid (hotel)*

el/la huésped   *guest*

el/la recepcionista
receptionist

Verbos y expresiones verbales

aterrizar   *to land*

bajar de   *to get off*

confirmar   *to confirm*

conseguir (i, i)   *to get, obtain*

dejar   *to leave*

despedirse (i, i) de
to say good-bye

despegar   *to take off*

disfrutar de   *to enjoy*

empacar   *to pack*

facturar
to check (baggage)

registrarse   *to register, check in*

subir a   *to get on, board*

volar (ue)   *to fly*

abrocharse el cinturón
to fasten one's seatbelt

hacer las maletas
to pack

parece que...
it seems that...

sacar los pasaportes
to get passports

tener prisa
to be in a hurry

Autoprueba y repaso WILEY PLUS ✓

I. The subjunctive and the indicative with impersonal expressions. Completa las oraciones combinando la información de las declaraciones con la expresión impersonal indicada.

Modelo: No llevo mi computadora portátil.
Es mejor que...

Es mejor que no lleve mi computadora portátil.

1. El avión llega tarde. Es una lástima que...
2. Tengo todo el equipaje. Es bueno que...
3. Vamos a la aduana. Es urgente que...
4. No puedo encontrar el boleto. Es horrible que...
5. No hay azafatas. Es extraño que...
6. No me gusta volar. Es cierto que...

II. More indefinite and negative words. Cambia las siguientes oraciones a la forma negativa.

Modelo: Conozco a algunos jugadores del equipo de baloncesto.

No conozco a ningún jugador del equipo de baloncesto.

1. O Jorge o Miguel te pueden ayudar a limpiar la casa.
2. El hotel tiene aire acondicionado y calefacción.
3. Muchos hoteles tienen televisores con pantalla grande.
4. Algunos estudiantes van a ir a Antigua.
5. Todos fueron a la discoteca.

III. The subjunctive with indefinite entities.

A. Estás en un hotel y pides varias cosas. Escribe oraciones con las palabras indicadas.

Modelo: necesitar una habitación / no costar mucho

Necesito una habitación que no cueste mucho.

1. necesitar una habitación / estar en la planta baja
2. preferir un cuarto / tener camas sencillas
3. querer un baño / ser más grande
4. necesitar una llave / abrir el mini-bar

B. Estás en un hotel y hablas con el recepcionista. Completa la conversación usando el verbo entre paréntesis en el subjuntivo o en el indicativo según la situación.

1. Tú: Busco una habitación que _____ (tener) vista al mar.
Recepcionista: Tenemos una habitación que _____ (tener) vista al mar. ¿Desea verla?

2. Tú: Prefiero una habitación que _____ (estar) cerca de la piscina.
Recepcionista: Lo siento, pero no tenemos ninguna habitación que _____ (estar) cerca de la piscina.

3. Tú: Busco una habitación que_____ (ser) económica.
Recepcionista: No hay habitaciones en este hotel que _____ (ser) económicas.

4. Tú: Prefiero cenar en un restaurante que _____ (servir) comida vegetariana.
Recepcionista: Pues, en el hotel hay un restaurante que _____ (servir) comida vegetariana.

IV. The future tense. Forma oraciones para hablar de lo que las siguientes personas harán este verano.

Modelo: yo / tomar clases

Tomaré clases este verano.

1. mi mamá / poder ir a la Florida
2. Luis / tener que trabajar
3. Carmen y sus amigos / querer visitar la Alhambra
4. mis abuelitos / venir a visitarnos
5. el profesor Vivar-Marín y su familia / viajar por México
6. yo / pasar los fines de semana en la playa

V. Repaso general. Contesta con oraciones completas.

1. En el aeropuerto, ¿qué información encontramos en el horario?
2. Al llegar al aeropuerto, ¿qué hacen los pasajeros?
3. ¿Qué tipo de hotel buscas para tus próximas vacaciones?
4. ¿Conoces algún lugar para ir de vacaciones que sea económico?
5. ¿Harás un viaje este verano? ¿Qué más harás?

VI. Cultura.

1. Nombra tres cosas que tienen en común El Salvador y Guatemala, y tres cosas que los hacen diferentes.
2. Describe qué son los *paradores*.
3. ¿Qué es una pupusa?
4. Describe uno de los símbolos comunes en la ropa tradicional maya.

Answers to the *Autoprueba y repaso* are found in **Apéndice 2**.

En la carretera

En la carretera
En la carretera
En la carretera
En la carretera
En la carretera
En la carretera
En la carretera

By the end of this chapter you will be able to:

- Talk about travel by car, train, and bus
- Make suggestions
- Express conditions and purpose
- React to past actions and events
- Talk about activities with a general or unknown subject

ENTRANDO AL TEMA

1. ¿Has viajado en la Ruta 66, la carretera famosa que atraviesa los Estados Unidos? ¿Sabes cuántas millas tiene?

2. ¿Has viajado a algún lugar donde se habla español? ¿Cómo llegaste?

En la carretera

MEXIBUSES
SEGUROS Y CÓMODOS

seguro

cómodo

PEMEX

la estación de servicio/ la gasolinera

el tráfico/ el tránsito

la carretera/ la autopista

el autobús

el aire

AIRE

AZTECA
La mejor agencia de viajes

el conductor

la agencia de viajes

el camino

la llanta (desinflada)

echar gasolina

la gasolina

llenar el tanque

el parabrisas

la llanta

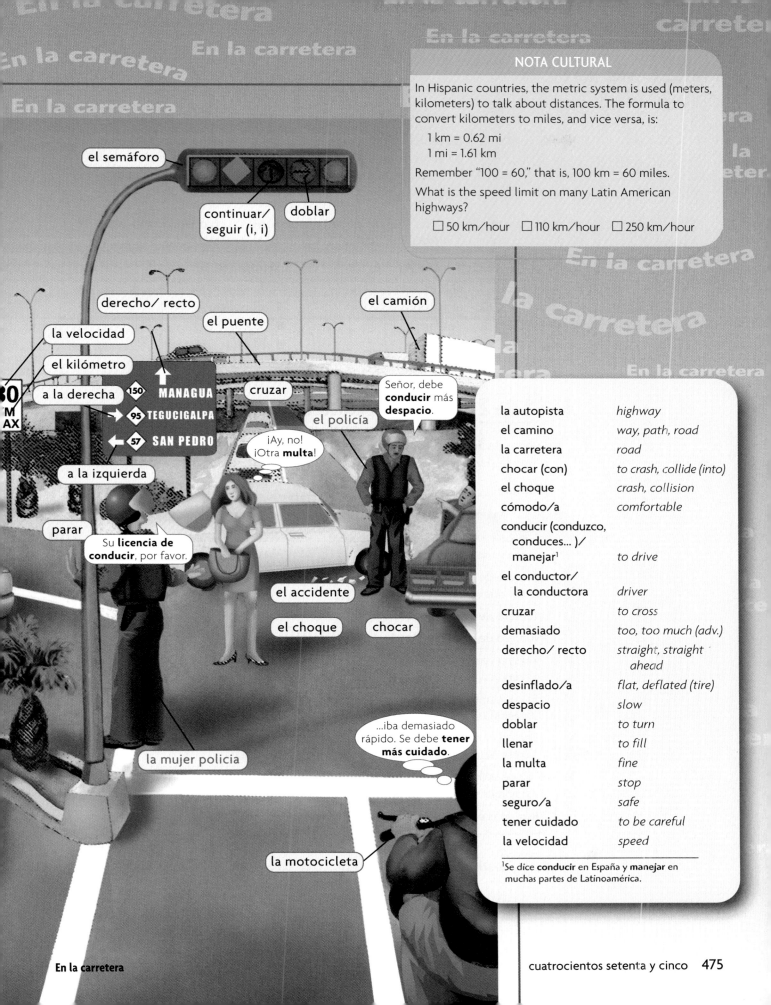

el semáforo

continuar/
seguir (i, i)

doblar

NOTA CULTURAL

In Hispanic countries, the metric system is used (meters, kilometers) to talk about distances. The formula to convert kilometers to miles, and vice versa, is:

1 km = 0.62 mi
1 mi = 1.61 km

Remember "100 = 60," that is, 100 km = 60 miles.

What is the speed limit on many Latin American highways?

□ 50 km/hour   □ 110 km/hour   □ 250 km/hour

derecho/ recto

la velocidad

el kilómetro

a la derecha

a la izquierda

parar

el puente

el camión

cruzar

150 MANAGUA

95 TEGUCIGALPA

57 SAN PEDRO

Señor, debe **conducir** más **despacio**.

el policía

¡Ay, no! ¡Otra **multa**!

Su **licencia de conducir**, por favor.

el accidente

el choque   chocar

...iba demasiado rápido. Se debe **tener más cuidado**.

la mujer policia

la motocicleta

la autopista	highway
el camino	way, path, road
la carretera	road
chocar (con)	to crash, collide (into)
el choque	crash, collision
cómodo/a	comfortable
conducir (conduzco, conduces...)/ manejar[1]	to drive
el conductor/ la conductora	driver
cruzar	to cross
demasiado	too, too much (adv.)
derecho/ recto	straight, straight ahead
desinflado/a	flat, deflated (tire)
despacio	slow
doblar	to turn
llenar	to fill
la multa	fine
parar	stop
seguro/a	safe
tener cuidado	to be careful
la velocidad	speed

[1]Se dice **conducir** en España y **manejar** en muchas partes de Latinoamérica.

Así se dice

14-1 **¿Qué es?** Trabajando en parejas, un/a estudiante define las palabras de su lista y/o da ejemplos basados en la escena de las páginas 474–475; el/la otro/a estudiante tiene que identificar la palabra. Atención: Cubre la lista de tu compañero/a con un papel o con la mano.

Modelo: llanta   **Es negra; el autobús tiene cuatro pero una está desinflada...**

Estudiante A:	**Estudiante B:**
1. el semáforo	6. la gasolinera
2. el autobús	7. el policía
3. doblar	8. seguir
4. el puente	9. el motocicleta
5. parar	10. la velocidad

14-2 **¿Qué clase de conductor eres?** Trabajen en parejas. Haz preguntas a tu compañero/a para completar el cuadro de abajo. Luego, decide si tu compañero/a presenta un riesgo (*risk*) alto, mediano o bajo, desde la perspectiva de una compañía de seguros.

Nombre: _____

Marca y modelo de carro²			
Número de años con licencia de conducir			
Número de accidentes			
Número de multas (*tickets*)			
¿Alguna vez se te ha acabado (*run out*) la gasolina?	☐ Nunca	☐ 1 o 2 veces	☐ Más de 2 veces
¿Sabes cambiar una llanta desinflada?	☐ Sí	☐ No	
¿Usas el cinturón de seguridad (*seat belt*)?	☐ Siempre	☐ A veces	☐ Nunca
¿Te pones impaciente cuando hay mucho tráfico?	☐ Siempre	☐ A veces	☐ Nunca
¿Respetas el límite de velocidad?	☐ Siempre	☐ A veces	☐ Nunca

Esta persona presenta un riesgo   ☐ alto   ☐ mediano   ☐ bajo

---

²Si no tienes carro, di la marca y modelo de un carro que manejas a veces (por ejemplo: el de tu familia, etc.).

14-3 **Señales (Signs) para los automovilistas.** Tu amigo/a está manejando por una ciudad latinoamericana y tú lo/la guías. Al ver cada letrero, dile lo que debe hacer. Usa mandatos de **tú.**

Velocidad máxima 90 km.

Modelo: No manejes/ conduzcas a más de 90 km. por hora.

Prohibido girar en U.

Prohibido doblar a la izquierda.

Prohibido seguir derecho.

Prohibido estacionar o detenerse.

Ceder el paso.

No tocar la bocina.

Pararse.

No cambiar de carril.

Los vehículos y los mecánicos

TALLER MECÁNICO URIBE

▶ LE **REVISAMOS** LA BATERÍA Y EL AIRE DE LAS LLANTAS.

▶ LE CAMBIAMOS EL ACEITE, LOS FILTROS Y LAS LLANTAS.

▶ LE **REPARAMOS** LOS **FRENOS** Y LE **AFINAMOS** EL **MOTOR.**

▶ SU AUTO **FUNCIONARÁ** COMO NUEVO.

Estamos en la **esquina** de la Calle 7 y la Avenida 6 a tres **cuadras** de la estación de autobuses.

Consultas y café **gratis**

No busque donde **estacionar.** Tenemos amplio **estacionamiento.**

Tel. 555-39 27

afinar (el motor)	to tune up (the motor)	**funcionar**	to work, run (machine)
la cuadra	block	**gratis**	(for) free
la esquina	corner	**el motor**	engine
estacionar	to park	**reparar**	to repair
el estacionamiento	parking	**revisar**	to check
el freno	brake	**el taller mecánico**	(repair) shop

Así se dice

14-4 **¿De qué se trata?** Empareja las palabras con las oraciones que mejor las describen.

1. Cuando el auto no funciona, lo llevas a este lugar.
2. Cuando llegas a tu destino, dejas el coche en este lugar.
3. En la intersección de dos calles, hay cuatro.
4. Es el "corazón" del auto.
5. No cuesta dinero.
6. Observar las partes del coche para ver si hay problemas.
7. Un grupo de edificios entre calles paralelas.
8. Hacer funcionar otra vez.

_____ a. el estacionamiento
_____ b. gratis
_____ c. reparar
_____ d. revisar
_____ e. el taller mecánico
_____ f. la cuadra
_____ g. la esquina
_____ h. el motor

14-5 **Se vende automóvil usado.** Viste un anuncio clasificado sobre un automóvil usado y decides llamar al vendedor del carro.

Paso 1. Completa la conversación telefónica.

Vendedor:	Bueno.
Cliente:	Buenas tardes. Con el Sr. Benavides, por favor.
Vendedor:	Con él habla.
Cliente:	Señor Benavides, vi su anuncio en el periódico y me interesa saber más sobre su carro.
Vendedor:	Es un _____ del año _____. Acabo de traerlo del taller. Ahí le afinaron _____, le _____ la batería, le cambiaron _____ y _____ y le _____ los frenos. Ahora está como nuevo.
Cliente:	¿Me puede dar su dirección para ver y probar el coche?
Vendedor:	Sí, es el número 2434 de la Calle Esmeralda, a dos _____ de la estación de autobuses.
Cliente:	¿Cuándo puedo verlo?
Vendedor:	Pues ahora mismo si quiere.

Paso 2. En parejas, un estudiante es el vendedor y el otro el cliente que viene para ver el carro. Conversen e intenten llegar a un acuerdo. Por supuesto, el comprador pregunta sobre los detalles e intenta encontrar "problemitas" para reducir el precio, pero el vendedor resiste... ¿Comprará el auto? ¿Cuál será el precio final?

El airbag ya estaba inventado. Los plásticos de BASF lo han hecho más seguro.

El "pez globo" se llena de aire y aumenta de volumen para evitar los ataques de sus depredadores (*predators*). ¿Hay una relación entre el pez globo y los *airbags* de los carros? ¿Tiene *airbags* tu carro? ¿Te sientes más seguro/a con *airbags*?

14-6 **Perdón, ¿cómo se dice?** Muchas palabras referidas a los transportes varían en países diferentes. Por ejemplo:

auto/ carro/ coche   aparcar/ estacionar/ parquear

autobús/ camión/ colectivo

HINT

Los nombres de las ciudades te ayudarán a identificar los dos países no mencionados.

En parejas, indiquen qué palabras se usan en tres países hispanos. Completen las tres columnas según la información que sigue.

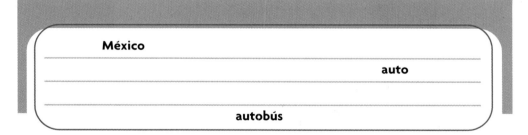

México		
		auto
	autobús	

- Para tomar un camión, tienes que ir a México.

- En Madrid no se toma ni colectivo ni camión.

- En Buenos Aires puedes tomar un colectivo.

- En el país donde hay carros también hay camiones.

- En un país estacionas el auto, en otro aparcas el coche y en otro parqueas el carro.

Así se dice

14-7 **Para ver un poco de Puebla.** Tú y tu amigo/a acaban de llegar a Puebla, México, y están planeando su visita.

Paso 1. Primero, lean la información sobre Puebla y decidan juntos qué lugares quieren visitar.

1. _____   4. _____

2. _____   5. _____

3. _____

LUGARES INTERESANTES EN PUEBLA

La Catedral
Su construcción comenzó en 1575. Es una joya de la arquitectura colonial. Sus torres° son las más altas del país.

La Biblioteca Palafoxiana
Está clasificada como un monumento histórico de México. Fue fundada en 1646.

Mercado El Parián
Es la antigua° plazuela de San Roque. Se construyó en 1801. Hoy es un mercado donde se puede encontrar artesanías, dulces°, téxtiles, etc.

Iglesia de la Compañía de Jesús
Otra de las iglesias famosas de la ciudad; es de estilo barroco; tiene torres blancas y un altar bello.

El barrio del Artista
Es una plazuela con una fuente° hermosa y muchos talleres de artistas.

La casa del Alfeñique
Esta casa del siglo XVIII tiene mucha ornamentación blanca y por eso se la llama *alfeñique*, un dulce poblano°.

La Capilla° del Rosario
Este ejemplo del arte barroco novohispano se considera una de las maravillas de México. El interior de la capilla es de estuco cubierto con lámina de oro de veintidós quilates.

La Plazuela de los Sapos°
Rodeada de casas típicas y bazares de antigüedades, tiene una fuente muy linda en el centro. Aquí se puede contratar a mariachis y tríos.

El Museo Amparo
Una de sus exhibiciones más importantes es sobre las culturas mesoamericanas.

torres *towers;* **antigua** *former;* **dulces** *candy;* **poblano** *from Puebla;* **fuente** *fountain;* **la Capilla** *chapel;* **Sapos** *toads*

Paso 2. Están listos para comenzar su visita y piden consejo al recepcionista del hotel. Él les da indicaciones para llegar a ciertos puntos de interés en la ciudad. Escuchen atentamente para identificar el lugar al que llevan estas indicaciones. Recuerden que ahora están en el Hotel Colonial ("E" en su mapa).

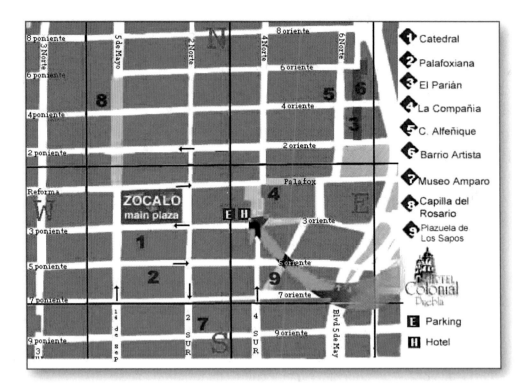

 Paso 3. Es tu segundo día en Puebla, y esta mañana fuiste solo/a a visitar dos de los lugares de tu lista (*Paso 1*). Ahora estás descansando en el hotel con tu amigo/a y le recomiendas que visite estos lugares. Usando el mapa del *Paso 2*, túrnense para dar instrucciones (sin mencionar el destino final) y escuchar. ¡Cuidado! Hay calles de una sola vía. ¿Qué lugares recomienda tu amigo/a?

1. _____   2. _____

NOTA CULTURAL

Many older cities in Spanish-speaking countries were formed spontaneously and somewhat disorderly. In such places, people normally **don't** use cardinal points (north, south, east, west) when giving directions. They are more likely to use expressions such as, "Go straight that way" and use points of reference such as, "Turn on the first street after passing the church."

Así se dice

¡Qué lío!

¡Reacciones!

¡Caramba!	*Oh, my gosh!*
¡Claro!/ ¡Por supuesto!	*Of course!*
¡Socorro!/ ¡Auxilio!	*Help!*
Lo siento mucho.	*I'm so sorry.*
¡Qué barbaridad!	*How awful!*
¡Qué lástima!	*What a shame!*
¡Qué lío!	*What a mess!*
¡Ay de mí!	*Poor me! (What am I going to do?)*
¡Qué suerte!	*What luck!/How lucky!*

  14-8 ¡Caramba! ¿Qué dices en las siguientes situaciones? Usa todas las reacciones de la lista. Hay más de una respuesta posible.

¿Qué dices cuando... ?

1. Un/a amigo/a de tu compañero/a de cuarto ha tenido un accidente y está en el hospital.

2. Estás en el centro de Managua y ¡tu coche tiene una llanta desinflada!

3. Llueve mucho, y los limpiaparabrisas no funcionan.

4. Estás manejando muy rápidamente por las calles de Tegucigalpa y descubres que ¡los frenos no funcionan!

5. Tu mejor amigo/a te cuenta que anoche le robaron su coche nuevo.

6. Un policía te para y te pide la licencia de conducir, pero no la tienes.

7. Abres la puerta del coche de tu amigo/a y ves que todo está muy sucio. Hay papeles, comida y ropa vieja por todas partes.

8. Tu tía rica te pregunta si quieres un coche nuevo para tu cumpleaños.

Cultura: Honduras y Nicaragua

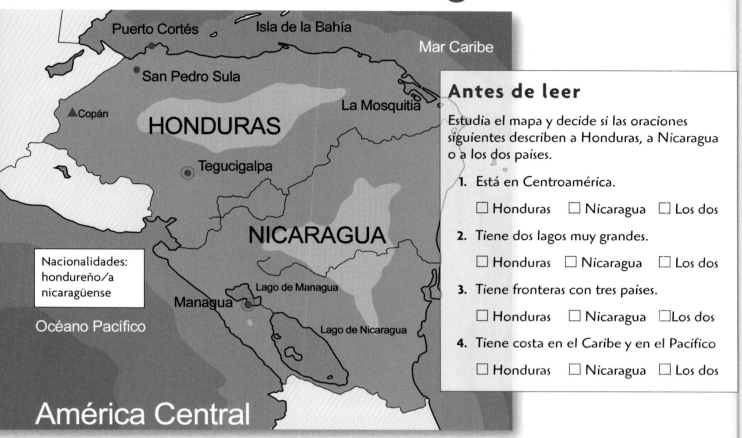

Puerto Cortés • Isla de la Bahía
Mar Caribe
• San Pedro Sula
▲ Copán
HONDURAS
La Mosquitia
⊙ Tegucigalpa

NICARAGUA

Nacionalidades:
hondureño/a
nicaragüense

Lago de Managua
Managua ⊙
Lago de Nicaragua

Océano Pacífico

América Central

Antes de leer

Estudia el mapa y decide si las oraciones siguientes describen a Honduras, a Nicaragua o a los dos países.

1. Está en Centroamérica.

   ☐ Honduras ☐ Nicaragua ☐ Los dos

2. Tiene dos lagos muy grandes.

   ☐ Honduras ☐ Nicaragua ☐ Los dos

3. Tiene fronteras con tres países.

   ☐ Honduras ☐ Nicaragua ☐ Los dos

4. Tiene costa en el Caribe y en el Pacífico

   ☐ Honduras ☐ Nicaragua ☐ Los dos

HONDURAS

Las dos ciudades más importantes de Honduras son San Pedro Sula, el centro industrial del país, y Tegucigalpa, la capital. Tegucigalpa está situada en la montañosa zona central.

A los hondureños se les puede llamar *catrachos* o *catrachas*. Esta palabra se deriva del apellido del general hondureño, Florencio Xatruch, que en 1857 dirigió a las fuerzas hondureñas en defensa contra una invasión del filibustero estadounidense William Walker.

Ésta es la Iglesia de Nuestra Señora de los Dolores en el centro de Tegucigalpa.

Cultura: Honduras y Nicaragua

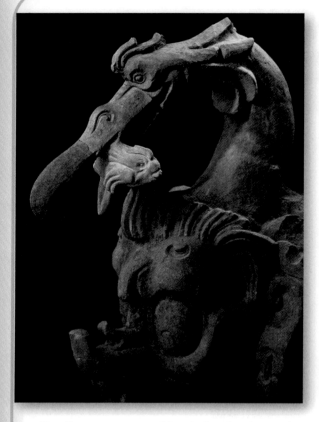

Un pájaro enorme, que mide más de ocho pies, en el museo de Copán.

Lee lo que ofrece este grupo para los turistas, con atención especial a las palabras en **negrita.**

En Honduras viven varios grupos étnicos. Los habitantes originales precolombinos eran los mayas y los lencas. Para el año 800 d.C., los mayas habían abandonado inexplicablemente sus ciudades. Cuando llegaron los españoles en 1523, sólo encontraron las ruinas de Copán, una gran ciudad de palacios y pirámides.

Una familia garífuna

El área más aislada y remota del país se llama la Mosquitia —vuelve al mapa para ver dónde se encuentra. Allí viven 50.000 indígenas miskitos. En la costa caribeña viven los garífuna, que llegaron a Honduras en el siglo XVIII. Se escaparon de la esclavitud[1] bajo las colonias inglesas del Caribe. Tienen relación cultural con otros descendientes africanos en el Caribe, como los de Jamaica.

[1]slavery

Garifuna tours

Se imagina usted caminando a través del **bosque tropical** rico en vida silvestre y con alrededores llenos de vistas coloridas y penetrantes sonidos corales, **buceando** entre una variedad de arrecifes coralinos inalcanzables para proteger las reservas marinas excepto llegando hasta ellos en lancha, haciendo **kayaking** a través de canales estrechos dentro de manglares intocables en el Río Plátano con una gran variedad de aves, mariposas, lagartos y monos aulladores, cargándose de adrenalina practicando **rafting** en las claras aguas del Río Cangrejal o simplemente descansando en una hamaca, desconectado del mundo después de **un almuerzo típico** garífuna en una playa tranquila…

NICARAGUA

Nicaragua, el país más grande de Centroamérica, se caracteriza por sus lagos hermosos y sus volcanes. Managua, la capital del país desde 1858, está a lado del lago del mismo nombre.

El gran Lago de Nicaragua tiene más de 8.000 km² y es el más grande de Centroamérica. En el lago está la isla de Ometepe, que es la isla más grande del mundo situada en un lago. Según la leyenda, los indígenas precolombinos, los nicarao, llegaron desde el norte cuando cayó la gran ciudad de Teotihuacán. Sus líderes religiosos les dijeron que viajaran hacia el sur hasta encontrar un lago con dos volcanes, y así se establecieron en Ometepe.

El Lago de Nicaragua

Después de leer

Decide si las oraciones siguientes describen a Honduras, a Nicaragua o a los dos países.

1. Tiene la isla más grande del mundo situada en un lago.
   ☐ Honduras   ☐ Nicaragua   ☐ Los dos
2. Hay una comunidad garífuna muy grande.
   ☐ Honduras   ☐ Nicaragua   ☐ Los dos
3. La bandera es azul y blanca.
   ☐ Honduras   ☐ Nicaragua   ☐ Los dos

Managua, Nicaragua

Así se forma

Sigamos la carretera 95 y tratemos de llegar a Managua antes de las cinco de la tarde.

1. *Nosotros (Let's)* commands: Making suggestions

To express a suggestion or command with *let's*, Spanish uses the **nosotros** form of the present subjunctive.

Revisemos la batería.	***Let's check*** the battery.
No **esperemos** más.	***Let's* not *wait*** any longer.

- In **nosotros** commands, as in other command forms, object and reflexive pronouns are attached to an affirmative command but placed before a negative command.

  Hagámos**lo** mañana.   No **lo** hagamos en este momento.

- To form the affirmative *let's* command of a reflexive verb, delete the final **-s** of the present subjunctive form before adding the pronoun **nos**. Note the written accent.

  levantemo**s** > levantemo– + **nos** = **¡Levantémonos!**

- The verbs **ir** and **irse** have irregular affirmative *let's* commands . . .

  ¡Vamos! or **¡Vámonos!**   *Let's go!*

  and an alternative form **vamos a** + *infinitive* . . .

  ¡Vamos a parar aquí! **Let's stop** here!

  but the negative counterparts do use the subjunctive form.

  ¡No vayamos allí!/ ¡No nos vayamos allí!   *Let's not go there!*

  ¡No paremos aquí!   *Let's not stop here!*

 (14-9) Un fin de semana en Tegucigalpa.

Paso 1. Vas a viajar de Managua a Tegucigalpa con unos amigos. Una persona del grupo es un poco mandona (*bossy*) y siempre insiste en organizarles la vida a todos. Determina el orden cronológico de sus sugerencias. Escribe el número al lado de cada oración.

_____ **a.** Desayunemos antes de salir.

_____ **b.** Levantémonos a las seis de la mañana.

_____ **c.** Durante el viaje, cambiemos de chofer cada dos horas.

_____ **d.** Salgamos a las siete en punto.

_____ **e.** Al llegar, estacionémonos en el Hotel Honduras Maya.

_____ **f.** Almorcemos en el camino.

_____ **g.** Hoy, llevemos el carro a la gasolinera para llenar el tanque y revisar las llantas.

_____ **h.** Y después, regresemos al hotel para descansar.

_____ **i.** Si todavía está abierta, podemos ir a ver la Iglesia de Nuestra Señora de los Dolores.

_____ **j.** Acostémonos temprano esta noche para estar en forma para el viaje mañana.

_____ **k.** Luego, busquemos un buen restaurante para cenar.

Paso 2. En general eres muy flexible pero no estás de acuerdo con todas las sugerencias de tu amigo/a. Responde a las sugerencias que no te gustan y ofrece una alternativa. Usa formas de mandato de **nosotros**.

Modelo: **No, no nos levantemos a las seis; mejor levantémonos a las ocho.**

14-10 **Planeando un itinerario.** Tú y dos amigos/as deciden continuar su viaje por Honduras dos días más, pero tienen preferencias diferentes. Usen los mandatos de nosotros para expresar sus sugerencias y acuerden (*agree on*) un plan interesante para todos.

Estudiante A: Te encanta la arquitectura, visitar museos o pasear por las calles de una ciudad para observar a la gente e ir de compras. También te gusta salir por la noche y te parece importante tener un hotel cómodo para descansar.

Estudiante B: A ti te fascina la naturaleza. Te encanta practicar deportes de aventura o tomar el sol en la playa. Por supuesto, al final del día prefieres dormir bajo las estrellas que bajo el techo de un hotel.

Estudiante C: ¡A ti te gusta todo! Ayuda a tus amigos/as a planear un viaje con algo para todos/as.

Piensen en:

1. cuándo quieren salir y regresar
2. adónde quieren ir
3. si van en moto, coche, autobús o tren
4. lo que quieren (o no quieren) hacer durante el viaje
5. lo que deben llevar (ropa, comida, etc.)
6. adónde van a dormir (acampar, moteles, etc.)
7. cuánto dinero van a llevar para los gastos (*expenses*)

Modelo: Estudiante A: **Quedémonos en Tegucigalpa un día más.**

Estudiante B: **No, no. Vayamos a la playa en la Mosquitia.**

Estudiante C: **Tengo una idea —vayamos a San Pedro Sula. Un día podemos visitar la ciudad y las ruinas mayas de Copán y otro día vamos a la playa...**

Escenas

Linda

Manuel

Hacia el Lago de Nicaragua

Unfortunately

Linda y Manuel alquilaron un carro y están camino al Lago de Nicaragua. Manuel conduce y Linda está a su lado. Desgraciadamente°, el carro no está en muy buenas condiciones.

Paso 1. En una escala de 1 (poco serio) a 5 (muy serio), ¿cómo consideras estos problemas mecánicos?

		Poco serio				Muy serio
a.	Los frenos no funcionan bien.	1	2	3	4	5
b.	El carro tiene poco aceite.	1	2	3	4	5
c.	El aire acondicionado hace ruido.	1	2	3	4	5
d.	Una llanta necesita aire.	1	2	3	4	5
e.	No puedes bajar y subir las ventanillas.	1	2	3	4	5
f.	El motor hace un ruido extraño.	1	2	3	4	5

Si estás viajando, ¿cuáles de estos problemas serían una razón para parar?

Paso 2. Escucha la conversación entre Linda y Manuel y escribe un resumen (*summary*) de la historia en dos líneas.

Paso 3. Lee estas preguntas. Después escucha la conversación otra vez y escribe tus respuestas.

1. ¿Adónde van Linda y Manuel?
2. ¿Quién está manejando el coche?
3. ¿Por qué está nerviosa Linda?
4. ¿En dónde se paran?
5. ¿Qué revisa el empleado?
6. ¿Qué le pasa al coche?

Paso 4. Escucha una vez más mientras lees el texto y comprueba (*check*) tus respuestas para el *Paso 3.*

Linda:	Manuel, vas muy rápido y casi no tenemos gasolina.
Manuel:	¡Ay, Linda! Todo está bien. Tenemos prisa por llegar al Lago de Nicaragua.
Linda:	¿Qué es ese ruido? ¿No lo oyes? Hay un ruido en la llanta.
Manuel:	Es tu imaginación, Linda. Es mejor que te duermas.
Linda:	Por favor. Paremos en esa estación de servicio para que revisen el coche. Si no, nunca vamos a llegar al lago.
Manuel:	Bueno, bueno... está bien. Voy a parar. *(Entran en la estación de servicio.)*
Manuel:	*(Al empleado.)* Buenas tardes, ¿puede llenar el tanque y revisar las llantas, por favor?
Empleado:	Sí, inmediatamente. *(El empleado echa la gasolina y revisa las llantas.)* ¿Quiere que le revise el motor y los frenos?
Manuel:	No, no es necesario.
Linda:	¡Sí! ¡Sí, es necesario!

(El empleado revisa el motor y los frenos.)

Empleado: *(A Manuel)* Señor, la llanta delantera° derecha está en muy malas   *front*
condiciones, el coche casi no tiene aceite, los frenos están
gastados°... Necesito por lo menos cuatro horas para repararlo   *worn out*
todo. Lo siento mucho.

Linda: *(A Manuel)* ¿Ves, Manuel?

Manuel: Es verdad, mi amor. Tenías razón°, como siempre. ¡Qué mala suerte   **Tenías...** *You were right*
hemos tenido con este carro!

Linda: Bueno, seamos pacientes, estamos de vacaciones...

Así se forma

> No podemos continuar el viaje a menos que encuentre cuál es el problema.

2. The subjunctive after conjunctions of condition or purpose: Expressing condition or purpose

The <u>subjunctive</u> is <u>always used</u> after the following conjunctions:

en caso de que *in case*

con tal (de) que *provided that*

a menos (de) que *unless*

para que *so that, in order that*

- These conjunctions denote purpose (*so that*) and condition/contingency (*unless, provided that, in case*). They indicate that the outcome of the actions they introduce is dependent on other actions. Since the speaker considers the outcomes to be indefinite or pending, they may or may not take place.

Trae tu tarjeta de crédito **en caso de que** la **necesites**.

*Bring your credit card **in case you need** it.*

Puedes alquilar un coche **con tal de que tengas** una licencia válida.

*You can rent a car **provided you have** a valid license.*

No alquiles el auto **a menos que no encuentres** asiento en el tren.

*Don't rent the car **unless you cannot find** a seat on the train.*

Vamos a la agencia **para que preguntes** sobre las opciones diferentes.

*Let's go to the agency **so that you can ask** about the different options.*

Así se forma

- When the subject does not change (the same person is the subject of the main verb and the verb after the conjunction), **para que** + *subjunctive* is usually replaced by the preposition **para** + *infinitive*.

Vamos a la estación de autobuses **para** que ella **compre** los boletos.	We are going to the bus station **so that** she **can buy** the tickets.
Vamos a la estación de autobuses **para comprar** los boletos.	We are going to the bus station **to (in order to) buy** the tickets.

14-11 **Un viaje a las ruinas mayas de Copán.** Estás en Tegucigalpa, haciendo los preparativos para un viaje en autobús a las ruinas de Copán. Lee cada declaración de la columna A y complétala con la frase apropiada de la columna B.

A

1. Vamos a la estación de autobuses...
2. Debemos llevar los pasaportes...
3. No podemos ver todas las ruinas...
4. Al llegar, debemos conseguir un mapa de las ruinas...
5. Carlos viene con nosotros...
6. Nos vamos a quedar en un hostal estudiantil...
7. Será difícil ver todo el museo...

B

a. en caso de que las autoridades quieran revisarlos.
b. con tal de que encontremos uno en la ciudad de Copán.
c. para buscar información acerca de los horarios.
d. a menos que lleguemos temprano.
e. a menos que nos quedemos varios días.
f. para que sea más fácil orientarnos.
g. con tal de que reciba el dinero que le mandó su tío.

Las ruinas de Copán, Honduras

14-12 **Un viaje de negocios y placer.** En parejas, imaginen que Uds. son los guías de dos profesores de Nicaragua que llegan a su universidad para asistir a una conferencia. Ustedes van a llevarlos a conocer la ciudad y les van a explicar por qué los llevan a los lugares indicados. Completen las oraciones.

Modelo: Vamos a llevarlos a un restaurante de comida rápida **en caso de que tengan hambre o sed.**

Vamos a llevarlos...

1. al centro comercial...
2. al banco...
3. a la oficina de correos...
4. al centro estudiantil
5. a Kinko's...
6. a... (un sitio importante de la ciudad)

14-13 **¿Para qué?** Alfonso decide separarse del grupo para visitar San Pedro Sula. Se prepara para su viaje. ¿Por qué o para qué lleva las siguientes cosas?

Modelo: Alfonso lleva un paraguas en caso de que llueva.

14-14 **¿Realmente necesitamos eso?** Están empacando y las maletas están muy pesadas porque ¡tienen demasiadas cosas! Trabajen en parejas.

Paso 1. Lee tu lista de tres objetos "cuestionables" que pusiste en tu equipaje. Tú piensas que es importante llevar estas cosas y que pueden ser útiles o importantes durante el viaje. Escribe tus razones. ¡Usa tu imaginación!

Estudiante A:
una flauta musical
unas cortinas
fotos de tu familia

Estudiante B:
una lámpara pequeña
una raqueta de tenis
un libro de biología

Paso 2. Ahora lee tu lista y tus razones a tu compañero/a. Háganse preguntas y respondan a las preguntas de su compañero/a.

¿Qué objetos van a llevar? ¿Cuáles van a dejar?

Así se dice

En la estación

los aseos/ el servicio	restroom(s)	el boleto/ billete	
el andén	platform	...de ida/ sencillo	one-way ticket
la taquilla	ticket window	...de ida y vuelta	round-trip ticket
perder (el tren/ autobús..)	to miss the train/bus . . .		

14-15 **¿Cierto o falso?** Escucha las siguientes afirmaciones e indica si son ciertas o falsas. Si son falsas, corrígelas para que sean ciertas.

Modelo: (Oyes:) La taquilla es el lugar donde subes al tren.
(Marcas:) Falso
(Escribes:) **El andén es el lugar donde subes al tren.**

	Cierto	Falso	
1.	☐	☐	_____
2.	☐	☐	_____
3.	☐	☐	_____
4.	☐	☐	_____
5.	☐	☐	_____
6.	☐	☐	_____

14-16 **En la estación del ferrocarril.**

Paso 1. Observa la ilustración de arriba durante un minuto.

Paso 2. Ahora cierra el libro. Tienes cinco minutos para describir la escena en un párrafo incluyendo todos los detalles que recuerdes.

14-17 Un viaje a Sevilla en el AVE.

En España existe un tren de alta velocidad llamado AVE (Alta Velocidad España). Ustedes quieren viajar en este tren y encuentran esta descripción en un anuncio publicitario de RENFE (Red Nacional del Ferrocarril de España). Léanlo.

Los trenes de alta velocidad AVE conectan Madrid con el sur y noreste de España. Estos trenes ofrecen servicios tales como cafetería, venta de artículos a bordo, canales para escuchar música, vídeos, pasatiempos para niños, aseos y facilidades para los minusválidos°. Puede viajar en clase Club, Preferente o Turista. La clase Club incluye aparcamiento, servicio de restaurante a la carta y hasta servicio de bar en el asiento. Puede usted viajar con su mascota (perros pequeños y gatos), transportar su bicicleta y llevar una maleta y un maletín.

handicapped

La Renfe promete extrema puntualidad con demoras de sólo minutos. Si su tren se demora más de quince minutos, puede obtener una devolución de parte del costo de su viaje.

Precios (en euros) de Madrid a:

	Ciudad Real	Córdoba	Sevilla	Zaragoza	Huesca	Lleida
Turista	27,10	52,10	69,80	39,60	47,90	55
Preferente	41,70	78,20	105,20	58,40	71,90	83,40
Clase Club	50	93,80	127,10	70,90	86,50	101,10

Parece interesante, ¿verdad? Ahora un/a estudiante hace el papel del empleado de la Renfe y el otro/la otra es el/la pasajero/a. Hagan las siguientes transacciones:

1. comprar un boleto para una de las ciudades que menciona el folleto
2. pedir información (sobre horario/ equipaje/ comida/ andenes/ aseos, etc.)
3. hablar de posibles demoras y tratar de resolver los problemas que puedan causar

Modelo:
Empleado/a de Renfe: **Buenos días. ¿En qué puedo servirle?**
Pasajero/a: **Deseo comprar...**
Empleado/a: **Muy bien, señor/señorita, aquí lo tiene. Cuesta...**

Investig@ en INTERNET

¿Cuántas millas hay entre Madrid y las siguientes ciudades? (Es posible que sea más fácil encontrar esta información en kilómetros y convertir en millas después.) ¿Cuánto tiempo dura el viaje en el AVE desde Madrid hasta cada una de ellas?

	¿Millas desde Madrid?	¿Tiempo de viaje en el AVE?
Ciudad Real		
Córdoba		
Sevilla		
Zaragoza		
Lleida		
Huesca		

¿Hay algún tren similar en Estados Unidos? ¿Sabes qué velocidad máxima alcanza (*reach*)?

SITUACIONES

Compraste un boleto de tren para viajar de Barcelona a Madrid. El revisor (*conductor*) te pide el boleto, y te das cuenta de (*realize*) que ¡lo has perdido! Ahora tendrás que comprar otro y pagar una multa —un gran inconveniente porque tienes poco dinero. Trata de explicarle tu situación al revisor:

Señor, le aseguro que compré un billete en Barcelona. Lo tenía en mi mochila....

Cultura: La Carretera Panamericana

Antes de leer

1. ¿Cuál es el viaje en carro más largo que has hecho?
2. ¿Has visto la película *Diarios de motocicleta*?

La Carretera
Panamericana

.... Pan American
Highway

La película *Diarios de motocicleta* (2004) muestra un viaje del revolucionario argentino Ché Guevara que recorrió partes de esta carretera en 1952.

¿Has pensado en recorrer Latinoamérica en carro? La Carretera Panamericana ofrece una aventura inigualable[1]. Comienza en Fairbanks, Alaska, y continúa hasta Ushuaia, Tierra del Fuego, en Argentina. Esta gran vía de 16,000 mi (25,750 km) conecta las culturas y los paisajes de las tres Américas, pasando por numerosas ciudades y pueblos, y cruzando las selvas y las montañas más importantes del continente. A veces es una autopista. Otras veces es una carretera de dos carriles[2].

El plan para su construcción comenzó en 1925 con un congreso celebrado en Buenos Aires. Los Estados Unidos y los países de Latinoamérica trabajaron juntos en la planificación y construcción de esta carretera, y actualmente sólo falta construir 160 km (casi 100 millas) en la densa selva del Darién, entre Panamá y Colombia. A causa de la importancia ecológica de la zona, es muy probable que nunca se termine de construir esta sección de la carretera. Al llegar a Darién, los viajeros transportan sus vehículos en barco hasta Venezuela o Colombia. Allí pueden retomar la Carretera Panamericana y continuar su viaje hacia el sur.

[1]*unequaled* [2]*lanes*

Después de leer

1. ¿Cierto o falso?
   a. La Carretera Panamericana tiene una extensión de 10,000 millas.
   b. Hay una interrupción corta en la Carretera Panamericana entre Panamá y Colombia.
2. ¿Cuál es la carretera más pintoresca de tu país o de tu región? ¿Por qué?

Así se forma

Me recomendaron que llevara la cámara para sacar fotos de las ruinas mayas.

3. The imperfect subjunctive: Reacting to past actions or events

You have studied various uses of the subjunctive and practiced the present subjunctive (relating actions that take place in the present or in the future) and the present perfect subjunctive (relating actions and events that have taken place in the immediate past).

Present subjunctive

Espero (que **se diviertan** en Copán).   *I hope that **they (will) have a good time** in Copán.*

Present perfect subjunctive

Me alegro de (que **se hayan divertido** en Copán).   *I am glad that **they have had a good time** in Copán.*

In the examples above, the verb of the *main clause* is in the present indicative, and the verb of the *subordinate clause*, in parentheses, is in the present subjunctive or the present perfect subjunctive.

In general, the imperfect (past) subjunctive is used in the same kinds of situations as the present subjunctive (after expressions of influence, emotion, doubt, etc.), but relates actions or events that took place in the past. When the verb of the *main clause* is in a past tense (usually preterit or imperfect), the **imperfect subjunctive** is used in the *subordinate clause*.

Main clause	Subordinate clause
Es bueno... *present indicative*	...que **hagas** las reservaciones. *present subjunctive* ...que **hayas hecho** las reservaciones. *present perfect subjunctive*
Les **recomendé**... *past indicative*	...que **hicieran** las reservaciones. *imperfect subjunctive*
Siempre les **recomendaba**... *past indicative*	...que **viajaran** en tren. *imperfect subjunctive*

Formation of the imperfect subjunctive

To form the imperfect subjunctive of all verbs, **-ar**, **-er**, and **-ir**:

- use the **ellos** form of the preterit indicative as a base: **compraron**

- delete the **-ron** ending from it: **compra-**

- add the following endings:
 -ra, -ras, -ra, -ramos, -rais, -ran[3].   **comprara**

---

[3]In Spain and in certain dialects of Spanish, the imperfect subjunctive has an alternate set of endings: -se, -ses, -se, -semos, -sen (**comprase, comprases**...) These forms are frequently found in writing.

Así se forma

The imperfect subjunctive thus automatically reflects all irregularities of the preterit.

<table>
<tr><td></td><td></td><td>compra<u>r</u></td><td>volv<u>er</u></td><td>sal<u>ir</u></td></tr>
</table>

	compr**ar**	volv**er**	sal**ir**
(Preterit) →	compr~~aron~~	volvi~~eron~~	sali~~eron~~
(yo)	compr**ara**	volvi**era**	sali**era**
(tú)	compr**aras**	volvi**eras**	sali**eras**
(Ud., él, ella)	compr**ara**	volvi**era**	sali**era**
(nosotros/as)	compr**áramos**	volvi**éramos**	sali**éramos**
(vosotros/as)	compr**arais**	volvi**erais**	sali**erais**
(Uds., ellos, ellas)	compr**aran**	volvi**eran**	sali**eran**

Other examples:

	(Preterit)		Imperfect subjunctive
estar	estuvieron	→	**estuviera, estuvieras,...**
leer	leyeron	→	**leyera, leyeras,...**
tener	tuvieron	→	**tuviera, tuvieras,...**
dormir	durmieron	→	**durmiera, durmieras,...**
ir/ ser	fueron	→	**fuera, fueras,...**
pedir	pidieron	→	**pidiera, pidieras,...**

- **Hubiera** is the imperfect subjunctive form of **haber**.

Nos alegrábamos de que **hubiera** un vagón-restaurante en el tren.	We were happy that **there was** a dining car on the train.

 14-18 **Jefes, profesores y amigos.** La semana pasada fue muy estresante; todos esperaban algo de ti. Según la situación, identifica quién o quiénes esperaban cada cosa.

> **a.** Tu jefe (*boss*) esperaba que...
> **b.** Tu compañero/a de cuarto esperaba que...
> **c.** Tu profesor/a de español esperaba que...

Modelo: ...hiciera todos los ejercicios.
Mi profesor/a esperaba que hiciera todos los ejercicios.

1. ...llegara a clase temprano
2. ...trabajara desde las nueve hasta las cinco
3. ...limpiara el cuarto
4. ...hiciera horas extra
5. ...lo/la ayudara con la tarea
6. ...fuera al cine con él/ella
7. ...hablara en español
8. ...aprendiera las formas del subjuntivo
9. ...no hablara tanto por teléfono
10. ...hiciera un trabajo muy profesional

14-19 **Una visita a mi consejero/a.** Esteban quiere mejorar sus notas este semestre y fue a ver a su consejero/a, pero... parece que no recuerda bien las recomendaciones que le hizo.

Paso 1. Escucha y anota las recomendaciones que Esteban dice que le dio su consejero/a. Si piensas que la recomendación es incorrecta, escribe la versión correcta.

Modelo: (Oyes:)   Me recomendó que estudiara en la biblioteca.
(Anotas:)   **Le recomendó que estudiara en la biblioteca.**
(Oyes:)   Me dijo que saliera más con mis amigos/as.
(Corriges y anotas:) **Probablemente le dijo que saliera menos con sus amigos/as.**

Paso 2. Tú también tenías algunos consejos para Esteban, ¿qué le recomendaste?

Le recomendé que... _____

Le sugerí que... _____

14-20 **Natalia de voluntaria.** Durante su semestre en Ecuador, Natalia trabajó como voluntaria en una clínica. Su amiga le dijo que en Los Nevados, un pueblo situado en la zona andina, necesitaban medicamentos. Natalia decidió ir al pueblo para llevarlos. ¿Qué le recomendó su amiga? Usa las expresiones siguientes.

llevar...

| ponerse   escalar   cruzar   dar   regresar   seguir   tomar   despertarse |

Modelo: Le recomendó que llevara...
Le recomendó que llevara su mochila, los medicamentos y comida.

14-21 **Hace unos años...** ¿Qué pasaba en tu vida durante los períodos indicados?

Paso 1. Completa las siguientes oraciones y compara con el presente.

Modelo: **Cuando tenía diez años, mis padres no querían que yo viera mucho la televisión...**

1. Cuando tenía diez años,
   a. yo esperaba que mis padres...
   b. quería que mis amigos/as...
   c. mis padres no querían que yo...

2. Cuando estaba en la escuela secundaria,
   a. yo buscaba un/a novio/a que...
   b. mis padres querían que yo...
   c. mis maestros me recomendaban...

3. Cuando vine a la universidad,
   a. yo temía que mi nuevo/a compañero/a de cuarto...
   b. yo esperaba que los profesores...
   c. yo esperaba que los otros estudiantes...

Paso 2. En parejas, comenten y comparen lo que pasaba en su vida durante los períodos indicados. Túrnense.

Al final, compartan algunos de sus deseos, temores y esperanzas con la clase.

14-22 **¿Qué hicieron en la clase?** Un/a compañero/a de clase estaba enfermo/a y te llama para saber lo que hicieron en clase. Completa la conversación. ¡Atención! Todos los verbos deben estar en el subjuntivo, unos en el presente del subjuntivo y otros en el imperfecto del subjuntivo.

Compañero/a: Hola,... ¿qué tal? Te llamo para saber lo que la profesora quiere que _____ (hacer) para el lunes.

Tú: Hola,... espero que _____ (sentirse) mejor. Pues, la profesora dijo que quería que _____ (estudiar) los verbos en el imperfecto del subjuntivo y que _____ (escribir) una composición sobre los aztecas.

Compañero/a: ¿Explicó cuánto tenemos que escribir?

Tú: Sí, dijo que quería dos párrafos y que recomendaba que
source _____ (usar) al menos una fuente° del Internet o de la biblioteca. Como siempre, insistió que _____ (tener) cuidado con los acentos y la ortografía. Ya conoces a la profesora.

Compañero/a:	¿Ya encontraste tu fuente adicional?
Tú:	No. Busqué en el Internet pero no encontré nada que me _____ (servir).
Compañero/a:	Pues, si tú no encontraste nada, dudo tener mejor suerte. Es mejor que (yo) _____ (ir) a la biblioteca.
Tú:	Creo que tienes razón. ¡Ojalá que nosotros _____ (encontrar) algo. ¡Ah!, se me olvidaba. También dijo que _____ (hacer) los ejercicios del manual, y claro, que _____ (usar) un lápiz o un bolígrafo de un color diferente para hacer las correcciones. Tú sabes.
Compañero/a:	Sí, por supuesto. Gracias otra vez. Te veo el lunes en clase.

4. The impersonal *se*: Talking about activities with a general or unknown subject

When the subject is not specific or general, English uses such words as *one, people, you, we, they*; when the subject is unknown or not mentioned the passive voice[4] is used. When there is no specific subject or the subject is not mentioned, Spanish commonly uses a construction with **se**.

se +	third-person singular verb + singular noun/verb
	third-person plural verb + plural noun

Not specific/general subject:

Se prohibe estacionar.	*Parking **is prohibited**.*
Se debe mostrar el pasaporte.	***You must** show your passport.*
¿Cómo **se dicen** los números en francés?	*How **do you say** the numbers in French?*

Unknown/not mentioned subject:

Se construyó el hotel sobre las rocas.	*The hotel **was built** on the rocks.*
Se habla inglés. (*sign on a store window*)	*English **is spoken**.*
Se venden mapas aquí.	*Maps **are sold** here.*

---

[4]The English passive voice is formed with the verb *to be* + *the past participle*: The house *was built* in 1821.

Can you guess what the following signs say?

 14-23 **¿Dónde están los siguientes letreros (*signs*)?** Asocia cada letrero con el lugar donde se ve.

Letrero

1. Se prohibe fumar.

2. No se aceptan tarjetas de crédito.

3. Se necesita secretaria.

4. Se vende computadora como nueva.

5. Se arreglan llantas.

6. Se necesita la llave para entrar a la piscina.

7. Se abre a las 9 A.M. y se cierra a las 6 P.M.

Lugar

a. en un hotel

b. en un periódico

c. en un restaurante

d. en un avión

e. en un taller mecánico

f. en una oficina en México

g. en un banco

14-24 ¿Qué lugar es?

Paso 1. En parejas, escojan uno de los lugares mencionados abajo. Describan qué se hace, se puede hacer o no se puede hacer en ese lugar. ¿Qué pareja puede hacer la descripción más completa?

Modelo: la clase de español

> **En este lugar se estudia y, algunas veces, también se juega. Se habla mucho, pero generalmente no se habla inglés porque se habla español...**

> en la biblioteca   en la estación de tren
>
> en la piscina   en el supermercado

Paso 2. Ahora vamos a adivinar. De forma individual, piensa en un lugar que es familiar para todos (la biblioteca, el cine, la playa, la iglesia, el restaurante...) y escríbelo aquí:

_____

Paso 3. En grupos, una persona contesta preguntas del resto del grupo sobre las cosas que **se hacen, se puede hacer** o no **se puede hacer** en el lugar que pensó. ¿Quién puede adivinar el lugar?

Modelo: **En este lugar, ¿se trabaja?/ ¿Se venden bebidas?/ ¿Se puede dormir?/ ¿Se necesita dinero?...**

14-25 ¿Qué nos ofrecen Honduras y Nicaragua?

En este capítulo han aprendido mucho sobre Honduras y Nicaragua. En parejas, escojan uno de estos países y escriban un anuncio publicitario turístico, enfatizando todo lo que se puede hacer allí.

Modelo: **Honduras/ Nicaragua es un país... No se ven muchos turistas y se puede vivir la cultura...**

Dicho y hecho

¡A ESCUCHAR!

¡Venga aquí a comprar su coche! Tres vendedores de coches (A, B y C) presentan anuncios en la televisión para promover (*promote*) sus modelos especiales. Aquí tenemos tres personas que desean comprar coches. Escucha los tres anuncios y decide a qué vendedor le va a comprar el coche cada persona. Indica A, B o C según la letra del vendedor.

Personas

___ **1.** Marcos, un ejecutivo de posición prestigiosa en su compañía.

___ **2.** Lidia, una persona joven, profesional, enérgica y aventurera.

___ **3.** Paco, un joven de dieciocho años que trabaja pero gana poco dinero.

Ahora, escucha los anuncios otra vez. Decide qué deseas comprar y por qué. Menciona dos o tres razones.

4. Marca el coche que deseas: ...

5. Por qué lo deseas comprar: ...

CONVERSANDO

Hablemos de viajes y de transportes. La clase se divide en dos filas (fila A y fila B), una frente a la otra. Cada pareja habla por tres minutos acerca del tema 1. Luego, la primera persona de la fila A va al final de la fila, y esa fila se mueve hacia adelante (*forward*). Las nuevas parejas hablan del tema 2, etc.

Temas:
1. un viaje que hicieron en carro, tren o autobús
2. un viaje que quieren hacer en el futuro
3. la importancia de conocer a lugares/ personas diferentes
4. las ventajas (*advantages*) de viajar en carro vs. en avión. **Se puede...**
5. las ventajas y desventajas de tener un carro
6. los problemas con el estacionamiento en su ciudad o su universidad

DE MI ESCRITORIO

Cartas a los "desesperados". Imagina que trabajas para el periódico *El Investigador*. Eres Victoria y aconsejas a los lectores. Escríbele una respuesta a una de estas personas, indicando tus reacciones y recomendaciones. Usa las expresiones indicadas como guía.

Te recomiendo que...	Debes...	con tal que...	En caso de que...
Te sugiero que...	No debes...	a menos que...	Mi recomendación final es...

Querida Victoria:

Salgo para la universidad en un mes. No te puedes imaginar cuántas ganas tengo de comprarme una motocicleta. ¡Me encanta volar por las autopistas y sentir el poder del motor en mi cuerpo! ¡Y he ahorrado suficiente dinero para comprármela! Pero mis padres quieren que compre un Volvo usado del año '99. ¡Qué aburrido! Pero dicen que es más seguro. ¿Qué debo hacer?

–"Frustrado en Managua"

Querida Victoria:

Me he enamorado de un coche. Es un convertible rojo, con un motor potente de 320 caballos de fuerza. Tiene una velocidad máxima de 250 kilómetros (155 millas) por hora. Mis amigos me recomiendan que no lo compre, porque cuesta 60.000 dólares. Yo tengo cinco tarjetas de crédito y hasta puedo pedir un préstamo° en el banco.

–"El soñador°"

loan

dreamer

Artes musicales: La música garífuna

Antes de leer

¿Conoces algún tipo de música que tenga influencia de ritmos africanos? ¿Cuál?

La música garífuna mantiene conocimiento de los cantos, bailes, y otras tradiciones artísticas que han caracterizado a su cultura por años. Se nota la fuerte influencia africana en los ritmos y los instrumentos. Un grupo internacionalmente conocido de la música garífuna se llama Lánigiü Müa, que quiere decir "Corazón de la tierra". El grupo es el resultado de la iniciativa del director hondureño de teatro, Rafael Murillo Selva. Lánigiü Müa ha podidio prosperar gracias al apoyo del Instituto Hondureño del Turismo.

A través de este y otros grupos, muchos cantantes, músicos, bailadores, y tamboristas garífunas han enriquecido a la cultura mundial con su herencia artística y su cosmovisión.

Después de leer

Mira la foto de los bailarines de la bomba y la plena en la página 62. ¿Ves alguna semejanza entre esa foto y ésta de los bailarines de la música garífuna?

¿Crees que la música también tiene semejanzas?

Bailadores del grupo Black Men Soul participando en la primera cumbre (*summit*) garífuna de 2005 en la Isla del Maíz, a 560 km (360 millas) al noreste de Managua, Nicaragua.

Repaso de vocabulario activo

Adjetivos

cómodo/a   *comfortable*

desinflado/a   *flat, deflated (tire)*

gratis   *free (does not cost money)*

seguro/a   *safe*

Adverbios y frases adverbiales

a la derecha   *to the right*

a la izquierda   *to the left*

demasiado   *too, too much*

derecho/ recto   *straight, straight ahead*

despacio   *slow, slowly*

Conjunciones

a menos (de) que   *unless*

con tal (de) que   *provided that*

en caso de que   *in case*

para que   *so that; in order that*

Expresiones útiles

¡Ay de mí!   *Poor me!*

¡Caramba!   *Oh, my gosh!*

¡Claro!/ ¡Por supuesto!   *Of course!*

Lo siento mucho.   *I'm so sorry.*

¡Qué barbaridad!   *How awful!*

¡Qué lástima!   *What a shame!*

¡Qué lío!   *What a mess!*

¡Qué suerte!   *What luck!/How lucky!*

¡Socorro!/ ¡Auxilio!   *Help!*

Sustantivos

El automóvil   *The automobile*

los frenos   *brakes*

la llanta   *tire*

el motor   *motor*

el parabrisas   *windshield*

el taller mecánico   *auto shop*

el tanque   *tank*

En la carretera, en el camino   *On the road*

el accidente   *accident*

el autobús   *bus*

la autopista   *highway/freeway*

el camión   *truck⁵*

la carretera/ el camino   *road, way*

el choque   *crash, collision*

la cuadra   *block (in a city)*

la esquina   *corner*

la estación (de tren/ autobuses)   *(train/bus) station*

la estación de servicio/ la gasolinera   *service/gas station*

el estacionamiento   *parking*

el kilómetro   *kilometer*

la moto(cicleta)   *motorcycle*

el puente   *bridge*

el semáforo   *traffic light*

el tráfico/ el tránsito   *traffic*

En la estación (del ferrocarril)   *In the (train) station*

el andén   *track*

los aseos/ el servicio   *bathroom*

el boleto/ billete   *ticket*

de ida/ sencillo   *one-way*

de ida y vuelta   *round-trip*

de primera/ segunda clase   *first/second class*

el maletero   *trunk*

la taquilla   *ticket window*

el tren   *train*

Otras palabras útiles

la agencia de viajes   *travel agency*

el aire   *air*

el conductor/la conductora   *(male/female) driver*

la gasolina   *gas*

la licencia de conducir   *driver's license*

la multa   *ticket; fine*

el policía   *police officer (male)*

la mujer policía   *police officer (female)*

la velocidad   *speed*

Verbos y expresiones verbales

conducir   *to drive*

continuar   *to continue*

chocar (con)   *to crash, collide (into)*

cruzar   *to cross*

doblar   *to turn*

estacionar   *to park*

funcionar   *to work, run (machine)*

llenar   *to fill*

manejar   *to drive*

parar   *to stop*

reparar   *to repair*

revisar   *to check over*

seguir (i, i)   *to follow, continue*

afinar el motor   *to tune up the motor*

echar gasolina   *to put gas (in the tank)*

hacer reservaciones/ reservas   *to make reservations*

llenar el tanque   *to fill the tank*

perder (ie) el tren   *to miss the train*

tener cuidado   *to be careful*

---

⁵In México, **camión** may also refer to a bus.

Autoprueba y repaso  WILEY PLUS ✓

I. *Nosotros* (Let's) commands. ¿Hacerlo o no hacerlo? Da la forma afirmativa y negativa de los siguientes mandatos.

1. levantarnos a las diez
2. salir para el centro
3. ir por la ruta más directa
4. parar en el supermercado
5. cruzar el nuevo puente
6. seguir recto por cuatro cuadras
7. explorar el sector histórico de la ciudad

II. The subjunctive after conjunctions of condition or purpose. Termina las respuestas.

Modelo: ¿Para qué llamas tanto a tus padres?
Los llamo tanto para que **no se preocupen por mí.**

1. ¿No ha llamado Marta todavía? No, voy a quedarme aquí en caso de que...
2. ¿José no sabe mi dirección? No, voy a mandársela para que (él)...
3. ¿Ya escribiste la carta? No, voy a escribirla en español con tal de que (tú)...
4. ¿Puedo alquilar un coche? Por supuesto, puedes alquilarlo con tal de que...
5. ¿Vas a salir esta noche? Sí, pienso salir a menos que...

III. The imperfect subjunctive. Indica los deseos de las personas.
Modelo: ¿Qué quería mamá que hiciera yo?
sacar la basura
Quería que sacara la basura.

1. ¿Qué quería Mamá que hiciera yo?
   a. limpiar mi cuarto
   b. ir al supermercado
   c. llamar a mis abuelos
   d. organizar mi clóset
2. ¿Qué nos sugirió la profesora de español?
   a. escribir los ejercicios del manual
   b. llegar a clase temprano
   c. hacer los ejercicios del laboratorio
   d. participar en clase

3. ¿Qué esperaban los abuelos?
   a. llamarlos para Navidad
   b. escribirles un mensaje electrónico
   c. visitarlos en verano
   d. invitarlos para la graduación

IV. *Se + verb.* Termina las siguientes oraciones.

Modelo: En España _____ castellano, catalán, vasco y gallego.
En España se hablan castellano, catalán, vasco y gallego.

1. En Centroamérica _____ gallopinto.
2. En un avión no _____ fumar.
3. En la biblioteca no _____ en voz alta.
4. _____ los billetes de tren en la taquilla.
5. Durante la semana de exámenes finales _____ mucho.

V. *Repaso general.* Contesta con oraciones completas.

1. Cuando vas a una gasolinera, ¿qué haces primero? ¿Y después?
2. ¿Qué dices cuando estás en el centro de la ciudad de Nueva York y tu coche no funciona? (¡...!)
3. ¿Has hecho un viaje en tren o en autobús? (¿Cuándo?) (¿Adónde?)
4. ¿Te gusta la idea de viajar en tren o en autobús? ¿Por qué?
5. ¿Qué cosas se puede hacer durante un viaje en tren?
6. Cuando eras niño/a, ¿hacías viajes en carro con tu familia? (¿Adónde iban?)
7. Cuando eras más joven, ¿qué querías que tus padres/ maestros/ amigos hicieran para mejorar tu vida?

VI. *Cultura.*
1. ¿Qué características tiene el Lago de Nicaragua?
2. ¿Qué es el gallopinto?
3. ¿Cómo es la música garífuna?

Answers to the *Autoprueba y repaso* are found in **Apéndice 2.**

El mundo en las noticias

By the end of this chapter you will be able to:

- Talk about major issues in today's global society
- Talk about pending actions
- Talk about what might or would happen
- Hypothesize
- Express hopes and wishes

UNIDAD
53

UNIVISION
CHICAGO

Illinois
204243 D
Land of Lincoln

FRONTLINE

Así se dice	Así se forma	Cultura	Dicho y hecho
• El mundo en las noticias • Tus opiniones sobre los problemas mundiales	**1.** The subjunctive with time expressions **2.** The conditional tense **3.** *If* clauses **4.** The imperfect subjunctive with **ojalá**	• El español en los medios de comunicación en los Estados Unidos • El servicio voluntario y el activismo estudiantil • Artes periodísticas: Jorge Ramos	• ¡Manos a la obra! • Un noticiero • Una entrevista

ENTRANDO AL TEMA

1. ¿Cuáles crees que son las cinco cadenas de televisión más populares de los Estados Unidos?

2. ¿Cuáles son algunas historias comunes en las telenovelas (*soap operas*) en los Estados Unidos?

3. ¿Alguna vez has hecho un servicio voluntario?

El mund

Así se dice

El mundo en las noticias

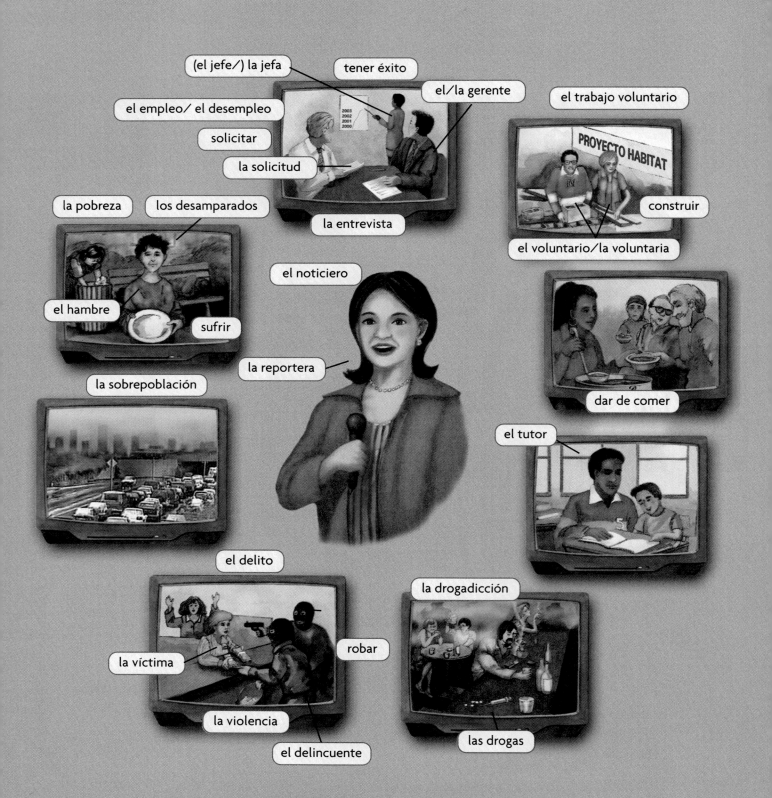

(el jefe/) la jefa

tener éxito

el/la gerente

el trabajo voluntario

el empleo/ el desempleo

solicitar

la solicitud

la entrevista

PROYECTO HABITAT

construir

el voluntario/la voluntaria

la pobreza

los desamparados

el noticiero

el hambre

sufrir

la sobrepoblación

la reportera

dar de comer

el tutor

el delito

la drogadicción

la víctima

robar

la violencia

las drogas

el delincuente

el acuerdo de paz	*peace treaty*	los derechos (humanos)	*(human) rights*	el hambre	*hunger*
apoyar	*to support*			el jefe/la jefa	*boss*
los/las ciudadanos/as	*citizens*	los desamparados	*the homeless*	la libertad	*freedom*
construir	*build*	la igualdad	*equality*	solicitar	*to apply (for a job)*
dar de comer	*feed*	la investigación	*research*		
el delincuente	*criminal*	el/la gerente	*manager*	la solicitud	*application*
el delito	*crime*	la guerra	*war*	tener éxito	*to be successful*

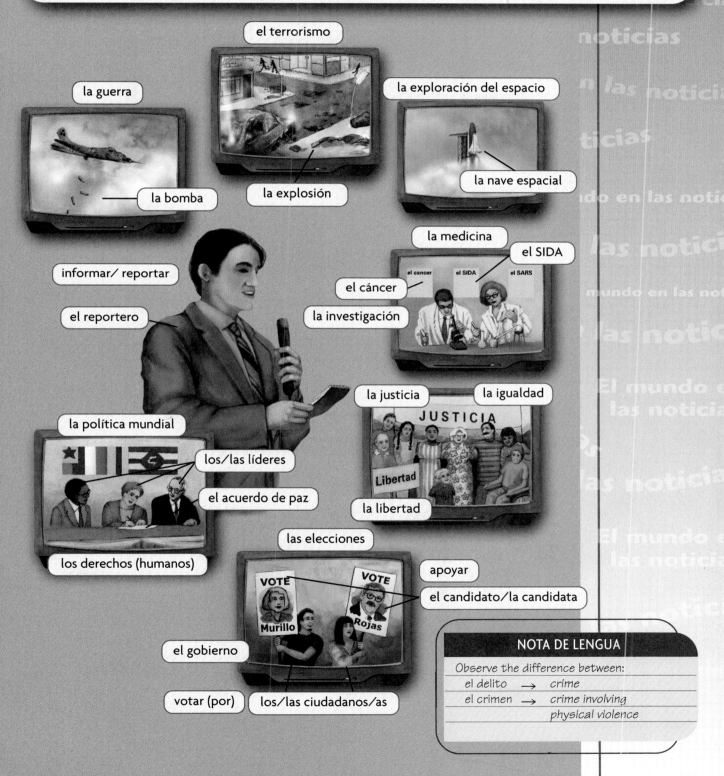

el terrorismo

la guerra

la exploración del espacio

la bomba

la explosión

la nave espacial

la medicina

el SIDA

informar/ reportar

el cáncer

la investigación

el reportero

la justicia

la igualdad

la política mundial

los/las líderes

el acuerdo de paz

la libertad

los derechos (humanos)

las elecciones

apoyar

el candidato/la candidata

el gobierno

votar (por)

los/las ciudadanos/as

NOTA DE LENGUA

Observe the difference between:

el delito	→	crime
el crimen	→	crime involving physical violence

Así se dice

15-1 ¿Persona, problema u objetivo?

Paso 1. Marca la columna apropiada para decidir si las siguientes palabras se refieren a una persona, a un problema o a un objetivo.

	Persona/s	Problema	Objetivo
el desempleo			
la guerra			
el delincuente			
la igualdad			
la drogadicción			
el líder			
la pobreza			
la libertad			
los ciudadanos			
la paz			

Paso 2. Escoge una de las palabras anteriores por su importancia, positiva o negativa, para ti. Explica brevemente (en dos o tres líneas) porque te parece algo o alguien importante.

15-2 ¿Cuáles son los problemas más graves de nuestra sociedad?

Paso 1. Haz una lista con los tres problemas más graves de nuestra sociedad, en orden de importancia.

1. _____
2. _____
3. _____

Paso 2. En grupos de tres o cuatro personas, comparen sus listas y expliquen los motivos de su elección. Decidan juntos una lista de cinco problemas graves y organícenlos por orden de importancia.

15-3 **Noticias actuales.** En parejas, escojan una de las pantallas de televisión de las páginas 508–509. Imaginen que Uds. son los reporteros; escriban la notica e inventen los detalles. Estén preparados para leer la noticia a la clase. Usen palabras del vocabulario.

Tus opiniones sobre los problemas mundiales

	Sí	No
¿Crees que es posible...		
• evitar las **guerras**/ mantener la **paz**?	☐	☐
• **eliminar** parte de la pobreza y el hambre del mundo?	☐	☐
• eliminar el **prejuicio** y la **discriminación**?	☐	☐
• prevenir el **narcotráfico** y la **drogadicción**?	☐	☐
• controlar la **sobrepoblación** del mundo?	☐	☐
¿**Estás a favor de** o **en contra de**...		
• el derecho a llevar **armas**?	☐	☐
• el derecho de la mujer a **escoger**[1] el **aborto**?	☐	☐
• la **pena de muerte**?	☐	☐
• **legalizar** la marihuana?	☐	☐
• darles amnistía a los inmigrantes indocumentados?	☐	☐
• expulsar a los que crucen la **frontera** ilegalmente?	☐	☐
¿Crees que debemos...		
• eliminar las **leyes** que **prohíben** el consumo de alcohol para	☐	☐
los menores de veintiún años?	☐	☐
• gastar más para la **exploración del espacio**?	☐	☐
... para ayudar a los **desamparados**?	☐	☐
... para encontrar curas para el **cáncer** y el **SIDA**?	☐	☐
... para educación?	☐	☐
... para **el ejército** y la defensa militar?	☐	☐
• **luchar por** los **derechos humanos** y la **libertad** de todos?	☐	☐

el arma	*weapon*	**el narcotráfico**	*drug trafficking*
escoger	*to choose*	**luchar por**	*to fight for*
el ejército	*army*	**la pena de muerte**	*death penalty*
la frontera	*border*	**prohibir**	*to forbid, prohibit*
la ley	*law*		

estar a favor de/ en contra de   *to be in favor of/against*

---

[1]**Escoger** changes the **g** to **j** to maintain the same pronunciation in the **yo** form of the present indicative (**escojo**) and in all forms of the present subjunctive (**escoja, escojas, escoja, escojamos, escojáis, escojan**).

15-4 **Organizaciones.** ¿Qué causas apoyan las siguientes organizaciones?

Paso 1. Combina la organización con la causa correspondiente.

Organización	Causa
__d__ **1.** Hábitat para la Humanidad	**a.** Lucha por los derechos humanos.
_____ **2.** Asociación Americana contra el Cáncer	**b.** Protege los mares, los animales en peligro de extinción, el medio ambiente, etc.
_____ **3.** Amnistía Internacional	**c.** Ayuda a los que sufren por catástrofes naturales, guerras, etc.
_____ **4.** PETA[2]	**d.** Construye[3] viviendas para los pobres y los desamparados.
_____ **5.** UNICEF[2]	**e.** Ayuda a los pobres y a los desamparados.
_____ **6.** Greenpeace[2]	**f.** Defiende los derechos de los animales.
_____ **7.** El Ejército de Salvación	**g.** Busca una cura para una enfermedad grave.
_____ **8.** La Cruz Roja	**h.** Defiende los derechos de los niños de todo el mundo.

Paso 2. ¿Hay alguna otra organización que te parece importante? ¿Por qué? ¿Eres miembro de esta organización? Compartan sus respuestas en grupos de cuatro o cinco personas.

15-5 **Así pensamos.** En grupos de cuatro, comparen sus respuestas a las preguntas del cuestionario sobre los problemas mundiales (en la página 511) y defiendan sus opiniones. Un/a secretario/a debe tomar apuntes. Algunos grupos van a presentar sus ideas a la clase.

Modelo: **Algunos/ La mayoría/ Todos estamos a favor de/ en contra de... porque...**

---

[2]The names of these organizations are not translated into Spanish, and their acronyms are read as words.
[3]The present indicative of **construir: construyo, construyes, construye, construimos, construís, construyen.**

15-6 **¿Qué le pasa al mundo?** En parejas, observen estas tiras cómicas de Mafalda, del humorista Quino (Argentina.) ¿Cómo las interpretan? ¿Les parecen efectivas?

Cultura: El español en los medios de comunicación en los Estados Unidos

Antes de leer

1. ¿Cuáles son las cinco cadenas de televisión más grandes de los Estados Unidos?
2. ¿Hay periódicos o emisoras de radio en español en el lugar donde vives? ¿Cómo se llaman?

En los Estados Unidos, los medios de comunicación en español se destacan por su aumento continuo e impresionante.

LA TELEVISIÓN

> **NOTA DE LENGUA**
>
> 1 billion (US Eng) = 1.000 millones (Sp.)
>
> 1 trillion (US Eng) = 1 billón (Sp.)

Las dos cadenas televisivas principales en español son Univisión y Telemundo. Univisión, la más grande de las dos, fue fundada en 1961 desde una emisora pequeña de San Antonio, Texas, y adquirió su forma actual cuando un grupo de inversores se la compró a Hallmark en 1992. El número de televidentes —unos 3 millones— hace a Univisión la quinta cadena más popular del país (después de Fox, ABC, NBC y CBS). Se transmite al 97% de las casas hispanas en el país.

En 2003, Univisión compró la gigante *Hispanic Broadcasting Corporation,* con sesenta y tres emisoras de radio, la mayoría en California, Texas y Florida. Esto ha convertido a Univisión en el gigante de los medios en español. En 2006 Univisión vendió por 12.3 mil millones de dólares a Broadcast Media Partners.

Telemundo empezó en 1986 cuando se unieron varias cadenas en Miami, Los Ángeles y Nueva York. Se vendió a Sony en 1998 y luego a NBC en 2002 por la suma impresionante de 1.98 mil millones de dólares dejando muy claro el valor y el potencial de la cadena. Una ventaja para los noticieros de Telemundo es que pueden hacer uso de las imágenes de satélite de NBC en sus programas.

Hay emisoras en español las 24 horas del día en las ciudades grandes pero también en sitios como Anchorage, Salt Lake City, Little Rock, Savannah y Oklahoma City.

LOS PERIÓDICOS

En 2001, la circulación de periódicos diarios en español era de 1,7 millones, más del triple que en 1990. A diferencia de las cadenas televisivas, los periódicos no se han consolidado en gran medida. Comenzaron como, y todavía son, productos comunitarios que sirven a los residentes locales.

LA CIRCULACIÓN DE VARIOS PERIÓDICOS EN ESPAÑOL (2006)

Título	Lugar	Circulación
La Opinión	Los Ángeles, CA	126.000
El Nuevo Herald	Miami, FL	86.000
El Diario/ La Prensa	Nueva York, NY	50.000
Hoy	Chicago, IL	40.000

Investig@ en INTERNET

Busca en Internet uno de los periódicos en español que se mencionan en el texto (o un periódico local en español) y toma notas sobre una notica interesante para compartir con la clase.

Los temas cubiertos por los medios en español, tanto por la televisión como en los periódicos, pueden variar sustancialmente de un lugar a otro, según el origen de los residentes locales. Por ejemplo, en Miami, donde hay una concentración fuerte de cubanos, las noticias suelen[1] cubrir temas caribeños. En Nueva York, con su muy diversa población hispana, las noticias son más cosmopolitas en general, pero con cierto enfoque en temas puertorriqueños y dominicanos. En el suroeste y en Los Ángeles, hay un interés particular en temas mexicanos.

Aún cuando un adulto aprenda un segundo idioma, hay cosas que prefiere hacer en su primer idioma, entre ellas recibir las noticias. Además, muchos reportajes de los medios en español cubren temas que los medios dominantes no tratan. Por ejemplo, si uno quiere saber sobre una huelga[2] de enfermeras en Honduras, un escándalo de corrupción en Perú o elecciones en Puerto Rico, sólo Univisión o Telemundo ofrece esta información.

[1]*tend to* [2]*strike*

LA PUBLICIDAD

En 2002, los ingresos[3] de la publicidad de los medios en español eran de 786 millones de dólares. El crecimiento[4] de la prensa hispana dio lugar a una consolidación nacional de recursos[5] publicitarios, llamado el *Latino Print Network,* que se dedica a vender anuncios a más de 200 publicaciones y 10 millones de suscriptores en más de 27 estados. También se ven mayores esfuerzos de parte de las empresas no hispanas por atraer a clientes hispanohablantes. Se estima que el poder adquisitivo del mercado hispano incrementará de 400 mil millones de dólares a un billón de dólares en el año 2010.

[3]*earnings* [4]*growth* [5]*resources*

Después de leer

1. ¿Por qué hay tanto interés en hacer publicidad dirigida a los hispanos en los Estados Unidos?
2. Busca un periódico en español en Internet y compara los reportajes con los de un periódico nacional en inglés. ¿Qué diferencias y similitudes hay?

Cuando termines la lección, podemos jugar al tenis.

1. The subjunctive with time expressions: Talking about pending actions

The subjunctive is used after the following conjunctions of time only when an action is pending, that is, when it has not yet occurred. In contrast, if the action is completed or habitual, the indicative is used.

cuando	*when*	hasta que	*until*
antes de que[4]	*before*	tan pronto como	*as soon as*
después de que	*after*		

action pending, yet to occur → subjunctive

Cuando llegue al orfanato, te llamaré.

When I arrive at the orphanage, I'll call you.

Compraré las medicinas **antes de que tú llegues.**

I will buy the medications before you arrive.

Los voluntarios saldrán **después de que terminen** el trabajo.

The volunteers will leave after they finish their work.

Me quedaré allí **hasta que el director me llame.**

I will stay there until the director calls me.

Tan pronto como reciba la llamada, recogeré a los niños.

As soon as I receive the call, I will pick up the children.

completed or habitual action → indicative

Mi amigo me llamó **cuando llegó** al orfanato.

My friend called me when he arrived at the orphanage. (completed)

No salí **hasta que paró** de llover.

I did not go out until it stopped raining. (completed)

Mi amigo siempre me llama **tan pronto como llega** a la ciudad.

My friend always calls me as soon as he arrives in town. (habitual)

When there is no change of subject, the conjunctions **antes de que, después de que**, and **hasta que** usually become **antes de** + *infinitive*, **después de** + *infinitive*, and **hasta** + *infinitive*.

---

[4]The conjunction **antes de que**, because it signals an action that has not yet occurred, is always followed by the subjunctive, even if the general event takes place in the past.

    Nos atacó antes de que lo viéramos. → the action of seeing is pending in relation to the moment when the attack took place.

(change of subject → subjunctive)	(no change of subject → infinitive)
Lo terminaremos **antes de que salgas.**	Lo terminaremos **antes de salir**.
Tomaremos la decisión **después de que hagas** la llamada.	Tomaremos la decisión **después de hacer** la llamada.
Nos quedaremos aquí **hasta que** lo **termines**.	Nos quedaremos aquí **hasta terminar**lo.

15-7 **Proyecciones hacia el futuro.** Indica las opciones que correspondan mejor a tus planes. También escribe una actividad nueva que no esté en la lista. Luego, lee tus respuestas a un/a compañero/a de clase. ¿Tienen mucho en común ustedes dos?

1. Antes de que **termine** este año escolar...
   ☐ hablaré con mis profesores de mis notas.
   ☐ estudiaré mucho y completaré mis trabajos escritos.
   ☐ saldré con todos mis amigos/as.
   ☐ iré a...
   ☐ ...

2. Después de que **termine** este año escolar...
   ☐ trabajaré.
   ☐ haré un viaje a...
   ☐ descansaré.
   ☐ volveré a casa.
   ☐ dejaré de fumar/ comer...
   ☐ me pondré a dieta.
   ☐ ...

3. Tan pronto como me **gradúe**...
   ☐buscaré empleo
   ☐haré estudios de posgrado.
   ☐me mudaré a...
   ☐ compraré un coche nuevo.
   ☐ ganaré mucho dinero.

4. En el futuro, ...
   ☐ viajaré a Europa/Sudamérica/...
   ☐ visitaré a todos mis parientes.
   ☐ seré voluntario/a.
   ☐ me casaré...
   ☐ ...

(15-8) ¿El pasado, el presente o el futuro de Univisión? Lee las oraciones sobre el canal de televisión estadounidense, Univisión. Elige la forma correcta del verbo —en el indicativo o en el subjuntivo— y <u>subráyalo</u>. Después, indica si la acción se refiere al pasado, al presente o al futuro.

Modelo: La cadena subió en popularidad cuando <u>contrataron</u>/ contraten a nuevos reporteros.

    ☒ pasado   ☐ presente   ☐ futuro

1. El canal adquirió el nombre "Univisión" cuando se venda / se vendió al grupo Hallmark.

    ☐ pasado   ☐ presente   ☐ futuro

2. El programa *Sábado Gigante* se hizo popular en los Estados Unidos cuando su anfitrión (*host*), Don Francisco, llegue / llegó a Miami.

    ☐ pasado   ☐ presente   ☐ futuro

3. Probablemente van a buscar a otra anfitriona para el *Show de Cristina* después de que Cristina Saralegui, la "Oprah del mundo hispano", se jubile / se jubila.

    ☐ pasado   ☐ presente   ☐ futuro

4. Univisión y Telemundo serán las cadenas en español más grandes hasta que lleguen / llegan cadenas competidoras.

    ☐ pasado   ☐ presente   ☐ futuro

5. Siempre comienza una nueva telenovela (*soap opera*) cuando otra termine / termina.

    ☐ pasado   ☐ presente   ☐ futuro

6. La cadena Univisión probablemente se va a vender otra vez cuando acaben / acaban las demandas (*lawsuits*) que existen contra la transacción.

    ☐ pasado   ☐ presente   ☐ futuro

Cristina Saralegui

Don Francisco

NOTA CULTURAL

Sábado Gigante

Sábado Gigante ("Giant Saturday") is the longest-running variety show in the history of television. It began in Chile in 1962 with its host Don Francisco, whose real name is Mario Kreutzberger. He wanted to create a mix of all the different shows he had seen in Argentina and the United States.

In 1986, Don Francisco and his show moved to Miami. Almost every Hispanic celebrity has appeared on *Sábado Gigante*. A new show has been recorded every single week—each one three hours long—without ever broadcasting a repeat. In 2001, Don Francisco was awarded a star on Hollywood's Walk of Fame, and Saturday, May 21, 2006 marked the 20th anniversary broadcast of *Sábado Gigante on* Univisión.

15-9 Mi futuro.

Paso 1. Usa las frases a continuación y un verbo en el subjuntivo para escribir oraciones sobre tu futuro.

Modelo: *Me graduaré de la universidad* tan pronto como *termine todas mis clases.*
Llevaré a mi mamá de vacaciones antes de que *se jubile.*

A	B
1. _____ ... hasta que...	_____ .
2. _____ ... después de que...	[otra persona] _____ .
3. _____ ... tan pronto como...	_____ .
4. _____ ... cuando...	_____ .
5. _____ ... antes de que...	[otra persona] _____ .

Paso 2. Lee tus frases de la columna A a un/a compañero/a. Vamos a ver si él/ella puede adivinar lo que escribiste en la columna B.

15-10 ¿Cuándo saldrán? Muy pronto, un grupo de amigos
universitarios se van de viaje en carro a hacer trabajo voluntario en Baja California. En parejas, indiquen cuándo saldrán. Sigan el modelo.

Modelo: Javier / llegar...
Saldrán tan pronto como Javier llegue a la universidad.

1. Javier / terminar el proyecto de...

3. Alfonso / devolver...

5. Esteban / reparar...

2. Rubén / llenar...

4. Carmen y Linda / comprar...

6. Pepita e Inés / hacer...

Escenas

Una entrevista

anchorwoman, host
Town Hall; mayor

Irene Piedras, reportera y presentadora° del noticiero "Verdad", está en el Ayuntamiento° de Buenavista para entrevistar a su alcalde° unos días antes de las elecciones.

Paso 1. Basándote en el título y la breve descripción de arriba, marca en las dos primeras columnas los temas que Irene Piedras probablemente mencione en la entrevista.

	es probable	no es probable	*Paso 2*
1. la delincuencia	_____	_____	_____
2. la guerra	_____	_____	_____
3. el cáncer y el SIDA	_____	_____	_____
4. el desempleo	_____	_____	_____
5. la corrupción	_____	_____	_____
6. la pobreza	_____	_____	_____
7. el terrorismo	_____	_____	_____
8. la drogadicción	_____	_____	_____

Paso 2. Escucha la conversación y marca en la última columna de arriba los temas que se mencionan.

Paso 3. Escucha la conversación otra vez y responde a las siguientes preguntas.

1. ¿Quiénes apoyan al alcalde en la lucha contra la drogadicción?
2. ¿Qué ha filmado el equipo del noticiero?
3. Según las estadísticas, ¿qué problemas tiene Buenavista respecto a...
   ... la delincuencia?
   ... la tasa° de desempleo?
   ... los desamparados?
   ... las empresas y compañías
4. ¿Qué responde el alcalde?
5. Finalmente, ¿qué les pide el alcalde a los ciudadanos de Buenavista?

rate

Paso 4. Escucha una vez más mientras lees el texto. Después, revisa tus respuestas.

Irene: Buenas tardes, Sr. Alcalde. Gracias por estar con nosotros hoy. Me gustaría que nos hablara de sus programas para luchar contra la drogadicción y el narcotráfico.

Alcalde: Con mucho gusto. Bajo mi dirección como alcalde, hemos desarrollado° un programa contra la delincuencia y ha aumentado

hemos... *we have developed*

el número de policías. Ahora espero el apoyo de los ciudadanos de Buenavista para librar° a nuestra bella ciudad de un problema tan grave.

to free

Irene: Sin embargo, Sr. Alcalde, ayer nuestro equipo filmó a traficantes de drogas frente al Ayuntamiento. ¿Qué tiene que decir al respecto°?

al... about the matter

Alcalde: Les aseguro° a los votantes que estamos trabajando en eso y cuando estos delincuentes sean detenidos, los llevaremos ante la justicia.

I assure

Irene: Bueno, pasando a otro tema. Según las estadísticas que tengo, la delincuencia ha aumentado en los últimos años, la tasa de desempleo ha subido, los desamparados sufren de hambre en nuestras calles y varias empresas y compañías han abandonado nuestra ciudad.

Alcalde: Pues sí, es cierto. Buenavista está pasando por un momento difícil, pero la situación era peor antes de que yo fuera alcalde.

Irene: ¿Hay algo más que quisiera decirles a los televidentes?

Alcalde: Que voten mañana por mí, ¡el mejor de todos los candidatos!

Irene: Bueno, ya lo oyeron de la boca del Sr. Alcalde. Gracias por sus palabras y ¡buena suerte!

Así se forma

Mi candidata dice que apoyaría la educación.

Mi candidato dice que protegería el medio ambiente.

2. The conditional tense: Talking about what would happen

The conditional tells what *would* potentially happen in certain circumstances. For example: I *would*[5] go to South America (*if I had the money*).

—¿**Solicitarías** empleo en esa compañía?
 ***Would* you *seek* a job with that company?**

—No, yo **buscaría** empleo en otra.
 *No, I **would look for** a job in another one.*

The conditional of all regular **-ar**, **-er**, and **-ir** verbs is formed by adding the following endings to the *entire infinitive*. Note that the conditional endings are identical to the imperfect tense endings of **-er** and **-ir** verbs.

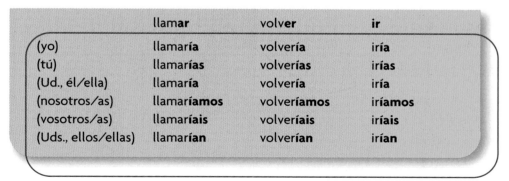

	llam**ar**	volv**er**	**ir**
(yo)	llamar**ía**	volver**ía**	ir**ía**
(tú)	llamar**ías**	volver**ías**	ir**ías**
(Ud., él/ella)	llamar**ía**	volver**ía**	ir**ía**
(nosotros/as)	llamar**íamos**	volver**íamos**	ir**íamos**
(vosotros/as)	llamar**íais**	volver**íais**	ir**íais**
(Uds., ellos/ellas)	llamar**ían**	volver**ían**	ir**ían**

---

[5]When *would* implies *used to* (*habitual past action*), the imperfect is used:
Every summer, I would go to South America. **Cada verano, iba a Sudamérica.**

- Verbs that have an irregular stem in the future tense form the conditional with that same irregular stem and regular conditional endings.

Infinitivo	Futuro	Formas del condicional
hacer	haré	haría, harías, haría, haríamos, haríais, harían
poder	podré	podría, podrías,...
poner	pondré	pondría, pondrías,...
querer	querré	querría, querrías,...
saber	sabré	sabría, sabrías,...
tener	tendré	tendría, tendrías,...
decir	diré	diría, dirías,...
salir	saldré	saldría, saldrías,...
venir	vendré	vendría, vendrías,...

—¿**Podrías** ayudarnos?　　***Would*** you **be able** to help us?
—Ella dijo que lo **haría**.　　*She said that she* ***would do*** *it.*

- The conditional of **hay** (*there is, there are*) is **habría** (*there would be*).

Dijo que no **habría** ningún problema.　　*He said that* ***there would be*** *no problem.*

(15-11) ¿Lo harías?

Paso 1. En grupos de tres personas, escriban sus nombres en la línea de arriba de la siguiente tabla. Después, háganse las preguntas y anoten las respuestas en las columnas.

	_____	_____	_____
1. ¿Votarías por una mujer para la presidencia del país? (¿Quién?)			
2. ¿Eliminarías la pena de muerte?			
3. ¿Apoyarías la prohibición de fumar en todos los espacios públicos (incluso bares)?			
4. ¿Cambiarías la edad legal para consumir bebidas alcohólicas? ¿Y para obtener una licencia de conducir? (¿Qué edad te parece apropiada?)			
5. ¿Apoyarías la explotación del petróleo en parques nacionales?			
6. ¿Trabajarías como voluntario/a en un pueblo remoto sin electricidad ni comodidades?			

	_____	_____	_____
7. ¿Adoptarías a un/a bebé de otro país?			
8. ¿Dedicarías el dinero de los programas de exploración espacial a otras cosas? ¿A qué?			
9. ¿Cambiarías las leyes sobre la investigación con células madre (*stem cells*)? ¿Cómo?			

 Paso 2. Compartan sus datos con la clase y calculen los porcentajes (*percentages*) de estudiantes a favor y en contra de cada pregunta.

 15-12 **Soluciones**. ¿Qué harían ustedes para empezar a resolver los problemas del mundo? En grupos de tres o cuatro personas, propongan una o dos soluciones para cada categoría usando el *condicional*. Un/a secretario/a escribe las ideas.

Categorías:

1. el desempleo
2. el hambre y la pobreza
3. el crimen
4. la drogadicción
5. las enfermedades graves
6. la discriminación

 15-13 **¿Qué tienen que decir sobre el récord?** Lee la información de acuerdo con el *Guinness Book of World Records* y contesta las preguntas. Después, comparte tus hipótesis con la clase.

1. Paul Crake de Australia subió los 1.576 escalones (*steps*) del edificio Empire State de Nueva York en 9 minutos y 33 segundos en 2003. ¿Cuántos escalones subirías en el mismo tiempo? Da tus razones.

2. Scott Day, de Londres, hizo girar (*spun*) una moneda durante 19,37 segundos en abril del 2004. ¿Cuánto tiempo podrías hacer girar tú una moneda de 25 centavos?

3. Hossein Rezazadeh de Irán levantó 212,5 kilos (468,5 libras) en los Juegos Olímpicos de Sydney el 26 de septiembre del año 2000. ¿Cuántos kilos/ libras levantarías? ¿Por qué crees eso?

4. Kimi Puntillo de los EE.UU. completó un maratón en cada uno de los siete continentes en 700 días, entre el 4 de noviembre de 1996 y el 4 de octubre de 1998. Comenzó en Nueva York y terminó en Argentina. ¿Participarías en un maratón? ¿Cuántas millas podrías correr? ¿Cuánto tiempo te tomaría?

5. El récord por comer más alacranes (*scorpions*) es del trabajador salvadoreño Rene Alvarenga "Comealacranes" que cada día caza y después come unos 20 a 30 y se calcula que ha comido unos 35.000 en su vida. Probablemente no te gusten mucho los alacranes... ¿con qué comida podrías tú obtener un récord?

6. Celia Porchas de Peña (México) tiene 5.533 tazas, que colecciona desde 1980. ¿Qué te gustaría coleccionar a ti?

7. ¿Qué podrías hacer para alcanzar un récord mundial? Sé creativo/a.

Cultura: El servicio voluntario y el activismo estudiantil

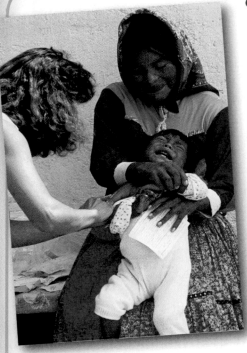

El voluntarismo en acción

Antes de leer

¿Haces algún servicio voluntario? ¿Cuál es?

En los países hispanos, los jóvenes forman organizaciones y participan activamente en ellas para servir al país en múltiples formas. Los universitarios, por ejemplo, encuentran en el trabajo voluntario y en el activismo oportunidades excelentes para educarse y contribuir al desarrollo[1] de la nación.

Algunos estudiantes voluntarios se dedican a la investigación y a la promoción del patrimonio cultural o al cuidado del medio ambiente. Otros se ocupan de gran parte de los programas de alfabetización en las zonas rurales. De igual importancia son los programas de salud y planificación familiar. Aunque los participantes son generalmente universitarios de las facultades de medicina o ciencias sociales, es común encontrar estudiantes de otras disciplinas y hasta[2] alumnos de escuelas secundarias.

La expresión política es también una parte de la vida estudiantil. Los universitarios tienden a defender ideas más izquierdistas que las de los gobiernos y a expresarlas públicamente en manifestaciones callejeras. Es frecuente ver grupos protestando contra el gobierno, la contaminación ambiental, las condiciones educativas en las universidades o el aumento del costo de la matrícula. Las huelgas[3] asociadas con estas protestas estudiantiles frecuentemente interrumpen las clases.

[1]development [2]even [3]strikes

Después de leer

¿Para qué causas es común que protesten los universitarios en Estados Unidos? ¿Y en Latinoamérica?

En las universidades de los Estados Unidos	En las universidades de Latinoamérica

Así se forma

> Si pudiera, eliminaría toda la pobreza del mundo.

3. *If* clauses: Hypothesizing

When the **si** (*if*) clause poses a situation that is <u>possible or likely to occur</u> (not obviously contrary-to-fact or hypothetical), the **si** clause is in the present indicative and the result is in the present indicative or future tense.

> **Possible situation:**
> **si** + *present indicative, (then) present/future*

> Si **tengo** tiempo, **voy/ iré**.   If I **have** time, I **go**/I'**ll go**.

When the **si** clause expresses a <u>hypothetical situation</u>, i.e., contrary-to-fact or very unlikely to occur, it is formed with the <u>past subjunctive</u>. The <u>conditional</u> is used to express the result, i.e., what *would occur* as a consequence.

> **Hypothetical situation:**
> **si** + *imperfect subjunctive, (then) conditional*

> Si **tuviera** el dinero, se lo **donaría**   If I **had** the money, I **would donate**
> a los pobres.   it to the poor.

Note that the clauses can appear in either order (hypothetical situation first or last).

> **Hablaría** con el presidente si él   I **would speak** with the president if
> **estuviera** aquí.   he **were** here.

NOTA DE LENGUA

Remember this about if clauses:

1. **Si** (*If*) clauses can be followed by present indicative or imperfect subjunctive, <u>never present subjunctive</u>.
2. Remember the connections: possible   → indicative – present
   hypothetical   → subjunctive – conditional
3. The **si** clause can be first or last. Use a comma only when the **si** clause is first.

15-14 **Emociones.** Empareja las situaciones y las consecuencias según tu opinión. Cuando termines, completa la situación que no tenga consecuencia.

1. Estaría muy triste si...
2. Estaría muy preocupado/a si...
3. Estaría sorprendido/a (*surprised*) si...
4. Estaría enojado/a si...
5. Estaría muy contento/a si...
6. Estaría muy nervioso/a si...
7. Estaría deprimido/a si...
8. Estaría más tranquilo/a si...
9. Tendría miedo si...

a. subiera la tasa de desempleo.
b. sacara A en todas mis clases.
c. no hubiera contaminación.
d. un/a amigo/a consumiera drogas.
e. fuera víctima de un robo.
f. los profesores no trataran a todos con igualdad.
g. escuchara una explosión.
h. el noticiero dijera que hay una cura para el cáncer.
i. ...

 15-15 **¿Qué harías?** En este capítulo hemos hablado de la actualidad en el mundo. Piensa ahora en tu universidad.

Paso 1. Completa las siguientes oraciones según tu opinión.

1. Si hubiera una manifestación contra/ a favor de _____, participaría en ella porque...
2. Si pudiera cambiar una cosa en el campus, cambiaría _____ porque...
3. Si pudiera añadir (*add*) un curso/ una especialización nueva, sería _____ porque...
4. Si se pudiera renovar o modernizar un espacio de la universidad, se debería renovar _____ porque...
5. Si la universidad ofreciera un nuevo servicio a los estudiantes, me gustaría tener...
6. Si pudiera pedirle una cosa al presidente de la Universidad, le diría/ pediría...

 Paso 2. Las elecciones para el comité de representantes estudiantiles están cerca, y tú y tus amigos/as forman un grupo para presentarse a las elecciones. En grupos de tres personas, comparen sus respuestas para el *Paso 1* y escojan cuatro o cinco problemas importantes que quieran resolver.

Modelo: **Queremos que no haya clases los viernes.**

 Paso 3. Escriban cinco oraciones explicando lo que harán si son elegidos.

Modelo: **Si nos eligen como representantes, pediremos que no haya clases los viernes.**

 15-16 **Aventuras por el mundo hispano.**

Paso 1. Completa las siguientes oraciones basándote en lo que has aprendido del mundo hispano.

1. Si pudiera visitar una ciudad hispana, visitaría _____.
2. Si quisiera visitar un espacio natural, iría a _____.
3. Si pudiera probar (*try*) una comida local, probaría _____.
4. Si pudiera visitar un edificio o museo, iría a _____.
5. Si pudiera conocer a un hispano famoso, me gustaría conocer a _____

   _____.

 Paso 2. Ahora, en grupos de cinco, cada estudiante hace un sondeo (*poll*) en el grupo sobre uno de los temas anteriores: ciudades, espacios naturales, etc. Anota las respuestas de tus compañeros/as.

Modelo: Si pudieras visitar una ciudad hispana, ¿cuál visitarías?
Si pudiera visitar una ciudad hispana, visitaría Buenos Aires.

 Paso 3. Formen nuevos grupos con estudiantes que tengan información sobre el mismo tema. Compartan sus datos para averiguar qué ciudades, espacios naturales, etc., son más populares. Informen a la clase.

NOTA CULTURAL

Las telenovelas hispanas

Telenovelas are mini-series on Latin-American and Brazilian television stations. There are numerous differences between *telenovelas* and U.S. soap operas. *Telenovelas*, or *novelas* for short, only last between eight and twelve months. They are also broadcast during prime time evening slots.

The plots of *novelas* are frequently one of four general types: a poor girl who falls in love with a rich man; the "epoch" *novela* of a given time period; teen *novelas* that represent the lives of young people; and the musical *novela* that follows aspiring musicians.

Latin-American *telenovelas* have fans all over the world. For example, the Colombian *novela* "Yo soy Betty la fea", which lasted two years from 2000 to 2001, was broadcast in at least 70 different countries and has been imitated in many places including Russia, India, Germany, Spain, and the United States.

La protagonista de la telenovela colombiana *Yo soy Betty la fea*

 15-17 La imaginación. Observa los dibujos e indica lo que harías en esas circunstancias. Intenta ser creativo/a.

Si / estar...

Modelo: Si estuviera en la selva, observaría la naturaleza, me escaparía de las serpientes, exploraría el río,...

Si / ser...

Si / vivir...

Si / ver un extraterrestre...

Si / ser invisible...

15-18 **Una cadena (*chain*) de posibilidades.** En grupos, escojan uno de los siguientes temas. En cinco minutos, escriban una cadena muy larga según el modelo. Después lean sus "creaciones" a la clase.

Modelo: Si tuviera mil dólares, **haría un viaje.**

Si hiciera un viaje, iría a México.

Si fuera a México, comería muchas tortillas.

Si comiera muchas tortillas,...

1. Si tuviera tiempo,...
2. Si tuviera novio/a,...
3. Si no estuviera aquí,...
4. Si pudiera conocer a un personaje de la historia,...
5. Si me quedara sólo un año de mi vida,...

15-19 **Una cápsula de tiempo.** Imaginen que se va a crear una cápsula de tiempo y pueden poner adentro diez objetos que representen nuestro mundo en el siglo XXI. En grupos de cuatro, decidan qué pondrían en la cápsula y por qué. Algunos grupos presentarán sus ideas a la clase.

15-20 **"Nuestros Pequeños Hermanos".** Lean sobre esta organización y luego completen las oraciones.

Elisabet, voluntaria del orfanato "NPH" en Honduras, es amiga de Nahum. ¿Participas tú en algún trabajo voluntario?

"Nuestros Pequeños Hermanos" es una organización que sirve a niños y jóvenes que viven en circunstancias difíciles en América Latina y el Caribe. Su misión es darles a los desamparados protección, comida, ropa, cuidados médicos y educación. Ofrece[6] a los huérfanos pobres una solución en un ambiente de familia y permite a las familias con gran número de hermanos permanecer juntos. Los voluntarios de NPH dan clases de inglés, ayudan a los niños con la tarea, les leen cuentos a los pequeños, juegan con los niños durante las horas de recreo, a veces ayudan a preparar la comida, y —lo más importante— les dan a los niños mucho cariño y amor. ¿Deseas ser voluntario/a? Busca más información: www.nphamigos.org.

1. Me parece muy bueno que... y que...
2. Es fenomenal que... y que...
3. Si fuera voluntario/a en NPH, (yo)...., ..., ...

---

[6]The present indicative **yo** form of **ofrecer** (*to offer*) is **ofrezco**; consequently the present subjunctive is **ofrezca, ofrezcas, ofrezca, ofrezcamos, ofrezcáis, ofrezcan.**

SITUACIONES

Durante tu primer día en el pueblecito donde vas a trabajar como voluntario/a, el líder del grupo te muestra la choza (*hut*) en la que vas a vivir, el retrete (*outhouse*),... Acostumbrado/a a todo confort moderno, estás a punto de abandonar el proyecto. Un/a compañero/a trata de convencerte de que te debes quedar.

Tú: **¡No hay ni baño!**
Compañero/a: **Sí, pero...**

4. The imperfect subjunctive with *ojalá*: Expressing hopes and wishes

In **Capítulo 11** you learned that **ojalá** or **ojalá que** is always followed by the subjunctive, since it expresses hope or desire.

¡Ojalá que pudiera viajar a la luna!

- **Ojalá** and **ojalá que** followed by the present subjunctive indicate that there is a possibility the situation will occur.

  Present subjunctive

  Ojalá (que) mi candidato **gane** la elección.

  I hope that my candidate wins the election.

- Followed by the imperfect subjunctive, they indicate that the situation is not likely to occur or is impossible.

  Imperfect subjunctive

  Ojalá (que) pudiéramos hacer el viaje a Washington.

  I wish (If only) we could take the trip to Washington (but we can't).

15-21 En un mundo ideal...

 Paso 1. Consideren los cinco problemas a continuación. ¿Qué cambios desean ustedes? Escriban sus deseos usando **Ojalá que** + *el presente del subjuntivo* cuando creen que es posible que ese deseo ocurra, y **Ojalá que** + *el pasado del subjuntivo* cuando opinan que el deseo es imposible.

El problema	*Posible*	*Improbable/Imposible*
El desempleo	Ojalá que haya menos desempleo.	Ojalá que todo el mundo tuviera un trabajo que pagara al menos $10 por hora.
La drogadicción		
La discriminación		
Las guerras		
La epidemia del SIDA		
La pobreza		

Paso 2. Ahora, compartan sus ideas con un/a compañero/a. ¿Qué ideas son más populares?

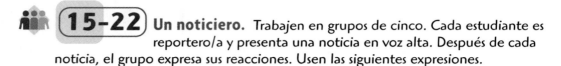

Así se forma

15-22 **Un noticiero.** Trabajen en grupos de cinco. Cada estudiante es reportero/a y presenta una noticia en voz alta. Después de cada noticia, el grupo expresa sus reacciones. Usen las siguientes expresiones.

> Ojalá que...   Una solución para el problema de... sería...
> Es muy bueno que...   Es trágico que... porque...

Mortalidad infantil y juvenil

Cuenca, Ecuador —La Organización Mundial de Salud (OMS) declara que seis enfermedades infecciosas (SIDA, tuberculosis, malaria, rubéola, diarrea e infecciones de las vías respiratorias) son responsables del 90% de las muertes de los niños del mundo. Más del 37% de las muertes infantiles ocurren durante los primeros veintiocho días de vida, en el período neonatal. La desnutrición es una causa subyacente en más de la mitad de las muertes antes de los cinco años.

Niños trabajadores

Ciudad de México, México —La Organización Internacional del Trabajo (OIT) estima en 218 millones el número de niños menores de dieciocho años que trabajan en el mundo. Esta cifra representa una disminución de un 11% respecto a las cifras del año 2000. Juan Somavia, Director General de la OIT, subrayó que "si bien la lucha contra el trabajo infantil sigue siendo un desafío de proporciones enormes, estamos en el camino correcto".

El calentamiento de la tierra

thawing
reached

greenhouse effect

Buenos Aires, Argentina —El derretimiento° del hielo y de los glaciares de Groenlandia y el polo ártico han alcanzado° niveles nunca vistos. Según los científicos, el hielo es mucho más delgado de lo habitual. Esto se debe al calentamiento provocado por las emisiones de dióxido de carbono que causa el efecto invernadero° en el planeta.

Poco a poco se va lejos

failure
cause, lead to

Buenos Aires, Argentina —El gobierno argentino ha modificado su plan de prevención contra el uso de las drogas. En las últimas décadas la lucha se basó fundamentalmente en explicar cuáles son los efectos que estas sustancias causan a quienes las consumen. Debido al fracaso° del método, se está usando un nuevo modelo. Ahora, la idea es atacar las razones socio-culturales, familiares o individuales que provocan° el uso de las drogas.

¡"No" al terrorismo!

headed

spreads

Bilbao, España —Más de 120.000 personas participaron en Bilbao de una manifestación encabezada° por personalidades del mundo político. El sentimiento general fue demostrar que estaban en contra del terrorismo y de la violencia que éste produce. Todos los presentes buscaban paz y querían decirle a ETA[7] que no quieren una organización que siembra° el terror y el sufrimiento en el pueblo.

---

[7]Euzkadi ta Azkatasuna—a militant terrorist organization that advocates the separation of the Basque region from the rest of Spain.

(15-23) Último ejercicio. Lean el epílogo y luego contesten las preguntas.

EPÍLOGO

Has llegado al final del libro. ¡Felicitaciones! Antes de la despedida, te ofrecemos a continuación el desenlace° de la historia.

outcome

El profesor **Marín-Vivar** y su colega, la profesora **Falcón**, están de regreso después de experiencias interesantes en Honduras y Guatemala.

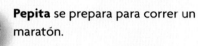

Camila sigue sus estudios de arte en Nueva York.

Pepita se prepara para correr un maratón.

Carmen descubrió que tiene parientes en Málaga y quiere viajar a España con sus hijas.

Alfonso se fue a Montreal a una escuela de arte culinario y va a combinar su gusto por la cocina con su interés en la informática.

Natalia volvió de Ecuador satisfecha de su labor como voluntaria y ahora está considerando servir en el Cuerpo de Paz.

Esteban conoció a una guatemalteca muy simpática y ahora se escriben mensajes electrónicos con frecuencia. Además le fascinó la cultura maya y ha decidido continuar sus estudios de posgrado en la ciudad de Guatemala.

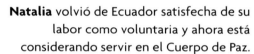

Javier sigue con el tenis y quiere hacer trabajo voluntario en un hospital.

Linda y **Manuel** encontraron trabajo y ya fijaron la fecha de la boda.

Inés sigue con sus conciertos de piano y piensa ir a Argentina a visitar a **Octavio**, que está en Mendoza trabajando con una compañía norteamericana.

¡Ah! Y por supuesto, **Rodolfo**, aunque ya ha usado varias de sus nueve vidas, sigue muy contento durmiendo junto a la chimenea con **Gitana** y sus tres gatitos.

1. ¿Cuáles son tus personajes favoritos y por qué? Inventa algunos detalles para agregarlos (*add them*) a sus vidas.
2. ¿Cuáles son tus planes profesionales para el futuro?

Dicho y hecho

¡A ESCUCHAR!

¡Manos a la obra (*Let's get to work*)! Escucha los siguientes anuncios de la estación de radio KZK 95FM que presenta oportunidades de trabajo voluntario en todas partes del mundo. Decide qué opción (A, B o C) corresponde mejor a cada uno de los tres estudiantes indicados.

Estudiantes:

____ 1. Elena, estudiante de biología, adora los animales y le encanta viajar.

____ 2. Jaime, estudiante de matemáticas, tiene siete hermanos menores, es muy extrovertido y practica varios deportes.

____ 3. María, estudiante de español, vivió en México por un año, le interesa la sociología y le gusta mucho conocer a personas de otros países.

Ahora, escucha los anuncios otra vez. Decide cuál de las tres opciones sería la mejor para ti y por qué.

Opciones:

____ **A.** El Paso (Centro de Auxilios Familiares)

____ **B.** Los Ángeles (Programa de Verano)

____ **C.** Galápagos (Centro Charles Darwin)

CONVERSANDO

Un noticiero. En grupos pequeños, preparen un noticiero para luego presentárselo a la clase. Primero, inventen un nombre original para el programa. Luego, cada uno/a de ustedes estará a cargo de una noticia. Pueden consultar el Internet en español para ayudarse con las noticias del país y del mundo.

DE MI ESCRITORIO

Una entrevista. Eres reportero/a y tu compañero/a es una persona famosa de la historia, de la literatura o del mundo de la política, la música, el cine, etc. Juntos, escriban una entrevista para luego presentársela a la clase. Incluyan cinco preguntas imaginativas y sus respuestas.

Artes periodísticas: Jorge Ramos

Antes de leer

Generalmente, ¿cuantos años, aproximadamente, tienen los presentadores de las noticias en las cadenas nacionales?

_____30 _____40 _____50

Jorge Ramos

Jorge Ramos es el periodista más visto de los medios hispanos en Estados Unidos. Estudió la carrera de comunicación en la Universidad Iberoamericana en la Cuidad de México. Inmigró a los Estados Unidos como estudiante en 1983 —su primer trabajo fue de mesero— e hizo sus estudios en la Universidad de California en Los Ángeles y más tarde obtuvo una maestría en relaciones internacionales en la Universidad de Miami.

Desde 1986, Ramos ha sido presentador en el programa *Noticiero Univisión*. De hecho, a la edad de veintiocho años, fue uno de los presentadores nacionales más jóvenes de la historia de la televisión estadounidense. En varios lugares, como Miami, Los Ángeles y Houston, el programa de Ramos y su co-presentadora, María Elena Salinas, consigue regularmente más televidentes[1] que sus competidores en cadenas[2] de lengua inglesa. Su noticiero se transmite en Estados Unidos y en trece países latinoamericanos.

[1]*viewers* [2]*networks*

Ramos ha cubierto cinco guerras —El Salvador, el Golfo Pérsico, Kosovo, Afganistán e Irak— numerosos eventos históricos como la caída del muro de Berlín, el fin del apartheid en Sudáfrica y la desintegración de la Unión Soviética. En total, ha ganado siete premios Emmy por su labor en *Noticiero Univisión*. Además de su noticiero televisivo, hace un programa diario por la radio en docenas de emisoras y escribe una columna semanal que se publica en más de cuarenta diarios del hemisferio.

Una parte del éxito de Ramos se debe a que es un entrevistador excelente. "La labor del periodista," dice Ramos, "es fiscalizar, monitorear a los poderosos y así evitar sus abusos." Varios personajes intelectuales le han admirado su periodismo, entre ellos:

"Jorge Ramos es en realidad un entrevistador implacable, un entrevistador incómodo, pero sobre todo, es un entrevistador valiente."
—*Guadalupe Loaeza, periodista mexicana*

"Creo que todos los latinoamericanos... lo apreciamos enormemente; por su puntualidad, su objetividad y el carácter cultural que da a su información."
—*Carlos Fuentes, escritor mexicano*

Ramos ha entrevistado a algunas de las figuras políticas y culturales más importantes de nuestros tiempo, como Fidel Castro de Cuba, los presidentes Clinton y Bush padre e hijo, la autora Isabel Allende y el presidente Hugo Chávez de Venezuela.

Ramos ha publicado seis libros, cuatro de los cuales se han traducido al inglés. En 2004, la *American Association of Publishers* le otorgó su Premio de Honor por la promoción de la lectura y los libros en Estados Unidos —el mismo premio que había ganado Oprah Winfrey el año anterior. También fue el primer hispano en ganar el premio David Brinkley a la excelencia periodística. En 2005, la revista *Time* calificó a Jorge Ramos como uno de los veinticinco hispanos más influyentes de Estados Unidos.

Después de leer

¿Cuáles de los premios siguientes ha ganado Jorge Ramos?

_____Emmy   _____Pulitzer

_____David Brinkley Award

_____American Association of Publishers Honor Award

Repaso de vocabulario activo

Conjunciones

antes de que   *before*
cuando   *when*
después de que   *after*
hasta que   *until*
tan pronto como   *as soon as*

Sustantivos

El empleo   *Job*

la entrevista   *interview*
el/la gerente   *(m./f.) manager*
el jefe/la jefa   *(m./f.) boss*
la solicitud   *application*

Las noticias   *News*

el noticiero   *news program*
el reportero/la reportera   *(m./f.) reporter*

La política y la sociedad   *Politics and society*

el acuerdo de paz   *peace agreement*
el candidato/la candidata   *(m./f.) candidate*
el ciudadano/la ciudadana   *(m./f.) citizen*
la cura   *cure*
los derechos (humanos)   *(human) rights*
el ejército   *army*
la elección   *election*
la exploración del espacio   *(outer) space exploration*
la frontera   *border*
el gobierno   *government*
la igualdad   *equality*
la investigación   *research*
la justicia   *justice*
la ley   *law*

la libertad   *freedom*
el/la líder   *leader*
la medicina   *medicine*
la nave espacial   *spaceship*
la paz   *peace*
la pena de muerte   *death penalty*
la política mundial   *world politics*
el trabajo voluntario   *volunteer work*
el tutor/la tutora   *tutor*
el voluntario/la voluntaria   *volunteer*

Los problemas humanos   *Human problems*

el aborto   *abortion*
el arma   *weapon*
la bomba   *bomb*
el cáncer   *cancer*
la corrupción   *corruption*
el delincuente   *delinquent, criminal*
el delito   *misdemeanor, crime*
los desamparados   *homeless people*
el desempleo   *unemployment*
la discriminación   *discrimination*
la droga   *drug*
la drogadicción   *drug addiction*
la explosión   *explosion*
la guerra   *war*
el hambre   *hunger*
el narcotráfico   *drug trafficking*
la pobreza   *poverty*
el prejuicio   *prejudice*
el SIDA   *AIDS*
la sobrepoblación   *overpopulation*
el terrorismo   *terrorism*
la víctima   *victim*
la violencia   *violence*

Verbos y expresiones verbales

apoyar   *to support*
construir   *to build*
eliminar   *to eliminate*
escoger   *to choose*
informar/ reportar   *to report*
legalizar   *to legalize*
luchar (por)   *to fight (for)*
prohibir   *to prohibit*
robar   *to rob, steal*
solicitar   *to apply*
sufrir   *to suffer*
votar (por)   *to vote (for)*

dar de comer   *to feed*
estar a favor/ en contra de   *to be for/against*
tener éxito   *to be successful*

Autoprueba y repaso WILEY PLUS ✓

I. The subjunctive with time expressions.
Completa las oraciones con la frase entre paréntesis. Usa el subjuntivo o el pretérito según la situación.

1. (yo / recibir el dinero)
   Te llamé tan pronto como...
   Te voy a llamar tan pronto como...

2. (tú / darme el número de teléfono del hotel)
   Haré las reservaciones cuando...
   Hice las reservaciones cuando...

3. (tú / llamarme)
   Fui a la agencia de viajes después de que...
   Iré a la agencia de viajes después de que...

4. (nosotros / regresar de la luna de miel)
   No anunciaré nuestro matrimonio hasta que...
   No anuncié nuestro matrimonio hasta que...

II. The conditional tense.
Di lo que harían las siguientes personas con un millón de dólares.

Modelo: Carlos / comprar una casa
   Carlos compraría una casa.

1. yo / viajar a muchos países
2. Pepe / poner el dinero en el banco
3. tú / darles dinero a los pobres
4. ustedes / gastar todo el dinero
5. nosotros / hacer un viaje a la Patagonia
6. mis amigas / ir a Chile a esquiar

III. If clauses.
Haz oraciones indicando la condición (**Si...**) y el resultado.

Modelo: encontrar un trabajo mejor / ganar más dinero
   Si encontrara un trabajo mejor, ganaría más dinero.

1. ganar más dinero / ahorrarlo
2. ahorrarlo / tener mucho dinero
3. tener mucho dinero / comprar un coche
4. comprar un coche / hacer un viaje
5. hacer un viaje / ir a Puerto Vallarta
6. ir a Puerto Vallarta / quedarme allí dos meses
7. quedarme allí dos meses / perder mi trabajo
8. perder mi trabajo / no tener dinero

IV. The imperfect subjunctive with *ojalá*.
Indica tus deseos en las siguientes situaciones. Sigue el modelo.

Modelo: Mi padre es muy conservador.
   Ojalá (que) mi padre no fuera tan conservador.

1. ¡El aire está tan contaminado!
2. Hay mucho desempleo en esta ciudad.
3. Muchas personas sufren del SIDA y del cáncer.
4. Tenemos muchos problemas que resolver.

V. *Repaso general.* Contesta con oraciones completas.

1. ¿Cuáles son algunos de los problemas más serios de nuestro país hoy en día?
2. Si pudieras cambiar una cosa de nuestro mundo, ¿qué cambiarías? ¿Por qué?
3. Cuando estabas en la escuela secundaria, ¿te preocupabas por algunos de los problemas del mundo? (¿Cuáles?) ¿Te preocupabas por otros problemas? (¿Cuáles?)
4. ¿Qué harás cuando te gradúes?

VI. *Cultura.*

1. ¿Cómo se llaman las dos emisoras televisivas en español más grandes de los Estados Unidos?
2. ¿Cuáles son las diferencias entre las telenovelas típicas en español y las *soap operas* en inglés?
3. ¿Quiénes son Cristina Saralegui, Jorge Ramos y Don Francisco?
4. Nombra dos actividades voluntarias que son comunes entre los jóvenes de Latinoamérica.

Answers to the *Autoprueba y repaso* are found in **Apéndice 2.**

Apéndice 1: *Verbos*

Regular Verbs: *Simple Tenses*

Infinitive Present Participle Past Participle	Indicative						Subjunctive		Imperative (commands)
	Present	Imperfect	Preterit	Future	Conditional		Present	Imperfect	
hablar *to speak* hablando hablado	hablo hablas habla hablamos habláis hablan	hablaba hablabas hablaba hablábamos hablabais hablaban	hablé hablaste habló hablamos hablasteis hablaron	hablaré hablarás hablará hablaremos hablaréis hablarán	hablaría hablarías hablaría hablaríamos hablaríais hablarían		hable hables hable hablemos habléis hablen	hablara hablaras hablara habláramos hablarais hablaran	habla/ no hables hable hablemos hablad/ no habléis hablen
comer *to eat* comiendo comido	como comes come comemos coméis comen	comía comías comía comíamos comíais comían	comí comiste comió comimos comisteis comieron	comeré comerás comerá comeremos comeréis comerán	comería comerías comería comeríamos comeríais comerían		coma comas coma comamos comáis coman	comiera comieras comiera comiéramos comierais comieran	come/ no comas coma comamos comed/ no comáis coman
vivir *to live* viviendo vivido	vivo vives vive vivimos vivís viven	vivía vivías vivía vivíamos vivíais vivían	viví viviste vivió vivimos vivisteis vivieron	viviré vivirás vivirá viviremos viviréis vivirán	viviría vivirías viviría viviríamos viviríais vivirían		viva vivas viva vivamos viváis vivan	viviera vivieras viva viviéramos vivierais vivieran	vive/ no vivas viva vivamos vivid/ no viváis vivan

Regular Verbs: Perfect Tenses

Indicative								Subjunctive			
Present Perfect		Past Perfect		Future Perfect		Conditional Perfect		Present Perfect		Past Perfect	
he has ha hemos habéis han	hablado comido vivido	había habías había habíamos habíais habían	hablado comido vivido	habré habrás habrá habremos habréis habrán	hablado comido vivido	habría habrías habría habríamos habríais habrían	hablado comido vivido	haya hayas haya hayamos hayáis hayan	hablado comido vivido	hubiera hubieras hubiera hubiéramos hubierais hubieran	hablado comido vivido

Stem-changing -ar and -er Verbs: e → ie; o → ue

Infinitive Present Participle Past Participle	Indicative					Subjunctive		Imperative (commands)
	Present	Imperfect	Preterit	Future	Conditional	Present	Imperfect	
pensar (ie) *to think* pensando pensado	**pienso** **piensas** **piensa** pensamos pensáis **piensan**	pensaba pensabas pensaba pensábamos pensabais pensaban	pensé pensaste pensó pensamos pensasteis pensaron	pensaré pensarás pensará pensaremos pensaréis pensarán	pensaría pensarías pensaría pensaríamos pensaríais pensarían	**piense** **pienses** **piense** pensemos penséis **piensen**	pensara pensaras pensara pensáramos pensarais pensaran	piensa/ no pienses piense pensemos pensad/ no penséis piensen
volver (ue) *to return* volviendo vuelto (irrreg.)	**vuelvo** **vuelves** **vuelve** volvemos volvéis **vuelven**	volvía volvías volvía volvíamos volvíais volvían	volví volviste volvió volvimos volvisteis volvieron	volveré volverás volverá volveremos volveréis volverán	volvería volverías volvería volveríamos volveríais volverían	**vuelva** **vuelvas** **vuelva** volvamos volváis **vuelvan**	volviera volvieras volviera volviéramos volvierais volvieran	vuelve/ no vuelvas vuelva volvamos volved/ no volváis vuelvan

Other verbs of this type are:

e → ie: cerrar, despertarse, empezar, entender, nevar, pensar, perder, preferir, querer, recomendar, regar, sentarse

o → ue: acordarse de, acostarse, almorzar, costar, encontrar, jugar, mostrar, poder, recordar, resolver, sonar, volar, volver

Stem-changing -ir Verbs: e → ie, i; e → i, i; e → ue, u

Infinitive Present Participle Past Participle	Indicative					Subjunctive		Imperative (commands)
	Present	Imperfect	Preterit	Future	Conditional	Present	Imperfect	
sentir (ie, i) *to feel, to regret* **sintiendo** sentido	**siento** **sientes** **siente** sentimos sentís **sienten**	sentía sentías sentía sentíamos sentíais sentían	sentí sentiste **sintió** sentimos sentisteis **sintieron**	sentiré sentirás sentirá sentiremos sentiréis sentirán	sentiría sentirías sentiría sentiríamos sentiríais sentirían	**sienta** **sientas** **sienta** **sintamos** **sintáis** **sientan**	**sintiera** **sintieras** **sintiera** **sintiéramos** **sintierais** **sintieran**	**siente**/ no **sientas** **sienta** **sintamos** sentid/ no **sintáis** **sientan**
pedir (i, i) *to ask (for)* **pidiendo** pedido	**pido** **pides** **pide** pedimos pedís **piden**	pedía pedías pedía pedíamos pedíais pedían	pedí pediste **pidió** pedimos pedisteis **pidieron**	pediré pedirás pedirá pediremos pediréis pedirán	pediría pedirías pediría pediríamos pediríais pedirían	**pida** **pidas** **pida** **pidamos** **pidáis** **pidan**	**pidiera** **pidieras** **pidiera** **pidiéramos** **pidierais** **pidieran**	**pide**/ no **pidas** **pida** **pidamos** pedid/ no **pidáis** **pidan**

Stem-changing -ir Verbs: e → ie, i; e → i, i; e → ue, u *(continued)*

Infinitive / Present Participle / Past Participle	Indicative					Subjunctive		Imperative (commands)
	Present	**Imperfect**	**Preterit**	**Future**	**Conditional**	**Present**	**Imperfect**	
dormir (ue, u) *to sleep* **durmiendo** dormido	**duermo** **duermes** **duerme** dormimos dormís **duermen**	dormía dormías dormía dormíamos dormíais dormían	dormí dormiste **durmió** dormimos dormisteis **durmieron**	dormiré dormirás dormirá dormiremos dormiréis dormirán	dormiría dormirías dormiría dormiríamos dormiríais dormirían	**duerma** **duermas** **duerma** **durmamos** **durmáis** **duerman**	**durmiera** **durmieras** **durmiera** **durmiéramos** **durmierais** **durmieran**	**duerme**/ no **duermas** **duerma** **durmamos** dormid/ no **durmáis** **duerman**

Other verbs of this type are:
e → ie, i: divertirse, invertir, preferir, sentirse, sugerir
e → i, i: conseguir, despedirse de, reírse, repetir, seguir, servir, vestirse
o → ue, u: morir(se)

Verbs with Spelling Changes

1. c → qu: tocar (model); buscar, explicar, pescar, sacar

Infinitive / Present Participle / Past Participle	Indicative					Subjunctive		Imperative (commands)
	Present	**Imperfect**	**Preterit**	**Future**	**Conditional**	**Present**	**Imperfect**	
tocar *to play (musical instr.), to touch* tocando tocado	toco tocas toca tocamos tocáis tocan	tocaba tocabas tocaba tocábamos tocabais tocaban	**toqué** tocaste tocó tocamos tocasteis tocaron	tocaré tocarás tocará tocaremos tocaréis tocarán	tocaría tocarías tocaría tocaríamos tocaríais tocarían	**toque** **toques** **toque** **toquemos** **toquéis** **toquen**	tocara tocaras tocara tocáramos tocarais tocaran	toca/ no **toques** **toque** **toquemos** tocad/ no **toquéis** **toquen**

2. z → c: abrazar; Also almorzar, cruzar, empezar (ie)

Infinitive / Present Participle / Past Participle	Indicative					Subjunctive		Imperative (commands)
	Present	**Imperfect**	**Preterit**	**Future**	**Conditional**	**Present**	**Imperfect**	
abrazar *to hug* abrazando abrazado	abrazo abrazas abraza abrazamos abrazáis abrazan	abrazaba abrazabas abrazaba abrazábamos abrazabais abrazaban	**abracé** abrazaste abrazó abrazamos abrazasteis abrazaron	abrazaré abrazarás abrazará abrazaremos abrazaréis abrazarán	abrazaría abrazarías abrazaría abrazaríamos abrazaríais abrazarían	**abrace** **abraces** **abrace** **abracemos** **abracéis** **abracen**	abrazara abrazaras abrazara abrazáramos abrazarais abrazaran	abraza/ no **abraces** **abrace** **abracemos** abrazad/ no **abracéis** **abracen**

3. g → gu: pagar; Also apagar, jugar (ue), llegar

	Present	Imperfect	Preterite	Future	Conditional	Present Subjunctive	Imperfect Subjunctive	Commands
pagar *to pay (for)*	pago	pagaba	pagué	pagaré	pagaría	**pague**	pagara	
pagando	pagas	pagabas	pagaste	pagarás	pagarías	**pagues**	pagaras	paga/ no **pagues**
pagado	paga	pagaba	pagó	pagará	pagaría	**pague**	pagara	**pague**
	pagamos	pagábamos	pagamos	pagaremos	pagaríamos	**paguemos**	pagáramos	**paguemos**
	pagáis	pagabais	pagasteis	pagaréis	pagaríais	**paguéis**	pagarais	pagad/ no **paguéis**
	pagan	pagaban	pagaron	pagarán	pagarían	**paguen**	pagaran	**paguen**

4. gu → g: seguir (i, i); Also conseguir

	Present	Imperfect	Preterite	Future	Conditional	Present Subjunctive	Imperfect Subjunctive	Commands
seguir (i, i) *to follow*	**sigo**	seguía	seguí	seguiré	seguiría	**siga**	siguiera	
siguiendo	sigues	seguías	seguiste	seguirás	seguirías	**sigas**	siguieras	sigue/ no **sigas**
seguido	sigue	seguía	siguió	seguirá	seguiría	**siga**	siguiera	**siga**
	seguimos	seguíamos	seguimos	seguiremos	seguiríamos	**sigamos**	siguiéramos	**sigamos**
	seguís	seguíais	seguisteis	seguiréis	seguiríais	**sigáis**	siguierais	seguid/ no **sigáis**
	siguen	seguían	siguieron	seguirán	seguirían	**sigan**	siguieran	**sigan**

5. g → j: recoger; Also escoger, proteger

	Present	Imperfect	Preterite	Future	Conditional	Present Subjunctive	Imperfect Subjunctive	Commands
recoger *to pick up*	**recojo**	recogía	recogí	recogeré	recogería	**recoja**	recogiera	
recogiendo	recoges	recogías	recogiste	recogerás	recogerías	**recojas**	recogieras	recoge/ no **recojas**
recogido	recoge	recogía	recogió	recogerá	recogería	**recoja**	recogiera	**recoja**
	recogemos	recogíamos	recogimos	recogeremos	recogeríamos	**recojamos**	recogiéramos	**recojamos**
	recogéis	recogíais	recogisteis	recogeréis	recogeríais	**recojáis**	recogierais	recoged/ no **recojáis**
	recogen	recogían	recogieron	recogerán	recogerían	**recojan**	recogieran	**recojan**

6. i → y: leer; Also caer, oír. Verbs with additional i → y changes (see below): construir; Also destruir

	Present	Imperfect	Preterite	Future	Conditional	Present Subjunctive	Imperfect Subjunctive	Commands
leer *to read*	leo	leía	leí	leeré	leería	lea	**leyera**	
leyendo	lees	leías	leíste	leerás	leerías	leas	**leyeras**	lee/ no leas
leído	lee	leía	**leyó**	leerá	leería	lea	**leyera**	lea
	leemos	leíamos	leímos	leeremos	leeríamos	leamos	**leyéramos**	leamos
	leéis	leíais	leísteis	leeréis	leeríais	leáis	**leyerais**	leed/ no leáis
	leen	leían	**leyeron**	leerán	leerían	lean	**leyeran**	lean
construir *to construct, to build*	**construyo**	construía	construí	construiré	construiría	**construya**	**construyera**	
construyendo	**construyes**	construías	construiste	construirás	construirías	**construyas**	**construyeras**	**construye**/ no **construyas**
construido	**construye**	construía	**construyó**	construirá	construiría	**construya**	**construyera**	**construya**
	construimos	construíamos	construimos	construiremos	construiríamos	**construyamos**	**construyéramos**	**construyamos**
	construís	construíais	construisteis	construiréis	construiríais	**construyáis**	**construyerais**	construid/ no **construyáis**
	construyen	construían	**construyeron**	construirán	construirían	**construyan**	**construyeran**	**construya**

Irregular Verbs

Infinitive Present Participle Past Participle	Indicative						Subjunctive		Imperative (commands)
	Present	Imperfect	Preterit	Future	Conditional		Present	Imperfect	
caer *to fall* **cayendo** caído	**caigo** caes cae caemos caéis caen	caía caías caía caíamos caíais caían	caí caíste **cayó** caímos caísteis **cayeron**	caeré caerás caerá caeremos caeréis caerán	caería caerías caería caeríamos caeríais caerían		caiga caigas caiga caigamos caigáis caigan	cayera cayeras cayera cayéramos cayerais cayeran	cae/ no caigas caiga caigamos caed/ no caigáis caigan
conocer *to know, to be acquainted with* conociendo conocido	conozco conoces conoce conocemos conocéis conocen	conocía conocías conocía conocíamos conocíais conocían	conocí conociste conoció conocimos conocisteis conocieron	conoceré conocerás conocerá conoceremos conoceréis conocerán	conocería conocerías conocería conoceríamos conoceríais conocerían		conozca conozcas conozca conozcamos conozcáis conozcan	conociera conocieras conociera conociéramos conocierais conocieran	conoce/ no conozcas conozca conozcamos conoced/ no conozcáis conozcan
conducir *to drive* conduciendo conducido	**conduzco** conduces conduce conducimos conducís conducen	conducía conducías conducía conducíamos conducíais conducían	**conduje** **condujiste** **condujo** **condujimos** **condujisteis** **condujeron**	conduciré conducirás conducirá conduciremos conduciréis conducirán	conduciría conducirías conduciría conduciríamos conduciríais conducirían		conduzca conduzcas conduzca conduzcamos conduzcáis conduzcan	condujera condujeras condujera condujéramos condujerais condujeran	conduce/ no conduzcas conduzca conduzcamos conducid/ no conduzcáis conduzcan
dar *to give* dando dado	**doy** das da damos dais dan	daba dabas daba dábamos dabais daban	**di** **diste** **dio** **dimos** **disteis** dieron	daré darás dará daremos daréis darán	daría darías daría daríamos daríais darían		**dé** **des** **dé** **demos** **deis** **den**	diera dieras diera diéramos dierais dieran	da/ no des dé demos dad/ no déis den
decir *to say, to tell* **diciendo** **dicho**	**digo** **dices** **dice** decimos decís **dicen**	decía decías decía decíamos decíais decían	**dije** **dijiste** **dijo** **dijimos** **dijisteis** **dijeron**	**diré** **dirás** **dirá** **diremos** **diréis** **dirán**	**diría** **dirías** **diría** **diríamos** **diríais** **dirían**		diga digas diga digamos digáis digan	dijera dijeras dijera dijéramos dijerais dijeran	di/ no digas diga digamos decid/ no digáis digan

Infinitivo / Gerundio / Participio	Presente	Imperfecto	Pretérito	Futuro	Condicional	Presente de subjuntivo	Imperfecto de subjuntivo	Mandatos
estar *to be* estando estado	estoy estás está estamos estáis están	estaba estabas estaba estábamos estabais estaban	estuve estuviste estuvo estuvimos estuvisteis estuvieron	estaré estarás estará estaremos estaréis estarán	estaría estarías estaría estaríamos estaríais estarían	esté estés esté estemos estéis estén	estuviera estuvieras estuviera estuviéramos estuvierais estuvieran	estés/ no estés esté estemos estad/ no estéis estén
haber *to have* habiendo habido	he has ha hemos habéis han	había habías había habíamos habíais habían	hube hubiste hubo hubimos hubisteis hubieron	habré habrás habrá habremos habréis habrán	habría habrías habría habríamos habríais habrían	haya hayas haya hayamos hayáis hayan	hubiera hubieras hubiera hubiéramos hubierais hubieran	
hacer *to do, to make* haciendo **hecho**	hago haces hace hacemos hacéis hacen	hacía hacías hacía hacíamos hacíais hacían	hice hiciste hizo hicimos hicisteis hicieron	haré harás hará haremos haréis harán	haría harías haría haríamos haríais harían	haga hagas haga hagamos hagáis hagan	hiciera hicieras hiciera hiciéramos hicierais hicieran	**haz**/ no hagas haga hagamos haced/ no hagáis hagan
ir *to go* **yendo** ido	voy vas va vamos vais van	iba ibas iba íbamos ibais iban	fui fuiste fue fuimos fuisteis fueron	iré irás irá iremos iréis irán	iría irías iría iríamos iríais irían	vaya vayas vaya vayamos vayáis vayan	fuera fueras fuera fuéramos fuerais fueran	**ve**/ no vayas vaya vayamos id/ no vayáis vayan
oír *to hear* **oyendo** **oído**	oigo oyes oye oímos oís oyen	oía oías oía oíamos oíais oían	oí oíste oyó oímos oísteis oyeron	oiré oirás oirá oiremos oiréis oirán	oiría oirías oiría oiríamos oiríais oirían	oiga oigas oiga oigamos oigáis oigan	oyera oyeras oyera oyéramos oyerais oyeran	oye/ no oigas oiga oigamos oíd/ no oigáis oigan

Infinitive Present Participle Past Participle	Indicative					Subjunctive		Imperative (commands)
	Present	Imperfect	Preterit	Future	Conditional	Present	Imperfect	
poder (ue) *to be able, can* podiendo podido	**puedo** **puedes** **puede** podemos podéis **pueden**	podía podías podía podíamos podíais podían	**pude** **pudiste** **pudo** pudimos pudisteis **pudieron**	**podré** **podrás** **podrá** **podremos** **podréis** **podrán**	**podría** **podrías** **podría** **podríamos** **podríais** **podrían**	pueda puedas pueda podamos podáis puedan	pudiera pudieras pudiera pudiéramos pudierais pudieran	
poner *to put, to place* poniendo **puesto**	**pongo** pones pone ponemos ponéis ponen	ponía ponías ponía poníamos poníais ponían	**puse** **pusiste** **puso** pusimos pusisteis **pusieron**	**pondré** **pondrás** **pondrá** **pondremos** **pondréis** **pondrán**	**pondría** **pondrías** **pondría** **pondríamos** **pondríais** **pondrían**	ponga pongas ponga pongamos pongáis pongan	pusiera pusieras pusiera pusiéramos pusierais pusieran	**pon**/ no pongas ponga pongamos poned/ no pongáis pongan
querer (ie) *to wish, to want, to love* queriendo querido	**quiero** **quieres** **quiere** queremos queréis **quieren**	quería querías quería queríamos queríais querían	**quise** **quisiste** **quiso** quisimos quisisteis **quisieron**	**querré** **querrás** **querrá** **querremos** **querréis** **querrán**	**querría** **querrías** **querría** **querríamos** **querríais** **querrían**	quiera quieras quiera queramos queráis quieran	quisiera quisieras quisiera quisiéramos quisierais quisieran	quiere/ no quieras quiera queramos quered/ no queráis quieran
saber *to know* sabiendo sabido	**sé** sabes sabe sabemos sabéis saben	sabía sabías sabía sabíamos sabíais sabían	**supe** **supiste** **supo** **supimos** **supisteis** **supieron**	**sabré** **sabrás** **sabrá** **sabremos** **sabréis** **sabrán**	**sabría** **sabrías** **sabría** **sabríamos** **sabríais** **sabrían**	**sepa** **sepas** **sepa** **sepamos** **sepáis** **sepan**	supiera supieras supiera supiéramos supierais supieran	sabe/ no sepas sepa sepamos sabed/ no sepáis sepan
salir *to leave, to go out* saliendo salido	**salgo** sales sale salimos salís salen	salía salías salía salíamos salíais salían	salí saliste salió salimos salisteis salieron	**saldré** **saldrás** **saldrá** **saldremos** **saldréis** **saldrán**	**saldría** **saldrías** **saldría** **saldríamos** **saldríais** **saldrían**	salga salgas salga salgamos salgáis salgan	saliera salieras saliera saliéramos salierais salieran	sal/ no salgas salga salgamos salid/ no salgáis salgan

Infinitivo	Presente	Imperfecto	Pretérito	Futuro	Condicional	Presente subjuntivo	Imperfecto subjuntivo	Mandatos
ser *to be* / siendo / sido	soy / eres / es / somos / sois / son	era / eras / era / éramos / erais / eran	fui / fuiste / fue / fuimos / fuisteis / fueron	seré / serás / será / seremos / seréis / serán	sería / serías / sería / seríamos / seríais / serían	sea / seas / sea / seamos / seáis / sean	fuera / fueras / fuera / fuéramos / fuerais / fueran	sé/ no seas / sea / seamos / sed/ no seáis / sean
tener *to have* / teniendo / tenido	tengo / tienes / tiene / tenemos / tenéis / tienen	tenía / tenías / tenía / teníamos / teníais / tenían	tuve / tuviste / tuvo / tuvimos / tuvisteis / tuvieron	tendré / tendrás / tendrá / tendremos / tendréis / tendrán	tendría / tendrías / tendría / tendríamos / tendríais / tendrían	tenga / tengas / tenga / tengamos / tengáis / tengan	tuviera / tuvieras / tuviera / tuviéramos / tuvierais / tuvieran	ten/ no tengas / tenga / tengamos / tened/ no tengáis / tengan
traer *to bring* / trayendo / traído	traigo / traes / trae / traemos / traéis / traen	traía / traías / traía / traíamos / traíais / traían	traje / trajiste / trajo / trajimos / trajisteis / trajeron	traeré / traerás / traerá / traeremos / traeréis / traerán	traería / traerías / traería / traeríamos / traeríais / traerían	traiga / traigas / traiga / traigamos / traigáis / traigan	trajera / trajeras / trajera / trajéramos / trajerais / trajeran	trae/ no traigas / traiga / traigamos / traed/ no traigáis / traigan
venir *to come* / viniendo / venido (also **prevenir**)	vengo / vienes / viene / venimos / venís / vienen	venía / venías / venía / veníamos / veníais / venían	vine / viniste / vino / vinimos / vinisteis / vinieron	vendré / vendrás / vendrá / vendremos / vendréis / vendrán	vendría / vendrías / vendría / vendríamos / vendríais / vendrían	venga / vengas / venga / vengamos / vengáis / vengan	viniera / vinieras / viniera / viniéramos / vinierais / vinieran	ven/ no vengas / venga / vengamos / venid/ no vengáis / vengan
ver *to see* / viendo / visto	veo / ves / ve / vemos / veis / ven	veía / veías / veía / veíamos / veíais / veían	vi / viste / vio / vimos / visteis / vieron	veré / verás / verá / veremos / veréis / verán	vería / verías / vería / veríamos / veríais / verían	vea / veas / vea / veamos / veáis / vean	viera / vieras / viera / viéramos / vierais / vieran	ve / no veas / vea / veamos / ved/ no veáis / vean

Capítulo 1

I.
1. PEPITA: (Muy) Bien, gracias.
PROFESORA:(Muy) Bien, gracias.
2. PROFESORA:¿Cómo te llamas?
3. CARMEN: ¿Cómo estás? (¿Qué tal?)
CARMEN: Muy bien, gracias. (Regular.)
4. PROFESORA:Mucho gusto. (Encantada.)
CARMEN: El gusto es mío. (Igualmente.)
5. MANUEL: Me llamo Manuel.
PEPITA: Me llamo Pepita.
PEPITA: Igualmente.
6. CARMEN: ¿Qué hora es?
PEPITA: Hasta luego. (Hasta pronto. Chao. Adiós.)

II.
1. Ellos son de Chile pero nosotras somos de México.
2. Tú eres de Colombia pero ustedes son de España.
3. Luis es de El Salvador pero Juan y Elena son de Honduras.

III.
1. (Los jeans cuestan) treinta y cinco dólares.
2. (El suéter cuesta) cincuenta y siete dólares.
3. (La chaqueta cuesta) setenta y dos dólares.
4. (El sombrero cuesta) veintiséis dólares.
5. (El video cuesta) quince dólares.
6. (El CD cuesta) nueve dólares.

IV.
1. los lunes, los miércoles, los viernes (los martes, los jueves)...
2. los sábados, los domingos (los viernes, los sábados)

V.
1. Es el catorce de febrero.
2. Es el primero de abril.
3. Es el cuatro de julio.
4. Es el veintitrés de noviembre.
5. Es el veinticinco de diciembre.

VI.
1. Es la una y cuarto (la una y quince) de la tarde.
2. Son las nueve y media (las nueve y treinta) de la noche.
3. Son las seis menos diez (las cinco y cincuenta) de la mañana.
4. Son las doce menos veinte (las once y cuarenta) de la noche.
5. Es (el) mediodía.

VII.
1. Me llamo...
2. Muy bien, gracias. (Regular.)
3. Sí, (No, no) soy inflexible y arrogante.
Sí, (No, no) soy responsable y generoso/a.
4. Soy de...
5. Es el... de...
6. Es lunes, etc.
7. Son las... (Es la...)
8. Es a las...

VIII.
1. With a light kiss on the right cheek in Argentina. With one kiss on each cheek in Spain.
2. It is the celebration of the Epiphany, on January 6th.
3. It is the day when the saint with your name is honored.

Capítulo 2

I. A. 1. el, los ejercicios
2. la, las lecciones
3. la, las páginas
4. el, los Capítulos

B. un, una, un, una, unas, una, unos

II.
1. Voy a la cafetería (al centro estudiantil).
2. Vamos al laboratorio (a la residencia estudiantil/al cuarto).
3. Vamos al gimnasio.
4. Van a la oficina del profesor.
5. Vas a la librería.
6. Va al cuarto (a la residencia estudiantil/a casa/al apartamento).

III.
1 Compro...
2. Llegan...
3. ¿Estudias...?

4. ¿Trabaja...?
5. Usamos...
6. Escucha...

IV.
1. Asistimos... aprendemos...
2. Vivo... estudio...
3. Comen... toman...
4. Leemos... escribimos...
5. Imprimes... usas...
6. Hago... salgo...

V.
1. Sí, (No, no voy) a clases todos los días.
2. Mi primera clase es a la (las)...
3. Hay... estudiantes en la clase de español.
4. Sí, (No, no) hay (mucha) tarea todas las noches.
5. Sí, (No, no) escribimos en el *Cuaderno de ejercicios* todas las noches.
6. Voy a la librería. Voy al laboratorio (al centro de computadoras).
7. Voy a...
8. Ceno a las...
9. Como en casa (en la cafetería/en mi apartamento/en un restaurante).

VI.
1. Most universities in Spanish-speaking countries are public and financed by the government so students only have to pay for their books and supplies. Programs of study are very rigid and specialized.
2. It is a small tree frog found in Puerto Rico and a symbol of the country.
3. Both combine Spanish and African influence. *Bomba* is older and comes directly from Africa, while *plena* was born in the early 1900's on the south coast of the island.

Capítulo 3

I.
1. tengo
2. tiene
3. tienen
4. tenemos
5. tienes

II.
1. Tengo mis fotos.
2. ¿Tienes tus libros?
3. Tiene su diccionario.
4. Tenemos nuestro televisor.
5. ¿Tienen (ustedes) sus calculadoras?

III.
1. Es la foto de Marta.
2. Son los cuadernos de José.
3. Son los exámenes de los estudiantes.

IV.
1. soy, son perezosos
2. son, es bajo
3. somos, somos... simpáticos
4. es, son difíciles

V.
1. Están en la librería.
2. Estamos en el gimnasio.
3. Estoy en la cafetería (en el centro estudiantil).
4. Está en la oficina de la profesora Falcón.

VI.
1. Estoy nervioso/a (preocupado/a).
2. Están (muy) ocupados.
3. Está (muy) enfermo.
4. Estamos contentos/as.

VII.
1. Tengo... años.
2. Mi madre es simpática, etc. o Mi padre es alto, etc.
3. Mis amigos/as son simpáticos/as, etc.
4. Mis amigos/as están bien (contentos/as), etc.
5. Sí, estamos preocupados/as por nuestras notas en la clase de... o No, no estamos preocupados/as por nuestras notas.
6. Tenemos clases los lunes, etc.
7. Nuestras clases son difíciles, etc.

VIII. 1. Traditional families have more children and the family includes grandparents (often they live with their children and grandchildren) uncles, cousins, etc.
2. Approximately 15% of the population in the USA is Hispanic. Most of them live in California, Texas, New York, and Florida.
3. Latin murals in California started in the 60s and 70s, they were painted by young Mexican artists to illustrate aspects of the Mexican-American history.

Capítulo 4

I. 1. ¿A tus padres les gusta tomar café? Sí, (No, no) les gusta tomar café.
2. ¿A ustedes les gusta la comida italiana? Sí, (No, no) nos gusta la comida italiana.
3. ¿A ustedes les gusta desayunar temprano? Sí, (No, no) nos gusta desayunar temprano.
4. ¿A tu abuela le gustan los postres? Sí, (No, no) le gustan los postres.
5. ¿A ti te gustan los frijoles negros? Sí, (No, no) me gustan los frijoles negros.

II. 1. ¿Pueden cocinar? Sí, (No, no) podemos cocinar.
2. ¿Quieren ir al supermercado? Sí, (No, no) queremos ir al supermercado.
3. ¿Almuerzan a las doce todos los días? Sí, (No, no) almorzamos a las doce todos los días.
4. ¿Prefieren cenar en un restaurante o en la cafetería? Preferimos cenar en un restaurante (en la cafetería).
5. ¿Normalmente piden postres en los restaurantes? Sí, normalmente pedimos postres en los restaurantes. o No, normalmente no pedimos...

III. A. 1. Dos cuestan doscientos cincuenta dólares.
2. Dos cuestan trescientos cuarenta dólares.
3. Dos cuestan novecientos dólares.
4. Dos cuestan dos mil ochocientos dólares.
5. Dos cuestan mil quinientos dólares.
6. Dos cuestan cincuenta mil dólares.

B. 1. mil cuatrocientos noventa y dos
2. mil quinientos ochenta y ocho
3. mil setecientos setenta y seis
4. mil novecientos ochenta y nueve
5. dos mil uno

IV. 1. ¿Qué bebe? o ¿Por qué no bebe vino?
2. ¿Cuál es su fruta favorita?
3. ¿Cuándo trabaja? o ¿Qué hace por la mañana?
4. ¿De dónde es?
5. ¿Cuántos años tiene?
6. ¿Dónde vive?
7. ¿Adónde va? o ¿Cuándo va?
8. ¿Cómo está?

V. 1. Como huevos, etc.
2. Mi postre favorito es el helado, etc.
3. Me gustan más las manzanas, etc.
4. Quiero cenar en...
5. Generalmente duermo... horas.
6. Sí, (No, no) podemos estudiar toda la noche sin dormir.

VI. 1. (*Answers may vary.*)
2. A Mexican tortilla is a thin corn or flour bread, while Spanish tortilla is an omelet typically made with potato, onion and eggs. Oil, tourism, and money sent back by emigrants. There is also developing industry and trade in the areas near the U.S. border.

Capítulo 5

I. MARTA: Sabes
PABLO: sé, conozco

MARTA: Sabes
PABLO: sé, conozco

II. 1. Tú vienes a clase todos los días. Yo vengo...
2. Nosotros decimos "hola" a los estudiantes al entrar en la clase. Yo digo "hola"...
3. Ellas traen la tarea a clase. Yo traigo...
4. Ana pone la tarea en el escritorio del profesor. Yo pongo...
5. Nosotros sabemos todo el vocabulario. Yo sé...
6. Ustedes hacen preguntas en clase. Yo hago...
7. Ella no sale de clase temprano. Yo no salgo...

III. 1. Marta va a jugar al tenis.
2. Luisa y Alberto van a montar en bicicleta.
3. Voy a ver un partido de fútbol.
4. Vas a preparar la paella.
5. Vamos a ir a la playa.

IV. 1. Está nevando.
2. El niño está durmiendo.
3. Estoy leyendo una novela.
4. Estamos viendo la tele.
5. Mis hermanos están preparando la cena.

V. es, Es, está, Es, es, está

VI. (*Answers may vary.*)
1. Estoy escribiendo los ejercicios de la *Autoprueba*.
2. Voy a estudiar, etc.
3. Hago tarea para la clase de..., salgo con mis amigos, etc.
4. Tengo que estudiar, etc.
5. Tengo ganas de dormir, etc.
6. Conozco muy bien a...
7. Traigo mis libros, etc.
8. Mi estación favorita es la primavera (el verano, etc.) porque...
9. Hace calor (buen tiempo/ frío/ viento/etc.).

VII. 1. In Caribbean countries baseball is more popular than soccer.
2. The story of a family during Rafael Trujillo's dictatorship in the Dominican Republic.
3. The islands' African heritage is present in the racial makeup of their inhabitants. There is also African influence in the music and dance of Dominicans and Cubans.

Capítulo 6

I. 1. Mi compañero/a de cuarto se despierta.
2. Me levanto.
3. Te bañas.
4. Pepita se cepilla los dientes.
5. Nos ponemos suéteres porque hace frío.
6. Octavio y Manual se visten.

II. 1. ...frecuentemente.
2. ...fácilmente.
3. ...recientemente.
4. ...inmediatamente.

III. A. 1. Me duché.
2. Pepita se peinó.
3. Te lavaste la cara.
4. Nos afeitamos.
5. Ellos se cepillaron los dientes.

B. 1. Llegué al trabajo a las nueve.
2. Dos colegas leyeron las noticias del día.
3. Mi colega y yo mandamos un mensaje...
4. Escribiste un memo muy importante.
5. Fuimos a un restaurante chino para almorzar.
6. En la tarde, mi colega llamó a varios de nuestros clientes.
7. Ella resolvió un problema serio.
8. Salimos del trabajo a las cinco de la tarde.

IV. A. 1. Pues, Camila va a invitarme. *o* Camila me va a invitar.
2. Pues, Camila va a invitarnos. *o* Camila nos va a invitar.
3. Pues, Camila va a invitarlos/las. *o* Camila los/las va a invitar.
4. Pues, Camila va a invitarlas. *o* Camila las va a invitar.
5. Pues, Camila va a invitarlos. *o* Camila los va a invitar.
6. Pues, Camila va a invitarla. *o* Camila la va a invitar.
7. Pues, Camila va a invitarte. *o* Camila te va a invitar.

B. 1. Sí, (No, no) quiero verlos/las. *o* Sí, (No, no) los/ las quiero ver.
2. Sí, (No, no) voy a llamarlos. *o* Sí, (No, no) los voy a llamar.
3. Sí, (No, no) estoy haciéndola ahora. *o* Sí, (No, no) la estoy haciendo ahora.
4. Sí, (No, no) los completé.
5. Sí, (No, no) voy a estudiarlo. *o* Sí, (No, no) lo voy a estudiar.

V. 1. Por la mañana después de levantarme, me ducho, etc.
2. Antes de acostarme, me cepillo los dientes, etc.
3. Ayer fui a... También...
4. El fin de semana pasado...
5. Sí, lo/ la llamé. Hablamos de... *o* No, no lo/ la llamé.

VI. 1. (*Answers will vary.*) Arabs lived in Spain for almost 800 years and left an important imprint in many aspects of Spanish culture; there was a militarydictatorship for 40 years; Spain has a king, Juan Carlos I...
2. (*Answers will vary.*) Spain belongs to the European Community; The Spanish currency is the euro; Barcelona hosted the Olympic Games in 1992; Spain is composed by different regions with their own cultural identities; there are four official languages in Spain.
3. *Azulejos* are ceramic tiles, which were first brought to Spain by the Arabs who settled there.

Capítulo 7

I. 1. La gente está dentro del cine (en el cine).
2. La iglesia está detrás del banco.
3. La estatua está cerca del centro de la ciudad.
4. En el quiosco, las revistas están encima de los periódicos.

II. 1. conmigo
2. contigo
3. ellos/ellas
4. nosotros

III. A. 1. Voy a visitar esa iglesia.
2. Voy a visitar este museo.
3. Quiero ver estas obras de arte.
4. Queremos ver aquellos rascacielos.

B. 1. No, prefiero ésas (aquéllas).
2. No, prefiero ésos (aquéllos).
3. No, prefiero ése (aquél).
4. No, prefiero ésa (aquélla).

IV. 1. —Carlos y Felipe, ¿pidieron ustedes ayuda a un tutor? Sí, (No, no) la pedimos.
2. —Alberto, ¿durmió usted bien después de volver del centro? Sí, (No, no) dormí bien después de volver del centro.
3. —Linda y Celia, ¿hicieron ustedes algo interesante en el centro? Sí, hicimos algo interesante. *o* No, no hicimos nada interesante.
4. Linda y Celia, ¿se divirtieron ustedes? Sí, (No, no) nos divertimos.
5. Sr. Sancho, ¿prefirió el director de la escuela la ópera o el ballet? El director de la escuela prefirió la ópera (el ballet).

V. 1. No, nadie fue conmigo.
2. No, no hice nada interesante (en el centro).
3. Tampoco la visité./ Yo no la visité tampoco.

VI. 1. —Los bancos abren a las... de la mañana. Los almacenes abren a las...
2. —Sí, gasté mucho dinero en restaurantes el mes pasado. Pedí... *o* No, no gasté...
3. Pedimos...
4. Sí, fuimos al centro para... *o* No, no fuimos al centro...
5. Dormí... horas.
6. Casi nunca (Casi siempre) duermo ocho horas porque...

7. Anoche estudié, etc. *o* No hice nada anoche.
8. El fin de semana pasado fuimos..., etc. *o* No hicimos nada.

VII. 1. Argentina, Chile
2. Los grupos europeos más numerosos que emigraron a Buenos Aires fueron grupos españoles, italianos, alemanes y armenios.
3. Salvador Allende (primer presidente socialista de Chile), Pinochet (dictador chileno), Juan Perón (dictador argentino), los mapuches (grupo indígena de Chile), Benito Quinquela Martín (pintor argentino), los gauchos (rancheros argentinos), Jorge Luis Borges (escritor argentino), Gabriela Mistral (Premio Nóbel de Literatura)

Capítulo 8

I. A. 1. —El abrigo es mío. Las botas son mías. Los guantes son míos. La gorra es mía.
2. —La ropa interior es nuestra. Los jeans son nuestros. Las corbatas son nuestras.
3. —La blusa es tuya. El vestido es tuyo. La camiseta es tuya. Las medias son tuyas.
4. —La ropa de verano es suya. Las faldas son suyas. Los trajes de baño son suyos.

B. 1. Mi primo va con unos amigos suyos.
2. Viviana va con un amigo suyo.
3. Mi hermana y yo vamos con un amigo nuestro.
4. Voy con unos amigos míos.

II. 1. Natalia y Linda trajeron las decoraciones.
2. Pusimos las flores en la mesa.
3. Javier quiso venir pero no pudo.
4. Casi todos los estudiantes vinieron.
5. Estuviste en la fiesta por cuatro horas.
6. Tuve que salir temprano.

III. 1. Me dio su reloj.
2. Le regaló un bolso de cuero.
3. Les compró una computadora nueva.
4. Nos mandó tarjetas postales del Perú.
5. Te prestó su cámara.

IV. 1. Se lo regalamos.
2. Se la regaló.
3. Se las regalaron.
4. Se la regalé.
5. Nos lo regaló.

V. 1. —Las mujeres llevan vestido, etc. Los hombres llevan chaqueta y corbata, etc.
2. —Debo llevar mi abrigo, mis suéteres, etc. a Alaska. Debo llevar mi traje de baño, mis pantalones cortos, etc. a la Florida.
3. —Sí, fui de compras el fin de semana pasado a Sears. Compré zapatos de tenis, etc. *o* No, no fui de compras...
4. Estuve en casa (en una fiesta, etc.). Estudié, etc.
5. Traje mis libros, etc.
6. —Sí, le di la tarea para hoy (se la di) a la profesora/al profesor. *o* No, no le di la tarea (se la di).

VI. 1. Quito (la capital de Ecuador), Cuzco (ciudad en Perú, la capital del Imperio Tahuantinsuyo), La Paz (la capital administrativa de Bolivia), Machu Picchu (antigua ciudad del Imperio Inca), el Lago Titicaca (el lago más grande de Sudamérica, el lago navegable más alto del mundo), las Islas Galápagos (islas a 960 millas de la costa ecuatoriana en las que coexisten especies de animales únicas en el mundo)
2. Huipil: vestido blanco de origen maya con un bordado de flores de colores vivos. Las mujeres lo llevan en la Península de Yucatán, en México; Polleras: vestidos panameños con encajes y bordados con hilo de oro; Guayaberas: camisas de telas livianas y bordadas de colores claros que se llevan en las regiones costeras del Caribe.
3. La cultura lambayeque se desarrolló en la costa norte de Perú entre los años 900 y 1100–1200 d.c. Los lambayeque creían en la vida después de la muerte.

Capítulo 9

I.
1. Tráiganmelos./No me los traigan.
2. Examínela./No la examine.
3. Descanse más./No descanse más.
4. Estudie las palabras./No estudie las palabras.
5. Lea el libro./No lea el libro.

II.
1. Mis hermanos y yo éramos niños muy buenos.
2. Íbamos a una escuela pequeña.
3. (Yo) Escuchaba a mis maestras.
4. José jugaba al vólibol durante el recreo.
5. Ana y Tere veían la tele por la tarde.
6. Comías galletas todos los días.

III.
1. llamó, habló
2. explicó, estaba
3. preguntó, tenía
4. explicó, dolía, tenía
5. quería, estaba
6. contestó
7. dijo, podía
8. aceptó, dio
9. se sentía, se durmió

IV. A.
1. Hace (*minutos/horas*) que estoy en clase.
2. Hace (*años/semanas/etc.*) que estudio español.
3. —Hace (*semanas/meses/años/etc.*) que conozco al/a la profesor/a de español.
4. —Hace (*semanas/meses/años/etc.*) que vivo en la misma casa (el mismo apartamento).
5. Hace (*meses/años/etc.*) que tengo permiso de conducir un auto.

B.
1. —Hablé con mi familia hace (*días/semanas/etc.*). *o* Hace (*días/semanas/etc.*) que hablé...
2. —Compré un regalo para alguien hace (*días/semanas/etc.*). *o* Hace (*días/semanas/etc.*) que compré...
3. Me hice un examen médico hace (*semanas/meses/años/etc.*). *o* Hace (*semanas/meses/años/etc.*) que me hice...
4. Visité un museo hace (*semanas/meses/años/etc.*). *o* Hace (*semanas/meses/años/etc.*) que visité...
5. —Llegué a la universidad hace (*semanas/meses/años/etc.*). *o* Hace (*semanas/meses/años/etc.*) que llegué...

V.
1. La última vez que fui al médico tenía fiebre (*dolor de cabeza, etc.*).
2. Hace (*semanas/meses/años, etc.*) que estudio en la universidad.
3. —Conocí a mi mejor amigo/a hace... años (*meses, etc.*). *o* Hace... años (*meses, etc.*) que conocí...
4. —En la escuela primaria mi maestro/a preferido/a era (*nombre*). Era muy simpático/a, inteligente, etc.
5. —Cuando ocurrió el ataque terrorista del 11 de septiembre (yo) estaba (*en casa, en la escuela/el trabajo/etc.*).
6. —Al oír las noticias me sentí (*deprimido/a, enojado/a, etc.*). Después (yo) (*llamé a.../fui a casa/etc.*).

VI.
1. Frontera con Colombia: Ecuador, Brasil, Panamá, Perú, Venezuela; Frontera con Venezuela: Colombia, Brasil, Guyana.
2. Venezuela significa "pequeña Venecia" porque en el año 1500 los españoles encontraron allí a los indios guajiros, que vivían en chozas suspendidas sobre unas islas muy pequeñas en el Lago Maracaibo.
3. Posibles respuestas de remedios caseros: limonada caliente con ron, whisky o miel para los resfriados o la gripe; hervir clavos de olor en agua para los orzuelos; dorar un ajo al fuego y aplicar al oído con un algodón para el dolor de oídos; asustar, poner jugo de limón en la lengua, poner un hilo rojo en la frente para el hipo; té de flores de naranjo, té de tilo para el nerviosismo; poner los pies en agua de sal tibia para el dolor de pies.
4. Gabriel García Márquez es un autor y periodista colombiano que ganó el Premio Nóbel de Literatura en 1982.

Capítulo 10

I.
1. Beatriz, ¡haz la cama!
2. María, ¡pasa la aspiradora!
3. Luis, ¡devuelve los libros al estante!
4. Laila, ¡pon la mesa!
5. Miguel, ¡limpia el baño!
6. Juanito, ¡saca la basura!

II.
1. No prendas el estéreo, por favor.
2. No uses mi computadora, por favor.
3. No toques mis cosas, por favor.
4. No salgas ahora, por favor.
5. No me digas mentiras, por favor.
6. No te preocupes, por favor.

III.
1. La abuela ha trabajado en el jardín.
2. Todos hemos lavado y secado la ropa.
3. Papá ha limpiado el garaje.
4. Mi hermana ha salido dos veces a bailar.
5. No has hecho nada.

IV.
1. Había apagado la computadora.
2. Habías imprimido tu trabajo escrito.
3. Mi compañero/a de cuarto había cerrado las ventanas.
4. Habíamos hecho la tarea para la clase de español.
5. Linda y Teresa habían leído la novela para la clase de inglés.

V.
1. —Los profesores son tan simpáticos como los estudiantes. *o* Los estudiantes son tan simpáticos como los profesores.
2. —El tailandés es tan difícil como el francés. *o* El francés es tan difícil como el tailandés.
3. —Susana tiene tanta paciencia como Ana. *o* Ana tiene tanta paciencia como Susana.
4. —Su hermano compró tantos libros como Alberto. *o* Alberto compró tantos libros como su hermano.

VI. A.
1. —El reloj Rolex es más caro que el reloj Timex. *o* El reloj Timex es menos caro que el reloj Rolex.
2. —Comprar una casa es menos económico que alquilar un apartamento. *o* Alquilar un apartamento es más económico que comprar una casa.
3. —Ir de vacaciones a la playa es mejor que ir de vacaciones a las montañas. *o* Ir de vacaciones a las montañas es mejor que ir de vacaciones a la playa.
4. —Limpiar la casa es menos divertido que ver la tele. *o* Ver la tele es más divertido que limpiar la casa.

B.
1. —La ciudad de Duluth es la más fría de las tres. *o* Duluth es la ciudad más fría de las tres.
2. Bill Gates es el hombre más rico de los tres.
3. El Honda (el Ford/el Subaru) es el mejor coche de los tres.
4. —La revista *National Geographic* (*Newsweek/Movie Line*) es la más interesante de las tres. *o* *National Geographic* (*Newsweek/Movie Line*) es la revista más interesante de las tres.

VII.
1. —Sí, soy tan generoso/a como (más generoso/a que) (menos generoso/a que) mi mejor amigo/a. *o* No, no soy más generoso/a que mi mejor amigo/a.
2. —Sí, tengo tantos amigos como (más amigos que) (menos amigos que) él/ella. *o* No, no tengo tantos amigos como él/ella.
3. Estudio más que (menos que) (tanto como) él/ella.
4. —La clase de... es la (clase) más interesante de la universidad porque...
5. —(*Nombre*) es el/la mejor profesor/a de esta universidad porque...
6. El apartamento era...
7. Este año he (viajado a.../estudiado en.../comprado.../etc.).
8. Antes de empezar mi carrera universitaria había (ido a.../conocido a.../estudiado.../etc.).

VIII.
1. La población de Paraguay es diversa (inmigrantes europeos y 25 tribus indígenas; el 95% de la población es de origen mestizo), mientras que la población de Uruguay es uniforme (casi un 90% desciende de inmigrantes europeos).
2. Cristina Peri Rossi es una escritora uruguaya.
3. El patio es un elemento representativo de muchas casas hispanas y tiene varias funciones importantes, como recibir visitas o dar una pequeña fiesta.
4. Pedro Figari fue un pintor uruguayo.

Capítulo 11

I.
1. Se enamoraron inmediatamente.
2. Se comprometieron seis meses más tarde.
3. Se casaron en secreto dos meses más tarde.
4. Aún hoy, después de veinticinco años, se aman mucho.

II.
1. Quiere que estudiemos más. Quiere que Ana y Linda estudien más.
2. Quiere que Esteban haga la tarea. Quiere que hagamos la tarea.
3. Quiere que Juan vuelva pronto. Quiere que volvamos pronto.
4. —Quiere que me divierta en clase. Quiere que nos divirtamos en clase.
5. —Quiere que los estudiantes sean puntuales. Quiere que seas puntual.
6. —Quiere que (yo) vaya a la biblioteca. Quiere que todos los estudiantes vayan a la biblioteca.

III.
1. Les sugiero que se vayan durante el invierno.
2. Prefiero que exploren las playas remotas.
3. Quiero que se diviertan mucho durante su visita a San Juan.
4. Quiero que visiten el bosque lluvioso.
5. —Les recomiendo a mis amigos que hablen en español todo el tiempo.
6. Les pido a todos que me compren un regalo.

IV.
1. Me alegro de que tengamos una cita esta noche.
2. Ojalá que me lleve a un buen restaurante.
3. Temo que llegue un poco tarde.
4. Espero que no se olvide de la cita.
5. Ojalá que podamos comunicarnos bien.

V.
1. —Vamos al cine (nos reunimos en.../etc.). Normalmente cenamos en un restaurante (escuchamos música/ bailamos/etc.).
2. Me llevo muy bien con (nombre de persona).
3. —Sí, hago muchas llamadas de larga distancia. Llamo a... Hablamos de... o No, no hago muchas llamadas de larga distancia.
4. Hablamos, bailamos, nos abrazamos, nos besamos, etc.
5. Quiero que mis amigos estudien, que no vean la tele, etc.
6. —Prefiero que limpie el cuarto (prepare la comida, etc.). Prefiero que no fume, (no hable por teléfono toda la noche/no lleve mi ropa/etc.).
7. —Espero que me dé una "A" en el curso (que me escriba una carta de recomendación, etc.).

VI.
1. Las dos monedas oficiales de Panamá son el dólar estadounidense y el balboa panameño.
2. El Canal de Panamá es el mayor canal navegable del continente con 82.6 kilómetros (50 millas) de largo. Su construcción comenzó en 1902. En 1999 los EE.UU. le entregaron el canal a los panameños.
3. Los "sombreros de Panamá" se fabrican en Ecuador.

Capítulo 12

I.
1. Nos fascinan los relámpagos.
2. Les molestan los mosquitos.
3. Le interesa la biología. o Le interesan los libros de biología.
4. Me encanta pescar.
5. (A Pablo) Le importa la familia.

II.
1. Trabajé para poder ir a Costa Rica.
2. Salí para Costa Rica el 6 de agosto.
3. Estuve allí por un mes.
4. Viajé por todo el país.
5. Compré un libro sobre los bosques nubosos para mi madre.
6. Lo compré por tres mil colones.
7. Mi madre me dijo, "Gracias por el libro".

III. A.
1. No creo que ustedes encuentren el remo.
2. No estoy seguro/a de que el guía sepa hablar español.
3. Dudo que los kayaks lleguen a tiempo.
4. No estoy seguro/a de que estemos remando bien.
5. No creo que puedas ir con nosotros.

B.
1. Creo que cuesta más de doscientos dólares.
2. No creo que haya un problema serio.
3. Dudo que sea muy larga.
4. No estoy seguro/a de que sean buenos.
5. Estoy seguro/a de que vienen con nosotros.

IV.
1. Me alegro de que mis amigos hayan llegado recientemente.
2. Me alegro de que mi mejor amiga me haya comprado un regalo.
3. Siento que hayas perdido tu cámara.
4. Me alegro de que mis amigos me hayan llamado.
5. Siento que hayan tenido un accidente.

V.
1. —Me fascinan (interesan) más las arañas, etc. Me molestan los mosquitos, etc.
2. Me encantan...
3. Me interesan más...
4. —Sí, creo que es muy bueno para la salud hacer ejercicio al aire libre. o No, no creo que sea muy bueno...
5. —Sí, dudo que hayamos hecho todo lo posible para proteger el medio ambiente. Para protegerlo más debemos... o No, no dudo que hemos hecho...
6. —Sí, he viajado mucho. Me alegro (No me alegro) de que haya viajado mucho. o No, no he viajado mucho. Siento (No siento) que no haya viajado más.

VI.
1. Los ticos son personas costarricenses de ascendencia española. También se usa "ticos" para describir a los costarricenses. Se dice que esta palabra viene del diminutivo y que se usa porque las personas en Costa Rica suelen usar mucho el diminutivo.
2. El "ecoturismo" se practica mucho en Costa Rica. Es el turismo a áreas naturales en las que se conserva el medio ambiente a la vez que se apoya a los residentes locales.
3. Las carretas es una forma de arte folklórico. Antes las carretas se usaban para transportar productos, como el café, en zonas rurales. Ahora se decoran y se usan principalmente en desfiles y festivales.

Capítulo 13

I.
1. Es una lástima que el avión llegue tarde.
2. Es bueno que tenga todo el equipaje.
3. Es urgente que vayamos a la aduana.
4. Es horrible que no pueda encontrar el boleto.
5. Es extraño que no haya azafatas.
6. Es cierto que no me gusta/guste volar.

II.
1. Ni Jorge ni Miguel te pueden ayudar a limpiar la casa.
2. —El hotel no tiene aire acondicionado y (ni) calefacción. o El hotel no tiene ni aire acondicionado ni calefacción. o El hotel ni tiene aire acondicionado ni calefacción.
3. Ningún hotel tiene televisor(es) con pantalla grande.
4. Ningún estudiante va a ir a Antigua. o Ninguno va...
5. Nadie fue a la discoteca. o Ninguno fue...

III. A.
1. Necesito una habitación que esté en la planta baja.
2. Prefiero un cuarto que tenga camas sencillas.
3. Quiero un baño que sea más grande.
4. Necesito una llave que abra el mini-bar.

B.
1. tenga, tiene
2. esté, esté

3. sea, sean
4. sirva, sirve

IV.
1. Mi mamá podrá ir a la Florida.
2. Luis tendrá que trabajar.
3. Carmen y sus amigos querrán visitar la Alhambra.
4. Mis abuelitos vendrán a visitarnos.
5. El profesor Marín-Vivar y su familia viajarán por México.
6. (Yo) Pasaré los fines de semana en la playa.

V.
1. Encontramos las horas de las salidas y llegadas de los vuelos.
2. Muestran sus pasaportes, facturan su equipaje, consiguen sus tarjetas de embarque, etc.
3. Busco un hotel que tenga... o Busco un hotel que sea...
4. —Sí, conozco algún lugar que es económico. o No, no conozco ningún lugar que sea económico.
5. Sí, haré un viaje este verano. También... o No, no haré un viaje este verano.

VI.
1. Tres cosas que tienen en común: 1. Tienen frontera con Honduras; 2. La capital tiene un nombre igual o muy similar al nombre del país; 3. Se habla español; Tres cosas que los hacen diferentes: 1. Guatemala tiene frontera con Belice, El Salvador no; 2. Guatemala es más grande que El Salvador; 3. Guatemala tiene costa con el Océano Pacífico y el Mar Caribe, El Salvador tiene costa sólo con el Océano Pacífico.
2. Los paradores son antiguos edificios convertidos en hospedajes para viajeros.
3. La pupusa es el plato nacional de El Salvador. Son dos tortillas de maíz rellenas de carne, frijoles y, a veces, queso.
4. Algunos de los símbolos son: los diamantes, el Dios de la Tierra, la cola del escorpión, la rana, el buitre. Los diamantes representan el universo y el movimiento diario del sol.

Capítulo 14

I.
1. Levantémonos a las diez. No nos levantemos...
2. Salgamos para el centro. No salgamos...
3. Vamos (Vayamos) por la ruta más directa. No vayamos...
4. Paremos en el supermercado. No paremos...
5. Crucemos el nuevo puente. No crucemos...
6. Sigamos recto por cuatro cuadras. No sigamos recto...
7. Exploremos el sector histórico de la ciudad. No exploremos...

II.
1. ...me llame.
2. ...la sepa (la tenga).
3. ...me ayudes (me des papel, etc.).
4. —...tenga(s) veintiún años, licencia de conducir y tarjeta de crédito. o ...haya uno disponible.
5. —...tenga que trabajar (estudiar, etc.). o ...llueva, etc. o ...mi(s) padre(s) (esposo/a) insista(n) que yo...

III.
1. —Quería que limpiara mi cuarto/ fuera al supermercado/ llamara a mis abuelos/ organizara mi clóset.
2. —Nos sugirió que escribiéramos los ejercicios del manual/ llegáramos a clase temprano/ hiciéramos los ejercicios del laboratorio/ participáramos en clase.
3. —Esperaban que los llamara (llamáramos) para Navidad/ les escribiera (escribiéramos) un mensaje electrónico/ los visitara (visitáramos) en verano/ los invitara (invitáramos) para la graduación.

IV.
1. se practica (se puede practicar)
2. se permite (se puede)
3. se habla (se permite hablar/se debe hablar)
4. se venden (se compran)
5. se estudia (se debe estudiar)

V.
1. Primero reviso el aceite; después...
2. Digo ¡Ay de mí!, etc.
3. Sí, he hecho un viaje en tren/autobús a... o No, no he hecho...
4. Sí, me gusta la idea porque... o No, no me gusta la idea porque...
5. Se puede dormir (leer, comer, descansar, ver el paisaje, etc.).

6. —Sí, hacía viajes en carro con mi familia. Íbamos a... o No, no hacía viajes en carro.
7. —Quería que mis padres/maestros/amigos (verbo: imperfecto del subjuntivo)...

VI.
1. El Lago de Nicaragua tiene más de 8.000 km² y es el más grande de Centroamérica.
2. El gallopinto es un plato típico de centroamérica y consiste de arroz y frijoles.
3. La música garífuna tiene una fuerte influencia africana en los ritmos y los instrumentos. Esta música mantiene los cantos, bailes y tradiciones artísticas que han caracterizado a la cultura por años.

Capítulo 15

I.
1. ...recibí el dinero., ...reciba el dinero.
2. —...me des el número de teléfono del hotel., ... me diste el número de teléfono del hotel.
3. ...me llamaste (llamaras), ...me llames.
4. ...regresemos de la luna de miel., ... regresamos de la luna de miel.

II.
1. (Yo) Viajaría a muchos países.
2. Pepe pondría el dinero en el banco.
3. Les darías dinero a los pobres.
4. Ustedes gastarían todo el dinero.
5. Haríamos un viaje a la Patagonia.
6. Mis amigas irían a Chile a esquiar.

III.
1. Si ganara más dinero, lo ahorraría.
2. Si lo ahorrara, tendría mucho dinero.
3. Si tuviera mucho dinero, compraría un coche.
4. Si comprara un coche, haría un viaje.
5. Si hiciera un viaje, iría a Puerto Vallarta.
6. Si fuera a Puerto Vallarta, me quedaría allí dos meses.
7. Si me quedara allí dos meses, perdería mi trabajo.
8. Si perdiera mi trabajo, no tendría dinero.

IV.
1. Ojalá (que) el aire no estuviera tan contaminado.
2. Ojalá (que) no hubiera mucho desempleo en esta ciudad.
3. Ojalá (que) muchas personas no sufrieran del SIDA y del cáncer.
4. Ojalá (que) no tuviéramos muchos problemas que resolver.

V.
1. (En mi opinión,) Algunos de los problemas más serios son...
2. Cambiaría... porque...
3. —Sí, me preocupaba por... o No, no me preocupaba por los problemas del mundo/otros problemas.
4. (Cuando me gradúe,) Trabajaré, haré un viaje, etc.

VI.
1. Univisión y Telemundo.
2. Las telenovelas duran entre ocho y doce meses, mientras que las soap operas pueden durar años. Las telenovelas se televisan a la hora punta, por las noches, mientras que las soap operas se televisan por la mañana o por la tarde.
3. Cristina Saralegui es la anfitriona del Show de Cristina; Jorge Ramos es el periodista más visto de los medios hispanos en Estados Unidos; Don Francisco es el presentador de Sábado Gigante, el show de variedades de más duración en la historia de la televisión.
4. Algunos jóvenes se dedican a la investigación y a la promoción del patrimonio cultural o al cuidado del medio ambiente. Otros participan en programas de alfabetización en las zonas rurales.

Afganistán (el) – afgano/a
Albania – albanés, albanesa
Alemania – alemán, alemana
Andorra – andorrano/a
Angola – angoleño/a
Antigua y Barbuda – antiguano/a
Arabia Saudí o Arabia Saudita – saudí
Argelia – argelino/a
Argentina (la) – argentino/a
Armenia – armenio/a
Australia – australiano/a
Austria – austriaco/a
Azerbaiyán – azerbaiyano/a

Bahamas (las) – bahameño/a
Bahréin – bahreiní
Bangladesh – bengalí
Barbados – barbadense
Bélgica – belga
Belice – beliceño/a
Benín – beninés, beninesa
Bielorrusia – bielorruso/a
Bolivia – boliviano/a
Bosnia-Herzegovina – bosnio/a
Botsuana – bostuano/a
Brasil (el) – brasileño/a
Brunéi Darussalam – bruneano/a
Bulgaria – búlgaro/a
Burkina Faso – burkinés, burkinesa
Burundi – burundés, burundesa
Bután – butanés, butanesa

Cabo Verde – caboverdiano/a
Camboya – camboyano/a
Camerún (el) – camerunés, camerunesa
Canadá (el) – canadiense
Chad – (el) – chadiano/a
Chile – chileno/a
China – chino/a
Chipre – chipriota
Ciudad del Vaticano – vaticano/a
Colombia – colombiano/a
Comoras – comorense/a
Congo (el) – congoleño/a
Corea del Norte – norcoreano/a
Corea del Sur – surcoreano/a
Costa Rica – costarricense
Costa de Marfil – marfileño/a
Croacia – croata
Cuba – cubano/a

Dinamarca – danés, danesa
Dominica – dominiqués/dominiquesa
uador (el) – ecuatoriano/a
Egipto – egipcio/a
Emiratos Árabes Unidos (los) – emiratense
Eritrea – eritreo/a
Eslovaquia – eslovaco/a
Eslovenia – esloveno/a
España – español/a
Estados Unidos de América (los) – estadounidense
Estonia – estonio/a
Etiopía – etíope

Filipinas – filipino/a
Finlandia – finlandés, finlandesa
Francia – francés, francesa
Fiyi – fiyiano/a

Gabón (el) – gabonés, gabonesa
Gambia – gambiano/a
Georgia – georgiano/a
Ghana – ghanés, ghanesa
Granada – granadino/a
Grecia – griego/a
Guatemala – guatemalteco/a
Guinea – guineano/a
Guinea-Bissáu – guineano/a
Guinea Ecuatorial (la) – guineano, ecuatoguineano/a
Guyana – guyanés, guyanesa

Haití – haitiano/a
Honduras – hondureño/a
Hungría – húngaro/a

India (la) – indio/a
Indonesia – indonesio/a
Irán – iraní
Iraq – iraquí
Irlanda – irlandés, irlandesa
Islandia – islandés, islandesa
Islas Cook (las) – cookiano/a
Islas Marshall (las) – marshalés, marshalesa
Islas Salomón (las) – salomonense
Israel – israelí
Italia – italiano/a

Jamaica – jamaicano/a
Japón (el) – japonés, japonesa
Jordania – jordano/a

Kazajstán – kazako/a
Kenia – keniata
Kirguistán – kirguís
Kiribati – kiribatiano/a
Kuwait – kuwaití

Laos – laosiano/a
Lesotho – lesothense
Letonia – letón, letona
Líbano (el) – libanés, libanesa
Liberia – liberiano/a
Libia – libio/a
Liechtenstein – liechtensteiniano/a
Lituania – lituano/a
Luxemburgo – luxemburgués, luxemburguesa

Macedonia – macedonio/a
Madagascar – malgache
Malasia – malayo/a
Malawi – malawiano/a
Maldivas – maldivo/a
Malí – malí
Malta – maltés, maltesa
Marruecos – marroquí
Mauricio – mauriciano/a
Mauritania – mauritano

México – mexicano/a
Micronesia – micronesio/a
Moldavia – moldavo/a
Mónaco – monegasco/a
Mongolia – mongol/a
Mozambique – mozambiqueño/a
Myanmar – birmano/a

Namibia – namibio/a
Nauru – nauruano/a
Nepal – nepalés, nepalesa
Nicaragua – nicaragüense
Níger – nigerino/a
Nigeria – nigeriano/a
Noruega – noruego/a
Nueva Zelanda o Nueva Zelandia – neocelandés, neozelandesa

Omán – omaní

Países Bajos (los) – neerlandés, neerlandesa
Pakistán (el) – pakistaní
Paláu – palauano/a
Panamá – panameño/a
Papúa Nueva Guinea – papú
Paraguay (el) – paraguayo/a
Perú (el) – peruano/a
Polonia – polaco/a
Portugal – portugués, portuguesa
Puerto Rico – puertorriqueño/a

Qatar – catarí

Reino Unido británico/a
República Centroafricana (la) – centroafricano/a
República Checa (la) – checo/a
República Democrática del Congo (la) – congoleño/a
República Dominicana (la) – dominicano/a
Ruanda – ruandés, ruandesa
Rumania o Rumanía – rumano/a
Rusia – ruso/a

Salvador (el) – salvadoreño/a
Samoa – samoano/a
San Cristóbal y Nieves – sancristobaleño/a
San Marino – sanmarinense
Santa Lucía – santalucense
Santo Tomé y Príncipe santotomense/a
San Vicente y las Granadinas sanvicentino/a
Senegal (el) – senegalés, senegalesa
Seychelles – seychellense
Sierra Leona – sierraleonés, sierraleonesa
Singapur – singapurense
Siria – sirio/a
Somalia – somalí
Sri Lanka cingalés, cingalesa
Suazilandia – suazi
Sudáfrica – sudafricano/a
Sudán (el) – sudanés, sudanesa
Suecia – sueco/a
Suiza – suizo/a
Surinam – surimanés, surimanesa

Tailandia – tailandés, tailandesa
Tanzania – tanzaniano/a
Tayikistán – tayiko/a

Togo (el) – togolés, togolesa
Tonga – tongano/a
Trinidad y Tobago – trinitense
Túnez – tunecino/a
Turkmenistán – turcomano/a
Turquía – turco/a
Tuvalu – tuvaluano/a

Ucrania – ucraniano/a
Uganda – ugandés, ugandesa
Uruguay (el) – uruguayo/a
Uzbekistán – uzbeko/a

Vanuatu – vanuatuense
Venezuela – venezolano/a
Vietnam – vietnamita

Yemen (el) – yemení
Yibuti – yibutano/a
Yugoslavia – yugoslavo/a

Zambia – zambiano/a
Zimbabue – zimbabuense

Más Profesiones

actor *actor m*
actress *actriz f*
administrator *administrador/a*
ambassador *embajador/a*
anchorperson *presentador/a (de radio y televisión)*
artist *artista m/f*
astrologer *astrólogo/a*
astronaut *astronauta m/f*
astronomer *astrónomo/a*
baker *panadero/a*
barber *barbero m*
bodyguard *guardaespaldas m/f*
bricklayer *albañil m*
butler *mayordomo m*
captain *capitán/a*
carpenter *carpintero/a*
cartographer *cartógrafo/a*
chauffeur *chofer*
consultant, advisor *consejero/a (en asuntos técnicos)*
cook *cocinero/a*
counselor *consejero/a (en asuntos personales)*
dancer *bailarín m/ f*
dentist *dentista m/f*
designer *diseñador/a*
diplomat *diplomático/a*
dishwasher *lavaplatos*
electrician *electricista m/f*
engineer *ingeniero/a*
farmer *agricultor/a*
firefighter *bombero/a*
fisherman, fisherwoman *pescador/a*
flight attendant *azafata f, sobrecargo m/f*
florist *florista m/f*
flower grower *floricultor/a*
foreman, forewoman *capataz/a*
forest ranger *guardabosque m/f*

gardener *jardinero/a*
geographer *geógrafo/a*
geologist *geólogo/a*
governor *gobernador/a*
hairdresser *peluquero/a*
historian *historiador/a*
janitor *conserje*
jeweler *joyero/a*
journalist *periodista m/f*
judge *juez m/f*
laborer, worker *obrero/a*
librarian *bibliotecario/a*
maid *sirvienta f*
make-up artist *maquillador/a*
male nurse, nurse *enfermero/a*
manager *gerente m/f*
manufacturer *fabricante m*
masseur, masseuse *masajista m/f*
mathematician *matemático/a*
mayor, mayoress *alcalde/sa*
mechanic *mecánico/a*
miner *minero/a*
minister *ministro/a*
musician *músico/a*
notary (public) *notario/a*
novelist *novelista m/f*
office worker *oficinista m/f*
painter *pintor/a*
parking attendant *guardacoches m/f*
pastry cook *pastelero/a*
philosopher *filósofo/a*
photographer *fotógrafo/a*
pianist *pianista m/f*
pilot *piloto m/f*
playwright, dramatist *dramaturgo/a*
plumber *plomero, fontanero m*
poet, female poet *poeta/isa*
police superintendent *comisario/a*
policeman, policewoman *policía*
politician *político/a*
priest *sacerdote*
psychiatrist *psiquiatra m/f*
psychologist *psicólogo/a*
radio announcer *locutor/a*
real estate agent *agente de bienes raíces*
sailor *marinero/a*
sculptor, sculptress *escultor/a*
shopkeeper *tendero*
singer *cantante m/f*
soldier *soldado/mujer soldado*
tailor *sastre/a*
technician *técnico/a*
teller *cajero/a (en banco)*
tour guide *guía m/f turístico*
tradesman, tradeswoman *comerciante m/f*
translator *traductor/a*
truck driver *camionero/a*
veterinarian *veterinario/a*
warder, jailer *carcelero/a*
wrestler *luchador/a*
writer *escritor/a*

Otras materias académicas

anatomy *anatomía*
anthropology *antropología*
architecture *arquitectura*
Arabic (language) *árabe*
astronomy *astronomía*
biochemistry *bioquímica*
botany *botánica*
business administration *administración de empresas*
Chinese (language) *chino*
civil engineering *ingeniería civil*
computer science *computación*
creative writing *escritura creativa*
dramatic arts *teatro, artes dramáticas*
drawing *dibujo*
electrical engineering *ingeniería eléctrica*
film *cine*
finance *finanzas*
genetics *genética*
geography *geografía*
geology *geología*
geometry *geometría*
gymnastics *gimnástica*
Hebrew (language) *hebreo*
industrial engineering *ingeniería industrial*
Italian (language) *italiano*
Japanese (language) *japonés*
journalism *periodismo*
jurisprudence *derecho*
Latin (language) *latín*
law *derecho*
linguistics *lingüística*
mechanical engineering *ingeniería mecánica*
microbiology *microbiología*
nursing *enfermería*
nutrition *nutrición*
obstetrics *obstetricia*
painting *pintura*
pharmacology *farmacología*
philology *filología*
physical education *educación física*
physiology *fisiología*
Russian (language) *ruso*
sculpture *escultura*
social work *trabajo social*
statistics *estadística*
swimming *natación*
theology *teología*
zoology *zoología*

A

a bit, a little, somewhat un poco 3
a bit, a little, somewhat un poco *adv.* 3
a quarter cuarto 1
a trip viaje *m* 14
A.M. (in the morning) de la mañana 1
a; one un/uno/una 1; 2
abortion aborto *m* 15
accident accidente *m* 14
accountant contador/a *m/f* 6
accounting contabilidad *f* 2
acid rain lluvia ácida 12
address dirección 7
admission ticket entrada *f* 7
adolescence adolescencia 10
adolescents adolescentes *m, pl.* 10
adulthood, maturity madurez *f* 11
adults adultos *m, pl.* 11
adventure aventura *f* 12
affectionate cariñoso/a 11
after después de que *conj* 15
after (class) después de (clase) 2
afternoon tarde *f* 1
afterwards, later después de *prep.* 7
ahead of time con... de anticipación 13
AIDS SIDA *m* 15
air aire *m* 14
air conditioning aire acondicionado 13
airline aerolínea *f* 13
airplane avión *m* 13
airport aeropuerto *m* 13
aisle (between rows of seats) pasillo *m* 13
alarm clock despertador *m* 6
algebra álgebra *f (but el* álgebra) 2
all afternoon toda la tarde 2
all day todos los días 2
all morning todo/a/os/as *adj.*: toda la mañana 2
all night toda la noche 2
all of a sudden, suddenly repente 9
allergy alergia *f* 9
(almost) always (casi) siempre 2
already ya 6
also también 4
ambulance ambulancia *f* 9
American (from the United States) estadounidense *m/f, n., adj.* 1
amusing, fun divertido/a *m/f* 3
and y 3
angry enojado/a 11
animal animal *m* 11
animal species especie animal *f* 12
ankle tobillo *m* 9
another otro/a 4
answer respuesta *f* 2
answering machine contestador automático *m* 11
any, some, someone algún (alguno/a/os/as) 13
apartment apartamento *m* 2
apple manzana *f* 4
application solicitud *f* 15
April abril 1
area code código *m* de área 11
Argentinian argentino/a *m/f, n., adj.* 1
arm brazo *m* 9
army ejército *m* 15
arrival llegada *f* 13
art arte *m (but las* artes) 2
as . . . as tan: tan... como 9
as much as tanto: tanto como 10
as much/ many . . . as tanto/a/os/as... como 10
as soon as tan pronto como 15
at home en casa 6
at work en el trabajo 3
at, to a 2
ATM machine cajero *m* automático 7
August agosto 1
aunt tía *f* 3
autumn, fall otoño *m* 5
avenue avenida *f* 7

B

baby bebé *m/f* 3
back espalda *f* 9
backpack mochila *f* 2
bacon tocineta *f* 4
bacon tocino *m* 4
bad malo/a 3
bad, badly mal 3
baggage claim reclamo de equipajes *m, pl.* 13
baked al horno 4
ball pelota *f* 5
banana banana *f* 4
banana plátano *m* 4
bandage venda *f* 9
bank; bench banco 7
bar bar *m* 7
baseball béisbol *m* 5
basement sótano *m* 10
basketball baloncesto *m* 5
basketball básquetbol *m* 5
bathing suit traje de baño 8
bathroom baño *m* 10
bathroom los aseos/el servicio *m* 14
bathtub bañera *f* 10
beach playa *f* 3
beans frijoles *m, pl.* 4
because porque 4
because of causa (a causa de) 12
bed cama *f* 6
bedroom dormitorio *m* 10
bedroom recámara *f* 10
beer cerveza *f* 4
before antes de que *conj* 15
before (class) antes de (clase) *prep* before
behind detrás de 7
beige beige 5
bellhop botones *m* 13
belt cinturón *m* 8
beneath, under debajo de 7
beside al lado de 7
beside lado: al... de 7
best mejor 7
best friend mejor amigo/a *m* 3
between, among entre 7
bicycle bicicleta *f* 5
big, large grande 3
bill, check; account cuenta *f* 7
biology biología *f* 2
bird pájaro *m* 12
birth nacimento *m* 11
birthday cumpleaños *m* 2
black negro/a 5
blanket cobija *f* 13
blanket manta *f* 13
blonde rubio/a 3
blouse blusa *f* 8
blue azul 5
boarding pass tarjeta de embarque 13
boat barco *m* 12
boat (small) bote *m* 12
body cuerpo *m* 9
Bolivian X boliviano/a *m/f, n., adj.*
bomb bomba 15
bone hueso *m* 9
book libro *m* 2
bookshelf, shelf estante *m* 10
bookstore librería *f* 2
boots botas *f, pl.* 8
border frontera *f* 15
bored/boring aburrido/a 3
boss jefa *f* 15
boss jefe *m* 15
boy chico *m* 3
boy muchacho *m* 3
boyfriend novio *m* 3
bracelet pulsera *f* 8
brakes frenos *m, pl.* 14
bread (toast) pan *m* (tostado) 4
breakfast desayuno *m* 3
bridge puente *m* 14
briefcase, carry-on bag maletín *m* 13
broccoli bróculi *m* 4
brother hermano *m* 2
brother-in-law cuñado *m* 3
brown marrón 5
brunette, dark-skinned moreno/a 3
brush cepillo *m* 6
building edificio *m* 7
bureau cómoda *f* 10
bus autobús *m* 7
bus station estación de autobuses 14
bus stop parada *f* de autobús 7
business empresa *f* 6
businessman hombre de negocios 6
businesswoman mujer de negocios 6
busy ocupado/a 3
but pero 3

butter mantequilla *f* 4
butterfly mariposa *f* 12
bye, so-long chao 1

C

cafeteria cafetería *f* 2
cake torta *f* 4
calculator calculadora *f* 2
calculus cálculo *m* 2
calling card tarjeta telefónica 11
calmly tranquilamente 6
camera cámara *f* 12
camp campamento *m* 12
campfire fogata *f* 12
cancer cancer *m* 15
candidate candidato/a *m/f* 15
cap gorra *f* 8
car auto *m* 3
car carro *m* 3
car coche *m* 3
card tarjeta *f* 7
carne de cerdo carne *f* de cerdo 4
carrot zanahoria *f* 4
cash efectivo *m* 7
cashier cajero/a *m/f* 6
cast yeso *m* 9
cat gato *m* 3
cathedral catedral *f* 7
CD, compact disk CD *m* 2
CD, compact disk disco compacto *m* 2
cell phone teléfono *m* celular 11
cereal cereal *m* 4
chain cadena *f* 8
chair silla *f* 2
chalk tiza *f* 2
chalkboard, board, blackboard pizarra *f* 2
change, small change, exchange cambio *m* 7
chapter capítulo *m* 2
check cheque *m* 7
cheese queso *m* 4
chemistry química *f* 2
cherry cereza **f** 4
chest, breast pecho *m* 9
chicken gallina *f* 12
chicken pollo *m* 4
child niña *f* 3
child niño *m* 3
childhood niñez 11
children niños *m, pl.* 11
Chilean chileno/a *m/f, n., adj.* 1
chill escalofrío *m* 9
church iglesia *f* 7
citizen ciudadano/a *m/f* 15
city ciudad *f* 3
city block cuadra *f* 14
class clase *f* 2
classroom aula *f* (*but el* aula) 1
clean limpio/a 8
clock; watch reloj *m* 2; 8

closed cerrado/a 3
closet clóset *m* 8
closet ropero/clóset *m* 8
clothes, clothing ropa *f* 8
clothing store tienda *f* de ropa 5
cloud nube *f* 5
cloudy está (muy) nublado 5
coat Abrigo *m* 8
coffee; coffee place café *m* 4
cold frío/a 5
cold resfriado *m* 9
college/university universidad *f* 2
Colombian colombiano/a *m/f, n., adj.* 1
comb peine *m* 6
comfortable cómodo/a 14
company compañía *f* 6
computer computadora *f* 2
computer programmer programador/a *m/f* 2
computer science computación *f* 2
computer science informática *f* 2
congratulations felicidades *f* 11
constantly constantemente 6
construct construir 15
contact lenses lentes *m* de contacto 8
cookie galleta *f* 4
corn maíz *m* 4
corruption corrupción *f* 15
Costa Rican costarricense *m/f, n., adj.* 1
cotton algodón *m* 8
cough tos *f* 9
country campo *m* 3
country país *m* 13
cousin primo/a *m/f* 3
cow vaca *f* 12
crash choque *m* 14
cream crema *f* 4
credit card tarjeta de crédito 7
crime crimen *m* 15
cruise ship crucero *m* 12
crutches muletas *f, pl.* 9
Cuban cubano/a *m/f, n., adj.* 1
cup taza *f* 10
cure cura *f* 15
currency, money, coin moneda *f* 7
curtain cortina *f* 10
customs aduana *f* 13

D

dangerous peligroso/a 12
date fecha *f* 1
date, appointment cita *f* 11
daughter hija *f* 3
day día *m* 1
day before yesterday anteayer 6
death muerte *f* 11
death penalty pena de muerte 15
December diciembre 1
deforestation desforestación *f* 12
delay demora *f* 13

delighted (to meet you) encantado/a 1
delinquent, offender, criminal delito *m* 15
delivery person repartidor/a *m/f* 6
deodorant desodorante *m* 6
department store almacén *m* 7
departure salida *f* 13
depressed deprimido/a 9
desert desierto *m* 12
dessert postre *m* 3
destroy destruir (y) 12
destruction destrucción *f* 12
diarrhea diarrea *f* 9
dictionary diccionario *m* 2
difficult, hard difícil 3
dining room comedor *m* 10
dirty sucio/a 8
disagreeable, unpleasant (persons) antipático/a 3
discrimination discriminación *f* 15
dish, course 3; *pl.* **ate** plato *m* 10
dishwasher lavaplatos *m* 10
divorce divorcio 11
divorced divorciado/a 11
do a blood test hacer un análisis de sangre 9
doctor doctor/a *m/f* 2
doctor médico/a *m/f* 2
doctor's office consultorio *m* del médico/de la médica 9
Does it hurt? ¿Te duele? 9
dog perro *m* 3
Dominican dominicano/a *m/f n., adj.* 1
door puerta *f* 2
double bed cama doble 6
double room habitación doble 13
dress vestido *m* 8
drink, beverage bebida *f* 4
driver conductor/a 14
driver's license licencia *f* de conducir 14
drought sequía *f* 12
drug addiction drogadicción *f* 15
drug trafficking narcotráfico *m* 15
drugs drogas *f, pl.* 14
dryer secadora *f* 10
dumb, silly tonto/a 3

E

each, every cada 9
ear (inner) oído *m* 9
ear (outer) oreja *f* 9
early temprano 2
earrings aretes *m, pl.* 8
earrings pendientes *m, pl.* 8
earth, land tierra *f* 12
easily fácilmente 6
easy fácil 3
easy chair sillón *m* 10
economics economía *f* 2
Ecuadorian ecuatoriano/a *m/f, n., adj.* 1

egg/fried eggs/scrambled eggs huevo *m*/huevos fritos/huevos revueltos 4
eighth octavo/a 13
elderly ancianos *m pl*./ la anciana *f* /el anciano *m* 11
election elección *f* 15
electric shaver máquina *m* de afeitar 6
elementary school escuela *f* 3
elevator ascensor *m* 13
e-mail correo *m* electrónico
e-mail address dirección *f* electrónica 2
e-mail message mensaje *m* electrónico 2
emergency *f, pl*. emergencias 9
employee empleado/a *m/f* 6
employment empleo *m* 15
English (language) inglés *m* 2
envelope sobre *m* 7
environment medio *m* ambiente 12
equality igualdad *f* 15
eraser borrador *m* 2
every afternoon todas las tardes 2
every day todo el día 2
every evening, night todas las noches 2
every morning todas las mañanas 2
exam examen *m* 2
exciting emocionante 13
exercise ejercicio *m* 2
expensive caro/a 8
explosion explosión *f* 15
extinction extinción *f* 12
eye ojo *m* 9
eyeglasses gafas *f, pl*. 8

F

face cara *f* 9
factory fábrica *f* 6
fair justo 13
faithful fiel 11
family familia *f* 2
family room sala familiar 10
far from lejos de 7
farm granja *f* 12
fashion moda *f* 8
fat gordo/a 3
father padre *m* 2
father-in-law suegro *m* 3
February febrero 1
fever fiebre *f* 9
few pocos/ as *m/f, adj*. 4
fifth quinto/a 13
film, movie película *f* 7
finally por fin 9
finally por fin 9
fine, well bien 3
fine, ticket multa *f* 14
finger dedo *m* 9
fingernail uña *f* 9
fire fuego *m* 12
fireplace, chimney chimenea *f* 10
first primer 13

first primero/a 6
first class de primera clase 14
first floor primer piso *m* 10
first/second class ticket boleto de primera/ segunda clase round trip ticket 14
fish pescado *m* 4
fish pez *m* (los peces) 12
flat tire llanta desinflada 14
flat, deflated (tire) desinflado/a 14
flight vuelo *m* 13
flight attendant (f) azafata *f* 13
flight attendant (m) auxiliar *m* de vuelo 13
floor suelo *m* 10
floor (of a building) piso *m* 10
flowers flores *f, pl*. 5
flu gripe *f* 9
fly mosca *f* 12
food, main meal comida *f* 3
foot pie *m* 9
football fútbol americano *m* 5
for, down, by, along, through por 7
for, in order to, toward, by para 14
forest bosque *m* 12
forest fires incendios *m, pl*. forestales 12
fork tenedor *m* 10
fourth cuarto/a 12
free gratis 14
freedom libertad *f* 15
French (language) francés *m* 2
french fries papas fritas 4
frequently frecuentemente 6
frequently con frecuencia 2
Friday viernes 1
fried frito/a 4
friend amigo/a *m/f* 3
friendly, kind amable 3
friendship amistad *f* 11
from where? ¿de dónde...? 4
fruit fruta *f* 3
full-time job trabajo *m* de tiempo completo 5
furniture muebles *m, pl*. 10

G

game, match partido *m* 5
garage garaje *m* 10
garbage basura *f* 12
garden jardín *m* 10
garlic ajo *m* 4
gas gasolina *f* 12
gas station gasolinera *f* 14
gate puerta de salida 13
generally generalmente 6
German (language) alemán *m* 2
gift regalo *m* 8
girl chica *f* 3
girl muchacha *f* 3
girlfriend novia *f* 3

glass (drinking) vaso *m* 10
global warming calentamento global *m* 12
gloves guantes *m, pl*. 8
Go to the pharmacy Vaya a la farmacia 9
goblet copa *f* 10
gold oro *m* 8
golf golf *m* 5
good bueno/a 3
good afternoon buenas tardes 1
good evening/night buenas noches 1
good morning buenos días 1
good-bye adiós 1
good-looking, pretty bonito/a 3
good-looking, pretty/handsome guapo/a 3
good-looking, pretty/handsome hermoso/a 3
government gobierno *m* 15
grade, score nota *f* 2
granddaughter nieta *f* 3
grandfather abuelo *m* 3
grandmother abuela *f* 3
grandparents abuelos *m, pl*. 3
grandson nieto *m* 3
grape uva *f* 4
grass hierba *f* 12
gray gris 5
great-grandfather bisabuelo *m* 3
great-grandmother bisabuela *f* 3
green verde 5
green bean judía *f* verde 4
grilled parrilla (a la parrilla) 4
Guatemalan guatemalteco/a *m/f, n., adj*. 1
guest huésped/a *m/f* 13
guitar guitarra *f* 4
gurney camilla *f* 9
gym, gymnasium gimnasio *m* 21

H

hair pelo *m* 9
hair dryer secador *m* de pelo 6
hair dryer secador *m* de pelo 6
half media *f* 1
half-brother medio hermano *m* 3
half-sister media hermana 3
ham jamón *m* 4
hamburger hamburguesa *f* 4
hand mano *f* 9
happy contento/a 3
hardworking trabajador/a 3
hat sombrero *m* 8
he; obj. *prep. pron.* him él *m, subj*. 6
head cabeza *f* 9
headache dolor *m* de cabeza 9
headache dolor *m* de cabeza *f* 9
headphones audífonos *m, pl*. 2
health salud *f* 8
heart corazón *m* 9

heating calefacción *f* 13
hello/hi hola 1
Help! ¡Auxilio! 14
Help! ¡Socorro! 14
here aquí 3
high school colegio *m* 3
highway autopista *f* 14
hill colina *f* 12
him, you, it lo *dir. obj. m* 5
his, her, its, your (formal), their su/sus 2
**(of) his, (of) hers, (of) theirs, (of) yours
   (formal)** suyo/a/os/as 8
history historia *f* 2
home, house casa 2
homeless desamparados *m, pl.* 15
homemaker amo/a *m/f* de casa 6
homework, assignment, task tarea *f* 2
Honduran hondureño/a *m/f, n., adj.* 1
honest, sincere sincero/a 11
honeymoon luna de miel 11
horse caballo *m* 12
hospital hospital *m* 9
hot (temperature, not spiciness)
   caliente 5
hotel hotel *m* 13
house keeper amo/a *m/f* de casa 2
How are you? (formal) Cómo está
   usted?
How are you? (informal) ¿Cómo estás? 1
how are you? (informal) ¿qué pasa? 1
How awful! ¡Qué barbaridad! 14
how many? ¿cuántos/as? 3
how much? ¿cuánto/a? 4
how? ¿cómo? 1
human rights derechos *m, pl.* humanos 15
hunger hambre *f (but el* hambre) 15
husband esposo *m* 3
husband marido *m* 3

I

I yo *subj. pron.* 1
I am sorry Disculpe 1
I hope ojalá que... 11
**I want to introduce . . . to you
   (informal); reflex. pron. yourself
   (informal)** te presento 1
I would like quisiera 4
I'm (so) sorry lo siento (mucho) 1
I'm (so) sorry lo siento (mucho) 1
I'm very sorry Lo siento mucho 14
ice hielo *m* 4
ice cream helado *m* 4
immediately inmediatamente 6
in case en caso de que 14
in front of delante de 7
in front of, opposite enfrente de 7
in front of, opposite, facing frente a 7
in order to (do something) para que 12
in style a la moda 8
in the afternoon por la tarde 2

in the afternoon; P.M. (in the afternoon)
   de la tarde; por/en la tarde 2
in the evening, at night por la noche 2
**in the evening, at night; P.M. (in the
   evening, at night)** por/en la noche 1
in the morning por/en la mañana 2
in the morning por la mañana 2
in, at; on en 2; 7
inexpensive barato/a 8
infancy infancia *f* 11
infection infección *f* 9
injection inyección *f* 9
insects insectos *m, pl.* 12
inside dentro de 7
instead of en vez de 7
intelligent inteligente 3
interview entrevista *f* 15
island isla *f* 12
it rains llueve 5
it seems that . . . parece que 13
it's (very) cloudy nublado 5
it's (very) cold hace (mucho) frío 5
it's (very) hot/cool/cold/sunny/windy
   hace (mucho) calor/fresco/frío/sol/
   viento 5
it's a pity ura lástima: es... 13
it's a shame lástima: es una... 13
it's better es mejor 13
it's good es bueno 13
it's horrible horrible: es... 13
it's important importante: es... 13
it's impossible imposible: es... 13
it's improbable improbable: es... 13
it's improbable improbable: es... 13
it's interesting interesante: es... 13
it's necessary necesario: es... 13
it's necessary preciso: es... 13
it's obvious obvio: es... 13
it's possible posible: es... 13
it's probable probable: es... 13
it's raining está lloviendo 5
it's ridiculous ridículo: es... 13
it's snowing está nevando 5
it's snowing nieva 5
it's strange extraño: es... 13
it's sunny hace sol 5
it's true verdad: es... 13
it's true, correct cierto: es... 13
it's unfair no es... 13
it's urgent urgente: es... 13
it's wonderful es fenomenal 13
Italian (language) italiano *m* 5

J

jacket chaqueta *f* 8
jam mermelada *f* 4
January enero 1
Japanese (language) japonés *m* 5
jealous celoso/a 11
jeans jeans *m, pl.* 8

jeans vaqueros *m, pl.* 8
jewelry joyas *f, pl.* 8
jewelry shop joyería *f* 7
juice jugo *m* 4
juice zumo *m* 4
July julio 1
June junio 1
jungle selva *f* 12
justice justicia *f* 15

K

kayak kayak *m* 12
key llave *f* 13
keyboard teclado *m* 2
kilometer kilómetro *m* 14
kitchen cocina *f* 10
knife cuchillo *m* 10

L

laboratory laboratorio *m* 2
lake lago *m* 5
lamp lámpara *f* 10
laptop/notebook (computer)
   computadora portátil *f* 13
last night anoche 6
last week semana *f* pasada 6
last weekend fin de semana pasado 6
last year/month/summer pasado: el
   año/ mes/ verano 6
later más tarde 2
law ley *f* 15
Lawyer abogado/a *m/f* 6
lazy perezoso/a 3
leader líder *m/f* 15
leather cuero *m* 8
leave, depart, to go away irse 11
leaves hojas *f, pl.* 5
leg pierna *f* 9
lemon limón *m* 4
less menos 4
lesson lección *f* 2
letter carta *f* 7
lettuce lechuga *f* 4
library biblioteca *f* 2
life vida *f* 11
light luz *f* 10
lightning relámpago *m* 12
line (of people or things) cola *f* 7
line (of people or things) fila *f* 7
lip labio *m* 9
literature literatura *f* 2
little (quantity) poco/a *m/f, adj.* 4
littles poco *adv.* 4
living room sala *f* 10
lobster langosta *f* 4
long largo/a 8
long distance call llamada de larga
   distancia 11
long-/short-sleeved de manga
   larga/corta 8

long-sleeved de manga larga 8
love amor *m* 11
love at first sight amor a primera vista 11
luggage equipaje *m* 13
lunch almuerzo *m* 4
lung pulmón *m* 9

M

magazine revista *f* 7
maid (hotel) camarera *f* 13
mailbox buzón *m* 7
main floor planta baja 13
makeup maquillaje *m* 6
mall, shopping center centro comercial 7
man hombre *m* 3
manager gerente/a *m/f* 15
map mapa *m* 2
March marzo 1
market mercado *m* 3
married casado/a 11
mathematics matemáticas *f, pl.* 2
May mayo 1
me mí *obj. prep. pron.* 6
me; *ind. obj.* me (to/for me); *refl. pron.* myself me *dir. obj.* 5
meat, beef carne *f* 4
medicine medicina *f* 15
metro, subway metro *m* 7
Mexican mexicano/a *m/f, n., adj.* 1
microwave microondas *m* 10
midnight medianoche *f* 1
milk leche *f* 4
mirror espejo *m* 10
misdemeanor, crime delincuente *m* 15
Monday lunes *m* 1
money dinero *m* 6
month mes *m* 1
moon luna *f* 12
more más 4
mosquito mosquito *m* 12
mother madre *f* 3
mother-in-law suegra *f* 3
motor motor *m* 14
motorcycle motocicleta *f* 14
mountain biking ciclismo *m* de montaña 12
mountain climbing alpinismo/el andinismo *m* 12
mountain climbing andinismo *m*, alpinismo *m* 11
mountains montañas *f, pl.* 3
mouse ratón *m* 2
mouth boca *f* 9
movie theater, cinema cine *m* 7
much, a lot; mucho/a/os/as *m/f* mucho *adv. adj.*
much, a lot, many times, often muchas veces *f* 8
museum museo *m* 7
music música *f* 2

my mi/mis 2
my name is . . . me llamo... 1
my soul mate, other half mi media naranja 11

N

napkin servilleta *f* 10
nasal congestion congestión *f* nasal 9
natural resources recursos *m, pl.* naturales 12
nature naturaleza *f* 12
nausea náuseas *f, pl.* 8
near cerca de 7
neck cuello *m* 9
necklace collar *m* 8
neighbor vecino/a *m/f* 10
neither . . . nor ni... ni 13
neither, not either tampoco 7
nephew sobrino *m* 3
nervous nervioso/a 3
never nunca 2
new nuevo/a 3
newlyweds recién casados *m, pl.* 11
news noticias *f, pl.* 7
newscast noticiero *m* 15
newspaper periódico *m* 7
newsstand quiosco *m* 7
next próximo/a 5
next month/year/summer el próximo mes/ año / verano 5
Nicaraguan nicaragüense *m/f, n., adj.* 1
nice meeting you too igualmente 1
nice, likeable simpático/a 3
niece sobrina *f* 3
night noche *f* 1
nightstand mesita *f* de noche 10
ninth noveno/a 13
no one, nobody nadie 7
no, none, no one ningún (ninguno/a) 13
noise ruido *m* 10
noon mediodía *m* 1
normally normalmente 6
nose nariz *f* 9
not, not even ni 13
notebook cuaderno *m* 2
notes apuntes *m, pl.* 2
nothing nada 7
November noviembre 1
now ahora 2
nurse enfermero/a *m/f* 6

O

ocean océano *m* 12
October octubre 1
Of course! ¡Claro! 14
Of course! ¡Por supuesto! 14
of mine mío/a/os/as 7
of yours (*informal*) tuyo/a/os/as 7
of, from de *prep* 1
office oficina *f* 2

Oh my gosh! ¡Caramba! 14
oil aceite *m* 4
OK, so-so regular 1
old viejo/a 3
old (elderly); older mayor 3
old age vejez 11
olive aceituna *f* 4
on sobre 7
on time a tiempo 2
on top of, above encima de 7
once, one time una vez 9
onion cebolla *f* 4
open abierto/a 3
open your mouth abrala boca 9
or o 3
or . . . either o... o 13
orange (color) anaranjado/a 5
orange (fruit) naranja *f* 4
other otros/as 4
ought to, should (do something) deber + *infinitive* 5
our; (of) ours nuestro/a/os/as 8
outdoors aire libre *m* 12
outer space exploration exploración *f* del espacio 15
outside fuera de 7
oven horno *m* 10
overpopulation sobrepoblación *f* 15
ozone layer capa *f* de ozono 12

P

package paquete *m* 7
page página *f* 2
pants pantalones *m, pl.* 8
paper papel *m* 2
paper (academic) trabajo *m* escrito 15
paramedics paramédicos *m, pl.* 9
pardon me, excuse me con permiso 1
pardon me, excuse me perdón 1
parents padres *m, pl.* 3
park parque *m* 7
parking estacionamiento *m* 14
partner, significant other, couple pareja *f* 11
part-time job trabajo de tiempo parcial 5
party fiesta *f* 2
passenger pasajero/a *m/f* 13
passport pasaporte *m* 13
pastry shop, bakery pastelería *f* 7
patient paciente *m/f* 9
pea guisante *m* 4
peace paz *f* 15
peace accord acuerdo *m* de paz *f* 15
peach durazno *m* 4
peach melocotón *m* 4
pear pera *f* 4
pen bolígrafo *m* 2
pen pluma *f* 2
pencil lápiz *m* 2
people gente *f* 7

pepper pimienta *f* 4
personally personalmente 6
pharmacy farmacia *f* 9
philosophy filosofía *f* 2
phone book guía *f* telefónica 11
physics física *f* 2
picture, painting cuadro *m* 4
pie, pastry pastel *m* 4
pig cerdo *m* 12
pillow almohada *f* 13
pilot piloto/a *m/f* 13
pineapple piña *f* 4
pink rosado/a 5
pizzeria pizzería *f* 7
place lugar *m* 7
planet planeta *m* 12
plant planta *f* 12
platform andén *m* 14
play obra *f* de teatro 7
plaza, town square plaza *f* 7
please favor (por favor) 1
please por favor 1
pleased to meet you mucho gusto 1
poisonous pesticide tóxico/pesticida *f* 12
policeman policía *m* 14
policewoman mujer policía 14
political science ciencias *f, pl.* políticas 2
pollution contaminación *f* 12
poor pobre 3
Poor me! (What am I going to do?) ¡Ay de mí! 14
pork carne de cerdo/puerco *f* 4
pork chop chuleta *f* de cerdo 4
pork chop chuleta *f* de cerdo/puerco 4
porter maletero *m* 14
possibly posiblemente 6
post card tarjeta postal 7
post office oficina de correos 8
poster póster *m* 10
potato papa *f* 4
potato patata *f* 4
poverty pobreza *f* 15
pregnant embarazada 9
prejudice prejuicio *m* 15
prescription receta *f* 9
price precio *m* 8
printer impresora *f* 2
private bath baño privado 13
probably probablemente 6
problem problema *m* 12
professor profesor/a *m/f* 2
provided that con tal (de) que 1
psychology psicología *f* 2
Puerto Rican puertorriqueño/a *m/f, n., adj.* 1
purple morado/a 5
purse, bag bolso/a *m* 8

Q

question pregunta *f* 2
quiz prueba *f* 2

R

raft balsa *f* 12
railroad station estación de ferrocarril 14
rain lluvia *f* 5
raincoat impermeable *m* 8
rapidly rápidamente 6
razor navaja *f* 6
recently recientemente 6
reception, front desk recepción *f* 9
receptionist recepcionista *m/f* 9
red rojo/a 5
refrigerator refrigerador *m* 10
relative pariente *m* 3
religion religión *f* 2
reporter reportero/a 15
research investigación *f* 15
reservation reservación *f* 13
responsible responsable 3
rest descanse 9
restaurant restaurante *m* 2
restroom aseos *m, pl.* 13
restroom servicio *m* 14
rice arroz *m* 4
rich rico/a 3
ring anillo *m* 8
river río *m* 15
road camino *m* 14
road carretera *f* 14
roof techo *m* 10
room cuarto *m* 2
room habitación *f* 9
room service servicio de habitación 13
roommate compañero/a *m/f* de cuarto 6
round trip ticket billete de ida y vuelta 13
rug, carpet alfombra *f* 10
Russian (language) ruso *m* 5

S

sad triste 3
safe seguro/a 14
salad ensalada *f* 4
sales rebajas *f* 8
salt sal *f* 4
sand arena *f* 12
sand castle castillo de arena *m* 12
sandals sandalias *f, pl.* 8
sandwich bocadillo *m* 4
sandwich sándwich *m* 4
Saturday sábado *m* 1
sausage chorizo *m* 4
sausage salchicha *f* 4
Say ah! Diga ¡ah! 9
scarf bufanda *f* 8
schedule horario *m* 13
scissors tijeras *f, pl.* 6
sea mar *m* 12
seafood marisco *m* 3

season estación *f* 4
seat asiento *m* 13
second segundo/a 13
second class de segunda clase 14
second floor segundo piso 10
secretary secretario/a *m/f* 6
see you soon hasta pronto 1
see you tomorrow hasta: hasta mañana 1
see you tomorrow hasta mañana 1
September septiembre 1
serious wound herida *f* grave 9
serious, dependable serio/a 3
service/gas station estación de servicio/la gasolinera 14
seventh séptimo/a 13
shaving cream crema de afeitar *f* 6
she obj. *of prep.* her ella *f, subj.* 1
sheet sábana *f* 13
sheet of paper hoja *f* de papel 2
shirt camisa *f* 8
shoe store zapatería *f* 7
shoes zapatos *m, pl.* 8
shop taller *m* mecánico 14
short bajo/a 3
short corto/a 8
short- sleeved de manga corta 8
shorts pantalones cortos 8
shoulder hombro *m* 9
shower ducha *f* 10
shrimp camarón *m* 4
sick enfermo/a 3
silk seda *f* 8
silver plata *f* 8
single soltero/a 11
single bed cama sencilla 6
single room habitación sencilla 13
sink (bathroom) lavabo *m* 10
sink (kitchen) fregadero *m* 10
sister hermana *f* 3
sister-in-law cuñada *f* 3
sixth sexto/a 13
size (clothing) talla *f* 8
skinny flaco/a 3
skirt falda *f* 8
sky cielo *m* 12
skyscraper rascacielos *m* 7
sleeping bag saco *m* de dormir 12
sleeve manga *f* 8
slow, slowly despacio 14
slowly lentamente 6
small, little pequeño/a 3
snack merienda *f* 3
snake serpiente *f* 12
snow nieve *f* 5
so that, in order that para + *infinitivo* 7
soap jabón *m* 6
soccer fútbol *m* 5
sociology sociología *f* 2
socks calcetines *m, pl.* 8
sofa sofá *m* 10
soft drink refresco *m* 4

some unos/unas 2
someone, somebody alguien 7
something algo 7
sometimes a veces 2
son hijo *m* 3
sore throat dolor de garganta *f* 9
sore throat dolor *m* de garganta 9
soup sopa *f* 4
space ship nave *f* espacial 15
Spanish español/española *m/f, n., adj.* 1
Spanish (language) español *m* 2
speed velocidad *f* 14
spider araña *f* 12
spoon cuchara *f* 10
sport deporte *m* 5
spring primavera *f* 5
stages of life etapas *f, pl.* de la vida 11
stairs escalera *f* 10
stamp estampilla *f* 7
stamp sello *m* 7
star estrella *f* 12
statue estatua *f* 7
steak bistec *m* 4
stepbrother hermanastro *m* 3
stepfather padrastro *m* 3
stepmother madrastra *f* 3
stepsister hermanastra *f* 3
stereo estéreo *m* 10
Stick out your tongue. Saque la lengua. 9
still, yet todavía 4
stockings, hose, socks medias *f, pl.* 8
stomach estómago *m* 9
stomach ache dolor de estómago *m* 9
stomachache dolor *m* de estómago 9
store clerk dependiente/a *m/f* 6
store, shop tienda *f* 6
storm tormenta *f* 12
stove estufa *f* 10
straight, straight ahead derecho 14
strawberry fresa *f* 4
street calle *f* 7
street corner esquina *f* 14
stressed estresado/a 3
strong fuerte 3
student alumno/a *m/f* 2
student estudiante *m/f* 2
student center centro estudiantil 2
student desk pupitre *m* 2
student dorm residencia *f* estudiantil 2
suddenly de repente 9
sugar azúcar *m* 4
suit traje *m* 8
suitcase maleta *f* 13
summer verano *m* 5
sun sol *m* 12
Sunday domingo *m* 1
sunglasses gafas de sol 8
supper, dinner cena *f* 3
sweater suéter *m* 8
swimming pool piscina *f* 13

T

table mesa *f* 2
Take a deep breath. Respire profundamente. 7
Take aspirin/the pills/the capsules. Tome aspirinas/las pastillas/las cápsulas. 9
Take liquids. Tome líquidos. 9
take out, to withdraw retirar 7
Take the prescription to the pharmacy. Lleve la receta a la farmacia. 9
tall alto/a 3
tank tanque *m* 14
taxi taxi *m* 7
tea té *m* 4
teacher maestro/a *m/f* 2
teacher's desk escritorio *m* 2
team equipo *m* 5
teaspoon cucharita *f* 10
telephone call llamada *f* telefónica 11
television set televisor *m* 2
tennis tenis *m* 5
tennis shoes zapatos de tenis 8
tent tienda de campaña 12
tenth décimo/a 13
terrific fenomenal 1
terrorism terrorismo *m* 15
thank you (very much) (muchas) gracias 1
thank you/thanks gracias 1
that aquel/aquella *adj.* 6
that ese/a *adj.* 6
that que 4
that on aquél/aquélla *pron.* 6
that one ése/a *pron.* 6
that which lo que 14
the el *m, definite article* 2
the las *f, pl. definite article* 2
the line is busy línea está ocupada 11
the pleasure is mine el gusto es mío 1
the weather is nice/bad hace buen/mal tiempo 5
the; *dir. obj.* her, you (*f*), it (*f*) la *f, definite article* 5
theater teatro *m* 7
them (*f*), you (*f, pl.*) las *dir. obj.* 5
them, you; *m, pl., definite article* the los *m, dir. obj.* 6; 2
then entonces 6
then luego 6
there allí 3
there is/are hay 2
thermometer termómetro *m* 9
these estos/as *adj.* 6
these estos/as *pron.* 6
they obj. *of prep.* them ellas *f, subj* 1
they obj. *of prep.* them ellos *m, subj* 1
thin delgado/a 3
thing cosa *f* 8
third tercero/a 13
this este/a *adj.* 6

this afternoon esta tarde 3
this morning esta mañana 2
this one éste/a *pron.* 6
this, that esta 6
those aquéllos/as *pron.*; aquellos/as *adj.* 6
those esos/as *adj.* 6
those ésos/as *pron.* 6
throat garganta *f* 9
Thursday jueves *m* 1
ticket billete *m* 13
ticket window taquilla *f* 14
tie corbata *f* 8
time hora *f* 1
tip propina *f* 13
tire llanta *f* 14
tired cansado/a 3
to advise aconsejar 11
to answer contestar 7
to apply (job) solicitar 15
to arrive llegar 2
to ask preguntar 8
to ask for, request, order pedir (i, i) 4
to attend asistir (a) 2
to avoid evitar 12
to backpack viajar de mochila 12
to be estar 3
to be ser 2
to be able, can poder (ue) 4
to be afraid tener miedo 12
to be against estar en contra de 15
to be annoying to, to bother molestar 12
to be born nacer 11
to be careful tener cuidado 14
to be engaged estar comprometido/a 11
to be engaged estar prometido/a 11
to be fascinating to, to fascinate fascinar 12
to be glad (about) alegrarse (de) 11
to be hot/cold tener calor/frío 5
to be hungry/thirsty tener hambre/sed 4
to be important to, to matter importar 12
to be in a hurry tener prisa 13
to be in favor of estar a favor de 15
to be in love (with) estar enamorado/a de 11
to be interesting to, to interest interesar 12
to be jealous tener celos 11
to be married (to) estar casado/a (con) 11
to be on vacation estar de vacaciones *f, pl.* 12
to be pregnant estar embarazada 11
to be ready estar listo 12
to be ready listo/a: estar... 11
to be seated estar sentado/a 9
to be sleepy, tired tener sueño 6

to be sorry, regret sentir (ie, i) 11
to be standing estar de pie 8
to be standing estar de pie 9
to be successful tener éxito 15
to be sure of estar seguro/a (de) 12
to be together estar juntos/as 11
to be together juntos/as: estar... 11
to begin empezar (ie) (a) 7
to believe creer 11
to break romper 10
to break one's (arm/leg) fracturar(se) (el brazo/ la pierna) 9
to break up (with) romper (con) 11
to bring traer 5
to brush one's hair cepillarse el pelo 6
to brush one's teeth cepillarse los dientes 6
to buy comprar 2
to call llamar 3
to camp acampar 12
to cash, to charge cobrar 7
to change, exchange cambiar 7
to check revisar 14
to check (baggage) facturar 13
to choose escoger 15
to clean limpiar 5
to clear the table quitar:... la mesa 10
to climb (the mountain) escalar (la montaña) 12
to close cerrar (ie) 7
to comb one's hair peinarse 6
to come venir (ie) 5
to communicate comunicarse 11
to complain about quejarse de 11
to confirm confirmar 13
to continue continuar 14
to continue, follow seguir (i, i) 14
to contribute contribuir (y) 12
to cook cocinar 4
to cost costar (ue) 4
to cough toser 9
to count 7, tell, narrate (a story or incident) contar (ue) 8
to crash, collide chocar 14
to cross cruzar 14
to cry llorar 11
to cut one's hair/nails/a finger cortarse el pelo/ las uñas/ el ded 6
to cut oneself cortarse 5
to cut the lawn cortar:... el césped 10
to dance bailar 5
to deposit depositar 7
to die morir (ue, u) 7
to do, make hacer 2
to doubt dudar 12
to draw blood sacar sangre 9
to drink beber 2
to drive conducir 14
to drive manejar 5
to dry (oneself) secarse 6
to dry the dishes secar:... los pl.atos 9

to eat comer 2
to eliminate eliminar 15
to enjoy (something) disfrutar de 13
to enter, go into entrar (en/a) 7
to examine examinar 9
to exercise, to do exercises hacer ejercicio 5
to exercise, work out, do exercises hacer ejercicio 5
to explain explicar 8
to fall in love (with) enamorarse (de) 11
to fasten one's seat belt abrocharse el cinturón 13
to fear, be afraid of temer 11
to feed dar de comer 15
to feel sentirse (ie, i) 9
to feel like (doing something) tener ganas de + infinitivo 5
to fight (for) luchar (por) 15
to fill (the tank) llenar (el tanque) 14
to find encontrar (ue) 7
to find out, inquire averiguar 6
to finish terminar 7
to fish pescar 12
to fix reparar 14
to fly volar (ue) 13
to forbid prohibir 15
to forget olvidar/ olvidarse de 11
to get (stand) in line hacer cola 7
to get (stand) in line hacer fila 6
to get a grade sacar una nota 2
to get along well/badly llevarse bien/mal 11
to get angry enojarse 11
to get divorced divorciarse 11
to get dressed vestirse (i) 6
to get engaged (to) comprometerse (con) 11
to get married (to) casarse (con) 11
to get off, to get out of . . . bajarse de 13
to get on, board subirse a 13
to get passports sacar los pasaportes 13
to get tired cansarse 9
to get up levantarse 6
to get, obtain conseguir (i, i) 13
to get/become sick enfermarse 9
to give dar 5
to give (as a gift) regalar 8
to give a shot/vaccination poner una inyección/ una vacuna 9
to give birth dar a lu 11
to go ir 2
to go down bajar 10
to go on a cruise, take a trip on a ship/boat/cruise ship hacer un viaje en crucero/ en barco 12
to go on vacation ir(se) de vacaciones 12
to go out (with), date salir (con) 11
to go parachute jumping saltar en paracaídas 12
to go parasailing practicar el parasail 12

to go shopping ir de compras 5
to go snorkeling hacer el esnórquel 12
to go to bed acostarse (ue) 6
to go to sleep, to fall asleep dormir (ue) 6
to go up subir 10
to go white-water rafting rafting: practicar el... 12
to go white-water rafting practicar el descenso de ríos 12
to have a good time divertirse (ie) 6
to have breakfast desayunar 2
to have dinner cenar 2
to have just (completed an action) acabar de + infinitivo 6
to have lunch almorzar (ue) 4
to have to . . . (do something) tener que + infinitivo 5
to hear oír 5
to help ayudar (a) 10
to hug abrazar 3
to hurt oneself lastimarse 9
to inform informar/ reportar 15
to insist (on) insistir (en) 11
to intend/plan (to do something) pensar (ie) + infinitivo 5
to invest invertir (ie, i) 7
to invite invitar (a) 7
to keep guardar 10
to kill matar 11
to kiss besar 3
to know (facts, information); to know how to (skills) saber 5
to land aterrizar 13
to laugh at reírse (de) 11
to learn aprender 2
to leave dejar 13
to leave a message dejar un mensaje 11
to leave behind dejarse 13
to leave, go out salir 2
to legalize legalizar 15
to lend prestar 8
to lie mentir 11
to lift weights levantar pesas 5
to like gustar 4
to listen to escuchar 2
to live vivir 2
to look at mirar 8
to look for buscar 2
to lose perder (ie) 7
to love amar 3
to make an appointment hacer una cita 9
to make reservations hacer reservaciones/ reservas 14
to make the bed hacer la cama 10
to meet up (with) (by chance) encontrarse (ue) (con) 11
to meet, get together reunirse (con) 11
to meet, know, be acquainted with conocer 5

to miss extrañar 11
to miss the train perder el tren 14
to move (from house to house) mudarse 10
to move (oneself) mover(se) (ue) 10
to need necesitar 4
to open abrir 7
to pack empacar 13
to pack hacer las maletas 13
to paint pintar 5
to park estacionar 14
to pay (for) pagar 7
to pick up, gather recoger 12
to play (instruments) tocar 5
to play/to play (sport) jugar (ue)/ jugar al (deporte) 5
to practice practicar 2
to prefer preferir (ie, i) 4
to prepare preparar 2
to prevent prevenir 12
to print imprimir 2
to protect proteger 12
to put gas (in the tank) echar gasolina 14
to put on (shoes, clothes, etc.) ponerse (los zapatos, la ropa, etc.) 6
to put on makeup maquillarse 6
to put, place poner 5
to rain llover (ue) 5
to read leer 2
to really like, love; to delight, to enchant encantar 12
to receive recibir 7
to recommend recomendar (ie) 11
to recycle reciclar 12
to reduce reducir 12
to register registrarse 13
to remember acordarse (ue) de 11
to remember recordar (ue) 11
to rent alquilar 10
to repeat repetir (i, i) 7
to report reportar 15
to rest descansar 5
to return regresar 2
to return (something) devolver (ue) 8
to return, to go back volver (ue) 4
to ride horseback montar a caballo 12
to ring, to sound sonar (ue) 6
to rob robar 15
to row remar 12
to run correr 5
to run, work, function (machine) funcionar 14
to save (money) ahorrar 7
to save, conserve conservar 12
to say good-bye despedirse (i, i) 13
to say, tell decir (i) 5
to scuba dive, skin dive bucear 12
to see ver 5
to sell vender 4
to send enviar 7
to send mandar 2

to separate separarse (de) 11
to serve servir (i, i) 4
to set the table poner la mesa 10
to shave afeitarse 6
to show mostrar (ue) 8
to sign firmar 7
to sing cantar 5
to sit down sentarse (ie, i) 9
to ski esquiar 5
to sleep dormirse (ue) 4
to smoke fumar 5
to sneeze estornudar 9
to snow nevar (ie) 5
to solve/resolve resolver (ue) 10
to speak hablar 2
to spend gastar 7
to spend (time), to happen, pass pasar 7
to sprain (one's ankle) torcer(se) (ue) 9
to stay quedarse 9
to stop (movement) parar 14
to study estudiar 2
to suffer sufrir 15
to suggest sugerir (ie, i) 11
to sunbathe tomar el sol 5
to support (a candidate/cause) apoyar 15
to surf hacer surf 12
to surf the Web navegar por la red 2
to swim nadar 12
to take a bath, bathe bañarse 6
to take a hike dar una caminata 12
to take a shower ducharse 6
to take a walk/stroll dar un paseo 5
to take care of cuidar 2
to take notes tomar apuntes m, pl. 2
to take off despegar 13
to take off (clothes, etc.) quitarse la ropa 6
to take one's blood pressure tomar la presión arterial 9
to take one's pulse tomar el pulso 9
to take one's temperature tomar la temperatura 9
to take out the garbage sacar la basura 10
to take photos sacar fotos f, pl. 11
to take photos tomar fotos f, pl. 12
to take, drink tomar 4
to the left izquierda f: a la... 14
to the right derecha: a la ... 14
to think pensar (ie) 4
to think about (someone or something) pensar (ie) en 11
to tidy (the room) ordenar (el cuarto) 10
to travel viajar 5
to try to (do something) tratar de + infinitivo 11
to tune the motor afinar el motor 14
to turn doblar 14
to turn off apagar 10
to turn on prender 10

to understand comprender 2
to understand entender (ie) 4
to use usar 2
to vacuum pasar la aspiradora 10
to visit visitar 3
to vomit vomitar 9
to vote (for) votar (por) 15
to wait (for); to hope, expect esperar 7; 11
to wake up despertarse (ie) 6
to walk caminar 5
to want, love querer (ie) 4
to wash one's hands/face lavarse las manos/ la cara 6
to wash oneself lavarse 5
to wash the dishes lavar:... los platos 10
to waste desperdiciar 12
to watch TV ver la tele(visión) 5
to wear llevar 8
to win, to earn, make money ganar 5; 6
to work; trabajar para... to work for trabajar 6
to worry (about) preocuparse (por) 9
to write escribir 2
to x-ray sacar una radiografía 9
today hoy 1
toilet inodoro m 10
toilet paper papel higiénico 6
tomato tomate m 4
tomorrow, morning Mañana f 1
tongue lengua f 9
tonight esta noche 2
too, too much demasiado adv. 14
tooth diente m 9
toothbrush cepillo de dientes 6
toothpaste pasta f de dientes 6
towel toalla f 6
traffic tráfico m 14
traffic tránsito m 14
traffic light semáforo m 14
train tren m 14
trash can cubo m de la basura 10
travel agency agencia f de viajes 14
traveler's check cheque de viajero 7
tree árbol m 5
truck camión m 14
T-shirt, undershirt camiseta f 8
Tuesday martes m 1
tune the motor afinar el motor 14
tutor tutor/a 15

U

ugly feo/a 3
umbrella paraguas m 8
uncle tío m 3
understanding comprensivo/a 11
underwear ropa f interior 8
unemployment desempleo m 15
unfortunately desafortunadamente 6
unless a menos (de) que 14

until hasta que 15
upon (doing something) al + *infinitivo* 7
Uruguayan uruguayo/a *m/f, n., adj.* 1
us; *ind. obj.* us (to/for us); *refl. pron.*
  ourselves nos *dir. obj.* 5

V

vacation vacaciones *f, pl.* 12
vaccination vacuna *f* 9
valley valle *m* 12
VCR, video VCR *m* 2
vegetable legumbre *f* 3
vegetable verdura *f* 3
very muy 3
very well muy bien 1
victim víctima *f* 15
vinegar vinagre *m* 4
violence violencia *f* 15
volleyball vólibol *m* 5
volunteer voluntario/a *m/f* 15
volunteerism trabajo voluntario *m* 15
vomit vómito *m* 9

W

waiter/waitress mesero/a *m/f* 6
waiting room sala de espera 9
wall pared *f* 10
wallet Billetera/la cartera *f* 8
wallet cartera *f* 8
want, wish desear 4
war guerra *f* 15
washer lavadora *f* 10
wastebasket papelera *f* 2
water agua *f* (*but el* agua) 4
waterfall cascada *f* 12
waterfall catarata *f* 12
watermelon sandía *f* 4
wave ola *f* 12
we; *obj. prep.* us nosotros/as *m/f,*
  subj. pron. 1
weak débil 3
weapon arma *f* 15
weather clima *m* 5
weather tiempo *m* 5
Web page página web 2
Web site sitio web *m* 2
wedding boda *f* 11

Wednesday miércoles *m* 1
week semana *f* 1
weekend fin *m* de semana 2
welcome bienvenido/a 13
well pues 1
what ¿qué? 4
What a mess! ¡Qué lío! 14
What a shame! ¡Qué lástima! 14
What luck!/ How lucky! ¡Qué suerte! 14
what, that which lo que 4
what's happening? (informal) ¿qué tal? 1
what's new? (*informal*) ¿qué hay de
  nuevo? 1
What's your name (*formal*)? ¿Cómo se
  llama usted? 1
What's your name? (*informal*) ¿Cómo te
  llamas? 1
wheel chair silla de ruedas 9
when cuando 4
when? ¿cúando 2
where ¿dónde? 3
(to) where? ¿adónde? 2
(to) where? ¿adónde? 2
which (one)? ¿cuál? 4
which (ones)? ¿cuáles? 4
while mientras 9
white blanco/a 5
who? ¿quién/quiénes? 3
whose? ¿de quién? 4
why? ¿por qué? 4
widower/widow viudo/a *m/f* 11
wife esposa *f* 3
window ventana *f* 2
window (airplane, train, car)
  ventanilla *f* 13
windshield parabrisas *m* 14
wine vino *m* 4
winter invierno *m* 5
with con 4;
without sin 4
woman, wife mujer *f* 3
wool lana *f* 8
work trabajo *m* 6
world mundo *m* 12
world politics política *f* mundial 15
worried preocupado/a 3
worse Peor 10

Y

year año *m* 4
years old tener... años 3
yellow amarillo/a 5
yesterday ayer 6
you (*formal*); *obj. prep.* you (*formal*)
  usted *subj. pron.* 1; 6
you (*informal*) ti *obj. prep.* 6
you (*informal*) tú *subj. pron.* 1
you (*informal*) ; *ind. obj.* you (to/for
  you) (*informal*) te *dir. obj.* 5
you (informal, pl., Sp.); *obj. prep.* you
  (*informal, pl., Sp.*) vosotros/as *m/f,*
  subj 6
you (*pl.*); *ind. obj.* you (to/for you); *refl.*
  pron. yourselves os *dir. obj.* 5
you (*pl.*); *obj. prep.* you (*pl.*) ustedes
  subj. pron. 1; 6
you, him, her (to/for . . .) le *ind. obj.* 8
you, them (to/for you, them) les *ind.*
  obj. 8
you're welcome de nada 1
young joven 3
young people, adolescents jóvenes *m,*
  pl. /los adolescentes 11
younger menor 3
your (*informal*) tu/tus 2
your (*informal*); (of) yours (*informal*)
  vuestro/a/os/as 7
yourself, himself, herself, themselves se
  reflex. pron. 5
youth juventud *f* 11

Vocabulario: *Spanish-English*

A

a at, to 2; **a veces** sometimes 2
abierto/a open 3
abogado/a *m/f* lawyer 6
aborto *m* abortion 15
abrala boca open your mouth 9
abrazar to hug 3
abrigo *m* coat 8
abril April 1
abrir to open 7
abrocharse el cinturón to fasten one's seat belt 13
abuela *f* grandmother 3
abuelo *m* grandfather 3
abuelos *m, pl.* grandparents 3
aburrido/a bored 3; boring 3
acabar de + *infinitivo* to have just (completed an action) 6
acampar to camp 12
accidente *m* accident 14
aceite *m* oil 4
aceituna *f* olive 4
aconsejar to advise 11
acordarse (ue) de to remember 11
acostarse (ue) to go to bed 6
acuerdo *m* **de paz** *f* peace accord 15
adiós good-bye 1
adolescencia adolescence 10
adolescentes *m, pl.* adolescents 10
¿adónde? (to) where? 2
aduana *f* customs 13
adultos *m, pl.* adults 11
aerolínea *f* airline 13
aeropuerto *m* airport 13
afeitarse to shave 6
afinar el motor tune the motor 14
agencia *f* **de viajes** travel agency 14
agosto August 1
agua *f* (**but el** agua) water 4
ahora now 2
ahorrar to save (money) 7
aire *m* air 14; **aire acondicionado** air conditioning 13; **aire libre** *m* outdoors 12
ajo *m* garlic 4
al + *infinitivo* upon (doing something) 7
al lado de beside 7
alegrarse (de) to be glad (about) 11
alemán *m* German (language) 2
alergia *f* allergy 9
alfombra *f* rug, carpet 10
álgebra *f* (**but el** álgebra) algebra 2
algo something 7
algodón *m* cotton 8
alguien someone, somebody 7
algún (alguno/a/os/as) any, some, someone 13
allí there 3
almacén *m* department store 7
almohada *f* pillow 13
almorzar (ue) to have lunch 4

almuerzo *m* lunch 4
alpinismo/el andinismo *m* mountain climbing 12
alquilar to rent 10
alto/a tall 3
alumno/a *m/f* student 2
amo/a *m/f* **de casa** homemaker 6
amable friendly, kind 3
amar to love 3
amarillo/a yellow 5
ambulancia *f* ambulance 9
amigo/a *m/f* friend 3
amistad *f* friendship 11
amor *m* love 11; **amor a primera vista** love at first sight 11
anaranjado/a orange (color) 5
ancianos *m/***la anciana** *f /***el anciano** *m pl.* elderly 11
andén *m* platform 14
andinismo *m*, **alpinismo** *m* mountain climbing 11
anillo *m* ring 8
animal *m* animal 11
año *m* year 4; **tener... años** to be . . . years old 3
anoche last night 6
anteayer day before yesterday 6
antes de (clase) *prep.* before (class) 2; **antes de que** *con.j* before 15
antipático/a disagreeable, unpleasant (persons) 3
apagar to turn off 10
apartamento *m* apartment 2
apoyar to support (a candidate/cause) 15
aprender to learn 2
apuntes *m, pl.* notes 2
aquel/aquella *adj.* that 6; **aquél/aquélla** *pron* that one 6
aquellos/as *adj.* those 6; **aquéllos/as** *pron* those 6
aquí here 3
araña *f* spider 12
árbol *m* tree 5
arena *f* sand 12
aretes *m, pl.* earrings 8
argentino/a *m/f, n., adj* Argentinian 1
arma *f* weapon 15
arroz *m* rice 4
arte *m* (**but las artes**) art 2
ascensor *m* elevator 13
aseos *m, pl.* restroom 13
asiento *m* seat 13
asistir (a) to attend 2
aterrizar to land 13
audífonos *m, pl.* headphones 2
aula *f* (**but el** aula) classroom 1
auto *m* car 3
autobús *m* bus 7; **parada** *f* **de autobús** bus stop 7
autopista *f* highway 14
auxiliar *m* **de vuelo** flight attendant (*m*) 13

¡Auxilio! ¡Help! 14
avenida *f* avenue 7
aventura *f* adventure 12
averiguar to find out, inquire 6
avión *m* airplane 13
ayer yesterday 6
ayudar (a) to help 10
azafata *f* flight attendant (f) 13
azúcar *m* sugar 4
azul blue 5

B

bailar to dance 5
bajar to go down 10; **bajarse de** to get off, to get out of . . . 13
bajo/a short 3
baloncesto *m* basketball 5
balsa *f* raft 12
banana *f* banana 4
bañarse to take a bath, bathe 6
banco *m* bank 7; bench 7
bañera *f* bathtub 10
baño *m* bathroom 10; **baño privado** private bath 13
bar *m* bar 7
barato/a inexpensive 8
barco *m* boat 12
básquetbol *m* basketball 5
basura *f* garbage 12
bebé *m/f* baby 3
beber to drink 2
bebida *f* drink, beverage 4
beige beige 5
béisbol *m* baseball 5
besar to kiss 3
biblioteca *f* library 2
bicicleta *f* bicycle 5
bien fine 1; well 3
bienvenido/a welcome 13
billete *m* ticket 13; **billete de ida y vuelta** round trip ticket 13
Billetera/la cartera *f* wallet 8
biología *f* biology 2
bisabuela *f* great-grandmother 3
bisabuelo *m* great-grandfather 3
bistec *m* steak 4
blanco/a white 5
blusa *f* blouse 8
boca *f* mouth 9
bocadillo *m* sandwich 4
boda *f* wedding 11
boleto *m* ticket 13; **boleto de ida y vuelta** round trip ticket 14; **boleto de primera/ segunda clase** *m* first/secon class ticket 14
bolígrafo *m* pen 2
boliviano/a *m/f, n., adj* Bolivian X
bolso/a *m* purse, bag 8
bomba bomb 15
bonito/a good-looking, pretty 3
borrador *m* eraser 2

bosque *m* forest 12
botas *f, pl.* boots 8
bote *m* boat (small) 12
botones *m* bellhop 13
brazo *m* arm 9
bróculi *m* broccoli 4
bucear to scuba dive, skin dive 12
bueno/a good 3; **es bueno** it's good 13
bufanda *f* scarf 8
buscar to look for 2
buzón *m* mailbox 7

C

caballo *m* horse 12
cabeza *f* head 9; **dolor** *m* **de cabeza** headache 9
cada each, every 9
cadena *f* chain 8
café *m* coffee 4; coffee place 7
cafetería *f* cafeteria 2
cajero *m* **automático** ATM machine 7
cajero/a *m/f* cashier 6
calcetines *m, pl.* socks 8
calculadora *f* calculator 2
cálculo *m* calculus 2
calefacción *f* heating 13
calentamento global *m* global warming 12
caliente hot (temperature, not spiciness) 5
calle *f* street 7
cama *f* bed 6; **cama doble** double bed 13; **cama sencilla** single bed 13
cámara *f* camera 12
camarera *f* maid (hotel) 13
camarón *m* shrimp 4
cambiar to change, exchange 7
cambio *m* change, small change, exchange 7
camilla *f* gurney 9
caminar to walk 5
camino *m* road 14
camión *m* truck 14
camisa *f* shirt 8
camiseta *f* T-shirt, undershirt 8
campamento *m* camp 12
campo *m* country 3
cancer *m* cancer 15
candidato/a *m/f* candidate 15
cansado/a tired 3
cansarse to get tired 9
cantar to sing 5
capa *f* **de ozono** ozone layer 12
capítulo *m* chapter 2
cara *f* face 9
¡Caramba! Oh my gosh! 14
cariñoso/a affectionate 11
carne *f* meat, beef 4; **carne de cerdo/ puerco** pork 4; **carne de res** beef 4
caro/a expensive 8
carretera *f* road 14

carro *m* car 3
carta *f* letter 7
cartera *f* wallet 8
casa *f* home, house 2; **amo/a** *m/f* **de casa** homemaker 6; **en casa** at home 3
casado/a married 11; **recién casados** *m, pl.* newlyweds 11
casarse (con) to get married (to) 11
cascada *f* waterfall 12
(casi) siempre (almost) always 2
castillo de arena *m* sand castle 12
catarata *f* waterfall 12
catedral *f* cathedral 7
causa (a causa de) because of 12
CD *m* CD, compact disk 2
cebolla *f* onion 4
celoso/a jealous 11
cena *f* supper, dinner 3
cenar to have dinner 2
centro comercial mall, shopping center 7; **centro estudiantil** student center 2
cepillarse el pelo to brush one's hair 6; **cepillarse los dientes** to brush one's teeth 6
cepillo *m* brush 6; **cepillo de dientes** toothbrush 6
cerca de near 7
cerdo *m* pig 12; **chuleta** *f* **de cerdo** pork chop 4; **carne** *f* **de cerdo** pork 4
cereal *m* cereal 4
cereza *f* cherry 4
cerrado/a closed 3
cerrar (ie) to close 7
cerveza *f* beer 4
chao bye, so-long 1
chaqueta *f* jacket 8
cheque *m* check 7; **cheque de viajero** traveler's check 7
chica *f* girl 3
chico *m* boy 3
chileno/a *m/f, n., adj* Chilean 1
chimenea *f* fireplace, chimney 10
chocar to crash, collide 14
choque *m* crash 14
chorizo *m* sausage 4
chuleta *f* **de cerdo/puerco** pork chop 4
ciclismo *m* **de montaña** mountain biking 12
cielo *m* sky 12
ciencias *f, pl.* **políticas** political science 2
cierto: es . . . it's true, correct 13
cine *m* movie theater, cinema 7
cinturón *m* belt 8; **abrocharse el cinturón** to fasten one's seat belt 13
cita *f* date, appointment 11
ciudad *f* city 3
ciudadano/a *m/f* citizen 15
¡Claro! Of course! 14
clase *f* class 2

clima *m* weather 5
clóset *m* closet 8
cobija *f* blanket 13
cobrar to cash, to charge 7
coche *m* car 3
cocina *f* kitchen 10
cocinar to cook 4
código *m* **de área** area code 11
cola *f* line (of people or things) 7
colegio *m* high school 3
colina *f* hill 12
collar *m* necklace 8
colombiano/a *m/f, n., adj* Colombian 1
comedor *m* dining room 10
comer to eat 2
comida *f* food, main meal 3
¿cómo? how? 4; **¿Cómo está usted?** How are you? (*formal*) 1; **¿Cómo estás?** How are you? (*informal*) 1; **¿Cómo se llama usted?** What's your name (*formal*)? 1; **¿Cómo te llamas?** What's your name? (*informal*) 1
cómoda *f* bureau 10
cómodo/a comfortable 14
compañero/a *m/f* **de cuarto** roommate 6
compañía *f* company 6
comprar to buy 2
comprender to understand 2
comprensivo/a understanding 11
comprometerse (con) to get engaged (to) 11
computación *f* computer science 2
computadora *f* computer 2; **computadora portátil** laptop/notebook computer) 13
comunicarse to communicate 11
con with 4; **con permiso** pardon me, excuse me 1; **con tal (de) que** provided that 14
con . . . de anticipación . . . ahead of time 13
conducir to drive 14
conductor/a driver 14
confirmar to confirm 13
congestión *f* **nasal** nasal congestion 9
conocer to meet, know, be acquainted with 5
conseguir (i, i) to get, obtain 13
conservar to save, conserve 12
constantemente constantly 6
construir construct 15
consultorio *m* **del médico/de la médica** doctor's office 9
contabilidad *f* accounting 2
contador/a *m/f* accountant 6
contaminación *f* pollution 12
contar (ue) to count 7, tell, narrate (a story or incident) 8
contento/a happy 3
contestar to answer 7

contestador automático *m* answering machine 11
continuar to continue 14
contribuir (y) to contribute 12
copa *f* goblet 10
corazón *m* heart 9
corbata *f* tie 8
correo *m* **electrónico** e-mail 2
correr to run 5
corrupción *f* corruption 15
cortar: ... el césped to cut the lawn 10; **cortarse** to cut oneself 5; **cortarse el pelo/ las uñas/ el ded** to cut one's hair/nails/a finger 6
cortina *f* curtain 10
corto/a short 8; de manga corta short-sleeved 8
cosa *f* thing 8
costar (ue) to cost 4
costarricense *m/f, n., adj.* Costa Rican 1
creer to believe 11
crema *f* cream 4; **crema de afeitar** shaving cream 6
crimen *m* crime 15
crucero *m* cruise ship 12
cruzar to cross 14
cuaderno *m* notebook 2
cuadra *f* (city) block 14
cuadro *m* picture, painting 4
¿cuál? which (one)? 4
¿cuáles? which (ones)? 4
cuando when 4; **¿cúando?** when? 2
¿cuánto/a? how much? 4
¿cuántos/as? how many? 3
cuarto a quarter 1
cuarto *m* room 2
cuarto/a fourth 12
cubano/a *m/f, n., adj.* Cuban 1
cubo *m* **de la basura** trash can 10
cuchara *f* spoon 10
cucharita *f* teaspoon 10
cuchillo *m* knife 10
cuello *m* neck 9
cuenta *f* bill, check 7; account 7
cuero *m* leather 8
cuerpo *m* body 9
cuidar to take care of 2
cumpleaños *m* birthday 2
cuñada *f* sister-in-law 3
cuñado *m* brother-in-law 3
cura *f* cure 15

D

dar to give 5; **dar a luz** to give birth 11
dar de comer to feed 15
dar un paseo to take a walk/stroll 5; **dar una caminata** to take a hike 12
de *prep* of, from 1; **de repente** suddenly 9
debajo de beneath, under 7
deber + *infinitive* ought to, should (do something) 5

débil weak 3
décimo/a tenth 13
decir (i) to say, tell 5
dedo *m* finger 9
desforestación *f* deforestation 12
dejar to leave 13; **dejarse** to leave behind 13; **dejar un mensaje** to leave a message 11
delante de in front of 7
delgado/a thin 3
delincuente *m* misdemeanor, crime 15
delito *m* delinquent, offender, criminal 15
demasiado *adv.* too, too much 14
demora *f* delay 13
dentro de inside 7
dependiente/a *m/f* store clerk 6
deporte *m* sport 5
depositar to deposit 7
deprimido/a depressed 9
derecha: a la ... to the right 14
derecho straight, straight ahead 14
derechos *m, pl.* **humanos** human rights 15
desafortunadamente unfortunately 6
desamparados *m, pl* homeless 15
desayunar to have breakfast 2
desayuno *m* breakfast 3
descansar to rest 5; **descanse** rest 9
desear want, wish 4
desempleo *m* unemployment 15
desierto *m* desert 12
desinflado/a flat, deflated (tire) 14
desodorante *m* deodorant 6
despacio slow, slowly 14
despedirse (i, i) to say good-bye 13
despegar to take off 13
desperdiciar to waste 12
despertador *m* alarm clock 6
despertarse (ie) to wake up 6
después de (clase) after (class) 2; afterwards, later 7; **después de** *prep* after 7; **después de que** *conj* after 15
destruir (y) destroy 12
destrucción *f* destruction 12
detrás de behind 7
devolver (ue) to return (something) 8
día *m* day 1; **buenos días** good morning 1
diarrea *f* diarrhea 9
diccionario *m* dictionary 2
diciembre December 1
diente *m* tooth 9
difícil difficult, hard 3
Diga ¡ah! Say ah! 9
dinero *m* money 6
dirección address 7; **dirección** *f* **electrónica** e-mail address 2
disco compacto *m* CD, compact disk 2
discriminación *f* discrimination 15
Disculpe I am sorry. 1
disfrutar de to enjoy (something) 13

divertido/a *m/f* amusing, fun 3
divertirse (ie) to have a good time 6
divorciado/a divorced 11
divorciarse to get divorced 11
divorcio divorce 11
doblar to turn 14
doctor/a *m/f* doctor 2
dolor *m* **de cabeza** *f* headache 9; **dolor de estómago** *m* stomachache 9
dolor de garganta *f* sore throat 9
domingo *m* Sunday 1
dominicano/a *m/f* *n., adj* Dominican 1
¿dónde? where 3; **¿adónde?** (to) where? 2; **¿de dónde...?** from where? 4
dormir (ue) to sleep 4; **dormirse (ue)** to go to sleep, to fall asleep 6
dormitorio *m* bedroom 10
drogadicción *f* drug addiction 15
drogas *f, pl* drugs 14
ducha *f* shower 10
ducharse to take a shower 6
dudar to doubt 12
durazno *m* peach 4

E

echar gasolina to put gas (in the tank) 14
economía *f* economics 2
ecuatoriano/a *m/f, n., adj* Ecuadorian 1
edificio *m* building 7
efectivo *m* cash 7
ejercicio *m* exercise 2; **hacer ejercicio** to exercise, to do exercises 5
ejército *m* army 15
el *m, definite article* the 2
él *m, subj* he 1; *obj. prep. pron.* him 6
elección *f* election 15
eliminar to eliminate 15
ella *f, subj* she 1; *obj. of prep.* her 6
ellas *f, subj* they 1; *obj. of prep.* them 6
ellos *m, subj* they 1; *obj. of prep.* them 6
embarazada pregnant 9
emergencias emergency f, pl. 9
emocionante exciting 13
empacar to pack 13
empezar (ie) (a) to begin 7
empleado/a *m/f* employee 6
empleo *m* employment 15
empresa *f* business 6
en in, at 2;on 7; **en caso de que** in case 14
en vez de instead of 7
enamorarse (de) to fall in love (with) 11
encantado/a delighted (to meet you) 1
encantar to really like, love 5; to delight, to enchant 12
encima de on top of, above 7
encontrar (ue) to find 7; **encontrarse (ue) (con)** to meet up (with) (by chance) 11

enero January 1
enfermarse to get/become sick 9
enfermero/a m/f nurse 6
enfermo/a sick 3
enfrente de in front of, opposite 7
enojado/a angry 11
enojarse to get angry 11
ensalada f salad 4
entender (ie) to understand 4
entonces then 6
entrada f (admission) ticket 7
entrar (en/a) to enter, go into 7
entre between, among 7
entrevista f interview 15
enviar to send 7
equipaje m luggage 13
equipo m team 5
escalar (la montaña) to climb (the
    mountain) 12
escalera f stairs 10
escalofrío m chill 9
escoger to choose 15
escribir to write 2
escritorio m (teacher's) desk 2
escuchar to listen to 2
escuela f elementary school 3
ese/a adj. that 6; ése/a pron. that one 6
esos/as adj. those 6; ésos/as pron.
    those 6
espalda f back 9
español m Spanish (language) 2
español/española m/f, n., adj. Spanish 1
especie animal f animal species 12
espejo m mirror 10
esperar to wait (for) 7; to hope, expect 11
esposa f wife 3
esposo m husband 3
esquiar to ski 5
esquina f (street) corner 14
esta this, that 6; esta mañana this
    morning 2; esta noche tonight 2; esta
    tarde this afternoon 2
estación f season 4; estación de
    autobuses bus station 14
estación de servicio/la gasolinera
    service/gas station 14
estación de ferrocarril railroad
    station 14
estacionamiento m parking 14
estacionar to park 14
estadounidense m/f, n., adj American
    (from the United States) 1
estampilla f stamp 7
estante m bookshelf, shelf 10
estar to be 3; estar a favor de to be in
    favor of 15
estar casado/a (con) to be married
    (to) 11
estar comprometido/a to be engaged 11
estar de pie to be standing 8
estar de vacaciones f, pl. to be on
    vacation 12

estar embarazada to be pregnant 11
estar enamorado/a de to be in love
    (with) 11
estar en contra de to be against 15
estar juntos/as to be together 11
estar listo to be ready 12
estar prometido/a to be engaged 11
estar seguro/a (de) to be sure of 12
estar sentado/a to be seated 9
estatua f statue 7
este/a adj. this 6; éste/a pron. this
    one 6
estéreo m stereo 10
estómago m stomach 9; dolor m de
    estómago stomachache 9
estornudar to sneeze 9
estos/as adj. these 6; estos/as pron.
    these 6
estrella f star 12
estresado/a stressed 3
estudiante m/f student 2
estudiar to study 2
estufa f stove 10
etapas f, pl. de la vida stages of life 11
evitar to avoid 12
examen m exam 2
examinar to examine 9
explicar to explain 8
exploración f del espacio (outer) space
    exploration 15
explosión f explosion 15
extinción f extinction 12
extrañar to miss 11
extraño: es . . . it's strange 13

F

fábrica f factory 6
fácil easy 3
fácilmente easily 6
facturar to check (baggage) 13
falda f skirt 8
familia f family 2
farmacia f pharmacy 9
fascinar to be fascinating to, to
    fascinate 12
favor (por favor) please 1
febrero February 1
fecha f date 1
felicidades f congratulations 11
fenomenal terrific 1; es fenomenal it's
    wonderful 13
feo/a ugly 3
fiebre f fever 9
fiel faithful 11
fiesta f party 2
fila f line (of people or things) 7
filosofía f philosophy 2
fin m de semana weekend 2; fin de
    semana pasado last weekend 6; por
    fin finally 9
firmar to sign 7

física f physics 2
flaco/a skinny 3
flores f, pl flowers 5
fogata f campfire 12
fracturar(se) (el brazo/ la pierna) to
    break one's (arm/leg) 9
francés m French (language) 2
frecuentemente frequently 6; con
    frecuencia frequently 2
fregadero m sink (kitchen) 10
frenos m, pl. brakes 14
frente a in front of, opposite, facing 7
fresa f strawberry 4
frijoles m, pl beans 4
frío/a cold 5; hace (mucho) frío it's
    (very) cold 5
frito/a fried 4
frontera f border 15
fruta f fruit 3
fuego m fire 12
fuera de outside 7
fuerte strong 3
fumar to smoke 5
funcionar to run, work, function
    (machine) 14
fútbol m soccer 5; fútbol americano
    football 5

G

gafas f, pl. eyeglasses 8; gafas de sol
    sunglasses 8
galleta f cookie 4
gallina f chicken 12
ganar to win 5; to earn, make money 6
garaje m garage 10
garganta f throat 9; dolor m de
    garganta sore throat 9
gasolina f gas 12
gasolinera f gas station 14
gastar to spend 7
gato m cat 3
generalmente generally 6
gente f people 7
gerente/a m/f manager 15
gimnasio m gym, gymnasium 2
gobierno m government 15
golf m golf 5
gordo/a fat 3
gorra f cap 8
gracias thank you/thanks 1
grande big, large 3
granja f farm 12
gratis free 14
gripe f flu 9
gris gray 5
guantes m, pl. gloves 8
guapo/a good-looking,
    pretty/handsome 3
guardar to keep 10
guatemalteco/a m/f, n., adj.
    Guatemalan 1

guerra *f* war 15
guía *f* **telefónica** phone book 11
guisante *m* pea 4
guitarra *f* guitar 4
gustar to like 4; **el gusto es mío** the pleasure is mine 1

H

habitación *f* room 9
habitación doble double room 13
habitación sencilla single room 13
hablar to speak 2
hace buen/mal tiempo the weather is nice/bad 5
hace (mucho) calor/fresco/frío/sol/viento it's (very) hot/cool/cold/sunny/windy 5
hace sol it's sunny 5
hacer to do, make 2
hacer la cama to make the bed 10
hacer cola to get (stand) in line 7
hacer ejercicio to exercise, work out, do exercises 5
hacer el *esnórquel* to go snorkeling 12
hacer fila to get (stand) in line 6
hacer las maletas to pack 13
hacer reservaciones/reservas to make reservations 14
hacer *surf* to surf 12
hacer un análisis de sangre do a blood test 9
hacer un viaje en crucero/en barco to go on a cruise, take a trip on a ship/boat/cruise ship 12
hacer una cita to make an appointment 9
hambre *f* (*but el* **hambre**) hunger 15
hamburguesa *f* hamburger 4
hasta: hasta mañana see you tomorrow. 1; **hasta pronto** see you soon 1; **hasta que** until 15
hay there is/are 2
helado *m* ice cream 4
herida *f* **grave** serious wound 9
hermana *f* sister 3
hermanastra *f* stepsister 3
hermanastro *m* stepbrother 3
hermano *m* brother 2
hermoso/a good-looking, pretty/handsome 3
hielo *m* ice 4
hierba *f* grass 12
hija *f* daughter 3
hijo *m* son 3
historia *f* history 2
hoja *f* **de papel** sheet of paper 2; **hojas** *f, pl.* leaves 5
hola hello/hi 1
hombre *m* man 3; **hombre de negocios** businessman 6
hombro *m* shoulder 9

hondureño/a *m/f, n., adj* Honduran 1
hora *f* time 1
horario *m* schedule 13
horno *m* oven 10; **al horno** baked 4
horrible: es . . . it's horrible 13
hospital *m* hospital 9
hotel *m* hotel 13
hoy today 1
hueso *m* bone 9
huésped/a *m/f* guest 13
huevo *m* egg 4; **huevos fritos** fried eggs 4; **huevos revueltos** scrambled eggs 4

I

iglesia *f* church 7
igualdad *f* equality 15
igualmente nice meeting you too 1
impermeable *m* raincoat 8
importante: es . . . it's important 13
importar to be important to, to matter 12
imposible: es . . . it's impossible 13
impresora *f* printer 2
imprimir to print 2
improbable: es . . . it's improbable 13
incendios *m, pl.* **forestales** forest fires 12
infancia *f* infancy 11
infección *f* infection 9
informar/reportar to inform 15
informática *f* computer science 2
inglés *m* English (language) 2
inmediatamente immediately 6
inodoro *m* toilet 10
improbable: es . . . it's improbable 13
insectos *m, pl.* insects 12
insistir (en) to insist (on) 11
inteligente intelligent 3
interesante: es . . . it's interesting 13
interesar to be interesting to, to interest 12
invertir (ie, i) to invest 7
investigación *f* research 15
invierno *m* winter 5
invitar (a) to invite 7
inyección *f* injection 9
ir to go 2
ir de compras to go shopping 5
ir(se) de vacaciones to go on vacation 12
irse leave, depart, to go away 11
isla *f* island 12
italiano *m* Italian (language) 5
izquierda *f:* **a la...** to the left 14

J

jabón *m* soap 6
jamón *m* ham 4
japonés *m* Japanese (language) 5
jardín *m* garden 10
jeans *m, pl.* jeans 8
jefa *f* boss 15

jefe *m* boss 15
joven young 3
jóvenes *m, pl.* **/los adolescentes** young people, adolescents 11
joyas *f, pl.* jewelry 8
joyería *f* jewelry shop 7
judía *f* **verde** green bean 4
jueves *m* Thursday 1
jugar (ue) to play 5; **jugar al (deporte)** to play (sport) 5
jugo *m* juice 4
julio July 1
junio June 1
juntos/as: estar . . . to be together 11
justicia *f* justice 15
justo fair 13; **no es . . .** it's unfair 13
juventud *f* youth 11

K

kayak *m* kayak 12
kilómetro *m* kilometer 14

L

la *f, definite article* the 2; *dir. obj.* her, you (f), it (f) 5
labio *m* lip 9
laboratorio *m* laboratory 2
lado: al . . . de beside 7
lago *m* lake 5
lámpara *f* lamp 10
lana *f* wool 8
langosta *f* lobster 4
lápiz *m* pencil 2
largo/a long 8; **de manga larga** long-sleeved 8
las *dir. obj.* them (f), you (f, pl.) 5
las *f, pl. definite article* the 2
lástima: es una ... it's a shame 13
lastimarse to hurt oneself 9
lavabo *m* sink (bathroom) 10
lavadora *f* washer 10
lavaplatos *m* dishwasher 10
lavar: . . . los platos to wash the dishes 10
lavarse to wash oneself 5; **lavarse las manos/la cara** to wash one's hands/face 6
le *ind. obj.* you, him, her (to/for . . .) 8
lección *f* lesson 2
leche *f* milk 4
lechuga *f* lettuce 4
leer to read 2
legalizar to legalize 15
legumbre *f* vegetable 3
lejos de far from 7
lengua *f* tongue 9
lentamente slowly 6
lentes *m* **de contacto** contact lenses 8
les *ind. obj.* you, them (to/for you, them) 8

levantar pesas to lift weights 5
levantarse to get up 6
ley f law 15
libertad f freedom 15
librería f bookstore 2
libro m book 2
licencia f **de conducir** driver's license 14
líder m/f leader 15
limón m lemon 4
limpiar to clean 5
limpio/a clean 8
línea está ocupada the line is busy 11
listo/a: estar . . . to be ready 11
literatura f literature 2
llamada f **telefónica** telephone call 11; **llamada de larga distancia** long distance call 11
llamar to call 3
llanta f tire 14; **llanta desinflada** flat tire 14
llave f key 13
llegada f arrival 13
llegar to arrive 2
llenar (el tanque) to fill (the tank) 14
llevar to wear 8
llevarse bien/mal to get along well/badly 11
Lleve la receta a la farmacia. Take the prescription to the pharmacy. 9
llorar to cry 11
llover (ue) to rain 5; **está lloviendo** it's raining 5; **llueve** it's raining, it rains 5
lluvia f rain 5; **lluvia ácida** acid rain 12
lo dir. obj. m him, you, it 5; **lo que** what, that which 4; **lo siento (mucho)** I'm (so) sorry 1
los m, dir. obj. them, you 6; m, pl., definite article the 2
los aseos/el servicio m bathroom 14
Lo siento mucho. I'm very sorry. 14
luchar (por) to fight (for) 15
luego then 6
lugar m place 7
luna f moon 12; **luna de miel** honeymoon 11
lunes m Monday 1
luz f light 10

M

madrastra f stepmother 3
madre f mother 3
madurez f adulthood, maturity 11
maestro/a m/f teacher 2
maíz m corn 4
mal bad, badly 3
maleta f suitcase 13
maletero m porter 14
maletín m briefcase, carry-on bag 13
malo/a bad 3
mañana tomorrow, morning f 1; **de la mañana** A.M. (in the morning) 1;

hasta mañana see you tomorrow 1; **por/en la mañana** in the morning 2
mandar to send 2
manejar to drive 5
manga f sleeve 8; **de manga larga/corta** long-/short-sleeved 8
mano f hand 9
manta f blanket 13
mantequilla f butter 4
manzana f apple 4
mapa m map 2
maquillaje m makeup 6
maquillarse to put on makeup 6
máquina m **de afeitar** electric shaver 6
mar m sea 12
marido m husband 3
mariposa f butterfly 12
marisco m seafood 3
marrón brown 5
martes m Tuesday 1
marzo March 1
más more 4; **más tarde** later 2
matar to kill 11
matemáticas f, pl mathematics 2
mayo May 1
mayor old (elderly) 3; older 3
me dir. obj. me 5; ind. obj. me (to/for me) 8; refl. pron. myself 5; **me llamo . . .** my name is . . . 1
media f half 1; **media hermana** half-sister 3; **mi media naranja** my soul mate, other half 11
medias f, pl. stockings, hose, socks 8
medianoche f midnight 1
médico/a m/f doctor 2
medicina f medicine 15
medio hermano m half-brother 3
medio m **ambiente** environment 12
mediodía m noon 1
mejor best 7; **mejor amigo/a** m/f best friend 3; **es mejor** it's better 13
melocotón m peach 4
menor younger 3
menos less 4; **a menos (de) que** unless 14
mensaje m **electrónico** e-mail message 2
mentir to lie 11
mercado m market 3
merienda f snack 3
mermelada f jam 4
mes m month 1
mesa f table 2
mesero/a m/f waiter/waitress 6
mesita f **de noche** nightstand 10
metro m metro, subway 7
mexicano/a m/f, n., ad.j Mexican 1
mí obj. prep. pron me 6; **¡Ay de mí!** Poor me! (What am I going to do?) 14
mi/mis my 2
microondas m microwave 10

mientras while 9
miércoles m Wednesday 1
mío/a/os/as (of) mine 7; **el gusto es mío** the pleasure is mine 1
mirar to look at 8
mochila f backpack 2
moda f fashion; **a la moda** in style 8
molestar to be annoying to, to bother 12
moneda f currency, money, coin 7
montañas f, pl. mountains 3
montar a caballo to ride horseback 12
morado/a purple 5
moreno/a brunette, dark-skinned 3
morir (ue, u) to die 7
mosca f fly 12
mosquito m mosquito 12
mostrar (ue) to show 8
motocicleta f motorcycle 14
motor m motor 14; **afinar el motor** to tune the motor 14
mover(se) (ue) to move (oneself) 10
muchacha f girl 3
muchacho m boy 3
mucho adv. much, a lot 4; **mucho/a/os/as** m/f adj much, a lot 4; **(muchas) gracias** thank you (very much) 1; **muchas veces** f pl. many times, often 8; **mucho gusto** pleased to meet you 1
mudarse to move (from house to house) 10
muebles m, pl. furniture 10
muerte f death 11; **pena de muerte** death penalty 15
mujer f woman, wife 3; **mujer de negocios** businesswoman 6
mujer policía policewoman 14
muletas f, pl. crutches 9
multa f fine, ticket 14
mundo m world 12
museo m museum 7
música f music 2
muy very 3; **muy bien** very well 1

N

nacer to be born 11
nacimento m birth 11
nada nothing 7; **de nada** you're welcome 1
nadar to swim 12
nadie no one, nobody 7
naranja f orange (fruit) 4
narcotráfico m drug trafficking 15
nariz f nose 9
naturaleza f nature 12
náuseas f, pl. nausea 8
navaja f razor 6
nave f **espacial** space ship 15
navegar por la red to surf the Web 2
necesario: es . . . it's necessary 13
necesitar to need 4

negro/a black 5
nervioso/a nervous 3
nevar (ie) to snow 5; **está nevando** it's snowing 5
ni not, not even 13
ni... ni neither . . . nor 13
nicaragüense m/f, n., ad.j Nicaraguan 1
nieta f granddaughter 3
nieto m grandson 3
nieva it's snowing 5
nieve f snow 5
ningún (ninguno/a) no, none, no one 13
niña f child 3
niñez childhood 11
niño m child 3
niños m, pl. children 11
noche f night 1; **buenas noches** good evening/night 1; **de la noche** p.m. (in the evening, at night) 1; **por/en la noche** in the evening, at night 2
normalmente normally 6
nos dir. obj. us 5; ind. obj. us (to/for us) 7; refl. pron. ourselves 5
nosotros/as m/f, subj. pron. we 1; obj. prep. us 6
nota f grade, score 2
noticias f, pl. news 7
noticiero m newscast 15
noveno/a ninth 13
novia f girlfriend 3
noviembre November 1
novio m boyfriend 3
nube f cloud 5
nublado cloudy 5; **está (muy) nublado** it's (very) cloudy 5
nuestro/a/os/as our 2;(of) ours 8
nuevo/a new 3
nunca never 2

O

o or 3; **o . . . o** either . . . or 13
obra f de teatro play 7
obvio: es . . . it's obvious 13
océano m ocean 12
octavo/a eighth 13
octubre October 1
ocupado/a busy 3
oficina f office 2; **oficina de correos** post office 8
ojo m eye 9
oído m ear (inner) 9
oír to hear 5
ojalá que . . . I hope 11
ola f wave 12
olvidar to forget 11; **olvidarse de** to forget 11
ordenar (el cuarto) to tidy (the room) 10
oreja f ear (outer) 9
oro m gold 8
os dir. ob.j you (pl.) 5; ind. obj. you (to/for you) 7; refl. pron. yourselves 5

otoño m autumn, fall 5
otro/a another 4
otros/as other 4

P

paciente m/f patient 9
padrastro m stepfather 3
padre m father 2
padres m, pl. parents 3
pagar to pay (for) 7
página f page 2; **página web** Web page 2
país m country 13
pájaro m bird 12
pan m **(tostado)** bread (toast) 4
pantalones m, pl pants 8; **pantalones cortos** shorts 8
papa f potato 4; **papas fritas** french fries 4
papel m paper 2; **papel higiénico** toilet paper 6
papelera f wastebasket 2
paquete m package 7
para for, in order to, toward, by 12; **para que** so that, in order that 14; **para + infinitivo** in order to (do something) 7
parabrisas m windshield 14
parada f de autobús bus stop 7
paraguas m umbrella 8
paramédicos m, pl. paramedics 9
parar to stop (movement) 14
parece que it seems that . . . 13
pared f wall 10
pareja f partner, significant other 3; couple 11
pariente m relative 3
parque m park 7
parrilla (a la parrilla) grilled 4
partido m game, match 5
pasado: el año/ mes/ verano . . . last year/ month/ summer 6
pasajero/a m/f passenger 13
pasaporte m passport 13
pasar to spend (time), to happen, pass, 7
pasar la aspiradora to vacuum 10
pasillo m aisle (between rows of seats) 13
pasta f de dientes toothpaste 6
pastel m pie, pastry 4
pastelería f pastry shop, bakery 7
patata f potato 4
paz f peace 15
pedir (i, i) to ask for, request, order 4
pecho m chest, breast 9
peinarse to comb one's hair 6
peine m comb 6
película f film, movie 7
peligroso/a dangerous 12
pelo m hair 9; **secador m de pelo** hair dryer 6
pelota f ball 5
pendientes m, pl earrings 8

pensar (ie) to think 4; **pensar (ie) +infinitivo** to intend/plan (to do something) 5; **pensar (ie) en** to think about (someone or something) 11
peor worse 10
pequeño/a small, little 3
pera f pear 4
perder (ie) to lose 7; **perder el tren** to miss the train 14
perdón pardon me, excuse me 1
perezoso/a lazy 3
periódico m newspaper 7
pero but 3
perro m dog 3
personalmente personally 6
pescado m fish 4
pescar to fish 12
pesticida f tóxico poisonous pesticide 12
pez m **(los peces)** fish 12
pie m foot 9; **estar de pie** to be standing 9
pierna f leg 9
piloto/a m/f pilot 13
pimienta f pepper 4
piña f pineapple 4
pintar to paint 5
piscina f swimming pool 13
piso m floor (of a building) 10
pizarra f chalkboard, board, blackboard 2
pizzería f pizzeria 7
planeta m planet 12
planta f plant 12
planta baja main floor 13
plata f silver 8
plátano m banana 4
plato m dish, course 3; plate 10
playa f beach 3
plaza f plaza, town square 7
pluma f pen 2
pobre poor 3
pobreza f poverty 15
poco adv. little 4; **un poco** adv a bit, a little, somewhat 3
poco/a m/f, adj. little (quantity) 4; **pocos/ as** m/f, adj. few 4
poder (ue) to be able, can 4
policía m policeman 14
política f mundial world politics 15
pollo m chicken 4
poner to put, place 5; **poner la mesa** to set the table 10
poner una inyección/una vacuna to give a shot/vaccination 9
ponerse (los zapatos, la ropa, etc.) to put on (shoes, clothes, etc.) 6
por for, down, by, along, through 7
por favor please 1
por fin finally 9
por la mañana in the morning 2
por la noche in the evening, at night 2
por la tarde in the afternoon 2

¿por qué? why? 4
¡Por supuesto! Of course! 14
porque because 4
posible: es . . . it's possible 13
posiblemente possibly 6
póster *m* poster 10
postre *m* dessert 3
practicar to practice 2
practicar el descenso de ríos to go white-water rafting 12
practicar el *parasail* to go parasailing 12
precio *m* price 8
preciso: es . . . it's necessary 13
preferir (ie, i) to prefer 4
pregunta *f* question 2
preguntar to ask 8
prejuicio *m* prejudice 15
prender to turn on 10
preocupado/a worried 3
preocuparse (por) to worry (about) 9
preparar to prepare 2
prestar to lend 8
prevenir to prevent 12
primavera *f* spring 5
primer first 13; **primer piso** *m* first floor, 10
primero *adv.* first 6; **primero/a** first 13; **de primera clase** first class 14
primo/a *m/f* cousin 3
probable: es . . . it's probable 13
probablemente probably 6
problema *m* problem 12
profesor/a *m/f* professor 2
programador/a *m/f* computer programmer 2
prohibir to forbid 15
propina *f* tip 13
proteger to protect 12
próximo/a next 5; **el próximo mes/ año / verano** next month/year/summer 5
prueba *f* quiz 2
psicología *f* psychology 2
puente *m* bridge 14
puerta *f* door 2; **puerta de salida** gate 13
puertorriqueño/a *m/f, n., adj* Puerto Rican 1
pues well 1
pulmón *m* lung 9
pulsera *f* bracelet 8
pupitre *m* (student) desk 2

Q

que that 4; **lo que** what, that which 4; **¿qué?** what?, which? 4; **¿qué hay de nuevo?** what's new? (*informal*) 1; **¿qué pasa?** what's happening? (*informal*) 1; **¿qué tal?** how are you? (*informal*) 1
¡Qué barbaridad! How awful! 14
¡Qué lástima! What a shame! 14
¡Qué lío! What a mess! 14

¡Qué suerte! What luck!/ How lucky! 14
quedarse to stay 9
quejarse de to complain about 11
querer (ie) to want, love 4
queso *m* cheese 4
¿quién/quiénes? who? 3; **¿de quién?** whose? 4
química *f* chemistry 2
quinto/a fifth 13
quiosco *m* newsstand 7
quisiera I would like 4
quitar: . . . la mesa to clear the table 10
quitarse la ropa to take off (clothes, etc.) 6

R

***rafting:* practicar el . . .** to go white-water rafting 12
rápidamente rapidly 6
rascacielos *m* skyscraper 7
ratón *m* mouse 2
rebajas *f* sales 8
recámara *f* bedroom 10
recepción *f* reception, front desk 9
recepcionista *m/f* receptionist 9
receta *f* prescription 9
recibir to receive 7
reciclar to recycle 12
recientemente recently 6
reclamo de equipajes *m, pl.* baggage claim 13
recoger to pick up, gather 12
recomendar (ie) to recommend 11
recordar (ue) to remember 11
recursos *m, pl.* **naturales** natural resources 12
reducir to reduce 12
refresco *m* soft drink 4
refrigerador *m* refrigerator 10
regalar to give (as a gift) 8
regalo *m* gift 8
registrarse to register 13
regresar to return 2
regular OK, so-so 1
reírse (de) to laugh at 11
relámpago *m* lightning 12
religión *f* religion 2
reloj *m* clock 2; watch 8
remar to row 12
reparar to fix 14
repartidor/a *m/f* delivery person 6
repente all of a sudden, suddenly 9
repetir (i, i) to repeat 7
reportar to report 15
reportero/a reporter 15
reservación *f* reservation 13
resfriado *m* cold 9
residencia f **estudiantil** student dorm 2
resolver (ue) to solve/resolve 10
Respire profundamente. Take a deep breath. 7

responsable responsible 3
respuesta *f* answer 2
restaurante *m* restaurant 2
retirar take out, to withdraw 7
reunirse (con) to meet, get together 11
revisar to check 14
revista *f* magazine 7
rico/a rich 3
ridículo: es . . . it's ridiculous 13
río *m* river 15
robar to rob 15
rojo/a red 5
romper to break 10; **romper (con)** to break up (with) 11
ropa *f* clothes, clothing 8; **ropa** *f* **interior** underwear 8
ropero/clóset *m* closet 8
rosado/a pink 5
rubio/a blonde 3
ruido *m* noise 10
ruso *m* Russian (language) 5

S

sábado *m* Saturday 1
sábana *f* sheet 13
saber to know (facts, information) 5; to know how to (skills) 5
sacar fotos *f, pl.* to take photos 11
sacar la basura to take out the garbage 10
sacar los pasaportes to get passports 13
sacar una nota to get a grade 2
sacar una radiografía to x-ray 9
sacar sangre to draw blood 9
saco *m* **de dormir** sleeping bag 12
sal *f* salt 4
sala *f* living room 10; **sala de espera** waiting room 9
sala familiar family room 10
salchicha *f* sausage 4
salida *f* departure 13
salir to leave, go out 2; **salir (con)** to go out (with), date 11
salud *f* health 8
saltar en paracaídas to go parachute jumping 12
sandalias *f, p.l* sandals 8
sandía *f* watermelon 4
sándwich *m* sandwich 4
Saque la lengua. Stick out your tongue. 9
se *reflex. pron.* yourself, himself, herself, themselves 5
secador *m* **de pelo** hair dryer 6
secadora *f* dryer 10
secar: . . . los platos to dry the dishes 9; **secarse** to dry (oneself) 6
secretario/a *m/f* secretary 6
seda *f* silk 8
seguir (i, i) to continue, follow 14

segundo/a second 13; **de segunda clase** second class 14

segundo piso second floor 10

seguro/a safe 14

sello *m* stamp 7

selva *f* jungle 12

semáforo *m* traffic light 14

semana *f* week 1; **semana** *f* **pasada** last week 6

sentarse (ie, i) to sit down 9

sentir (ie, i) to be sorry, regret 11; **lo siento (mucho)** I'm (so) sorry 1; **sentirse (ie, i)** to feel 9

separarse (de) to separate 11

septiembre September 1

séptimo/a seventh 13

sequía *f* drought 12

ser to be 2

serio/a serious, dependable 3

serpiente *f* snake 12

servicio m restroom 14; **servicio de habitación** room service 13

servilleta *f* napkin 10

servir (i, i) to serve 4

sexto/a sixth 13

SIDA *m* AIDS 15

silla *f* chair 2; **silla de ruedas** wheel chair 9

sillón *m* easy chair 10

simpático/a nice, likeable 3

sin without 4

sincero/a honest, sincere 11

sitio web *m* Web site 2

sobre on 7; **sobre** *m* envelope 7

sobrepoblación *f* overpopulation 15

sobrina *f* niece 3

sobrino *m* nephew 3

sociología *f* sociology 2

¡Socorro! ¡Help! 14

sofá *m* sofa 10

sol *m* sun 12

solicitar to apply (job) 15

solicitud *f* application 15

soltero/a single 11

sombrero *m* hat 8

sonar (ue) to ring, to sound 6

sopa *f* soup 4

sótano *m* basement 10

su/sus his, her, its, your (*formal*), their 2

subir to go up 10; **subirse a** to get on, board 13

sucio/a dirty 8

suegra *f* mother-in-law 3

suegro *m* father-in-law 3

suelo *m* floor 10

suéter *m* sweater 8

sufrir to suffer 15

sugerir (ie, i) to suggest 11

suyo/a/os/as (of) his, (of) hers, (of) theirs, (of) yours (*formal*) 8

T

talla *f* size (clothing) 8

taller *m* **mecánico** shop 14

también also 4

tampoco neither, not either 7

tan: tan . . . como as . . . as 9; **tan pronto como** as soon as 15

tanque *m* tank 14

tanto: tanto como as much as 10; **tanto/a/os/as . . . como** as much/ many . . . as 10

taquilla *f* ticket window 14

tarde *f* afternoon 1; **buenas tardes** good afternoon 1; **de la tarde** P.M. (in the afternoon) 1; **por/en la tarde** in the afternoon 2

tarea *f* homework, assignment, task 2

tarjeta *f* card; **tarjeta de crédito** credit card 7

tarjeta de embarque boarding pass 13

tarjeta postal post card 7

tarjeta telefónica calling card 11

taxi *m* taxi 7

taza *f* cup 10

te *dir. obj.* you (*informal*) 5; *ind. obj.* you (to/for you) (*informal*) 8; **¿Te duele?** Does it hurt? 9

te presento (*informal*) I want to introduce . . . to you 1; *reflex. pron.* yourself (*informal*) 5

té *m* tea 4

teatro *m* theater 7

techo *m* roof 10

teclado *m* keyboard 2

teléfono *m* **celular** cell phone 11

televisor *m* television set 2

temer to fear, be afraid of 11

temprano early 2

tenedor *m* fork 10

tener calor/frío to be hot/cold 5

tener celos to be jealous 11

tener cuidado to be careful 14

tener éxito to be successful 15

tener ganas de + *infinitivo* to feel like (doing something) 5

tener hambre/sed to be hungry/thirsty 4

tener miedo to be afraid 12

tener prisa to be in a hurry 13

tener que + *infinitivo* to have to . . . (do something) 5

tener sueño to be sleepy, tired 6

tenis *m* tennis 5

tercero/a third 13

terminar to finish 7

termómetro *m* thermometer 9

terrorismo *m* terrorism 15

ti *obj. prep.* you (*informal*) 6

tía *f* aunt 3

tiempo m weather 5; **a tiempo** on time 2

tienda *f* store, shop 6; **tienda de campaña** tent 12

tienda *f* **de ropa** clothing store 5

tierra *f* earth, land 12

tijeras *f, pl* scissors 6

tío *m* uncle 3

tiza *f* chalk 2

toalla *f* towel 6

tobillo *m* ankle 9

tocar to play (instruments) 5

tocineta *f* bacon 4

tocino *m* bacon 4

todo/a/os/as *adj.* **toda la mañana** all morning 2; **toda la noche** all night 2; **toda la tarde** all afternoon 2; **todas las mañanas** every morning 2; **todas las noches** every evening, night 2; **todas las tardes** every afternoon 2; **todo el día** all day 2; **todos los días** every day 2

todavía still, yet 4

tomar to take, drink 4; **tomar apuntes** *m, pl.* to take notes 2; **tomar el sol** to sunbathe 5; **tomar fotos** *f, pl.* to take photos 12

tomar la temperatura to take one's temperature 9; **tomar la presión arterial** to take one's blood pressure 9; **tomar el pulso** to take one's pulse 9

tomate *m* tomato 4

Tome aspirinas/las pastillas/las cápsulas. Take aspirin/the pills/the capsules. 9

Tome líquidos. Take liquids. 9

tonto/a dumb, silly 3

torcer(se) (ue) to sprain (one's ankle) 9

tormenta *f* storm 12

torta *f* cake 4

tos *f* cough 9

toser to cough 9

trabajador/a hardworking 3

trabajar to work 2; **trabajar para . . .** to work for 6

trabajo *m* work 6; **trabajo** *m* **de tiempo completo** full-time job 5; **trabajo de tiempo parcial** part-time job 5; **trabajo** *m* **escrito** paper (academic) 2; **trabajo voluntario** *m* volunteerism 15; **en el trabajo** at work 3

traer to bring 5

tráfico *m* traffic 14

traje *m* suit 8; **traje de baño** bathing suit 8

tranquilamente calmly 6

tránsito *m* traffic 14

tratar de + *infinitivo* to try to (do something) 11

tren *m* train 14

triste sad 3

tú *subj. pron.* you (*informal*) 1

tu/tus your (*informal*) 2
tutor/a tutor 15
tuyo/a/os/as (of) yours (*informal*) 7

U

un/uno/una a 2; one 1; **un poco** *adv.* a bit, a little, somewhat 3; **una vez** once, one time 9
ura lástima: es . . . it's a pity 13
unos/unas some 2
universidad *f* college/university 2
uña *f* fingernail 9
urgente: es . . . it's urgent 13
uruguayo/a *m/f, n., adj.* Uruguayan 1
usar to use 2
usted *subj. pron.* you (*formal*) 1; *obj. prep.* you (*formal*) 6
ustedes *subj. pron.* you (*pl.*) 1; *obj. prep.* you (*pl.*) 6
uva *f* grape 4

V

vaca *f* cow 12
vacaciones *f, pl.* vacation 12
vacuna *f* vaccination 9
valle *m* valley 12
vaqueros *m, pl.* jeans 8
vaso *m* glass (drinking) 10
Vaya a la farmacia. Go to the pharmacy. 9
VCR *m* VCR, video 2
vecino/a *m/f* neighbor 10
vejez old age 11
velocidad *f* speed 14
venda *f* bandage 9
vender to sell 4
venir (ie) to come 5
ventana *f* window 2
ventanilla *f* window (airplane, train, car) 13
ver to see 5; **ver la tele(visión)** to watch TV 5
verano *m* summer 5
verdad: es . . . it's true 13
verde green 5
verdura *f* vegetable 3
vestido *m* dress 8
vestirse (i) to get dressed 6
viajar to travel 5; **viajar de mochila** to backpack 12
viaje *m* a trip 14
víctima *f* victim 15
vida *f* life 11
viejo/a old 3
viernes Friday 1
vinagre *m* vinegar 4
vino *m* wine 4
violencia *f* violence 15
visitar to visit 3
viudo/a *m/f* widower/widow 11

vivir to live 2
volar (ue) to fly 13
vólibol *m* volleyball 5
voluntario/a *m/f* volunteer 15
volver (ue) to return, to go back 4
vomitar to vomit 9
vómito *m* vomit 9
vosotros/as *m/f, subj.* you (*informal, pl., Sp.*) 1; *obj. prep.* you (*informal, pl., Sp.*) 6
votar (por) to vote (for) 15
vuelo *m* flight 13
vuestro/a/os/as your (*informal*) 2; (of) yours (*informal*) 7

Y

y and 3
ya already 6
yeso *m* cast 9
yo *subj. pron.* I 1

Z

zanahoria *f* carrot 4
zapatería *f* shoe store 7
zapatos *m, pl.* shoes 8; **zapatos de tenis** tennis shoes 8
zumo *m,* juice 4

Índice

PHOTO CREDITS

Preface
Digital Vision

Chapter 1
Page 2: PhotoAlto/Laurence Mouton/SUPERSTOCK. Page 8 (top right): Robert Frerck/Odyssey Productions. Page 8 (top left): Herman Agopian/Taxi/Getty Images, Inc. Page 8 (bottom right): Robert Frerck/Odyssey Productions. Page 12 (top left): Francis M. Roberts/Alamy Images. Page 12 (top right): Alamy Images. Page 12 (bottom left): Nancy Kaszerman/NewsCom. Page 12 (bottom right): IT Stock/Age Fotostock America, Inc. Page 12 (left): Gamma-Presse, Inc. Page 12 (center left): Scott Gries/Getty Images, Inc. Page 12 (center right): Al Tielemans/SI/IPN/Aurora Photos. Page 12 (right): Vince Bucci/Getty Images, Inc. Page 15 (left): Carlos S. Pereyra/Age Fotostock America, Inc. Page 15 (center): Apis/Abramis/Alamy Images. Page 15 (right): Glow Images/Age Fotostock America, Inc. Page 21: North Wind Photo/Alamy Images. Page 27 (top left): Photodisc/Getty Images, Inc. Page 27 (bottom left): Blend Images/SUPERSTOCK. Page 27 (bottom right): Thomas Barwick/Riser/Getty Images, Inc. Page 27 (top right): Digital Vision/Punchstock.

Chapter 2
Page 32: Superstock/Punchstock. Page 38 (top): SUPERSTOCK. Page 38 (bottom): George Brice/Alamy Images. Page 39 (top left): Andres Leighton/©AP/Wide World Photos. Page 39 (bottom): Jerry and Marcy Monkman/Danita Delimont. Page 39 (right): Courtesy Kim Potowski. Page 42 (top center): Courtesy Kim Potowski. Page 42 (top left): iStockphoto. Page 42 (top right): Floyd Anderson/iStockphoto. Page 42 (bottom left): Vladimir Dmitriev/iStockphoto. Page 42 (bottom right): Francisco Roman Photography. Page 50 (left): Robert Frerck/Odyssey Productions. Page 50 (right): Francisco Roman Photography. Page 54 (left): Nicholas Pitt/Alamy Images. Page 54 (right): Kim Karpeles/Alamy Images. Page 60: David R. Frazier Photolibrary, Inc./Alamy. Page 62: Bob Krist/Corbis. Page 63 (left): Arturo Limon/iStockphoto. Page 63 (right): John Rodriguez/iStockphoto.

Chapter 3
Page 66: Ariel Skelly/Age Fotostock America, Inc. Page 71: Reportage/Gamma Presse, Inc. Page 72: Photo by Alfonzo Fernandez, San Antonio, Texas. Page 73 (top): Mario Algaze/The Image Works. Page 72 (bottom): dieter Spears/iStockphoto. Page 73 (bottom): Rudi Von Briel/PhotoEdit. Page 75 (bottom): John Neubauer/PhotoEdit. Page 75 (top right): Ralf-Finn Hestoft/Corbis. Page 75 (center right): ©AP/Wide World Photos. Page 79: Odyssey Productions. Page 85 (top): Polka Dot Images/SUPERSTOCK. Page 90: Michael Newman/PhotoEdit. Page 91 (top): Digital Vision/Getty Images. Page 91 (top left): William Howard/Stone/Getty Images, Inc. Page 91 (center left): Nossa Productions/Getty Images, Inc. Page 91 (center right): John and Lisa Merrill/Danita Delimont. Page 91 (bottom right): Robert Frerck/Woodfin Camp & Associates. Page 91 (bottom center): Bill Frymire/Masterfile. Page 91 (bottom left): David McNew/Getty Images News and Sport Services. Page 95: Jose L. Palaez/Corbis Stock Market. Page 97 (bottom): John Pugh, "Siete Punto Uno". Photo courtesy of John Pugh. Page 97 (top): Yreina Cervantez, "La Ofrenca". Mural, Toluca Street under 1st Street Bridge, Los Angeles. A Neighborhood Pride: Great Walls Unlimited project. ©SPARC.

Chapter 4
Page 100: Kayte M. Deioma/PhotoEdit. Page 105: San Rosto/Age Fotostock America, Inc. Page 109 (bottom): David Crockett Photography/Alamy Images. Page 109 (top): Mary Evans Picture Library. Page 110 (top left): Robert Frerck/Odyssey Productions. Page 110 (bottom left): Hugh Rogers. Page 110 (bottom right): Russell Cheyne/Stone/Getty Images, Inc. Page 110 (top right): ©Everton/The Image Works. Page 111: Courtesy Laila Dawson. Page 118 (right): Courtesy Laila Dawson. Page 118 (left): xela/Alamy Images. Page 125: Chad Slattery/Stone/Getty Images. Page 126 (bottom right): Zev Robinson/Jupiter Images. Page 126 (top left): Erik Rank/Foodpix. Page 126 (center right): John Lei/Stock, Boston. Page 126 (top right): Matthew Klein/Photo Researchers. Page 126 (center left): David Simson/Stock, Boston. Page 126 (bottom left): Courtesy Laila Dawson. Page 130: Jeff Oshiro/Jupiter Images. Page 133: Hulton Archive/Getty Images. Page 137: D. Donne Bryant Stock.

Chapter 5
Page 140: Schultheiss Selection GmbH & CoKG/Getty Images, Inc. Page 146 (center): Tomas Bravo/Reuters/Landov LLC. Page 146 (bottom right): Enrique Marcarian/Reuters/Landov LLC. Page 146 (top right): Daniel Garcia/AFP/Getty Images, Inc. Page 146 (bottom left): Marcelo Del Pozo/Reuters/Landov LLC. Page 146 (top left): Pablo la Rosa/Reuters/Landov LLC. Page 150: John Grieshop/Getty Images, Inc. Page 151 (left): Guido Alberto Rossi/The Image Bank/Getty Images. Page 151 (right): Fred Prouser/Reuters/Landov LLC. Page 151 (bottom right): Max & Bea Hunn/D. Donne Bryant Stock Photography. Page 151 (bottom left): Ralph Notaro/Getty Images, Inc. Page 153 (center): Max Morse/Reuters/Landov LLC. Page 153 (right): Jon Buckle/PA Photos/Landov LLC. Page 153 (left): Nikki Boertman/Reuters/Landov LLC. Page 154: Bill Eichner. Page 164 (top right): Art Wolfe/Stone/Getty Images. Page 164 (center): Courtesy Laila Dawson. Page 164 (top left): ©AP/Wide World Photos. Page 164 (bottom center): ©Everton/The Image Works. Page 164 (bottom right): Chip and Rosa Maria Peterson. Page 164 (bottom left): Michael Busselle/Stone/Getty Images. Page 165: Raymond Forbes/Age Fotostock America, Inc. Page 166 (bottom right): Alamy Images. Page 166 (top right): Pablo Corral Vega/Corbis Images. Page 166 (top left): Owen Franken/Corbis Images. Page 166 (center right): Art Rickerby/Time Life/Getty Images, Inc. Page 166 (center): Jose Luis Roca/Getty Images, Inc. Page 166 (bottom right): Simon Bruty/Getty Images, Inc. Page 166 (center left): Rodrigo Arangua/AFP/Getty Images, Inc. Page 173: Prensa Latina/Getty Images News and Sport Services. Page 150: Corbis/SUPERSTOCK.

Chapter 6
Page 176: AA World Travel Library/Alamy Images. Page 182 (right): Peter Bowater/Age Fotostock America, Inc. Page 182 (left): J.d. Dallet/Age Fotostock America, Inc. Page 183 (bottom): Age fotostock/SUPERSTOCK. Page 183 (bottom left): Don Quixote, 1955 (gouache on paper), Picasso, Pablo (1881–1973)/Private Collection, © DACS /Peter Willi/The Bridgeman Art Library International. Page 183 (top left): Ian Waldie/Getty Images, Inc. Page 183 (top right): MC/EFOQUE/SIPA/NewsCom. Page 184: Peter Holmes/Age Fotostock America, Inc. Page 184 (bottom): age fotostock/SUPERSTOCK. Page 185 (top): Factoria Singular/Age Fotostock America, Inc. Page 185 (center right): Robert Frerck/Odyssey Productions. Page 185 (center left): Ina Peters/iStockphoto. Page 185 (top right): ©AP/Wide World Photos. Page 185 (bottom right): Matthew Klein/Photo Researchers. Page 207 (right): Orban Thierry/Corbis Sygma. Page 207 (left): AFP/Getty Images News and Sport Services. Page 207 (bottom): Robert Frerck/Odyssey Productions. Page 213 (left): Robert Frerck/Odyssey Productions. Page 213 (right): Courtesy Laila Dawson.

Chapter 7
Page 216: Kord.com/SUPERSTOCK. Page 222 (right): Icon Sports Media. Page 223 (top): Chad Ehlers/Stone/Getty Images. Page 223 (bottom right): Robert Frerck/Odyssey Productions. Page 223 (bottom left): Richard Mildenhall/ArenaPAL/Topham/The Image Works. Page 224 (top left): Kit Houghton/Corbis Images. Page 224 (center): Loren McIntyre. Page 222 (left): Joel Robine/AFP/Getty Images, Inc. Page 224 (bottom right): Steve Benbow/Woodfin Camp & Associates. Page 225 (top left): Alex Stewart/The Image Bank/Getty Images. Page 225 (top right): Barnabas Bosshart/Corbis Images. Page 225 (bottom left): Leo Rosenthal/Getty Images, Inc. Page 225 (bottom right): Larissa Skinner/iStockphoto. Page 228 (left): Alamy Images. Page 228 (right): Bobbi Fabian/Jupiter Images. Page 232: SUPERSTOCK. Page 235 (top): Courtesy Laila Dawson. Page 235 (bottom): Frank Scherschel/Getty Images News and Sport Services. Page 241: Martin Thomas/Reuters/NewsCom. Page 249: ©AP/Wide World Photos.

Chapter 8
Page 252: Blend Images/SUPERSTOCK. Page 265 (top): Robert Frerck/Odyssey Productions. Page 265 (center left): Ira Block/National Geographic Society. Page 265 (bottom right): Robert Frerck/Odyssey Productions. Page 266 (top left): George Holton/Photo Researchers. Page 266 (top): John Maier/The Image Works. Page 266 (center left): Richard Smith/Corbis Sygma. Page 266 (bottom right): Yoshio Tomii/SUPERSTOCK. Page 267 (top right): Christopher Leggett/Age Fotostock America, Inc. Page 267 (top left): Courtesy Laila Dawson. Page 267 (center right): Ken Biggs. Page 267 (bottom): David Mercado/Reuters/Landov LLC. Page 274 (top): Suzanne Murphy/D. Donne Bryant Stock Photography. Page 274 (center left): Jeff Greenberg/Alamy. Page 274 (center right): Bryon Augustin/D. Donne Bryant Stock Photography. Page 274 (bottom): Chip Peterson and Rosa Maria de la Cueva Peterson. Page 287 (bottom left): Courtesy Laila Dawson. Page 287 (bottom right): Courtesy Laila Dawson. Page 287 (top): Courtesy Laila Dawson.

Chapter 9

Page 291: Blend Images/SUPERSTOCK. Page 294: Yellow Dog Productions/The Image Bank/Getty Images. Page 295: Mug Shots/Corbis Stock Market. Page 296 (top left): Glowimages/Age Fotostock America, Inc. Page 296 (top center): Jose Luis Pelaez/Age Fotostock America, Inc. Page 296 (top right): Glowimages/Age Fotostock America, Inc. Page 296 (bottom left): Jon Feingersh Photogr/Age Fotostock America, Inc. Page 296 (bottom center): Jose Luis Pelaez, Inc/Age Fotostock America, Inc. Page 296 (bottom right): Photodisc/Age Fotostock America, Inc. Page 297: Image Bank/Getty Images. Page 298 (top left): Alexander Rieser/Alamy. Page 298 (center right): Joe Standart. Page 298 (bottom left): Carlos Alvarez/Getty Images News and Sport Services. Page 299 (top left): Loris Barbazza/Stone/Getty Images. Page 299 (right): ©AP/Wide World Photos. Page 299 (bottom left): M. Algaze/The Image Works. Page 305: Lynn Johnson/Aurora Photos. Page 306: Stephan Wallgren/AFP/Getty Images. Page 313 (right): Felicia Martinez/PhotoEdit. Page 313 (left): Jim Parkin/iStockphoto.

Chapter 10

Page 326: Alamy Images. Page 336 (top left): Victor Englebert. Page 336 (top right): Robert Fried/D. Donne Bryant Stock Photography. Page 336 (bottom left): E. Caldwell/D. Donne Bryant/PO. Page 336 (bottom right): Punchstock. Page 337 (top): Robert Harding Picture Library/Alamy. Page 337 (bottom): Gary M. Prior/Getty Images News and Sport Services. Page 337 (top left): Sartoroti/Ministry of Tourism of Uruguay. Reproduced with permission. Page 337 (bottom center): Thomas Colchie Literary Agent. Page 343 (top): Thomas Northcut/Getty Images. Page 343 (bottom left): Mike Randolphe/Masterfile. Page 343 (bottom right): Jean-Yves Bruel/Masterfile. Page 348: Timothy Ross/The Image Works. Page 351: DPPI/Icon Sports Media. Page 356 (top left): Alamy Images. Page 356 (top right): Jose L. Palaez/Corbis Stock Market. Page 356 (top center): WireImageStock/ Masterfile. Page 356 (center left): Courtesy Laila Dawson. Page 356 (center): Courtesy Laila Dawson. Page 356 (center right): John A. Rizzo/Digital Vision/Punchstock. Page 356 (bottom left): Adalberto Ríos Szalay/Age Fotostock America, Inc. Page 356 (bottom center): Courtesy Laila Dawson. Page 356 (bottom right): Courtesy Laila Dawson. Page 357: Pedro Figari, Baile Criollo; 61x82 cm, oil on canvas. Photo courtesy Museo Virtual de Artes El País. ©1997El País.

Chapter 11

Page 366: corbis/Media Bakery. Page 374 (right): Danny Lehman/Corbis Images. Page 374 (bottom left): Dixon Hamby/Alamy. Page 375 (top left): Gonzalo Azumendi/Age Fotostock America, Inc. Page 375 (top right): Alfredo Maiquez/Age Fotostock America, Inc. Page 375 (center left): Will & Deni McIntyre/Photo Researchers. Page 375 (bottom): ©AP/Wide World Photos. Page 380: Juan Barreto/AFP/Getty Images. Page 385: Rony Liang/Bruce Coleman, Inc. Page 389: Gonzalo Azumendi/Age Fotostock America, Inc. Page 397 (right): Kevin Schafer/Corbis Images. Page 397 (left): Kevin Schafer/Corbis Images.

Chapter 12

Page 400: Stockbyte/SUPERSTOCK. Page 404: Gallo Images/Getty Images. Page 405 (top right): Andoni Canela/Aurora Photos. Page 405 (center left): Kenneth Garrett/Danita Delimont. Page 405 (center right): Digital Vision/SUPERSTOCK. Page 405 (bottom left): imagebroker/Alamy. Page 405 (bottom right): Courtesy Laila Dawson. Page 409: M. Algaze/The Image Works. Page 411 (top): Age Fotostock/SUPERSTOCK. Page 411 (bottom): Courtesy Laila Dawson. Page 414: Sylvain Grandadam/Age Fotostock America, Inc. Page 416: Courtesy Costa Rica Expeditions, www.costaricaexpeditions.com. Page 417 (right): Jon Arnold/Danita Delimont. Page 417 (left): Reinhard Dirscherl/Age Fotostock America, Inc. Page 418: Sue Cunningham/Danita Delimont. Page 421 (left): Ken Graham/Stone/Getty Images. Page 421 (right): Peter Christopher/Masterfile. Page 421 (bottom): UNEP. Page 422: Michael Fogden/Animals Animals. Page 427 (top): ©AP/Wide World Photos. Page 427 (bottom): age fotostock/SUPERSTOCK. Page 433: Jeff Greenberg/Danita Delimont.

Chapter 13

Page 437: Sylvain Grandadam/Age Fotostock America, Inc. Page 444 (top left): Carsten Reisinger/Alamy. Page 444 (bottom left): Ken Welsh/Age Fotostock America, Inc. Page 444 (top right): Donne Bryant/D. Donne Bryant Stock Photography. Page 444 (center right): Jorge Mujica/NewsCom.

Page 444 (center left): Michael & Patricia Fogden/Minden Pictures/Getty Images. Page 444 (bottom right): Man W. Hunn/SUPERSTOCK. Page 445 (top left): IT Stock Free/SUPERSTOCK. Page 445 (top right): SUPERSTOCK. Page 445 (bottom): Richard Bradley/Alamy. Page 447: Robert Fried/Alamy. Page 449: Museo Ixchel del Traje Indígena. Page 456: Peter Horre/Alamy. Page 460: ADD World Wide Travel Images/Alamy. Page 461 (bottom): Pablo Corral V/Corbis Images. Page 461 (top): Parador Hacienda Gripiñas. Page 467: Guenter Wamser/Age Fotostock America, Inc. Page 469 (top): Courtesy The Textile Museum, Washington, D.C. Page 469 (bottom): Courtesy The Textile Museum, Washington, D.C.

Chapter 14

Page 472: Robert Fried/Alamy. Page 483: Courtesy Laila Dawson. Page 484 (top left): Kenneth Garrett/Danita Delimont. Page 484 (top right): Courtesy Laila Dawson. Page 485 (bottom): Peter Chartrand/D. Donne Bryant Stock Photography. Page 485 (top): A. Farnsworth/The Image Works. Page 489: La Prensa. Page 490: AGE fotostock/SUPERSTOCK. Page 494: Focus Features/Photofest. Page 499: Somos/Age Fotostock America, Inc. Page 489: Esteban Felix/©AP/Wide World Photos.

Chapter 15

Page 506: Kim Karpeles/Digital Railroad, Inc. Page 514 (right): NewsCom. Page 514 (left): NewsCom. Page 518 (bottom): Reuters/Landov LLC. Page 518 (top): ©AP/Wide World Photos. Page 524: Courtesy Michael Navarro. Page 527: Newsmakers/NewsCom. Page 533: Tania Humaran/NewsCom. All other flags IT Stock/SuperStock.

TEXT CREDITS

Page 173: **Herederos de Nicolás Guillén** for "Sensemayá" by Nicolás Guillén. Reprinted by permission.

Page 323: **Programa Editorial de la Universidad del Valle** for "El Amigo." By Miguel Fernando Caro G. from *Antología del cuento corto colombiano.* Reprinted by permission.

REALIA CREDITS

CHAPTER 2 *Page 37:* Reprinted by permission of Telmex.

CHAPTER 4 *Page 107:* ©Chef Merito 1998, all rights reserved. Reprinted by permission; *Page 135:* Printed by permission of Lario's Restaurant.

CHAPTER 6 *Page 181:* Created by Siboney U.S.A., International Hispanics Communications, Copyright Colgate-Palmolive Company.

CHAPTER 8 *Page 258:* Reprinted by permission of Buenhogar.

CHAPTER 9 *Page 303:* Printed by permission of Lario's Restaurant.

CHAPTER 10 *Page 328:* Permission requested; *Page 360:* Adapted by permission of Richard López at Puntaweb.

CHAPTER 11 *Page 393:* Reprinted by permission of Revista IMAGEN.

CHAPTER 12 *Page 421:* World Environment Day logo 2007, The United Nations Environment Programme; *Page 425:* Reprinted by permission of SAETA, Inc.; *Page 426:* Adapted by permission of Kempery Tours CIA, LTDA.; *Page 428:* Reprinted by permission of Teatro Lope de Vega; *Page 429:* Reprinted by permission el Parque de Atracciones-Madrid; *Page 429:* Reprinted by permission of Arrocería Puerto de Atocha y Restaurante Redondela; *Page 432:* Permission requested.

CHAPTER 13 *Page 479:* Reprinted by permission of BASF Española S.A.; *Page 481:* Reprinted by permission of Maria Luisa O. de Montellano.

CHAPTER 14 *Page 513:* Permission has been requested.

Every attempt has been made to locate the copyright holder for the campus map located on page 49.

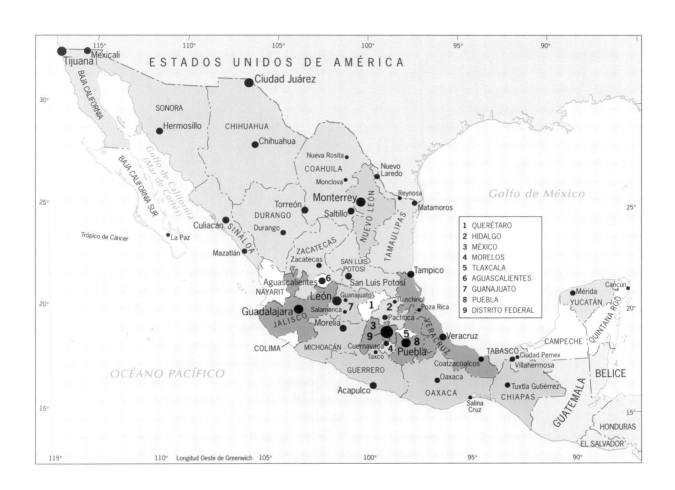

ESTADOS UNIDOS DE AMÉRICA

Tijuana
Mexicali
115°
110°
105°
100°
95°
90°

Ciudad Juárez

30°

BAJA CALIFORNIA

SONORA

Hermosillo

CHIHUAHUA

Chihuahua

Nueva Rosita

COAHUILA

Nuevo Laredo

Monclova

Reynosa

Golfo de México

25°

Golfo de California (Mar de Cortés)

BAJA CALIFORNIA SUR

Torreón

Monterrey

Matamoros

DURANGO

Saltillo

NUEVO LEÓN

25°

Culiacán

SINALOA

Durango

Trópico de Cáncer

La Paz

ZACATECAS

TAMAULIPAS

Mazatlán

Zacatecas

SAN LUIS POTOSÍ

Tampico

Aguascalientes

6

San Luis Potosí

NAYARIT

León

Guanajuato

20°

Tlanchinol

Poza Rica

Salamanca

7

1

2

Guadalajara

JALISCO

Morelia

3

Pachuca

Veracruz

Cuernavaca

9

5

8

VERACRUZ

COLIMA

MICHOACÁN

Taxco

4

Puebla

Mérida

Cancún

YUCATÁN

QUINTANA ROO

20°

CAMPECHE

Coatzacoalcos

TABASCO

Ciudad Pemex

Villahermosa

BELICE

OCÉANO PACÍFICO

GUERRERO

Oaxaca

CHIAPAS

Tuxtla Gutiérrez

GUATEMALA

Acapulco

OAXACA

Salina Cruz

15°

HONDURAS

EL SALVADOR

15°

115°
110°
Longitud Oeste de Greenwich 105°
100°
95°
90°

1 QUERÉTARO
2 HIDALGO
3 MÉXICO
4 MORELOS
5 TLAXCALA
6 AGUASCALIENTES
7 GUANAJUATO
8 PUEBLA
9 DISTRITO FEDERAL

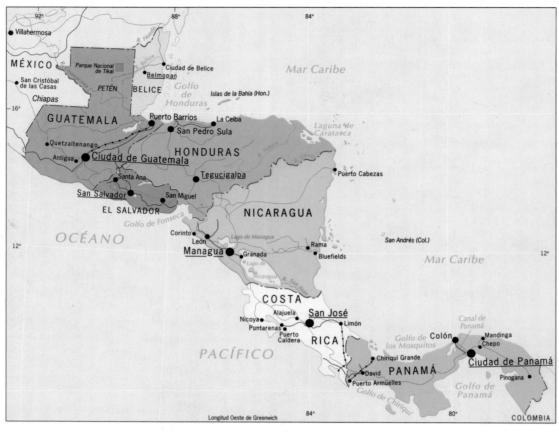
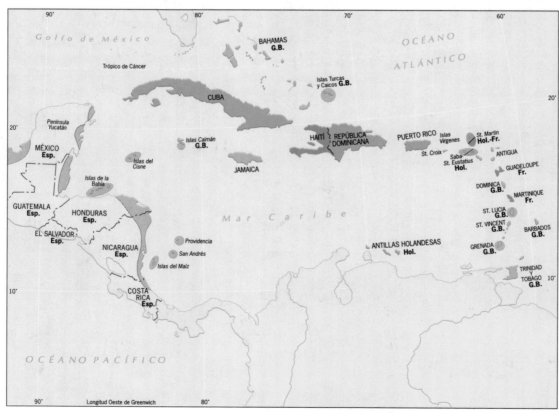